Lecture Notes in Computer Science 16693

The series Lecture Notes in Computer Science (LNCS), including its subseries Lecture Notes in Artificial Intelligence (LNAI) and Lecture Notes in Bioinformatics (LNBI), has established itself as a medium for the publication of new developments in computer science and information technology research, teaching, and education.

LNCS enjoys close cooperation with the computer science R & D community, the series counts many renowned academics among its volume editors and paper authors, and collaborates with prestigious societies. Its mission is to serve this international community by providing an invaluable service, mainly focused on the publication of conference and workshop proceedings and postproceedings. LNCS commenced publication in 1973.

Lieven Eeckhout · Chao Li · Zhibin Yu ·
Avi Mendelson
Editors

Advanced Parallel Processing Technologies

17th International Symposium, APPT 2026
Brussels, Belgium, July 27, 2026
Proceedings

Springer

Editors
Lieven Eeckhout
Ghent University
Ghent, Belgium

Chao Li
Shanghai Jiao Tong University
Shanghai, China

Zhibin Yu
Chinese Academy of Sciences
Beijing, China

Avi Mendelson
Israel Institute of Technology
Haifa, Israel

ISSN 0302-9743 ISSN 1611-3349 (electronic)
Lecture Notes in Computer Science
ISBN 978-981-92-4804-9 ISBN 978-981-92-4805-6 (eBook)
https://doi.org/10.1007/978-981-92-4805-6

This Springer imprint is published by the registered company Springer Nature Singapore Pte Ltd.
The registered company address is: 152 Beach Road, #21-01/04 Gateway East, Singapore 189721, Singapore

Preface

It is our great pleasure to welcome you to the 17th International Symposium on Advanced Parallel Processing Technology (APPT 2026) in Brussels, the vibrant heart of Europe and a crossroads of cultures. In much the same spirit, APPT serves as a dynamic confluence of diverse research domains, spanning chip design, computer architecture, systems, and emerging paradigms in computing. Over the years, APPT has matured into a premier international forum—a place where bold ideas are debated, conventions are challenged, and the evolving frontiers of parallel computing are continually redrawn. This year, we embraced the theme "Computing Evolved," reflecting both the relentless pace of innovation and the transformative shifts ahead. To bring this vision to life, we put together a rich and immersive four-day program, featuring the main conference, specialized workshops, hands-on tutorials, technical and young scholar forums, a student research challenge, and work-in-progress sessions. Highlighting the program were four distinguished academic keynote addresses, each poised to inspire new perspectives and ignite forward-looking dialogue across our global community.

We received 142 submissions this year, which doubles that of last year (2025). Reviewing was done in one round. Each paper received at least 3 double-blind reviews and a few papers received 4 reviews. Seven papers were "desk-rejected" by the program co-chairs for egregious formatting violations or double-blind violations. The review process was modeled as a "fixed-capacity slot competition" model, in which the goal was to identify papers which are really of high quality. Thirty-six of the 142 submissions were accepted as regular papers, for an acceptance rate of 25%. Fourteen and four of the submissions were accepted as posters and work-in-progress (WIP) papers, respectively. The accepted papers cover a wide range of topics, including high-performance computing, cloud computing, deep learning accelerators, large language model systems, parallel architecture simulation, microarchitecture, and more.

The Program Committee consisted of 37 full PC members and the External Review Committee (ERC) contained 23 members. The 60 reviewers came from 8 countries and 35 universities/research institutes. Each reviewer was assigned 6~10 papers. This workload variation across PC and ERC members was due to the need to match reviewer expertise with the topic of the submissions. We are deeply grateful to all the reviewers who devoted the precious time from their busy schedules to review the papers and provide valuable feedback and suggestions. In addition, we are extremely grateful to many people who helped us in this process. Yunji Chen, Chair of the Technical Committee on Computer Architecture (TCArch), China Computer Federation (CCF), provided wise advice when unforeseen issues arose. Thirty-one members of the APPT preparation committee discussed strategies on difficult issues such as types of accepted papers, and patiently answered innumerable questions about the process. The Submission Chairs, Songwen Pei and Yangjie Zhou, did a great job of helping with paper assignments and configuring the submission system. The Publication Chairs, Xiaoli Gong and Jinyi Deng, did a fantastic job of working with the authors to get the accepted papers, posters, and work-in-progress (WIP) papers into the proceedings. Shuang Chen, Yu Feng, and Shuibing He helped invite some PC and ERC members. The Artifact Evaluation Committee Chairs, Mingyu Gao and Haiyu Mao, did the hard work to create the Artifact Evaluation Committee and ensure the quality of the artifacts that were recognized at APPT. The Web Chairs, Jing Wang and Chengzhi Lu, did a great job managing and updating the conference website. Our Executive Chairs, Yi Wang and Xiaofeng Hou, did a remarkable job handling the myriad essential tasks that kept the conference running smoothly. Our Tech Forum Chairs, Xuehai Qian and Zidong Du, organized an exciting Tech Forum program that strengthened interactions between academia and industry. The Award Chairs, Gongxuan Zhang and Weizhi Meng, carefully coordinated the conference awards selection process. The Workshop Chairs, Zhuoran Song and Hao Zheng, and the Tutorial Chairs, Youwei Zhuo and Fengbin Tu, put together excellent workshop and tutorial programs. The PhD Forum Chairs, Shuwen Deng and Amelie Chi Zhou, organized a vibrant forum for student researchers, while the Poster Chairs, Zichen Xu and Xin Fu, coordinated the poster session and helped showcase ongoing research. The Student Competition Chairs, Yu Feng and Yanan Guo, organized an engaging student competition that encouraged innovation and participation. We also thank the Travel Grant Chairs, Xiaohang Wang and Amit Singh, for coordinating travel support, and the Registration Chairs, Meng Zhang and Xueqi Li, for ensuring a smooth registration process for all attendees. The APPT Steering Committee provided guidance on many matters and supported our vision for how to run the process.

We hope that you enjoyed APPT 2026!

July 2026

Lieven Eeckhout
Chao Li
Zhibin Yu
Avi Mendelson

Organization

General Co-chairs

Lieven Eeckhout	Ghent University, Belgium
Chao Li	Shanghai Jiao Tong University, China

Program Co-chairs

Zhibin Yu	Shenzhen Institutes of Advanced Technology, China
Avi Mendelson	Technion, Israel

Program Committee

Bo Yuan	Rutgers University, USA
Stijn Eyerman	Intel, USA
Xulong Tang	University of Pittsburgh, USA
Jian Huang	University of Illinois Urbana-Champaign, USA
David Kaeli	Northeastern University, USA
Bingyao Li	University of California, Riverside, USA
Bo Wu	Colorado School of Mines, USA
Jeeho Ryoo	Fairleigh Dickinson University, USA
Zheng Wang	University of Leeds, UK
Almutaz Adileh	Huawei, China
Georgios Vavouliotis	Huawei Zurich Research Center, Switzerland
Yuan Wen	University of Aberdeen, UK
Yuhao Zhu	University of Rochester, USA
Jie Zhang	Peking University, China
Jiayi Huang	Hong Kong University of Science and Technology (Guangzhou), China
Dong Du	Shanghai Jiao Tong University, China
Guangyu Sun	Peking University, China
Huimin Cui	Institute of Computing Technology, CAS, China
Lei Liu	Beihang University, China
Lixin Zhang	Sudo Information Technology, China
Meng Li	Peking University, China

Mingyu Gao	Tsinghua University, China
Rui Hou	Institute of Information Engineering, CAS, China
Youwei Zhuo	Peking University, China
Yu Hua	Huazhong University of Science and Technology, China
Zhan Shi	Huawei, China
Jingwen Leng	Shanghai Jiao Tong University, China
Liqiang Lu	Zhejiang University, China
Chao Wang	University of Science and Technology of China, China
Libo Huang	National University of Defense Technology, China
Suzhen Wu	Xiamen University, China
Mattan Erez	University of Texas at Austin, USA
Artemiy Margaritov	Huawei, China
Jie Zhou	George Washington University, USA
Yang (Katie) Zhao	University of Minnesota, USA
Xin Xin	University of Central Florida, USA
Jian Weng	King Abdullah University of Science and Technology, Saudi Arabia

External Review Committee

Mingyu Liang	Google, USA
Ping Chen	Zhejiang University, China
Siling Yang	Zhejiang University, China
Shiyi Li	Harbin Institute of Technology, Shenzhen, China
Chencheng Ye	Huazhong University of Science and Technology, China
Xia Zhao	Academy of Military Science, China
Zhen Wang	Shenzhen Institute of Advanced Technology, Chinese Academy of Science, China
Chao Chen	Shenzhen Institute of Advanced Technology, Chinese Academy of Science, China
Yongkui Yang	Shenzhen Institute of Advanced Technology, Chinese Academy of Science, China
Lu Wang	Academy of Military Science, China
Jiacheng Zhao	Institute of Computing Technology, Chinese Academy of Science, China
Tianyi Liu	Institute of Computing Technology, Chinese Academy of Science, China
Weiwei Chen	Huawei, China

Lei Dai	Huawei, China
Shiqing Zhang	Academy of Military Science, China
Rui Wang	Beihang University, China
Yitao Hu	Tianjin University, China
Renhai Chen	Huawei, China
Xueliang Li	Shenzhen University, China
Yaohua Wang	National University of Defense Technology, China
Bo Mao	Xiamen University, China
Zhibo Xuan	Beihang University, China
Han Zhao	Shanghai Jiao Tong University, China

Steering Committee

Jack Dongarra (Co-chair)	University of Tennessee, USA
Yunji Chen (Co-chair)	Chinese Academy of Sciences, China
Ahmed Louri	George Washington University, USA
Albert Zomaya	University of Sydney, Australia
Anand Sivasubramaniam	Penn State University, USA
Bingsheng He	National University of Singapore, Singapore
Dean Tullsen	University of California, San Diego, USA
Dimitris Gizopoulos	University of Athens, Greece
Hai Jin	Huazhong University of Science and Technology, China
Jean-Luc Gaudiot	University of California, Irvine, USA
Jiwu Shu	Tsinghua University, China
Josep Torrellas	University of Illinois Urbana-Champaign, USA
Lieven Eeckhout	Ghent University, Belgium
Minyi Guo	Shanghai Jiao Tong University, China
Per Stenstrom	Chalmers University of Technology, Sweden
Rajkumar Buyya	University of Melbourne, Australia
Schahram Dustdar	Vienna University of Technology, Austria
Weisong Shi	Wayne State University, USA
Xian-He Sun	Illinois Institute of Technology, USA
Yiran Chen	Duke University, USA
Yuan Xie	Hong Kong University of Science and Technology, China

Executive Co-chairs

Yi Wang	Shenzhen University, China
Xiaofeng Hou	Shanghai Jiao Tong University, China

Tech Forum Co-chairs

Xuehai Qian	Tsinghua University, China
Zidong Du	ICT/CAS, China

Award Co-chairs

Gongxuan Zhang	Nanjing University of Science and Technology, China
Weizhi Meng	Lancaster University, UK

Submission Co-chairs

Songwen Pei	Shanghai Institute of Technology, China
Yangjie Zhou	National University of Singapore, Singapore

Publication Co-chairs

Xiaoli Gong	Nankai University, China
Jinyi Deng	Tsinghua University, China

Workshop Co-chairs

Zhuoran Song	Shanghai Jiao Tong University, China
Hao Zheng	University of Central Florida, USA

Tutorial Co-chairs

Youwei Zhuo	Peking University, China
Fengbin Tu	Hong Kong University of Science and Technology, China

PhD Forum Co-chairs

Shuwen Deng	Tsinghua University, China
Amelie Chi Zhou	Hong Kong Baptist University, China

Poster Co-chairs

Zichen Xu	Nanchang University, China
Xin Fu	University of Houston, USA

Artifact Evaluation Co-chairs

Mingyu Gao	Tsinghua University, China
Haiyu Mao	King's College London, UK

Student Competition Co-chairs

Yu Feng	Shanghai Jiao Tong University, China
Yanan Guo	University of Rochester, USA

Travel Grant Co-chairs

Xiaohang Wang	Zhejiang University, China
Amit Singh	University of Essex, UK

Registration Co-chairs

Meng Zhang	Huazhong University of Science and Technology, China
Xueqi Li	ICT/CAS, China

Web/Social Media Co-chairs

Jing Wang	East China Normal University, China
Chengzhi Lu	Nanyang Technological University, Singapore

Publicity Committee

Shuang Chen (Chair)	Huawei, China
Amro Awad	University of Oxford, UK
Hyokeun Lee	Ajou University, South Korea
Huanle Xu	University of Macau, China
Jian Weng	King Abdullah University of Science and Technology, Saudi Arabia
Kaoru Ota	Tohoku University, Japan
Maolin Wang	Hong Kong University of Science and Technology, China
Shanquan Tian	Google, USA
Stéphane Zuckerman	CY Cergy Paris University, France
Tiziano De Matteis	Vrije Universiteit Amsterdam, Netherlands
Wei Li	University of Sydney, Australia

Contents

Serving Systems

LLM Workflows

AI Design Automation

Scalable Computing

AI Accelerators

Kernel Acceleration

Featured Articles

ZIPPer: A Fine-Grained Co-design of ZeRO-DP and Pipeline Parallelism for LLM Training on Heterogeneous GPUs

Lang Yuan[1], Linbo Qiao[1](✉), Yu Tang[2](✉), Mingxiang Zhu[1], Wei Shang[1], and Dongsheng Li[1]

[1] National Key Laboratory of Parallel and Distributed Processing, College of Computer Science and Technology, National University of Defense Technology, Changsha, China
{yuanlang,qiao.linbo,zhumingxiang,shangwei,dsli}@nudt.edu.cn
[2] Information Support Force Engineering University, Wuhan, China
tangyu14@alumni.nudt.edu.cn

Abstract. Training large language models with hybrid pipeline and data parallelism suffers from severe memory redundancy and load imbalance on heterogeneous clusters. Existing ZeRO integrations operate at coarse granularities, forcing local gradient accumulation that critically inflates memory pressure and restricts efficiency. To address these challenges, we present **ZIPPer**, a fine-grained co-design of ZeRO-DP and pipeline parallelism tailored for LLM training on heterogeneous GPUs. To alleviate the memory redundancy, ZIPPer eliminates gradient redundancy by performing an in-place Reduce-Scatter communication immediately after each micro-batch backward pass. This scales down the gradient memory proportionally to the data-parallel degree. An asynchronous dual-stream scheme largely hides this communication overhead. Furthermore, to resolve the load imbalance caused by cluster heterogeneity, ZIPPer employs a topology-aware joint cost model and a simulator-driven algorithm. By framing pipeline partitioning as a minimax optimization, it intelligently balances execution times and memory constraints across heterogeneous GPUs. Experimental results on GPT and LLaMA models show that tailored ZIPPer configurations significantly outperform existing baselines. Specifically, ZIPPer improves training throughput by up to 66.8% and reduces peak memory usage by up to 46% under different optimization strategies.

Keywords: Distributed Training · Large Language Models · Pipeline Parallelism · ZeRO · Heterogeneous Clusters · Memory Optimization

1 Introduction

The rapid growth of large language models (LLMs) [2,3,5,7,12,31] has driven the need for increasingly scalable and memory-efficient training systems. Modern models with tens or hundreds of billions of parameters are commonly trained

L. Eeckhout et al. (Eds.): APPT 2026, LNCS 16693, pp. 3–17, 2027.
https://doi.org/10.1007/978-981-92-4805-6_1

using hybrid parallelism that combines pipeline parallelism (PP) and data parallelism (DP) [20,24,26,29]. While this hybrid strategy enables scaling across hundreds or thousands of GPUs, it introduces two fundamental challenges in modern clusters. First, significant memory redundancy exists within each pipeline stage. Parameters, gradients, and optimizer states are replicated across data-parallel replicas, which occupies tens of gigabytes of GPU memory and limits feasible micro-batch sizes. Second, real-world GPU clusters are inherently heterogeneous, consisting of devices with different memory capacities, compute throughputs, and interconnect bandwidths [22,32]. Such heterogeneity leads to severe pipeline imbalance and even out-of-memory (OOM) failures under naive or uniform partitioning strategies.

While ZeRO [24] effectively removes redundancy in pure data-parallel training, integrating it with pipeline parallelism remains difficult. Existing frameworks [26,28] typically operate at the global batch granularity, which is misaligned with the micro-batch execution semantics of pipeline scheduling [8,20]. Consequently, gradients must be accumulated locally, causing memory usage to grow linearly with the number of micro-batches. Furthermore, existing partitioning methods mostly assume homogeneous hardware, failing to balance the intricate trade-offs between memory footprint and compute efficiency in heterogeneous environments.

To overcome these limitations, we propose **ZIPPer**, a fine-grained, co-designed framework that jointly optimizes memory efficiency and pipeline scheduling for LLM training on heterogeneous GPUs. ZIPPer unifies two core components: an efficient micro-batch execution component and a heterogeneity-aware pipeline partitioning component.

At the execution level, ZIPPer integrates ZeRO Stage-2 with pipeline parallelism at the micro-batch level. Instead of accumulating full gradients locally, it performs an in-place, buffer-free Reduce-Scatter immediately after each micro-batch backward pass. This design effectively eliminates gradient replication—scaling down the gradient memory footprint within each stage by a factor of N_{dp}. Furthermore, we introduce an asynchronous dual-stream execution scheme that overlaps communication with subsequent forward computation, thereby reducing communication overhead while maintaining high pipeline utilization.

At the partitioning level, ZIPPer extends beyond execution optimizations by employing a *topology-aware joint cost model.* This model mathematically captures heterogeneous device bandwidths and compute capabilities, explicitly accounting for the temporal overlap between ZeRO communication and computation. Driven by this model, ZIPPer utilizes a lightweight boundary adjustment algorithm to formulate pipeline partitioning as a minimax optimization. This ensures strict memory feasibility on limited devices while minimizing the overall execution bottleneck.

In summary, this paper makes the following contributions:

- We propose **ZIPPer**, a comprehensive co-designed framework that tightly couples micro-batch ZeRO-2 execution with heterogeneity-aware pipeline partitioning.

- We design a highly efficient execution engine within ZIPPer, featuring an in-place Reduce-Scatter mechanism and an asynchronous dual-stream overlap scheduler. This eliminates gradient redundancy and scales down the peak memory footprint by a factor of N_{dp} without sacrificing throughput.
- We develop a topology-aware joint cost model and a simulator-driven partitioning algorithm for ZIPPer, effectively balancing memory usage and computation loads across complex heterogeneous clusters.

2 Related Work

2.1 ZeRO

To mitigate memory bottlenecks in large model training, ZeRO [24] partitions optimizer states, gradients, and parameters across data-parallel workers. While ZeRO-Offload [27] and ZeRO-Infinity [25] further utilize host memory. Orthogonal optimizations include gradient checkpointing [4], sequence parallelism [14], FlashAttention [6], and activation balancing via BPIPE [13]. However, ZeRO is fundamentally designed for global data-parallel training. Its native communication patterns clash with the fine-grained micro-batch semantics of pipeline parallelism, causing severe memory pressure without a careful execution co-design.

2.2 Pipeline Parallelism

Pipeline parallelism improves scalability via layer partitioning and micro-batch execution. Foundational schedules like GPipe [11] and PipeDream [10,18] have been refined by DAPPLE [8], PipeDream-2BW [19], and interleaved 1F1B [20] to reduce pipeline bubbles and memory footprints. Recent approaches, including Zero Bubble [23], Chimera [15], and Hanayo [17], further enhance efficiency through advanced computation-communication overlap. Nevertheless, these methods predominantly assume homogeneous hardware. They overlook the integration of ZeRO memory sharding and fail to address the complex communication costs inherent in heterogeneous environments.

2.3 Heterogeneity-Aware Training

Addressing hardware disparity requires balancing memory, computation, and communication across heterogeneous clusters. Existing literature explores topology-aware cost modeling [9,16,32,33,35] or adapts specific parallelism dimensions (e.g., PP, DP, or ZeRO) for heterogeneous devices [22,34]. However, prior efforts typically optimize a single parallelism strategy in isolation or focus purely on compute load. Crucially, they lack a comprehensive framework that jointly co-designs pipeline scheduling, ZeRO-based micro-batch memory sharding, and asynchronous communication overlap under stringent heterogeneous bandwidth and capacity constraints.

2.4 Positioning of ZIPPer

Table 1 contrasts ZIPPer with representative systems along five dimensions central to memory-efficient hybrid-parallel training. Existing approaches either neglect memory sharding under pipeline parallelism (Megatron-LM), apply ZeRO or FSDP only at global-batch granularity (DeepSpeed, TorchTitan), or address heterogeneity without integrating ZeRO-style sharding into the pipeline schedule (HetPipe). ZIPPer's novelty lies not in any single component, but in unifying *micro-batch-level* ZeRO-2 sharding, asynchronous computation–communication overlap, and a heterogeneity-aware joint cost model into a single co-design.

Table 1. Qualitative comparison of ZIPPer with representative large-model training systems.

System	Pipeline parallel	Memory sharding (ZeRO/FSDP)	Hetero.-aware partitioning	Comm–comp verlap	MB-level sharding
Megatron-LM [20]	✓	–	–	Partial	–
DeepSpeed [26]	✓	ZeRO-1/2/3 (global)	–	–	–
TorchTitan (PP-FSDP)	✓	FSDP (global)	–	Partial	–
HetPipe [22]	✓	–	✓	–	–
ZIPPer (ours)	✓	ZeRO-2 (per micro-batch)	✓	✓	✓

3 Micro-Batch-Level ZeRO-2 Pipeline Training

3.1 Micro-Batch-Level ZeRO-2 Enhanced Pipeline Architecture

Existing training frameworks provide limited support for combining pipeline parallelism with ZeRO-2. Naively integrating ZeRO-2 into pipeline training often leads to inefficient gradient communication and additional memory overhead [1, 26]. To address this limitation, ZIPPer integrates ZeRO-2 into the 1F1B pipeline schedule at the micro-batch granularity.

Figure 1 compares PP-ZeRO-1 and our design. PP-ZeRO-1 delays gradient synchronization until all micro-batches complete, causing memory to grow linearly with N_{mb}. In contrast, our method performs a Reduce-Scatter after each micro-batch backward pass, immediately partitioning and releasing full gradients. As illustrated in Fig. 2, this design reduces the peak gradient memory from $O(M)$ to $O(M/N_{dp})$.

We adopt ZeRO-2 instead of ZeRO-3 to balance memory efficiency and throughput. While ZeRO-3 further shards parameters, it requires frequent All-Gather operations that compete with pipeline P2P communication, leading to pipeline stalls under micro-batch scheduling.

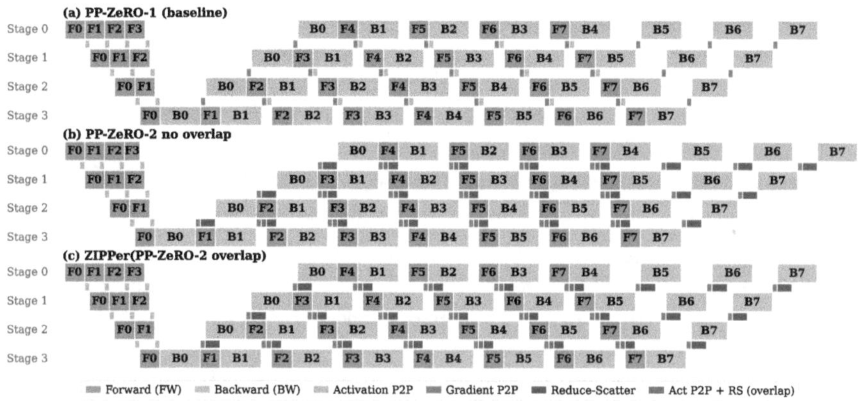

Fig. 1. Execution timelines of three pipeline training designs. (a) **PP+ZeRO-1**: delayed global gradient synchronization. (b) **PP+ZeRO-2 no overlap**: per-micro-batch Reduce-Scatter blocks compute. (c) **ZIPPer**: asynchronous Reduce-Scatter overlapped with the next forward pass.

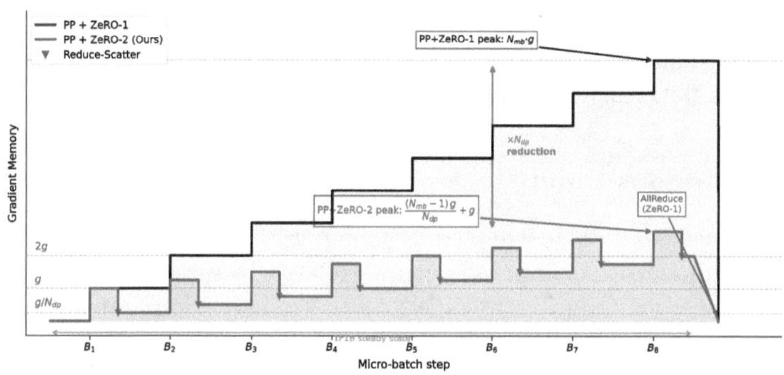

Fig. 2. Gradient memory usage over time across pipeline micro-batches under different ZeRO strategies.

3.2 In-Place Micro-Batch Communication

Conventional ZeRO-2 implementations rely on bucket-based communication, where gradients are first accumulated into buffers before being synchronized. While effective for standard data-parallel training, this design becomes inefficient under pipeline micro-batch execution.

First, bucket construction requires additional transient buffers. This inflates peak memory usage, especially when activations already dominate. Second, bucket communication operates at a coarse granularity. It struggles to align perfectly with pipeline execution, especially on heterogeneous GPUs, leading to substantial performance loss. Let M_{Bucket} denote the bucket size. The communication time can be approximated as

$$T_{comm} = N_{mb} \cdot L_p \cdot \frac{\|\mathbf{g}_l^{(m)}\|}{M_{Bucket}} \left(\alpha + \frac{M_{Bucket}}{B} \right), \tag{1}$$

where N_{mb} is the number of micro-batches, L_p is the number of layers assigned to a pipeline stage, and $\mathbf{g}_l^{(m)}$ denotes the gradient tensor of layer l for micro-batch m. The term $\|\mathbf{g}_l^{(m)}\|$ represents its size in bytes. M_{Bucket} is the bucket size used for gradient aggregation, while α and B denote communication latency and effective bandwidth, respectively. Small buckets incur large startup overhead due to frequent communication launches, while large ones delay communication and lead to excessive gradient accumulation, severely exacerbating memory pressure.

To address these issues, we propose a fine-grained in-place reduction mechanism. Instead of copying gradients into communication bucket, Reduce-Scatter is performed directly on the gradient tensors produced by each micro-batch

$$\mathbf{s}^{(m)} \leftarrow \Psi_{\text{reduce-scatter}}(\mathbf{g}^{(m)}). \tag{2}$$

This design eliminates buffer duplication and bounds communication memory overhead while naturally aligning communication with micro-batch execution.

3.3 Asynchronous Computation–Communication Overlap

Micro-batch-level Reduce-Scatter reduces memory footprint but introduces fragmented communication. Compared with ZeRO-1, which performs a single global synchronization, our design triggers N_{mb} fine-grained communications, leading to frequent kernel launches and communication overheads that interrupt the compute stream and create pipeline bubbles.

To eliminate these bubbles, we adopt a dual-stream execution scheme. Once the backward computation of micro-batch i (BW_i) completes, its communication Comm_i is immediately dispatched to a dedicated communication stream. At the same time the compute stream proceeds with the forward pass of the next micro-batch j (FW_j). This creates a natural overlap:

$$\text{BW}_i \rightarrow \begin{cases} \text{Comm}_i \text{ (comm stream)} \\ \text{FW}_j \text{ (compute stream)} \end{cases}$$

Empirical profiling on mainstream Transformer models shows that forward computation typically dominates communication cost, so communication can often be hidden behind computation and removed from the critical path. This asynchronous design eliminates blocking synchronization and reduces communication-induced pipeline bubbles.

4 Heterogeneity-Aware Pipeline Partitioning

Memory consumption in pipeline-parallel Transformer training is inherently imbalanced, as early stages must buffer activations for multiple in-flight micro-batches. This front-heavy memory footprint frequently causes out-of-memory (OOM) failures. Heterogeneous clusters exacerbate this phenomenon, as varying memory capacities and compute capabilities make uniform partitioning severely suboptimal—risking OOMs on memory-limited devices while wasting high-performance compute. To address this, we propose a heterogeneity-aware pipeline partitioning method. It strictly prioritizes memory feasibility to prevent OOMs, while strategically distributing workloads to fully exploit heterogeneous compute power. The method consists of three components: A **Lightweight Memory Simulator** that efficiently estimates per-stage peak memory under different partitions; A **Topology-Aware Joint Cost Model** that captures memory, computation, and communication costs under heterogeneous hardware; An **Iterative Boundary Shifting Algorithm** that searches for a balanced partition guided by bottleneck analysis.

4.1 Lightweight Memory Simulation

Evaluating the memory usage of different pipeline partitions through real training runs is expensive. This makes iterative partition search impractical. To address this issue, we employ a lightweight memory simulator based on PyTorch's *FakeTensor* [1] mechanism. Instead of executing real GPU computations, the simulator performs a virtual training pass that tracks tensor lifetimes and memory allocation events during forward and backward propagation.

By replaying the operator execution trace and recording allocation and release events along the timeline, the simulator estimates the peak memory usage of each pipeline stage. Specifically, this peak memory footprint is obtained by tracking the lifecycles of all tensors and calculating the maximum sum of the sizes of concurrently active tensors at any point during execution. Since the simulation avoids real tensor allocation and GPU execution, the memory profiling process completes within seconds, enabling efficient exploration of pipeline partition strategies.

4.2 Topology-Aware Joint Cost Model

Memory-only partitioning is insufficient in heterogeneous clusters with diverse compute and interconnect characteristics. To capture both communication heterogeneity and computation–communication overlap in micro-batch ZeRO-2, we develop a topology-aware joint cost model for per-stage execution.

P2P Communication. For adjacent stages k and $k+1$, we model point-to-point communication using the α-β model to account for heterogeneous latency and bandwidth:

$$T^{\mathrm{p2p}}_{k\to k+1} = \alpha^{\mathrm{p2p}}(k, k+1) + \frac{V}{B^{\mathrm{p2p}}(k, k+1)} \tag{3}$$

where α^{p2p} and B^{p2p} denote the startup latency and bandwidth, respectively. The payload volume V represents either the activations or the corresponding activation gradients. The total P2P cost $T^{\text{p2p}}(k)$ aggregates transfers with neighboring stages.

ZeRO-2 Communication with Overlap. Each micro-batch triggers a Reduce-Scatter:

$$T^{\text{rs}}(k) = \alpha^{\text{dp}}(k) + \frac{N_{dp} - 1}{N_{dp}} \cdot \frac{G_k}{B^{\text{dp}}(k)}, \tag{4}$$

where N_{dp} is the data parallel degree, G_k is the per micro-batch gradient size of stage k, and $\alpha^{\text{dp}}(k)$ and $B^{\text{dp}}(k)$ denote the latency and bandwidth of the data-parallel communication group associated with stage k. Since communication overlaps with forward computation, only the non-overlapped portion extends the total execution time:

$$T^{\text{exposed}}(k) = \max\left(0, T^{\text{rs}}(k) - T^{\text{fwd}}(k)\right). \tag{5}$$

Stage Cost. We first define the per-micro-batch execution cost:

$$T^{\text{unit}}(k) = T^{\text{fwd}}(k) + T^{\text{bwd}}(k) + T^{\text{p2p}}(k) + T^{\text{exposed}}(k) \tag{6}$$

The total stage time under pipeline execution is then approximated as

$$\tilde{T}(k) = N_{mb} \cdot T^{\text{unit}}(k) + T^{\text{stall}}(k), \tag{7}$$

where $T^{\text{stall}}(k)$ captures idle time caused by pipeline imbalance and scheduling dependencies. Pipeline throughput is determined by $\max_k \tilde{T}(k)$.

In practice, $T^{\text{fwd}}(k)$ and $T^{\text{bwd}}(k)$ are obtained via lightweight profiling, where representative operators are benchmarked and scaled according to the number of layers assigned to each stage.

Joint Cost Model. In the heterogeneous clusters, the pipeline throughput is determined by the slowest stage, while each stage must also satisfy device memory constraints. We formulate layer partitioning as a constrained minimax problem. Let $\tilde{T}(k)$ denote the per-iteration exposed time of stage k. The objective minimizes the critical-path latency with a hard memory feasibility constraint:

$$\min_{\mathcal{B}} \max_{k} \mathcal{S}(k), \tag{8}$$

$$\mathcal{S}(k) = \begin{cases} \tilde{T}(k), & \text{if } M_{\text{peak}}(k) \leq C_k, \\ +\infty, & \text{otherwise}, \end{cases} \tag{9}$$

where C_k is the memory capacity of the device hosting stage k. Any partition violating memory constraints is deemed infeasible. Among all feasible partitions, the optimizer selects the one that minimizes the maximum stage time, i.e., the pipeline bottleneck.

In practice, we implement the feasibility check as a large penalty to enable gradient-free search:

$$\mathcal{S}(k) = \tilde{T}(k) + \Lambda \cdot \mathbf{1}[M_{\text{peak}}(k) > C_k], \tag{10}$$

where $\Lambda \gg \max_k \tilde{T}(k)$ is a sufficiently large constant (we use $\Lambda = 10^6$ in all experiments). This equation guarantees that any memory-feasible partition is preferred over any infeasible one, while among feasible partitions the bottleneck stage time is minimized.

Algorithm 1 Heterogeneity-Aware Joint-Score Boundary Shifting

Input: Total layers L_{total}, stages N, device capacities $\mathcal{K}$, topology bandwidth $\mathcal{W}$, simulator $\Psi(\cdot)$, weights w_1, w_2
Output: Partition boundaries $\mathcal{B}$

Initialize $\mathcal{B}$ with uniform partition
$\mathcal{M} \leftarrow \Psi(\mathcal{B})$ {peak memory per stage}
$\mathcal{T}[k] \leftarrow \tilde{T}(k;\, \mathcal{B},\, \mathcal{W})$ for each k
$\mathcal{S}(k) = \tilde{T}(k) + \Lambda \cdot \mathbf{1}[M_{\text{peak}}(k) > C_k]$
while true **do**
    $k_{src} \leftarrow \arg\max_k\ \mathcal{S}[k]$
    $k_{dst} \leftarrow \arg\min_k\ \mathcal{S}[k]$
    Propose $\mathcal{B}'$ by shifting one layer from k_{src} toward k_{dst}
    $\mathcal{M}' \leftarrow \Psi(\mathcal{B}')$
    $\mathcal{T}'[k] \leftarrow \tilde{T}(k;\, \mathcal{B}',\, \mathcal{W})$
    $\mathcal{S}'[k] \leftarrow \tilde{T}(k) + \Lambda \cdot \mathbf{1}[M_{\text{peak}}(k) > C_k]$
    if $\max_k\ \mathcal{S}'[k] < \max_k\ \mathcal{S}[k]$ **then**
        $\mathcal{B} \leftarrow \mathcal{B}',\ \mathcal{M} \leftarrow \mathcal{M}',\ \mathcal{T} \leftarrow \mathcal{T}',\ \mathcal{S} \leftarrow \mathcal{S}'$
    else
        break
    end if
end while
return $\mathcal{B}$

4.3 Heterogeneity-Aware Iterative Boundary Shifting

Pipeline partitioning is a discrete optimization problem under contiguity constraints. Given L_{total} layers and N stages, the partition is defined by boundaries $\mathcal{B} = \{b_1, \ldots, b_{N-1}\}$, which split the model into contiguous segments $S_k = [b_k, b_{k+1})$. For a given partition, the simulator $\Psi(\cdot)$ estimates memory $M_{\text{peak}}(k)$ and the cost model computes $\tilde{T}(k)$, yielding the joint score $\mathcal{S}(k)$ in Eq. (8).

At each iteration, we identify the bottleneck stage $k_{src} = \arg\max_k \mathcal{S}(k)$ and the least loaded stage $k_{dst} = \arg\min_k \mathcal{S}(k)$, and shift one layer from k_{src} toward k_{dst} to form a candidate partition $\mathcal{B}'$. The update is accepted only if it strictly reduces the global peak score $\max_k \mathcal{S}'(k) < \max_k \mathcal{S}(k)$. The process terminates when no further improvement is possible.

Our greedy partitioner is not guaranteed to find the global optimum. However, the contiguity and memory-feasibility constraints prune most infeasible partitions, so the local optimum is sufficient in practice. Stronger global search methods are left as future work.

5 Experiments

5.1 Experimental Setup

Hardware. All of these experiments are conducted on a two-node heterogeneous GPU cluster. One node contains 8 NVIDIA H100 GPUs (80 GB), while the other contains 8 NVIDIA RTX A6000 GPUs (48 GB). These two nodes are connected via InfiniBand.

Models. We evaluate **ZIPPer** on representative Transformer-based large language models, including GPT-3 and LLaMA [21,30] architectures. The detailed model configurations are summarized in Table 2.

Table 2. Model configurations used in experiments.

Model	Params	Layers	Hidden	Heads	FFN
GPT-3	2.7B	32	2560	32	10240
GPT-3	6.7B	32	4096	32	16384
LLaMA	2.7B	32	2560	32	6912
LLaMA	7B	32	4096	32	11008

We compare the proposed **ZIPPer** framework against two baselines: (a) **DeepSpeed (PP-ZeRO-1)**: employs pipeline parallelism combined with ZeRO-1 optimizer state partitioning. (b) **TorchTitan (PP-FSDP)**: integrates pipeline parallelism with Fully Sharded Data Parallel (FSDP) to shard gradients and optimizer states. To thoroughly evaluate our co-design, we test three variants of **ZIPPer**: (c) **ZIPPer (Memory-Only)**: minimizes absolute peak memory, where the score is defined as $\mathcal{S}(k) = M_{\text{peak}}(k)$. (d) **ZIPPer (Memory-Balanced)**: minimizes peak memory utilization, using $\mathcal{S}(k) = M_{\text{peak}}(k)/C_k$. (e) **ZIPPer (Throughput-Balanced)**: optimizes throughput under memory constraints, using Eq. (10). For both baselines, we use their default partitioning and communication configurations.

5.2 Throughput Comparison

Our method consistently achieves higher training throughput across all configurations and model architectures. As shown in Fig. 3, the ZIPPer(Throughput-Balanced) delivers the best performance in all settings, significantly outperforming both the DeepSpeed (PP-ZeRO-1) and TorchTitan (PP-FSDP) baselines.

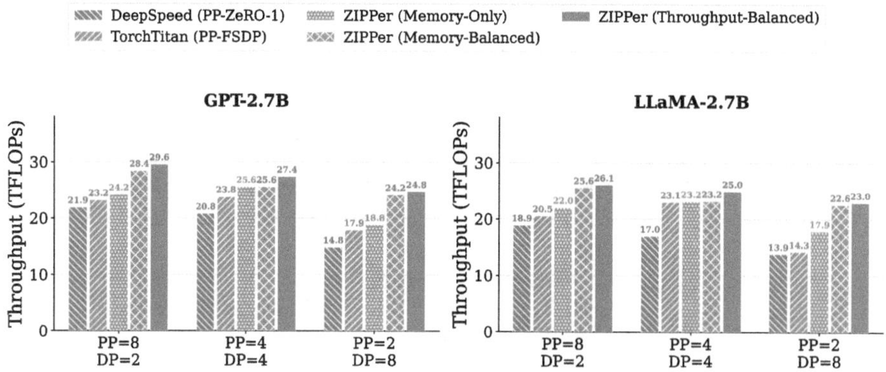

Fig. 3. Training throughput (TFLOPs) of GPT-2.7B under different parallel configurations.

To be more specific, on the GPT-2.7B model, ZIPPer improves throughput over DeepSpeed by 34.9% (PP = 8), 31.8% (PP = 4), and 66.8% (PP = 2). Compared to the highly optimized TorchTitan baseline, ZIPPer still achieves substantial gains of 27.4%, 15.2%, and 38.4% in the respective configurations. Similar trends are observed on the LLaMA architectures.

These improvements stem from two core mechanisms. First, ZIPPer's asynchronous computation–communication overlap substantially hides communication overhead. Second, its topology-aware cost model overcomes the critical-path bottlenecks of uniform partitioning by optimally mapping compute and communication workloads to the underlying heterogeneous hardware.

Notably, ZIPPer yields the most profound throughput gains at smaller pipeline depths (e.g., PP = 2/DP = 8) because assigning more layers per stage provides finer load-balancing granularity. Furthermore, the larger data-parallel group at PP = 2 generates massive ZeRO communication volumes, which maximizes the performance gap between ZIPPer's asynchronous overlap mechanism and naive synchronous baselines.

5.3 Memory Efficiency

Figure 4 illustrates the peak memory allocation and utilization. DeepSpeed (PP-ZeRO-1) exhibits high memory usage (39.2–42.9 GB across both models) with utilization reaching up to 96.5%. While TorchTitan (PP-FSDP) slightly mitigates the absolute footprint (36.0–41.0 GB), its utilization still remains critically high at 82.0–90.6%.

In contrast, the **ZIPPer** (Memory-Only) strategy slashes peak memory by up to 46.0% (GPT-3 2.7B) and 46.5% (LLaMA 2.7B) compared to DeepSpeed, lowering the maximum utilization to a much safer 42.9–76.5% range. Furthermore, the Memory-Balanced and Throughput-Balanced variants strategically trade a marginal amount of memory for substantial throughput gains. They maintain an exceptionally safe utilization margin (38.9–56.8%).

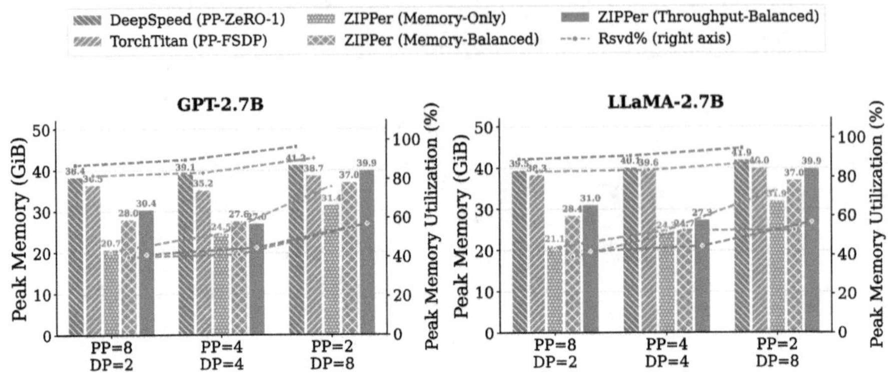

Fig. 4. Peak GPU memory usage and utilization of GPT-2.7B across parallel configurations.

5.4 Compatibility with Tensor Parallelism

To evaluate architectural generality, we extend **ZIPPer** to 3D parallelism by integrating Tensor Parallelism (TP). Because ZIPPer operates strictly at the pipeline and data-parallel levels, it is orthogonal to intra-layer TP partitioning and can be seamlessly applied (Figs. 5 and 6).

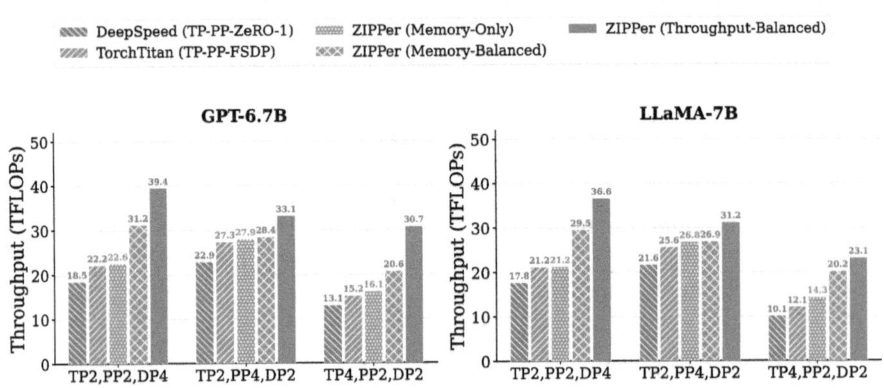

Fig. 5. Training throughput of GPT-6.7B and LLaMA-7B under 3D parallelism.

Across various TP-enabled configurations, ZIPPer consistently outperforms both baselines. On LLaMA-7B, the Throughput-Balanced variant delivers up to 2.29× and 1.91× the training throughput of DeepSpeed and TorchTitan, respectively. Simultaneously, the Memory-Only variant reduces peak memory allocation by up to 26.5% compared to DeepSpeed, successfully lowering the memory utilization from 67.2–73.6% down to a safe 38.8–64.0% range.

These robust improvements mirror the trends observed on GPT-6.7B, where ZIPPer achieves up to 2.35× throughput speedups and up to 21.9% memory

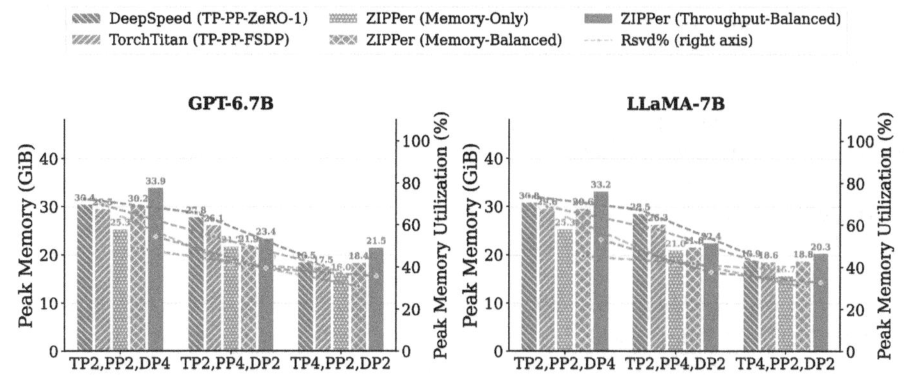

Fig. 6. Peak GPU memory usage and utilization of GPT-6.7B and LLaMA-7B under 3D parallelism

reduction. These results clearly demonstrate that our co-design principles remain highly effective and extensible under complex 3D parallel environments.

5.5 Training Capacity Analysis

We evaluate the maximum trainable sequence length before out-of-memory (OOM) occurs under fixed hardware constraints. As shown in Table 3, **ZIPPer** consistently supports significantly longer contexts than both DeepSpeed and TorchTitan. By reducing peak memory and balancing distributions, ZIPPer achieves up to a 1.9× (vs. DeepSpeed) and 1.8× (vs. TorchTitan) context length extension, substantially improving the effective training capacity on the same hardware.

Table 3. Maximum supported sequence length before OOM.

Config	GPT-6.7B				LLaMA-7B			
	DS	TT	ZIPPer	Gain	DS	TT	ZIPPer	Gain
PP4/DP4	2048	2176	3584	1.8×/1.6×	2048	2176	3712	1.8×/1.7×
PP8/DP2	2176	2304	4096	1.9×/1.8×	2304	2304	4096	1.8×/1.8×
PP2/DP8	2048	2048	3072	1.5×/1.5×	2048	2048	3072	1.5×/1.5×

Note: DS = DeepSpeed (PP-ZeRO-1), TT = TorchTitan (PP-FSDP). Gain is shown as (vs. DS)/(vs. TT).

6 Conclusion

In this paper, we present **ZIPPer**, a co-designed framework that integrates micro-batch ZeRO-2 with heterogeneity-aware pipeline partitioning. With in-place Reduce-Scatter and an asynchronous dual-stream scheduler, ZIPPer eliminates gradient redundancy and largely hides communication overhead. Guided by a topology-aware joint cost model, our partitioning algorithm balances memory and compute loads across heterogeneous GPUs. Evaluations on GPT and LLaMA models demonstrate that ZIPPer improves training throughput by up to 66.8% and reduces peak memory by up to 46% under different configurations compared to existing baselines.

Acknowledgments. This work was supported by the Natural Science Foundation of Hubei Province, China (Grant No. 2026AFB445).

Statement on AI Usage. The technical solution and experimental design presented in this paper were independently completed by the authors. AI tools were used solely for language polishing and formatting optimization, and did not participate in the development of the research ideas or core content.

References

1. Ansel, J., et al.: Pytorch 2: faster machine learning through dynamic python bytecode transformation and graph compilation. In: Proceedings of the 29th ACM International Conference on Architectural Support for Programming Languages and Operating Systems, vol. 2, pp. 929–947 (2024)
2. Bai, J., et al.: Qwen technical report. arXiv:2309.16609 (2023)
3. Brown, T.B., et al.: Language models are few-shot learners. In: Advances in Neural Information Processing Systems (NeurIPS) (2020)
4. Chen, T., Xu, B., Zhang, C., Guestrin, C.: Training deep nets with sublinear memory cost. arXiv:1604.06174 (2016)
5. Chowdhery, A., et al.: PaLM: scaling language modeling with pathways. J. Mach. Learn. Res. **24**(240), 1–113 (2023)
6. Dao, T., Fu, D.Y., Ermon, S., Rudra, A., Ré, C.: FlashAttention: fast and memory-efficient exact attention with IO-awareness. In: Advances in Neural Information Processing Systems (NeurIPS) (2022)
7. DeepSeek-AI: DeepSeek-R1: Incentivizing reasoning capability in LLMs via reinforcement learning. arXiv:2501.12948 (2025)
8. Fan, S., et al.: DAPPLE: a pipelined data parallel approach for training large models. In: PPoPP (2021)
9. Guo, J., et al.: Adaptis: reducing pipeline bubbles with adaptive pipeline parallelism on heterogeneous models (2025). https://arxiv.org/abs/2509.23722
10. Harlap, A., et al.: PipeDream: fast and efficient pipeline parallel DNN training. arXiv:1806.03377 (2018)
11. Huang, Y., et al.: GPipe: efficient training of giant neural networks using pipeline parallelism. In: NeurIPS (2019)
12. Jiang, A.Q., et al.: Mistral 7B. arXiv:2310.06825 (2023)
13. Kim, T., Kim, H., Yu, G.I., Chun, B.G.: BPIPE: memory-balanced pipeline parallelism for training large language models. In: International Conference on Machine Learning (ICML) (2023)
14. Korthikanti, V.A., et al.: Reducing activation recomputation in large transformer models. In: Proceedings of Machine Learning and Systems (MLSys) (2023)
15. Li, S., Hoefler, T.: Chimera: efficiently training large-scale neural networks with bidirectional pipelines. In: SC (2021)

16. Liang, P., Qiao, L., Lai, Z., Li, D.: Parallelsim: an accurate, generic, and efficient simulator for distributed deep learning. CCF Trans. High Perform. Comput. **8** (2026). https://doi.org/10.1007/s42514-025-00271-w
17. Liu, Z., Cheng, S., Zhou, H., You, Y.: Hanayo: harnessing wave-like pipeline parallelism for enhanced large model training efficiency. In: SC (2023)
18. Narayanan, D., et al.: PipeDream: generalized pipeline parallelism for DNN training. In: SOSP (2019)
19. Narayanan, D., Phanishayee, A., Shi, K., Chen, X., Zaharia, M.: Memory-efficient pipeline-parallel DNN training. In: ICML (2021)
20. Narayanan, D., et al.: Efficient large-scale language model training on GPU clusters using Megatron-LM. In: SC (2021)
21. OpenAI: GPT-4 technical report. Technical report, OpenAI (2023). https://arxiv.org/abs/2303.08774
22. Park, J.H., et al.: HetPipe: enabling large DNN training on (whimpy) heterogeneous GPU clusters through integration of pipelined model parallelism and data parallelism. In: USENIX ATC (2020)
23. Qi, P., Wan, X., Huang, G., Lin, M.: Zero bubble pipeline parallelism. In: ICLR (2024)
24. Rajbhandari, S., Rasley, J., Ruwase, O., He, Y.: ZeRO: memory optimizations toward training trillion parameter models. In: SC (2020)
25. Rajbhandari, S., Ruwase, O., Rasley, J., Smith, S., He, Y.: ZeRO-infinity: breaking the GPU memory wall for extreme scale deep learning. In: SC (2021)
26. Rasley, J., Rajbhandari, S., Ruwase, O., He, Y.: DeepSpeed: system optimizations enable training deep learning models with over 100 billion parameters. In: KDD (2020)
27. Ren, J., et al.: ZeRO-offload: democratizing billion-scale model training. In: USENIX ATC (2021)
28. Shoeybi, M., Patwary, M., Puri, R., LeGresley, P., Casper, J., Catanzaro, B.: Megatron-LM: training multi-billion parameter language models using model parallelism. arXiv:1909.08053 (2019)
29. Tang, Y., et al.: Koala: efficient pipeline training through automated schedule searching on domain-specific language. ACM Trans. Archit. Code Optim. **22**(2) (2025). https://doi.org/10.1145/3722113
30. Touvron, H., et al.: LLaMA: open and efficient foundation language models. arXiv:2302.13971 (2023)
31. Touvron, H., et al.: Llama 2: open foundation and fine-tuned chat models. arXiv:2307.09288 (2023)
32. Um, T., et al.: Metis: fast automatic distributed training on heterogeneous GPUs. In: USENIX ATC, pp. 563–578 (2024)
33. Zhang, S., Diao, L., Wu, C., Cao, Z., Wang, S., Lin, W.: HAP: SPMD DNN training on heterogeneous GPU clusters with automated program synthesis. In: EuroSys (2024)
34. Zhang, W., Hu, Y., Shi, J., Bai, X.: Poplar: efficient scaling of distributed DNN training on heterogeneous GPU clusters. In: Proceedings of the AAAI Conference on Artificial Intelligence, vol. 39, no. 21, pp. 22587–22595 (2025). https://doi.org/10.1609/aaai.v39i21.34417
35. Zheng, L., et al.: Alpa: automating inter- and intra-operator parallelism for distributed deep learning. In: 16th USENIX Symposium on Operating Systems Design and Implementation (OSDI) (2022)

obliv-clang: Real-World Oblivious Programming in C++

Yunqian Luo[1] and Mingyu Gao[1,2](✉)

[1] Tsinghua University, Beijing, China
luoyq23@mails.tsinghua.edu.cn, gaomy@tsinghua.edu.cn
[2] Shanghai Qi Zhi Institute, Shanghai, China

Abstract. Side-channel vulnerabilities, particularly timing and access-pattern-based attacks, have become critical issues for confidential data processing in trusted environments. Oblivious programming is an effective approach to alleviate these attacks by making program execution not leak any secret through execution time and data access traces. To facilitate oblivious programming in practice, we propose a compilation-time checking tool, obliv-clang, which can comprehensively check the obliviousness of a program written in C++. It is designed to support the rich language features in C++, including the complicated concept of arbitrarily nested pointers, in order to seamlessly work with existing industry-level codebases and produce high-performance compiled binaries with minimum compilation overheads. We design a set of rules in obliv-clang and formally prove their soundness in the presence of complicated C++ language features. We also implement several non-trivial oblivious algorithms as case studies to demonstrate the expressiveness of obliv-clang, and show that programs compiled using obliv-clang can outperform previous solutions.

Keywords: Compiler · Trusted Execution Environment · Oblivious Programming

1 Introduction

Confidential data processing in trusted environments, such as trusted execution environments (TEEs), remains vulnerable to various side-channel attacks exploiting shared caches [10], OS-controlled page tables [4,22], branch predictors [12], and speculative execution [31]. These attacks succeed because certain sensitive execution properties leak through timing observation and shared hardware units, even when data are architecturally isolated. The major defenses to these side-channel attacks can be categorized into hardware changes and software techniques. They complement each other—timing and I/O pattern issues are best avoided by software, while speculation-based vulnerabilities require hardware fixes. This work focuses on the software solutions, among which the most prominent approach is *oblivious programming*: making execution traces (timing, I/O patterns) independent of secrets.

L. Eeckhout et al. (Eds.): APPT 2026, LNCS 16693, pp. 18–33, 2027.
https://doi.org/10.1007/978-981-92-4805-6_2

Existing methods for oblivious programming each have drawbacks. Domain-specific languages (DSLs) [5,15,33] require costly toolchain integration, especially in industrial environments with complicated software projects. Separate modeling tools [25,34] face consistency issues between models and implementations. Compiler transformations [19,24] lack high-level application semantics and can only be done conservatively, resulting in performance degradation.

In this work[1], we present obliv-clang, a compiler plugin for the widely used, industry-class C++ language, which checks the obliviousness of a program statically at the compilation time. It is implemented using the popular clang and LLVM infrastructure. As the key principle, obliv-clang is designed to work directly with C++ and support its rich language features, including pointers and references, function calls, compound types, object-oriented programming, templates, and more. Therefore, it can seamlessly work with existing codebases with minimum porting effort, eliminating the extra burden of using a new domain-specific language in previous work. In addition, obliv-clang is implemented directly in the compiler, so it avoids the consistency issue between separate modeling and implementation. Finally, using a familiar, mature, and industry-class language like C++ allows developers to conveniently write their code, and also able to retain high performance for the developed oblivious programs.

The key challenge of designing a compilation-time checker like obliv-clang is its soundness, meaning that the check must be comprehensive so that if a program passes, it should be considered safe to execute. The major difficulty is to handle the arbitrarily nested pointers (like "a pointer to a pointer to a pointer") in C++, which can be dereferenced, taken-address, and assigned in many ways. In particular, we find that assigning a secret pointer with a public pointer value, which seems benign, could sometimes be unsafe and leak sensitive data (see Example 2 in Sect. 3.2). To address this problem, obliv-clang formally introduces the concept of oblivious levels (`olevels`), together with a set of rules to deduce each variable's `olevel` along the program dataflow and to forbid unsafe operations accordingly. These rules are extended beyond simple operations to support also function calls, compound types, and templates. In such a way, obliv-clang is able to provide verifiable security with formal proofs.

Since obliv-clang is a front-end checker, we also need to ensure that the backend compiler optimization passes do not break the obliviousness property. We thoroughly analyze the relevant optimization passes in LLVM and suppress the ones that may compromise obliviousness. Furthermore, we apply an extra double-check on the generated assembly code using existing tools [8], which ensure end-to-end obliviousness.

We have implemented several non-trivial oblivious algorithms, including PathORAM [28] and Oblivious BFS [3], using our obliv-clang tool, in order to demonstrate its good expressiveness. We also quantitatively evaluate obliv-clang, showing that the extra obliviousness check incurs minor overheads (less than 18%) to the compilation time, and it produces relatively high-performance

[1] An extended version of this paper is available at [16].

compiled binaries. When compared to previous tools, the programs compiled with obliv-clang run 27.8% faster than Jasmin [1] and 66.9% faster than FaCT [5] on average. The implementation of obliv-clang has been open sourced at github.com/tsinghua-ideal/obliv-clang.

Our contributions in this paper are summarized below:

- The design and implementation of a program obliviousness check tool, obliv-clang, as a compiler plugin working seamlessly with the C++ language.
- A set of obliviousness check rules that support the rich set of C++ language features, including arbitrarily nested pointers, function calls, compound types, templates, etc.
- A formal proof about the soundness of our obliviousness check rules.
- The case studies and evaluation experiments to demonstrate the expressiveness and performance advantages of obliv-clang.

2 Background and Motivation

2.1 Oblivious Programming

Program obliviousness prevents attackers from learning sensitive information through execution traces (timing, memory, and I/O patterns). Attackers extract traces either directly (through privileged access) or indirectly via shared hardware [4,10,22]. Oblivious programming requires branch conditions, memory, and I/O patterns to remain independent of sensitive data. Common techniques include redundant branch execution, oblivious memory scanning, and cmove-like instructions. Researchers have developed efficient algorithms including ORAM [28], oblivious BFS [3], and oblivious data structures [32].

Oblivious programming is tricky and subtle—developers can easily break obliviousness through overlooked details. Thus, automatic tools are essential to facilitate correct oblivious programming.

2.2 Tradeoffs and Limitations of Existing Tools

Previous work can be classified along two dimensions: (1) whether behaviors are modified, i.e., check-only [1,20,25] vs. transforming [5,14,15,19,23,24]; and (2) at which level to perform analysis, e.g., the frontend abstract syntax tree (AST) [5,14,24,25] vs. the backend intermediate representation (IR) [19,23]. Automatic transformations could introduce performance overheads due to conservative handling. Frontend approaches offer better analysis but backend optimizers may undermine their security. Additionally, many designs rely on DSLs, which require costly toolchain development and lack standard features.

2.3 Our Approach

We build upon C++ and the `clang` compiler, verifying obliviousness directly on source code at compilation time. C++ is widely used in industry. It offers well-defined semantics in its specification [29], a minimal runtime with close hardware control, and compatibility with numerous software interfaces and libraries. The `clang` compiler offers a friendly, extensible plugin interface used by many tools [6, 7], enabling non-intrusive checker implementation. The `clang` frontend processes C++ and C code in a unified AST format, allowing obliv-clang to handle C code seamlessly—important since many system and cryptographic libraries are written in C. While our tool is a checker, we also implement backend mechanisms to guarantee obliviousness during code generation (Sect. 5).

Challenges. Working directly with C++ presents challenges due to its rich semantics. First, expressing secrecy for arbitrarily nested pointers requires a precise scheme. Second, function calls across translation units need obliviousness-aware interfaces. Third, object-oriented features require handling relationships between class instances, members, and methods. Fourth, templates may instantiate with both sensitive and non-sensitive data. Finally, external libraries require annotations invisible to the compiler. Our design in Sect. 3 addresses these.

2.4 Security Model

Our security model focuses on timing and access-pattern-related attacks in two scenarios:

1. The victim program executes in a TEE enclave, where adversaries with hardware access can perform access-pattern-based attacks, including timing, cache [10], and page-table [4,22] attacks.
2. The victim program executes on normal hardware, where adversaries without hardware access can interact with the program and observe timing.

Side-channel attacks based on power [13], electromagnetism [21], speculative execution [31], rowhammer [11], and similar vectors are beyond our scope.

To ensure security under these assumptions, programs must satisfy the following properties in Theorems 1 and 2. Formal definitions of object secrecy will be provided in Sect. 3.

Theorem 1 (Secrecy). *For a program P with no undefined behaviors, and any external input x, let $v_{pub}(x)$ be the set of values of its public objects during execution, $\mathsf{Trace}(P, x)$ be the execution trace. There exists a probabilistic polynomial time (p.p.t.) simulator Simu such that no p.p.t. adversary $\mathcal{A}$ can distinguish $\mathsf{Trace}(P, x)$ and $\mathsf{Simu}(v_{pub}(x))$. Formally:*

$$\forall x, \left| \Pr[\mathcal{A}(v_{pub}(x), \mathsf{Trace}(P, x))] - \Pr[\mathcal{A}(v_{pub}(x), \mathsf{Simu}(v_{pub}))] \right| < \epsilon(n), \tag{1}$$

where n is a security parameter, and ϵ is a negligible function.

Theorem 2 (Dataflow (informal)). *There is no data flow from secret objects to public objects.*

3 Design

We designed obliv-clang, a C++ compiler plugin for clang that verifies program obliviousness directly on source code at compilation time. As a checker, obliv-clang's primary goal is *soundness*: programs passing its checks should be considered safe. This section details obliv-clang's semantics, including the required programmer annotations to indicate protected data and the comprehensive rules enforced to ensure obliviousness. We focus on addressing challenges of supporting flexible C++ semantics—pointers, references, function calls, and compound types—while maintaining compatibility with external libraries. The formal soundness proof is provided in the extended version of this paper [16].

3.1 Getting Started: Oblivious Variables

The basic information required by obliv-clang is the knowledge of which variables should be treated as secret. Since a compiler cannot inherently determine which objects are sensitive, we require programmer annotations in the source code to provide this information. We believe such annotations only add moderate burden to programmers, as programmers typically well understand the purposes and secrecy requirements of their variables.

Beginning with a minimal language subset (no references, no nested pointers, only plain values), an object's secrecy can be described by a boolean flag. obliv-clang requires secret variables to be annotated with the custom `obliv` attribute. C++ specifications allow compilers to define custom attributes as language extensions [29, Chapter 9.12], which can be applied to declarations, statements, translation units, and other elements. Furthermore, with the `clang` toolchain, parsing attributes can be easily done using plugins, without intrusive changes to the compiler's internal core logic (Sect. 4).

To satisfy the Secrecy and Dataflow properties from Sect. 2.4, the following rules are required:

Rule 1 (Basic Arithmetic). Any expression depending on an oblivious object is also oblivious. Note that we only consider value dependencies; comma expressions, compilation-time constant expressions (e.g., `sizeof`, `alignof`), and take-address operations are not considered dependencies.

Rule 2 (Basic Casting). It is forbidden to cast an oblivious expression to a non-oblivious expression.

Rule 3 (Basic Dereference). It is forbidden to dereference an oblivious pointer. Similarly, it is forbidden to take an oblivious object as the base address or index in an array subscript expression.

Rule 4 (Allocation). It is forbidden to create an object whose size is oblivious (e.g., `new[]` with oblivious length).

Rule 5 (Condition). The condition in any conditional clause (`if`, `while`, `for`, `switch`, ternary expressions, short-circuit boolean expressions) must not be an oblivious expression.

Note that "cast" in Rule 2 refers to both explicit and implicit casting. In assignments, the right side is first cast into the target type before assignment to the left side, so this can also be considered as an assignment rule.

The following code snippet demonstrates these rules:

Example 1.

```
#define OBLIV [[obliv]]  // to make it look less cumbersome

// declare an oblivious variable
OBLIV int x = 1729;
// error: cannot assign oblivious value to public variable
int y = x + 3;
// ok
OBLIV int z = x * 10;
// error: cannot take oblivious value as control-flow condition
if (x > 0) x = x - 1;
// error: cannot take oblivious value as array subscript
int *arr = new int[16]; int w = arr[x % 16];
```

3.2 Obliviousness Levels

For a pointer, obliviousness has dual meanings: the pointer's own value (which memory address it points to) and its dereferenced value (content at that address). With arbitrarily nested pointers in C++, this becomes increasingly complex.

We propose the concept of *obliviousness level* (`olevel`) to describe multi-level obliviousness. An expression's `olevel` is a binary string where the i-th digit (counting from the right, starting from 0) represents the obliviousness after dereferencing it i times. An expression whose `olevel` ends with 1 is considered oblivious. In our discussion, an expression is less/more oblivious if its last `olevel` digit is less/more than another's; an expression has no greater/smaller `olevel` if every digit of its `olevel` is no greater/smaller than the corresponding digit of another; "greater/smaller" is defined as the contrary of "no greater/smaller."

Dataflow occurs with assignment expressions. To satisfy the dataflow property, we should not allow assigning an expression with another of a greater `olevel`. However, assignments with smaller `olevel` can also be dangerous. In Example 2, `ppc` of `olevel 100` is assigned with `&public_c` of smaller `olevel 0`:

While assignments between different `olevels` appear unsafe, some cases with smaller `olevels` seem benign. For example, assigning a public value to a secret value, is clearly safe—we can not pass any secret information into public by this assignment. But when pointer nests get deeper, it is much less oblivious whether an assignment is safe.

Example 2.

```
char public_c = 'p';
[[obliv("1")]] char secret_c = 'x';
[[obliv("10")]] char *pc = &secret_c;
[[obliv("100")]] char **ppc = &pc;

// if obliv("00") to obliv("10") is allowed
*ppc = &public_c;
*pc = secret_c;  // 'x' flows to public_c!
```

To formalize the dataflow property, we distinguish between the `olevel` in an expression's type and the *inherent* `olevel` of the underlying memory location. In C++, lvalues correspond to memory areas; their inherent `olevel` is defined by the allocation site (variable declarations for stack/static allocations, or `new` expressions for heap allocations). We call lvalues corresponding to allocations *primitive lvalues.* Two lvalues *alias* when they refer to the same memory area. In a well-formed program, every lvalue aliases with a primitive lvalue. We formalize Theorem 2 as:

Theorem 3 (Dataflow of Assignment). *There is no execution of an assignment statement whose assignee (which must be an lvalue) is aliasing a non-oblivious lvalue, but the assigner is an oblivious value.*

Theorem 4 (Dataflow of Value Dependency). *An expression whose value depends on oblivious values is also oblivious.*

We use the following notations: $x \downarrow^k$ denotes dereferencing x by k times; $\texttt{const}(x)$ and $\texttt{obliv}(x)$ denote the constantness and obliviousness of x.

Now we specify the `olevel` rules to satisfy Theorem 3. The danger in Example 2 occurs because an oblivious expression `**ppc` aliases with a non-oblivious expression `public_c`, but `*ppc` is not constant and can be assigned a secret value which flows to the non-oblivious `public_c`. To avoid this, we restrict "non-oblivious to oblivious" assignments by ensuring the ancestors in the pointer hierarchy are constant:

Rule 6 (Casting). Consider two expressions, a and b. b can be implicitly cast to a if and only if, in addition to C++'s cast rules, the following *oblivious cast rules* hold:

1. For a $k > 0$, if $\texttt{const}(a \downarrow^k) = 0$, for any $k' \geq k$,

$$\texttt{const}(a \downarrow^{k'}) = \texttt{const}(b \downarrow^{k'}) \tag{2}$$

$$\texttt{obliv}(a \downarrow^{k'}) = \texttt{obliv}(b \downarrow^{k'}). \tag{3}$$

2. For any $k \geq 0$,

$$\texttt{obliv}(a \downarrow^{k}) \geq \texttt{obliv}(b \downarrow^{k}). \tag{4}$$

For an assignment $a \leftarrow b$, if a is a reference type, the assignment is allowed when b can be implicitly converted to the `olevel` and type of a according to the above casting rules. If a is a value type, b only needs to be converted to the `olevel` and type of constant a, i.e., with $\texttt{const}(a)$ set to 1 but other `olevel` and type unchanged.

Intuitively, condition 2 in Rule 6 prevents assigning oblivious values to non-oblivious targets, e.g., assigning an oblivious b to a non-oblivious a. Condition 1 parallels C++'s implicit conversion rule for `const`-modifiers [29, Chapter 7.3.6], preventing inherent-constant memory from being overwritten. When $\texttt{const}(a\downarrow^k) = 0$ and $\texttt{obliv}(a\downarrow^{k'}) \neq \texttt{obliv}(b\downarrow^{k'})$ for some $k' \geq k$, assigning an oblivious value to $a\downarrow^{k'}$ would also assign it to the non-oblivious $b\downarrow^{k'}$, violating the dataflow theorem.

To satisfy Theorem 4, we have:

Rule 7 (Arithmetic). For an arithmetic operator expression, if any operands are oblivious, the total expression is also oblivious. Note that we only consider arithmetic expressions; comma expressions, compilation-time constant expressions (e.g., `sizeof`, `alignof`), and pointer reference/dereference operators are not considered dependencies.

Rule 8 (Dereference). It is forbidden to dereference an oblivious pointer (the array indexing expression `p[i]` is interpreted as `*(p + i)`). The result of a dereference operator shifts the `olevel` right by one digit, while the result of a take-address operator shifts the `olevel` left by one digit.

Rule 9 (Pointer Arithmetic). For the arithmetic of pointers, the only allowed type is the addition of a pointer `p` and an integer `i` (including the equivalent `&p[i]`). The 0th digit of the result `olevel` is the logical-OR of the operands' obliviousnesses, and the remaining digits are the same as `p`.

These rules ensure the theorems stated earlier. Note that Rules 6 to 8 replace their "basic" versions (Rules 1 to 3). The following example demonstrates how oblivious assignment rules work:

Example 3.

```
// [[obliv]] is the abbreviation of [[obliv("1")]]
[[obliv]] int x = 1;
[[obliv("10")]] int *xp = &x;
[[obliv("100")]] int **xpp = &xp;
// error, 2nd digit of olevel differs
[[obliv("110")]] int **ypp = xpp;
// ok, 2nd level is constant
[[obliv("110")]] int *const *const ypp = xpp;
// ok, the first level is passed by value
[[obliv("101")]] int **ypp = xpp;
```

3.3 Function Calls

Since callers typically only see function declarations in headers while their implications could exist in other translation units, obliviousness must be expressed in function signatures. We interpret function calls as series of assignments:

Rule 10 (Function Call). When checking a function, the following rules should be enforced:

1. Each parameter of a function can be annotated with an `olevel`.
2. When checking the function body, the parameters are treated as variables with their annotated `olevel`s.
3. The function itself can be annotated with an `olevel`, which indicates the `olevel` of its return value.
4. When checking the function body, every expression returned in a `return` statement should be able to be cast to the annotated `olevel` of the function, according to Rule 6.
5. When calling a function, for each parameter, the given argument should be able to be cast to the `olevel` of the declared parameter, according to Rule 6.

3.4 Classes

C++ classes (`struct`, `union`) declare compound types with methods, inheritance, and polymorphism, requiring additional rules:

Rule 11 (Class). For a class type (`struct` and `union` types also included), the following rules are enforced:

1. In the declaration of a class type, its members can be annotated with an `olevel`. The difference from a normal `olevel` declaration is that the last digit of class member `olevel` can be `"x"` besides `0` and `1`. If not specified, a class member has an `"x"` `olevel`.
2. In a class member access expression (e.g., `c.member` or `c->member`), if the `olevel` of the member declaration ends with `"x"`, the `olevel` of the expression is the `olevel` of the member declaration with the last digit changed to the `olevel` of the class instance (`c` or `*c`). Otherwise the `olevel` of the expression is the same as the member declaration.
3. A method can be annotated with `obliv_this`. In the presence of this annotation, `this` is interpreted as a pointer to an oblivious instance. An oblivious instance can only call `obliv_this` methods. A public instance can call all methods.
4. When a method is overridden during inheritance, the `olevel` annotations should be identical to the annotations in the original declaration.
5. Virtual methods should not be called from a pointer to an oblivious polymorphic pointer.

By default, a member's obliviousness inherits from the instance (`olevel` ending with `"x"`), analogous to C++'s `const`/`mutable` distinction. Virtual calls on oblivious polymorphic pointers are forbidden as the VPTR would be oblivious.

3.5 Templates

A single template could generate multiple instantiations. Since template parameters may carry `olevel` information (via function return values or parameters), obliv-clang checks each instantiation rather than the template declaration itself. This is straightforward as `clang` generates separate AST for each instantiation.

3.6 Unsafe Code Blocks

We provide the `obliv_unsafe` attribute to mark code blocks as unsafe, bypassing obliviousness checks. This approach, inspired by Rust's `unsafe` keyword, is necessary in several cases:

- Inspecting internal secret values when debugging;
- Implementing subroutines whose obliviousness requires sophisticated mathematics beyond automatic checking (e.g., extracting public values from oblivious variables through encryption/hashing with secret keys, or asserting on execution paths that should not trigger);
- Working with third-party libraries whose implementations are in separate translation units invisible to the compiler.

Like Rust's unsafe blocks, this feature indicates areas requiring special programmer attention and human auditing. We anticipate that in the future, more expressive semantics will reduce the need for unsafe blocks.

3.7 Known Limitations

When using external libraries, the compiler cannot determine the obliviousness of symbols without `olevel` annotations in library headers. Programmers must add these annotations, though this is typically a moderate burden. Another limitation involves function overloading. Since `olevel` is not part of C++ types, overloading by `olevel` alone is prohibited unless encoded in the ABI.

4 Implementation

obliv-clang is implemented in approximately 800 lines of C++ code. It registers an annotation handler to parse `obliv`-related annotations and a frontend plugin that executes after `clang` parses the source code into an AST. The plugin scans the AST and raises compilation errors for code violating our rules.

obliv-clang works like other `clang` plugins: it compiles into a dynamic library loaded during compilation, requiring only one additional compiler option to load the plugin. Our implementation targets a wide range of LLVM monorepo versions (tested on both LLVM 13 and LLVM 20). `clang`'s AST data structure remains relatively stable, so minimal maintenance is needed to support newer versions.

5 Compiler Optimization Suppression

Modern compilers perform aggressive performance optimizations that reorganize program structures. While obliv-clang ensures obliviousness at the AST level, the LLVM optimizer may apply transformations that undermine these guarantees.

Consider this example from [26]:

```
// Select an element from an array in constant time
uint64_t constant_time_lookup(
        const size_t secret_idx, const uint64_t table[16]) {
    uint64_t result = 0;
    for (size_t i = 0; i < 16; i++) {
        const bool cond = i == secret_idx;
        const uint64_t mask = (-(int64_t)cond);
        result |= table[i] &mask;
    }
    return result;
}
```

This function uses bit operations to extract `table[secret_idx]`, without revealing `secret_idx` through side channels. However, LLVM's optimizer can detect this pattern and bypass the protection. When compiled with `clang` 21.1.0 targeting x86-64 Linux using `-O3 -fno-unroll-loops -fno-vectorize`, the compiler generates a branch depending on whether `i` equals to `secret_idx`, allowing attackers to learn information about `secret_idx` by observing control flow, violating the intended obliviousness.

This issue arises because current compiler optimizers prioritize correctness without considering obliviousness. Reconstructing LLVM to be obliviousness-aware would require enormous engineering effort. Instead, we adopt a simpler approach. When our plugin loads, it disables optimization passes that could produce unsafe changes. We manually inspected all `clang` optimization passes to determine their safety. Here is the list: ReassociatePass, LoopInstSimplifyPass, LoopSimplifyCFGPass, LoopRotatePass, IndVarSimplifyPass, LoopDeletionPass, LoopInterchangePass, LoopFlattenPass, X86CmovConverterPass.

To ensure the completeness of necessary passes to disable, obliv-clang provides an extra double-check step that applies rigorous obliviousness verification to the generated assembly code using existing tools [8]. The performance impact of disabling these optimization passes is insignificant, as evaluated in Sect. 6.2.

6 Evaluation

We evaluate obliv-clang's expressiveness through case studies, and assess its performance through compilation and runtime benchmarks.

6.1 Case Studies

PathORAM. PathORAM [28] provides an oblivious random access interface with $O(\log^3 N)$ overhead. Our non-recursive implementation is 251 lines of code (LOCs). The position map requires `obliv_unsafe` blocks since positions read from the secret map must become public for tree traversals.

Oblivious BFS. Oblivious BFS [3] performs BFS traversals such that an attacker cannot learn the graph structure from the execution trace. It shuffles the graph randomly and chooses each next vertex with equal probability. Our implementation uses 158 LOCs.

Real-World Cryptographic Vulnerabilities. CVE-2024-13176 (the Minerva attack) is a timing side channel in OpenSSL's ECDSA: a ∼300 ns signal leaks when the inverted nonce's top word is zero, enabling private key recovery on NIST P-521. The root cause was that `BN_mod_exp_mont()` lacked constant-time protection for its secret base and result, despite protecting the exponent. With obliv-clang, this flaw is caught automatically:

```
int BN_mod_exp_mont(BIGNUM *r, const BIGNUM *a, const BIGNUM *p,
                    const BIGNUM *m, BN_CTX *ctx, BN_MONT_CTX *m_ctx);
static int ec_field_inverse_mod_ord(const EC_GROUP *group,
        OBLIV_PTR BIGNUM *r, OBLIV_PTR const BIGNUM *x, BN_CTX *ctx) {
    if (!BN_mod_exp_mont(r, x, ...))  // ERROR: OBLIV_PTR to non-OBLIV_PTR
        goto err;
}
```

obliv-clang's explicit dataflow tracking catches secret values flowing into unannotated functions, demonstrating robustness over naming conventions alone.

Others. We have also tested obliv-clang on several other algorithms, including oblivious shuffle [18] and tree-based data structures [32]. We also write some standard library wrappers to assist in using standard libraries. The adoption of these programs is straightforward. The only requirement is to mark variables and function parameters with appropriate `olevels`.

To quantify the migration effort, we measure the LOCs requiring `[[obliv]]` annotations compared to the total LOCs. For example, we annotated 32 out of 190 LOCs in PathORAM, 10 out of 94 LOCs in Oblivious BFS, and 25 out of 311 LOCs in Poly1305 (see later). This demonstrates that the annotation burden is modest—typically just 8% to 17% of the codebase requires modifications, and these modifications are localized to variable declarations and function signatures involving secret data.

6.2 Performance

All experiments run an Intel Xeon Gold 5218R processor with 256 GB DDR4 memory, with Ubuntu 22.04. Programs are compiled with `clang` 13.0.1 at `-O3`; with obliv-clang, optimization passes mentioned in Sect. 5 are disabled.

Compilation Overheads. We evaluate compilation overheads on five benchmarks: PathORAM (251 LOCs, Sect. 6.1), Oblivious BFS (158 LOCs, Sect. 6.1), tiny_jpeg (1306 LOCs, JPEG encoding) [9], monocypher (3277 LOCs, cryptography library) [30], and sqlite3 (250815 LOCs) [27]. All programs are compiled (but not linked) with and without our obliv-clang plugin. Results are shown in Fig. 1a (average of 10 runs after 3 warm-ups). Without the double-check step (Sect. 5), overheads are below 11%; with it, below 18%. Overheads decrease for larger programs, making obliv-clang suitable for real-world codebases.

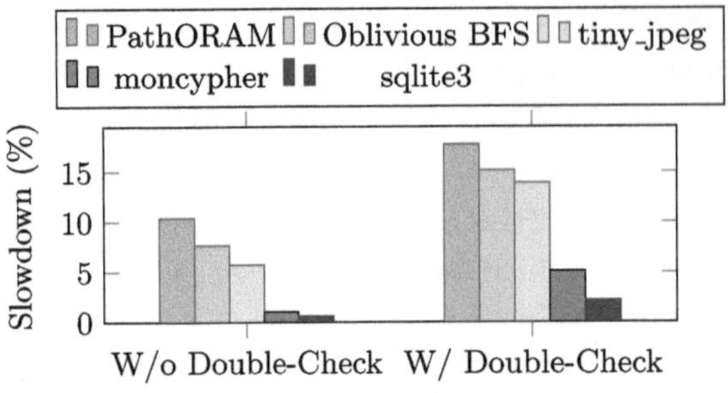

(a) Compilation time overheads.

Testcase	Slowdown
PathORAM	29.5%
Oblivious BFS	0.91%
tiny_jpeg	1.27%
lz4	−2.72%

(b) Optimization suppression overheads.

Fig. 1. Overheads from compilation process and optimization suppression.

Optimization Suppression Overheads. We measure execution time with and without suppression on: PathORAM with randomly generated operations on size 2^{20}, Oblivious BFS on a 4096-node graph, tiny_jpeg encoding a 1000×1000 image, and lz4 [17] with compression level 3. Figure 1b shows the results. Most benchmarks see negligible slowdown, with lz4 even slightly faster. PathORAM slows down by 29.5%, likely because the suppressed passes could reorganize its loops for better performance.

Runtime Performance. We compare obliv-clang against FaCT [5] (a DSL that verifies and transforms oblivious code) and Jasmin [1] (a DSL with formally verified compilation) on six algorithms: AES128, poly1305, salsa20, secretbox, siphash [2], and PathORAM. Both FaCT and Jasmin lack usability features (e.g., limited loop constructs, manual register allocation), restricting comparison to simple microbenchmarks. The results are shown in Fig. 2. obliv-clang is 27.8% faster than Jasmin and 66.9% faster than FaCT on average. For poly1305, the obliv-clang implementation is 29.8% slower than Jasmin. The reason might be that the main body of poly1305 calculation is 128-bit integer arithmetic, and the code generation of 128-bit arithmetic in Jasmin is more optimized.

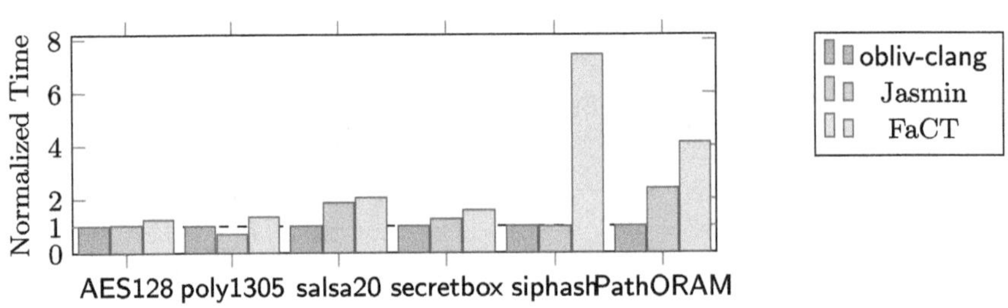

Fig. 2. Performance comparison of oblivious programs using different tools.

7 Conclusion

We present obliv-clang, a compiler plugin for the C++ language that performs static checks for oblivious programming. It is specifically implemented using the clang and LLVM infrastructures. Compared to previous work, obliv-clang aims to provide natural semantics and maximum compatibility with widely used industry-level programming languages and workflow while being able to provide a verifiable soundness guarantee even in the presence of complex language features. Our experiments show that obliv-clang leads to low compilation overheads and can achieve better performance on the compiled oblivious programs compared to previous tools.

Acknowledgments. The authors thank the anonymous reviewers for their valuable suggestions, and the Tsinghua IDEAL group members for constructive discussion. The technical solution and experimental design presented in this paper were independently completed by the authors. AI tools were used solely for language polishing and formatting optimization, and did not participate in the development of the research ideas or core content.

References

1. Almeida, J.B., et al.: Jasmin: high-assurance and high-speed cryptography. In: ACM SIGSAC Conference on Computer and Communications Security (CCS), pp. 1807–1823 (2017)
2. Aumasson, J.-P., Bernstein, D.J.: SipHash: a fast short-input PRF. In: Galbraith, S., Nandi, M. (eds.) INDOCRYPT 2012. LNCS, vol. 7668, pp. 489–508. Springer, Heidelberg (2012). https://doi.org/10.1007/978-3-642-34931-7_28
3. Blanton, M., Steele, A., Alisagari, M.: Data-oblivious graph algorithms for secure computation and outsourcing. In: ACM SIGSAC Symposium on Information, Computer and Communications Security (ASIA CCS), p. 207 (2013)
4. Bulck, J.V., Weichbrodt, N., Kapitza, R., Piessens, F., Strackx, R.: Telling your secrets without page faults: stealthy page table-based attacks on enclaved execution. In: USENIX Security Symposium, pp. 1041–1056 (2017)
5. Cauligi, S., et al.: FaCT: a DSL for timing-sensitive computation. In: ACM SIGPLAN Conference on Programming Language Design and Implementation (PLDI), pp. 174–189 (2019)
6. Clang-Tidy — Extra Clang Tools 18.0.0git Documentation (2023). https://clang.llvm.org/extra/clang-tidy/
7. What is Clangd? (2023). https://clangd.llvm.org/
8. Disselkoen, C., Cauligi, S., Tullsen, D., Stefan, D.: Finding and eliminating timing side-channels in crypto code with pitchfork. In: SRC TECHCON (2020)
9. Gonzalez, S.: TinyJPEG (2022)
10. Götzfried, J., Eckert, M., Schinzel, S., Müller, T.: Cache attacks on intel SGX. In: European Workshop on Systems Security (EuroSec), pp. 1–6 (2017)

11. Jang, Y., Lee, J., Lee, S., Kim, T.: SGX-Bomb: locking down the processor via rowhammer attack. In: Workshop on System Software for Trusted Execution (SysTEX), pp. 1–6 (2017)
12. Lee, S., Shih, M.W., Gera, P., Kim, T., Kim, H., Peinado, M.: Inferring fine-grained control flow inside SGX enclaves with branch shadowing. In: USENIX Security Symposium, pp. 557–574 (2017)
13. Lipp, M., et al.: PLATYPUS: software-based power side-channel attacks on X86. In: IEEE Symposium on Security and Privacy (S&P), pp. 355–371 (2021)
14. Liu, C., Hicks, M., Shi, E.: Memory trace oblivious program execution. In: IEEE Computer Security Foundations Symposium (CSF), pp. 51–65 (2013)
15. Liu, C., Wang, X.S., Nayak, K., Huang, Y., Shi, E.: ObliVM: a programming framework for secure computation. In: IEEE Symposium on Security and Privacy (S&P), pp. 359–376 (2015)
16. Luo, Y., Gao, M.: obliv-clang: Real-World Oblivious Programming in C++ (Extended Version). arXiv preprint cs.PL/2606.16187 (2026). https://arxiv.org/abs/2606.16187
17. LZ4 - Extremely Fast Compression (2023). https://lz4.org/
18. Ohrimenko, O., Goodrich, M.T., Tamassia, R., Upfal, E.: The Melbourne Shuffle: Improving Oblivious Storage in the Cloud (2014)
19. Rane, A., Lin, C., Tiwari, M.: Raccoon: closing digital side-channels through obfuscated execution. In: USENIX Security Symposium, pp. 431–446 (2015)
20. Reparaz, O., Balasch, J., Verbauwhede, I.: Dude, is My Code Constant Time? (2016)
21. Sayakkara, A., Le-Khac, N.A., Scanlon, M.: A survey of electromagnetic side-channel attacks and discussion on their case-progressing potential for digital forensics. Digit. Investig. **29**(1), 43–54 (2019)
22. Shih, M.W., Lee, S., Kim, T., Peinado, M.: T-SGX: eradicating controlled-channel attacks against enclave programs. In: Network and Distributed System Security Symposium (NDSS). Internet Society, San Diego, CA (2017)
23. Shinde, S., Chua, Z.L., Narayanan, V., Saxena, P.: Preventing page faults from telling your secrets. In: ACM Asia Conference on Computer and Communications Security (ASIA CCS), pp. 317–328 (2016)
24. Sinha, R., Rajamani, S., Seshia, S.A.: A compiler and verifier for page access oblivious computation. In: Joint Meeting on Foundations of Software Engineering (ESEC/FSE), pp. 649–660 (2017)
25. Son, J., Prechter, G., Poddar, R., Popa, R.A., Sen, K.: ObliCheck: efficient verification of oblivious algorithms with unobservable state. In: USENIX Security Symposium (2021)
26. Sprenkels, D.: LLVM Provides No Side-Channel Resistance (2019). https://dsprenkels.com/cmov-conversion.html
27. SQLite Home Page (2023). https://www.sqlite.org/index.html
28. Stefanov, E., et al.: Path ORAM: an extremely simple oblivious RAM protocol. J. ACM (JACM) **65**(4), 1–26 (2018)
29. The C++ Standards Committee: C++ Standard Draft Sources (2022). https://github.com/cplusplus/draft
30. Vaillant, L.: Monocypher (2023). https://monocypher.org/
31. Van Bulck, J., et al.: Foreshadow: extracting the keys to the intel SGX kingdom with transient out-of-order execution. In: USENIX Security Symposium, pp. 991–1008 (2018)
32. Wang, X.S., et al.: Oblivious data structures. In: ACM SIGSAC Conference on Computer and Communications Security (CCS), pp. 215–226 (2014)

33. Zahur, S., Evans, D.: Obliv-C: A Language for Extensible Data-Oblivious Computation (2015)
34. Zhang, Z., Barthe, G.: CT-LLVM: Automatic Large-Scale Constant-Time Analysis. Cryptology ePrint Archive, Report 2025/338 (2025)

Uni-Winograd: A Massively Resource-Efficient and Unified Radix-4 NTT Architecture for PQC Algorithms

Danni Wang[1], Hao Yu[1], Zili Zhou[1], Sizhao Li[1(✉)], Guisheng Yin[1], and Donghui Guo[2]

[1] College of Computer Science and Technology, Harbin Engineering University, Harbin, China
{wangdanni,yuhaoo,lizi_zhou,sizhao.li,yinguisheng}@hrbeu.edu.cn

[2] School of Electronic Science and Engineering, Xiamen University, Xiamen, China
dhguo@xmu.edu.cn

Abstract. With the ongoing standardization of post-quantum cryptography (PQC), efficient hardware implementations of schemes such as ML-DSA and ML-KEM have become increasingly important. The Number Theoretic Transform (NTT) remains the primary computational bottleneck. Although Winograd-based approaches reduce multiplicative complexity, existing high-radix designs still rely on diverse constant multiplications and algorithm-specific data paths, limiting hardware reuse and overall efficiency. This work presents Uni-Winograd, a unified and resource-efficient radix-4 Winograd NTT architecture. Through a multi-level Kronecker-product formulation, we reveal that after four levels of nesting, the set of multiplication constants converges to only four discrete values. This constant-set discretization enables all non-trivial multiplications to be mapped onto a small set of shared operations, eliminating the need for general-purpose multipliers and algorithm-specific data paths, and thereby enabling a fully unified design. Based on this insight, the proposed architecture employs a reusable Winograd computation core that supports NTT for both ML-DSA and ML-KEM. A pipelined scheduling strategy combined with real-time address generation further ensures efficient execution and high resource utilization. FPGA implementation results show that Uni-Winograd significantly reduces hardware cost while achieving a 52% DSP and 72% BRAM reduction at comparable latency, and an 88% DSP reduction in the resource-efficient configuration, compared with state-of-the-art designs, along with improved area-time efficiency.

Keywords: Post-Quantum Cryptography · Winograd NTT · Hardware Acceleration · FPGA Implementation

1 Introduction

With the continued progress of post-quantum cryptography (PQC) standardization, efficient hardware designs for practical deployment have become an

L. Eeckhout et al. (Eds.): APPT 2026, LNCS 16693, pp. 34–48, 2027.
https://doi.org/10.1007/978-981-92-4805-6_3

important research topic. Among the major PQC candidates, lattice-based cryptographic schemes have emerged as a mainstream direction due to their strong security and favorable performance. Representative algorithms such as ML-KEM [16] and ML-DSA [15] rely heavily on polynomial arithmetic, making the efficiency of underlying arithmetic modules crucial to overall system performance.

The Number Theoretic Transform (NTT) serves as the core technique for accelerating polynomial convolution over finite fields and constitutes one of the principal computational bottlenecks in hardware accelerators. Conventional NTT implementations are mainly based on Cooley-Tukey (CT) or Gentleman-Sande (GS) decompositions with radix-2 or radix-4 structures. Although these approaches provide regular dataflow and simple control logic, they still require numerous modular multiplications across multiple decomposition stages [4,11], which leads to high DSP usage, long latency, and considerable memory-access overhead. Consequently, it remains challenging to achieve both high throughput and high energy efficiency on resource-constrained platforms. Considering the trade-offs among iteration depth, memory access overhead, and control complexity, this work adopts radix-4 as the basic decomposition granularity.

Winograd can be combined with multiplier design to accelerate polynomial operations [19,20]. Moreover, Winograd techniques were introduced into DFT computation in [1] by reformulating the transform into permutations, additions/subtractions, and a few non-trivial constant multiplications, thereby reducing the reliance on general-purpose multipliers at the cost of a moderate increase in linear operations. Subsequent research further constructed recursively generated recursive matrices and butterfly units for power-of-two transform sizes [17] and applied for NTT [3,9]. Building on these efforts, Mandal and Basu Roy [14] derived higher-radix Winograd NTT structures, such as radix-8 and radix-16, providing an alternative to CT- and GS-based schemes, whose critical paths are typically longer in high-radix implementations. From a hardware perspective, such structures are attractive because they facilitate constant sharing, shift-add replacement, pipelined scheduling, and on-chip memory reuse, exhibiting strong potential for resource-constrained PQC accelerators.

Despite these advances, existing studies still exhibit three levels of critical limitations. First, conventional NTT architectures remain heavily dependent on modular multiplication, while the associated multipliers and twiddle factors operations incur substantial area and latency overheads [13,21]. Second, existing Winograd [14] or high-radix NTT [4,13] designs mainly improve efficiency through data scheduling, parallel butterfly organization, and conflict-free memory mapping. Although these techniques enhance scalability and parallelism, they do not exploit the discretized structure of Winograd constants to reduce multiplier diversity or constant-multiplication complexity. Third, most prior designs are optimized for a single algorithm [5,12,18] lacking a unified cross-algorithm design methodology and thus limiting general-purpose PQC accelerators. A few studies that support both ML-KEM and ML-DSA still adopt conventional NTT structures, where frequent and modular multiplications consume valuable hardware resources [2,10,13]. This issue becomes particularly critical on edge devices with limited DSP, BRAM, and power budgets. Deploying separate accelerators for the two algorithms is often impractical, creating an urgent need for a unified lightweight NTT architecture that can reuse the same datapath.

To address these issues, this paper proposes Uni-Winograd, a unified radix-4 Winograd NTT architecture for PQC algorithms. The main contributions of this work are summarized as follows.

- We propose a unified radix-4 Winograd formulation based on multi-level Kronecker-product expansion, and reveal that the multiplication constants converge to only four discrete values after four levels of nesting, establishing the theoretical foundation for a unified hardware design.
- Based on this property, we develop a unified radix-4 Winograd NTT processor that integrates a shared computation core, pipelined scheduling, real-time address generation, and conflict-free memory mapping, enabling efficient hardware reuse across ML-DSA and ML-KEM with a hybrid mapping strategy for compatibility.
- FPGA results demonstrate that the proposed architecture significantly reduces DSP and BRAM usage and improves area-time efficiency while maintaining competitive performance, despite latency increase in the HP configuration. Two design points are evaluated: a resource-efficient (RE) configuration (6 DSPs, 286 cycles) and a high-performance (HP) configuration (24 DSPs, 68 cycles).

2 Background

2.1 Number Theoretic Transform

The Number Theoretic Transform (NTT) is a fundamental technique for efficient polynomial convolution over finite fields. It can be viewed as the finite-field counterpart of the Discrete Fourier Transform (DFT), and is widely used in lattice-based post-quantum cryptography to accelerate operations in the ring $R_q = \mathbb{Z}_q[x]/(x^N + 1)$. For a sequence $\mathbf{x} = (x_0, x_1, \ldots, x_{N-1})$ of length N, the NTT maps it into the transform domain using an N-th primitive root of unity modulo q, denoted as $X_k = \sum_{n=0}^{N-1} x_n \omega_N^{nk} \pmod q, k = 0, 1, \ldots, N-1$, enabling polynomial multiplication to be converted into point-wise multiplication. As a result, the computational complexity is reduced from $O(N^2)$ to $O(N \log N)$.

Conventional NTT implementations usually adopt CT or GS decompositions offer regular dataflow and simple control, but require many modular multiplications across recursive butterfly stages. As the major source of resource and latency overhead, conventional radix-2 and radix-4 structures are not well suited to resource-constrained FPGA platforms or lightweight PQC accelerators.

2.2 Winograd NTT

The design of Winograd NTT evolves from DFT to Winograd DFT and then to Winograd NTT. The N-point DFT of the input sequence x_n is defined as $Y_k =$

$\sum_{n=0}^{N-1} x_n e^{-j2\pi nk/N}, k = 0, 1, \ldots, N-1$. In matrix form, it can be expressed as $\mathbf{Y} = \mathbf{E}_N\mathbf{X}$, where $\mathbf{E}_N$ represents the Fourier matrix. Direct calculation requires quadratic complexity. To reduce this cost, the Winograd method restructures the DFT of power-of-2 length into a recursive matrix decomposition [17]. When $N = 2^{i+1}$, the DFT matrix can be recursively decomposed into $E_{2^{i+1}} = (H_2 \otimes I_{2^i})(E_{2^i} \oplus Q_{2^i})P_\pi$ where H_2 is a 2-order Hadamard matrix, I_{2^i} is the identity matrix, P_π is a permutation matrix, and Q_{2^i} serves as a prefix matrix containing the transformation-related rotation factors. This decomposition separates the transform into permutation, Hadamard-type additions/subtractions, and a small number of non-trivial multiplications. As an example, suppose that N=4. Then $\mathbf{Y_{4\times 1}} = \mathbf{E}_4\mathbf{X_{4\times 1}}$ can be written as $\mathbf{Y}_{4\times 1} = (\mathbf{H}_2 \otimes \mathbf{I}_2)(\mathbf{E}_2 \oplus \mathbf{Q}_2)\mathbf{P}_4^{(\pi_4)}\mathbf{X}_{4\times 1}$, where

$$\mathbf{E}_2 = \begin{bmatrix} a_4 & a_4 \\ a_4 & -a_4 \end{bmatrix} = (a_4 \oplus a_4)\mathbf{H}_2, \qquad \mathbf{Q}_2 = \begin{bmatrix} a_4 & a_4 \\ b_4 & -b_4 \end{bmatrix} = (a_4 \oplus b_4)\mathbf{H}_2$$

$$\mathbf{H}_2 \otimes \mathbf{I}_2 = \begin{bmatrix} 1 & 1 \\ 1 & -1 \end{bmatrix} \otimes \begin{bmatrix} 1 & 0 \\ 0 & 1 \end{bmatrix} = \begin{bmatrix} 1 & 0 & 1 & 0 \\ 0 & 1 & 0 & 1 \\ 1 & 0 & -1 & 0 \\ 0 & 1 & 0 & -1 \end{bmatrix} = \mathbf{M}_4^{(0)}$$

Taking into account the above factorization schemes, the transform can be rewritten as $\mathbf{Y}_{4\times 1} = \mathbf{M}_4^{(0)}\mathbf{D}_4\mathbf{M}_4^{(1)}\mathbf{P}_4^{(\pi_4)}\mathbf{X}_{4\times 1}$, where

$$\mathbf{M}_4^{(1)} = \begin{bmatrix} 1 & 1 \\ 1 & -1 \end{bmatrix} \oplus \begin{bmatrix} 1 & 1 \\ 1 & -1 \end{bmatrix} = \begin{bmatrix} 1 & 1 & 0 & 0 \\ 1 & -1 & 0 & 0 \\ 0 & 0 & 1 & 1 \\ 0 & 0 & 1 & -1 \end{bmatrix}$$

$$\mathbf{D}_4 = \mathrm{diag}(\eta_0, \eta_1, \eta_2, \eta_3), \qquad \eta_0, \eta_1, \eta_2 = a_4 = 1, \quad \eta_3 = b_4 = -j$$

Compared with conventional BFU structures, Winograd mainly reduces costly multiplications at the expense of a moderate increase in additions, which is more favorable for hardware implementation.

Applying this idea to NTT decomposes a length-N transform into smaller minimum-multiplication sub-transforms. In radix-4 Winograd NTT, the length-N transform is first divided into four length-$N/4$ subproblems and then recombined through permutations, Kronecker-product sub-transform matrices, and staged twiddle factors. Moreover, each 4-point block is factorized into three stages: pre-addition, constant multiplication, and post-addition. This concentrates nontrivial multiplications into a few diagonal positions, which is beneficial for constant sharing, shift-add replacement, and parameterized hardware mapping.

3 Methodology

3.1 Layered Representation of Radix-4 NTT

To construct a unified formulation for Winograd NTT, we consider the length-N NTT matrix $\mathbf{F}_N$ with $N = 4^m$, which (k,n)-th entry is defined as $[F_N]_{k,n} =$

$\omega_N^{kn}, 0 \leq k, n < N$. By expanding the input and output indices in radix-4 form, the exponent term can be decomposed hierarchically, allowing the full transform to be rewritten as a multi-stage radix-4 structure:

$$\mathbf{F}_N = \mathbf{P}_{\text{out}} \left(\prod_{s=0}^{m-1} \mathbf{T}_s \right) \mathbf{P}_{\text{in}}$$

where $\mathbf{P}_{\text{in}}$ and $\mathbf{P}_{\text{out}}$ are input/output permutation matrices, and $\mathbf{T}_s$ denotes the radix-4 transform operator of stage s. Each stage can be expressed as

$$\mathbf{T}_s = \mathbf{I}_{4^{m-s-1}} \otimes \mathbf{B}_4^{(s)} \otimes \mathbf{I}_{4^s}$$

where $\mathbf{B}_4^{(s)}$ denotes the embedded 4-point basic block associated with its corresponding twiddle factors, and $\otimes$ denotes the Kronecker product. This formulation reveals that a length-N radix-4 NTT can be interpreted as a hierarchical composition of small 4-point modules with identical topology across stages.

3.2 Four-Level Kronecker Nesting and Constant-Set Discretization

Building upon the hierarchical representation of the radix-4 NTT, we further consider the 4-point sub-transform arising in an arbitrary stage, which match the transform size used in ML-KEM and ML-DSA. For each 4-point local transform, the basic module can be written as $\mathbf{W}_4 = \mathbf{A}_4\mathbf{D}_4\mathbf{B}_4$, where $\mathbf{A}_4$ and $\mathbf{B}_4$ are sparse matrices mainly composed $\{0, \pm 1\}$ and $\mathbf{D}_4$ is a diagonal matrix containing the nontrivial constant multiplications. Since the linear operations in $\mathbf{A}_4$ and $\mathbf{B}_4$ are hardware-friendly, the implementation cost of the 4-point module is dominated by the constant set in $\mathbf{D}_4$.

Then the overall transform can be written as a four-layer composition of radix-4 Winograd blocks

$$\mathbf{F}_{256} = \mathbf{P}_{\text{out}} \cdot \boldsymbol{\Theta}_3 \cdot \boldsymbol{\Theta}_2 \cdot \boldsymbol{\Theta}_1 \cdot \boldsymbol{\Theta}_0 \cdot \mathbf{P}_{\text{in}}$$

where the radix-4 transform operator at stage s is given by $\boldsymbol{\Theta}_s = \mathbf{I}_{4^{3-s}} \otimes (\mathbf{A}_4\mathbf{D}_4\mathbf{B}_4) \otimes \mathbf{I}_{4^s}$ Using the distributive property of Kronecker products $(\mathbf{X} \otimes \mathbf{Y})(\mathbf{U} \otimes \mathbf{V}) = (\mathbf{XU}) \otimes (\mathbf{YV})$, this four-level structure can be reorganized into the unified form

$$\mathbf{F}_{256} = \mathbf{P}_{\text{out}} \cdot \mathbf{A}_{\text{glob}} \cdot \mathbf{D}_{\text{glob}} \cdot \mathbf{B}_{\text{glob}} \cdot \mathbf{P}_{\text{in}}$$

where $\mathbf{A}_{\text{glob}}$ and $\mathbf{B}_{\text{glob}}$ preserve the sparse linear structure of the transform, and $\mathbf{D}_{\text{glob}}$ aggregates all constant multiplications arising from the diagonal terms and inter-stage twiddle factors. Therefore, the key to a unified architecture is the analysis of the construction and distribution of the constant set in $\mathbf{D}_{\text{glob}}$.

Under the Winograd factorization, most linear combinations are absorbed into $\mathbf{A}_4$ and $\mathbf{B}_4$, so actual multipliers are required only for a limited number of diagonal constants and their combinations with stage twiddle factors. If the diagonal constant set of the 4-point block is denoted by $C_0 = \{c_1, c_2, \ldots, c_r\}$, then the constant set at stage s can be expressed as $\mathcal{C}_s = \{c \cdot t \pmod q \mid c \in \mathcal{C}_{s-1},\ t \in \mathbf{T}_s\}$. Focusing on ML-KEM and ML-DSA, the constants generated through four-level nesting satisfy a discrete closure property. As a result, all required hardware multiplications can be reduced to a common finite set $C^\star = \{\gamma_0, \gamma_1, \gamma_2, \gamma_3\}$. This means that, regardless of whether the transform is NTT or INTT, the hardware only needs to support four types of constant-multiplication structures, while the difference between algorithms lies only in the specific parameter values. This discretization property is the mathematical foundation of the proposed unified hardware design.

It should be noted that the "four-level nesting" refers to the full radix-4 expansion of the target 256-point transform, rather than to a universal convergence depth of Winograd NTT. Since both ML-DSA and ML-KEM use $N = 256 = 4^4$, the complete radix-4 decomposition contains exactly four stages. In general, for a radix-4 Winograd NTT of length $N = 4^m$, whether the union of the constant set $\mathcal{C}_s$ can be mapped to a small number of hardware-equivalent constants depends on the modulus q, the selected roots of unity, the stage twiddle factors, and the normalization of the Winograd factorization. Thus, for other PQC algorithms, lengths or moduli, the same closure condition must be checked separately.

3.3 Unified Radix-4 Winograd NTT for ML-KEM and ML-DSA

According to the design, the radix-4 Winograd NTT core we proposed is depicted as shown in Algorithm 1. The operator H denotes the Hadamard transform, which is represented by the matrix $\begin{bmatrix} 1 & 1 \\ 1 & -1 \end{bmatrix}$. Given two input operands a and b, this operation produces two outputs corresponding to modular addition and modular subtraction, respectively, $(a + b) \bmod q$ and $(a - b) \bmod q$, where q denotes the modulus. This design effectively reduces the multiplicative complexity and provides the structural basis for hardware unification.

Algorithm 1 Radix-4 Winograd NTT Core Algorithm

```
1: Input: x_i, ω, q where, i = 0, 1, 2, 3
2: Output: y_i where, i = 0, 1, 2, 3
3: u_0, u_2 = H_2(x_0, x_2)
4: u_1, u_3 = H_2(x_1, x_3)
5: φ_0 = φ_1 = φ_2 = 1, φ_3 = ω
6: attr_1 = [u_0, u_1, u_2, u_3],    attr_2 = [φ_0, φ_1, φ_2, φ_3]
7: for i ← 0 to 3 do
8:     v_i = (attr_1[i] × attr_2[i])
9: end for
10: y_0, y_2 = H_2(v_0, v_1)
11: y_1, y_3 = H_2(v_2, v_3)
12: return y_i where, i = 0, 1, 2, 3
```

For ML-DSA, the 256-point NTT decomposes naturally into four radix-4 stages and is implemented via the unified radix-4 Winograd core. For ML-KEM, the modulus constraint prevents the final stage from using the same 4-point decomposition; a hybrid mapping is adopted: the preceding stages use the radix-4 Winograd core, while the final stage uses a conventional radix-2 butterfly. Before this last stage, most linear transforms and multiplication reductions have been completed by the Winograd cores; intermediate results are then re-indexed for radix-2 access, and precomputed twiddle factors fetched from ROM. Since only the final stage requires special handling, the performance benefit of the Winograd reduction is largely preserved while maintaining compatibility with both schemes.

4 Architecture

4.1 Overall Architecture

Figure 1 illustrates the proposed unified radix-4 Winograd NTT processor, consisting of a controller, address generator, contants ROM, conflict-free memory-mapping module, coefficient memory, and a radix-4 Winograd NTT unit. The controller coordinates stage execution, data movement, and memory access; the address generator and contants ROM provide stage-dependent addresses and precomputed constants. Coefficients are mapped into four memory banks for parallel access, while substitution and reorder logic rearrange intermediate results for the next stage. In a complete ML-KEM/ML-DSA accelerator, the radix-4 Winograd NTT can serve as a shared computing unit within the polynomial arithmetic module, with its datapath reused across both schemes. For ML-DSA, all NTT stages are implemented using the unified radix-4 Winograd structure. For ML-KEM, the preceding stages reuse the same radix-4 core, while the final stage is performed by an additional radix-2 butterfly unit due to the modulus-dependent root-of-unity constraint. With this strategy, unified support for both ML-DSA and ML-KEM can be achieved while maintaining a high degree of hardware reuse.

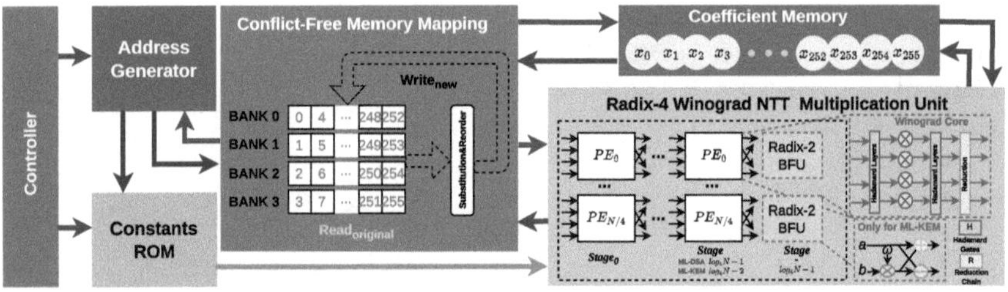

Fig. 1. Overview of Uni-Winograd.

4.2 Radix-4 Winograd NTT Unit

The proposed radix-4 Winograd NTT unit is the fundamental computing block of the whole architecture. It performs 4-point local NTT operations and serves as the core module for multi-stage pipelined execution. As illustrated in the Fig. 2(a), the internal dataflow follows the Winograd decomposition and is divided into three stages: an initial Hadamard transform, an intermediate multiplication stage, and a final Hadamard recombination stage. During the multiplication stage, we only need to read the corresponding precomputed constants from the constants ROM as designed and then perform the computation. This organization reduces the number of nontrivial modular multiplications while preserving a regular and reusable data path.

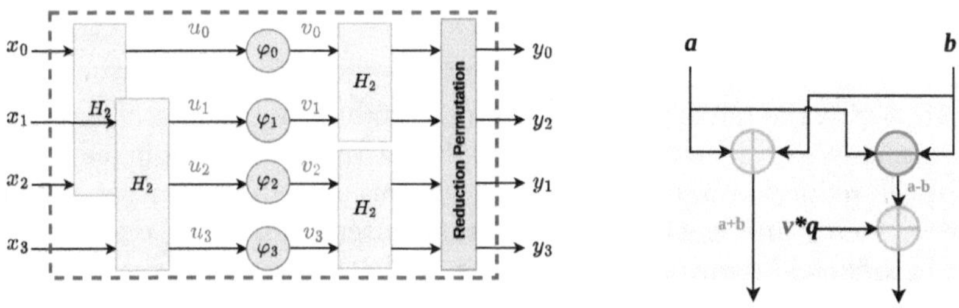

(a) Core Unit (b) Hadamard Gate

Fig. 2. Radix-4 Winograd NTT unit.

The Hadamard gate is the most basic linear-operation module in the proposed core. As Fig. 2(b) shown, we have designed the Hadamard gate to perform $a+b$ and $a-b+q$ where a and b of $\lceil \log_2 q \rceil$-bits produces outputs $a+b$ and $a-b+vq$ of dimension $(\lceil \log_2 q \rceil + 1)$-bits at most. The reason for using $a-b+vq$ instead of direct subtraction is that the latter may generate negative intermediate values, which are undesirable for pipelined inter-stage transmission and unified processing. Assume that the input ranges at a given stage are known and that B_{max} is the maximum possible value of b. To guarantee $a-b+vq \geq 0$ for all cases, it is sufficient to consider the worst case $a=0$ and $b=B_{\text{max}}$, which leads to $v=\lceil b_{\text{max}}/q \rceil$.

In radix-4 Winograd NTT, Hadamard gates appear both before and after multiplication. Before multiplication, the inputs are original coefficients with $0 \leq a, b \leq q-1$. Hence, $B_{\text{max}} = q-1, v_{\text{before}} = \left\lceil \frac{q-1}{q} \right\rceil = 1$. After multiplication, the inputs come from the multiplier output. In a partially reduced implementation for ML-DSA, since $2^{23} < q < 2^{24}$, the datapath is typically 24-bit unsigned, giving $0 \leq a, b \leq 2^{24}-1$. Thus, $B_{\text{max}} = 2^{24}-1, v_{\text{after}} = \lceil 2^{24} - 1/q \rceil$. For $q = 8380417$, $v_{\text{after}} \approx 2.002 = 3$.

In summary, the compensation factor in radix-4 Winograd NTT is determined by the maximum input range of each stage: $v=1$ before multiplication and $v=3$ after multiplication. This guarantees a non-negative subtraction output and enables an efficient unsigned hardware datapath.

4.3 Modular Multiplication Unit for ML-KEM and ML-DSA

The modular multiplication unit computes $(a \times b) mod\ q$. Considering both reduction efficiency and hardware cost, the design adopts K-RED(Algorithm 2) as the primary reduction method. The K-RED can be implemented mainly with shift and add/subtract operations rather than more expensive general division logic.

Algorithm 2 K-RED Algorithm

1: **Input:** $C = a \times b$
2: **Output:** $K \times C \bmod q$
3: $d_0 = C[m:0],\ d_1 = C \gg m$
4: **return** $(K \times d_0 - d_1)$

For ML-DSA, the radix-4 Winograd core introduces a Hadamard stage before multiplication, which increases the operand bitwidth. Accordingly, as shown in Fig. 3(a), the reduction unit is tailored to support multiplication between a 23-bit twiddle factor and a 24-bit data operand after Hadamard expansion. The resulting product is then processed by the K-RED flow to obtain the reduced output. This design allows the wider intermediate precision introduced by the Winograd structure to be handled without disrupting the pipeline.

For ML-KEM, since the incomplete NTT, its computation is more complex than that of ML-DSA. Therefore, we incorporates a Montgomery-based reduction method in addition to K-RED. Specifically, it outputs $a \times b \times R^{-1}$, where R is a power of two greater than q. By properly selecting R and preprocessing the twiddle factors with corresponding constants, the domain conversion is absorbed into the constant design, thereby reducing datapath overhead and making the method more suitable for ML-KEM hardware implementation.

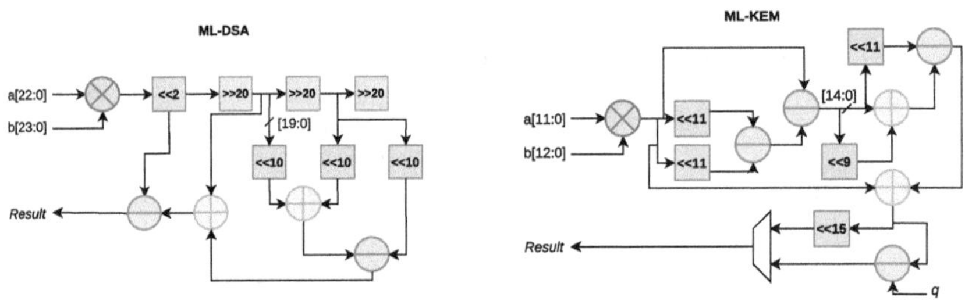

Fig. 3. K-RED Reduction for ML-DSA and ML-KEM.

4.4 Conflict-Free Memory Mapping

To sustain one radix-4 operation per cycle in a pipelined design, the architecture uses a four-bank conflict-free memory, with each bank implemented by true dual-port RAM and storing 64 coefficients. At each stage, four coefficients are read in parallel, processed by the radix-4 Winograd core, and then rearranged before being written back so that accesses in the next stage also remain conflict-free.

This organization matches the parallelism of the computation core and is crucial for high throughput.

Since the polynomial dimensions of both ML-KEM and ML-DSA are $N = 256 = 4^4$, each coefficient index is represented as a four-digit radix-4 number, $n = (d_3 d_2 d_1 d_0)_4$, $d_i \in \{0, 1, 2, 3\}$. The mapping scheme uses one radix-4 digit as the bank index, while the remaining three digits form the intra-bank address. If the intra-bank digits are denoted by $(x, y, z)_4$, the corresponding linear address can be expressed as $addr = 16x + 4y + z$.

For the read mapping, the digit expanded at stage s is chosen as the bank index $bank_{\text{read}} = d_s$, while the remaining three digits determine the intra-bank address. Hence, the four coefficients participating in one radix-4 butterfly differ only in and are naturally distributed across four banks, enabling conflict-free parallel reads. To preserve in-place storage without overwriting coefficients that have not yet been consumed, scheduling is performed on a 4×4 tile rather than on individual butterflies. For two adjacent radix-4 stages s and $s + 1$, a tile is defined by fixing all radix-4 digits except $r = d_{s+1}$ and $c = d_s$. Under this formulation, each row of the tile corresponds to one radix-4 butterfly in stage s, and each column to one butterfly in stage $s + 1$. The tile therefore forms the smallest closed data unit spanning two adjacent stages.

During execution, the entire 4×4 tile is first loaded from the main memory into an on-chip register buffer, and radix-4 butterfly operations are then performed row-wise to produce the intermediate result $\mathbf{Y} = [y_{r,c}]$. Subsequently, a local transpose is carried out as $z_{r,c} = y_{c,r}$, yielding a new tile $\mathbf{Z} = [z_{r,c}]$, which is written back to the physical address range originally occupied by the tile. Since all old data in the tile have been read before write-back starts, in-place overwrite does not corrupt unread inputs. After the transpose, the coefficients are also reorganized along the new bank dimension required by the next stage, so conflict-free parallel access is preserved. The process of conflict-free read/write mapping from stage 0 to stage 1 is shown in the left of Fig. 4. The complete mapping process for N=256 is summarized in the right of Fig. 4. In this way, the proposed method achieves both safe in-place write-back and conflict-free memory access for high-throughput radix-4 NTT hardware.

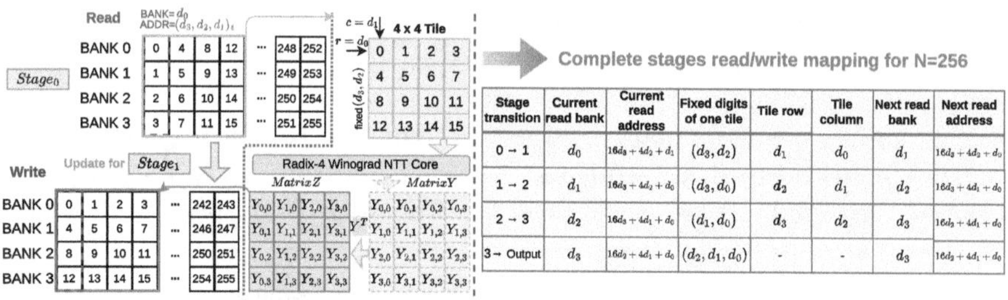

Fig. 4. Conflict-free read/write mapping. The left side of the dashed line shows the mapping from Stage 0 to Stage 1, while the right side presents the complete stage mapping pattern for $N = 256$.

5 Experiment and Evaluation

5.1 Experimental Setup

The design is implemented in C++, synthesized via Vitis HLS 2022.2, and evaluated on a Xilinx Zynq-7000 FPGA (xc7z020clg484-1) using Vivado 2022.2. All metrics are obtained from post-place-and-route (Post-PnR) results. Two NIST PQC schemes are evaluated: ML-KEM ($N = 256$, $q = 3329$) and ML-DSA ($N = 256$, $q = 8380417$).

5.2 Implementation Results and Comparative Analysis

Table 1 summarizes the resource utilization and performance of the proposed Uni-Winograd architecture for ML-DSA, alongside representative state-of-the-art NTT accelerators. Table 2 presents the corresponding results for ML-KEM. For fair comparison, all baseline designs target comparable FPGA platforms and support polynomial length $N = 256$. Slice counts of prior works are estimated as LUT/4 (or LUT/8 for UltraScale+ devices) to enable consistent cross-platform comparison. The area-time product (AT) is reported in the AT column as LUT count multiplied by latency. The proposed architecture provides two design points: a resource-efficient (RE) and a high-performance (HP), both requiring only 4 BRAMs.

For ML-DSA (Table 1), the HP configuration reduces DSP and BRAM usage by 52% and 72% over the baseline [14] at comparable latency (68 vs. 58 cycles); the RE configuration achieves an 88% DSP reduction at higher latency (286 vs. 58 cycles). For ML-KEM (Table 2), DSP and BRAM usage drop by 79% and 67%, respectively, relative to the same baseline. Both configurations outperform conventional radix-2/4 architectures in resource-latency trade-off, demonstrating the cross-algorithm efficiency of the unified design.

5.3 Performance Analysis and Discussion

Resource Efficiency. These resource reductions follow directly from the constant-set discretization property. By mapping all non-trivial multiplications to four shared constants, general-purpose modular multipliers are eliminated: the HP configuration requires only 24 DSPs versus 50 for the baseline [14] at comparable latency, while the RE configuration uses just 6 DSPs at higher latency. The conflict-free memory mapping further enables a compact 4-bank BRAM organization (64-deep each), reducing BRAM usage from 14.5 to 4 blocks. For ML-KEM, DSP and BRAM usage drop by 79% and 67%, respectively.

Unification and Reusability. A key advantage of Uni-Winograd is its zero-reconfiguration-cost support for both ML-DSA and ML-KEM. The same hardware instance can be reused by updating modular reduction parameters and the corresponding Winograd constants. For ML-KEM, a hybrid mapping (radix-4 Winograd in early stages and radix-2 butterfly in the final stage) enables direct

Table 1. Comparison results for ML-DSA implementation.

NTT Type	Design	Board	LUT	Slice	FFs	BRAM	DSP	Latency	Freq. (MHz)	AT
Radix-2	[5]	Artix-7	9018	2255	6292	2	16	256	250	3948
Radix-4	[22]	Zynq-7000	2386	597	932	2	8	256	217	1648
Radix-2	[6]	Artix-7	11000	2750	5182	12	64	156	140	10196
			63000	15750	18000	48	256	103	126	33802
Radix-2	[11]	Kintex-U+	26520	3315	15171	24	48	113	194	4727
Radix-16 (Winograd)	[14]	Zynq-7000	12141	3664	7941	14.5	50	58	254	1978
		ZCU102	11963	1813	7187				297	1330
		Artix-7	12720	3667	7834				183	2747
Radix-4(RE)	**Ours**	Zynq-7000	3009	753	4427	4	6	286	270	1433
Radix-4(HP)	**Ours**	Zynq-7000	11362	2840.5	18841	4	24	68	270	1319

Table 2. Comparison results for ML-KEM implementation.

NTT Type	Design	Board	LUT	Slice	FFs	BRAM	DSP	Latency	Freq. (MHz)	AT
Radix-2/4	[7]	Zynq-7000	5293	1323	5518	-	34	127	265	2263
	[8]	Artix-7	1740	575	643	5	4	224	200	1092
Radix-2	[11]	Kintex-U+	24186	3023	14756	24	48	100	200	3912
Radix-8/16 (Winograd)	[14]	Zynq-7000	9824	2745	4752	12	29	58	181	1809
		ZCU102	9083	1520	3839				252	1017
		Artix-7	9985	2983	4580				132	2585
Radix-4 (RE)	**Ours**	Zynq-7000	3009	753	4427	4	6	286	270	1433
Radix-4 (HP)	**Ours**	Zynq-7000	11362	2840.5	18841	4	24	68	270	1319

reuse of the same datapath. The logic reuse rate exceeds 90% across all supported modes. In contrast, prior flexible designs (e.g., [11]) rely on duplicated datapaths or multiplexed arithmetic units, resulting in higher resource overhead (e.g., 48 DSPs and 24 BRAMs on Kintex-U+). This unified design is particularly suitable for multi-standard PQC systems under strict area constraints.

Overall Efficiency. The area-time product (AT) results further validate the efficiency of the proposed design. Using the [14] design (1978) as a reference, the proposed RE configuration achieves AT = 1433 (0.72×), while the HP configuration achieves 1319 (0.67×). For ML-KEM, the corresponding improvements are from 1809 to 1433 (0.79×) and 1319 (0.73×), respectively. Moreover, when normalized per DSP, Uni-Winograd exhibits significantly higher efficiency than prior designs, highlighting its suitability for DSP-constrained FPGA platforms.

Throughput per DSP, defined as $f/(\text{Latency} \times \text{DSP})$, further confirms this trend: the HP and RE configurations achieve 1.89× and 1.80× higher throughput per DSP than the baseline [14], respectively. Taken together, these normalized metrics place both configurations on the resource-efficiency Pareto frontier: HP achieves superior DSP efficiency at comparable latency, while RE defines the low-DSP extreme for $N = 256$ NTT designs.

Design Trade-Off. Compared with the [14] design, Uni-Winograd achieves a more balanced design trade-off. While [14] minimizes latency (58 cycles), it requires substantially higher DSP and BRAM resource. In contrast, the HP configuration (24 DSPs, 68 cycles) introduces only a modest latency overhead while reducing DSP usage by more than 50% and BRAM usage to 4 blocks. For applications without strict sub-200 ns latency constraints (e.g., IoT gateways for signature verification or key encapsulation), the RE configuration (6 DSPs, 286 cycles) offers significantly improved resource efficiency while still meeting practical performance requirements (e.g., $< 2\,\mu\text{s}$ per NTT).

Table 3. Post-implementation power and energy estimates.

Configuration	Total (W)	Dynamic (W)	Static (W)	Energy/NTT (nJ)
RE	0.321	0.215	0.106	459
HP	0.513	0.404	0.109	174

* Energy/NTT = Total Power × $\text{Latency}_{\text{cycles}}/f_{\text{clk}}$. Includes full block-design overhead.

Power and Energy Efficiency. Table 3 reports the post-implementation power estimates obtained from Vivado on the Zynq-7000 xc7z020clg484-1 device. The RE configuration consumes 37.5% less power than HP (0.321 W vs. 0.513 W) due to its lower DSP and logic utilization. However, its 4.2× longer latency yields higher energy per NTT (459 nJ vs. 174 nJ), as the shorter execution time of the HP configuration reduces static energy accumulation. Thus, RE suits thermally constrained scenarios, while HP favors energy-sensitive applications such as battery-powered devices.

6 Conclusion

This paper presents Uni-Winograd, a unified and resource-efficient radix-4 Winograd NTT architecture for ML-DSA and ML-KEM. Through a hierarchical Kronecker-product analysis, we prove that the set of multiplication constants collapses to only four discrete values after four levels of nesting, thereby establishing a constant-set discretization property that enables a unified datapath design. Based on this insight, we construct a reusable Winograd computation core and integrate pipelined scheduling with conflict-free memory mapping to achieve efficient cross-algorithm hardware reuse. FPGA implementation results show that the proposed architecture achieves a 52% DSP and 72% BRAM reduction at comparable latency, and up to 88% DSP reduction in the RE configuration, while maintaining a competitive resource-latency trade-off. Overall, this work introduces a constant-structure-driven design methodology that provides a general and scalable framework for efficient and reusable PQC hardware accelerators.

Acknowledgments. This work is supported by the National Key R&D Program of China (No.2022YFB4400703), the National Key R&D Program of Heilongjiang Province (2024ZXDXA12) and the Fundamental Research Funds for the Central Universities (3072026XK0801).

Disclosure of Interests. All authors disclosed no relevant relationships.

References

1. Agnello, J.S.: An introduction to the winograd discrete fourier transform. Ph.D. thesis, Iowa State University (1979). https://stars.library.ucf.edu/rtd/392, retrospective Theses and Dissertations
2. Aikata, A., Mert, A.C., Imran, M., Pagliarini, S., Roy, S.S.: Kali: a crystal for post-quantum security using kyber and dilithium. IEEE Trans. Circuits Syst. I Regul. Pap. **70**(2), 747–758 (2023). https://doi.org/10.1109/TCSI.2022.3219555
3. Bailey, D.: Winograd's algorithm applied to number-theoretic transforms. Electron. Lett. **13**(18) (1977). https://doi.org/10.1049/el:19770394
4. Chen, X., Yang, B., Yin, S., Wei, S., Liu, L.: CFNTT: scalable radix-2/4 NTT multiplication architecture with an efficient conflict-free memory mapping scheme. IACR Trans. Cryptogr. Hardw. Embed. Syst. **2022**(1), 94–126 (2022). https://doi.org/10.46586/tches.v2022.i1.94-126
5. Cui, Y., Zhong, J., Wang, B., Xu, T., Wang, C., Liu, W.: High-performance hardware implementation of crystals-dilithium based on improved MDC-NTT. IEEE Trans. Comput. **74**(9), 2896–2908 (2025). https://doi.org/10.1109/TC.2025.3576934
6. Derya, K., Mert, A.C., Öztürk, E., Savaş, E.: CoHA-NTT: a configurable hardware accelerator for NTT-based polynomial multiplication. Microprocess. Microsyst. **89**(C) (2022). https://doi.org/10.1016/j.micpro.2022.104451
7. Duong-Ngoc, P., Lee, H.: Configurable mixed-radix number theoretic transform architecture for lattice-based cryptography. IEEE Access **10**, 12732–12741 (2022). https://doi.org/10.1109/ACCESS.2022.3145988
8. Guo, W., Li, S.: Highly-efficient hardware architecture for crystals-kyber with a novel conflict-free memory access pattern. IEEE Trans. Circuits Syst. I Regul. Pap. **70**(11), 4505–4515 (2023). https://doi.org/10.1109/TCSI.2023.3306347
9. Hua, J.Y., Gao, Z., Yu, J.W., Tang, S., Yu, X.T.: A low complexity realisation of winograd number theoretic transform and its application. Int. J. Electron. **102**(2), 248–259 (2015). https://doi.org/10.1080/00207217.2014.896045
10. Kundi, D.E.S., Mera, J.M.B., Strub, P.Y., Hutter, M.: High-performance NTT hardware accelerator to support ML-KEM and ML-DSA. In: ASHES 2024: Proceedings of the 2024 Workshop on Attacks and Solutions in Hardware Security, pp. 100–105 (2024). https://doi.org/10.1145/3689939.3695785

11. Li, B., Yan, Y., Wei, Y., Han, H.: Scalable and parallel optimization of the number theoretic transform based on FPGA. IEEE Trans. Very Large Scale Integr. (VLSI) Syst. **32**(2), 291–304 (2024). https://doi.org/10.1109/TVLSI.2023.3312423
12. Li, M., Tian, J., Hu, X., Wang, Z.: Reconfigurable and high-efficiency polynomial multiplication accelerator for crystals-kyber. IEEE Trans. Comput. Aided Des. Integr. Circuits Syst. **42**(8), 2540–2551 (2023). https://doi.org/10.1109/TCAD.2022.3230359
13. Li, S., Zhai, C., Wang, X., Guo, Z., He, S., Guo, D.: RePM: reconfigurable elastic computing for polynomial multiplier with hybrid NTT algorithm. In: 2025 IEEE/ACM International Conference on Computer Aided Design (ICCAD), pp. 1–9 (2025). https://doi.org/10.1109/ICCAD66269.2025.11240941
14. Mandal, S., Basu Roy, D.: Winograd for NTT: a case study on higher-radix and low-latency implementation of NTT for post quantum cryptography on FPGA. IEEE Trans. Circuits Syst. I Regul. Pap. **71**(12), 6396–6409 (2024). https://doi.org/10.1109/TCSI.2024.3470335
15. National Institute of Standards and Technology: Module-lattice-based digital signature standard. In: Federal Information Processing Standards Publication (FIPS) NIST FIPS 204 (2024). https://doi.org/10.6028/NIST.FIPS.204
16. National Institute of Standards and Technology: Module-lattice-based key encapsulation mechanism standard. In: Federal Information Processing Standards Publication (FIPS) NIST FIPS 203 (2024). https://doi.org/10.6028/NIST.FIPS.203
17. Raciborski, M., Cariow, A.: On the derivation of winograd-type DFT algorithms for input sequences whose length is a power of two. Electronics **11**, 1342 (2022). https://doi.org/10.3390/electronics11091342
18. Tu, Y., Xie, J.: Eminem: efficient FPGA implementation of mixed-radix NTT hardware accelerators for NIST post-quantum cryptography falcon, dilithium, and hawk. ACM Trans. Reconfigurable Technol. Syst. **18**(4) (2025). https://doi.org/10.1145/3771287
19. Wang, J., Hou, J., Zhang, F., Meng, Y., Su, Y., Yang, C.: An efficient and parallelism-scalable large integer multiplier architecture using least-positive form and winograd fast algorithm. IEEE Trans. Circuits Syst. II Express Briefs **72**(1), 248–252 (2025). https://doi.org/10.1109/TCSII.2024.3457494
20. Wang, J., Yang, C., Zhang, F., Meng, Y., Xiang, S., Su, Y.: A high-throughput toom-cook-4 polynomial multiplier for lattice-based cryptography using a novel winograd-schoolbook algorithm. IEEE Trans. Circuits Syst. I Regul. Pap. **71**(1), 359–372 (2024). https://doi.org/10.1109/TCSI.2023.3332880
21. Xu, Y., Ding, L., He, P., Lu, Z., Zhang, J.: Meta: a memory-efficient tri-stage polynomial multiplication accelerator using 2D coupled-bfus. IEEE Trans. Circuits Syst. I Regul. Pap. **72**(2), 647–660 (2025). https://doi.org/10.1109/TCSI.2024.3461736
22. Zhao, C., et al.: A compact and high-performance hardware architecture for crystals-dilithium. IACR Trans. Cryptogr. Hardw. Embed. Syst. 270–295 (2021). https://doi.org/10.46586/tches.v2022.i1.270-295

Barbell: An Extensible Generator of On-demand Loads for Interactive Cloud Services

Yuxuan Liu[1], Yeh-Ching Chung[1], and Shuang Chen[2](✉)

[1] School of Data Science, The Chinese University of Hong Kong, Shenzhen, China
yuxuanliu1@link.cuhk.edu.cn, ychung@cuhk.edu.cn
[2] Shuhai Lab, Huawei Cloud, Hangzhou, China
chenshuang0804@gmail.com

Abstract. Interactive cloud service developers and infrastructure designers heavily rely on load generators to optimize service performance and infrastructure architecture. However, existing load generators are far from meeting their demands, for two reasons. First, they can only generate loads of peak or stable intensity in request rate, whereas our analysis of real-world traces shows that complicated load fluctuations are common and traces are often dumped in server resource utilization. Second, they are *tightly coupled* with their designated service type. This blocks the load generator development from keeping up with the needs of emerging cloud services such as large language model (LLM) inference.

To address these two issues, we propose an extensible load generator dubbed Barbell to generate load patterns on demand, with two innovations accordingly. First, we propose a multi-pass load intensity generation method to generate loads with a configurable pipeline of modular passes. A segment-wise aggregation pass is devised to generate loads with segments of distinct patterns by merging segment-specific passes. A profile-guided conversion pass is designed to convert loads in resource utilization to request rates. Second, Barbell designs a *decoupled* architecture where the load generation is decoupled from the service type with hook and callback interfaces. Four service extension models are proposed to extend to services with various types of clients and protocols.

Evaluation results show that Barbell achieves comparable accuracy of performance measures obtained by service type-specific load generators. It can generate loads that mimic real load patterns in the cloud. We have extended Barbell to six popular interactive services, including LLM inference, with only a few hundred lines of code for each service type.

Keywords: Load Generation · Workload Characterization · Performance Evaluation · Cloud Computing

1 Introduction

Cloud data centers host a large number of interactive services such as web search and social media [14,16]. Via these services, end users send requests to cloud

L. Eeckhout et al. (Eds.): APPT 2026, LNCS 16693, pp. 49–63, 2027.
https://doi.org/10.1007/978-981-92-4805-6_4

servers where the requests are processed and sent back to the users in a timely manner. Cloud servers experience significantly variant loads, depending on the number of end users, the request rate of each user, and the service type. Besides the existing ones, new interactive services such as large language model (LLM) inference [6] are *rapidly emerging* in the cloud, imposing new load patterns.

Load generators are widely used by service developers and infrastructure designers to test the performance of these services. They act as clients and emulate end user behaviors by generating synthetic loads [19]. It is critical to generate representative loads because the user heavily relies on them to understand and improve the performance of their services [15]. However, existing load generators are far from meeting their demands, specifically due to two challenges.

Challenge 1. Existing load generators are insufficient in emulating complicated but realistic load patterns. This makes them inappropriate to evaluate services hosted in real cloud. Most like sysbench [28] and memtier_benchmark [5] (memtier in short) can only generate peak loads or limit to a stable request rate. However, analysis of real cloud traces [18,35] has shown that the services they work for barely operate at full or stable load. Mutilate [32] and OLTP-Bench [21] generate load variation with a single distribution or with step-wise fixed rates. Nevertheless, our analysis of CloudX traces shows that most periodic loads are diurnal, exhibiting distinct fluctuation patterns in different time periods. Facebook flashback [24] generates highly varying loads by replaying a given RPS trace, but fails when real traces are unavailable or when traces are not in request rate.

Challenge 2. Prior work also suffers from limited extensibility to various service types. Most existing load generators are designed to measure a specific service type with a specific load. For example, memtier [5] tests KV store services only, sysbench [28] tests relational database services only, and wrk [9,10] tests web services only. Even for a single service, it has been proved that the incomplete support of request control policies [37] leads to limited extensibility and intolerable evaluation cost [27]. Take Memcached, for instance, it can be tested using memtier [5], mutilate [32], mutated [12], YCSB [17], etc. Memtier only supports stress testing; mutilate only supports closed-loop; while mutated and YCSB can operate in open-loop but not closed-loop. The performance measured by different policies are incomparable due to the coordination emission issue [39].

Our Work. In this paper, we first analyze the limitations of prior work with concrete trace examples in Sect. 2. In Sect. 3, we extensively study load patterns of three diverse interactive services in CloudX, and find that unstable load is prevalent. Then, we propose Barbell in Sect. 4, which greatly improves the flexibility of load pattern generation and extensibility. We evaluate Barbell under various interactive cloud services to show its accuracy of measurement, flexibility of load pattern generation, and simplicity of extensibility in Sect. 5.

In summary, we make the following contributions:

1. We find that most cloud interactive services exhibit common load characterizations, calling for an extensible load generator to generate loads for them.

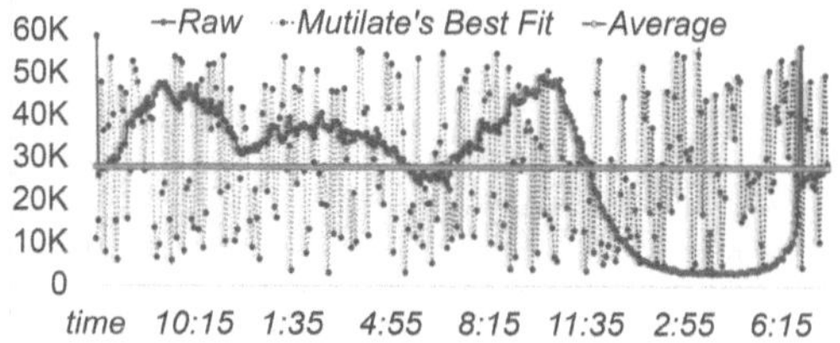

Fig. 1. A 24h RPS trace segment with diurnality in CloudX.

70% of VMs are unstable, but they exhibit common fluctuation patterns, including periodicity, diurnality, oscillation, and combinations of them.

2. We propose a multi-pass load intensity generation method to generate loads with a pipeline of passes that models elementary patterns, passes that aggregate them to generate combinatorial or load-segment-wise patterns, and passes that converts loads in resource utilization to RPS guided by profiling.
3. We design an extensible system architecture by decoupling general load generation functionality from service-specific ones. The general functionality has full support of request control policies and latency measurement, and we propose a methodology for each kind of interactive service to extend from it.
4. By putting it all together, we implement an extensible load generator named Barbell that can generate any desired load for any interactive cloud services.

2 Prior Work Limitation

2.1 Single-Pass Load Intensity Generation

Existing load generators fail to generate complicated load patterns because they model them in a single-pass way, trying to fit all patterns within an entire trace with a single model. The easiest model is to limit request rate to the peak or average. Many contemporary load generators, such as sysbench [28] and memtier [5], implement stress testing by issuing requests as fast as possible. Most of them can limit to a fixed rate, but cannot generate load fluctuation at all. To address this issue, mutilate [32] and OLTP-Bench [21] generates load variation with a single distribution or step-wise fixed rates. However, they fail to fit common load patterns like diurnality. Figure 1 shows a typical RPS trace segment with diurnality in CloudX. Mutilate's best-fitted distributions completely loses the diurnality.

Time series [22,25,41] models can fit complicated load variations, but the parameters (e.g., Hurst coefficient [36]) are obscure for users without expertise to tune. Besides, they require long (quadratic) time to generate large traces [40]. Facebook flashback [24] can model any load patterns by replaying a given RPS trace. Nevertheless, when the trace is not in RPS, the user has to do a manual transformation for every load on every server under test.

Table 1. Feature of VM's Load Pattern

Feature	Description
Stability	Range of the original series < 5%
Periodicity	ACF of the denoised series > 0.5
Fluctuation	CV of the residual series > 10%

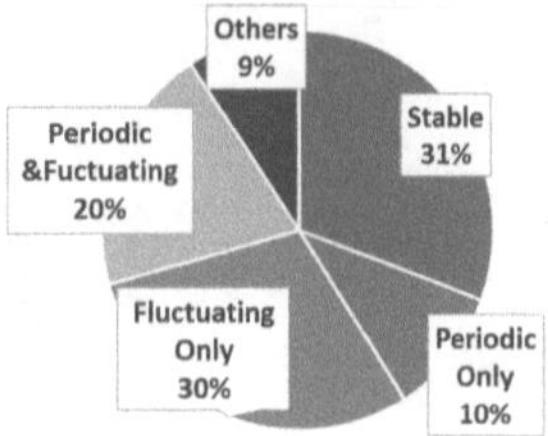

Fig. 2. Percentage of each type of VM.

2.2 Coupled General and Service-Specific Functionality

Existing load generators have limited extensibility to service types because they tightly couple general functionality to service-specific ones. Most of them are designated for a specific service type with specific interfaces. For example, mutilate [32] only implements get/set for KV store services, and sysbench [28] only implements SQL queries like select/insert for relational database services. The tight coupling lowers the development cost, but leads to significant heterogeneity across programming languages (C/C++, Java, Go), configuration methods (CLI, XML, Lua), and request control policies (closed-loop, open-loop, and partly-open-loop [37]). The heterogeneity causes intolerable cost in deployment and configuration, and incomparable measurements for a comprehensive evaluation [27].

Tailbench [26] and lancet [27] have pioneered the design of extensible load generators for general interactive services, by forcibly serializing all requests into socket streams. It works well for services with simple and stateless protocols like Redis, but fails for services with complicated or stateful protocols like MySQL. Developers have to manage every protocol detail, and cannot use off-the-shelf clients and connectors. Sysbench does similar thing by manually defining all SQL data structures and member fields, but it takes hundreds to thousands LoC, and the developers have to continuously fix compatibility issues [?, ?, ?].

3 Workload Characterization

3.1 Dataset and Feature Extraction

Our dataset includes three thousand VMs and about six million data points from twenty tenants and three cloud interactive services hosted in CloudX, namely, Relational Database Service (RDS, such as MySQL), Distributed Caching Service (DCS, such as Memcache), and Distributed Message Service (DMS, such as Kafka). For each VM, we perform the following steps to extract its load pattern:

1. Calculate the minimum, mean, and maximum. This gives us a general view of how large the VM's load is, and how large the load variation range is.

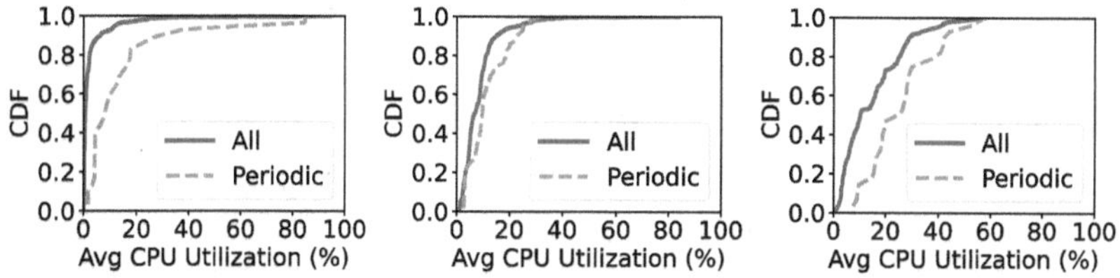

(a) DCS (b) RDS (c) DMS

Fig. 3. CDF of average CPU utilization of all and periodic VMs for three services.

2. Apply Autoregressive Integrated Moving Average (ARIMA) model [38] for time series analysis. Specifically, we decompose one load time series into three: trend, seasonality, and residuals. Combining trend and seasonality, we obtain the denoised and the residual series. The goal is to exclude the impact of residual when analyzing periodicity, and better understand fluctuations.
3. Calculate the autocorrelation function (ACF) [3,31] of the denoised series. ACF reflects how periodic the time series is. An absolute value closer to 1 represents stronger periodicity. We do not obtain ACF of the original load time series to exclude the impact of unpredictable spikes or fluctuations.
4. Divide the standard deviation of the residual series by the mean of the denoised series. Intuitively, this calculates the coefficient of variation (CV) [11] of the load and represents how fluctuated it is.
5. Categorize VMs based on the metrics calculated above, as shown in Table 1. The percentage of each type of VM is plotted in Fig. 2).

3.2 Load Characteristics in the Cloud

In summary, we observe two key characteristics: load intensity is mostly small to medium, and load variation shows periodic and fluctuating behavior.

Load Intensity Characteristics. It is well known that resource utilization is low in the cloud [18,20,23,33]. However, after categorizing VMs by their stability, we find that unstable VMs have much higher loads than stable VMs. Figure 3 shows the distribution of the average CPU utilization of all VMs and periodic VMs for each interactive service. The average of DCS, RDS, and DMS VMs is 2.7%, 8.4%, and 14.8%, respectively. DCS has the lowest average CPU utilization among them because it (i.e., KV store) is a memory-intensive service.

All stable VMs have an average CPU utilization under 10%. 64% of them even have loads lower than 3%, signaling that no workload is running inside. Since most cloud service providers provide monthly or yearly subscriptions cheaper than on-demand pricing [1,2], many users almost never release their resources even when their VMs are completely idle. Contrarily, periodic VMs have fluctuating loads, meaning that they are actively in use and, therefore, have a higher load, as shown in Fig. 3. CDF means cumulative distribution function.

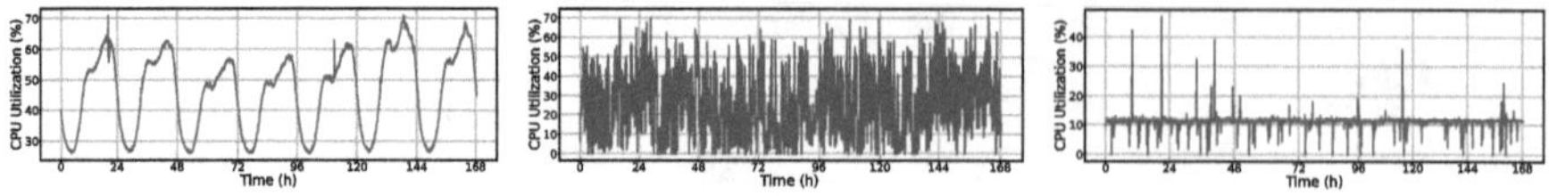

(a) Purely Periodic VM with Diurnal Loads (b) Fluctuating VM with Oscillating Load (c) Fluctuating VM with Bursty Load

Fig. 4. Load traces with different variation patterns in CloudX.

Load Variation Characteristics. Most periodic VMs have diurnal load patterns. Figure 4a is purely periodic with clear diurnality in a repeating period of 24 h. Fluctuating VMs have various fluctuating patterns. Figure 4b shows an oscillating pattern, while Fig. 4c is more bursty.

The best fitting distributions for unstable VMs are generalized normal distribution (gennorm), alpha distribution (alpha), and exponentially modified Gaussian distribution (exponorm).

4 Barbell Design

4.1 System Overview

Given the limitations of prior work (Sect. 2) and the load patterns in the real cloud (Sect. 3), we design Barbell, an extensible load generator to generate on-demand loads for interactive cloud services. Figure 5 shows the overall system design of Barbell, highlighting three key design choices:

- **Flexible load pattern generation** is realized through multi-pass load intensity generation with a custom pipeline of modular passes.
- **Request control policies are fully supported** in general functionality by managing the number of concurrent in-flight requests in each connection.
- **Extensibility** is realized through decoupling general and service-specific functionalities (extension in short) with the hook and callback interface.

4.2 Multi-pass Load Intensity Generator

The core of multi-pass load intensity generator is a pipeline of multiple passes, where each pass scans the entire trace from the previous pass, performs some adjustments, and output a new trace to the next pass or directly to the load executor. All intermediate results (IR) are time series (not necessarily in RPS), so the passes are modular and pluggable. Users can easily develop new passes to identify desired load patterns and apply them in the custom pass pipeline.

Entrance Pass (Synthesis/Replay)
The pass pipeline starts with an entrance pass (either a synthesis pass or a replay pass) to generate traces with raw patterns for all following passes. The *synthesis* pass fills the trace with random intensity generated by the specified distribution. The *replay* pass fills the trace with data points of an input trace, which can be collected from real clouds, public datasets, or third-party trace fitters.

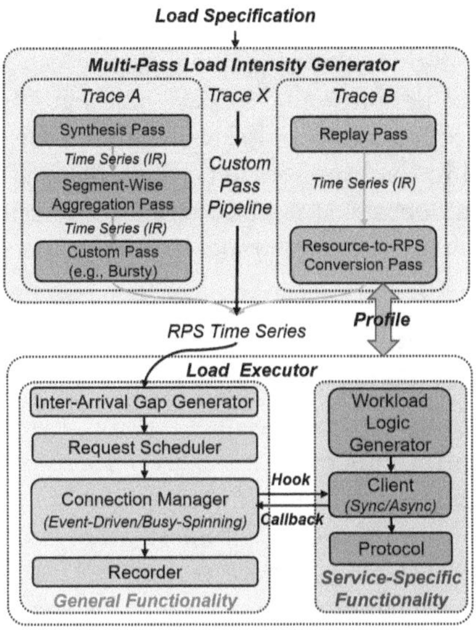

Fig. 5. System overview of Barbell.

Segment-Wise Load Aggregation Pass

This pass aggregates input traces with distinct load patterns to an output trace of multiple segments. Each segment exhibits the load pattern of an input trace. Take diurnal loads in Fig. 1 for instance, it exhibits distinct patterns during daytime and nighttime, so the pass aggregates traces from two synthesis passes. These two passes are configured with best fitted distribution to retain load patterns of daytime and nighttime separately. Finally, the pass aggregates input traces into one according to the duration of each segment and output it.

Similar to segment-wise load aggregation, passes can be easily developed to generate other load patterns in a modular fashion. For example, there can be a pass to generate load periodicity, and another pass to generate bursty loads of specified interval and intensity upon input traces.

Profile-Guided Resource to RPS Load Conversion Pass

Unlike above passes that work with static configuration, converting traces from resource utilization to RPS requires approximating RPS through interpolation of dynamically profiled data on the server under test. Among all common resource utilization, Barbell implements the prevalent scaled CPU load, and others can be implemented similarly. The pass first determines several representative CPU loads as targets to profile. These targets are the samples for interpolation, and the accuracy of approximation increases with finer-grained target selection. Test runs are then launched to approach each target gradually.

The initial test run works as stress testing to get the first RPS-CPU mapping without prior knowledge of the server. The pass then iteratively generates loads of fixed RPS, gets stabilized average CPU load, and update RPS for a new test run. A target is profiled successfully when a test run produces CPU load close enough to it within an error tolerance, which determines confidence of profiling. It is configurable and the default value is ±2% balancing both profiling time and accuracy. After all the targets are profiled successfully, the pass approximates the RPS of every CPU load in the input trace through piecewise linear interpolation. The profiling is efficient because its time complexity is linear to the range of scaled CPU load to profile, and is irrelevant to the length of the input sequence.

4.3 General Functionality

Request Scheduler

It manages a state machine for every request during load generation. A request initiates at the waiting state once the inter-arrival gap generator determines its arrival time. It then transits to the scheduled state when its arrival time arrives. There is a request queue in each connection to store in-flight requests that are sent out but have not received complete responses. Requests in the scheduled state sustain client-side waiting until an in-flight request completes.

The three request control policies are then controlled by the number of concurrent in-flight requests. Closed-loop policy allows only one global in-flight request among all connections. Open-loop policy supports unlimited concurrent in-flight requests, and the queue should have no size limit. Partly-open-loop policy lies in between. The larger the number of concurrent in-flight requests is, the more similar it behaves like open-loop, and vice versa (Fig. 6).

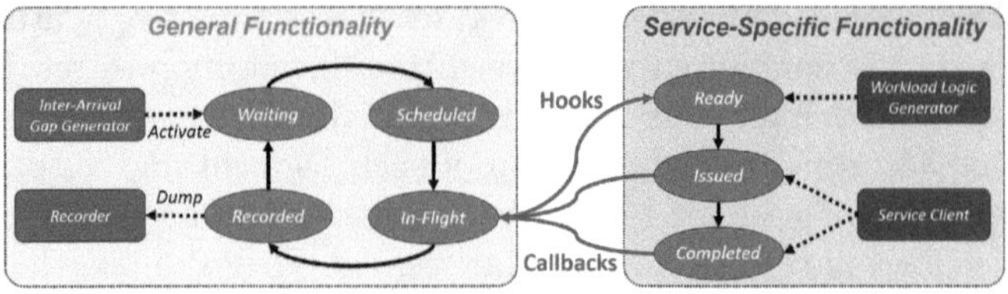

Fig. 6. State transition diagram of a request in Barbell.

Connection Manager

It ensures immediate issue of requests in the scheduled state whenever the request queue is not full to avoid latency underestimation due to coordination emission [39]. For closed-loop policy, it adopts the event-driven model to issue requests and receive responses in a single event loop. The interleaved execution produces accurate measurements because senders and receivers never overlap. When it comes to (partly-)open-loop policy, the event-driven model suffers from missed sends and receives because concurrent senders and receivers overlap. Barbell solves the issue by hosting the sender and receiver with separate threads. Both threads use busy-spinning to reduce client-side jitters when loads are heavy.

Hook and Callback Interface

Whenever a request enters the request queue, the connection manager notifies the service extension via *issue_req* hook. The request first transits to the ready state when the workload logic generator determines its request body (more details in Sect. 4.4). Then, the service client issues the request to the server (the issued state) and receives the response (the completed state) later, triggering *issued_cb* and *recv_cb* callbacks to notify the connection manager to measure client-side waiting time, end-to-end latency, and service-specific statistics if attached.

4.4 Service-Specific Functionality

Models for Service Extension

We categorize service extensions as four models (see Fig. 7) for services with different types clients and protocols. Currently, the six popular interactive cloud services that Barbell implements demonstrate the usage of all four models.

- **Direct Socket I/O** [*Redis, Memcached*]. The extension issues requests as I/O streams through built-in socket (TCP/UDP), and the developers issues requests and parses responses as streams following the service protocol. The *issued_cb* and *recv_cb* are triggered when the streams are loaded to the write buffer, and responses arrive at the read buffer separately.
- **Sync Client with Thread Interleaving** [*MySQL*]. The extension issues requests through client APIs in a synchronous way. The client manages protocol details and issues multiple requests simultaneously by launching multiple interleaved threads as a thread pool. Each incoming request fits an idle thread, and the pool size limits the number of concurrent in-flight requests.
- **Async Client with Stateless Protocol** [*Nginx, vLLM*]. Requests can be issued in a mutually independent way. The client issues them asynchronously through I/O multiplexing, and its built-in callbacks are implicitly triggered when it finishes issuing a request and receiving the response.
- **Async Client with Stateful Protocol** [*Kafka (Producer and Consumer)*]. The client must manage session history, request ordering and execution status. The extension still issues requests asynchronously, but has to explicitly pool the client occasionally to activate the I/O event and callbacks.

Workload Logic Generator

It determines the number and type of requests to issue along with all associated arguments. For *request-based* loads, where requests/transactions are mutually independent, it only generates the request body (e.g., key and value streams for KV store and web URLs for HTTP). It takes service-specific configurations generate workload logic that adheres desired features (e.g., hot key space and temporal locality). Barbell also supports generating *session-based* loads, where inter-request dependency exists [13]. An example is YCSB's core workload F of read-modify-write transactions [17]. The user reads a key, and updates it with a modified value. Barbell allows users to write a Lua script to program the request flow, then it loads and executes the script during runtime. Sysbench proposed similar configuration method, but they only work for relational database service.

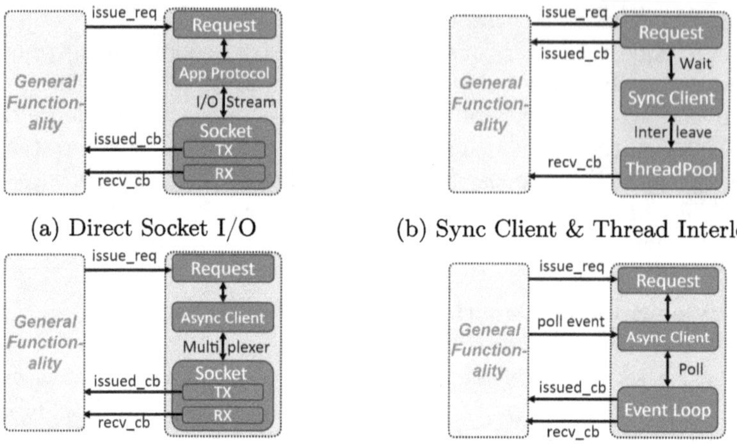

(a) Direct Socket I/O

(b) Sync Client & Thread Interleave

(c) Async Client & Stateless Protocol

(d) Async Client & Stateful Protocol

Fig. 7. Four models of service extension in Barbell.

5 Evaluation

We evaluate Barbell's accuracy of measurement in Sect. 5.2, flexibility of load pattern generation in Sect. 5.3, and simplicity of extensibility in Sect. 5.4.

5.1 Methodology

We use two Intel Xeon Silver 4210 machines running Ubuntu 20.04, each with 20 physical cores (40 threads) in 2 sockets and 96GB memory. The machines have hyper-threading and turbo boost enabled. We launch the latest stable release of each load generator in a 16-core docker container on one machine as client and each service in a 4-core docker container on the other machine as server. There is no difference between VM and docker to host the service as long as the overall resource consumption is under proper constraint. All containers are pinned to a fixed set of physical cores in the same socket, and use `-network host` to ensure stable performance measurement. Table 2 shows the dataset and load generators for each test service. Unless otherwise specified, load generators and services are instantiated with 8 and 4 threads/workers, separately. Each test lasts for 120 s. 30B and 200B are average key/value sizes among CloudX's DCS loads.

Table 2. Service Throughput Comparison with SOTA Load Generators

Service	Dataset	Load Generator	Maximum RPS
Memcached	10k key range, SET:GET=1:9 <Key(30B), Value(200B)>	Mutilate v0.1 Barbell	363452 368494 (+1.39%)
Nginx	GET method on files 10KB file size	wrk2 v4.0.0 Barbell	11403 11396 (−0.06%)
MySQL	OLTP read-only transactions 4 tables, each with 10k entries	Sysbench v1.0.20 Barbell	2345 2007 (−14.41%)

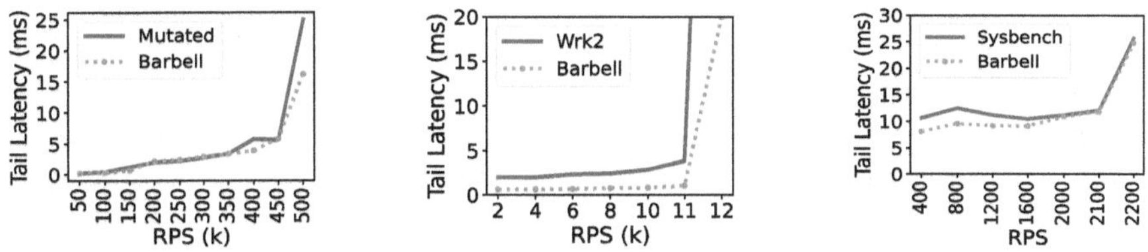

(a) Memcached (b) Nginx (c) MySQL

Fig. 8. 99th percentile of latency (tail latency) with increasing RPS.

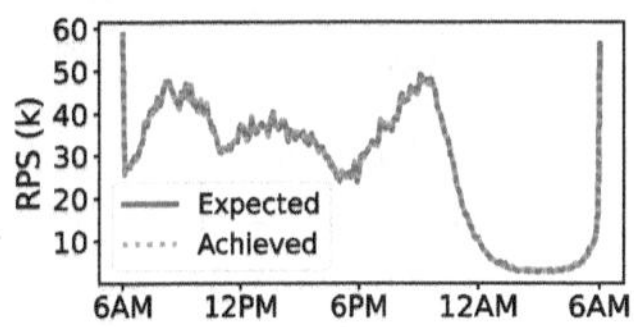

Fig. 9. The replay pass precisely replays trace in Fig. 1.

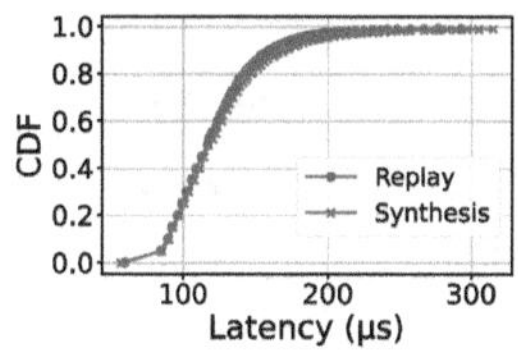

Fig. 10. Latency CDF under replay and synthesis pass pipeline.

5.2 Accuracy of Measurements

We evaluate Barbell's accuracy in throughput and latency measurement and show that Barbell can achieve comparable capability with other service-specific load generators that have limited request control policy support.

The maximum throughput under closed-loop policy reflects load generators' ability for typical stress testing. As Table 2 shows, Barbell achieves similar throughput with SOTA service-specific load generators for Memcached and Nginx with difference less than 2%. Compared with sysbench, Barbell underperforms by 14% in MySQL transaction throughput because Barbell implements the extension with off-the-shelf C++ connectors [8] and high-level LuaBridge [34] for Lua binding. It trades off some performance loss for considerably greater robustness due to complete encapsulation of protocol details.

Table 3. Decomposition of Barbell's LoC. 73% of LoC is in general functionality.

Functionality	General	Service Extension					
		Memcached	Redis [7]	Nginx	vLLM [30]	Kafka [29]	MySQL
LoC	6,431	579	566	229	246	496	284

Latency under open-loop policy reflects load generators' ability of faithful latency measurement by efficiently managing concurrent in-flight requests with minimal client-side jitters. Figure 8 shows that tail latency measured by Barbell shows the same trend to other load generators with increasing RPS. Latency remains stable at low load and increases dramatically after a specific RPS because of exponentially growing server-side queuing delay. Generally, Barbell reports tail latency similar to or closer to that measured by others before and after reaching the maximum closed-loop throughput.

5.3 Flexibility of Load Pattern Generation

We prove it by using two pass pipelines to generate trace in Fig. 1. The first pipeline consists of a single replay pass, and the other consists of a synthesis pass and a segment-wise load aggregation pass. The effectiveness of the Resource-to-RPS load conversion is trivial because it is guided by server-specific profiling.

Barbell Can Generate Fine-Grained Fluctuating Loads. Figure 9 shows the expected RPS (i.e., the input RPS) and the achieved RPS (i.e., the RPS that the server actually receives). It is clear that Barbell faithfully replays the trace; R^2 [4] of the achieved RPS is 0.99995 (the closer to 1, the better).

Barbell Can Generate Complicated Load Patterns in Real Traces. The synthesis pass generates loads of each segment with best-fitted `gennorm` and `alpha` distributions. The Kullback-Leibler (KL) divergence reduces to 0.049 (smaller the better) and 0.171 for daytime and nighttime, compared to 0.475 by fitting the entire trace. Although it cannot retain every rise and fall, Fig. 10 shows that latency CDF is almost the same to that of trace replaying.

5.4 Simplicity of Extensibility

Barbell is extensible to various interactive cloud services, including traditional ones running on CPUs and emerging ones running on GPUs and accelerators like LLM inference. The majority of codes (73%) are spent enriching the reusable general functionality, such as complete support of request control policies and latency measurement. Extending to a new service only takes 200-600 LoC (Table 3), which is much less than developing a new load generator from scratch.

Both service-agnostic (Server IP & port, etc.) and service-specific attributes are configured via one YAML file. Figure 11 shows the vLLM-specific fields in

```
RequestContentCustomization:
  vLLM:
    DataSetPath: /root/work/dataset/Qwen2-0.5B_dataset.json
    PromptLengthMax: 1024
    PromptLengthMin: 1024
    DecodeLengthMax: 32
    DecodeLengthMin: 32
    RandomSeed: 33
    UrlPath: http://150.1.68.169:8080/generate
```


Fig. 11. vLLM-specific configurations in YAML.

the YAML file, including the path to the dataset, the interested range of prompt and decode lengths, and the URL to the vLLM API server.

6 Conclusion and Future Work

We presented Barbell, a multi-threaded extensible load generator for interactive cloud services. It can generate loads with complicated but real patterns to emulate end user behavior through its multi-pass load intensity generation method. It fully decouples general and service-specific functionalities. New services can be easily extended with its powerful and complete general functionality.

Future work will focus on workload logic characterization and improving Barbell's ability to generate OLAP workloads with complex analytical logic.

Availability

To help further research on fluctuating load in the cloud, We open-source some load traces in CloudX, including one-week CPU utilization time series for 20 selected representative VMs. For Barbell, we prepare a docker image open for download and trial. Please visit https://anonymous.4open.science/r/Barbell-39CE.

Acknowledgment. We sincerely thank Zhibin Yu, Lv Chen and Zhangcheng Liang from Huawei Cloud for their extensive feedback on this work. This work was supported in part by an industry-university collaboration research project between Huawei Cloud and CUHK (Shenzhen).

Statements on AI Use. The technical solution and experimental design presented in this paper were independently completed by the authors. AI tools were used solely for language polishing and formatting optimization, and did not participate in the development of the research ideas or core content.

References

1. Alibaba cloud elastic compute service. https://www.alibabacloud.com/product/ecs

2. Amazon EC2. https://aws.amazon.com/ec2/
3. Class statsmodels.tsa.stattools.acf. https://www.statsmodels.org/stable/generated/statsmodels.tsa.stattools.acf.html
4. Coefficient of determination. https://en.wikipedia.org/wiki/Coefficient_of_determination
5. Memtier_benchmark. https://github.com/RedisLabs/memtier_benchmark
6. Openai API. https://platform.openai.com/
7. Redis: The real-time data platform. https://redis.io
8. Mysqlconnectorcpp (2008). https://github.com/mysql/mysql-connector-cpp
9. WRK (2015). https://github.com/wg/wrk
10. WRK2 (2015). https://github.com/giltene/wrk2
11. Abdi, H.: Coefficient of variation. Encyclopedia Res. Des. **1**(5), 169–171 (2010)
12. Belay, A., Terei, D.: Mutated (2015). https://github.com/scslab/mutated
13. Bahga, A., Madisetti, V.K., et al.: Synthetic workload generation for cloud computing applications. J. Softw. Eng. Appl. **4**(07), 396 (2011)
14. Barroso, L.A., Clidaras, J., Hölzle, U.: The datacenter as a computer: an introduction to the design of warehouse-scale machines. Synth. Lect. Comput. Archit. **8**(3), 1–154 (2013)
15. Beitch, A., Liu, B., Yung, T., Griffith, R., Fox, A., Patterson, D.A.: Rain: a workload generation toolkit for cloud computing applications. UC Berkeley Technical Publications (2010). UCB/EECS-2010-14
16. Chen, S., Delimitrou, C., Martínez, J.F.: Parties: QoS-aware resource partitioning for multiple interactive services. In: Proceedings of the Twenty-Fourth International Conference on Architectural Support for Programming Languages and Operating Systems, pp. 107–120 (2019)
17. Cooper, B.F., Silberstein, A., Tam, E., Ramakrishnan, R., Sears, R.: Benchmarking cloud serving systems with YCSB. In: Proceedings of the 1st ACM Symposium on Cloud Computing, pp. 143–154 (2010)
18. Cortez, E., Bonde, A., Muzio, A., Russinovich, M., Fontoura, M., Bianchini, R.: Resource central: understanding and predicting workloads for improved resource management in large cloud platforms. In: Proceedings of the 26th Symposium on Operating Systems Principles, pp. 153–167 (2017)
19. Curiel, M., Pont, A.: Workload generators for web-based systems: characteristics, current status, and challenges. IEEE Commun. Surv. Tutor. **20**(2), 1526–1546 (2018)
20. Delimitrou, C., Kozyrakis, C.: Quasar: resource-efficient and QoS-aware cluster management. ACM SIGPLAN Not. **49**(4), 127–144 (2014)
21. Difallah, D.E., Pavlo, A., Curino, C., Cudre-Mauroux, P.: OLTP-bench: an extensible testbed for benchmarking relational databases. Proc. VLDB Endow. **7**(4), 277–288 (2013)
22. Feitelson, D.G.: Workload modeling for performance evaluation. In: IFIP International Symposium on Computer Performance Modeling, Measurement and Evaluation, pp. 114–141. Springer (2002)
23. Guo, J., et al.: Who limits the resource efficiency of my datacenter: an analysis of alibaba datacenter traces. In: Proceedings of the International Symposium on Quality of Service, pp. 1–10 (2019)
24. Flashback (2015). https://github.com/facebookarchive/flashback
25. Kant, K., Tewari, V., Iyer, R.K.: Geist: a web traffic generation tool. In: Proceedings of the 12th International Conference on Computer Performance Evaluation, Modelling Techniques and Tools, TOOLS 2002, pp. 227–232. Springer, Heidelberg (2002)

26. Kasture, H., Sanchez, D.: Tailbench: a benchmark suite and evaluation methodology for latency-critical applications. In: 2016 IEEE International Symposium on Workload Characterization (IISWC), pp. 1–10 (2016). https://doi.org/10.1109/IISWC.2016.7581261
27. Kogias, M., Mallon, S., Bugnion, E.: Lancet: a self-correcting latency measuring tool. In: 2019 USENIX Annual Technical Conference (USENIX ATC 2019), pp. 881–896. USENIX Association, Renton, WA (2019). https://www.usenix.org/conference/atc19/presentation/kogias-lancet
28. Kopytov, A.: Sysbench manual. MySQL AB, pp. 2–3 (2012)
29. Kreps, J., Narkhede, N., Rao, J., et al.: Kafka: a distributed messaging system for log processing. In: Proceedings of the NetDB, vol. 11, pp. 1–7. Athens, Greece (2011)
30. Kwon, W., et al.: Efficient memory management for large language model serving with pagedattention. In: Proceedings of the ACM SIGOPS 29th Symposium on Operating Systems Principles (2023)
31. Legendre, P.: Spatial autocorrelation: trouble or new paradigm? Ecology **74**(6), 1659–1673 (1993)
32. Leverich, J., Kozyrakis, C.: Reconciling high server utilization and sub-millisecond quality-of-service. In: EuroSys 2014. Association for Computing Machinery, New York, NY, USA (2014). https://doi.org/10.1145/2592798.2592821
33. Lo, D., Cheng, L., Govindaraju, R., Ranganathan, P., Kozyrakis, C.: Heracles: improving resource efficiency at scale. In: Proceedings of the 42nd Annual International Symposium on Computer Architecture, pp. 450–462 (2015)
34. Reed, N., Atkinson, N.: Luabridge (2007). https://github.com/vinniefalco/LuaBridge
35. Reiss, C., Tumanov, A., Ganger, G.R., Katz, R.H., Kozuch, M.A.: Towards understanding heterogeneous clouds at scale: Google trace analysis. Intel Science and Technology Center for Cloud Computing. Technical Report, vol. 84, pp. 1–21 (2012)
36. Rose, O.: Estimation of the Hurst parameter of long-range dependent time series, vol. 137. Report (1996)
37. Schroeder, B., Wierman, A., Harchol-Balter, M.: Open versus closed: a cautionary tale (2006)
38. Shumway, R.H., Stoffer, D.S., Shumway, R.H., Stoffer, D.S.: Arima models. Time series analysis and its applications: with R examples, pp. 75–163 (2017)
39. Tene, G.: How not to measure latency. Low Latency Summit **68** (2013)
40. Wang, M., Madhyastha, T., Chan, N.H., Papadimitriou, S., Faloutsos, C.: Data mining meets performance evaluation: fast algorithms for modeling bursty traffic. In: Proceedings 18th International Conference on Data Engineering, pp. 507–516. IEEE (2002)
41. Yin, J., Lu, X., Zhao, X., Chen, H., Liu, X.: Burse: a bursty and self-similar workload generator for cloud computing. IEEE Trans. Parallel Distrib. Syst. **26**(3), 668–680 (2014)

LLM Inference

JSQKV: Joint Sparsification and Quantization for KV-Cache Compression and Decode Acceleration

Hao Zhang[1], Xiaoli Gong[1(✉)], Haoran Li[1], Huayou Su[2], Qingxia Chen[3], and Jin Zhang[1]

[1] College of Computer Science, Nankai University, Tianjin, China
{2120230710,gongxiaoli,wanch_lhr,nkzhangjin}@nankai.edu.cn
[2] National University of Defense Technology, Changsha, China
shyou@nudt.edu.cn
[3] Qian Xuesen Laboratory of Space Technology, Beijing, China

Abstract. As long-context large language models become increasingly widespread, autoregressive decoding is increasingly bottlenecked by KV-cache footprint and memory bandwidth. Existing KV-cache compression methods typically rely on sparsification or low-bit quantization, but simply combining the two often fails to simultaneously preserve model quality and deliver real end-to-end speedup, since sparsification changes how compressed KV-cache states are represented and executed during decoding. To address this issue, we present JSQKV, a joint sparse-quant framework for KV-cache compression and decode acceleration that co-designs compression policy, compressed format, and execution path. Specifically, JSQKV combines attention-score-based differential sparsification with a dual-window online mechanism, Per-Token-Tile quantization with Hadamard rotation, and a bitmap-based sparse-quant format with a matching decode kernel. Through this joint design, compressed KV-cache data remains compact in memory and is more effectively translated into reduced memory traffic and end-to-end speedup. Experimental results show that, under matched compression budgets, JSQKV generally outperforms the sequential MUSTAFAR+KIVI baseline on representative LongBench tasks, with larger gains under more aggressive sparse-quant settings. On Llama-3-8B-Instruct, JSQKV improves the average score on six representative LongBench tasks from 39.83 to 43.12, while also improving end-to-end throughput by 44.2% over dense decoding and increasing the KV-cache compression ratio to 3.48×.

Keywords: KV-cache compression · Sparsity · Quantization

1 Introduction

As context windows continue to grow in large language models, autoregressive decoding is increasingly bottlenecked by KV-cache footprint and memory bandwidth [7]. Since the KV cache grows linearly with context length and is repeatedly accessed during decoding, this stage is more memory-bound than prefill and

L. Eeckhout et al. (Eds.): APPT 2026, LNCS 16693, pp. 67–81, 2027.
https://doi.org/10.1007/978-981-92-4805-6_5

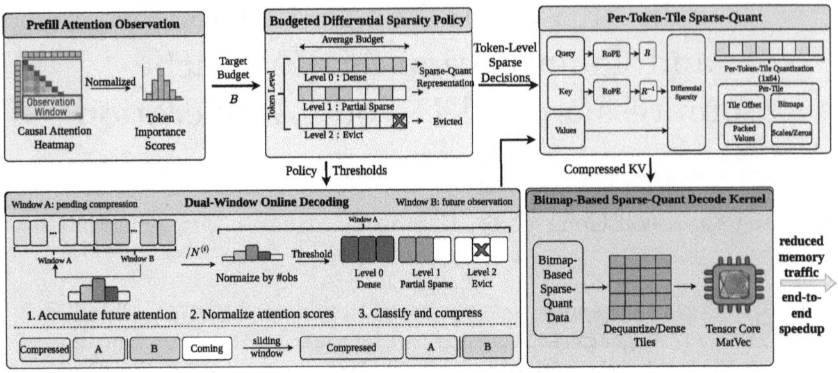

Fig. 1. Overview of JSQKV. The framework combines differential sparsity, dual-window online execution, Per-Token-Tile quantization with Hadamard rotation, and a bitmap-based sparse-quant decode path.

increasingly limits throughput, batch size, and deployment efficiency in long-context settings [1,14].

Prior work on KV-cache compression mainly follows two directions: sparsification and low-bit quantization. Token eviction and sparsification reduce retained history or prune redundant KV states [4,13,15,17,23,24,27], while quantization lowers the numerical precision of retained cache elements [2,5,10,16]. Although both are effective, existing studies still largely treat them as separate components.

In practice, joint sparse-quant KV-cache compression is not a simple sparse-then-quantize pipeline. Sparsification changes not only how much KV data is kept, but also the retained token and feature layout, which in turn affects quantization granularity, compressed data layout, and decode-time execution. As a result, algorithm-level compression gains do not automatically translate into lower memory traffic or real end-to-end speedup during decoding [1,13,28]. Moreover, token-differential compression is easy to estimate in prefill, where future attention is observable, but difficult to apply online during autoregressive decoding, where a token must be cached before its future importance can be known. Thus, the key challenge is twofold: preserving model quality under aggressive compression and keeping the compressed representation directly executable for practical decode-time acceleration.

To address these challenges, we propose JSQKV, a joint sparse-quant framework for KV-cache compression and decode acceleration. Rather than treating sparsification and quantization as separate post-processing steps, JSQKV co-designs compression policy, compressed representation, and runtime execution in a unified decode-stage pipeline, as illustrated in Fig. 1. Section 3.1 introduces an attention-score-based differential sparsification policy that allocates different compression budgets to historical tokens according to estimated future importance. Since such token-differential decisions are easy to estimate in prefill but not directly available when tokens are generated online, Sect. 3.2 presents a dual-window mechanism that accumulates future observations before compression and makes the differential policy applicable during autoregressive decoding. After sparse decisions are made, the remaining KV states still require a low-bit representation that is both robust and compatible with token-level sparse execution. To this end, Sect. 3.3 introduces Hadamard-based Per-Token-Tile quantization to mitigate key outliers and align quantization granularity with downstream computation. Finally, Sect. 3.4 presents a bitmap-based sparse-quant format and a matching decode kernel that keep the KV cache compact in memory and convert compression savings into reduced memory traffic and practical end-to-end decoding speedup. Together, these components form a unified sparse-quant decode pipeline for accurate and efficient KV-cache compression, and our evaluations show that JSQKV compares favorably with sequential sparse-quant baselines while also delivering practical end-to-end decoding speedup.

The main contributions of this paper are as follows:

- We propose an attention-score-based differential sparsification policy that assigns different sparsity levels to historical tokens under a fixed average compression budget, instead of applying a uniform compression ratio to all tokens.
- We design a dual-window online execution mechanism that makes this differential policy usable in autoregressive decoding, where future attention evidence is unavailable when a token is first generated.
- We propose Hadamard-based Per-Token-Tile quantization for the retained KV states to stabilize low-bit representation and align quantization granularity with token-level compression decisions.
- We design a bitmap-based sparse-quant format and matching decode kernel so that compressed KV-cache representations can be translated into reduced memory traffic and practical decode-time speedup.

2 Background and Related Work

KV Sparsification. KV-cache sparsification reduces memory cost by removing less useful history or pruning retained states during decoding. Token-level retention and eviction methods, such as StreamingLLM [23], H_2O [27], SnapKV [15], and PyramidKV [4], exploit the unequal contribution of historical tokens to future decoding. Finer-grained sparsification further explores redundancy within retained KV states. ThinK [24] prunes key channels using query-dependent importance, KVPruner [17] studies structured pruning of KV blocks, and MUSTAFAR [13] shows that unstructured per-token sparsity can be practical when paired with a bitmap-based sparse format and a matching attention kernel.

KV-Cache Quantization. KVQuant [10] studies ultra-low-bit KV-cache quantization for long-context inference, KIVI [16] uses asymmetric quantization with different granularities for Keys and Values, and QuaRot [2] and

RotateKV [5] improve low-bit robustness by reshaping activation distributions before quantization. These methods differ in quantization granularity, metadata cost, and execution compatibility.

Systems and Kernels for Attention. PagedAttention [14] improves KV-cache management through block-based memory organization, while FlashDecoding [9] and FlashInfer [26] optimize decode-stage attention in memory-bound settings. Loki [19] leverages low-rank keys to reduce data movement and computation, Flash-LLM [22] supports unstructured sparsity on Tensor Cores through a load-as-sparse and compute-as-dense framework, and Coruscant [12] further co-designs GPU kernels and sparse tensor cores for efficient unstructured sparse LLM inference.

3 Method

3.1 Budgeted Differential Sparsity Policy

A fixed sparsity ratio treats all historical tokens equally, wasting budget on unimportant tokens and over-compressing important ones. To address this issue, JSQKV estimates token importance from prefill attention and instantiates a three-level sparsity policy under an explicit average-budget constraint.

We use the attention distribution in prefill to estimate the relative importance of historical tokens. Let $\mathbf{A} \in \mathbb{R}^{T_q \times T_k}$ denote the causal attention matrix of the prompt. Following the observation-window idea in SnapKV [15], we use the last L_{obs} prompt tokens as an observation window. For a prefix token $j \leq T_k - L_{\text{obs}}$, its importance score is defined as

$$s_j = \frac{T_k}{L_{\text{obs}}} \sum_{i=T_k-L_{\text{obs}}+1}^{T_k} A_{i,j}. \tag{1}$$

This score measures how much token j is attended by queries in the observation window; tokens inside the observation window are preserved by construction, and the factor T_k/L_{obs} makes scores more comparable across prompts of different lengths.

Given the importance scores $\{s_j\}$, JSQKV assigns each token to one of three compression levels. Let $[p_0, p_1, p_2]$ denote the target proportions of Level 0, Level 1, and Level 2 tokens, where

$$p_0 + p_1 + p_2 = 1. \tag{2}$$

We compute two percentile thresholds,

$$\tau_{\text{high}} = \text{Percentile}(s, 1 - p_0), \tag{3}$$

$$\tau_{\text{low}} = \text{Percentile}(s, p_2), \tag{4}$$

and assign

$$\text{level}(j) = \begin{cases} 0, & s_j \geq \tau_{\text{high}}, \\ 1, & \tau_{\text{low}} \leq s_j < \tau_{\text{high}}, \\ 2, & s_j < \tau_{\text{low}}. \end{cases} \tag{5}$$

The three levels correspond to different compression strengths. Level 0 tokens are kept dense. Level 2 tokens are fully removed from the cache. Level 1 tokens use feature-level sparsity and keep only the largest-magnitude features in their key and value vectors. For a key vector $\mathbf{k}_j \in \mathbb{R}^d$, we apply

$$\tilde{k}_{j,i} = \begin{cases} k_{j,i}, & i \in \text{TopK}(|\mathbf{k}_j|, \lfloor(1-\rho_1)d\rfloor), \\ 0, & \text{otherwise}, \end{cases} \tag{6}$$

where ρ_1 is the feature-level sparsity ratio for Level 1 tokens. The same rule is applied to $\mathbf{v}_j$. In this way, important tokens retain more information, while less important tokens absorb more of the compression budget.

A fixed average sparsity budget does not uniquely determine the three-level policy: different dense/partial/evict allocations can share the same average compression ratio but lead to different accuracy outcomes. We therefore instantiate the policy under an explicit budget constraint. With $\rho_0 = 0$ for Level 0 and $\rho_2 = 1$ for Level 2, the target average sparsity budget B satisfies

$$B = p_0\rho_0 + p_1\rho_1 + p_2\rho_2 = p_1\rho_1 + p_2. \tag{7}$$

For a given target budget B, we search over a small feasible set of (p_0, ρ_1) pairs, recover the remaining proportions analytically, and select the final configuration on a small calibration split. This keeps the overall compression target fixed while allowing more careful allocation across dense, partially sparse, and evicted tokens.

3.2 Dual-Window Online Execution Mechanism

The policy in Sect. 3.1 relies on future attention, which is available in prefill but unavailable when a token is first generated during decoding. To make the same policy work online, JSQKV organizes the decode-stage KV cache into two consecutive windows of size W: Window A stores tokens waiting to be compressed, while Window B stores newly generated tokens whose queries provide additional attention observations for Window A, as illustrated in Fig. 2.

When a new query $\mathbf{q}_t$ is produced at decoding step t, we compute its attention to the tokens in Window A:

$$\boldsymbol{\alpha}_t = \text{softmax}\left(\frac{\mathbf{q}_t\mathbf{K}_A^\top}{\sqrt{d}}\right), \tag{8}$$

where $\mathbf{K}_A$ denotes the key states of Window A. These scores are accumulated across subsequent decoding steps in an attention buffer $\mathbf{Acc}$, whose i-th entry

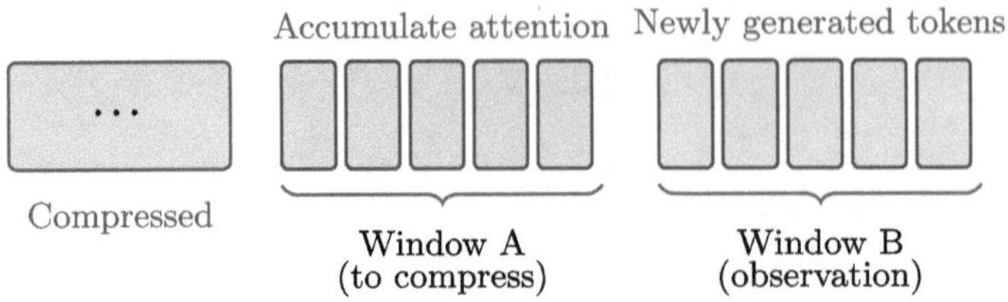

Fig. 2. Dual-window online execution during decoding. Window A accumulates attention statistics before compression, while Window B collects newly generated tokens and provides future observations.

stores the total future attention received by the i-th token in Window A while the current Window B is being filled.

Because earlier tokens in Window A are visible to more later queries, accumulated attention must be normalized before thresholding. For the token at position $i \in \{0, \ldots, W-1\}$ in Window A, the number of observations is

$$N^{(i)} = 2W - 1 - i, \tag{9}$$

which gives the normalized score

$$\bar{\alpha}^{(i)} = \frac{\mathbf{Acc}[:,:,i]}{N^{(i)}}. \tag{10}$$

We then compare the normalized scores against the thresholds $(\tau_{\text{high}}, \tau_{\text{low}})$ from Sect. 3.1 and assign each token in Window A to Level 0, Level 1, or Level 2. The empirical stability of these prefill-estimated thresholds is examined in Appendix 1.

After classification, Level 0 tokens remain dense, Level 1 tokens are partially pruned, and Level 2 tokens are removed. The compressed Window A is merged into the historical compressed region, Window B becomes the new Window A, the accumulator is reset, and decoding continues with a new empty Window B. In this way, each token is observed before compression while the number of uncompressed tokens remains bounded by $O(W)$.

3.3 Per-Token-Tile Quantization with Hadamard Rotation

The remaining nonzero KV states still require a low-bit representation. We therefore adopt *Per-Token-Tile* quantization, which aligns the quantization unit with token-level compression decisions and the tile-based decode path while providing a fine-grained low-bit representation.

For a token vector $\mathbf{x}_t \in \mathbb{R}^d$ (either key or value), the feature dimension is partitioned into $M = d/g$ contiguous tiles of size g:

$$\mathbf{x}_t = [\mathbf{x}_{t,1}, \mathbf{x}_{t,2}, \ldots, \mathbf{x}_{t,M}], \qquad \mathbf{x}_{t,m} \in \mathbb{R}^g. \tag{11}$$

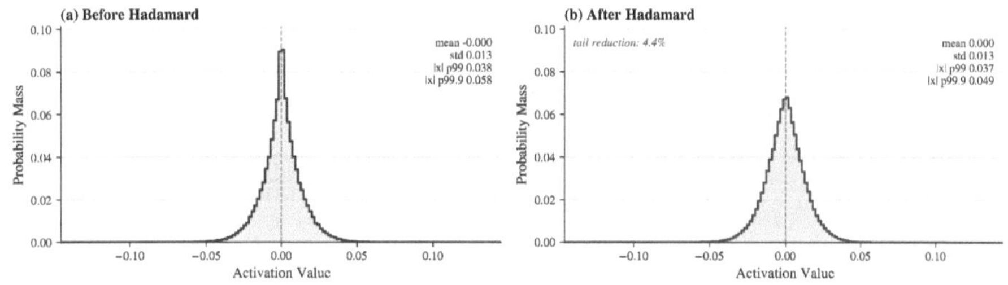

Fig. 3. Key-state activation distribution before and after Hadamard rotation on a Llama-2-7B sample. The rotation suppresses heavy tails while preserving enough variation for feature-level sparsification.

Table 1. PPL of RTN and Hadamard rotation (*Rotate*) on WikiText-2 under quantization-only and sparse-quant settings. Hadamard rotation improves low-bit quantization stability, while remaining compatible with subsequent KV sparsification.

Setting	4-bit		3-bit		2-bit	
	RTN	Rotate	RTN	Rotate	RTN	Rotate
Quant only	5.22	**5.14**	6.57	**5.28**	115.55	**5.35**
+50% KV sparsity	**5.27**	5.69	6.57	**6.35**	115.55	**6.65**

Each tile is quantized independently with its own scale $s_{t,m}$ and zero point $z_{t,m}$:

$$\mathbf{q}_{t,m} = \text{clip}\Big(\text{round}\Big(\frac{\mathbf{x}_{t,m} - z_{t,m}}{s_{t,m}}\Big), 0, 2^b - 1\Big), \tag{12}$$

where b is the quantization bitwidth.

Since key states may contain outliers that destabilize aggressive low-bit quantization, JSQKV applies Hadamard rotation to queries and keys before quantization. Let $\mathbf{H} \in \mathbb{R}^{d \times d}$ denote the normalized Hadamard matrix. We rotate

$$\tilde{\mathbf{q}}_i = \frac{1}{\sqrt{d}}\mathbf{H}\mathbf{q}_i, \qquad \tilde{\mathbf{k}}_j = \frac{1}{\sqrt{d}}\mathbf{H}\mathbf{k}_j. \tag{13}$$

Because the Hadamard matrix is orthogonal, the attention score is preserved:

$$\tilde{\mathbf{q}}_i^\top \tilde{\mathbf{k}}_j = \mathbf{q}_i^\top \mathbf{k}_j. \tag{14}$$

Figure 3 and Table 1 show that Hadamard rotation suppresses heavy tails and improves low-bit robustness, especially at lower bitwidths.

3.4 Sparse-Quant Format and Decode Kernel

We co-design a sparse-quant format and a matching decode kernel so that compressed KV-cache representations reduce not only storage cost but also decode-time memory traffic.

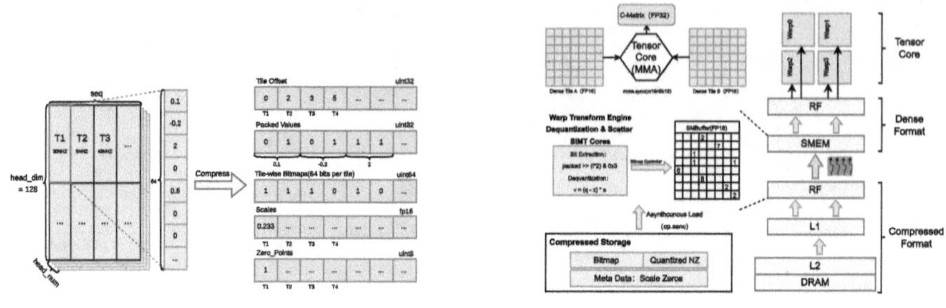

(a) bitmap-based sparse-quant format (b) Sparse-quant decode kernel

Fig. 4. Sparse-quant format and decode kernel. The format stores bitmap metadata and packed low-bit values, while the kernel follows a load-as-compressed, compute-as-dense execution path.

Figure 4 summarizes this design. Each 1×64 tile stores a bitmap for nonzero positions, packed low-bit values, a per-tile offset, and quantization metadata such as scales and zero points. During decode, the kernel follows a *load-as-compressed, compute-as-dense* strategy: it loads compressed tiles from memory, reconstructs dense shared-memory tiles through unpacking and dequantization, and then invokes Tensor Core matrix-vector computation. In this way, sparsity is handled along the loading path while the compute stage remains dense and regular.

This design is particularly useful for decode-stage attention, which is strongly memory-bound: keeping the KV cache compressed in memory reduces memory traffic, while reconstructing dense tiles only on the compute path avoids irregular accesses and control-flow divergence.

4 Experiments

4.1 Experimental Setup

Our implementation uses Python 3.10, PyTorch 2.6.0, CUDA 12.4, and custom CUDA/Triton kernels. All experiments are conducted on a single NVIDIA A100 80GB PCIe GPU with an Intel Xeon CPU and 252GB host memory.

For accuracy, we use the official LongBench [3] pipeline on six representative tasks: NarrativeQA, Qasper, MultiFieldQA-EN, HotpotQA, TREC, and LCC. We use Llama-3-8B-Instruct [8] as the main model and additionally test Llama-2-7B [20], Mistral-7B-v0.1 [11], and Qwen2.5-7B-Instruct [25]. Inputs are truncated to 8192 tokens via head-tail truncation when needed. We compare against dense decoding, a matched-budget uniform sparsity baseline based on MUSTAFAR [13], and a sequential MUSTAFAR+KIVI baseline [16] (denoted as **M+K**). Sparse-only settings use 50% and 70% average sparsity, while joint sparse-quant settings use 50/50 and 70/70 K/V sparsity with 4-bit and 2-bit quantization. Differential policies are selected on a small calibration split and re-checked on a disjoint validation split before final evaluation on these tasks.

Table 2. Sparse-only results on six representative LongBench tasks for Llama-3-8B-Instruct.

Method	NarrativeQA	Qasper	MultiFieldQA-EN	HotpotQA	TREC	LCC	Avg.
Dense	23.45	42.18	43.14	46.06	74.00	57.12	47.66
Uniform-50	23.44	43.73	42.93	45.94	73.50	56.03	47.59
Differential-50	23.44	43.73	42.93	45.94	**74.00**	**57.08**	**47.85**
Uniform-70	23.94	40.89	40.91	44.93	70.00	54.12	45.80
Differential-70	23.94	**41.03**	**41.61**	**45.12**	**72.50**	**55.45**	**46.61**

Table 3. Joint sparse-quant results on six representative LongBench tasks for Llama-3-8B-Instruct.

Setting	NarrativeQA	Qasper	MultiFieldQA-EN	HotpotQA	TREC	LCC	Avg.
M+K, 50/50 + 4-bit	21.61	**40.70**	**47.62**	41.13	**70.50**	53.83	45.90
JSQKV, 50/50 + 4-bit	**21.92**	39.38	46.77	**41.38**	**70.50**	**55.64**	**45.93**
M+K, 50/50 + 2-bit	**21.97**	38.96	**46.11**	40.39	68.00	44.86	43.38
JSQKV, 50/50 + 2-bit	21.16	**39.54**	44.49	**41.19**	**71.50**	**46.26**	**44.02**
M+K, 70/70 + 4-bit	20.94	37.32	44.90	**41.22**	68.00	52.71	44.18
JSQKV, 70/70 + 4-bit	**21.86**	**38.81**	**46.52**	40.64	**70.00**	**54.23**	**45.34**
M+K, 70/70 + 2-bit	**21.34**	35.43	43.43	39.21	63.00	36.59	39.83
JSQKV, 70/70 + 2-bit	19.70	**39.49**	**44.31**	**40.15**	**70.00**	**45.04**	**43.12**

For efficiency, we use Llama-3-8B-Instruct with 4096 input tokens, 256 generated tokens, and batch sizes from 1 to 8, and report end-to-end throughput, compression overhead, compressed KV-cache size, and compression ratio. We compare dense decoding, the MUSTAFAR [13] sparse kernel, and the proposed sparse-quant runtime path.

4.2 Accuracy Results

Differential Sparsity Alone. We first study differential sparsity without quantization or Hadamard rotation to isolate the effect of budget allocation, comparing JSQKV against dense decoding and a matched-budget uniform sparsity baseline at 50% and 70% average sparsity. Table 2 shows that differential sparsity remains non-negative and yields larger gains at 70% sparsity than at 50%, suggesting that token-level budget allocation becomes more valuable under tighter sparsity budgets.

Joint Sparsity-Quantization Results. Table 3 reports joint sparse-quant results on six representative LongBench tasks for Llama-3-8B-Instruct [8]. Across all four settings, JSQKV achieves higher average scores than the sequential

Table 4. Cross-model joint sparse-quant averages on six representative LongBench tasks.

Model	50/50 + 4-bit		50/50 + 2-bit		70/70 + 4-bit		70/70 + 2-bit	
	M+K	JSQKV	M+K	JSQKV	M+K	JSQKV	M+K	JSQKV
Llama-2-7B	31.34	**31.37**	**31.51**	30.23	30.57	**30.97**	29.92	**30.09**
Mistral-7B-v0.1	32.84	**32.90**	31.70	**32.37**	32.43	**32.71**	30.14	**32.35**
Qwen2.5-7B-Instruct	31.17	**37.08**	**26.10**	23.48	33.00	**39.67**	25.51	**35.20**

M+K baseline, with the largest gain at 70/70 + 2-bit, where the average score improves from 39.83 to 43.12. This supports jointly aligning sparsity, quantization, and runtime execution under tighter compression budgets. A quantization-only comparison isolating the contribution of the proposed low-bit representation is reported in Appendix 2.

Table 4 shows a generally favorable but non-uniform cross-model trend over M+K: gains are more consistent under tighter compression budgets, while a few milder settings remain neutral or slightly negative. This suggests that the benefit of JSQKV mainly comes from the joint design itself, although its magnitude still depends on model family and compression setting.

4.3 Efficiency Results

In efficiency experiments, we compare JSQKV against dense decoding and the executable MUSTAFAR sparse kernel [13], since the sequential **M+K** baseline does not provide a unified end-to-end runtime path.

End-to-End Throughput. Figure 5 reports end-to-end decoding throughput on Llama-3-8B-Instruct [8]. Dense decoding is strongest at batch size 1, where compression overhead is not yet amortized. As batch size increases, the compressed paths become more favorable, with the clearest sparse-quant advantage in the small-to-medium batch regime. Under 70/70 + 2-bit, JSQKV reaches 80.38 tokens/s at batch size 6, improving over dense decoding by 41.5% and over MUSTAFAR-70 by 3.0%. At larger batch sizes, the gap narrows, suggesting that unpacking and dequantization overheads are less effectively amortized once the workload becomes more compute-heavy.

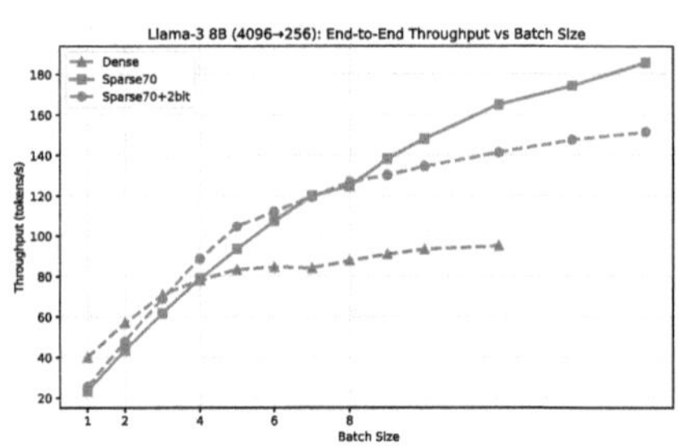

Fig. 5. End-to-end decoding throughput on Llama-3-8B. The clearest gain appears in the small-to-medium batch regime.

Table 5. Compression statistics at input length 4096.

Method	BS = 1			BS = 8		
	KV (MB)	Ratio	Time (ms)	KV (MB)	Ratio	Time (ms)
Sparse-50	2720.2	1.51×	740.8	2720.2	1.51×	5688.2
Sparse-70	1964.3	2.09×	716.3	1964.3	2.09×	5411.3
Sparse-50 + 2b	1261.2	3.25×	545.2	1261.2	3.25×	4317.9
Sparse-70 + 2b	1176.3	3.48×	552.9	1176.3	3.48×	4293.2

Compression Overhead. Table 5 reports representative compression statistics on Llama-3-8B-Instruct. Compared with sparsity-only baselines, the sparse-quant path achieves higher compression ratios while keeping compression time competitive. At batch size 8, JSQKV under 70/70 + 2-bit reduces the KV cache from 1964.3MB to 1176.3MB relative to MUSTAFAR-70, improving the compression ratio from 2.09× to 3.48× and reducing compression time from 5411.3ms to 4293.2ms. This suggests that the more compact sparse-quant representation also lowers compression-side write-back cost.

5 Conclusion

JSQKV reduces KV-cache cost through differential sparsification, stabilized low-bit quantization, and a bitmap-based sparse-quant decode kernel. Evaluation results show that, under matched compression budgets, JSQKV generally compares favorably with a sequential sparsity-plus-quantization baseline, with larger gains under more aggressive sparse-quant settings. These results further show that compression savings can translate into practical throughput gains during decoding. Overall, these findings support treating KV-cache compression as a systems-and-algorithms co-design problem rather than as a simple composition of independent post-processing steps.

Acknowledgments. This work was supported in part by the Natural Science Foundation of China (62372254), the Innovative Development Joint Fund Key Projects of Shandong NSF (ZR2023LZH003), and the Beijing-Tianjin-Hebei Basic Research Cooperation Project of Hebei Natural Science Foundation under Grant F2024203115 (24JCZXJC00160 in Tianjin).

Disclosure of Interests. The authors have no competing interests to declare that are relevant to the content of this article.

Use of Artificial Intelligence Tools. The technical solution and experimental design presented in this paper were independently completed by the authors. AI tools were used solely for language polishing and formatting optimization, and did not participate in the development of the research ideas or core content.

1 Threshold Stability for Prefill-to-Decode Reuse

Section 3.1 estimates the token-importance thresholds $(\tau_{\text{high}}, \tau_{\text{low}})$ from normalized prefill attention, and Sect. 3.2 reuses the same thresholds during decoding after normalizing the accumulated attention by the number of available future observations. This reuse strategy relies on a simple layer-wise stability assumption: under the same normalization rule, the importance-score scale of a fixed layer should remain sufficiently consistent for prefill-estimated thresholds to remain meaningful during online decoding.

We test this assumption using the same threshold definition as JSQKV. We compute normalized attention-derived importance scores from the observed attention statistics and derive the corresponding thresholds $(\tau_{\text{high}}, \tau_{\text{low}})$. The evaluation is conducted on Llama-3-8B-Instruct [8] using seven datasets: WikiText-2 [18], GSM8K [6], MuSiQue [21], and four LongBench tasks: Qasper, MultiFieldQA-EN, NarrativeQA, and HotpotQA [3]. Each dataset contributes 10 samples, and we evaluate layers 10 and 20 as representative layers.

Table 6. Cross-dataset stability of the normalized attention thresholds used by the prefill-to-decode reuse path. CV is computed from the per-dataset median thresholds.

Layer	Threshold	Median range	Median CV (%)
10	τ_{high}	0.67120–0.92427	10.21
10	τ_{low}	0.04243–0.06552	14.37
20	τ_{high}	0.35568–0.61690	19.40
20	τ_{low}	0.01732–0.02890	19.82

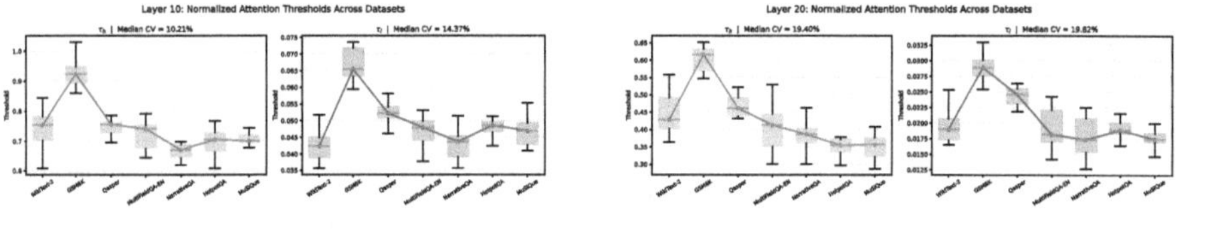

Fig. 6. Cross-dataset distributions of the normalized attention thresholds used by the prefill-to-decode reuse path. Left: Layer 10. Right: Layer 20. The thresholds remain stable at a fixed layer, while their absolute scale is layer dependent.

Table 6 reports the resulting cross-dataset statistics. For Layer 10, the median CV is 10.21% for τ_{high} and 14.37% for τ_{low}; for Layer 20, the corresponding values are 19.40% and 19.82%. Figure 6 shows the full distributions. Two observations matter most. First, for a fixed layer, both thresholds remain concentrated within a bounded range across datasets. Second, the threshold scale is clearly layer dependent, so the supported claim is reuse of *fixed per-layer thresholds*, not a single global threshold shared by all layers.

These results are sufficient for the reuse mechanism in Sect. 3.2. The decoder does not require decode-time scores to match prefill thresholds exactly for every sample; it only requires the normalized scores to stay on a comparable layer-wise scale. Taken together, Table 6 and Fig. 6 support estimating $(\tau_{\text{high}}, \tau_{\text{low}})$ once in prefill and reusing them during decoding without step-wise re-calibration.

2 Additional Quantization-Only Comparison

To isolate the contribution of the numerical representation in JSQKV, we compare a quantization-only instantiation of the JSQKV quantizer against a matched KIVI baseline [16]. This appendix keeps the same per-token-tile low-bit representation used by JSQKV but removes differential sparsity and the bitmap-based sparse runtime path.

Unless otherwise noted, both methods use a residual window of 128 tokens. The KIVI baseline uses channel-wise key quantization, per-token-head value quantization, and group size 128, whereas the JSQKV quantizer uses per-token-tile quantization with tile-wise Hadamard rotation (tile size 64 and Hadamard group size 64).

Table 7 reports quantization-only results on representative LongBench tasks for Llama-3-8B-Instruct [8]. At 4-bit and 3-bit, the two methods remain close in average score. At 2-bit, however, the JSQKV quantizer is noticeably stronger, improving the average over the representative tasks from 25.83 to 28.39, with especially visible gains on HotpotQA and LCC. This pattern suggests that the tile-aligned design is most helpful in the aggressive low-bit regime.

Table 8 summarizes the same comparison on additional model families using representative LongBench tasks. It is intended to show whether the quantization trend transfers under comparable representative-task settings, rather than

Table 7. Quantization-only comparison on representative LongBench tasks for Llama-3-8B-Instruct. Avg. is computed over the reported representative tasks.

Setting	Bit	NarrativeQA	HotpotQA	GovReport	TREC	PCount	LCC	Avg.
KIVI	4-bit	**24.26**	46.06	29.53	**74.00**	**6.50**	54.07	39.07
JSQKV quantizer	4-bit	22.47	**46.07**	**30.03**	73.50	5.50	**57.20**	**39.13**
KIVI	3-bit	20.81	45.64	**29.35**	**74.00**	6.75	**60.94**	**39.58**
JSQKV quantizer	3-bit	**21.64**	**46.62**	29.16	73.50	**7.00**	53.66	38.60
KIVI	2-bit	16.55	27.50	23.91	**58.00**	2.00	27.03	25.83
JSQKV quantizer	2-bit	**17.90**	**37.93**	**25.63**	55.50	**3.00**	**30.37**	**28.39**

Table 8. Cross-model quantization-only averages on representative LongBench tasks. Δ is "JSQKV quantizer minus KIVI".

Model	Protocol	KIVI 4-bit	JSQKV 4-bit	Δ	KIVI 3-bit	JSQKV 3-bit	Δ	KIVI 2-bit	JSQKV 2-bit	Δ
Llama-3-8B-Instruct	representative LongBench tasks	39.07	**39.13**	**+0.06**	**39.58**	38.60	-0.98	25.83	**28.39**	**+2.56**
Llama-2-7B	representative LongBench tasks	28.09	**28.33**	**+0.24**	**28.23**	27.82	-0.41	**24.33**	24.17	-0.16
Mistral-7B-v0.1	representative LongBench tasks	**31.19**	30.78	-0.41	**30.16**	29.52	-0.64	23.91	**25.72**	**+1.81**

to support strict cross-row ranking under an identical task set. The JSQKV quantizer remains competitive on Llama-2-7B and becomes favorable at 2-bit on Mistral-7B-v0.1, suggesting that its main benefit is improved robustness under aggressive low-bit quantization.

References

1. Agrawal, A., Kedia, N., Panwar, A., et al.: Taming throughput-latency tradeoff in LLM inference with sarathi-serve. arXiv preprint arXiv:2403.02310 (2024). https://arxiv.org/abs/2403.02310
2. Ashkboos, S., et al.: Quarot: outlier-free 4-bit inference in rotated LLMs. arXiv preprint arXiv:2404.00456 (2024)
3. Bai, Y., et al.: Longbench: a bilingual, multitask benchmark for long context understanding. arXiv preprint arXiv:2308.14508 (2023). https://arxiv.org/abs/2308.14508
4. Cai, Z., et al.: Pyramidkv: dynamic KV cache compression based on pyramidal information funneling. arXiv preprint arXiv:2406.02069 (2024). https://arxiv.org/abs/2406.02069
5. Chen, Z., et al.: Rotatekv: accurate and robust 2-bit kv cache quantization for LLMs via outlier-aware adaptive rotations (2025). https://arxiv.org/abs/2501.16383
6. Cobbe, K., et al.: Training verifiers to solve math word problems. arXiv preprint arXiv:2110.14168 (2021). https://arxiv.org/abs/2110.14168
7. Ding, Y., et al.: Longrope: extending LLM context window beyond 2 million tokens. arXiv preprint arXiv:2402.13753 (2024). https://arxiv.org/abs/2402.13753
8. Grattafiori, A., Dubey, A., Jauhri, A., Pandey, A., Kadian, A.: The llama 3 herd of models. arXiv preprint arXiv:2407.21783 (2024)
9. Hong, K., et al.: FlashDecoding++: faster large language model inference with asynchronization, flat GEMM optimization, and heuristics. In: Proceedings of Machine Learning and Systems (2024)
10. Hooper, C., et al.: Kvquant: towards 10 million context length LLM inference with kv cache quantization. arXiv preprint arXiv:2401.18079 (2024)
11. Jiang, A.Q., et al.: Mistral 7b. arXiv preprint arXiv:2310.06825 (2023). https://arxiv.org/abs/2310.06825
12. Joo, D., Hosseini, H., Hadidi, R., Asgari, B.: Coruscant: co-designing GPU kernel and sparse tensor core to advocate unstructured sparsity in efficient LLM inference. In: Proceedings of the 58th IEEE/ACM International Symposium on Microarchitecture, pp. 232–245 (2025). https://doi.org/10.1145/3725843.3756065
13. Joo, D., Hosseini, H., Hadidi, R., Asgari, B.: Mustafar: promoting unstructured sparsity for kv cache pruning in LLM inference. arXiv preprint arXiv:2505.22913 (2025). https://arxiv.org/abs/2505.22913
14. Kwon, W., et al.: Efficient memory management for large language model serving with pagedattention. In: Proceedings of the ACM SIGOPS 29th Symposium on Operating Systems Principles (2023). https://arxiv.org/abs/2309.06180
15. Li, Y., et al.: Snapkv: LLM knows what you are looking for before generation. arXiv preprint arXiv:2404.14469 (2024). https://arxiv.org/abs/2404.14469, version 2, June 17, 2024
16. Liu, Z., et al.: Kivi: a tuning-free asymmetric 2bit quantization for kv cache. arXiv preprint arXiv:2402.02750 (2024)

17. Lv, B., Zhou, Q., Ding, X., Wang, Y., Ma, Z.: Kvpruner: structural pruning for faster and memory-efficient large language models. arXiv preprint arXiv:2409.11057 (2024). https://arxiv.org/abs/2409.11057
18. Merity, S., Xiong, C., Bradbury, J., Socher, R.: Pointer sentinel mixture models. arXiv preprint arXiv:1609.07843 (2016). https://arxiv.org/abs/1609.07843
19. Singhania, P., Singh, S., He, S., et al.: Loki: low-rank keys for efficient sparse attention. arXiv preprint arXiv:2406.02542 (2024). https://arxiv.org/abs/2406.02542
20. Touvron, H., et al.: Llama 2: open foundation and fine-tuned chat models. arXiv preprint arXiv:2307.09288 (2023). https://arxiv.org/abs/2307.09288
21. Trivedi, H., Balasubramanian, N., Khot, T., Sabharwal, A.: Musique: multihop questions via single-hop question composition. Trans. Assoc. Comput. Linguist. **10**, 539–554 (2022). https://aclanthology.org/2022.tacl-1.31/
22. Xia, H., et al.: Flash-LLM: enabling cost-effective and highly-efficient large generative model inference with unstructured sparsity. arXiv preprint arXiv:2309.10285 (2023). https://arxiv.org/abs/2309.10285
23. Xiao, G., Tian, Y., Chen, B., Han, S., Lewis, M.: Efficient streaming language models with attention sinks. arXiv preprint arXiv:2309.17453 (2024). https://arxiv.org/abs/2309.17453
24. Xu, Y., et al.: Think: thinner key cache by query-driven pruning. In: International Conference on Learning Representations (2025). https://arxiv.org/abs/2407.21018, spotlight
25. Yang, A., et al.: Qwen2.5 technical report. arXiv preprint arXiv:2412.15115 (2024). https://arxiv.org/abs/2412.15115
26. Ye, Z., et al.: Flashinfer: efficient and customizable attention engine for LLM inference serving. In: Proceedings of Machine Learning and Systems (2025)
27. Zhang, Z., et al.: H_2o: heavy-hitter oracle for efficient generative inference of large language models. arXiv preprint arXiv:2306.14048 (2023). https://arxiv.org/abs/2306.14048
28. Zhong, Y., Liu, S., Chen, J., et al.: Distserve: disaggregating prefill and decoding for goodput-optimized large language model serving. In: 18th USENIX Symposium on Operating Systems Design and Implementation (OSDI 2024) (2024). https://www.usenix.org/conference/osdi24/presentation/zhong-yinmin

LocalKV: Leveraging Sparse Attention Locality for Efficient Long-Context LLM Inference

Chengwei Li[1], Guangda Liu[1], Jieru Zhao[1](✉), Quan Chen[1], and Minyi Guo[1,2]

[1] School of Computer Science, Shanghai Jiao Tong University, Shanghai, China
{exia,gd.liu,zhao-jieru}@sjtu.edu.cn, {chen-quan,guo-my}@cs.sjtu.edu.cn
[2] Guizhou Provincial Laboratory of Big Data, Guizhou University, Guiyang, China

Abstract. As the context window of Large Language Models expands to accommodate increasingly complex tasks, the KV cache emerges as a performance bottleneck. While existing compression methods reduce the memory footprint and access, they either suffer severe accuracy degradation, or incur substantial global selection overhead that scales linearly with context length. To address this dilemma, we propose **LocalKV**, a sparse decoding framework for efficient long-context LLM inference that preserves accuracy, leveraging algorithm-system co-optimization. On the algorithm side, LocalKV leverages the locality of sparse attention to identify important tokens only from the neighbors of previously selected tokens, avoiding costly global selection. On the system side, LocalKV eliminates the local tracking overhead by fusing it into the sparse Flash Attention kernel, and utilize asynchronous CPU-to-GPU prefetching to completely overlap the KV transfer latency. Extensive experiments show that LocalKV maintains near-lossless generation quality, while delivering a 1.6× decoding speedup over state-of-the-art methods.

Keywords: KV Cache · Sparse Attention · Co-optimization

1 Introduction

Large Language Models (LLMs) have achieved remarkable success across diverse tasks, leading to their widespread deployment in applications such as document analysis, chatbots, and coding assistants [4,13]. To support increasingly complex tasks like long-document QA, multi-turn dialogue, and repository-level code understanding, the context windows of LLMs are rapidly expanding: mainstream models now routinely support 128K tokens [7,19], with frontier models reaching up to 1 million tokens [5,24].

While larger context windows unlock new capabilities, they introduce significant deployment challenges, primarily stemming from the Key-Value (KV)

C. Li and G. Liu—Equal contribution.

L. Eeckhout et al. (Eds.): APPT 2026, LNCS 16693, pp. 82–96, 2027.
https://doi.org/10.1007/978-981-92-4805-6_6

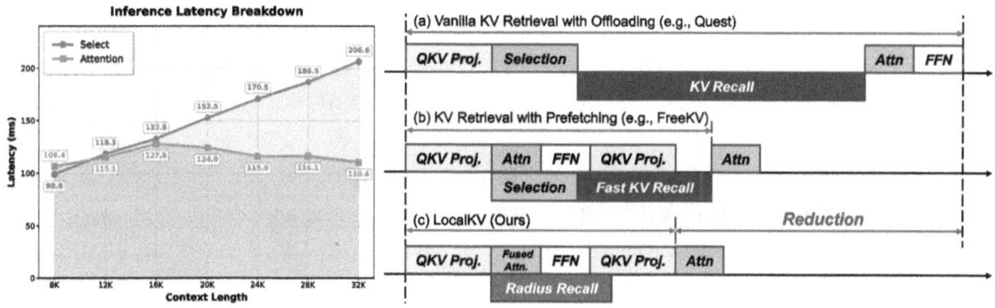

Fig. 1. Left: Latency of selection and sparse attention computation in Quest, using block size 32 and token budget 512, tested on Llama-3.1-8B. Right: Timeline of LOCALKV, compared against KV retrieval methods with and without prefetching.

cache, which stores the states of previous tokens to avoid redundant recomputation during inference. As KV cache grows linearly with context length, it creates a severe dual bottleneck. On the one hand, this massive memory footprint can easily exceed GPU capacity, and a single Llama-3-70B request with a 128K context can require roughly 40GB of VRAM. On the other hand, since autoregressive decoding is memory-bound, continuously loading this extensive cache at each generation step significantly degrades overall decoding speed.

To address this challenge, recent literature has explored sparse attention mechanisms to compress the KV cache. One prominent paradigm, KV dropping [22,25,30], restricts memory usage by retaining only a subset of important tokens and permanently evicting the rest. However, this strategy inherently overlooks the dynamic nature of token importance: tokens deemed irrelevant at early stages may suddenly become critical in subsequent decoding steps. Such permanent eviction inevitably leads to irreversible accuracy degradation. To mitigate this issue, another line of work, KV retrieval [16,17,23], has emerged as a highly effective alternative. Instead of suffering from irreversible token eviction, this paradigm offloads the complete KV cache to the host CPU memory, circumventing GPU out-of-memory (OOM) errors. During autoregressive decoding, the system dynamically evaluates token importance and retrieves only a sparse, critical subset of entries back to the GPU for the current token's generation.

Despite their superior accuracy, KV retrieval methods face severe efficiency challenges that hinder their practical deployment. On the one hand, dynamically identifying critical KV tuples from the entire context requires a **global selection**, incurring substantial computation overhead. Existing methods such as Quest [23] adopt block-wise selection to mitigate the cost, however, **it still grows linearly with the context length**. As demonstrated in Fig. 1, we compare the costs of selection with sparse attention computation in Quest, using block size of 32 and a retrieval budget of 512 tokens. The results reveal that the selection costs scale linearly with the context length, and exceed the sparse attention computation costs for context lengths above 16K. On the other hand, due to the limited bandwidth of the PCIe interconnect, recalling the selected KV tuples from CPU memory to GPU incurs costly transfer overhead. While state-of-the-art methods such as FreeKV attempt to overlap the transfer with inference, the linear growth of the selection cost ultimately breaks the pipeline, since the selection would become bottleneck under long context and hinder overlapping.

To address these fundamental challenges, we propose LocalKV, a sparse decoding framework for efficient long-context LLM inference, leveraging algorithm-system co-optimization. On the algorithmic side, we reveal and exploit **temporal and spatial locality** in sparse attention: neighbors of critical tokens at the current decoding step tend to remain important in subsequent steps. Based on the locality, LocalKV identifies important tokens only from the neighbors of previously selected tokens, avoiding costly global selection. To escape local optima, LocalKV periodically performs global updates with minimal overhead. On the system side, LocalKV further eliminates the local tracking overhead by fusing it directly into the sparse Flash Attention kernel. In addition, the algorithmic nature of LocalKV enables asynchronously prefetch KV cache from CPU memory, fully overlapping the transfer with computation. Extensive experiments demonstrate that LocalKV maintains near-lossless generation quality across diverse scenarios and models, delivering up to a 1.6× decoding speedup over state-of-the-art KV retrieval methods.

2 Background and Related Work

2.1 Problem Formulation

During the autoregressive decoding phase, the attention mechanism for a single head computes the output for the current token as $\mathbf{o} = \text{softmax}(\mathbf{q}\mathbf{K}^\top/\sqrt{d})\mathbf{V}$. Here, $\mathbf{q}, \mathbf{o} \in \mathbb{R}^{1\times d}$ denote the query vector and the corresponding attention output, while $\mathbf{K}, \mathbf{V} \in \mathbb{R}^{L\times d}$ represent the cached key and value states from the L preceding tokens. To optimize inference efficiency, contemporary LLMs frequently adopt Grouped Query Attention (GQA) [1]. Assuming the model possesses n_{qo} query heads and n_{kv} KV heads, the query heads are partitioned into groups of size $G = \frac{n_{qo}}{n_{kv}}$, where all heads within the same group share a single KV head. Consequently, the attention output for the h-th query head is formulated as $\mathbf{o}_h = \text{softmax}(\mathbf{q}_h\mathbf{K}_{\bar{h}}^\top/\sqrt{d})\mathbf{V}_{\bar{h}}$, where $\bar{h} = \lfloor\frac{h}{G}\rfloor$ indicates the index of the assigned KV head.

KV retrieval methods select a subset of KV tuples for attention computation based on attention weights derived from $\mathbf{q}$ and $\mathbf{K}$, defined as $I^h = \text{Sel}(\mathbf{q}^h, \mathbf{K}^h)$. Our primary goal is to select tokens which contribute most to the attention weights, thereby approximating the original dense computation as closely as possible. Specifically, the optimal index set I^h is $\text{argmax}_{I,|I|=B} \sum_{i\in I} \mathbf{q}^h(\mathbf{k}_i^h)^\top$, which mathematically corresponds to selecting tokens with the top-B largest attention weights. In practice, retrieval methods consistently retain KV tuples for S sink tokens at the beginning and W tokens within the local window, leaving exactly $B - S - W$ tuples available for this dynamic selection.

Table 1. Comparison of KV cache compression methods.

	RaaS	Quest	ClusterKV	FreeKV	LocalKV
Select Cost	$O(B)$	$O(\alpha L)$	$O(\alpha L)$	$O(\alpha L)$	Zero-Overhead
Group-Consistent	✓	×	✓	✓	✓
Offload	KV Drop	No Offload	Offload	Offload	Offload
Prefetch	No Prefetch	No Prefetch	No Prefetch	No Full Overlap	Full Overlap

For GQA models, retrieval efficiency relies on a *group-consistent* policy, where for any given KV head m, all G query heads sharing this KV head select identical indices (i.e., $I^{(m-1)G+1} = \cdots = I^{mG}$). This alignment ensures an optimal KV cache allocation of $O(B \times n_{kv})$. Conversely, divergent selections within a group force the system to allocate $O(B \times n_{qo})$ space, inflating both memory footprint and access overhead by a factor of G.

2.2 Related Work

KV Dropping. KV cache dropping policies can be broadly classified as static or dynamic. Static methods rely on eviction patterns defined prior to inference. For instance, StreamingLLM [26] preserves only sink and local window tokens. Building upon this, RazorAttention [22] and DuoAttention [25] apply aggressive eviction to a majority of heads, preserving the full cache solely for critical retrieval heads. Although computationally lightweight with memory scaling at $O(s \times L)$ for a preset sparsity ratio s, their inability to adapt to dynamic inference contexts often compromises model accuracy. In contrast, dynamic methods continuously evict KV tuples guided by online attention scores [15,30]. For long-generation scenarios, RaaS [10] addresses context overflow by discarding tokens that persistently receive low attention. Ultimately, dynamic dropping methods retain and score only a fixed KV cache budget, maintaining strong efficiency despite the additional online scoring overhead.

KV Retrieval. The inherent nature of KV dropping—whether static or dynamic—inevitably causes permanent and irrecoverable information loss, resulting in significant accuracy penalties that are especially pronounced during long-context decoding. In contrast, retrieval-based sparsity methods keep the full cache but only attend to a selected subset at each decoding step. While preserving accuracy, retrieval methods introduce significant efficiency challenges. First, **applying selection across the entire context by scoring over every token leads to unacceptable overhead**. To mitigate this, existing methods generally reduce the scoring granularity through grouped selection strategies. The dominant approach is **page-wise selection**, which summarizes contiguous keys within a fixed block and scores only these *page summaries*. For example, both Quest and FreeKV utilize min-max pooled keys to represent page-level statistics, while ArkVale [3] employs bounding volumes. Alternatively, departing from strict positional chunking, methods like ClusterKV [17] adopt a **cluster-based selection** paradigm, alleviating the overhead by aggregating and scoring KV tuples based on their semantic feature clusters rather than rigid page boundaries. Moreover, **accommodating the complete KV cache presents a critical systemic bottleneck**. Quest statically retains the entire KV cache in GPU memory, which severely constrains the maximum context length and batch scalability. Furthermore, its non-group-consistent selection policy incurs a G-fold penalty in memory access overhead. Conversely, methods like ArkVale and ClusterKV address these limitations by using group-consistent retrieval and offloading the full KV cache to the host CPU memory, fetching sparse KV subsets on-demand. However, despite these architectural optimizations, the inherent latency of Host-to-Device (H2D) data transfers across the PCIe bus remains prohibitively expensive, fundamentally throttling the overall inference throughput. To mitigate these latency bottlenecks, recent work such as FreeKV introduces an asynchronous speculative retrieval mechanism. By leveraging the high similarity of query vectors between adjacent decoding steps, FreeKV employs *speculative retrieval* to decouple the selection and recall processes, shifting them out of the critical inference path via step-wise KV reuse. On the system side, FreeKV designs a hybrid KV cache layout (CPU: HND, GPU: NHD, where H, N, and D denote n_{kv}, L, and d) and a custom Streamed Recall kernel to accelerate KV recall and prevent inference blocking. However, despite these system-level advancements, FreeKV inevitably inherits the fundamental flaw of existing retrieval methods: **a linearly growing token selection time**. Although retrieval methods successfully reduce the attention computation complexity from $O(L)$ to $O(B)$, the selector itself typically necessitates near-linear scans across the historical context (e.g., block-wise scoring or dynamic clustering). This introduces an unavoidable selection overhead of approximately $O(\alpha L)$ with a constant factor $\alpha < 1$. Consequently, as the context length L scales, this selection process eclipses the computational benefits of sparse attention and emerges as the primary inference bottleneck.

The features of KV dropping and retrieval methods are summarized in Table 1. As illustrated, LocalKV optimizes inference efficiency by combining zero-overhead tracking, group-consistent selection, and fully overlapped prefetching.

3 Observation

Prior work reports strong temporal locality in sparse decoding: token sets selected at adjacent generation steps overlap substantially. This pattern suggests that selection states can be reused instead of recomputed from scratch.

Beyond temporal locality, we observe *spatial locality*: tokens selected at the current step frequently appear near those selected at the previous step. To empirically validate this observation, we track the top-1024 highly attended tokens, denoted as I_t, during the inference of Llama-3.1-8B-Instruct on long-generation tasks and DeepSeek-R1-Qwen-7B on long-reasoning tasks. Specifically, we quantify this spatial proximity by measuring the minimal distance of each selected

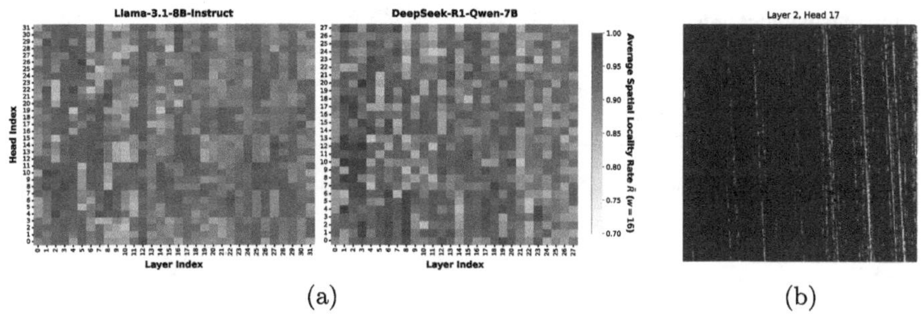

Fig. 2. (a) Spatial locality distribution. Each cell visualizes the average spatial locality rate ($\bar{R}$ at $w = 16$) for an individual attention head. (b) Attention map of Llama-3.1-8B-Instruct on GovReport tasks.

token $i \in I_t$ to the prior selection set I_{t-1} as $D_i = \min_{j \in I_{t-1}} |i - j|$. We then compute the generation-averaged spatial locality rate $\bar{R} = \frac{1}{N}\sum_{t=1}^{N} \frac{|\{i \in I_t | D_i \leq w\}|}{|I_t|}$ across N decoding steps, where w denotes a predefined distance threshold.

Setting the threshold $w = 16$, Fig. 2(a) demonstrates that $\bar{R}$ consistently exceeds 0.8 across all attention heads during diverse generation ($N = 512$) and reasoning ($N = 16384$) tasks, with the vast majority of heads surpassing 0.9. This exceptionally high spatial locality is observed across different layers, models, and tasks, likely driven by position embeddings [21] and the localized semantic continuity of adjacent tokens [29]. This quantitative observation aligns with the splash patterns in attention maps, as visualized in Fig. 2(b) and supported by prior studies [12,27,28], where critical tokens reside near the tokens selected in the preceding step. This locality of sparse attention indicates that localized tracking around previously critical tokens, serving as tracking anchors, can recover most high-value tokens at a significantly lower selection cost. Consequently, this insight renders exhaustive global scanning redundant and directly motivates our **anchor-based local tracking** mechanism.

4 Algorithm Design

4.1 Prefill Stage: Anchor Initialization

The algorithm of LocalKV is proposed based on the temporal and spatial locality of sparse attention. Specifically, we introduce a local tracking mechanism based on the fact that if a token is important at step $t-1$, its neighboring tokens also tend to have high importance at step t.

The tracking process is illustrated in Fig. 3. First, we identify the initial important tokens by utilizing the attention scores of the last prompt token $\mathbf{q}_{\text{last}}\mathbf{K}^\top$, where $\mathbf{q}_{\text{last}} \in \mathbb{R}^{1 \times d}$ is the query vector of the last prompt token, and $\mathbf{K} \in \mathbb{R}^{L \times d}$ denotes the cached key states of the preceding L tokens. We select the top-k tokens with the highest scores to form our initial important tokens. These tokens are referred to *anchors*, denoted as $\mathcal{A}^{(0)} = \{a_1^{(0)}, a_2^{(0)}, \dots, a_k^{(0)}\}$, which

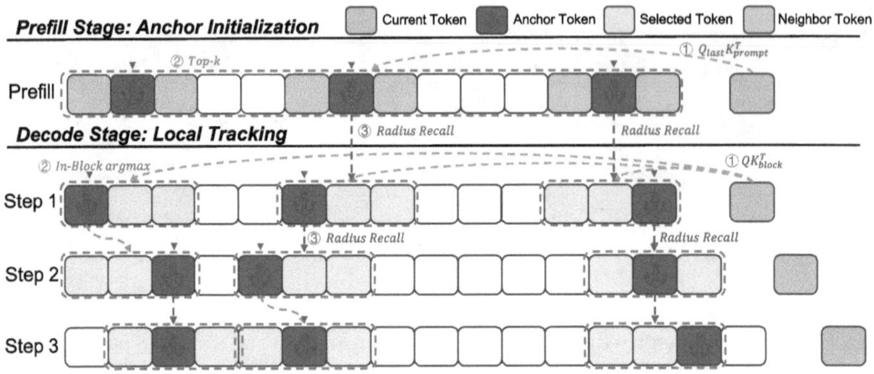

Fig. 3. Overview of the LocalKV's tracking algorithm. In this example, the decoding budget is set to $B = 9$ and the recall radius is set to $r = 1$.

represent the most critical contextual landmarks before the decoding stage. The $2 \times r$ neighbor tokens of the anchors are selected as token blocks for attention computation during the first decoding step.

Overhead. The complexity of identifying the initial anchors is restricted to $O(L)$, as it requires only a lightweight vector-matrix multiplication and incurring minimal overhead compared to the $O(L^2)$ prefill.

4.2 Decode Stage: Local Tracking

Instead of rescanning the entire context, at a given decoding step t, LocalKV seamlessly inherits the active anchor set $\mathcal{A}^{(t-1)}$ from the preceding step to guide its local tracking, effectively eliminating redundant global selection operations.

Local Neighborhood Retrieval. As shown in Fig. 3, LocalKV retrieves a localized block for each anchor $a_i^{(t-1)}$ based on a recall radius r, forming a baseline symmetric interval $[a_i^{(t-1)} - r, a_i^{(t-1)} + r]$. To guarantee zero budget waste, we introduce two adaptive spatial constraints. First, when boundary collisions occur at the global context boundaries, such as the Step 2 in Fig. 3, the conflicting retrieval block is dynamically shifted inward, ensuring fully valid token retrieval. Second, to prevent redundant memory access, as shown in Step 3 in Fig. 3, we strictly enforce interval disjointness: any overlap between adjacent retrieval blocks is resolved by pushing the subsequent block towards higher indices. Ultimately, these two adaptive spatial shifts ensure that attention is exclusively computed over strictly disjoint and globally valid contextual blocks.

Dynamic Anchor Update. As the decoding steps increase, the model's attention naturally shifts across the sequence to capture new contextual dependencies. Locking the anchors statically would fail to accommodate these shifts, leading to degraded performance. Therefore, LOCALKV continuously updates its anchors to track the attention flow. As shown in Fig. 3, after computing the local attention scores within the retrieved blocks, we identify the specific token index that yields the maximum attention score within each local block. This locally dominant token is then designated as the new anchor $a_i^{(t)}$ for the next decoding step. However, in long-decoding scenarios such as reasoning tasks, the attention distribution may exhibit abrupt shifts. Relying exclusively on localized tracking may fail to capture globally critical information. To escape local optima, LOCALKV periodically (e.g., every 128 steps) performs a global Top-K selection across all current tokens to update the anchors.

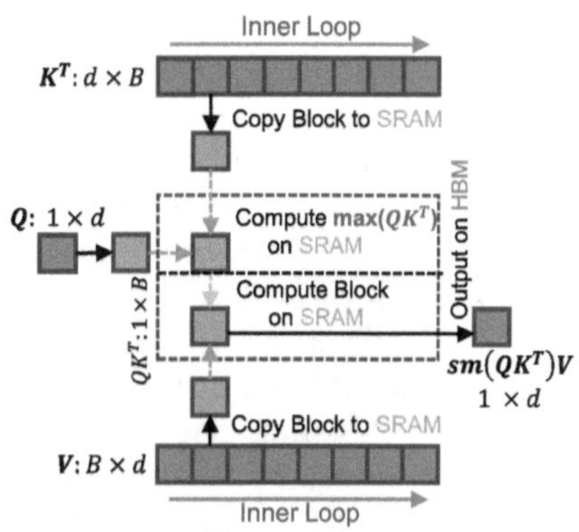

Fig. 4. Attention kernel with fused tracking. B denotes the token budget, and d represents the head dimension.

Algorithm 1: Attention with Fused Tracking
Input: Query $\mathbf{q} \in \mathbb{R}^{1\times d}$, KV Cache $\mathbf{K}, \mathbf{V} \in \mathbb{R}^{B\times d}$ in HBM, Block size B_c.
Output: Attn output $\mathbf{o} \in \mathbb{R}^{1\times d}$, Anchors $\mathbf{A} \in \mathbb{Z}^{T_c}$.
Initialize: $\mathbf{O} \leftarrow \mathbf{0} \in \mathbb{R}^{1\times d}$, $l \leftarrow 0$, $A_{idx} \leftarrow 0$.

Load $\mathbf{q}$ to SRAM.
Split $\mathbf{K}, \mathbf{V}$ into $T_c = \lceil B/B_c \rceil$ blocks.
for $j = 1$ to T_c **do**
  Load $\mathbf{K}_j, \mathbf{V}_j \in \mathbb{R}^{B_c\times d}$ to SRAM.
  $\mathbf{S}_j = \mathbf{q}\mathbf{K}_j^\top/\sqrt{d} \in \mathbb{R}^{1\times B_c}$
  # Local Anchor Update Operation
  $A_j = \arg\max(\mathbf{S}_j)$ {New anchor for block j}
  $m_{\text{new}} = \max(m, m_j)$
  $\mathbf{P}_j = \exp(\mathbf{S}_j - m_{\text{new}}) \in \mathbb{R}^{1\times B_c}$
  $l_{\text{new}} = \exp(m - m_{\text{new}}) \cdot l + \sum(\mathbf{P}_j)$
  $\mathbf{O} = \exp(m - m_{\text{new}}) \cdot \mathbf{O} + \mathbf{P}_j\mathbf{V}_j$
  $m = m_{\text{new}}$
  $l = l_{\text{new}}$
end for
$\mathbf{o} = \mathbf{O}/l$
Write $\mathbf{o}$ and $\mathbf{A}$ to HBM.

5 Kernel Design and System Implementation

5.1 Anchor-Shift Fused in Flash Attention

To eliminate the $O(\alpha L)$ selection overhead in current retrieval methods, we design a **Fused Tracking** kernel that seamlessly integrates the anchor update mechanism into the standard FlashAttention kernel. As illustrated in Fig. 4 and detailed in Algorithm 1, our approach achieves *zero-overhead* anchor updating by exploiting the data residency within the ultra-fast on-chip SRAM.

Specifically, the tiling mechanism of FlashAttention perfectly aligns with our block-wise anchor update strategy. During execution, the block-sized KV cache ($\mathbf{K}_j, \mathbf{V}_j \in \mathbb{R}^{B_c\times d}$) is loaded into SRAM to compute the pre-softmax attention scores $\mathbf{S}_j = \mathbf{q}\mathbf{K}_j^\top/\sqrt{d}$, which are subsequently passed through an online softmax and multiplied by $\mathbf{V}_j$ to update the final output block $\mathbf{O}$. Our method simply piggybacks on this mandatory computational flow. After computing $\mathbf{S}_j$, we perform an ultra-lightweight anchor extraction: $A_j = \arg\max(\mathbf{S}_j)$, before the online softmax reduction. By reusing this intermediate result, we update the local anchors without incurring extra HBM I/O overhead.

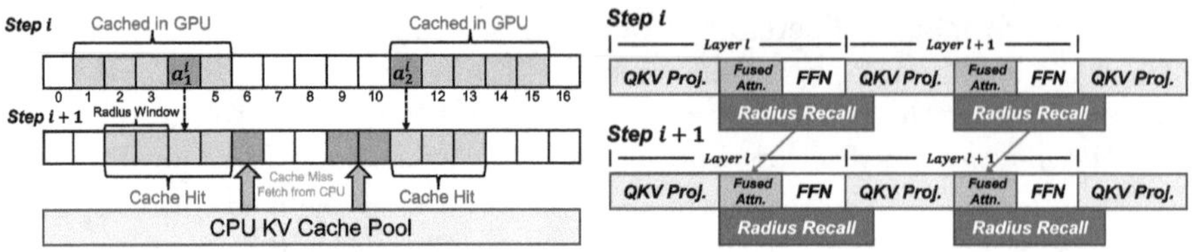

Fig. 5. Left: Radius recall where at most a half KV block is fetched. Right: The radius recall is executed asynchronously for prefetching the KV tuples for the next step.

5.2 Cache-Aware Prefetch

Radius Recall. Since the full KV cache is stored in host CPU memory (i.e., local DRAM), the required KV blocks must be transferred to the GPU during attention computation, incurring unavoidable H2D transfer overhead. However, in LocalKV, each new anchor is generated within the current block, and the recalled tokens are symmetrically distributed around it. As a result, the KV tuples recalled by the new anchor share a massive overlap with those recalled by the previous anchor, which are already cached in GPU memory. In particular, the tokens recalled by the new anchor theoretically share at least a 50% overlap with those fetched by the previous anchor. Exploiting this property, we design the **Radius Recall** mechanism (Fig. 5 left). During the recall phase, LocalKV exclusively fetches the cache-missed tokens, reducing the H2D transfer volume by at least half.

Asynchronous Prefetching. While Radius Recall halves the H2D traffic, the inherently slow CPU-GPU transfers may still block the primary decoding process. To resolve this stall, we propose **Asynchronous Prefetching**. Since the anchor updated in the current step is used to fetch KV tuples for the next step, we can immediately trigger the H2D transfer upon obtaining the new anchor. As shown in Fig. 5, our design enables the recall operation to overlap with attention and FFN computations of the current layer, as well as the QKV projections of the next layer. The recalled KV tuples during step i will then be reused in step $i+1$, continuing the process iteratively. By coupling this prefetching design with Radius Recall, LocalKV completely hides the H2D transfer latency, achieving a full overlap between computation and memory I/O.

6 Evaluation

6.1 Experimental Setup

Datasets and Models. We evaluate LocalKV across various models and tasks. For accuracy evaluation, we select LongBench [2] and NIAH [14] to cover general long-input and long-retrieval scenarios. In addition, we assess LocalKV on long reasoning tasks, including MATH500 [8], AIME24 [11], and GPQA [20]. For

Table 2. Accuracy results of LongBench and NIAH.

Methods	LongBench							NIAH		
	SD-QA	MD-QA	Sum.	FS	Syn.	Code	Avg.	16K	32K	64K
Llama-3.1-8B	48.14	43.48	26.04	63.74	66.59	60.10	51.35	100.00	100.00	100.00
RaaS	46.32	40.58	23.76	61.63	65.76	49.32	47.90	63.33	60.83	62.50
Quest	44.97	42.14	24.39	61.00	64.06	57.10	48.94	93.33	91.67	86.25
FreeKV	48.06	42.97	25.57	63.08	65.68	50.74	49.35	100.00	100.00	87.50
ClusterKV	48.04	**43.16**	**25.76**	63.23	66.12	59.48	50.96	88.33	87.50	84.75
LocalKV	**48.54**	42.44	25.33	**63.66**	**66.45**	**59.59**	**51.00**	**100.00**	**100.00**	**95.00**
Qwen-3-8B	47.71	40.70	24.34	63.44	70.17	66.10	52.08	100.00	100.00	100.00
RaaS	44.36	38.90	22.76	62.40	**70.50**	54.54	48.91	67.50	46.66	57.50
Quest	43.15	38.10	24.21	50.57	65.80	61.73	47.26	96.67	86.00	73.33
FreeKV	46.95	40.35	24.07	63.17	69.83	55.78	50.02	100.00	90.00	88.33
ClusterKV	**47.36**	40.52	**24.54**	63.18	69.67	**66.18**	**51.91**	94.17	90.00	87.08
LocalKV	47.08	**40.64**	24.09	**63.41**	70.17	65.92	51.89	**100.00**	**100.00**	**92.08**
Qwen-3-14B	48.67	46.30	24.32	64.73	69.33	66.53	53.31	100.00	100.00	100.00
RaaS	46.00	44.79	22.88	64.05	69.17	54.20	50.18	73.33	59.17	60.00
Quest	46.20	43.38	**24.39**	62.25	68.33	60.81	50.89	100.00	100.00	95.00
FreeKV	48.64	46.18	23.99	**64.73**	**69.83**	55.52	51.48	100.00	100.00	100.00
ClusterKV	48.30	46.25	24.07	64.35	69.33	65.76	53.01	100.00	100.00	96.25
LocalKV	**48.80**	**46.28**	23.84	64.66	69.17	**66.06**	**53.14**	**100.00**	**100.00**	**100.00**

LongBench and NIAH, we use general models including Llama-3.1-8B-Instruct [18], Qwen-3-8B [19], Qwen-3-14B [19]. For reasoning tasks, we use DeepSeek-R1-Llama-8B [6], DeepSeek-R1-Qwen-7B, Qwen-3-8B. Detailed metrics for each dataset are provided in the corresponding sections.

Baselines. We compare LocalKV against SOTA methods, including dynamic KV dropping methods like RaaS [10], and KV retrieval methods, including Quest [23], ClusterKV [17] and FreeKV [16]. The token budget B for all methods is consistently set to 2048. The sink size S and local window size W of LocalKV vary depending on the task. Additionally, the global update interval of LocalKV is set to 512 decoding steps. Following standard practice, KV Cache compression is not applied to the first layer and last layer in any of the methods. We consistently set the block size to 32 for LocalKV, Quest, FreeKV, and RaaS. For ClusterKV, we dynamically configure the number of clusters as $C = L/80$, where L denotes the context length. Other hyperparameters of the baselines, such as the update threshold for RaaS and the correction threshold of FreeKV, are retained as specified in their original configurations.

Table 3. Accuracy results of long reasoning tasks.

Methods	MATH500		AIME24		GPQA	
	pass@k	avg@k	pass@k	avg@k	pass@k	avg@k
DS-Llama-8B	92.00	83.00	63.33	50.00	62.00	39.00
RaaS	84.00	75.50	66.67	42.50	42.00	28.50
Quest	88.00	79.50	70.00	44.16	46.00	30.00
FreeKV	88.00	79.50	70.00	45.00	**74.00**	**40.50**
ClusterKV	88.00	78.00	70.00	**50.00**	62.00	37.00
LocalKV	**92.00**	**83.00**	**70.00**	48.34	62.00	37.50
DS-Qwen-7B	92.00	87.00	73.33	51.66	48.00	33.00
RaaS	86.00	81.50	70.00	48.33	44.00	31.00
Quest	89.00	85.00	73.33	51.67	51.00	34.00
FreeKV	88.00	86.00	73.33	50.00	**56.00**	**34.50**
ClusterKV	90.00	84.00	73.33	**53.33**	46.00	33.00
LocalKV	**92.00**	**86.50**	**73.33**	52.50	52.00	33.00
Qwen-3-8B	94.00	89.00	80.00	64.16	74.00	53.00
RaaS	84.00	81.00	66.67	56.67	66.00	49.50
Quest	86.00	84.50	70.00	62.50	72.00	53.00
FreeKV	86.00	83.50	73.33	58.33	70.00	53.00
ClusterKV	92.00	85.00	73.33	**63.33**	70.00	51.00
LocalKV	**94.00**	**87.00**	**76.67**	60.00	**78.00**	**57.00**

6.2 Model Accuracy

LongBench. We evaluate long-context capabilities using LongBench, reporting overall averages and specific scores across its six categories (Single-Doc QA, Multi-Doc QA, Summarization, Few-shot learning, Synthetic tasks, and Code). For all evaluated methods, input sequences are truncated to 32K tokens, with $S = W = 128$ under greedy decoding.

As shown in Table 2, for all models, the overall performance of LocalKV deviates by at most 0.35 points compared to the dense baseline, while achieving the best or second-best results across most metrics. Furthermore, the evaluated KV dropping baseline, RaaS, although exhibiting moderate performance degradation on this long-input benchmark, consistently underperforms compared to KV retrieval approaches.

Needle In A Haystack. To evaluate long-context retrieval, we employ the Needle In A Haystack (NIAH) benchmark. In this task, a target string (needle) is inserted into a long background text (haystack) at 10 different depths distributed from the beginning to the end of the text. We report the accuracy across input lengths of 16K, 32K, and 64K tokens. For all evaluated methods, we set $S = W = 128$ and applied greedy decoding.

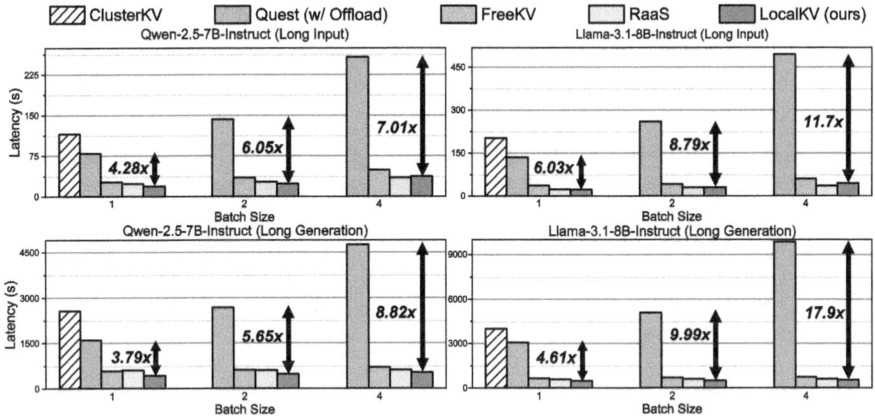

Fig. 6. End-to-end latency comparison between KV compression methods.

As shown in Table 2, for all models, LocalKV achieves lossless performance compared to the dense baseline at both 16K and 32K context lengths. Concurrently, as the sequence length extends to 64K, LocalKV secures the highest scores among all compressed methods.

Reasoning. To evaluate the prolonged, autonomous thinking processes of reasoning models like DeepSeek-R1, we use AIME24 and 50-problem subsets from MATH500 and GPQA. Since the outputs of reasoning models are highly sensitive to random seeds [9], we generate $k = 4$ different samples for each problem. We report two metrics: **pass@**k, measuring the likelihood of finding at least one correct solution among the k samples, and **avg@**k, representing the overall average accuracy. For all evaluated methods, we set $S = W = 512$ and the maximum generation length to 16K, and apply stochastic sampling with a temperature of 0.6 and a top-p value of 0.95, following the DeepSeek-R1 setup.

As shown in Table 3, LocalKV delivers accuracy comparable to models with full KV cache and outperforms other compression methods across most datasets. Baselines such as RaaS exhibit significant accuracy losses, particularly on AIME24, which involves more complex problems. Moreover, LocalKV consistently outperforms other KV retrieval methods in most cases, demonstrating the effectiveness of locally tracking important tokens.

6.3 Inference Efficiency

Setup. Experiments were conducted on an NVIDIA Ada 6000 (48GB), connected to Intel Xeon 6530 CPUs via PCIe Gen4. The evaluation covers Qwen-2.5-7B and Llama-3.1-8B models under both long-input (32K input, 512 output) and long-generation scenarios (600 input, 16K output). We set $B = 2048$ and $S = W = 512$ for all evaluated methods. Notably, since ClusterKV does not support multi-batch inference, we report its end-to-end latency only at a batch size of 1.

End-to-End Latency. As shown in Fig. 6, LocalKV demonstrates significant efficiency gains over state-of-the-art KV retrieval methods, achieving speedups of up to 17.9× and 1.6× compared to Quest and FreeKV. Moreover, LocalKV attains efficiency comparable to dropping methods like RaaS, which do not involve I/O offloading or recall. Specifically, LocalKV achieves 7.01× and 8.82× speedups over Quest under long-input and long-generation scenarios on Qwen-2.5-7B, and 11.7× and 17.9× on Llama-3.1-8B. The improvements become more pronounced for large batch sizes and in long-generation scenarios, where massive recall operations are required. In addition, the speedups are amplified for Llama-3.1-8B, which has a larger KV cache capacity compared to Qwen-2.5-7B.

7 Conclusion

We present LocalKV, an algorithm-system co-optimization sparse decoding framework. On the algorithm side, LocalKV fully exploits the inherent locality of sparse attention. On the system side, we design a fused kernel to eliminate overhead of tracking important tokens, coupled with radius recall and KV prefetching. LocalKV achieves near-lossless generation quality, and delivers a 1.6× decoding speedup over state-of-the-art methods.

Acknowledgments. This work was supported by the National Natural Science Foundation of China under Grant 62472273 and Grant 62232015.

Disclosure of Interests. The authors have no competing interests to declare that are relevant to the content of this article.
Artificial intelligence tools, if used, were used only for language organization and figure/table polishing, and did not participate in the generation of the core ideas or technical content.

References

1. Ainslie, J., Lee-Thorp, J., de Jong, M., Zemlyanskiy, Y., Lebron, F., Sanghai, S.: GQA: training generalized multi-query transformer models from multi-head checkpoints. In: Bouamor, H., Pino, J., Bali, K. (eds.) Proceedings of the 2023 Conference on Empirical Methods in Natural Language Processing, pp. 4895–4901. Association for Computational Linguistics, Singapore (2023). https://doi.org/10.18653/v1/2023.emnlp-main.298. https://aclanthology.org/2023.emnlp-main.298
2. Bai, Y., et al.: Longbench: a bilingual, multitask benchmark for long context understanding. arXiv preprint arXiv:2308.14508 (2023)
3. Chen, R., et al.: Arkvale: efficient generative LLM inference with recallable key-value eviction. In: Globerson, A., et al. (eds.) Advances in Neural Information Processing Systems, vol. 37, pp. 113134–113155. Curran Associates, Inc. (2024). https://proceedings.neurips.cc/paper_files/paper/2024/file/cd4b49379efac6e84186a3ffce108c37-Paper-Conference.pdf

4. Chew, R., Bollenbacher, J., Wenger, M., Speer, J., Kim, A.: LLM-assisted content analysis: using large language models to support deductive coding (2023). https://arxiv.org/abs/2306.14924
5. DeepMind, G.: Gemini 2.5: our most intelligent AI model (2025)
6. Guo, D., et al.: Deepseek-r1: incentivizing reasoning capability in LLMs via reinforcement learning (2025). https://arxiv.org/abs/2501.12948
7. Liu, A., et al.: Deepseek-v2: a strong, economical, and efficient mixture-of-experts language model (2024). https://arxiv.org/abs/2405.04434
8. Hendrycks, D., et al.: Measuring mathematical problem solving with the math dataset. In: Vanschoren, J., Yeung, S. (eds.) Proceedings of the Neural Information Processing Systems Track on Datasets and Benchmarks, vol. 1 (2021). https://datasets-benchmarks-proceedings.neurips.cc/paper_files/paper/2021/file/be83ab3ecd0db773eb2dc1b0a17836a1-Paper-round2.pdf
9. Hochlehnert, A., Bhatnagar, H., Udandarao, V., Albanie, S., Prabhu, A., Bethge, M.: A sober look at progress in language model reasoning: pitfalls and paths to reproducibility (2025). https://arxiv.org/abs/2504.07086
10. Hu, J., et al.: Efficient long-decoding inference with reasoning-aware attention sparsity (2025). https://arxiv.org/abs/2502.11147
11. Huggingface: Maxwell-jia/aime_2024 (2025). https://huggingface.co/datasets/Maxwell-Jia/AIME_2024
12. Jiang, H., et al.: Minference 1.0: accelerating pre-filling for long-context LLMs via dynamic sparse attention (2024). https://arxiv.org/abs/2407.02490
13. Jiang, J., Wang, F., Shen, J., Kim, S., Kim, S.: A survey on large language models for code generation (2024). https://arxiv.org/abs/2406.00515
14. Kamradt, G.: Needle in a haystack - pressure testing LLMs (2023). https://github.com/gkamradt/LLMTest_NeedleInAHaystack
15. Li, Y., et al.: Snapkv: LLM knows what you are looking for before generation (2024). https://arxiv.org/abs/2404.14469
16. Liu, G., Li, C., Ning, Z., Guo, M., Zhao, J.: Freekv: boosting kv cache retrieval for efficient LLM inference (2025). https://arxiv.org/abs/2505.13109
17. Liu, G., Li, C., Zhao, J., Zhang, C., Guo, M.: Clusterkv: manipulating LLM kv cache in semantic space for recallable compression (2024). https://arxiv.org/abs/2412.03213
18. Meta: The llama 3 herd of models (2024). https://arxiv.org/abs/2407.21783
19. Qwen: Qwen3: Think deeper, act faster (2025)
20. Rein, D., et al.: GPQA: a graduate-level google-proof Q&A benchmark (2023). https://arxiv.org/abs/2311.12022
21. Su, J., Lu, Y., Pan, S., Murtadha, A., Wen, B., Liu, Y.: Roformer: enhanced transformer with rotary position embedding (2023). https://arxiv.org/abs/2104.09864
22. Tang, H., et al.: Razorattention: efficient kv cache compression through retrieval heads (2024). https://arxiv.org/abs/2407.15891
23. Tang, J., Zhao, Y., Zhu, K., Xiao, G., Kasikci, B., Han, S.: Quest: query-aware sparsity for efficient long-context LLM inference. In: ICML (2024)
24. xAI: Grok 3 beta — the age of reasoning agents (2025). https://x.ai/news/grok-3
25. Xiao, G., et al.: Duoattention: efficient long-context LLM inference with retrieval and streaming heads (2024). https://arxiv.org/abs/2410.10819
26. Xiao, G., Tian, Y., Chen, B., Han, S., Lewis, M.: Efficient streaming language models with attention sinks. In: ICLR (2024)

27. Xie, X., Yu, Z., Liao, Y., Wang, T., Toh, K.C., Yan, S.: Slow-Fast Inference: Training-Free Inference Acceleration via Within-Sentence Support Stability (2026). https://doi.org/10.48550/arXiv.2603.12038
28. Xu, R., Xiao, G., Huang, H., Guo, J., Han, S.: XAttention: Block Sparse Attention with Antidiagonal Scoring (2025). https://doi.org/10.48550/arXiv.2503.16428
29. Yuan, J., et al.: Native sparse attention: hardware-aligned and natively trainable sparse attention (2025). https://arxiv.org/abs/2502.11089
30. Zhang, Z., et al.: H2o: heavy-hitter oracle for efficient generative inference of large language models. In: Oh, A., Naumann, T., Globerson, A., Saenko, K., Hardt, M., Levine, S. (eds.) Advances in Neural Information Processing Systems, vol. 36, pp. 34661–34710. Curran Associates, Inc. (2023)

MOCAP: Wafer-Scale-Chip-Oriented Memory-Orchestrated Chunked Pipelining Framework for Prefill-Only LLM Inference

Zichuan Wang[1], Huizheng Wang[1], Yuheng Xiao[1], Haonan Zuo[1], Taiquan Wei[1], Jinyi Deng[1], Chao Li[2], Yang Hu[1(✉)], and Shouyi Yin[1,3]

[1] School of Integrated Circuits, BNRist, Tsinghua University, Beijing 100084, China
hu_yang@tsinghua.edu.cn

[2] School of Computer Science and Engineering, Shanghai Jiao Tong University, Shanghai 200240, China

[3] Shanghai Artificial Intelligence Laboratory, Shanghai 200433, China

Abstract. Large language models (LLMs) are increasingly used in prefill-only workloads, where end-to-end latency is dominated by the prefill phase. For long-context prefill, communication overhead grows with sequence length and quickly becomes a bottleneck on conventional GPU systems, making wafer-scale chips (WSCs) a promising substrate due to their high communication bandwidth and large aggregate compute and memory capacity. A natural way to accelerate prefill is to partition a long input sequence into multiple chunks and execute them in a finer-grained pipeline across devices. However, directly applying this idea to long-context prefill on WSCs remains challenging. First, causal dependency across chunks causes KV cache to accumulate unevenly across pipeline stages, creating severe memory imbalance and limiting the feasible sequence length. Second, later chunks require more attention computation because each chunk depends on preceding chunks, leading to chunk-level latency imbalance.

To address these challenges, we present MOCAP, a memory-orchestrated chunked pipelining framework for prefill-only LLM inference on WSCs. MOCAP introduces Memory-Balanced KV Reallocation (MBKR) to alleviate memory imbalance by redistributing KV cache across pipeline stages, thereby extending the feasible sequence length. It further incorporates Latency-Balanced Chunk Partitioning (LBCP) to balance chunk execution cost under both attention-cost growth and KV reallocation overhead, improving pipeline efficiency. Experimental results show that, compared with GPipe, MOCAP achieves 76.4% lower end-to-end latency and 3.24× higher throughput on average. MOCAP also extends the maximum supported sequence length by up to 1.31× compared with Terapipe.

Keywords: Wafer-Scale Chips · KV Cache Management · Prefill-Only LLM Inference

---

Z. Wang and H. Wang—Contributed equally.

L. Eeckhout et al. (Eds.): APPT 2026, LNCS 16693, pp. 97–111, 2027.
https://doi.org/10.1007/978-981-92-4805-6_7

1 Introduction

Large language models (LLMs) have transformed AI across a broad range of applications. Beyond generative applications [41], LLM-style transformer inference is increasingly used in prefill-only scenarios [1,40], where the system only needs to process the input context and produce one output token, as shown in Fig. 1(b). In these workloads, the end-to-end latency is largely determined by the prefill phase, making prefill optimization essential.

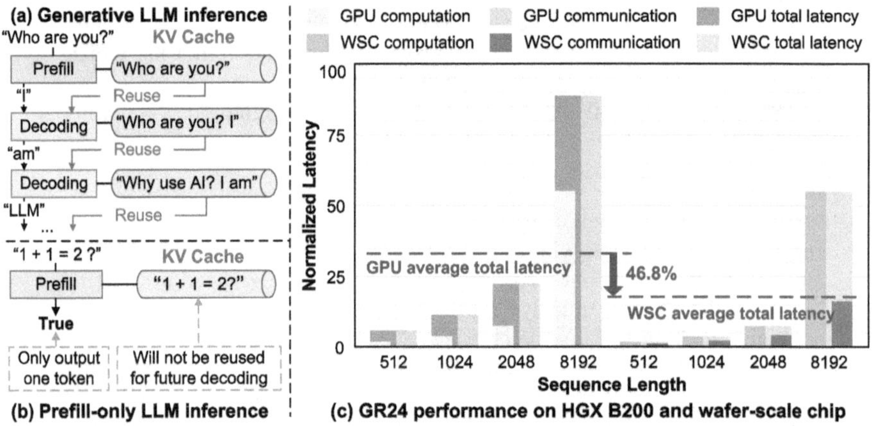

Fig. 1. (a) (b) LLM inference process. (c) End-to-end latency comparison between HGX B200 GPU systems and wafer-scale chips under equivalent compute and memory capacity on the GR24 [40].

However, since the communication volume in prefill grows proportionally with sequence length, communication becomes the dominant bottleneck on widely deployed GPU systems, as illustrated in Fig. 1(c). Recently, chip integration has advanced toward wafer-scale chips (WSCs) [4,10,11,18,21,22], which provide much higher compute density, memory capacity, and communication bandwidth. This makes WSCs a promising substrate for communication-intensive prefill. As shown in Fig. 1(c), the communication advantage of WSCs reduces end-to-end latency by 46.8% compared with GPU systems. However, existing studies [3,37] mainly focus on general inference, and do not specifically optimize prefill-only execution.

Terapipe [9] proposes a token-wise pipeline for the forward pass of LLM training, which exploits the causal dependency along the token dimension to enable token-wise pipelined execution across devices. Inspired by this idea, prefill can similarly partition the sequence into multiple chunks and execute them as a fine-grained chunked pipeline to reduce pipeline bubbles and improve utilization.

However, directly extending such a pipeline to prefill remains challenging. First, causal dependency across chunks causes the KV cache to accumulate unevenly across pipeline stages, and the resulting memory pressure quickly becomes a bottleneck, limiting the feasible sequence length. Second, the execution cost of different chunks is inherently imbalanced: later chunks incur higher attention latency due to their longer prefixes, so uniform chunk partitioning creates pipeline bubbles and degrades pipeline efficiency. Therefore, making the chunked prefill pipeline effective requires jointly addressing both KV cache accumulation and chunk-level latency imbalance.

To this end, we present MOCAP, a memory-orchestrated chunked pipelining framework for efficient prefill-only LLM inference on wafer-scale chips. First, MOCAP introduces Memory-Balanced KV Reallocation, which redistributes KV cache across pipeline stages to mitigate memory imbalance and relieve KV cache buildup at earlier stages, thereby enabling longer sequence execution under limited memory. Second, MOCAP incorporates Latency-Balanced Chunk Partitioning, which adaptively partitions the input sequence into non-uniform chunks to balance KV cache reallocation overhead and reduce pipeline bubbles caused by the increasing attention latency of later chunks. Together, MOCAP transforms the chunked pipeline into a scalable and efficient execution paradigm for prefill-only LLM inference on WSCs.

Our contributions are summarized as follows:

(1) We propose MOCAP, a memory-orchestrated chunked pipelining framework for prefill-only LLM inference on wafer-scale chips. **To the best of our knowledge, this is the first work to systematically optimize prefill-only LLM inference on WSCs.**
(2) We develop Memory-Balanced KV Reallocation, which mitigates stage-wise KV cache accumulation by redistributing KV cache across pipeline stages, improving memory utilization and enabling longer sequence execution.
(3) We design Latency-Balanced Chunk Partitioning, which balances KV cache reallocation overhead and compute imbalance through non-uniform partitioning.
(4) On average, MOCAP reduces end-to-end latency by 76.4% and improves throughput by 3.24× over GPipe. It also extends the maximum supported sequence length by up to 1.31× compared with Terapipe.

2 Background

2.1 Prefill-Only LLM Inference

Prefill-only LLM inference [1,40] represents an emerging class of workloads where the model processes the entire input sequence to produce only one token, without long autoregressive decoding. Unlike generative inference, which repeatedly reuses the KV cache during decoding, as shown in Fig. 1(a), prefill-only inference does not require the generated KV cache to be reused for future long decoding. Because the output is produced immediately after prefilling, the overall service latency is largely determined by the prefill phase.

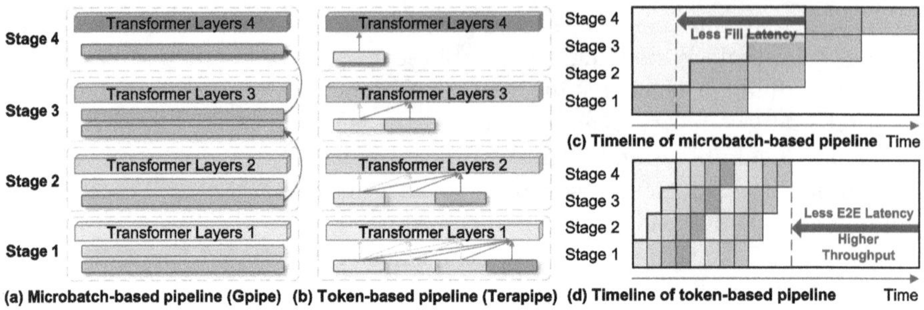

Fig. 2. Overview of microbatch-based pipeline and token-based pipeline.

This execution pattern leads to several distinctive system characteristics. First, although the KV cache is generated during prefilling, it does not need to be persistently stored for future decoding reuse, fundamentally changing the role of KV-cache management. Second, practical prefill-only workloads often involve long input contexts of up to 10^5 [40], so the system bottleneck shifts from iterative decoding efficiency to efficient processing of long sequences.

2.2 Chunked Pipeline

Terapipe [9] introduces chunked pipeline to alleviate the coarse granularity of microbatch-based pipeline parallelism. Unlike GPipe [5], which pipelines microbatches across stages as shown in Fig. 2(a), Terapipe pipelines token chunks across stages (Fig. 2(b)), thereby shortening pipeline fill time and improving throughput, as illustrated in Fig. 2(c)(d). Inspired by this idea, prefill can likewise partition the input sequence into chunks and execute them in a chunked pipeline.

Chunked pipeline induces a cross-chunk dependency through causal attention. As shown in Fig. 2(b), each chunk must attend to the key-value tensors generated by all preceding chunks. This dependency has two implications: 1) KV caches from earlier chunks must remain live for subsequent computation, causing progressive accumulation over the pipeline lifetime. 2) Later chunks face longer prefixes and therefore higher attention latency, which can manifest as pipeline bubbles.

2.3 Wafer-Scale Chips

Wafer-scale chips (WSCs) [4,10,21,22] extend chip integration beyond the conventional reticle limit through advanced packaging technologies. As illustrated in Fig. 3(a), WSCs consist of an interposer and multiple known-good dies (KGDs). The interposer provides dense on-package interconnects, in which die-to-die spacing is minimized to satisfy signal integrity constraints and maximize communication bandwidth. To preserve ultra-short inter-die links while maintaining scalable routing complexity, wafer-scale chips commonly adopt a nearest-neighbor

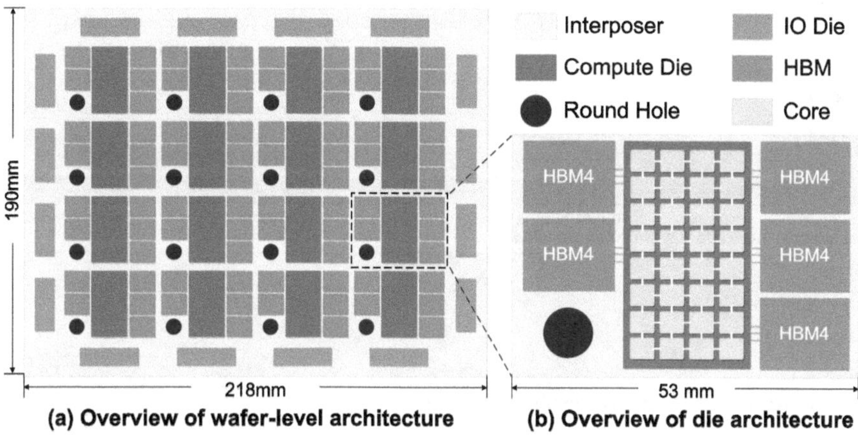

Fig. 3. Overview of wafer-scale chip architecture.

2D mesh topology, where each die physically connects to adjacent neighbors. Figure 3(b) further shows a representative die architecture, where each compute die contains an array of compute cores equipped with distributed SRAM for local buffering, while HBM stacks are placed around the compute die to provide large-capacity off-die storage and high memory access bandwidth.

A key architectural distinction between wafer-scale chips and conventional GPU systems lies in the communication fabric. **1)** Wafer-scale chips provide up to 10 TB/s die-to-die bandwidth, which is sufficient to largely mask KV-cache transfer overhead compared with the 900 GB/s NVLink [17] bandwidth in widely deployed GPU systems. **2)** The same communication interface can also be used by edge IO dies, extending the high-bandwidth domain beyond a local package region. **3)** D2D bandwidth becomes comparable to HBM bandwidth, making cross-die data movement a practical option.

3 Motivation

3.1 Memory Imbalance Limits Feasible Sequence Length

Challenge: As the sequence length grows, stage-wise KV-cache accumulation becomes increasingly imbalanced, eventually limiting the feasible sequence length. As illustrated in Sect. 2.2, earlier stages start accumulating KV cache earlier and keep it for longer, while later stages experience a much shorter accumulation window. This asymmetric KV-cache lifetime causes the peak memory occupancy to concentrate on the earliest stages. As illustrated in Fig. 4(a), the system is effectively bounded by the earliest-stage memory bottleneck: once the earliest stage reaches its memory limit, the execution can no longer scale to longer sequences, even though substantial memory capacity on later stages remains unused. In other words, the feasible sequence length is constrained by the peak per-stage occupancy rather than by the aggregate memory

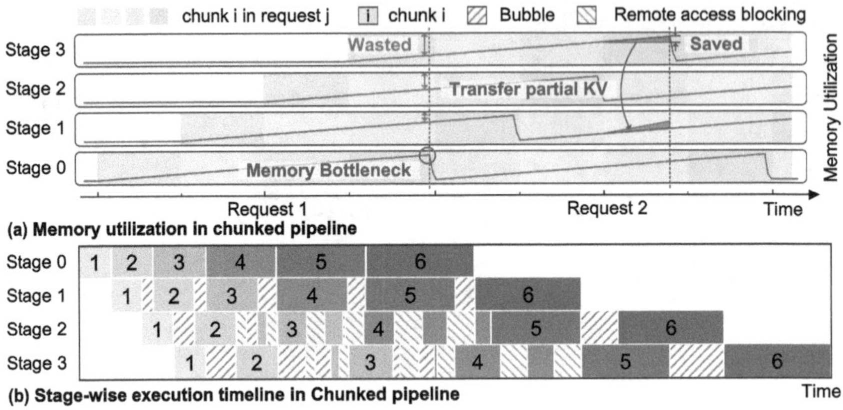

Fig. 4. Stage-wise memory and execution latency imbalance introduced by chunked pipeline.

capacity of the system, leaving a large fraction of memory stranded on non-bottleneck stages.

Insight: Such skewed memory utilization creates an opportunity to extend sequence headroom through stage-aware KV-cache reallocation. Although KV-cache accumulation is highly skewed, the memory pressure is not simultaneously saturated across all stages. In particular, when the earliest stage approaches its memory limit, later stages may still have substantial available space. As highlighted by the *wasted* and *saved* regions in Fig. 4(a), transferring part of the accumulated KV cache away from the bottleneck stage can reduce the peak memory occupancy and convert otherwise wasted memory on other stages into effective sequence headroom. Motivated by this opportunity, we propose Memory-Balanced KV Reallocation (MBKR) to mitigate memory imbalance and extend the feasible sequence length without requiring additional hardware memory.

3.2 Latency Imbalance Limits Compute Utilization

Challenge: Chunk latency becomes increasingly imbalanced as execution progresses, which limits the compute utilization of the chunked pipeline. The latency of each chunk consists of two major components: the attention latency and the GEMM latency, where the latter includes the QKV projection, the output projection, and the FFN computation. For the i-th chunk with length c_i, these two components can be approximated as

$$T_{i,\text{attn}} \propto c_i(p_i + c_i), p_i = \sum_{j=1}^{i-1} c_j \qquad T_{i,\text{gemm}} \propto c_i, \tag{1}$$

where p_i denotes the prefix length preceding the i-th chunk. This decomposition reveals the source of imbalance: as execution proceeds, the prefix length grows monotonically, causing later chunks to incur increasingly higher attention latency, while the GEMM latency only scales with the chunk size itself. As shown in Fig. 4(b), uniformly partitioned chunks therefore exhibit increasingly imbalanced execution time, which manifests as visible pipeline bubbles. Moreover, once KV cache is reallocated across stages, some stages must fetch KV data from remote stages during execution. These remote fetches do not merely add communication overhead; the accessed stage must spend time serving the request, which can delay its own local computation and thereby extend the critical path. As shown by the blue shaded blocks in Fig. 4(b), this additional blocking further aggravates chunk-level latency imbalance.

Insight: This inefficiency can be mitigated by reshaping chunk boundaries to compensate for both prefix-induced attention growth and reallocation-induced blocking. Since later chunks are inherently more expensive, assigning them the same size as earlier chunks is suboptimal. Instead, later chunks can be made smaller while earlier chunks take relatively larger portions of the sequence, so that the reduction in chunk size offsets the growth of attention latency as well as the additional delay caused by remote KV accesses. As suggested by the reduced bubbles and blocking intervals in Fig. 4(b), such latency-aware partitioning can better balance chunk execution time, shorten the critical path, and improve effective overlap across stages. To address this issue, we propose Latency-Balanced Chunk Partitioning (LBCP) to mitigate latency imbalance and improve compute utilization in chunked pipeline execution.

4 MOCAP Framework

4.1 Memory-Balanced KV Reallocation

As discussed in Sect. 3.1, the chunked pipeline creates a predictable stage-wise KV-cache imbalance. Exploiting this opportunity faces two challenges: (1) identifying a stage-pairing strategy that maximizes usable memory capacity, and (2) minimizing the communication cost introduced by KV-cache transfers. Therefore, an effective reallocation scheme must jointly optimize memory utilization and transfer overhead.

To this end, we propose *Memory-Balanced KV Reallocation* (MBKR). MBKR first identifies a stage placement strategy that maximizes memory utilization, and then applies a runtime reallocation policy. To describe this interaction, we refer to stages under excessive memory pressure as *debtor stages*, since they need to spill part of their KV cache, and stages with sufficient residual capacity as *creditor stages*, since they host spilled KV data and serve remote KV requests.

For stage placement, prior work on LLM training [6,29] adopts a head-to-tail pairing strategy, which pairs the stage with the highest memory pressure with the stage that has the lowest memory pressure, as shown in Fig. 5 (b, left). Such a placement is effective when the memory-pressure pattern remains stable. However, in chunked pipeline execution, the imbalance pattern changes during request transitions, causing the pairing to become mismatched. In particular, when the hotspot shifts to Stage 3, its original paired stage, Stage 4, differs from

```
(a) The proposed SCKP strategy:
Input: chunk scheme {c1,c2,···,cM}, stage
count N, thresholds p1, p2, memory
occupancy of stage_i s_i
 1 for each stage i do
 2     compute KV_i^new
       // local only state
 3     if s_i < p1 then
 4         load KV_i^local
       // creditor state
 5     else if s_i < p2 then
 6         store KV_{i+N/2}^new to local
 7         load KV_i^local
 8         send KV_{i+N/2}^global to stage_{i-N/2}
       // debtor state
 9     else
10         load KV_i^global from stage_{i+N/2}
11         load KV_i^local from stage_i
12     end if
13 end for
```

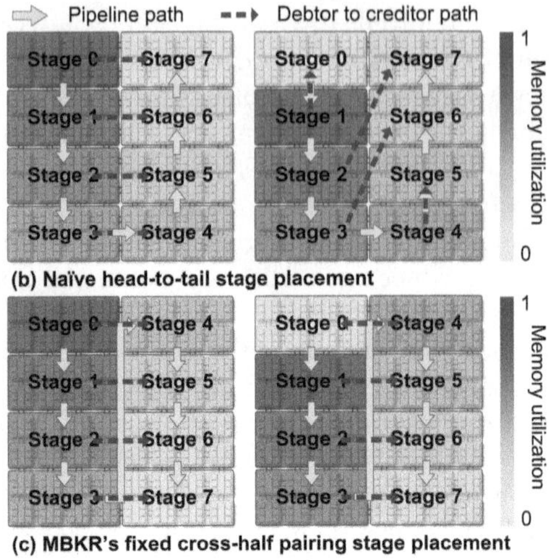

Fig. 5. Overview of memory-balanced KV reallocation.

it by only one chunk in memory occupancy, which means this head-to-tail strategy provides at most half a chunk of additional usable space. Figure 5(b, right) illustrates a natural remedy to dynamically rematch debtor and creditor stages according to instantaneous memory usage, so that the most heavily loaded stage is always paired with the least loaded one. However, such dynamic rematching would require previously spilled KV cache to be migrated again whenever the pairing changes, introducing substantial extra communication and severe link contention.

To avoid this overhead, MBKR adopts a fixed cross-half pairing, i.e., Stage i is paired with Stage $i + \frac{N}{2}$, and allows each paired stage to dynamically assume debtor or creditor roles according to runtime memory pressure. As shown in Fig. 5 (c, left), this pairing is effective in the steady phase because the two paired stages consistently differ by $\frac{N}{2}$ chunks in memory pressure, thereby preserving the maximum spill capacity. More importantly, the same relation remains valid in the switching phase. As shown in Fig. 5 (c, right), although the memory hotspot shifts across stages during request transitions, each stage is still paired with another stage whose pressure differs by $\frac{N}{2}$ chunks, so the fixed pairing continues to provide sufficient spill space without online rematching. In addition, MBKR places stage i adjacent to stage $i+\frac{N}{2}$, so that KV-cache transfers between paired stages traverse the shortest path. This minimizes communication overhead and reduces link contention caused by spill and remote-access traffic. In this way, MBKR simultaneously maximizes usable spill space and minimizes transfer cost under a fixed pairing strategy.

Figure 5(a) further illustrates the runtime policy of MBKR in an SPMD form. At the beginning of the chunked pipeline, every stage computes the newly generated KV cache (lines 1–2). If $s_i < p_1$, the stage remains local-only and

Algorithm 1: Latency-balanced Chunk Partitioning Scheme

```
   Input: #Stage N, #Chunk M, sequence length S
   Output: Optimal batch size B*, chunk slice scheme ss*, E2E latency T*
1  for m ← M to 1 do
2      for s ← S − 1 to 0 do
3          for k ← 1 to S − s − (M − m) do
4              t ← EvaluateChunk(k, s);
5              t'_max ← max(t_max[m + 1][s + k], t), t'_Σ ← t_Σ[m + 1][s + k] + t;
6              if t'_Σ + (N − 1)t'_max < t_Σ[m][s] + (N − 1)t_max[m][s] then
7                  t_max[m][s] ← t'_max, t_Σ[m][s] ← t'_Σ, ss[m][s] ← k;
8  while Temp > Temp_min do
9      for r ← 1 to R do
10         ss' ← Perturb(ss);
11         (B', T'_pre) ← EvaluatePrefill(ss'), T' ← EvaluateE2E(B', T'_pre);
12         if T' < T or Rand(0, 1) < exp(−(T' − T)/Temp) then
13             ss ← ss', B ← B', T ← T';
14         if T < T* then
15             ss* ← ss, B* ← B, T* ← T;
16     Temp ← α · Temp;
```

loads all required KV cache locally (lines 3–4). If $p_1 \leq s_i < p_2$, the stage acts as a creditor: it stores newly spilled KV cache from its paired stage while still serving its own local accesses, and sends the globally visible remote portion to the corresponding debtor stage when needed (lines 5–8). Otherwise, when $s_i \geq p_2$, the stage acts as a debtor and splits its KV accesses into a remote portion loaded from stage $i + \frac{N}{2}$ and a local portion loaded from itself (lines 9–11). In this way, MBKR turns a fixed cross-half pairing into a threshold-driven runtime KV-reallocation policy, without incurring the migration cost of online rematching.

4.2 Latency-Balanced Chunk Partitioning

As illustrated in Sect. 2.2, chunked pipeline suffers from two sources of chunk-level latency imbalance: the monotonic growth of attention latency with prefix length, and the additional KV reallocation overhead introduced by remote KV accesses. Together, these factors make chunk latency depend not only on the chunk size, but also on the chunk position and cross-stage KV reallocation. Under this coupled effect, end-to-end latency depends on the full chunk slice scheme and therefore no longer admits the local optimal substructure required by exact dynamic programming.

To address this challenge, we propose *Latency-Balanced Chunk Partitioning* (LBCP). LBCP first derives a compute-balanced chunk slicing scheme as an

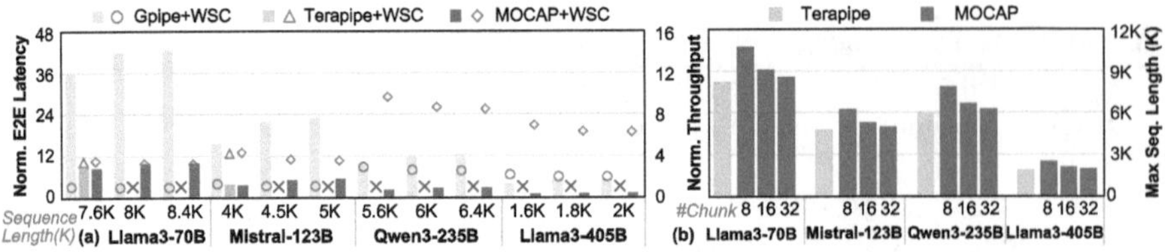

Fig. 6. (a) Performance of GPipe, Terapipe and MOCAP on WSCs. Red crossed marks indicate that the corresponding prefill jobs fail to run due to out-of-memory errors. (b) Maximum sequence length of Terapipe and MOCAP across different models and number of chunks. (Color figure online)

initialization, and then refines it under the full MBKR-enabled execution model, allowing it to efficiently optimize chunk boundaries for end-to-end latency.

In the first stage, LBCP uses dynamic programming to derive a compute-balanced chunk slice scheme, which serves as the initialization for the subsequent search for the partition that minimizes end-to-end latency (lines 1–7 in Algorithm 1). The loops enumerate the chunk index m, the current position s, and the candidate chunk size k (lines 1–3). EVALUATECHUNK returns the compute latency t (line 4), which is combined with the suffix state at $(m+1, s+k)$ to form $t'_{\max}$ and t'_{Σ} (line 5). The algorithm selects the candidate that minimizes $t'_{\Sigma} + (N-1)t'_{\max}$ and records the corresponding k in the chunk slice scheme ss (lines 6–7). This proxy yields a compute-balanced partition that provides a robust initialization for the second-stage search. Since it captures only deterministic compute cost, varying the batch size does not affect the relative ranking of candidate partitions.

In the second stage, LBCP refines the partition via simulated annealing under the full MBKR-enabled execution model (lines 8–16 in Algorithm 1). Each iteration perturbs one chunk boundary while preserving S and M (lines 8–10). EVALUATEPREFILL returns the maximum feasible batch size B' and prefill latency T'_{pre}. EVALUATEE2E then computes the corresponding end-to-end latency T' based on B' and T'_{pre} (line 11). Better candidates are accepted directly, while worse ones are accepted with a temperature-controlled probability (lines 12–13). The algorithm updates the best solution and gradually cools the temperature (lines 14–16). This refinement captures the coupled effect of compute growth and KV reallocation overhead ignored by the first-stage proxy, and further improves the partition for end-to-end latency. In this way, LBCP efficiently optimizes chunk boundaries for end-to-end latency under both compute growth and KV reallocation overhead.

5 Evaluation

5.1 Experimental Setup

Hardware Configuration: We configure each die in the WSC to be equivalent to an NVIDIA Blackwell GPU [17] capable of 4.5 PFLOPS, equipped with

180GB HBM featuring 7.7 TB/s access bandwidth. According to SoW-X [21], D2D bandwidth and cross-wafer bandwidth are both set at 5 TB/s. A 4×4 WSC configuration delivers 72 PFLOPS and 2.8TB memory capacity.

Workload: Given that model size is a key factor influencing performance, we select a series of models from 70B to 405B for our experiments, including Llama3-70B [13], Mistral-123B [15], Qwen3-235B [19], and Llama3-405B [14].

Methodology: To evaluate our proposed strategies, we develop a custom event-driven simulator built upon ASTRA-sim 2.0 [35]. We adopt end-to-end (E2E) latency and throughput as our primary evaluation metrics. E2E latency denotes the average time elapsed per request from arrival to completion, encompassing queuing delays and prefill execution latency. Throughput is defined as the total number of requests processed per second (req/s).

5.2 Performance on Wafer-Scale Chips

Performance compared with GPipe and Terapipe. We first evaluate MOCAP against two baselines, GPipe [5] and Terapipe [9]. GPipe serves as a conventional microbatch-based pipeline, while Terapipe represents a chunked pipeline. We perform this comparison on a 4×4 WSC across four representative LLMs and vary the sequence length. This setting allows us to jointly evaluate MOCAP under diverse model scales and attention characteristics.

Figure 6(a) presents the performance comparison among MOCAP, GPipe, and Terapipe on the WSC across multiple LLM models and sequence lengths. MOCAP consistently achieves the lowest normalized end-to-end latency and the highest normalized throughput across all evaluated settings. On average, compared with GPipe, MOCAP reduces end-to-end latency by 76.4% and improves throughput by 3.24×. These gains mainly arise from two factors: 1) KV reallocation recovers memory headroom under severe KV accumulation, allowing chunked pipelining to remain effective in the long-context regime; and 2) imbalance-aware partitioning reduces pipeline bubbles and mitigates the performance impact of the additional reallocation overhead. Furthermore, the results reveal two additional insights: 1) MOCAP's gain is shaped not only by nominal model size, but also by model architecture. Qwen3-235B is an MoE model, whose sparse activation lowers effective per-token compute, while Llama3-405B adopts a larger GQA ratio, which reduces KV-cache footprint and weakens the memory bottleneck from KV accumulation. 2) MOCAP's relative gain decreases with sequence length, indicating that the increasing KV reallocation overhead gradually offsets a larger fraction of the benefit from chunked pipeline.

Maximum Sequence Length Compared with Terapipe. We further evaluate the maximum feasible sequence length of MOCAP relative to Terapipe, and observe an average improvement of up to 1.31×, as shown in Fig. 6(b). We also find that using fewer chunks generally allows longer feasible sequences. Under a fixed sequence length, fewer chunks imply a larger chunk size, which enlarges the memory imbalance across stages: earlier stages accumulate KV cache more aggressively, while later stages leave more memory space unused. This stronger stage-wise imbalance creates more reallocation headroom for MBKR and thus supports a larger amount of spilled KV cache. However, larger chunks increase pipeline fill time, reducing pipeline efficiency. This reveals a fundamental trade-off in chunked pipeline: fewer chunks favor longer feasible sequences, while more chunks favor higher pipeline efficiency.

6 Related Work

Prior studies [2–4, 8, 11, 20, 23, 29, 31–34, 36–38] have explored architecture–system co-design for wafer-scale AI systems across LLM training and inference. Representative efforts such as WSC-LLM [37] jointly optimize LLM inference serving and wafer-scale architectures, whereas WATOS [29] co-explores LLM recomputation strategies and wafer-scale architectures for training. Nevertheless, these studies focus on general serving or training scenarios, rather than the unique memory-access and scheduling challenges of prefill-only inference.

Beyond WSCs, prior LLM accelerators [12, 24–28, 30, 39] improve Transformer inference at the operator or standalone-accelerator scale through attention sparsity [24, 28], bit-level compute–memory co-optimization [25, 30], and data compression [7, 16]. Nevertheless, they do not address orchestration and scheduling for multi-die parallel execution. In contrast, MOCAP targets prefill-only LLM inference on WSCs with a memory-orchestrated chunked pipelining framework.

7 Conclusion

This paper presents MOCAP, a memory-orchestrated chunked pipelining framework for prefill-only LLM inference on wafer-scale chips. By combining MBKR and LBCP, MOCAP jointly mitigates memory imbalance and compute imbalance in chunked pipeline execution, thereby extending the feasible sequence length and improving compute utilization. Compared with GPipe, MOCAP achieves 76.4% lower end-to-end latency and 3.24× higher throughput on average. Compared with Terapipe, MOCAP extends the maximum supported sequence length by up to 1.31×.

Acknowledgments. This work was supported in part by the National Science and Technology Major Project under Grant 2022ZD0115200; by NSFC under Grant 92464302, Grant 62125403, Grant U24B20164, Grant U24A20234 and Grant 62502255; in part by the Beijing S&T Project Z251100008425010; Shanghai Municipal Science and Technology Major project; the Natural Science Foundation of Jiangsu Province Basic Research Program under Grant BK20243042; the BNRist; and the Beijing Advanced Innovation Center for Integrated Circuits.

Declaration on the Use of Artificial Intelligence. Artificial intelligence tools, if used, were used only for language organization and figure/table polishing, and did not participate in the generation of the core ideas or technical content.

References

1. Du, K., Wang, B., Zhang, C., Cheng, Y., Lan, Q., Sang, H.: Prefillonly: an inference engine for prefill-only workloads in large language model applications. In: Proceedings of the ACM SIGOPS 31st Symposium on Operating Systems Principles, pp. 399–414 (2025)
2. Fang, J., Wang, H., Yang, Q., Kong, D., Dai, X., Deng, J.: PALM: a efficient performance simulator for tiled accelerators with large-scale model training. arXiv preprint arXiv:2406.03868 (2024)
3. He, C., Huang, Y., Mu, P., Miao, Z., Xue, J., Ma, L.: WaferLLM: large language model inference at wafer scale. arXiv preprint arXiv:2502.04563 (2025)
4. Hu, Y., Lin, X., Wang, H., He, Z., Yu, X., Zhang, J., et al.: Wafer-scale computing: advancements, challenges, and future perspectives. IEEE Circuits Syst. Mag. **24**(1), 52–81 (2024)
5. Huang, Y., et al.: Gpipe: efficient training of giant neural networks using pipeline parallelism. In: Advances in Neural Information Processing Systems, vol. 32 (2019)
6. Kim, T., Kim, H., Yu, G.I., Chun, B.G.: Bpipe: memory-balanced pipeline parallelism for training large language models. In: International Conference on Machine Learning, pp. 16639–16653. PMLR (2023)
7. Lee, S., Kim, B., Park, J., Jeon, D.: Clat: a clustering-based attention transformer accelerator for low-latency text generation in LLMs. IEEE Trans. Circ. Syst. I Reg. Pap. (2025)
8. Li, C., et al.: Rethermal: co-design of thermal-aware static and dynamic scheduling for LLM training on liquid-cooled wafer-scale chips. In: 2026 IEEE International Symposium on High Performance Computer Architecture (HPCA), pp. 1–15. IEEE (2026)
9. Li, Z., Zhuang, S., Guo, S., Zhuo, D., Zhang, H., Song, D.: Terapipe: token-level pipeline parallelism for training large-scale language models. In: International Conference on Machine Learning, pp. 6543–6552. PMLR (2021)
10. Lie, S.: Cerebras architecture deep dive: first look inside the HW/SW co-design for deep learning: cerebras systems. In: 2022 IEEE Hot Chips 34 Symposium (HCS), pp. 1–34. IEEE Computer Society (2022)
11. Liu, Y., et al.: Ouroboros: wafer-scale sram cim with token-grained pipelining for large language model inference. In: Proceedings of the 31st ACM International Conference on Architectural Support for Programming Languages and Operating Systems, vol. 2, pp. 1349–1365 (2026)
12. Lu, L., et al.: Sanger: a co-design framework for enabling sparse attention using reconfigurable architecture. In: MICRO-54: 54th Annual IEEE/ACM International Symposium on Microarchitecture, pp. 977–991 (2021)
13. Meta: Meta-Llama-3-70B (2024). https://huggingface.co/meta-llama/Meta-Llama-3-70B
14. Meta AI: Llama-3.1-405B (2024). https://huggingface.co/meta-llama/Llama-3.1-405B
15. Mistral AI: Mistral-Large-Instruct-2407 (2024). https://huggingface.co/mistralai/Mistral-Large-Instruct-2407
16. Moon, S., Li, M., Chen, G.K., Knag, P.C., Krishnamurthy, R.K., Seok, M.: T-REX: a 68-to-567μs/token 0.41-to-3.95 μJ/token transformer accelerator with reduced external memory access and enhanced hardware utilization in 16nm FinFET. In: 2025 IEEE International Solid-State Circuits Conference (ISSCC). vol. 68, pp. 406–408. IEEE (2025)

17. NVIDIA: NVIDIA DGX Vera Rubin NVL72 (2026). https://www.nvidia.com/en-us/data-center/dgx-vera-rubin-nvl72/
18. Pal, S., Liu, J., Alam, I., Cebry, N., Suhail, H., Bu, S.: Designing a 2048-chiplet, 14336-core waferscale processor. In: 2021 58th ACM/IEEE Design Automation Conference (DAC), pp. 1183–1188. IEEE (2021)
19. Qwen: Qwen3-235B-A22B (2025). https://huggingface.co/Qwen/Qwen3-235B-A22B
20. Rashidi, S., Won, W., Srinivasan, S., Gupta, P., Krishna, T.: FRED: flexible reduction-distribution interconnect and communication implementation for wafer-scale distributed training of DNN models. arXiv preprint arXiv:2406.19580 (2024)
21. Shih, P.C., Su, A.J., Tam, K.H., Huang, T.C., Chuang, K., Yeh, J.: SoW-X: a novel system-on-wafer technology for next generation AI server application. In: 2025 IEEE 75th Electronic Components and Technology Conference (ECTC), pp. 1–6. IEEE (2025)
22. Talpes, E., Williams, D., Sarma, D.D.: Dojo: the microarchitecture of Tesla's exa-scale computer. In: 2022 IEEE Hot Chips 34 Symposium (HCS), pp. 1–28. IEEE Computer Society (2022)
23. Tang, X., Hou, J., Jiang, D., Wei, T., Liu, J., Deng, J.: Moentwine: unleashing the potential of wafer-scale chips for large-scale expert parallel inference. In: 2026 IEEE International Symposium on High Performance Computer Architecture (HPCA), pp. 1–15. IEEE (2026)
24. Wang, H., Fang, J., Tang, X., Yue, Z., Li, J., Qin, Y.: SOFA: a compute-memory optimized sparsity accelerator via cross-stage coordinated tiling. In: 2024 57th IEEE/ACM International Symposium on Microarchitecture (MICRO), pp. 1247–1263. IEEE (2024)
25. Wang, H., et al.: Pade: a predictor-free sparse attention accelerator via unified execution and stage fusion. In: 2026 IEEE International Symposium on High Performance Computer Architecture (HPCA), pp. 1–19. IEEE (2026)
26. Wang, H., Wang, H., Wei, S., Hu, Y., Yin, S.: Bitstopper: an efficient transformer attention accelerator via stage-fusion and early termination. In: 2026 31st Asia and South Pacific Design Automation Conference (ASP-DAC), pp. 162–169. IEEE (2026)
27. Wang, H., Wang, H., Wei, S., Hu, Y., Yin, S.: Lapa: log-domain prediction-driven dynamic sparsity accelerator for transformer model. In: 2026 31st Asia and South Pacific Design Automation Conference (ASP-DAC), pp. 154–161. IEEE (2026)
28. Wang, H., et al.: BETA: a bit-grained transformer attention accelerator with efficient early termination. IEEE Trans. Circ. Syst. II Exp. Briefs (2025)
29. Wang, H., et al.: Watos: efficient LLM training strategies and architecture co-exploration for wafer-scale chip. In: 2026 IEEE International Symposium on High Performance Computer Architecture (HPCA), pp. 1–19. IEEE (2026)
30. Wang, H., et al.: MCBP: a memory-compute efficient LLM inference accelerator leveraging bit-slice-enabled sparsity and repetitiveness. In: Proceedings of the 58th IEEE/ACM International Symposium on Microarchitecture®, pp. 1592–1608 (2025)
31. Wang, H., et al.: Designing spatial architectures for sparse attention: star accelerator via cross-stage tiling. IEEE Trans. Comput. (2025)
32. Wang, H., et al.: Temp: a memory efficient physical-aware tensor partition-mapping framework on wafer-scale chips. In: 2026 IEEE International Symposium on High Performance Computer Architecture (HPCA), pp. 1–18. IEEE (2026)

33. Wang, H., Yang, Q., Wei, T., Yu, X., Li, C., Fang, J.: TMAC: training-targeted mapping and architecture co-exploration for wafer-scale chips. Integr. Circ. Syst. (2024)
34. Wei, T., Wang, H., Wang, Z., Yin, S., Hu, Y.: Spatial-aware orchestration of LLM attention on waferscale chips. In: International Symposium on Advanced Parallel Processing Technologies, pp. 386–391. Springer (2025)
35. Won, W., Heo, T., Rashidi, S., Sridharan, S., Srinivasan, S., Krishna, T.: Astra-sim2.0: modeling hierarchical networks and disaggregated systems for large-model training at scale. In: 2023 IEEE International Symposium on Performance Analysis of Systems and Software (ISPASS), pp. 283–294. IEEE (2023)
36. Xu, Z., Kong, D., Liu, J., Jiang, D., Dai, X., Deng, J.: Face: fully overlapped pd scheduling and multi-level architecture co-exploration on wafer. In: 2026 IEEE International Symposium on High Performance Computer Architecture (HPCA), pp. 1–16. IEEE (2026)
37. Xu, Z., Kong, D., Liu, J., Li, J., Hou, J., Dai, X.: WSC-LLM: efficient LLM service and architecture co-exploration for wafer-scale chips. In: Proceedings of the 52nd Annual International Symposium on Computer Architecture, pp. 1–17 (2025)
38. Yang, Q., Wei, T., Guan, S., Li, C., Shang, H., Deng, J.: PD constraint-aware physical/logical topology co-design for network on wafer. In: Proceedings of the 52nd Annual International Symposium on Computer Architecture, pp. 49–64 (2025)
39. Yue, Z., Wang, H., Fang, J., Deng, J., Lu, G., Tu, F.: Exploiting similarity opportunities of emerging vision AI models on hybrid bonding architecture. In: 2024 ACM/IEEE 51st Annual International Symposium on Computer Architecture (ISCA), pp. 396–409. IEEE (2024)
40. Zhai, J., Liao, L., Liu, X., Wang, Y., Li, R., Cao, X.: Actions speak louder than words: trillion-parameter sequential transducers for generative recommendations. arXiv preprint arXiv:2402.17152 (2024)
41. Zhang, C., You, Y., Wang, N., Park, J., Zhang, L.: Generative AI through CAS lens: an integrated overview of algorithmic optimizations, architectural advances, and automated designs. IEEE J. Emerg. Sel. Top. Circ. Syst. (2025)

Window-Diffusion: Accelerating Diffusion Language Model Inference with Windowed Token Pruning and Caching

Fengrui Zuo[1], Zhiwei Ke[1], Yiming Liu[1], Cheng Tang[1], Wenqi Lou[2(✉)], Teng Wang[2], Lei Gong[1], Chao Wang[1], and Xuehai Zhou[1]

[1] University of Science and Technology of China, Hefei, China
{vhicr,kzw17613940379}@mail.ustc.edu.cn, cswang@ustc.edu.cn
[2] Suzhou Institute of Advanced Research, University of Science and Technology of China, Suzhou, China
louwenqi@ustc.edu.cn

Abstract. Diffusion language models (DLMs) generate text through iterative denoising, but at each denoising step the model still performs attention over the full sequence, including many tokens that remain masked, resulting in substantial redundant computation. Existing acceleration methods typically require retraining the DLM and imposing constrained update patterns to reduce inference cost, which limits their direct applicability to pretrained DLMs. Our token-level analysis reveals pronounced structural locality in DLM inference. In practice, only a small set of tokens near the undecoded prefix tends to drive decoding, while distant undecoded tokens have limited influence and the retained local context can be effectively reused. Motivated by these observations, we propose **Window-Diffusion** (Code repository: https://github.com/vhicrgit/Window-Diffusion), a window-based token pruning and caching method for inference. We maintain a local computation window that slides rightward as denoising progresses, and partition undecoded tokens into: (i) *active tokens* that are computed online, (ii) *buffer tokens* whose KV states are cached and periodically refreshed, and (iii) *far-field tokens* that are pruned outside the window. Computation is restricted to active and buffer tokens within the window, while far-field tokens are omitted at each stage. Extensive experiments across diverse benchmarks and model scales demonstrate the effectiveness of our method. Our approach achieves up to 6.6× speedup with negligible quality degradation.

1 Introduction

Large language models (LLMs) have become the foundation of modern generative AI, yet the growing scale and inference cost of autoregressive LLMs place heavy demands on computing hardware [14,30,31], motivating hardware acceleration and more parallel generation paradigms [15,24,26,34]. Recently, diffusion Language Models (DLMs) have gained attention as a promising alternative

L. Eeckhout et al. (Eds.): APPT 2026, LNCS 16693, pp. 112–125, 2027.
https://doi.org/10.1007/978-981-92-4805-6_8

to autoregressive generation [12]. Instead of producing tokens strictly from left to right, DLMs formulate text generation as iterative denoising over the full sequence: inference begins with the prompt and a set of mask tokens, which are progressively refined into coherent text over multiple iterations. This sequence-level formulation enables parallel decoding and global modeling, allowing DLMs to achieve competitive performance in language modeling, code generation, and reasoning [21,29,35].

Despite these advantages, DLM inference incurs substantial latency [8,22,32]. A key bottleneck is that each denoising step performs bidirectional attention over the entire sequence up to a fixed maximum length. Although prior studies have developed effective optimization techniques for conventional Transformer and autoregressive LLM inference [6,7,10,11], these methods are not directly transferable to DLMs due to their full-sequence bidirectional denoising process. Some prior work improves DLM inference efficiency through model quantization [13,28,33] and KV caching [17,19], yielding measurable speedups. However, quantization reduces arithmetic and communication overhead but does not shorten the computed sequence. KV caching reuses the key/value states of decoded tokens to avoid recomputation, but it likewise cannot eliminate the redundant attention and feed-forward cost caused by large numbers of mask tokens. Recent approaches have sought to reduce per-step cost by restructuring generation (e.g., block diffusion [1], which combines inter-block autoregression with intra-block diffusion to limit computed tokens). However, they often require costly retraining and require block-by-block decoding, thereby sacrificing diffusion's flexible update order. Consequently, eliminating per-step redundancy from full-sequence computation on pretrained DLMs without retraining remains a key challenge.

To address this challenge, we revisit DLM inference from a token-level perspective and conduct a systematic analysis of decoding behavior and representation dynamics. Our analysis reveals two recurring empirical patterns in mask-based DLM inference that expose substantial redundancy in full-sequence denoising. More concretely, we observe that: (i) tokens likely to be updated consistently concentrate near the prefix of the undecoded region, dominating the decoding process; (ii) the effective dependency of active tokens on undecoded context is limited, with contributions from distant undecoded tokens rapidly diminishing, while non-active tokens in the retained local context exhibit stable intermediate representations that admit caching. Together, these observations indicate that full-sequence recomputation at every denoising step is unnecessary, and that DLM inference can be substantially accelerated through token-level selective computation and reuse of cached intermediate states.

Based on these insights, we propose Window-Diffusion, a training-free windowed token pruning and caching strategy for inference in standard DLMs, requiring no architectural or training modifications. Window-Diffusion adopts a dual-window mechanism at each diffusion step, pruning redundant tokens and separating tokens that require accurate online updates from those that primarily serve as context. For the latter, we employ cyclic KV caching with periodic refresh, reusing their key/value states across consecutive steps to avoid repeated low-yield attention computation while intermittently refreshing to bound approximation error.

Experimental results show that Window-Diffusion markedly accelerates DLM inference across diverse tasks with negligible impact on generation quality, delivering up to 2.3×–6.6× speedup over the original model and consistently outperforming prior acceleration baselines. Moreover, the same windowed pruning framework naturally supports adaptive-length inference by avoiding redundant computation beyond the effective decoding frontier. Since it operates at the inference level without modifying model architecture or training, Window-Diffusion is also compatible with complementary acceleration techniques such as quantization and parallel decoding.

2 Related Work

Diffusion Language Models. Diffusion models were first developed for continuous domains and later extended to discrete sequence modeling. D3PM introduced a general discrete diffusion framework for categorical data [2], while SEDD improved training stability with a score-entropy objective [18]. Subsequent work showed that masked diffusion can match autoregressive language modeling and scale favorably to large text models [20,23]. More recently, LLaDA and Dream extended masked diffusion to billion-parameter language models and achieved competitive results across diverse tasks [21,29].

Block Diffusion Paradigm. To reduce the inference cost of diffusion models, Block Diffusion adopts an autoregressive-over-blocks and diffusion-within-blocks paradigm [1]. Fast-dLLM, D2F, and SDLM further improve efficiency through KV reuse, distillation, and unified next-token/next-block prediction [16,25,27]. However, these methods typically require retraining, and block-wise decoding partially sacrifices the flexible update order of standard diffusion models.

KV-Cache in Diffusion Language Models. Applying KV-cache to diffusion models is challenging due to bidirectional attention and flexible decoding order. dKV-Cache addresses this by selectively caching decoded tokens with delayed updates, achieving substantial acceleration on 7B-scale models [19]. Block diffusion methods can also facilitate KV reuse through block-level causal structure [1,16,25,27]. Nevertheless, existing caching methods do not shorten the masked sequence being computed and thus cannot fundamentally remove the cost of full-sequence computation.

3 Empirical Motivation for Efficient DLM Inference

3.1 Preliminary: DLM Inference Paradigm

Mask-based DLMs generate discrete text through an **iterative denoising** process. Unlike autoregressive models that decode tokens strictly from left to right,

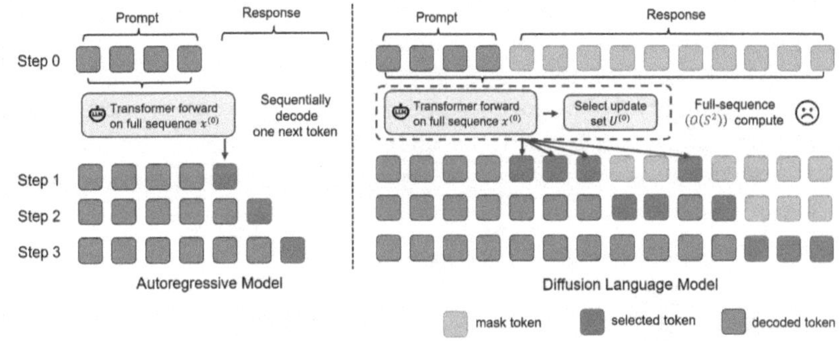

Fig. 1. Illustration of mask-based DLM inference.

they maintain a fixed-length sequence state containing both decoded tokens and undecided positions, and progressively refine the undecided positions over multiple diffusion steps. This work focuses on the inference behavior of such models and examines where redundant computation arises during denoising.

During inference, the model maintains a fixed-length sequence state

$$\mathbf{x}^{(t)} = (x_1^{(t)}, \dots, x_S^{(t)}), \qquad t = 0, 1, \dots, T,$$

which contains both decoded tokens and undecided positions. Inference begins from a highly masked initial state, where all non-prompt positions are set to a special placeholder (e.g., [MASK]), and progressively refines the sequence over T diffusion steps.

As illustrated in Fig. 1, each diffusion step performs a Transformer forward pass over the *entire sequence*, although only a small subset of positions is updated while the remaining tokens stay unchanged as conditioning context. Let $\mathcal{U}^{(t)} \subseteq \{1, \dots, S\}$ denote the updated positions at step t, where typically $|\mathcal{U}^{(t)}| \ll S$. Nevertheless, full-sequence computation is still performed at every step. Let L denote the number of Transformer layers. Without causal masking, the dominant cost of each diffusion step comes from full self-attention, yielding an overall inference complexity of

$$\mathcal{O}(T \cdot L \cdot S^2).$$

Thus, although computation scales with the full sequence length, only a small fraction of tokens undergo state changes at each step. This mismatch between full-sequence computation and sparse token updates is a major source of redundancy in mask-based DLM inference, motivating token-level selective computation and reuse.

3.2 Not All Tokens Need to Be Recomputed

To identify where redundant computation arises in mask-based DLM inference, we perform a token-level analysis from two perspectives: where the tokens selected for update are located and how much undecoded context these tokens actually need. We distinguish *active tokens*, which are likely to be updated at the current step and therefore require fresh prediction, from *context tokens*, which mainly provide conditioning information. The following results reveal a common empirical pattern in mask-based DLM inference.

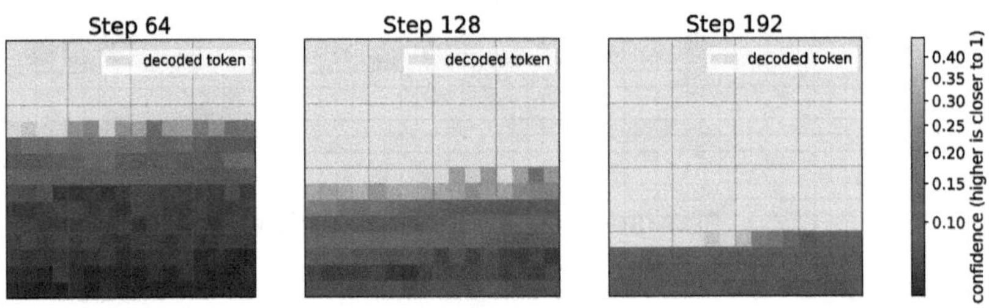

Fig. 2. Token-wise prediction confidence over undecoded positions at different diffusion steps in mask-based DLM inference.

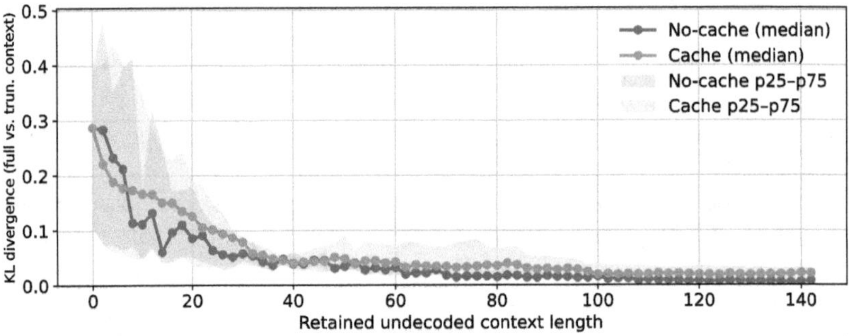

Fig. 3. KL divergence relative to the full-sequence no-cache reference under different retained undecoded context lengths; shaded bands show the 25th–75th percentiles over observation steps 30–60.

Observation 1. ***Active tokens exhibit pronounced prefix locality.***
At each diffusion step, we compute prediction confidence for all undecoded positions and visualize its distribution along the sequence, while excluding positions that have already been decoded. As shown in Fig. 2, at different diffusion steps (e.g., $t = 64, 128, 192$), high-confidence positions are not uniformly distributed across the undecoded region; instead, they consistently concentrate near its prefix. This indicates that, although mask-based DLMs can in principle update arbitrary positions in parallel, practical decoding is predominantly driven by a localized set of prefix-near tokens, while more distant positions are rarely selected

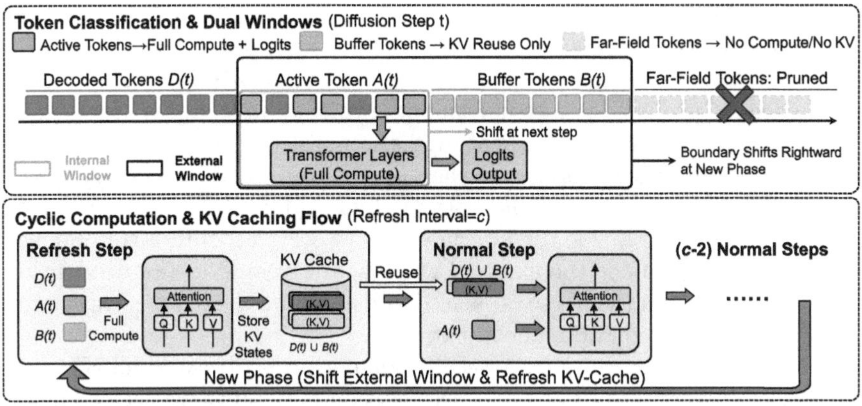

Fig. 4. Window-Diffusion inference framework. Top: In each phase, pre-phase decoded tokens are retained as context, active tokens are fully computed, buffer tokens provide context only, and far-field tokens are pruned. **Bottom:** A phase starts with one refresh step and is followed by normal steps that reuse cached KV states.

for update. Consequently, recomputing those distant undecoded tokens at every diffusion step incurs substantial redundant computation.

Observation 2. ***Active-token prediction mainly relies on a short local undecoded context, and the remaining retained context can be effectively reused via caching.***

To test how much undecoded context active-token prediction requires, we fix an observation step $t = t_0$, keep all decoded tokens, select a small prefix-near active set, and restrict the remaining undecoded context to a prefix of length W. For each W, we compare truncation-only inference and truncation with KV reuse of non-active undecoded tokens against the full-sequence no-cache reference using KL divergence on active-token predictions. As shown in Fig. 3, increasing W rapidly reduces the KL divergence before saturating, indicating that distant undecoded tokens provide little additional benefit. With caching enabled, predictions remain close to the reference, showing that the retained local undecoded context is highly reusable. These results suggest that distant undecoded tokens can be pruned, while non-active retained local context can be reused via caching.

4 Method: Window-Diffusion

4.1 Overview

We propose **Window-Diffusion**, a training-free inference acceleration framework for mask-based DLMs. It is motivated by the two observations in Sect. 3: decoding is mainly driven by a small set of prefix-near active tokens, and useful undecoded context is largely concentrated in a short local prefix.

As shown in Fig. 4, Window-Diffusion partitions denoising into a sequence of fixed-length **inference phases**. Within each phase, it applies a **dual-window** organization over the undecoded region: an **external window** retains only a local undecoded prefix as contextual support, while an **internal window** selects the most critical positions for current prediction. Tokens inside the internal window are called **active tokens**, and they are the only undecoded positions for which logits are computed at the current step. Undecoded tokens inside the external window but outside the internal window serve as **buffer tokens**, while undecoded tokens outside the external window are treated as **far-field tokens** and are pruned within the phase. Tokens decoded before the phase always remain in attention as fixed conditional context.

On top of this structure, Window-Diffusion performs **phase-level KV reuse with periodic refresh**. Prior DLM acceleration methods have shown that KV reuse for decoded or slowly changing tokens can be an effective approximation during denoising [19,27]. Building on this practical premise, we reuse KV states for stable contextual tokens, while continuing to update active tokens and tokens newly decoded within the current phase. At each phase boundary, the cache is refreshed to limit approximation drift.

4.2 Dual-Window Inference Mechanism

Consider inference phase p. Let $\mathcal{D}^{(<p)}$ denote the set of tokens that have already been decoded before phase p begins. These tokens are always retained in attention as fixed conditional context throughout the phase.

The dual-window mechanism applies only to tokens that remain undecoded at the beginning of the phase. We first define an **external window** $\mathcal{W}_{\text{ex}}^{(p)}$ as a fixed-length prefix of the current undecoded region. This window determines which undecoded tokens are kept as local context during phase p. Undecoded tokens outside $\mathcal{W}_{\text{ex}}^{(p)}$ are excluded from computation within the phase and are referred to as **far-field tokens**. This design is motivated by Observation 2, which shows that distant undecoded tokens provide limited additional benefit once a short local prefix is retained.

Within the external window, we further define a smaller **internal window** $\mathcal{W}_{\text{in}}^{(t)} \subseteq \mathcal{W}_{\text{ex}}^{(p)}$ at diffusion step t. It contains the undecoded positions most likely to be decoded next, and we denote this set by $\mathcal{A}^{(t)} := \mathcal{W}_{\text{in}}^{(t)}$, where $\mathcal{A}^{(t)}$ is the set of **active tokens**. At step t, logits are computed only for $\mathcal{A}^{(t)}$.

Let $\mathcal{D}_p^{(t)}$ denote the set of tokens that have been decoded within phase p up to step t. The remaining undecoded tokens inside the external window form the **buffer-token** set

$$\mathcal{B}^{(t)} = \mathcal{W}_{\text{ex}}^{(p)} \setminus \left(\mathcal{A}^{(t)} \cup \mathcal{D}_p^{(t)}\right).$$

Buffer tokens do not produce logits, but remain available as local contextual support for active tokens. As decoding progresses, newly decoded active tokens are moved into $\mathcal{D}_p^{(t)}$, and the internal window shifts rightward to keep covering the undecoded prefix. In contrast, the external window remains fixed within a phase and is updated only when the next phase begins.

Adaptive Termination. Window-Diffusion also naturally supports adaptive-length generation. Since the external window always tracks only the undecoded prefix, positions beyond the effective decoding frontier are automatically ignored. Once `<eos>` is generated, the internal window stops advancing and the remaining positions stay in the far-field region, avoiding unnecessary computation.

4.3 KV Reuse with Phase-Level Refresh

Under the dual-window structure, active tokens must still attend to contextual tokens from three sources at each diffusion step: pre-phase decoded tokens $\mathcal{D}^{(<p)}$, tokens decoded earlier within the current phase $\mathcal{D}_p^{(t)}$, and buffer tokens $\mathcal{B}^{(t)}$. Recomputing all of their Key/Value states at every step would still be wasteful.

Prior work on DLM caching has shown that decoded tokens or slowly changing contextual tokens can often be reused approximately across denoising steps. Following this line of work, Window-Diffusion treats KV reuse as a practical approximation for stable context, while keeping unstable tokens online-updated. Concretely, each phase consists of one **refresh step** followed by multiple **normal steps**, as illustrated in Fig. 4.

At the refresh step of phase p, denoted by $t_{\mathrm{ref}}^{(p)}$, we perform a full forward pass over all tokens retained in the phase, namely $\mathcal{D}^{(<p)} \cup \mathcal{W}_{\mathrm{ex}}^{(p)}$, and write their layer-wise KV states into cache:

$$(K,V)_{\mathcal{D}^{(<p)}\cup\mathcal{W}_{\mathrm{ex}}^{(p)}}^{(t_{\mathrm{ref}}^{(p)})} \leftarrow \mathrm{Forward}_\theta\left(\mathbf{x}^{(t_{\mathrm{ref}}^{(p)})}\right).$$

During the subsequent normal steps in the same phase, different token groups follow different computation rules in a fully structured manner. Active tokens $\mathcal{A}^{(t)}$ are fully recomputed and used for logit prediction. Tokens in $\mathcal{D}_p^{(t)}$, namely those decoded within the current phase, continue to receive representation and KV updates, but no longer produce logits. Buffer tokens $\mathcal{B}^{(t)}$ are used only as context, with their KV states directly reused from the latest refresh.

A key point is that tokens decoded within the current phase are *not* frozen immediately after decoding. Instead, they remain online-updated until the next refresh, which helps reduce inconsistency introduced by premature caching. When phase p ends, a new refresh is performed using the updated decoding state, and the same procedure repeats in the next phase. Overall, this phase-level reuse strategy avoids repeated computation on stable contextual tokens while preserving fresh updates for the tokens that most strongly affect current decoding.

5 Experiments

5.1 Experimental Setup

We evaluate Window-Diffusion on two state-of-the-art diffusion language models, LLaDA and Dream, across four widely used benchmarks: GSM8K-CoT [5],

MATH [9], HumanEval [4], and MBPP [3]. We first compare it with representative DLM acceleration methods to assess its overall efficiency–quality trade-off, and then conduct component-wise ablations on its key designs, including window-based pruning, decoded-token KV caching, and local undecoded-context reuse within the external window. All experiments are conducted on a single NVIDIA A6000 GPU.

5.2 Main Results

Table 1 compares Window-Diffusion with representative DLM acceleration methods, including DKV-Cache [19] and Fast-dLLM [27]. For fairness, we disable parallel decoding in Fast-dLLM and report accuracy, decoding throughput (tokens/s), and relative speedup over the original model. Unless otherwise specified, Window-Diffusion uses an internal window size of $L = 16$, a cache refresh cycle of 32, and fixed-length inference.

Overall, Window-Diffusion achieves consistent acceleration across tasks while largely preserving performance. On LLaDA-Base and Dream-Instruct, it reaches up to 5.9× and 6.6× speedup, respectively, while maintaining competitive accuracy. Compared with prior methods, it also offers a stronger efficiency–quality trade-off. DKV-Cache improves efficiency by reusing decoded tokens, but does not reduce computation on masked tokens, limiting its speedup. Fast-dLLM extends caching further, but often incurs greater accuracy degradation. In contrast, Window-Diffusion combines window-based pruning with phase-level KV reuse, reducing computation on undecoded tokens while preserving useful local context. As a result, it consistently delivers higher speedups than prior methods while maintaining competitive accuracy on both LLaDA-Base and Dream-Instruct.

Adaptive Termination Improves Efficiency with Minimal Accuracy Impact. Table 2 compares fixed-length inference (Dream, WD-Static) and adaptive-length inference (WD-Adaptive) on Dream-Instruct across four tasks. Unlike fixed-length decoding, which always runs to a predefined maximum length, WD-Adaptive stops once `<eos>` is generated and thus avoids redundant computation after sequence completion. As shown in Table 2, this strategy consistently reduces latency across all tasks, with especially large gains on code generation benchmarks such as HumanEval and MBPP, while maintaining accuracy close to the fixed-length setting. These results show that adaptive-length inference is an effective way to further improve DLM inference efficiency.

5.3 Ablations and Analysis

Component-Wise Ablation Study. To quantify the contribution of each component, we conduct a component-wise ablation on LLaDA-Base and Dream-Instruct, as shown in Table 3. We compare five configurations: Base; + Pruning, which restricts computation to a local undecoded region; + Prefix Cache, which reuses KV representations only for decoded tokens; + Pruning + Prefix Cache,

Table 1. Benchmark results of acceleration methods on LLaDA-Base and Dream-Instruct over four tasks. Each cell reports accuracy and throughput with relative speedup. The same cell format is used in the following tables.

	LLaDA-Base				Dream-Instruct			
Method	GSM8K	MATH	HumanEval	MBPP	GSM8K	MATH	HumanEval	MBPP
Base	70.7 4.49 (1.0×)	30.1 5.06 (1.0×)	32.9 6.59 (1.0×)	39.2 4.18 (1.0×)	81.0 14.4 (1.0×)	39.2 8.7 (1.0×)	55.5 6.1 (1.0×)	58.8 4.7 (1.0×)
DKV-Cache	68.7 8.07 (1.80×)	27.8 8.79 (1.74×)	**31.7** 9.08 (1.38×)	**38.2** 6.61 (1.58×)	82.7 17.4 (1.2×)	39.0 11.2 (1.3×)	33.5 8.1 (1.3×)	53.2 6.4 (1.4×)
Fast-dLLM (Prefix-Cache)	**68.8** 14.71 (3.28×)	**28.5** 15.39 (3.04×)	30.5 12.03 (1.83×)	37.8 10.37 (2.48×)	81.0 24.9 (1.7×)	39.2 17.4 (2.0×)	54.9 12.9 (2.1×)	48.6 10.0 (2.1×)
Fast-dLLM (Dual-Cache)	67.9 17.28 (3.85×)	25.5 18.37 (3.63×)	27.4 20.25 (3.07×)	36.0 16.71 (4.00×)	81.4 26.7 (1.8×)	**39.6** 27.2 (3.1×)	23.8 25.9 (4.2×)	50.2 24.9 (5.3×)
Window-Diffusion	68.5 25.14 (5.60×)	26.2 25.93 (5.12×)	28.0 27.91 (4.24×)	**38.2** 24.63 (5.90×)	**82.9** 32.5 (2.3×)	38.5 33.9 (3.9×)	**58.5** 32.3 (5.3×)	**55.4** 31.1 (6.6×)

which combines both; and Window-Diffusion, which further retains and reuses local undecoded context within the external window. Each entry reports task performance, throughput, and relative speedup over baseline.

The results show a clear pattern. + Pruning alone improves throughput, with larger speedup but also more noticeable degradation on Dream-Instruct, suggesting that pruning is more effective yet more aggressive in the Instruct setting. + Prefix Cache preserves performance better while still providing consistent acceleration on both models, indicating that decoded-token KV reuse is a stable source of efficiency gain. Combining the two strategies further improves throughput but also makes the performance drop more evident, especially on Dream-Instruct, implying that overly restricting undecoded context can remove useful conditioning information. By contrast, Window-Diffusion substantially alleviates this degradation while maintaining comparable acceleration, showing that local undecoded-context reuse within the external window is critical to a better efficiency–performance trade-off.

Effect of External Window Length. Figure 5(a) studies the effect of the external window length on accuracy and inference throughput using Dream-Base on HumanEval (0-shot), with the cache refresh cycle fixed at 32, the internal

Table 2. Performance and inference efficiency of Dream-Instruct under fixed-length and adaptive-length inference over four tasks.

Task	Length	Dream	Window-Diffusion	
			WD-Static	WD-Adaptive
GSM8K	256	81.0 / 17.8 (1.0×)	82.9 / 7.9 (2.3×)	82.4 / 3.5 (5.1×)
MATH	512	39.2 / 58.8 (1.0×)	38.5 / 15.1 (3.9×)	38.9 / 6.4 (9.2×)
HumanEval	768	55.5 / 125.9 (1.0×)	58.5 / 23.8 (5.3×)	57.9 / 2.9 (43.4×)
MBPP	1024	58.8 / 217.8 (1.0×)	55.4 / 32.9 (6.6×)	55.6 / 2.2 (99.0×)

Table 3. Component-wise ablation results of pruning and caching strategies on LLaDA-Base and Dream-Instruct over four tasks.

Method	LLaDA-Base				Dream-Instruct			
	GSM8K	MATH	HumanEval	MBPP	GSM8K	MATH	HumanEval	MBPP
Base	70.7	30.1	32.9	39.2	81.0	39.2	55.5	58.8
	4.49	5.06	6.59	4.18	14.4	8.7	6.1	4.7
	(1.0×)	(1.0×)	(1.0×)	(1.0×)	(1.0×)	(1.0×)	(1.0×)	(1.0×)
+ Pruning	67.7	**27.2**	33.5	39.4	51.2	32.2	27.4	50.8
	4.84	5.51	10.78	4.81	21.5	14.7	11.0	8.9
	(1.1×)	(1.1×)	(1.6×)	(1.2×)	(1.5×)	(1.7×)	(1.8×)	(1.9×)
+ Prefix Cache	**69.1**	26.4	**34.1**	**39.6**	80.4	38.0	**59.1**	50.2
	18.37	18.87	13.70	12.53	25.8	15.4	11.9	9.1
	(4.1×)	(3.7×)	(2.1×)	(3.0×)	(1.8×)	(1.8×)	(2.0×)	(1.9×)
+ Pruning + Prefix Cache	65.6	25.5	29.9	38.6	54.4	29.9	40.9	44.4
	25.19	25.93	28.02	24.73	33.8	34.2	33.0	31.7
	(5.6×)	(5.1×)	(4.3×)	(5.9×)	(2.3×)	(3.9×)	(5.4×)	(6.7×)
Window-Diffusion	68.5	26.2	28.0	38.2	**82.9**	**38.5**	58.5	**55.4**
	25.14	25.93	27.91	24.63	32.5	33.9	32.3	31.1
	(5.6×)	(5.1×)	(4.2×)	(5.9×)	(2.3×)	(3.9×)	(5.3×)	(6.6×)

window length set to 16, and the generation length set to 512. As the external window grows, model performance improves and then gradually saturates, indicating the rapidly diminishing marginal contribution of masked tokens, while inference throughput decreases only moderately due to the larger context. Balancing efficiency and performance, we set the external window length to 128.

Effect of Cache Refresh Cycle. Figure 5(b) studies the cache refresh cycle on LLaDA-Base for HumanEval (0-shot), with internal window length 16 and external window length 128. As the refresh cycle increases, throughput improves

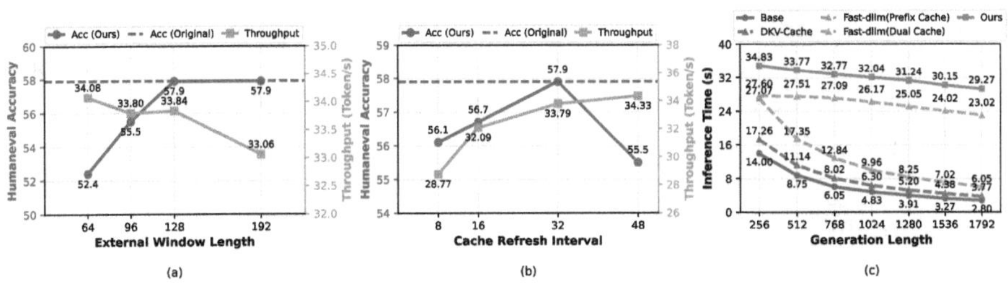

Fig. 5. (a) **Ablation study on the external window length.** (b) **Ablation study on the cache refresh interval.** (c) Inference time comparison across **generation lengths.**

and then saturates, while accuracy first improves and then declines. This reflects a trade-off: longer cycles reduce cache-update overhead but force newly decoded tokens to be recomputed for more steps before refresh, whereas shorter cycles cache them earlier, before their KV states become sufficiently stable. We therefore set the refresh cycle to 32 to balance efficiency and performance.

Effect of Generation Length. Figure 5(c) compares the inference time of the original model, DKV-Cache, Fast-dLLM, and Window-Diffusion under increasing generation lengths for a fixed input instance. As generation length increases, inference becomes substantially more expensive for all methods, with the original model showing the steepest growth. DKV-Cache and Fast-dLLM (Prefix-Cache) provide only limited gains because they reuse decoded tokens only and do not reduce computation on masked tokens. Fast-dLLM (Dual-Cache) further alleviates repeated computation, but periodic cache refresh still incurs substantial full-sequence processing. In contrast, Window-Diffusion consistently achieves strong speedup across different generation lengths by pruning masked tokens at the token level, and its advantage remains clear in long-generation settings.

6 Conclusion

We present Window-Diffusion, a training-free inference acceleration framework for diffusion language models. Motivated by our token-level analysis of DLM inference, it combines dual-window token organization with phase-level KV reuse to reduce redundant computation while preserving useful local context. Experiments across multiple tasks and model settings show that Window-Diffusion achieves consistent inference speedups with minimal quality degradation, demonstrating its practical value for efficient diffusion-based text generation.

Acknowledgments. This work was supported in part by the Strategic Priority Research Program of the Chinese Academy of Sciences under Grant Nos. XDB0660101, XDB0660000, and XDB0660100, in part by the National Natural Science Foundation of China under Grant No. 62502489, and in part by the Jiangsu Provincial Natural Science Foundation under Grant Nos. BK20241818 and BK20250479.

Disclosure of Interests. The technical solution and experimental design presented in this paper were independently completed by the authors. AI tools were used solely for language polishing and formatting optimization, and did not participate in the development of the research ideas or core content.

References

1. Arriola, M., et al.: Block diffusion: interpolating between autoregressive and diffusion language models. In: International Conference on Learning Representations, vol. 2025, pp. 50726–50753 (2025)
2. Austin, J., Johnson, D.D., Ho, J., Tarlow, D., Van Den, Berg, R.: Structured denoising diffusion models in discrete state-spaces. In: Advances in Neural Information Processing Systems, pp. 17981–17993 (2021)
3. Austin, J., et al.: Program synthesis with large language models. arXiv preprint arXiv:2108.07732 (2021)
4. Chen, M., et al.: Evaluating large language models trained on code. arXiv preprint arXiv:2107.03374 (2021)
5. Cobbe, K., et al.: Training verifiers to solve math word problems. arXiv preprint arXiv:2110.14168 (2021)
6. Dao, T., Fu, D., Ermon, S., Rudra, A., R'e, C.: Flashattention: fast and memory-efficient exact attention with io-awareness. In: Advances in Neural Information Processing Systems, vol. 35, pp. 16344–16359 (2022)
7. Dong, J., et al.: Moe-sched: enabling efficient FPGA deployment of mixture-of-experts vision transformers via coordinated scheduling. IEEE Trans. Very Large Scale Integr. VLSI Syst. **34**, 104–117 (2026)
8. Feng, G.: Theoretical benefit and limitation of diffusion language model. arXiv abs/2502.09622 (2025)
9. Hendrycks, D., et al.: Measuring mathematical problem solving with the math dataset. arXiv preprint arXiv:2103.03874 (2021)
10. Kwon, W., et al.: Efficient memory management for large language model serving with pagedattention. In: Proceedings of the 29th Symposium on Operating Systems Principles, pp. 611–626 (2023)
11. Leviathan, Y., Kalman, M., Matias, Y.: Fast inference from transformers via speculative decoding. In: Proceedings of the 40th International Conference on Machine Learning. ICML 2023. JMLR.org (2023)
12. Li, T., Chen, M., Guo, B., Shen, Z.: A survey on diffusion language models. arXiv preprint arXiv:2508.10875 (2025)
13. Lin, H., et al.: Quantization meets dLLMs: a systematic study of post-training quantization for diffusion LLMs. arXiv preprint arXiv:2508.14896 (2025)
14. Liu, F., et al.: Earth: an efficient MOE accelerator with entropy-aware speculative prefetch and result reuse. In: Proceedings of the 31st ACM International Conference on Architectural Support for Programming Languages and Operating Systems, vol. 2, pp. 633–646 (2026)
15. Liu, J., et al.: A survey on inference optimization techniques for mixture of experts models. ACM Comput. Surv. **58**(10), 1–37 (2026)
16. Liu, Y., et al.: Sequential diffusion language models. arXiv preprint arXiv:2509.24007 (2025)
17. Liu, Z., et al.: dLLM-cache: accelerating diffusion large language models with adaptive caching. arXiv preprint arXiv:2506.06295 (2025)

18. Lou, A., Meng, C., Ermon, S.: Discrete diffusion modeling by estimating the ratios of the data distribution. In: Proceedings of the 41st International Conference on Machine Learning, pp. 32819–32848 (2024)
19. Ma, X., Yu, R., Fang, G., Wang, X.: dKV-cache: the cache for diffusion language models. Adv. Neural. Inf. Process. Syst. **38**, 149009–149033 (2026)
20. Nie, S., et al.: Scaling up masked diffusion models on text. In: International Conference on Learning Representations, vol. 2025, pp. 82974–82997 (2025)
21. Nie, S.: Large language diffusion models. arXiv abs/2502.09992 (2025)
22. Peng, H., et al.: How efficient are diffusion language models? A critical examination of efficiency evaluation practices. arXiv preprint arXiv:2510.18480 (2025)
23. Sahoo, S.S., et al.: Simple and effective masked diffusion language models. In: Advances in Neural Information Processing Systems, pp. 130136–130184 (2024)
24. Song, Y., Mi, Z., Xie, H., Chen, H.: Powerinfer: fast large language model serving with a consumer-grade GPU. In: Proceedings of the ACM SIGOPS 30th Symposium on Operating Systems Principles, pp. 590–606 (2024)
25. Wang, X., et al.: Diffusion LLMs can do faster-than-AR inference via discrete diffusion forcing. arXiv abs/2508.09192 (2025)
26. Wen, H., et al.: QLlama: an FPGA-based microscaling quantization accelerator for energy-efficient llama2 inference. IEEE Embed. Syst. Lett. **17**(5), 337–340 (2025)
27. Wu, C., et al.: Fast-dLLM: training-free acceleration of diffusion LLM by enabling KV cache and parallel decoding. arXiv preprint arXiv:2505.22618 (2025)
28. Xu, C., Yang, D.: Dllmquant: quantizing diffusion-based large language models. arXiv preprint arXiv:2508.14090 (2025)
29. Ye, J., et al.: Dream 7b: diffusion large language models. arXiv preprint arXiv:2508.15487 (2025)
30. Yu, Z., et al.: Cambricon-LLM: a chiplet-based hybrid architecture for on-device inference of 70b LLM. In: 57th IEEE/ACM International Symposium on Microarchitecture (MICRO), pp. 1474–1488. IEEE (2024)
31. Zeng, S., et al.: Flightllm: efficient large language model inference with a complete mapping flow on FPGAs. In: Proceedings of the 2024 ACM/SIGDA International Symposium on Field Programmable Gate Arrays, pp. 223–234 (2024)
32. Zhang, S., Zhao, Y., Geng, L., Cohan, A., Tuan, L.A., Zhao, C.: Diffusion vs. autoregressive language models: a text embedding perspective. In: Proceedings of the 2025 Conference on Empirical Methods in Natural Language Processing, pp. 4273–4303 (2025)
33. Zhang, T., Li, Z., Yan, X., Qin, H., Guo, Y., Zhang, Y.: Quant-dLLM: post-training extreme low-bit quantization for diffusion large language models. arXiv preprint arXiv:2510.03274 (2025)
34. Zheng, Z., et al.: Lora: a latency-oriented recurrent architecture for large language model on multi-FPGA platform with communication optimization. IEEE Trans. Comput.-Aided Des. Integr. Circ. Syst. (2025)
35. Zhu, F., et al.: LLADA 1.5: variance-reduced preference optimization for large language diffusion models. arXiv preprint arXiv:2505.19223 (2025)

Serving Systems

TokenSimV2: Accurate and Fast LLM Inference on GPUs via Dynamic Graph Modeling

Zhuohang Bian, Feiyang Wu, Zhuoran Li, Yibo Zhao, Junchi Wu, Xuxiao Yang, and Youwei Zhuo(✉)

Peking University, Beijing, China
22373017@buaa.edu.cn,
{fywu25,2200012710,yibozhao,jcwu25,2300017833}@stu.pku.edu.cn,
youwei@pku.edu.cn

Abstract. LLM inference on GPUs mixes dense computation, KV Cache traffic, variable sequence lengths, and dynamic batching. Existing simulators either sacrifice accuracy by ignoring these stage-level dynamics or sacrifice speed by resorting to cycle-level detail. This paper presents TokenSimV2, a modeling methodology that achieves both high accuracy and fast evaluation for LLM inference on GPUs. TokenSimV2 pairs a token-level event-driven simulator with a Transformer Roofline Model that decomposes execution into prefill projection, prefill attention, decode projection, decode attention, and off-card communication. Validation against vLLM on real hardware shows sub-1% geometric-mean error for throughput and request latency. We use TokenSimV2 to study continuous batching, admission control, disaggregated worker allocation, decode hardware substitution, and platform sensitivity, demonstrating that accurate serving analysis requires both dynamic runtime modeling and stage-aware architectural diagnosis.

Keywords: Large language models · inference serving · modeling · roofline model · disaggregated serving

1 Introduction

LLM inference [10,20,26] is rapidly becoming one of the most important workloads [25] in modern datacenters, yet it defies simple modeling because multiple resources bottleneck execution at the same time. Prefill performs large dense matrix multiplications that stress compute throughput. Decode reads the KV Cache at every step and is dominated by memory bandwidth and capacity. Communication cost grows when stages span multiple devices or when the serving system places prefill and decode on separate hardware [27]. A single roofline number or a single end-to-end latency figure cannot reveal which resource is the true limit at a given operating point. Understanding and optimizing this complex interplay is essential for GPU architects [4,22], system designers [5–7,9,21], and

L. Eeckhout et al. (Eds.): APPT 2026, LNCS 16693, pp. 129–141, 2027.
https://doi.org/10.1007/978-981-92-4805-6_9

serving operators [8, 12, 13, 15] alike, yet no existing tool provides the necessary combination of accuracy, speed, and architectural visibility.

Existing simulators and analytical models each capture only part of this picture. Analytical models such as GenZ [2] and LLMCompass [24] expose hardware limits for individual operators or single batches, but they do not model the dynamic interplay of batching, preemption, and queueing that shapes real serving behavior. System-level simulators such as Vidur [1] reproduce end-to-end latency distributions, but they rely on regression-based timing models that obscure the underlying architectural bottleneck and require costly retraining for each new hardware or model configuration. LLMServingSim [3] attempts hardware–software co-simulation but suffers from slow execution and limited model coverage. The result is a fundamental gap: no existing methodology combines accurate dynamic modeling of serving-level behaviors with stage-aware architectural diagnosis that keeps compute, bandwidth, capacity, and communication limits simultaneously visible.

This paper presents TokenSimV2, a framework that closes this gap by achieving both high accuracy and fast evaluation for LLM inference on GPUs. TokenSimV2 combines two complementary views in one tool. A token-level event-driven simulator models dynamic request arrival, continuous batching [23], KV Cache allocation with paged memory, preemption [10], and inter-device communication [27] under realistic workload traces. TokenSimV2 enables accurate and fast modeling of LLM inference on GPUs via dynamic graph modeling, where nodes represent requests, token steps, KV Cache blocks, and workers, and edges encode batching, memory residency, preemption, and transfer dependencies. A Transformer Roofline Model decomposes execution into prefill projection, prefill attention, decode projection, decode attention, and off-card communication, mapping each component to its compute, bandwidth, capacity, and communication limits for a given model, workload, and hardware assignment. Together, these two components turn TokenSimV2 from a prediction tool into an architectural exploration tool: the simulator measures *what happens* under a given configuration, and the Transformer Roofline Model explains *why*.

We validate TokenSimV2 against vLLM on real hardware and observe sub-1% geometric-mean error for throughput and request latency. We compare TokenSimV2 with Vidur and LLMServingSim and show that it achieves higher accuracy in every case, with maximum deviation of 3.0% versus 6.6% for the best prior simulator. We then use TokenSimV2 to study three classes of design questions that span the space of LLM serving optimization. First, we examine dynamic serving behaviors that static batch-level models cannot capture, including continuous batching and admission control under memory pressure. Second, we analyze disaggregated serving, including prefill-to-decode worker ratio selection and decode hardware substitution with PIM devices. Third, we sweep compute, bandwidth, and capacity parameters to study platform sensitivity and use the Transformer Roofline Model to explain why the bottleneck shifts. These studies demonstrate that accurate LLM serving analysis requires both dynamic runtime modeling and stage-aware architectural diagnosis, and that TokenSimV2 provides both in a single, lightweight framework.

2 Background and Motivation

2.1 Serving System Optimizations

Real serving systems layer several runtime optimizations on top of two-stage execution. Continuous batching [23] inserts new requests between decode iterations to fill idle compute slots. Paged KV Cache management [10] partitions device memory into fixed-size blocks, reducing fragmentation and delaying preemption. Disaggregated execution [27] separates prefill and decode onto different devices to match each stage to appropriate hardware. These optimizations interact: a batching decision changes memory pressure, a memory limit triggers preemption, and a stage split introduces communication cost that depends on link type and KV Cache volume. Any modeling tool that ignores these interactions will mispredict throughput and latency under realistic serving conditions.

2.2 Limitations of Existing Modeling Approaches

Existing approaches fall into two categories, each with a fundamental limitation.

Analytical Hardware Models. GenZ [2] and LLMCompass [24] model individual operators or single iterations under static batch sizes and fixed sequence lengths. They cannot model continuous batching, preemption, or request queueing—the mechanisms that dominate real serving behavior. Their single-kernel roofline analysis collapses prefill and decode into one aggregate arithmetic intensity, hiding the fact that prefill projection can be compute-bound while decode attention remains bandwidth-bound at the same operating point.

System-level Simulators. Vidur [1] supports continuous batching and produces latency distributions, but it uses regression models trained on profiling data to estimate per-iteration time. This approach does not expose which stage or resource limits performance, and the regression model must be retrained when the hardware or model changes—a process that takes approximately 400 s per configuration. LLMServingSim [3] provides hardware–software co-simulation but runs slower than real time and cannot handle prompts longer than a few tens of tokens.

Neither category provides the combination that serving-oriented architecture studies require: accurate dynamic modeling and stage-aware diagnosis that keeps compute, bandwidth, capacity, and communication limits visible at the same time.

3 Methodology

TokenSimV2 consists of two tightly coupled components: a token-level event-driven simulator and a Transformer Roofline Model.

3.1 Event-Driven Simulator

The simulator is built on the discrete-event framework SimPy [17] and advances simulated time across all workers in a serving cluster. A two-level scheduler dispatches requests: the global scheduler assigns requests to workers, and each worker's local scheduler forms batches and decides when to run, preempt, or transfer requests. Each worker maintains a paged memory manager that tracks KV Cache allocation at block granularity, matching production systems such as vLLM [10]. When a batch is formed, the engine queries the Transformer Roofline Model for the iteration time. For inter-device transfers (e.g., KV Cache migration in disaggregated serving), a communication model computes transfer latency based on link type, data size, and overlap strategy.

3.2 Stage Decomposition

The Transformer Roofline Model decomposes each iteration into five components: prefill projection (PRF-PRJ), prefill attention (PRF-ATT), decode projection (DCD-PRJ), decode attention (DCD-ATT), and off-card communication (COMM). Projection and attention exhibit different scaling behaviors and stress different hardware resources, so collapsing them into one aggregate kernel hides the true bottleneck.

Let B denote batch size, N the number of layers, d the model dimension, h the number of attention heads, $d_h = d/h$ the per-head dimension, d_{ff} the feed-forward hidden dimension, and w the number of weight matrices in the MLP. For a request with prompt length L_p and decode length L_g, the average KV context length over decode steps is $\bar{L}_{kv} = L_p + L_g/2$.

Compute volume. Prefill and decode projection perform the same per-token work—multiplying through all linear layers—but prefill processes L_p tokens in parallel while decode processes one token per step over L_g steps. Prefill attention scales quadratically in prompt length; decode attention scales linearly in context length per step. Table 1 summarizes the FLOP count and memory traffic for each component.

Table 1. Compute volume (F_c) and memory traffic (M_c) for each stage component. $W_{proj} = 4d^2 + 2w \cdot d \cdot d_{ff}$ is the total projection weight count, and g is the number of KV groups.

Component	FLOPs (F_c)	Memory traffic (M_c)
PRF-PRJ	$B \cdot N \cdot L_p \cdot 2W_{proj}$	$N \cdot W_{proj} \cdot 2$ bytes
PRF-ATT	$B \cdot N \cdot 4h \cdot d_h \cdot L_p^2$	negligible (on-chip)
DCD-PRJ	$B \cdot N \cdot L_g \cdot 2W_{proj}$	$L_g \cdot N \cdot W_{proj} \cdot 2$ bytes
DCD-ATT	$B \cdot N \cdot L_g \cdot 4h \cdot d_h \cdot \bar{L}_{kv}$	$B \cdot N \cdot L_g \cdot 4g \cdot d_h \cdot \bar{L}_{kv}$ bytes

Key Scaling Differences. Prefill projection has high arithmetic intensity because $B \cdot L_p$ tokens share the same weight tensor; the intensity grows with batch size and prompt length. Decode projection has low intensity because only one token is processed per weight load. Decode attention has intensity close to 1 FLOP/byte regardless of batch size, because each FLOP requires reading the corresponding KV entry from device memory. Prefill attention traffic is negligible for typical prompt lengths because the KV tensors fit in on-chip SRAM.

3.3 From Arithmetic Intensity to Stage Time

The arithmetic intensity $I_c = F_c/M_c$ determines whether each component is compute-bound or bandwidth-bound. Given peak compute throughput Π (TFLOP/s) and memory bandwidth β (TB/s), the time for component c is:

$$T_c = \begin{cases} F_c/\Pi & \text{if } I_c \geq \Pi/\beta, \\ M_c/\beta & \text{if } I_c < \Pi/\beta. \end{cases} \tag{1}$$

Each stage can run on a different device with its own Π and β, supporting both homogeneous and heterogeneous deployments (e.g., decode on PIM devices). Communication time T_{COMM} covers inter-stage activation transfers, intra-stage allreduce, and KV Cache migration, using measured allreduce tables indexed by message size and link type. The total iteration time is:

$$T_{\text{iter}} = T_{\text{PRF-PRJ}} + T_{\text{PRF-ATT}} + T_{\text{DCD-PRJ}} + T_{\text{DCD-ATT}} + T_{\text{COMM}}. \tag{2}$$

This additive form models the iteration critical path at stage granularity. It includes communication overlap through the communication model, but it does not explicitly model CUDA-stream overlap between projection and attention kernels. When such kernel overlap is substantial, TokenSimV2 may overestimate the isolated iteration time, so we rely on end-to-end validation to confirm that the abstraction is accurate for the evaluated serving stacks.

3.4 Capacity and Serving Constraints

Device memory must hold three components: model weights (C_w), KV Cache (C_{KV}), and activations (C_a). Weight capacity is fixed for a given model. KV Cache capacity grows with batch size and context length: $C_{\text{KV}} = B \cdot N \cdot 2g \cdot d_h \cdot L \cdot 2$ bytes, where L is the total sequence length. Activation capacity is $C_a = B \cdot d \cdot L_p \cdot 2$ bytes. The capacity-feasible batch size B_{cap} is the largest B for which $C_w + C_{\text{KV}} + C_a$ fits in device memory.

However, capacity alone does not determine the useful batch size for interactive serving. The Transformer Roofline Model derives two additional ceilings: the *first-response bound* B_{TTFT} (largest B for which prefill latency meets a time-to-first-token target) and the *decode-rate bound* $B_{\text{tok/s}}$ (largest B for which per-step decode time meets a tokens-per-second target). The serving-feasible batch size is:

$$B_{\max} = \min\left(B_{\text{cap}},\ B_{\text{TTFT}},\ B_{\text{tok/s}}\right). \tag{3}$$

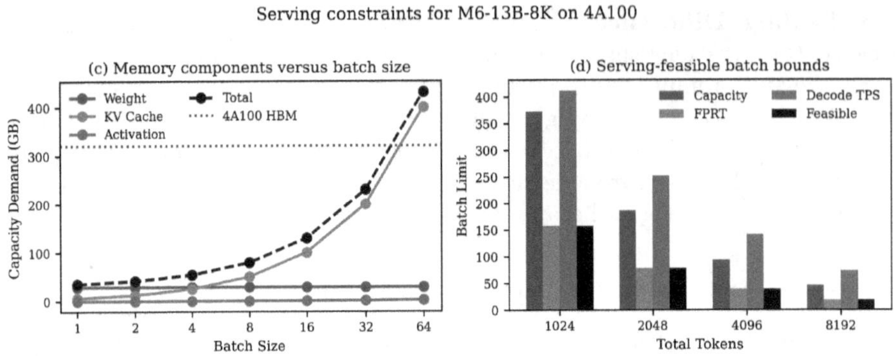

Fig. 1. Serving constraints derived by the Transformer Roofline Model for M6-13B-8K on 4×A100. (a) Memory demand breakdown as batch size increases (prompt ratio 0.5, total length 8192). (b) Capacity, first-response, and decode-rate batch ceilings across total lengths, with the serving-feasible minimum marked.

Figure 1 shows this analysis for M6-13B-8K on 4×A100. Raw capacity allows batch sizes from 372 down to 46 as total length grows from 1024 to 8192 tokens, but the serving-feasible limit is much smaller and is set by the first-response bound at every point. Capacity-only analysis systematically overestimates the feasible batch size for interactive serving.

4 Evaluation

4.1 Goals and Setup

This evaluation asks three questions. (1) Does TokenSimV2 match measured hardware behavior and improve on prior simulators? (2) Can TokenSimV2 capture dynamic serving effects that static analyses miss? (3) Does the Transformer Roofline Model explain why the bottleneck shifts across policies, workloads, and hardware choices?

Unless noted otherwise, experiments use the LLaMA2-7B model [18,19] on NVIDIA A100 GPUs (80 GB) with requests sampled from the ShareGPT dataset [16]. We compare against vLLM v0.6.2 on real hardware for validation, and against Vidur [1] and LLMServingSim [3] for simulator comparison.

4.2 Validation and Prior Simulator Comparison

Accuracy Against Real Hardware. We run 2000 ShareGPT requests on an A100 GPU and vary the request rate from low load to saturation. Figure 2 compares throughput and latency percentiles between TokenSimV2 and vLLM. The two curves overlap across all QPS values: the geometric mean error is 0.109% for throughput and 0.6%, 0.254%, and 0.337% for P50, P99, and maximum request latency.

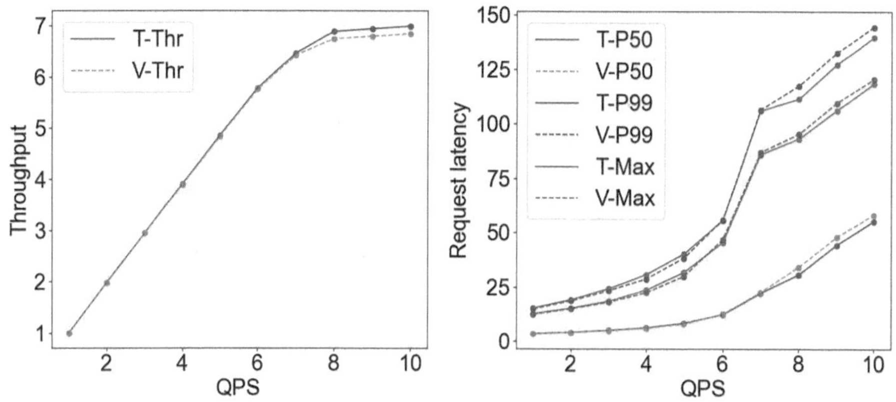

Fig. 2. Throughput and latency validation against vLLM (2000 ShareGPT requests, A100). "V-" / "T-": vLLM / TokenSimV2. Geometric mean errors: throughput 0.109%; P50 0.6%; P99 0.254%; Max 0.337%.

Accuracy Against Prior Simulators. Table 2 compares total elapsed time at 40 QPS on an A100 as request count grows from 100 to 500. TokenSimV2 achieves the smallest error in every column. The margin over LLMServingSim is small in this short-output setting, but TokenSimV2 preserves the stage-decomposed timing needed by the Transformer Roofline Model while matching or improving prior simulator accuracy.

Table 2. Total latency (seconds) for 10 output tokens across different request counts at 40 QPS on A100. Lower difference from real hardware is better.

Request Count	100	200	300	400	500
Real Hardware	2.756	5.246	7.819	10.371	12.981
Vidur	2.371	4.698	7.246	9.935	12.122
LLMServingSim	2.556	5.056	7.557	10.056	12.556
TokenSimV2	**2.592**	**5.089**	**7.587**	**10.095**	**12.593**

Disaggregated Serving Accuracy. We validate against DistServe [27] on two A100 GPUs (64 input tokens, 64 output tokens, request counts 1000–10000). As Fig. 3 shows, TokenSimV2 tracks DistServe's end-to-end latency with errors below 0.6% at $QPS = 8$ and below 3.4% at $QPS = 12$, confirming that stage boundaries and communication costs are preserved. The residual gap stems from bus-level KV transmission fluctuation and minor operator differences between DistServe's SwiftTransformer backend and TokenSimV2's model.

The close alignment across throughput, latency distribution, and disaggregated serving gives the subsequent design-space studies a measured anchor.

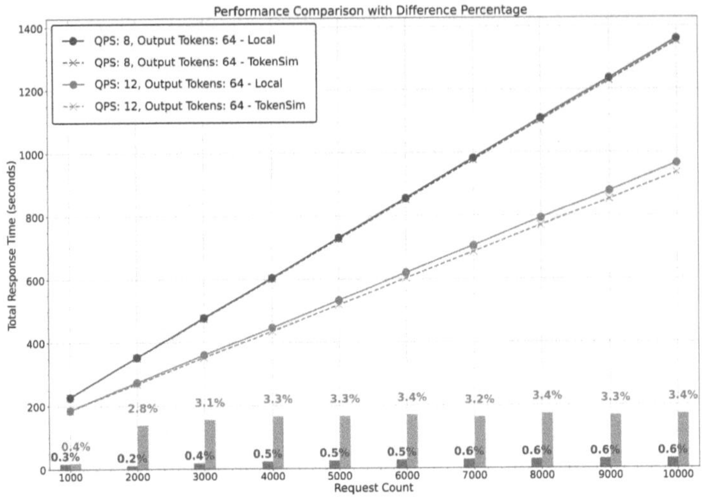

Fig. 3. Latency comparison with DistServe (2×A100, 64 input / 64 output tokens). Bar annotations show per-point error: ≤0.6% at $QPS = 8$, ≤3.4% at $QPS = 12$.

4.3 Disaggregated Serving Design Space

Prefill-to-Decode Worker Ratio. Disaggregated architectures [14,27] place prefill and decode on separate GPUs, but the optimal ratio depends on workload shape. Figure 4 sweeps input and output lengths on an 8×A100 node for LLaMA2-7B and OPT-13B. Two trends are visible: longer outputs shift the optimum toward more decode devices (e.g., at output length 2048 the best split is 2P/6D for LLaMA), while shorter inputs at the same output length further favor decode. The Transformer Roofline Model explains both: short outputs make prefill compute the binding constraint, so additional prefill devices help; long outputs make decode bandwidth the bottleneck, so decode devices become the limiting factor. The best stage split is therefore a function of workload shape, not a fixed deployment rule.

Decode Hardware Substitution. Since decode is bandwidth-bound, cheaper or higher-bandwidth devices are natural candidates for decode workers. We evaluate four decode device types—A100, V100 (∼1/4 cost), GDDR6-AiM [11] (∼1/2 cost), and a hypothetical A100 at 1/4 peak FLOPS—constrained to eight total devices.

Figure 5 reveals three findings. First, PIM devices are cost-effective under tight budgets: one A100 prefill + seven GDDR6-AiM achieves throughput comparable to a full A100 deployment at roughly half the cost. Second, PIM cannot fully replace A100 decode workers, because decode projection still requires meaningful compute throughput and the small per-device capacity limits batch size. Third, the reduced-FLOPS A100 variant performs worse than the original, showing that the A100's compute is not excessive even for decode—projection work

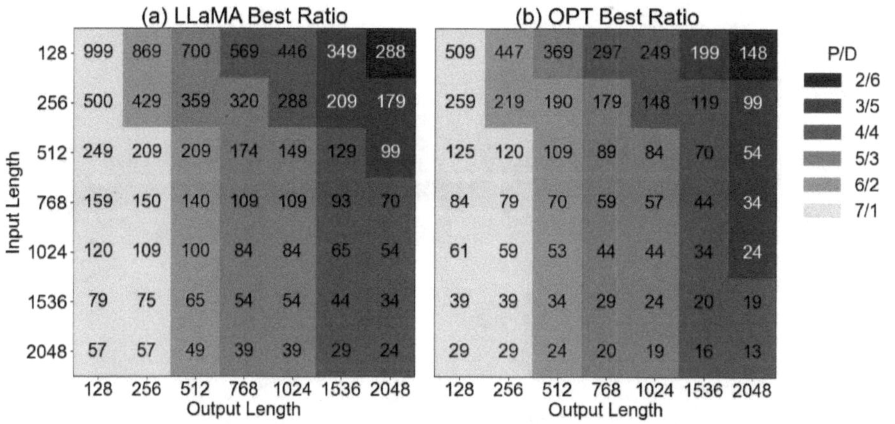

Fig. 4. Optimal prefill-to-decode ratio on 8×A100 across input/output length combinations (LLaMA2-7B and OPT-13B). Color encodes the P/D split; cell values are maximum SLO-attained throughput.

is non-trivial. This last observation would be invisible to any model that treats decode as purely bandwidth-bound.

4.4 Platform Sensitivity

We sweep compute, memory bandwidth, and memory capacity of the prefill GPU while processing 50000 ShareGPT requests in a disaggregated deployment. Figure 6 shows throughput for 1, 2, and 3 prefill devices. Scaling capacity (1/4×–4×) or bandwidth (1/8×–4×) relative to the A100 baseline has negligible effect on prefill throughput. Scaling compute, in contrast, produces proportional gains until the system hits the decode-side bottleneck—visible as the throughput plateau in the P1-D7 panel at 4× compute. The Transformer Roofline Model confirms this: prefill projection lies above the hardware ridge point in this configuration, so it is compute-bound, and neither bandwidth nor capacity relaxes that constraint. System-level throughput saturates when cumulative prefill compute exceeds what the decode workers can consume, shifting the bottleneck from prefill compute to decode bandwidth.

5 Discussion

5.1 Combining Dynamic and Analytical Modeling

The evaluation shows that neither dynamic runtime modeling nor stage-aware analytical modeling alone suffices. The simulator captures batching, preemption, and queueing effects that no static analysis can predict. The Transformer Roofline Model reveals *which* resource—compute, bandwidth, capacity, or communication—is the true bottleneck, a diagnosis invisible in end-to-end

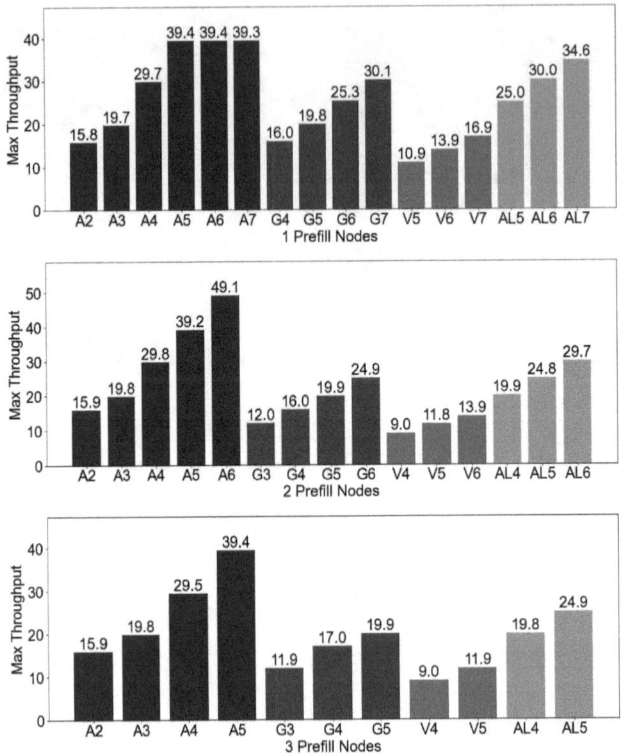

Fig. 5. Throughput with heterogeneous decode hardware (8 total devices). "V"/"A"/"G"/"AL": V100 / A100 / GDDR6-AiM / A100 at 1/4 FLOPS; trailing digit is decode device count.

latency numbers. Together, they turn TokenSimV2 from a prediction tool into an architectural exploration tool: the simulator measures what happens under a given configuration, and the Transformer Roofline Model explains why.

5.2 Scope and Limitations

The Transformer Roofline Model assumes each stage runs at peak throughput or bandwidth and does not model kernel-level effects (warp scheduling, bank conflicts, memory coalescing). This abstraction is accurate for the dense projection and attention operations studied, but may widen for custom fused kernels. The simulator does not model intra-iteration memory fragmentation or network congestion under multi-tenant deployment. Validation against real hardware (Sect. 4.2) confirms these abstractions are sufficient for the scenarios studied, but users should verify accuracy when applying TokenSimV2 to significantly different operator implementations or network topologies.

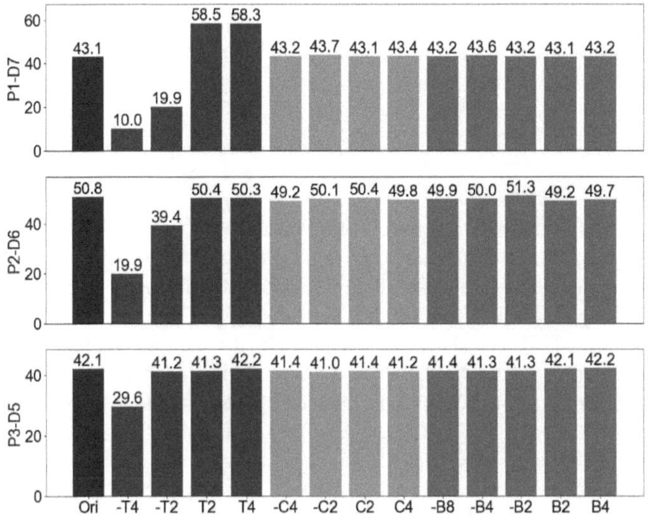

Fig. 6. Prefill throughput under hardware parameter sweeps (50000 ShareGPT requests, disaggregated deployment). "Ori": A100 baseline. "-Tn"/"Tn": compute $\div n$ / $\times n$. "-Cn"/"Cn": capacity scaling. "-Bn"/"Bn": bandwidth scaling. Compute scaling dominates; capacity and bandwidth scaling have <2% effect.

6 Conclusion

TokenSimV2 combines token-level dynamic modeling with a Transformer Roofline Model for accurate and fast evaluation of LLM inference on GPUs. The simulator captures continuous batching, paged KV Cache management, preemption, and disaggregated execution under realistic request streams. The Transformer Roofline Model decomposes transformer execution into five stage components, maps each to its compute, bandwidth, capacity, or communication limit, and derives serving-feasible batch ceilings under latency and throughput constraints. Validation against vLLM on real hardware shows sub-1% geometric-mean error for throughput and request latency. The combined methodology enables design-space studies—covering admission control, disaggregated worker allocation, decode hardware substitution, and platform sensitivity—that identify and explain bottleneck shifts across workloads, policies, and hardware configurations. These results show that accurate LLM serving analysis requires both dynamic runtime modeling and stage-aware architectural diagnosis, and that TokenSimV2 provides both in a single, lightweight framework.

Acknowledgments. This work is supported by National Key R&D Program of China under Grant No. 2024YFB4504300. Youwei Zhuo is the corresponding author.

Disclosure of Interests. The authors have no competing interests to declare that are relevant to the content of this article.

Artificial Intelligence Tools. Artificial intelligence tools, if used, were used only for language organization and figure/table polishing, and did not participate in the generation of the core ideas or technical content.

References

1. Agrawal, A., et al.: Vidur: a large-scale simulation framework for LLM inference. In: Proceedings of Machine Learning and Systems, vol. 6, pp. 351–366 (2024)
2. Bambhaniya, A., et al.: Demystifying platform requirements for diverse LLM inference use cases. arXiv:2406.01698 arXiv preprint (2024)
3. Cho, J., Kim, M., Choi, H., Heo, G., Park, J.: Llmservingsim: a HW/SW co-simulation infrastructure for LLM inference serving at scale. In: 2024 IEEE International Symposium on Workload Characterization (IISWC), pp. 15–29 (2024)
4. Dao, T., Fu, D., Ermon, S., Rudra, A., Ré, C.: Flashattention: fast and memory-efficient exact attention with io-awareness. Adv. Neural. Inf. Process. Syst. **35**, 16344–16359 (2022)
5. Gao, B., et al.: Cost-efficient large language model serving for multi-turn conversations with cachedattention (2024). https://arxiv.org/abs/2403.19708
6. Gao, S., Chen, Y., Shu, J.: Fast state restoration in LLM serving with HCACHE. In: Proceedings of the Twentieth European Conference on Computer Systems, pp. 128–143 (2025)
7. Gim, I., Chen, G., Lee, S.s., Sarda, N., Khandelwal, A., Zhong, L.: Prompt cache: modular attention reuse for low-latency inference. In: Gibbons, P., Pekhimenko, G., Sa, C.D. (eds.) Proceedings of Machine Learning and Systems. vol. 6, pp. 325–338 (2024). https://proceedings.mlsys.org/paper_files/paper/2024/file/a66caa1703fe34705a4368c3014c1966-Paper-Conference.pdf
8. Hu, C., et al.: Memserve: context caching for disaggregated LLM serving with elastic memory pool. arXiv preprint arXiv:2406.17565 (2024)
9. Hu, J., et al.: Epic: efficient position-independent caching for serving large language models. arXiv preprint arXiv:2410.15332 (2024)
10. Kwon, W., et al.: Efficient memory management for large language model serving with pagedattention. In: Proceedings of the 29th Symposium on Operating Systems Principles, pp. 611–626 (2023)
11. Kwon, Y., et al.: System architecture and software stack for gddr6-aim. In: 2022 IEEE Hot Chips 34 Symposium (HCS), pp. 1–25 (2022)
12. Lee, W., Lee, J., Seo, J., Sim, J.: InfiniGen: Efficient generative inference of large language models with dynamic KV cache management. In: 18th USENIX Symposium on Operating Systems Design and Implementation (OSDI 24), pp. 155–172 (2024)
13. Liu, Y., et al.: Cachegen: KV cache compression and streaming for fast large language model serving. In: Proceedings of the ACM SIGCOMM 2024 Conference, pp. 38–56 (2024)
14. Patel, P., et al.: Splitwise: efficient generative LLM inference using phase splitting. arXiv:2311.18677 arXiv preprint (2024)
15. Qin, R., et al.: Mooncake: a kvcache-centric disaggregated architecture for LLM serving. ACM Trans. Storage (2024)
16. ShareGPT Team: Sharegpt (2023). https://www.sharegpt.com/
17. SimPy Contributors: Simpy: Discrete event simulation for python (2026). https://simpy.readthedocs.io/. Accessed 11 Apr 2026

18. Touvron, H., et al.: Llama: Open and efficient foundation language models. arXiv:2302.13971 arXiv preprint (2023)
19. Touvron, H., et al.: Llama 2: open foundation and fine-tuned chat models. arXiv:2307.09288 arXiv preprint (2023)
20. Vaswani, A., et al.: Attention is all you need. In: Advances in Neural Information Processing Systems, vol. 30 (2017)
21. Yao, J., et al.: Cacheblend: fast large language model serving for rag with cached knowledge fusion. In: Proceedings of the Twentieth European Conference on Computer Systems, pp. 94–109 (2025)
22. Ye, Z., et al.: Flashinfer: efficient and customizable attention engine for LLM inference serving. Proc. Mach. Learn. Syst. **7** (2025)
23. Yu, G.I., Jeong, J.S., Kim, G.W., Kim, S., Chun, B.G.: Orca: A distributed serving system for Transformer-Based generative models. In: 16th USENIX Symposium on Operating Systems Design and Implementation (OSDI 22), pp. 521–538 (2022)
24. Zhang, H., Ning, A., Prabhakar, R., Wentzlaff, D.: A hardware evaluation framework for large language model inference. arXiv:2312.03134 arXiv preprint (2023)
25. Zhang, Y., et al.: To see is not to master: teaching LLMs to use private libraries for code generation. arXiv preprint arXiv:2603.15159 (2026)
26. Zheng, L., et al.: Sglang: efficient execution of structured language model programs. Adv. Neural. Inf. Process. Syst. **37**, 62557–62583 (2024)
27. Zhong, Y., et al.: Distserve: disaggregating prefill and decoding for goodput-optimized large language model serving. arXiv preprint arXiv:2401.09670 (2024)

TierServe: Revenue-Maximizing LLM Inference Scheduling Across Multiple Subscription Tiers

Chang Liu[1], Jiacheng Liu[2], Xiaofeng Hou[1(✉)], and Minyi Guo[1,3(✉)]

[1] Shanghai Jiao Tong University, Shanghai, China
chocobi@sjtu.edu.cn, {hou-xf,guo-my}@cs.sjtu.edu.cn
[2] The Hong Kong University of Science and Technology, Hong Kong, China
jiachengliu@ust.hk
[3] Guizhou Provincial Laboratory of Big Data, College of Computer Science and Technology,Guizhou University, Guiyang, China

Abstract. Large language model (LLM) inference systems serve clients across multiple subscription tiers with heterogeneous latency requirements and revenue contributions. Existing schedulers optimize throughput or service-level objectives (SLO) attainment, treating all requests as equally valuable. In multi-tier settings, this leads to a fundamental mismatch: a scheduler that maximizes goodput may allocate substantial resources to low-tier requests while high-tier requests miss their stricter SLOs, resulting in suboptimal operator revenue.

We present **TierServe**, a revenue-driven LLM inference scheduler that jointly leverages both subscription-tier priority and per-request SLO slack. TierServe prioritizes high-value requests while dynamically utilizing available slack to improve overall efficiency, aligning scheduling decisions with both business value and latency urgency. We evaluate TierServe across a range of workloads and load conditions. Results show that TierServe consistently improves system revenue over state-of-the-art baselines while maintaining competitive per-tier latency.

Keywords: LLM inference serving · revenue maximization · multi-tier scheduling

1 Introduction

Large language model (LLM) inference has rapidly become a dominant workload in modern cloud systems [12]. Unlike offline training, inference is inherently latency-sensitive: users interact with models in real time, and perceived service quality degrades sharply when responses arrive too slowly. As a result, production systems enforce latency service-level objectives (SLOs) [3,7,10,16], typically measured by time-to-first-token (TTFT) and time-per-output-token (TPOT), to guarantee an acceptable user experience.

L. Eeckhout et al. (Eds.): APPT 2026, LNCS 16693, pp. 142–156, 2027.
https://doi.org/10.1007/978-981-92-4805-6_10

Beyond latency constraints, real-world LLM services exhibit a second, equally important dimension of heterogeneity: requests originate from clients across multiple subscription tiers (e.g., free, professional, and enterprise), each associated with different revenue contributions and latency expectations. High-tier clients pay for stronger performance guarantees, while low-tier clients are served on a best-effort basis. This raises a fundamental systems question: *how should limited compute resources be allocated across heterogeneous requests to maximize operator revenue?*

Existing LLM schedulers do not account for this revenue heterogeneity. Throu-ghput-oriented and SLO-driven policies [10,18–20] aim to maximize the number of requests that meet their deadlines, treating all requests as equally valuable. However, in a multi-tier setting, SLO attainment is not aligned with business value. A scheduler may achieve high goodput by serving a large volume of low-tier requests with relaxed deadlines while allowing a smaller number of high-tier requests to miss their stricter SLOs, resulting in substantial revenue loss.

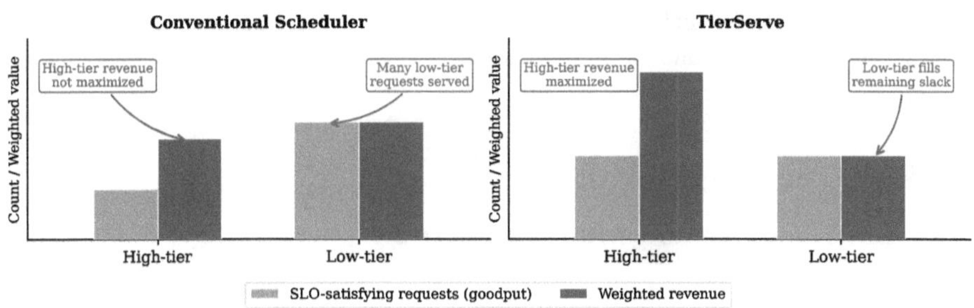

Fig. 1. In multi-tier LLM serving, goodput does not equate to revenue. Conventional schedulers prioritize request volume, often sacrificing high-value requests to satisfy low-value ones.

Figure 1 illustrates this mismatch. Under identical system capacity, two scheduling policies can achieve comparable aggregate SLO attainment yet yield drastically different revenue outcomes, because the policies differ in *which* requests they choose to satisfy. A goodput-maximizing scheduler favors whichever requests are easiest to serve on time, irrespective of their business value, whereas a revenue-aware scheduler directs resources toward the requests whose successful completion contributes the most to operator revenue. This gap is not an edge case but a structural consequence of optimizing SLO satisfaction instead of revenue, and it widens as the disparity in tier weights and SLO strictness grows.

To address this challenge, we present **TierServe**, a revenue-driven LLM inference scheduler that jointly leverages subscription-tier priority and per-request SLO slack. TierServe prioritizes high-value requests while dynamically reallocating surplus capacity from less urgent requests, aligning resource allocation with both business value and latency urgency. We formulate LLM inference scheduling as an online revenue maximization problem with heterogeneous deadlines and unknown job sizes, and design TierServe as a structured approximation that enforces two key principles: (i) *revenue dominance*, where higher-tier requests are prioritized at comparable urgency, and (ii) *slack efficiency*, where available SLO slack is fully utilized to avoid idle capacity. We evaluate TierServe using the Vidur simulator across a range of workloads and load conditions.

In summary, this paper makes the following contributions:

- **Revenue-driven scheduling formulation.** We identify the mismatch between conventional SLO-based objectives and operator revenue in multi-tier LLM serving, and formulate scheduling as a weighted revenue maximization problem.
- **Tier-slack joint scheduling.** We design TierServe, a scheduler that jointly leverages subscription-tier priority and per-request SLO slack to allocate resources, ensuring that high-value requests are prioritized while surplus capacity is efficiently utilized.
- **Empirical evaluation.** We implement TierServe in the Vidur simulator and show that it consistently outperforms state-of-the-art baselines across a wide range of workloads and load conditions.

2 Background and Motivation

2.1 LLM Inference and Multi-tier Serving

Modern LLM serving systems use continuous batching to interleave requests at the iteration level, allowing newly arrived requests to join an in-progress batch without waiting for all existing requests to complete [19]. Within this framework, latency is governed by two SLO metrics: TTFT, which measures the elapsed time from request arrival to the first output token, and TPOT, which measures the average interval between successive decode tokens. TPOT directly determines the streaming latency perceived by users during the decode phase and is the primary scheduling target in continuous batching systems, as the token budget allocated to each request per iteration is the main lever for controlling it.

In practice, LLM services operate under multi-tier subscription models, where requests originate from clients with heterogeneous revenue contributions and latency expectations. High-tier users pay for stronger performance guarantees, while low-tier users are served on a best-effort basis. As a result, requests are not interchangeable: allocating compute to different requests has fundamentally different implications for operator revenue.

2.2 Limitations of Existing Schedulers

Existing LLM inference schedulers can be broadly categorized into two classes: (i) length-based policies [18] [5] that prioritize short requests to improve average latency, and (ii) deadline-driven policies [20] [3] [10] that prioritize requests with urgent SLO deadlines. While effective at improving SLO attainment, both classes implicitly treat all requests as equally valuable.

Both classes lead to a fundamental mismatch in multi-tier settings. A scheduler that maximizes SLO satisfaction may allocate substantial resources to low-tier requests with relaxed deadlines, while high-tier requests with stricter SLOs miss their targets. As illustrated in Fig. 1, such behavior can yield high goodput but significantly lower revenue.

A natural alternative is to enforce strict tier isolation, reserving a fixed fraction of the token budget for each tier. While this avoids cross-tier interference, it fails to utilize surplus SLO slack: when high-tier requests carry ample slack, their reserved capacity sits idle rather than being redirected to generate additional revenue from lower tiers. Consequently, strict isolation sacrifices system efficiency without fully maximizing revenue.

These limitations motivate the need for a scheduler that jointly accounts for subscription-tier priority and per-request SLO slack, directing resources toward high-value requests while reclaiming surplus capacity from less urgent ones.

3 Design

TierServe is a revenue-driven LLM inference scheduler designed to allocate GPU resources across heterogeneous requests. As shown in Fig. 2, TierServe organizes requests into per-tier queues and constructs each batch by jointly considering subscription-tier priority and SLO slack.

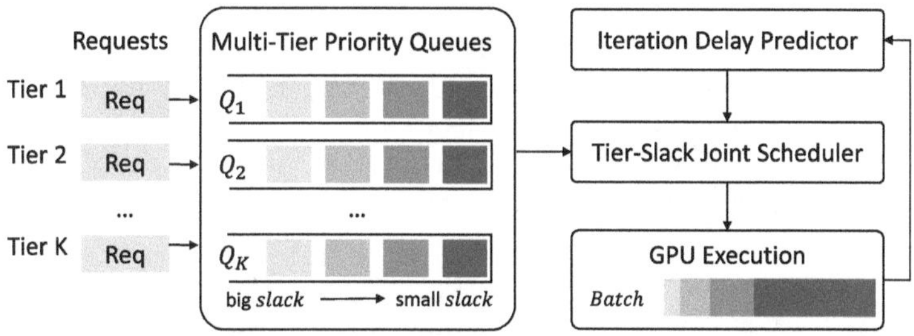

Fig. 2. Overview of TierServe. Incoming requests are organized into K per-tier priority queues. At each iteration, TierServe computes per-request SLO slack and applies a tier-slack joint scheduling algorithm to construct the next batch. The scheduler prioritizes high-tier requests at equal urgency while utilizing surplus slack to improve overall efficiency.

3.1 Revenue Maximization Objective

We model the tier heterogeneity by assigning each request r a priority weight $w_{p_r} > 0$ based on its subscription tier p_r, and define system revenue as the weighted count of SLO-satisfying requests:

$$V(R) = \sum_{r \in R} w_{p_r} \cdot L_r \cdot \mathbf{1}[\text{TPOT}(r) \leq \tau_{p_r}], \tag{1}$$

where τ_{p_r} is the TPOT SLO threshold for tier p_r and L_r is the total number of tokens of request r. This formulation captures the key objective of multi-tier LLM serving: maximizing the total weighted value of completed requests.

This objective prioritizes high-value requests when resources are constrained, and generalizes conventional goodput by incorporating heterogeneous business value.

We use tier-level weights as an abstraction of request revenue contribution. This abstraction reflects the common practice of offering differentiated service levels through subscription plans while keeping the scheduling objective tractable.

Although TierServe currently derives weights from subscription tiers, the framework does not depend on a particular pricing model. More sophisticated revenue formulations, such as token-based charging, dynamic pricing, or spot-capacity discounts, can be incorporated by replacing the weight assignment function. Since TierServe operates on abstract request weights rather than tier identities themselves, the scheduling algorithm remains unchanged.

3.2 Iteration Time Estimation

TierServe estimates the duration of each decoding iteration to convert a request's remaining latency budget into slack levels. Since iteration time varies with workload characteristics such as batch composition and output lengths, a static estimate may lead to inaccurate slack computation under changing workloads.

To capture runtime dynamics, TierServe maintains a sliding-window average over recent decoding iterations. Let t_i denote the duration of iteration i. The estimated iteration time $\hat{t}_i$ is computed as:

$$\hat{ti} = \frac{1}{W} \sum_{j=\max\{i-W,0\}}^{i-1} t_j, \tag{2}$$

where W is the window size. The estimate is updated once per iteration and used for subsequent slack calculations.

We intentionally adopt a lightweight estimator rather than a sophisticated prediction model. TierServe does not require precise completion-time forecasting; instead, the estimate is only used to determine the relative urgency of requests through slack levels. Consequently, the estimator should be sufficiently responsive to workload changes while remaining robust to transient runtime fluctuations.

To determine an appropriate window size, we evaluated $W \in 1, 2, 4, 8, 16, 32$. Smaller windows react quickly to workload variations but exhibit high variance due to short-term execution noise. Larger windows produce smoother estimates but respond more slowly to changes in workload conditions, resulting in stale slack calculations. Across all evaluated workloads, $W = 8$ provided the best trade-off between responsiveness and stability and therefore serves as the default configuration in TierServe.

3.3 Per-Tier Queues and SLO Slack

TierServe maintains K priority queues $Q_1 \succ Q_2 \succ \cdots \succ Q_K$, one for each subscription tier. Incoming requests are assigned to queues based on their tier, ensuring that higher-tier requests are always considered before lower-tier ones.

For each active decode request r, we define its SLO slack $\delta_r(t)$ as the number of future iterations it can be deferred without violating its TPOT SLO:

$$\delta_r(t_r^{\text{elapsed}}) = \frac{\tau_{p_r} \cdot L_r^{\text{decoded}} - t_r^{\text{elapsed}}}{\hat{\tau}_{\text{iter}}}, \tag{3}$$

where $\hat{\tau}_{\text{iter}}$ is the estimated iteration time and L_r^{decoded} is the decoded number of tokens of request r. A smaller δ_r indicates higher urgency, and $\delta_r < 1$ implies that the request must be scheduled in the next iteration to meet its SLO.

Within each queue, requests are ordered by increasing δ_r, so that the most urgent requests are considered first.

The core of TierServe is a tier-slack joint scheduling algorithm (Sect. 3.4), which determines how requests are selected from these queues to form each batch.

3.4 Tier-Slack Joint Scheduling

At each iteration, TierServe constructs the next batch by jointly considering tier priority and slack urgency. Algorithm 1 describes the procedure.

The scheduler performs a progressive scan over slack thresholds. Starting from the most urgent requests, it iterates over queues in priority order, admitting requests whose slack is below the current threshold, subject to batch capacity. If no additional requests can be admitted, the slack threshold is increased and the scan repeats until the batch is full or all queues are exhausted.

The tier-slack joint scan algorithm can be viewed as enforcing a *lexicographic priority* over (tier, slack), and satisfies two key properties simultaneously. *First* (tier priority guarantee): at any slack threshold level s, all requests in Q_k with $\delta_r \leq s$ are admitted before any request in Q_{k+1} with $\delta_r \leq s$. Higher-tier requests are therefore systematically preferred over lower-tier requests at the same urgency level, regardless of their arrival times or lengths. *Second* (resource efficiency): capacity left over after all requests at the current threshold have been admitted is not wasted; the threshold is raised and less urgent or lower-tier requests fill the remaining slots. Surplus SLO slack held by high-tier requests thus becomes available to lower-tier requests without any explicit redistribution mechanism or static budget reservation. The slack threshold is increased by

Algorithm 1 Tier-Slack Joint Scan

Require: Queues $Q_1, \ldots, Q_K$, each sorted by δ_r ascending; batch capacity B; current batch $\mathcal{B} \leftarrow \emptyset$

$s \leftarrow 1$
repeat
  added $\leftarrow 0$
  for $k = 1$ **to** K **do**
    for each request $r \in Q_k$ with $\delta_r \le s$, in queue order **do**
      if $|\mathcal{B}| < B$ **and** CanAllocate(r) **then**
        $\mathcal{B} \leftarrow \mathcal{B} \cup \{r\}$; Allocate($r$); added $\leftarrow$ added $+ 1$
      end if
    end for
  end for
  if added $= 0$ **then**
    $s \leftarrow s + 1$
  end if
until $|\mathcal{B}| = B$ **or** all queues are empty
return $\mathcal{B}$

one iteration at a time. This design is intentional rather than a tunable optimization parameter. Since slack is measured in iteration units, each slack value corresponds to a discrete urgency level. Expanding the threshold from s to s+1 preserves the ordering of urgency levels and ensures that requests with smaller slack are always considered before requests with larger slack. Using larger increments (e.g., s+2 or s+4) would skip intermediate urgency levels, potentially admitting less urgent requests before more urgent ones. Such behavior weakens the urgency guarantees underlying slack-based scheduling and may unnecessarily increase the risk of SLO violations for requests closer to their deadlines.

4 Evaluation

4.1 Experimental Setup

Simulator and Hardware. We evaluate TierServe using the Vidur simulation framework [1], which models LLM inference performance via operator-level profiling. All simulations target a single-replica deployment on one NVIDIA A100 80 GB GPU.

Model. We serve Meta-Llama-3-8B [4], an 8-billion-parameter decoder-only transformer with grouped-query attention (GQA) and a 128 K-token context window. The model is representative of widely deployed interactive LLM services and fits within a single A100 without quantization.

Workload Traces. We evaluate TierServe on two real-world production traces that exhibit distinct request length distributions.

AzureTrace [13] is a publicly released trace of LLM inference requests from Microsoft Azure, capturing conversation-style workloads with moderately long inputs and variable output lengths.

ShareGPT [14] is a dataset of real user conversations collected from the ShareGPT platform, widely used in LLM serving research. It features a heavy-tailed output length distribution with a higher decode-to-prefill ratio than AzureTrace.

For each trace, we replay requests at a series of scaled arrival rates (RPS) using a Poisson inter-arrival process, covering a range from resource-abundant operation to overloaded conditions. The RPS range for each trace is determined by a capacity probing step: we first run FCFS across a coarse RPS grid and identify the lowest RPS at which any tier's SLO attainment begins to degrade (lower bound of the interesting region) and the RPS at which all tiers suffer substantial violations (upper bound). We then select 7 evenly spaced RPS values within this range for the main experiments.

Baselines. We compare TierServe against four baselines: (1) **FastServe** [18], a scheduler that prioritizes short requests to improve TPOT, eliminating head-of-line blocking; (2) **vLLM**, the vLLM [11] scheduler with FCFS ordering; (3) **Tier-First**, which allocates token budget based on the subscription tiers and allows low-tier requests to be batched only when high-tier requests are all batched; (4) **JITServe** [20], a deadline-driven scheduler, which prioritizes requests with urgent deadlines.

4.2 End-to-End Revenue

Figure 3 plots the revenue ratio (revenue per token relative to the optimal value) against RPS for TierServe and the four baselines on both workload traces. We identify three distinct load regimes and analyze each in turn.

Offline Upper Bound. The offline scheduler has access to the entire request trace, including arrival times, output lengths, and execution durations. It therefore represents an oracle scheduler that can make globally optimal admission and scheduling decisions.

The offline bound is computed by solving a revenue-maximization scheduling problem over the complete trace. Requests that cannot be completed before their SLO deadlines are excluded, while the scheduler selects the subset of feasible requests that maximizes total revenue.

Low Load. Below the system's saturation point, all strategies achieve similar revenue: the GPU has sufficient capacity to serve every request within its TPOT SLO, so the scheduling policy has little effect on which requests complete successfully. All curves therefore converge near the Optimal Offline bound, and the revenue grows approximately linearly with RPS at a slope proportional to the average priority weight.

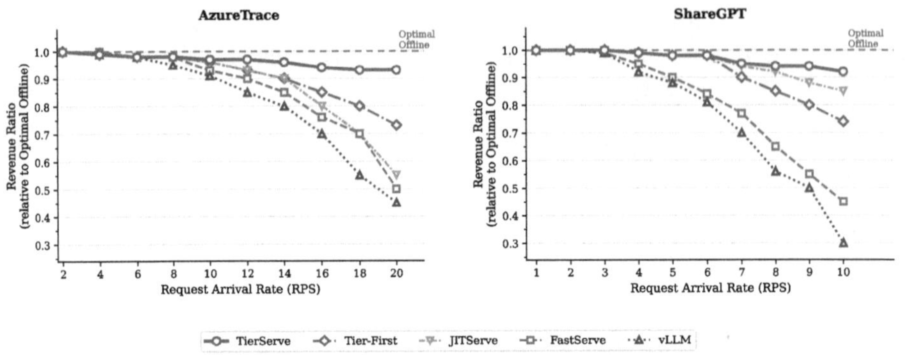

Fig. 3. Revenue ratio (revenue per token relative to optimal value) vs. request arrival rate (RPS) for TierServe and four baselines on AzureTrace (left) and ShareGPT (right). The dashed line denotes the Optimal Offline upper bound. Shaded regions indicate the load range over which each baseline exhibits its primary failure mode.

Moderate Load. As RPS approaches the saturation point, the strategies begin to diverge. vLLM-FCFS is the first to degrade: without any awareness of tier priority or deadline urgency, high-tier requests queue behind lower-value ones, causing Tier 1 SLO violations to appear at an RPS lower than TierServe's saturation point. FastServe degrades next: its preference for short requests improves TPOT on average but systematically deprioritizes long high-tier requests, diverting weighted capacity toward low-tier short ones. On AzureTrace, where request length and tier are largely uncorrelated, FastServe's revenue remains close to that of vLLM-FCFS. On ShareGPT, whose heavy-tailed output length distribution amplifies the length-priority mismatch, the gap between FastServe and TierServe widens. Tier-First and JITServe both outperform the length-agnostic baselines in this regime. Tier-First protects Tier 1 SLO attainment through strict budget reservation, yielding a revenue close to TierServe. However, its rigid inter-tier isolation prevents surplus SLO slack accumulated by Tier 1 requests from being reallocated to lower tiers, suppressing the revenue contribution of Tier 2 and Tier 3. JITServe's deadline-driven scheduling achieves comparable revenue to Tier-First by concentrating resources on requests whose deadlines are imminent; however, because it does not distinguish between tiers at equal urgency levels, it occasionally allocates capacity to low-tier requests whose TPOT deadlines happen to be tighter than those of high-tier requests with more slack, leading to a modest but consistent revenue shortfall relative to TierServe. Overall, TierServe improves revenue over the strongest moderate-load baseline on both AzureTrace and ShareGPT.

High Load. Under overload, the ranking of baselines shifts. Tier-First becomes the strongest baseline: it concentrates resources on high-tier requests, which do not constitute the majority of all requests but contribute significant weights. FastServe and vLLM-FCFS collapse to near-zero high-tier revenue: FastServe continues to fill batches with short low-tier requests, while FCFS ordering causes cascading deadline violations across all tiers. The advantage stems from the tier-slack joint scan: at slack threshold $s = 1$, TierServe first admits all Tier 1 requests whose deadlines are imminent before considering any Tier 2 or Tier 3 request at the same urgency level, whereas JITServe treats requests from different tiers interchangeably once their deadline distances are equal. As a result, TierServe concentrates the revenue gain from the most valuable clients even when the system cannot serve everyone.

4.3 Per-Tier TPOT

Figure.4 shows the mean TPOT per tier as a function of RPS. Each subplot corresponds to one subscription tier, and the horizontal dashed line marks the TPOT SLO threshold for that tier. A scheduler meets the SLO if its curve lies below this threshold.

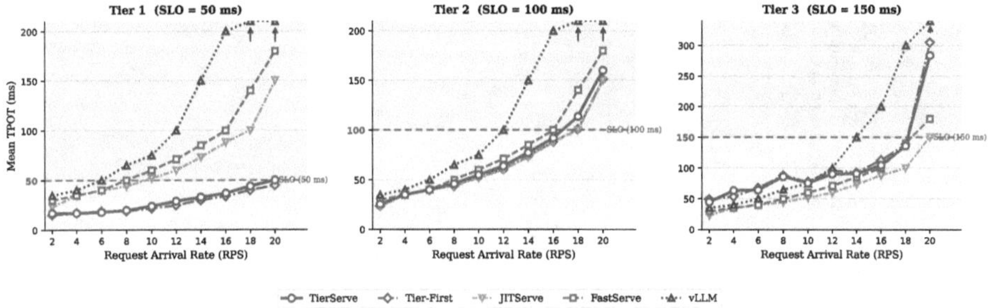

Fig. 4. Mean TPOT per subscription tier vs. RPS. The horizontal dashed line in each subplot marks the tier's SLO threshold. A scheduler satisfies the SLO when its curve remains below the threshold.

Tier 1 (SLO = 50 ms). TierServe and Tier-First are the only schedulers that keep Tier 1 TPOT below the 50 ms threshold across the full RPS range tested. TierServe stays within 50 ms up to RPS = 20, while Tier-First achieves slightly lower TPOT at moderate load owing to its strict budget reservation for Tier 1 requests. JITServe violates the Tier 1 SLO from RPS = 10 onward: although its deadline-driven policy is urgency-aware, it does not distinguish between tiers at equal urgency levels, allowing Tier 2 and Tier 3 requests with coincidentally tight deadlines to consume capacity that should be reserved for Tier 1. FastServe and vLLM degrade more severely: FastServe's preference for short requests diverts resources away from potentially long Tier 1 requests, and vLLM's FCFS ordering provides no latency protection whatsoever. At RPS = 20, FastServe and vLLM reach Tier 1 TPOT values of 180 ms and 450 ms respectively—3.6× and 9× the SLO threshold.

Tier 2 (SLO = 100 ms). The ordering of schedulers for Tier 2 largely mirrors Tier 1, but the contrasts between strategies are less pronounced because the 100 ms SLO affords more scheduling flexibility. TierServe and JITServe both satisfy the Tier 2 SLO up to approximately RPS = 14, after which both exceed 100 ms. TierServe's Tier 2 TPOT closely tracks that of JITServe throughout the load range, reflecting the fact that Tier 2 requests are served from the surplus capacity left over after Tier 1 requests at the current slack threshold have been admitted. Tier-First achieves Tier 2 TPOT values nearly identical to JITServe, as its fixed budget allocation for Tier 2 happens to match the capacity released by Tier 1 under this workload. FastServe and vLLM again show the highest TPOT for Tier 2.

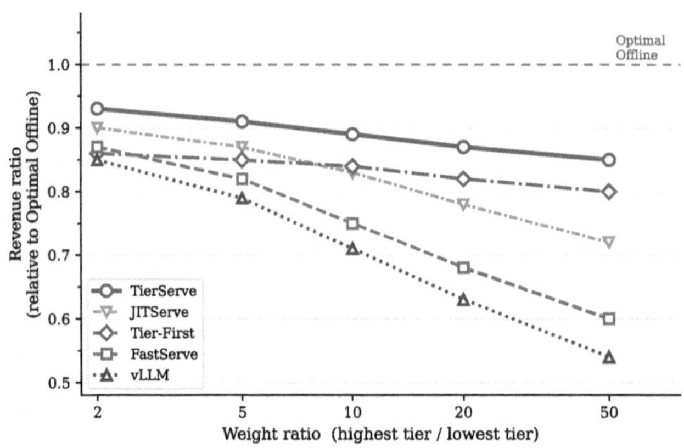

Fig. 5. Sensitivity to Weights.

Tier 3 (SLO = 150 ms). The Tier 3 results reveal the most differentiated behavior across schedulers, and expose the key trade-off between tier isolation and resource efficiency. TierServe serves Tier 3 requests using the capacity released by higher-tier requests with ample SLO slack, naturally improving Tier 3 TPOT without compromising Tier 1 or Tier 2 guarantees. Notably, JITServe achieves the lowest Tier 3 TPOT among all schedulers because its pure deadline-driven policy does not discriminate against low-tier requests: once a Tier 3 request's deadline becomes sufficiently urgent, it receives the same treatment as any other request. This benefit for Tier 3, however, comes at the cost of the Tier 1 SLO violations observed above. FastServe shows unexpectedly low Tier 3 TPOT as well, since its preference for short requests happens to serve many Tier 3 requests early; the improvement in Tier 3 TPOT is thus incidental rather than the result of deliberate priority management. Neither JITServe nor FastServe satisfy the system-level revenue objective, because their favorable Tier 3 performance is achieved by sacrificing high-weight Tier 1 and Tier 2 requests.

Summary. TierServe is the only scheduler that simultaneously satisfies the Tier 1 SLO across all tested RPS values, maintains competitive Tier 2 TPOT, and serves Tier 3 requests with lower TPOT than Tier-First. The tier-slack joint scan achieves this by admitting high-tier requests first at each urgency level, while converting their surplus SLO slack into additional capacity for lower-tier requests—a balance that none of the four baselines can strike.

4.4 Sensitivity to Weights

We vary the weight ratio between Tier 1 and Tier 3 from 2 : 1.5 : 1 (small gap) to 50 : 7 : 1 (large gap), with Tier 2 weight set to the geometric mean of the other two in each case. Figure 5 shows results at the saturation RPS. TierServe's revenue advantage over JITServe grows monotonically with the weight ratio: when high-tier requests are worth substantially more than low-tier ones, the ability to enforce strict tier ordering at equal urgency levels yields larger revenue gains. At the small ratio 2 : 1 : 1, TierServe and JITServe converge to each other, as the revenue difference between serving a Tier 1 versus a Tier 3 request is small enough that tier-agnostic deadline scheduling incurs only a marginal revenue penalty.

4.5 Ablation Study

To understand the contribution of TierServe's key design components, we conduct an ablation study that isolates the effects of subscription-tier priority, SLO slack, and queue structure.

We compare four variants: (1) **Tier-Only**, which enforces strict priority across tiers but does not use slack information (equivalent to Tier-First); (2) **Slack-Only**, which prioritizes requests solely based on urgency (equivalent to deadline-driven scheduling such as JITServe); (3) **TierServe-SQ**, which jointly

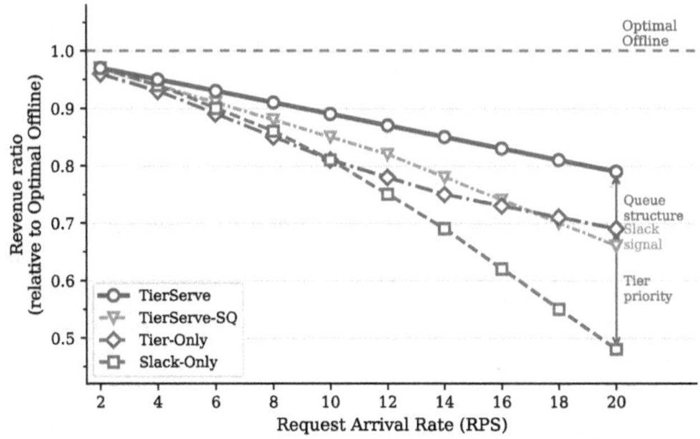

Fig. 6. Ablation Study.

considers both tier priority and slack but organizes all requests into a single priority queue, ranking requests by $\frac{K+1-\text{tier}}{\delta_r}$; and (4) **TierServe**, which maintains per-tier queues and applies the tier-slack joint scheduling algorithm.

Figure 6 shows the revenue ratio under varying load. Tier-Only protects high-tier requests but suffers from underutilization, as surplus slack in higher tiers cannot be exploited by lower tiers. Slack-Only improves efficiency by utilizing slack, but fails to prioritize high-value requests, leading to revenue loss when high-tier requests compete with lower-tier ones.

TierServe-SQ improves over both Tier-Only and Slack-Only by combining tier priority and slack into a unified priority score. However, it still falls short of TierServe. By collapsing all requests into a single queue, TierServe-SQ cannot enforce strict tier dominance at equal urgency levels, and its scalar priority may lead to suboptimal trade-offs between tier and slack. Note that although TierServe-SQ outperforms Tier-Only in most cases, Tier-Only surpasses it at extremely high load, because high-tier requests can saturate a single batch in this case.

In contrast, TierServe consistently achieves the highest revenue by explicitly structuring scheduling as a lexicographic policy over (tier, slack), ensuring that high-value requests are always prioritized while surplus capacity is efficiently utilized.

These results demonstrate that both signals (tier and slack) and the queue structure are critical: combining them in a single scalar priority is insufficient to achieve optimal revenue in multi-tier LLM serving.

5 Related Work

LLM Inference Serving. Early LLM serving systems focus on maximizing goodput or minimizing latencies through continuous batching and efficient memory management [17]. Orca [19] introduces iteration-level scheduling for continuous batching. vLLM [11] proposes PagedAttention to eliminate KV cache fragmentation. Sarathi-Serve [2]uses chunked prefill to reduce prefill–decode interference. DistServe [21] disaggregates the two phases across separate GPU pools. These systems optimize throughput or goodput uniformly across all requests, with no awareness of differential client revenue contribution.

Latency-aware and SLO-driven Scheduling. Several recent works incorporate latency constraints into scheduling [8,9]. Niyama [6] interpolates between EDF and SRPF across QoS classes. JITServe [20] schedules purely by deadline proximity. While these methods improve SLO attainment, they optimize the *count* of satisfied requests rather than weighted revenue, and do not distinguish between tiers at equal urgency levels.

Priority and Multi-class Scheduling. FastServe [18] uses multi-level feedback queues based on input length to approximate SJF and reduce head-of-line blocking. LTR [5] learns to rank requests by predicted output length to improve average job completion time. Both approaches use request length as a proxy for scheduling priority, which does not correlate with client revenue. DynamoLLM [15] addresses heterogeneous SLOs in the context of energy efficiency, dynamically scaling GPU frequency and instance count based on workload type. TierServe differs from all the above by treating subscription tier as an explicit, first-class scheduling dimension and optimizing weighted revenue as the primary objective.

6 Conclusion

We presented TierServe, a revenue-driven scheduler for multi-tier LLM inference. We showed that conventional schedulers optimize SLO attainment rather than operator revenue, leading to suboptimal resource allocation across heterogeneous clients. TierServe addresses this gap by jointly leveraging subscription-tier priority and per-request SLO slack, aligning scheduling decisions with both business value and latency urgency. Experimental results demonstrate that TierServe consistently improves revenue over state-of-the-art baselines across a wide range of workloads and load conditions. We believe that revenue maximization deserves greater attention as a first-class objective in LLM serving research, alongside the throughput and goodput metrics that currently dominate the field.

Acknowledgment. We sincerely thank all the anonymous reviewers for their valuable comments and feedback. This work was supported by the National Natural Science Foundation of China (No. U24A20234 & No.62502302). Corresponding authors are Minyi Guo and Xiaofeng Hou.

The technical solution and experimental design presented in this paper were independently completed by the authors. AI tools were used solely for language polishing and formatting optimization, and did not participate in the development of the research ideas or core content.

References

1. Agrawal, A., et al.: Vidur: a large-scale simulation framework for LLM inference. In: Proceedings of Machine Learning and Systems (MLSys), vol. 6, pp. 351–366 (2024)
2. Agrawal, A., et al.: Taming throughput-latency tradeoff in LLM inference with Sarathi-Serve. In: 18th USENIX Symposium on Operating Systems Design and Implementation (OSDI 24), pp. 117–134. USENIX Association (2024)
3. Bari, A.: Optimal Scheduling Algorithms for LLM Inference: Theory and Practice (2025)
4. Dubey, A., Jauhri, A., Pandey, A., Kadian, A., Al-Dahle, A., Letman, A., et al.: The Llama 3 herd of models (2024). https://arxiv.org/abs/2407.21783
5. Fu, Y., et al.: Efficient LLM scheduling by learning to rank. In: Advances in Neural Information Processing Systems (NeurIPS) (2024)
6. Goel, K., Mohan, J., Kwatra, N., Anupindi, R.S., Ramjee, R.: Niyama: breaking the silos of LLM inference serving (2025)

7. Hong, K., et al.: SOLA: optimizing SLO attainment for large language model serving with state-aware scheduling. In: Eighth Conference on Machine Learning and Systems (MLSys) (2025)
8. Hou, X., Li, C., Liu, J., Zhang, L., Hu, Y., Guo, M.: Ant-man: towards agile power management in the microservice era. International Conference for High Performance Computing, Networking, Storage and Analysis (SC), pp. 1–14 (2020)
9. Hou, X., et al.: Alphar: learning-powered resource management for irregular, dynamic microservice graph. In: IEEE International Parallel and Distributed Processing Symposium (IPDPS), pp. 797–806 (2021)
10. Huang, J., Xiong, Y., Yu, X., Huang, W., Li, E., Zeng, L., Chen, X.: SLO-aware scheduling for large language model inferences (2025)
11. Kwon, W., et al.: Efficient memory management for large language model serving with PagedAttention. In: Proceedings of the 29th ACM Symposium on Operating Systems Principles (SOSP '23), pp. 611–626. ACM (2023)
12. Liu, J., et al.: A survey on inference optimization techniques for mixture of experts models. ACM Comput. Surv. **58**(10), 1–37 (2026)
13. Microsoft Azure: AzureLLMInferenceTrace2023. Azure Public Dataset (2023). https://github.com/Azure/AzurePublicDataset
14. ShareGPT Contributors: ShareGPT_Vicuna_unfiltered. Hugging Face Datasets (2023). https://huggingface.co/datasets/anon8231489123/ShareGPT_Vicuna_unfiltered
15. Stojkovic, J., Zhang, C., Goiri, Í., Torrellas, J., Choukse, E.: Dynamollm: designing LLM inference clusters for performance and energy efficiency. In: 2025 IEEE International Symposium on High Performance Computer Architecture (HPCA), pp. 1348–1362. IEEE (2025)
16. Sun, B., et al.: Llumnix: dynamic scheduling for large language model serving. In: 18th USENIX Symposium on Operating Systems Design and Implementation (OSDI 24), pp. 173–192. USENIX Association (2024)
17. Tang, P., et al.: Moe-apex: an efficient MOE inference system with adaptive precision expert offloading. In: Proceedings of the 31st ACM International Conference on Architectural Support for Programming Languages and Operating Systems (ASPLOS) (2026)
18. Wu, B., Zhong, Y., Zhang, Z., Huang, G., Liu, X., Jin, X.: Fast distributed inference serving for large language models (2023)
19. Yu, G.I., Jeong, J.S., Kim, G.W., Kim, S., Chun, B.G.: Orca: a distributed serving system for transformer-based generative models. In: 16th USENIX Symposium on Operating Systems Design and Implementation (OSDI 22), pp. 521–538. USENIX Association (2022)
20. Zhang, W., et al.: Jitserve: Slo-aware LLM serving with imprecise request information. arXiv:2504.20068 arXiv preprint (2025)
21. Zhong, Y., et al.: DistServe: disaggregating prefill and decoding for goodput-optimized large language model serving. In: 18th USENIX Symposium on Operating Systems Design and Implementation (OSDI 24), pp. 193–210. USENIX Association (2024)

Identifying Iso-Cost Sweet Spot Configurations for Cloud OLAP Queries

Weitao Wan[1], Huanchen Zhang[1,2], and Mingyu Gao[1,2](✉)

[1] Tsinghua University, Beijing, China
wwt22@mails.tsinghua.edu.cn, {huanchen,gaomy}@tsinghua.edu.cn
[2] Shanghai Qi Zhi Institute, Shanghai, China

Abstract. Cloud-native OLAP systems run queries on virtual machine clusters. While pricing scales linearly with the virtual core count, query performance does *not*. Therefore it is critical to identify the best performing sweet spot among many iso-cost configurations, e.g., 4 nodes of 32 cores each vs. 64 nodes of 2 cores each. In this work, we aim to comprehensively understand what are the key factors of the underlying hardware and the executing query that determine the performance trade-off, and use them to help identify the iso-cost sweet spot configuration. We conduct extensive experiments using Presto, running dozens of queries across five AWS EC2 instance families. We empirically find that mid-range instances usually outperform both extremes. But the exact profile is highly dependent on instance families, determined by the hardware chiplet organization as well as the available network bandwidth. Furthermore, certain query-level characteristics, including data skewness, plan complexity, and shuffle intensity, can shift the sweet spots. Finally, we distill these findings into insightful lessons for future query engine design, including chiplet-aware parallelism planning, cluster sizing as a skew mitigation lever, and structural isolation of straggler propagation.

Keywords: cloud computing · OLAP · resource configuration · performance analysis

1 Introduction

Cloud-native online analytical query processing (OLAP) systems have recently emerged as a cost-efficient way to host database applications [5,8,17]. The query engine can leverage parallel computing resources in the form of virtual machine (VM) clusters, while data reside in object stores that are disaggregated from the computing [14,22]. This approach offers many unique advantages including high elasticity, high availability, on-demand cost, etc. when compared to traditional database infrastructures.

On current cloud platforms such as AWS EC2, the per-hour VM pricing scales linearly with the virtual CPU (vCPU) count. For example, in the AWS `r7i` family, 4 × `r7i.8xlarge` (32 vCPUs each) costs the same per hour as 64 × `r7i.large`

L. Eeckhout et al. (Eds.): APPT 2026, LNCS 16693, pp. 157–171, 2027.
https://doi.org/10.1007/978-981-92-4805-6_11

(2 vCPUs each); both configurations hold 128 total vCPUs and identical total memory. We call such VM clusters *iso-cost configurations*. As a result, spending the same budget can purchase VM clusters of very different configurations, among which some run substantially faster than the others for specific OLAP queries. Choosing the wrong configurations would waste substantial budget and also risk missing strict user-facing latency targets [27].

It thus remains an important question *how to choose the most appropriate cluster for a given query among the iso-cost configurations*. This decision is non-trivial because no single choice fits all. The performance profile is highly dependent on specific query behaviors as well as hardware types; any fixed policy would likely leave performance on the table for a certain portion of thousands of daily queries. Existing approaches either predict good configurations without explaining why they work [1,7,12], or characterize hardware effects in isolation without connecting them to query-level configuration choices [10,15]. What is missing is a comprehensive study about *which underlying mechanisms of the query and the hardware* actually govern the performance trade-off.

In this paper, we conduct such a study using a state-of-the-art engine Presto [22], running TPC-H [23] and TPC-DS [24] across five AWS EC2 instance families. We draw several insightful findings (Sect. 3). First, we observe a general pattern: for most queries, mid-range instances usually outperform both extremes. We call this optimum the *iso-cost sweet spot*. Second, the exact location of the sweet spot is dependent on hardware instance families. This is mainly due to *different microarchitecture designs, particularly the chiplet hierarchy within each processor*. On AMD instance families like `r7a` and `r6a`, a sharp per-core bandwidth drop at the chiplet boundary pushes the sweet spot to smaller instances, while Intel's tiled design (e.g., `r7i`) produces an architecturally milder boundary, and the iso-cost sweet spot profile resembles monolithic processors like `r6i`. Besides, network-enhanced instances like `r6in` differ from the general pattern: large instances are the fastest, while small instances exhibit elevated instability. Third, when fixing the instance family and executing different queries, some query-level characteristics may also shift the sweet spots: *data skewness and plan complexity* favor larger instances, while *shuffle intensity* favors smaller ones.

We distill the above findings into lessons for future query engine design guidelines and cluster-sizing tools (Sect. 4). We argue that, the chiplet topology should be considered to inform parallelism decisions beyond the raw vCPU count; cluster sizing should be treated as a first-class skew mitigation lever; and engine-level design changes can reduce the impact of straggler cascades. The indicators identified in our findings can further serve as extra decisive features for machine-learning-based configuration advisor methods.

2 Experimental Methodology

Our experiments use Presto [22], a representative SQL query engine, with the Prestissimo/Velox C++ backend [19], on AWS EC2 cloud. We use five memory-optimized instance families, covering two AMD chiplet architectures (AMD

Table 1. AWS EC2 `r6in` iso-cost configurations at 128 total vCPUs.

Instance Type	vCPUs	Memory	Baseline BW	Burst BW	Nodes
`r6in.large`	2	16 GiB	3.125 Gbps	Up to 25 Gbps	64
`r6in.xlarge`	4	32 GiB	6.25 Gbps	Up to 30 Gbps	32
`r6in.2xlarge`	8	64 GiB	12.5 Gbps	Up to 40 Gbps	16
`r6in.4xlarge`	16	128 GiB	25 Gbps	Up to 50 Gbps	8
`r6in.8xlarge`	32	256 GiB	50 Gbps	50 Gbps	4

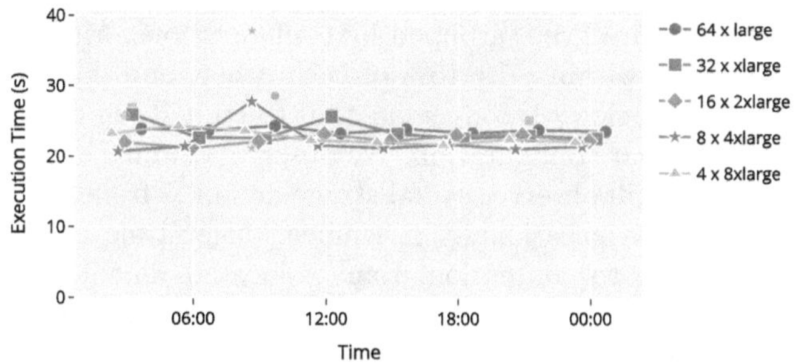

Fig. 1. Execution time of TPC-DS Q23-pruned on `r7i` with multiple executions over 24 h. Each point is one measured run, grouped by configurations.

Genoa `r7a`, AMD Milan `r6a`), an Intel tiled architecture (Sapphire Rapids `r7i`), an Intel monolithic architecture (Ice Lake `r6i`), and a network-enhanced monolithic variant (`r6in`). Within each family we build five iso-cost clusters at 128 total vCPUs, from 64 nodes of `large` to 4 nodes of `8xlarge`. Table 1 shows the `r6in` family as a representative example; other families have similar specifications at roughly half the absolute network bandwidth.

We run TPC-H [23] and TPC-DS [24], at the scale factor 1000 (∼295 GB in the Parquet file format) with data from Amazon S3. We restrict our analysis to queries whose physical plans remain identical across all the five iso-cost configurations in each family. Depending on resources such as per-node memory, Presto's optimizer may choose different join strategies (e.g., broadcast vs. partitioned) across configurations. By keeping the plan fixed, we focus on the hardware and query factors that determine performance. Comparing different configurations, each with its own best plan, is outside our scope. After filtering, 12 of 22 TPC-H queries and 29 of 60 TPC-DS queries are kept.

We perform parameter tuning on the Presto engine to avoid several performance pitfalls when it runs on our used instances. We find three engine parameters need adjustments. First, we reduce the output batch size of inter-worker data exchange from 10 MB to 2 MB. Smaller batches distribute received data across more threads and reduce per-batch initialization overhead. Second, we reduce the maximum data partition (split) size from 256 MB to 32 MB. The finer granularity reduces data-dependent load imbalance across workers. Third, we enable task-level split scheduling to replace the default node-level accounting. Under the default policy, a large scan stage occupies the node's global split counter and starves other stages of the same query that share the node; task-level scheduling eliminates this interference.

We verify the tuned baseline with TPC-DS Q23-pruned (Appendix A), a hand-simplified probe query with balanced data, low shuffle volume, and simple plan. These nice characteristics should produce nearly identical performance across our iso-cost configurations. To account for temporal variation, we launch fresh clusters every few hours over a 24-h window, perform warm-up runs, and record at least five measured runs per session. Figure 1 shows the result on `r7i`: each point is one measured run, grouped by configurations. Medians across the five configurations fall within ~10–15% of each other, and no configuration is systematically fastest or slowest, confirming that the tuned engine does not inherently favor any particular configuration. We observe a similar trend on `r7a` and `r6i`. Nevertheless, we still observe several straggler spikes from the experiments, where an individual run occasionally has much longer time than the median. We suspect this is due to contention from co-located tenants or unfavorable task placement on physical servers. When a single worker degrades, the penalty does not stay local: Presto's shared `PartitionedOutput` buffer back-pressures all producers uniformly, so the degradation cascades into a cluster-wide stall. Shuffle-heavy queries exhibit a second source of instability, network burst credit depletion, analyzed later in Sect. 3.3. As a result, a single run may produce misleading results. All reported numbers throughout the paper are medians across sessions with interquartile range (IQR) error bars.

3 Observation and Analysis of Iso-Cost Sweet Spot

In this section, we describe the key observations regarding the sweet-spot configurations across the 41 queries running on the well-tuned query engine from Sect. 2, using multiple hardware instance families at iso cost. We first summarize a general observation in Sect. 3.1. Then we compare different instance families (Sect. 3.2), as well as different queries on the same instance family (Sect. 3.3), and analyze their deviations from the general pattern.

3.1 General Pattern

Figure 2 shows the normalized execution time for the 12 TPC-H queries on `r7i`; the 29 TPC-DS queries exhibit the same pattern with similar magnitudes, and are omitted due to space limit. Every query exhibits measurable configuration sensitivity. Even Q04, the least sensitive query here, runs 11% slower on its worst configuration than on its best. For 10 of the 12 TPC-H queries, the optimum sits at 16 × `2xlarge` or 32 × `xlarge`, while the two extremes are consistently the slowest. Therefore the iso-cost sweet spot is clear: *both the small-node and large-node extremes are inferior to the middle, and the advantage of the mid-range holds across the full query set rather than appearing on one or two queries only.*

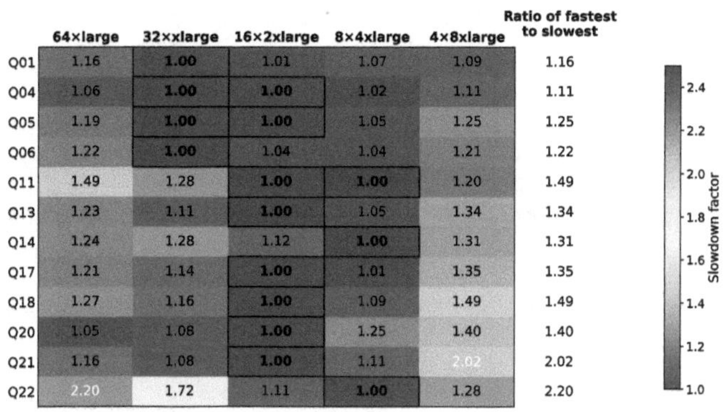

Fig. 2. Normalized execution time of TPC-H queries on `r7i`. Each row is a query. The fastest configuration for each query is marked as 1.00.

3.2 Differences Among Instance Families

Although the sweet spot pattern appears on every family we tested, its shape and the sweet-spot location differ widely; i.e., *the sweet-spot profile is family-specific.* In Fig. 3, we vary the instance family used, while keeping the same query of Q23-full (a complex multi-stage TPC-DS query). On AMD `r7a`, the optimum is $16 \times$ `2xlarge`, and larger instances become worse. On Intel `r7i` and `r6i`, the optimum shifts to $8 \times$ `4xlarge` with fewer but larger instances. Network-enhanced `r6in` breaks this pattern entirely.

We attribute these variations among instance families to their microarchitecture differences, particularly the *chiplet boundaries.* Table 2 summarizes the architecture for each family. Specifically, on AMD `r7a`, the individual cores within a single physical socket are distributed into multiple chiplets, a.k.a., core complex dies (CCDs) in AMD's terminology. Each CCD has a fixed link to the off-chip memory controllers. The CCD boundary of `r7a` falls at 8 physical cores, i.e., `2xlarge`. Doubling from `xlarge` to `2xlarge` activates a full CCD, saturates the link to memory, and drops per-vCPU bandwidth by nearly half, as shown in Fig. 4(a). In contrast, on Intel `r7i` in Fig. 4(b), a milder drop occurs at `8xlarge`, where the instance spans two or more tiles and cross-tile accesses incur additional latency. The two monolithic families not shown (`r6i` and `r6in`) have per-vCPU bandwidth roughly constant across sizes.

The MLC measurement establishes what the hardware delivers in isolation. To connect it to query-level behaviors, we further look into actual CPU time of query execution. If the per-vCPU throughput were constant across iso-cost configurations, the total CPU time across workers would be equal, because the configurations share the same number of total vCPUs and process the same data. Any deviations point to per-vCPU efficiency loss. Figure 5 applies this test to TPC-DS Q28, a shuffle-intensive query, on four families. Both AMD families show a staircase: on `r7a` (hyperthreading off), the CPU time rises from `2xlarge`, coinciding with the CCD boundary; on `r6a` (hyperthreading on), the

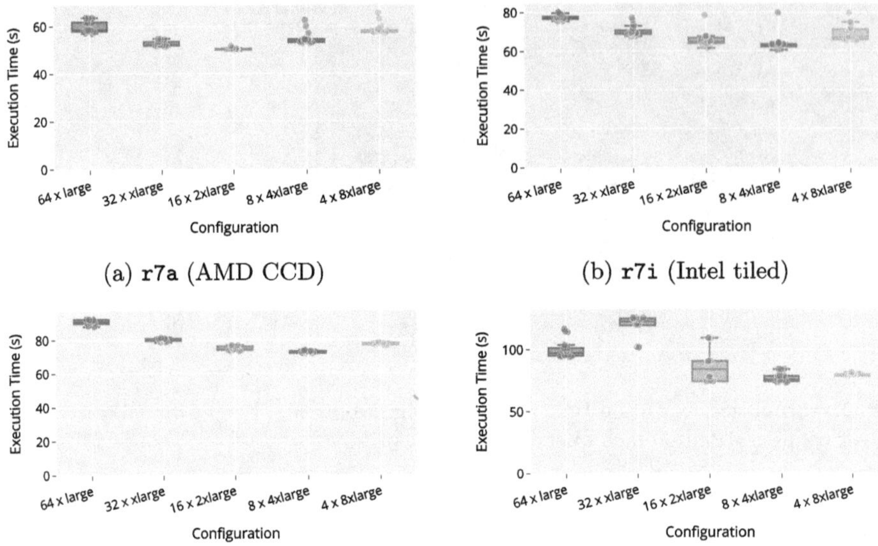

(a) **r7a** (AMD CCD) (b) **r7i** (Intel tiled)

(c) **r6i** (Intel monolithic) (d) **r6in** (network-enhanced)

Fig. 3. Execution time of TPC-DS Q23-full on four instance families.

rise starts at `4xlarge`, shifted by one size because hyperthreading doubles the vCPUs per CCD. On Intel tiled `r7i` and monolithic `r6i`, the CPU time stays flat. The difference between AMD and Intel chiplet designs is consistent with their memory-controller placement: AMD routes all memory traffic through a shared I/O die, so crossing a CCD boundary increases contention sharply, whereas Intel Sapphire Rapids integrates memory controllers into each tile, producing a more homogeneous bandwidth distribution [10]. Intel's tile boundary, although visible in MLC throughput as a mild per-vCPU drop (Fig. 4(b)), does not translate into significant per-vCPU efficiency loss at the query level. The staircase is also query-dependent on AMD: TPC-DS Q09, another shuffle-intensive query, shows flat CPU time on both `r7a` and `r6a`, just as it does on `r7i`. The difference likely

Table 2. Microarchitecture and chiplet boundary of the instance families. The L3 cache capacity per core is reported at `8xlarge`.

Family	Architecture	Hyperthreading	Chiplet Boundary	L3/core
`r7a`	AMD CCD (8c)	Off	`2xlarge` (CCD sat.)	4.0 MB
`r6a`	AMD CCD (8c)	On	`4xlarge` (CCD sat.)	4.0 MB
`r7i`	Intel tiled (12c)	On	`8xlarge` (cross-tile)	6.6 MB
`r6i`	Intel monolithic	On	-	3.4 MB
`r6in`	Intel monolithic	On	-	3.4 MB

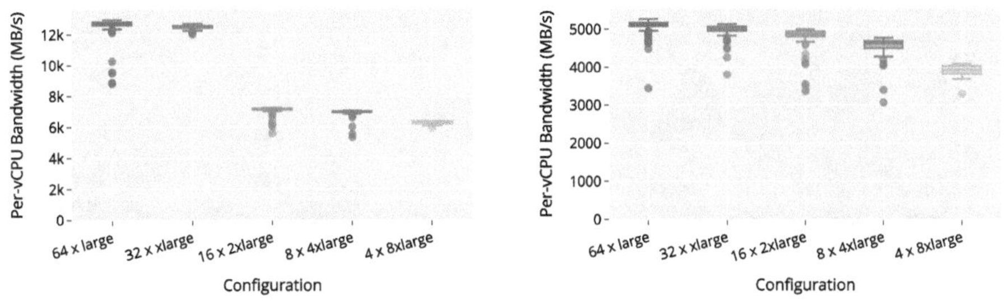

(a) `r7a` (AMD CCD) (b) `r7i` (Intel tiled)

Fig. 4. Per-vCPU memory bandwidth on two instance families. Measured using Intel Memory Latency Checker (MLC) [13], with a 2:1 read-to-write ratio, a 1 GB buffer that bypasses all caches.

reflects operator mix, as Q28's operators are more memory-bandwidth sensitive than Q09's. We investigate more query-specific behaviors in Sect. 3.3.

The families above all use standard network bandwidth. Network-enhanced `r6in` shares `r6i`'s monolithic Ice Lake die, but provides roughly twice the baseline bandwidth at every size (Table 1). Figure 3(d) shows that, the performance of Q23-full on `r6in` improves monotonically (with abnormal `xlarge`) toward larger instances, breaking the general sweet-spot pattern. Figure 6 confirms the trend on two additional queries. On all the three queries, the two smallest configurations are consistently the slowest; on Q23-full, `xlarge` burns ~30% more aggregate CPU time than `4xlarge` despite the monolithic die. This instability does not appear on `r6i`, which shares the same Ice Lake die, pointing to the network-enhanced Nitro configuration rather than the CPU as the likely cause.

3.3 Differences Among Queries

Next we examine why some individual queries deviate from the common pattern of each instance family. We discover two key factors: *data skewness and plan complexity* may push the optimum of a query toward larger instances, while *shuffle intensity* can push it toward smaller instances.

Small-Instance Penalties: Data Skewness and Plan Complexity. With a distributed query engine spanning multiple nodes like ours, the data partitions (splits) that are initially of comparable byte sizes may develop into vastly different sizes at downstream. For example, a date-range filter can eliminate most rows from some partitions, but almost none from others; a hash repartition may concentrate data onto a few receivers if the data distribution is highly skewed.

Such data skew could lead to significantly different performance impacts on different configurations. With many small workers each receiving few partitions, a worker that draws a disproportionately heavy one becomes a straggler. With fewer large workers each receiving many partitions, statistical averaging could potentially flatten out the imbalance.

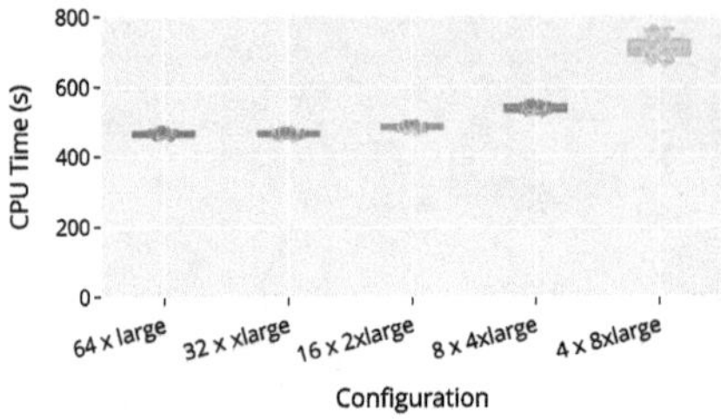

(a) **r7a** (AMD CCD, HT off)

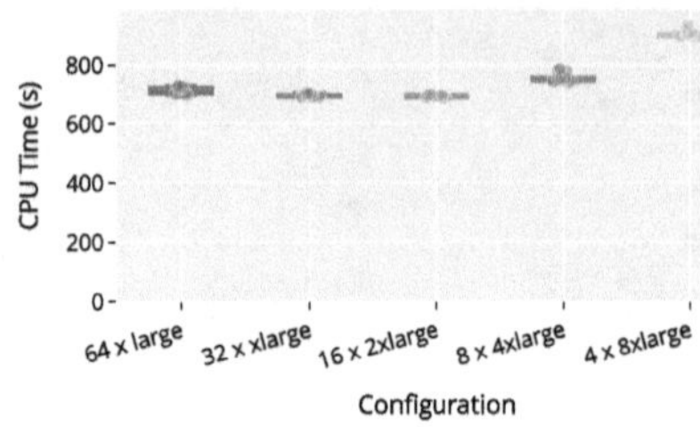

(b) **r6a** (AMD CCD, HT on)

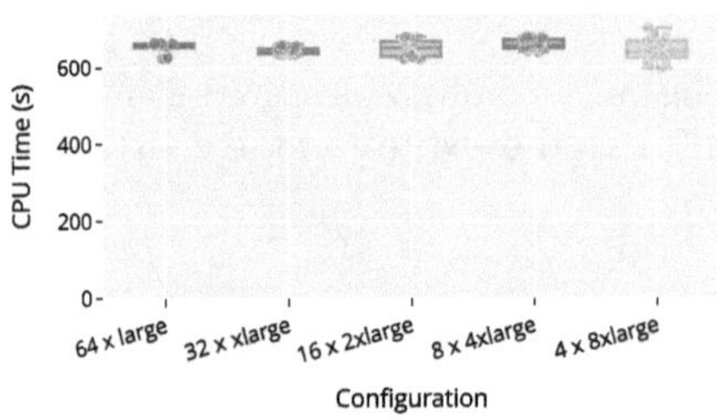

(c) **r7i** (Intel tiled)

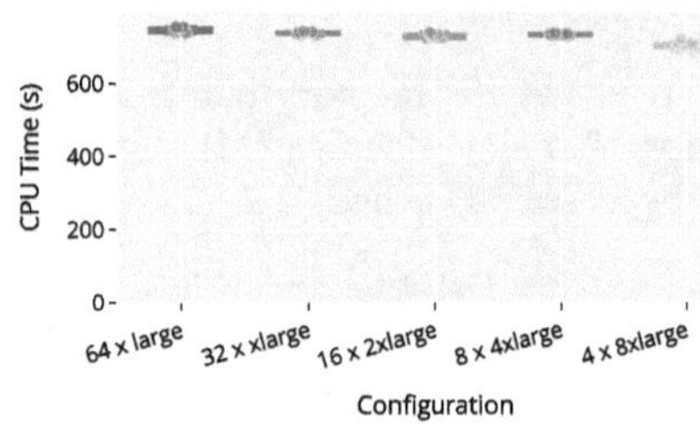

(d) **r6i** (Intel monolithic)

Fig. 5. CPU time of TPC-DS Q28 on four instance families.

Figure 7(a) shows TPC-DS Q22 on `r7i`. Q22 scans a fact table filtered to a 12-month date range. The data generator produces rows in chronological order, so row groups overlapping the target period retain nearly all their rows, while others produce almost nothing, yielding per-task output variation of $\sim$80$\times$ on `xlarge`. Execution time improves monotonically from 64 $\times$ `large` to 4 $\times$ `8xlarge`, a 2.5$\times$ speedup at identical cost. The run-to-run variance also shrinks at the same time, because each worker now averages over enough splits to stabilize against unlucky assignments. Figure 7(b) shows the same query on `r7a`. Performance improves through `2xlarge` but plateaus beyond it, and `8xlarge` is marginally slower than `4xlarge`. The plateau coincides with the CCD boundary, where per-vCPU memory bandwidth drops and offsets the skew absorption gain. On `r7i`, where the bandwidth drop is milder, Q22 improves all the way to `8xlarge`.

Q22's skew is statistical: random split assignment determines per-worker load, so more splits per worker always helps. On the other hand, TPC-DS Q67 has a different structure: a Window operator partitions by the product category, of which TPC-DS defines only 10 categories. The improvement saturates once the worker count approaches the key-space size, and the optimum on `r7i` falls at 8 $\times$ `4xlarge` rather than at the largest instance.

Besides data skewness, query plan complexity produces another independent small-instance penalty. Presto schedules each pipeline stage as a set of drivers on a per-node thread pool. When the plan has many concurrent stages, the total driver count exceeds the available threads and some drivers must be queued for execution. The penalty is severe on small instances: on 64 $\times$ `large`, each node

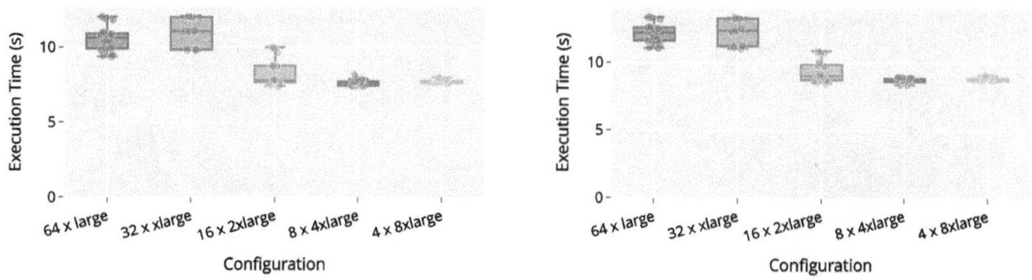

(a) Q28 (b) Q09

Fig. 6. Execution time of TPC-DS Q28 and Q09 on `r6in`, both of which do not follow the sweet-spot pattern.

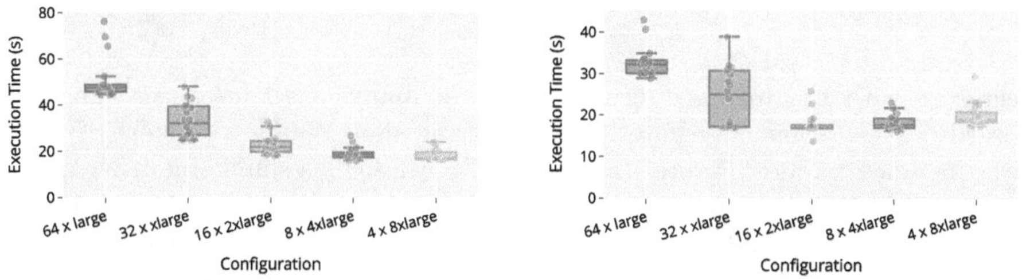

(a) Q22 on `r7i` (b) Q22 on `r7a`

Fig. 7. Execution time of TPC-DS Q22 on `r7i` (a) and `r7a` (b).

has only 2 vCPUs, and the thread pool is tiny. As a concrete example, Q23-full and Q23-pruned share the same data and core query logic, but differ in the plan structure: Q23-full has many concurrent pipeline stages, while Q23-pruned has few. While Q23-pruned achieves near iso-performance across configurations (only ~10–15% difference, Fig. 1), Q23-full on `r7i` is roughly 30% slower on 64 × `large` than on 8 × `4xlarge`. Figure 8 shows the diagnostic: on Q23-full, critical-path stages spend ~25% of their non-blocked time queued for a CPU thread on 64 × `large`, falling to ~15% on 4 × `8xlarge`; on Q23-pruned the corresponding waiting is below 1% at all sizes. The queuing also cascades: stages that progress slowly consume exchange buffer data at a reduced rate, eventually blocking upstream stages due to full buffers. The aggregate CPU time confirms this diagnosis. On Q23-full, the highest CPU time is on the largest instances (per-vCPU memory overhead from Sect. 3.2), while the longest wall-clock time is on the smallest. The two metrics point in opposite directions, confirming that queuing, not extra computation, is what penalizes small-instance configurations on complex plans.

Large-Instance Penalties: Shuffle and Network Tier. Shuffle-heavy queries push in the opposite direction. As shown in Table 1, iso-cost configurations share the same aggregate *baseline* network bandwidth, but the *burst* bandwidth per vCPU

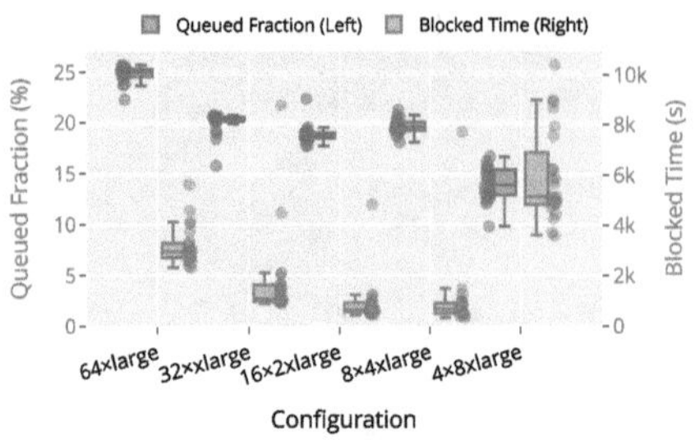

(a) Q23-full, critical-path stages

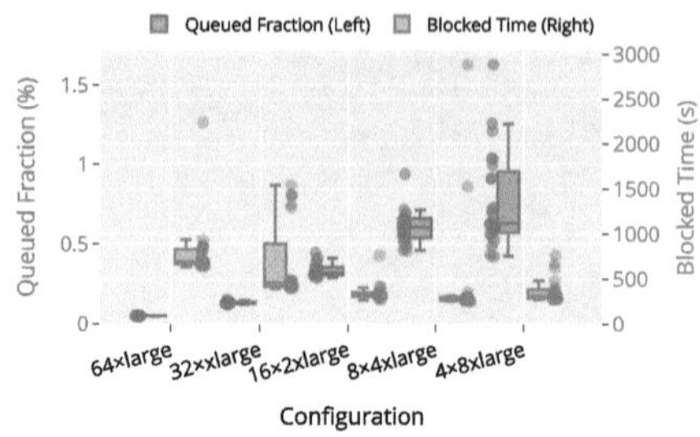

(b) Q23-pruned, corresponding stages

Fig. 8. Queued time fraction (left axis) and blocked time (right axis) of critical-path pipeline stages in TPC-DS Q23-full (a) and Q23-pruned (b) on `r7i`.

decreases with the instance size. Clusters of many small instances can temporarily exceed their aggregate baseline during short shuffles; clusters of a few large instances cannot. Figure 9(a) shows TPC-DS Q80, a shuffle-intensive query, on `r7i`. Table 1 shows that `8xlarge` is the only size whose baseline bandwidth equals its burst one and hence has no burst headroom; for Q80's shuffle volume, this fixed bandwidth is insufficient, making $4 \times$ `8xlarge` consistently the slowest when comparing the best runs of each configuration. Smaller configurations can burst above their baselines, but the burst capacity is governed by a credit mechanism: credits accumulate during low-traffic periods and deplete under sustained shuffle. Figure 10a shows the consequence over 24 h, plotting per-run execution time in (a) alongside aggregate cluster network throughput in (b). The two plots are complementary: latency spikes coincide with throughput drops. The effect is most visible on `xlarge` and `2xlarge`, whose burst headroom is large enough that credit depletion causes pronounced swings. TPC-DS Q28, Q80, and TPC-H Q17, along with seven other queries across both benchmarks, exhibit this pattern on standard-bandwidth families.

Large instances are slow on shuffle-heavy queries because their aggregate baseline bandwidth is too low, not because they are large. On network-enhanced `r6in`, which is of the same size but provides roughly twice the baseline network bandwidth (e.g., reaching 50 Gbps at `8xlarge`), the bottleneck disappears. Figure 9(b) shows Q80 on `r6in`: the bimodality is absent and performance improves monotonically with instance size.

4 Lessons and Discussions

From the observations and analyses in the previous section, we draw several insightful lessons that can potentially guide future cloud OLAP system designs.

Parallelism Planners Should be Aware of Hardware Chiplet Topology. On AMD families the chiplet boundary dominates the sweet-spot profile (Sect. 3.2), yet existing query engines set their parallelism based on vCPU count

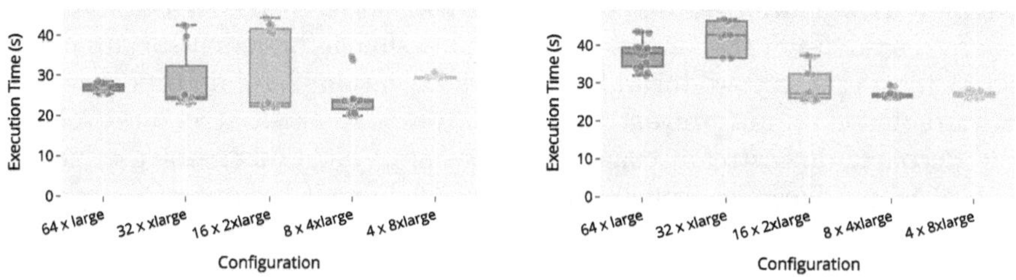

(a) r7i (standard) (b) r6in (network-enhanced)

Fig. 9. Execution time of TPC-DS Q80 on standard r7i (a) and network-enhanced r6in (b).

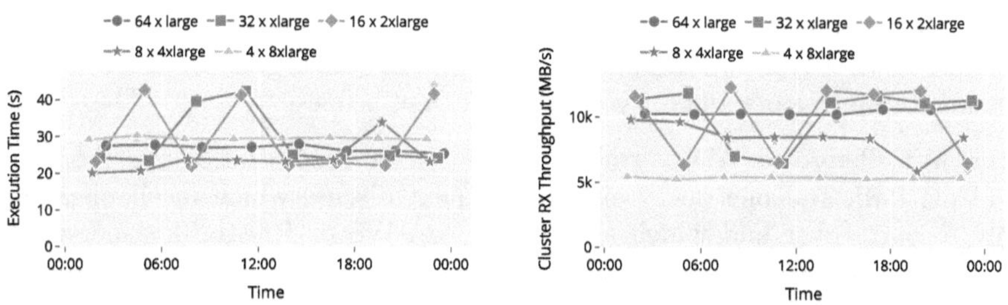

(a) Q80 latency time series (b) Aggregate cluster network RX

Fig. 10. Latency time series (a) and aggregate network throughput (b) of TPC-DS Q80 on r7i over 24 h.

alone. The chiplet boundary is a fixed, readable property of the instance family. So the engine can easily inspect this information at startup, and choose worker count and per-worker parallelism accordingly, extending the single-machine observation of Fogli et al. [10] to cluster sizing.

Node Instability Should be an Input To Placement, not Just a Dashboard Metric. Both burst credit depletion (Sect. 3.3) and memory-side contention straggler cascades (Sect. 2) are observable at runtime, yet existing engines log these signals without acting on them. Feeding them into an online, dynamic scheduler could avoid assigning shuffle-heavy stages to credit-depleted nodes and memory-sensitive operators to degraded workers.

Cluster Sizing is a First-Class Lever for Skew Mitigation. Prior skew mitigation approaches [2,21] work inside the engine. Figure 7 has shown that simply reducing the worker count of Q22 from 64 to 4 yields a 2.5× speedup at iso cost with no engine-side adaptation. Consequently, we argue that skew mitigation should not be confined to engine-internal algorithms; future research could also incorporate cluster-sizing knobs.

Straggler Isolation Should be Structural, not Statistical. The back-pressure cascade in Sect. 2 shows that shared exchange buffers associate cluster progress to the slowest producer. Speculative execution [2,20] detects slow tasks afterwards but does not prevent the buffer from stalling. A structural solution would decouple downstream consumers from any single upstream producer so that healthy producers continue while a degraded one is bypassed.

Machine-Learning-based Configuration Advisors can Use our Newly Discovered Mechanisms as Extra Model Features. Current advisors [1,7,12] treat configuration selection as a black box with vCPU count and price as the only features, limiting transfer across workloads and families. Our results supply four concrete features: (1) chiplet boundary location, (2) network bandwidth tier, (3) skewness profile, and (4) shuffle intensity. Among them, (1) and (2) are readable from the instance family, while (3) and (4) are computable from the query plan. We have not built such an advisor, but argue that these features, combined with certain machine learning methods, would give predictive tools a principled way to generalize beyond their current scopes.

Generality Beyond AWS and Presto. Our current results come from one cloud platform and one query engine. We next discuss which mechanisms are likely to carry over and which are specific to AWS or Presto. The per-vCPU memory-bandwidth cliff is not specific to AWS, because it comes from the processor architecture: the same AMD EPYC and Intel Xeon chips are used by other cloud providers [11,18]. The VM performance instability is not AWS-specific, either, as prior studies report similar variability across providers [6,16]. For network behavior, size-dependent bandwidth limits and a network-enhanced tier are common across major clouds [9]. However, the burst-credit instability is specific to AWS's network credit mechanism. For engine behavior, skew can interact with cluster sizes in any partition-parallel engine, but the effect is weaker when the engine repartitions skew at runtime. Spark does so through adaptive query execution [3,4,26], whereas Presto does not perform comparable runtime repartitioning. The plan-complexity penalty and the straggler cascade, however, are more specific to Presto and may not appear in other engines.

5 Related Work

This work investigates the efficiency of various cloud instance configurations when running OLAP queries. Two categories of prior research are relevant to our study. The first is cloud configuration selection. Predictive tools [1,7,12] sample configurations and model the latency-cost surface but do not explain why one configuration outperforms another, limiting their generalization across workloads and families. Analytical frameworks [15,25] characterize trade-off dimensions in closed-form models but do not connect them to query-level behaviors on a real engine. Neither approach has connected microarchitectural mechanisms to query-level outcomes. The second category is infrastructure characterization. Fogli et al. [10] characterize chiplet effects on OLAP processing on a single physical machine; our analysis extends theirs to a cloud setting where the instance size is the tunable parameter. Data skewness mitigation via adaptive partitioning [21] or speculative execution [2,20] treats skewness as a query-level symptom; our observation that skewness interacts with granularity is complementary.

6 Conclusion

Given a fixed budget for a query, should a cloud-native OLAP system use fewer large VMs or many small ones? We study this question by running two benchmark suites on a Presto tenant across five families of AWS EC2 instances. We find that the answer depends on the hardware: mid-range instances usually outperform both extremes on standard-bandwidth instances, with AMD's chiplet boundary noticeably shifting the optimum toward smaller instances, while on network-enhanced families, larger instances are faster. Query-level characteristics, such as data skewness, plan complexity, and shuffle intensity, also affect the sweet spot. The above indicators of the hardware and the query should be leveraged in cluster sizing decisions, potentially with the help of machine learning.

Acknowledgments. The authors thank the anonymous reviewers for their valuable suggestions, and the Tsinghua IDEAL group members for constructive discussion. Mingyu Gao is the corresponding author. The technical solution and experimental design presented in this paper were independently completed by the authors. AI tools were used solely for language polishing and formatting optimization, and did not participate in the development of the research ideas or core content.

A TPC-DS Q23-Pruned: Baseline Validation Query

Q23-pruned is a hand-simplified version of TPC-DS Q23 used as the baseline validation query in Sect. 2. The original Q23 contains two near-identical subquery patterns; Q23-pruned extracts the core scan, aggregation, and shuffle logic from one of them. The resulting query has balanced data, low shuffle volume, and a simple plan with few concurrent pipeline stages.

```
SELECT Count(*) AS total_rows,
       Sum(cnt) AS total_cnt
FROM   (SELECT Count(*) cnt
        FROM   store_sales, date_dim, item
        WHERE  ss_sold_date_sk = d_date_sk
               AND ss_item_sk = i_item_sk
               AND d_year IN (1999, 2000, 2001, 2002)
        GROUP  BY Substr(i_item_desc, 1, 30),
                  i_item_sk,
                  d_date
        HAVING Count(*) > 4);
```

References

1. Alipourfard, O., Liu, H.H., Chen, J., Venkataraman, S., Yu, M., Zhang, M.: CherryPick: adaptively unearthing the best cloud configurations for big data analytics. In: 14th USENIX Symposium on Networked Systems Design and Implementation (NSDI), pp. 469–482 (2017)
2. Ananthanarayanan, G., Ghodsi, A., Shenker, S., Stoica, I.: Effective straggler mitigation: attack of the clones. In: 10th USENIX Symposium on Networked Systems Design and Implementation (NSDI), pp. 185–198 (2013)
3. Apache Spark: Performance Tuning: Adaptive Query Execution (2026). https://spark.apache.org/docs/latest/sql-performance-tuning.html. Apache Spark Documentation. Accessed 2026
4. Armbrust, M., et al.: Spark SQL: relational data processing in spark. In: 2015 International Conference on Management of Data (SIGMOD), pp. 1383–1394 (2015)
5. Armenatzoglou, N., et al.: Amazon redshift re-invented. In: 2022 International Conference on Management of Data (SIGMOD), pp. 2205–2217 (2022)
6. Baresi, L., Dolci, T., Quattrocchi, G., Rasi, N.: A multi-faceted analysis of the performance variability of virtual machines. Softw. Practice Exp. **53**(11), 2067–2091 (2023)
7. Bilal, M., Canini, M., Rodrigues, R.: Finding the right cloud configuration for analytics clusters. In: 11th ACM Symposium on Cloud Computing (SoCC), pp. 208–222 (2020)
8. Dageville, B., et al.: The snowflake elastic data warehouse. In: 2016 International Conference on Management of Data (SIGMOD), pp. 215–226 (2016)
9. De Sensi, D., De Matteis, T., Taranov, K., Di Girolamo, S., Rahn, T., Hoefler, T.: Noise in the clouds: influence of network performance variability on application scalability. In: Proceedings of the ACM on Measurement and Analysis of Computing Systems (POMACS), vol. 6, no. 3, pp. 49:1–49:27 (2022)
10. Fogli, A., Zhao, B., Pietzuch, P.R., Bandle, M., Giceva, J.: OLAP on modern chiplet-based processors. Proc. VLDB Endowment (PVLDB) **17**(11), 3428–3441 (2024)
11. Google Cloud: Compute Engine: CPU Platforms (2026). https://cloud.google.com/compute/docs/cpu-platforms. Google Cloud Documentation. Accessed 2026
12. Hsu, C.J., Nair, V., Freeh, V.W., Menzies, T.: Arrow: low-level augmented Bayesian optimization for finding the best cloud VM. In: 38th IEEE International Conference on Distributed Computing Systems (ICDCS), pp. 660–670 (2018)
13. Intel Corporation: Intel Memory Latency Checker (MLC) (2025). https://www.intel.com/content/www/us/en/developer/articles/tool/intelr-memory-latency-checker.html. version 3.12. Accessed 2026
14. Kornacker, M., et al.: Impala: a modern, open-source SQL engine for hadoop. In: 7th Biennial Conference on Innovative Data Systems Research (CIDR) (2015)
15. Leis, V., Kuschewski, M.: Towards cost-optimal query processing in the cloud. Proc. VLDB Endowment (PVLDB) **14**(9), 1606–1612 (2021)
16. Leitner, P., Cito, J.: Patterns in the chaos—a study of performance variation and predictability in public IaaS clouds. ACM Trans. Internet Technol. (TOIT) **16**(3), 15:1–15:23 (2016)
17. Melnik, S., et al.: Dremel: a decade of interactive SQL analysis at web scale. Proc. VLDB Endowment (PVLDB) **13**(12), 3461–3472 (2020)
18. Microsoft Azure: Sizes for Virtual Machines in Azure (2026). https://learn.microsoft.com/azure/virtual-machines/sizes. Microsoft Azure Documentation. Accessed: 2026

19. Pedreira, P., et al.: Velox: meta's unified execution engine. Proc. VLDB Endowment (PVLDB) **15**(12), 3372–3384 (2022)
20. Perron, M., Fernandez, R.C., DeWitt, D.J., Madden, S.: Starling: a scalable query engine on cloud functions. In: 2020 International Conference on Management of Data (SIGMOD), pp. 131–141 (2020)
21. Rödiger, W., Idicula, S., Kemper, A., Neumann, T.: Flow-Join: adaptive skew handling for distributed joins over high-speed networks. In: 32nd IEEE International Conference on Data Engineering (ICDE), pp. 1194–1205 (2016)
22. Sethi, R., et al.: Presto: SQL on everything. In: 35th IEEE International Conference on Data Engineering (ICDE), pp. 1802–1813 (2019)
23. Transaction Processing Performance Council: TPC-H Benchmark Specification (2022). https://www.tpc.org/tpch/. revision 3.0.1.
24. Transaction Processing Performance Council: TPC-DS Benchmark Specification (2024). https://www.tpc.org/tpcds/. revision 4.0.0.
25. Wang, Z., Adamiak, E., Aiken, A.: A model for query execution over heterogeneous instances. In: 14th Conference on Innovative Data Systems Research (CIDR) (2024)
26. Zaharia, M., et al.: Apache spark: a unified engine for big data processing. Commun. ACM (CACM) **59**(11), 56–65 (2016)
27. Zhang, H., Liu, Y., Yan, J.: Cost-intelligent data analytics in the cloud. In: 14th Conference on Innovative Data Systems Research (CIDR) (2024)

LLM Workflows

Characterizing and Mitigating Context Redundancy in LLM Agent Workflows

Rongyu Luo, Lingxiao Zhao, and Yuezhi Che(✉)

Wuhan University, Wuhan, China
{rongyuluo,lingxiaozhao,cheyuezhi}@whu.edu.cn

Abstract. Large Language Models (LLMs) have recently become a prominent foundation for constructing autonomous agents and are increasingly widely adopted for their impressive capabilities in complex reasoning and decision-making. However, these agent workflows rely on iterative multi-turn interactions that repeatedly include system instructions, tool descriptions, and growing histories, leading to significant context redundancy. To understand and mitigate this inefficiency, we systematically characterize context redundancy in agent workflows and propose a lightweight Context-Aware Planner (CAP) that dynamically manages prompt construction during agent execution. CAP consists of three complementary components. First, a Prompt Builder adopts a merge-before-send strategy to aggregate temporally adjacent user inputs, reducing turn fragmentation. Second, a History Pruner truncates irrelevant past observations once prompt length exceeds a threshold, improving prefix cache reuse effectiveness. Third, a Tool Selector employs a small model to dynamically filter required tool schemas; crucially, an asynchronous pipeline overlaps this small model inference with environment execution to eliminate latency overhead. Together, these mechanisms reduce redundant context while preserving agent behavior. Evaluated on the BFCL benchmark using vLLM engine, our strategy reduces total prompt tokens by 55.8% and Time-To-First-Token (TTFT) by 16.6%, while maintaining steady system throughput. Furthermore, end-to-end task integrity, validated via an LLM-as-a-judge, remains preserved.

Keywords: LLM Agent · Token Redundancy · Prompt Optimization

1 Introduction

LLMs [8] are evolving into autonomous agents that reason, invoke tools, and interact with the environments through iterative *thought-action-observation* cycles [14,17]. Modern agent runtimes [1,15] implement this cycle as a sophisticated systems stack comprising query engines, tool registries, and session memory. In each turn, the runtime assembles a composite context—integrating static system prompts, tool schemas [12], and monotonic interaction history [13]—and resubmits it to the model for the next decision.

L. Eeckhout et al. (Eds.): APPT 2026, LNCS 16693, pp. 175–188, 2027.
https://doi.org/10.1007/978-981-92-4805-6_12

While functionally necessary, this execution paradigm introduces a fundamental systems inefficiency: structural context redundancy. Because the runtime repeatedly serializes largely unchanged context across turns, a substantial portion of tokens processed during inference correspond to previously computed states. To quantify this phenomenon, we first introduce a new metric, the Token Reuse Factor (TRF), which measures how many times tokens are redundantly reprocessed across turns. Our empirical profiling on the Berkeley Function Calling Leaderboard (BFCL) [9] reveals that a baseline agent exhibits a TRF of 3.25, meaning nearly 70% of processed prompt tokens are redundant replays of previously computed states.

From a systems perspective, this redundancy significantly amplifies the cost of the prefill phase, inflates the Key-Value (KV) cache footprint, and degrades TTFT. While engine-level optimizations like PagedAttention [6] and prefix caching improve memory management, they treat prompts as opaque streams and cannot eliminate the structural redundancy continuously regenerated by the agent runtime. To understand this inefficiency, we systematically characterize prompt evolution in multi-turn agent workflows. Our analysis reveals two dominant forms of structural redundancy: (1) *constant redundancy* arising from repeatedly serialized tool schemas that remain largely unchanged across turns, and (2) *growing redundancy* from accumulated interaction history that monotonically inflates prompt length over time.

Motivated by these findings, we propose a lightweight runtime planner, namely Context-Aware Planner (CAP), that dynamically manages prompt construction during agent execution. CAP introduces three complementary mechanisms: (1) a Prompt Builder that aggregates temporally adjacent user inputs to reduce turn fragmentation, (2) a History Pruner that removes low-utility historical context, and (3) a Tool Selector that dynamically filters required tool schemas.

In summary, this paper makes the following contributions:

- **Characterization of context redundancy.** We systematically analyze prompt evolution in multi-turn LLM agent workflows and identify three dominant structural sources of redundancy: turn fragmentation, constant prefix overhead, and monotonically growing history. We further introduce the TRF to quantitatively measure redundant token processing.
- **CAP planner for redundancy mitigation.** Guided by the characterization, we design a lightweight runtime planner that dynamically optimizes prompt construction using three complementary mechanisms: Prompt Builder, History Pruner, and Tool Selector, reducing redundant context.
- **Implementation and evaluation.** We implement our approach on the `vLLM` [6] serving stack and evaluate it on the BFCL benchmark. Our method reduces total prompt tokens by 55.8% and improves TTFT by 16.6%.

2 Background

LLM Inference as a Two-Phase Systems Pipeline. Autoregressive LLM inference consists of two phases: *prefill* and *decode*. During prefill, the model processes the entire prompt to construct initial KV states, scaling quadratically with sequence length and dominating TTFT. During decode, the model incrementally generates tokens conditioned on these cached KV states. The KV cache stores intermediate attention states for previously processed tokens, allowing subsequent decoding steps to reuse prior computation instead of recomputing the full sequence. As generation proceeds, the KV cache grows with the sequence length, increasing memory consumption and affecting the number of concurrent sequences that can be served on a fixed-memory GPU. Consequently, prompt length and generated output length both directly influence latency, memory usage, and overall system throughput [10].

LLM Agents as Closed-Loop Runtime Systems. Practical LLM agents operate as complex closed-loop *runtime architectures* [9,11,15,17,18] that iteratively execute a *thought–action–observation* cycle. In each turn, the runtime assembles a structured prompt from heterogeneous components: static instructions, massive tool schemas, permission constraints, and session history. After the model chooses an action, the resulting observation is written back into the session state before the next turn begins.

Tools in LLM agents are external functions defined by structured schemas (name, arguments, description) [11]. The runtime serializes these schemas into the prompt, allowing the model to select a tool. When a tool is invoked, the runtime executes it and appends the returned observation to the interaction context.

Interaction history records user inputs, model outputs, and tool observations across turns. This history is appended to the prompt to preserve short-term context and support multi-step reasoning, growing as the session progresses. Memory mechanisms provide additional context for long-term memory, which may be retrieved from external storage.

The runtime combines tools, history, and memory to construct prompts for each step, enabling iterative reasoning and tool-assisted execution. Figure 1 illustrates the overall closed-loop architecture of such an LLM agent.

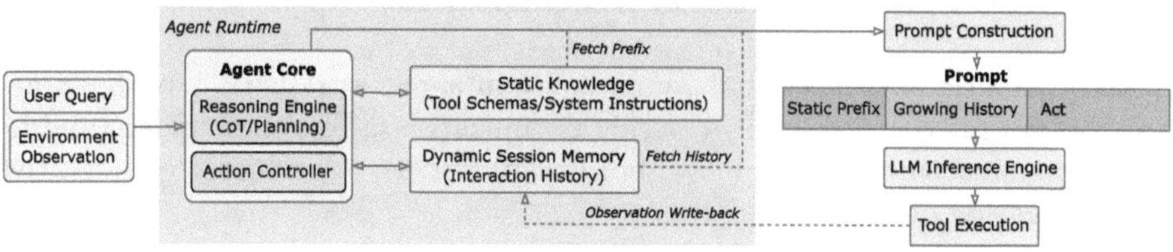

Fig. 1. Overall architecture of LLM Agent.

3 Motivation

Agent Runtime Causes Redundancy. Although LLM agents enable multi-step reasoning and tool-assisted execution, their runtime architecture introduces significant inefficiencies during multi-turn interactions. In each step, the runtime aggregates multiple components, including system instructions, tool schemas, and accumulated interaction history, before invoking the model again. While this orchestration paradigm is essential for controllability and multi-step reasoning, it introduces inherent redundancy [5,7].

First, static control context such as tool schemas and system instructions is repeatedly serialized at every turn to maintain execution fidelity. These components remain largely unchanged but must still be reprocessed. Second, the dynamic session context grows monotonically as past actions and observations are appended to the prompt. Over time, the majority of prompts correspond to historical information that has already been processed in previous turns.

Consequently, the dominant cost in agent inference shifts from processing new information to repeatedly re-materializing previously seen runtime states. As the interaction depth increases, the ratio of redundant tokens [4] grows, leading to inflated prefill latency and increased memory consumption. A detailed quantitative analysis and measurement methodology are presented in Sect. 4.

Prefix Caching Limitation. Modern inference engines attempt to mitigate repeated computation through memory-management mechanisms like PagedAttention [6]. Building on this, *prefix caching* [3] reuses precomputed KV states for identical prompt prefixes.

Prefix caching strictly assumes leading-sequence stability. However, in real agent runtimes, tool registries are modified by task-dependent routing, and unstructured history growth continuously shifts the sequence footprint. Because serving engines treat prompts as opaque token streams, they cannot prevent the runtime from regenerating redundant structures. They reduce the cost of stable prefixes, but cannot eliminate the structural redundancy continuously generated by the application layer. As a result, prefix caching can only partially reduce redundant computation and cannot prevent the repeated serialization of runtime state inherent in agent architectures.

4 Characterizing Context Redundancy

These observations suggest that redundancy in agent workflows is both significant and not fully addressed by existing optimizations. To better understand its underlying structure and guide system design, we next conduct a quantitative characterization of context redundancy.

Profiling Methodology and the TRF Metric. We profile a standard ReAct-style agent [17] executing 30 multi-turn tasks from the Berkeley Function Calling

Leaderboard (BFCL) [9]. To isolate runtime-layer context behavior from external network jitter, we deploy `Qwen2.5-7B-Instruct` using the `vLLM` alongside deterministic mock tools.

The fundamental inefficiency in LLM agents is the repetitive re-processing of known states. To quantify this, we introduce the **Token Reuse Factor (TRF)**. Consider a multi-turn agent session $\mathcal{S}$ consisting of T turns. At turn t, the assembled prompt P_t can be decomposed into three semantic segments:

$$P_t = P^{sys}_{static} \oplus H_t \oplus F_t \tag{1}$$

where P^{sys}_{static} is the constant control prefix (instructions and tool schemas), H_t is the monotonically growing session history, and F_t is the active decision frontier (the immediate user query and the newest observation).

While the serving engine must process the entire length $|P_t|$ during each prefill phase, only the initial system prompt and newly introduced frontiers contribute unique information. We therefore define TRF as:

$$\mathrm{TRF}(\mathcal{S}) = \frac{\sum_{t=1}^{T} |P_t|}{|P^{sys}_{static}| + \sum_{t=1}^{T} |F_t|} \tag{2}$$

A TRF of 1.0 indicates perfect efficiency with no redundant processing. TRF > 1.0 reflect repeated computation introduced by multi-turn agent.

Empirical Profiling. Our profiling reveals substantial redundancy during agent execution. Over 101 aggregate turns across the 30 tasks, the engine processed a total of **125,023 prompt tokens**. However, the actual unique tokens present in the final session states amounted to only **38,447**. This yields a macro **TRF of 3.25**, indicating that about 69.3% of the prompt-side computation is entirely redundant.

Figure 2 shows an example of the token composition breakdown: (1) **Constant Intercept (60.6%):** Static instructions and tool schemas consistently consume over half of the computational budget. (2) **Growing Slope (34.1%):** Accumulated assistant and observation histories continuously inflate the context. (3) **Useful Frontier (5.3%):** The genuinely new information driving the agent's current decision—user queries and current observations—constitutes less than 10% of the processed tokens. In summary, over 90% of the engine's prefill cycles are spent reprocessing static prefixes and accumulated history rather than new information.

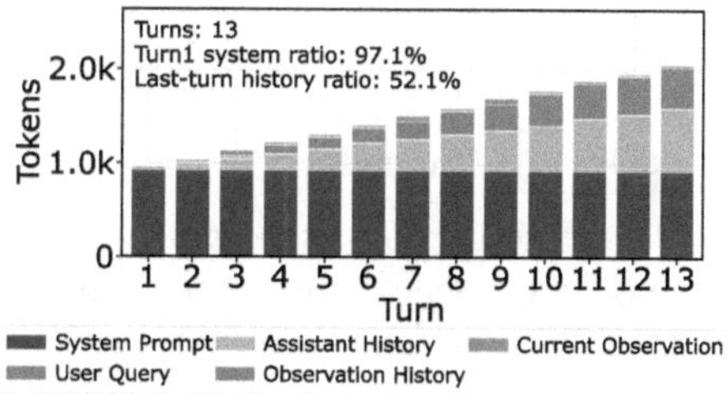

Fig. 2. Per-turn token breakdown for a representative long-chain task.

Case Study: Late-Stage Context Collapse. To illustrate the impact of redundancy, we examine a long-horizon task (`multi_turn_base_0`) at Turn 13. At this late boundary, the prompt length $|P_{13}|$ reaches 2,061 tokens. The composition is highly skewed: 929 tokens are locked in the static system prefix, and 1,073 tokens belong to the massive historical accretion. The actual new observation returned by the environment ($|F_{13}|$) is merely 59 tokens. Consequently, to process 59 tokens of new information, the inference engine is forced to allocate memory and compute attention across **2,002 redundant tokens**—a catastrophic transient repetition ratio of over **34:1**. This rapid growth increases KV cache usage, elevates TTFT, and reduces the capacity for concurrent requests.

Overall, the characterization reveals that context redundancy in agent workflows is structured and dominated by static prefixes and monotonically growing history. These observations motivate runtime mechanisms that reduce repeated prefix processing, control history growth, and minimize redundant invocations.

5 Design

The characterization in Sect. 4 reveals that context redundancy in LLM agents arises from three structural sources: constant prefix overhead, monotonically growing history, and turn fragmentation. These redundancy patterns are not independent but jointly inflate prompt length and repeatedly trigger redundant prefill computation.

To address this problem, we propose the Context-Aware Planner (CAP), a lightweight runtime module that dynamically manages prompt construction during agent execution. CAP operates at the agent runtime layer and introduces three complementary mechanisms: (1) Prompt Builder mitigates turn fragmentation by merging temporally adjacent user inputs. (2) History Pruner controls monotonically growing context by removing low-utility historical content. (3) Tool Selector reduces constant prefix overhead by dynamically filtering tool schemas.

5.1 Design Overview

A typical production-style agent executes a closed loop: input, context assembly, model inference, tool execution, observation write-back, next turn. While structurally necessary, this loop introduces severe hardware-level bottlenecks.

Figure 3 presents the overall CAP runtime workflow. CAP integrates three complementary controls coordinated through an asynchronous pipeline spanning compute, memory, and scheduling levels:

- **Compute-Level Control (Interaction):** Turn fragmentation repeatedly triggers expensive $O(N^2)$ prefill operations [2]. CAP reduces unnecessary turn creation to amortize repetitive prefill computation.
- **Memory-Level Control (Context):** Static tool schemas and monotonically growing interaction history consume KV-cache capacity. CAP selectively prunes redundant tool schemas and compacts low-utility history to bound context growth.

- **Scheduling-Level Control (System):** Context optimization may introduce auxiliary latency. CAP executes context selection asynchronously and overlaps it with non-critical intervals to avoid additional delay.

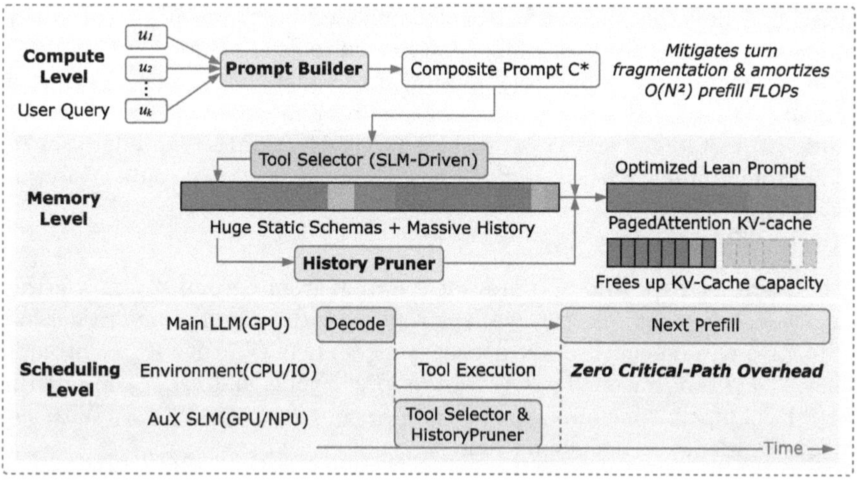

Fig. 3. CAP framework overview.

5.2 CAP Runtime Control

Strategy 1 Prompt Builder: Mitigating Turn Fragmentation. Prompt Builder targets a serving-side pattern in which multiple user requests are queued before the agent starts execution, such as batched user submissions or grouped subtasks. In this setting, issuing a separate model invocation for each request repeatedly processes nearly identical prefixes; we refer to this pattern as *turn fragmentation*, which inflates redundant prefill computation. To mitigate this inefficiency, Prompt Builder applies a merge-before-send strategy that combines these pending requests into a single composite frontier while preserving chronological order and explicit sub-task boundaries. CAP does not merge across an agent response, tool execution, or observation boundary. Formally, for a burst of requests $u_1, u_2, \ldots, u_k$ arriving within window τ, the serving engine traditionally processes k separate prompts $C_1, \ldots, C_k$. Prompt Builder transforms these into a single composite prompt: $C^* = \mathcal{M}(u_1, u_2, \ldots, u_k; H, S)$, where H is the history, S is the static context, and $\mathcal{M}(\cdot)$ is the merge operator.

Strategy 2 Tool Selector: Reducing Constant Prefix Overhead. The static prompt prefix often contains vast tool schemas and usage instructions, inflating the constant per-turn cost even when only a fraction of tools are activated. Tool Selector reduces this redundancy by dynamically identifying the subset of tools relevant to the current task frontier. CAP employs a lightweight small language model (SLM) to predict which tools are likely to be invoked.

SLM-Driven Prediction and Fallback. The SLM predicts the subset of tools likely required for the immediate task frontier using the user query, the active frontier, and function metadata. Selected tools retain their full JSON schemas and few-shot demonstrations, while non-selected tools are reduced to lightweight names-only metadata. To preserve task integrity under ambiguous or overlapping tool descriptions, CAP uses a conservative fallback hierarchy: (1) SLM semantic routing, (2) metadata- and keyword-based expansion of the candidate set, and (3) full-prompt fallback when confidence is low or the predicted route is internally inconsistent.

Asynchronous Pipeline. To prevent the SLM from becoming a new critical-path bottleneck, Tool Selector overlaps routing with existing non-critical intervals (e.g., environment I/O or decode times). Let T_{env} denote environment latency, T_{SLM} tool-routing latency, $T_{prefill}$ prefill time, and T_{decode} decode time. A sequential pipeline incurs $T_{step} = T_{env} + T_{SLM} + T_{prefill} + T_{decode}$. With asynchronous overlap, the latency becomes:

$$T_{step} = \max(T_{SLM}, T_{decode\_prev} + T_{env}) + T_{prefill} + T_{decode}. \quad (3)$$

When $T_{SLM} \leq T_{decode\_prev} + T_{env}$, the routing latency is fully hidden, converting structural token reduction into pure, user-visible TTFT acceleration. In our implementation, the router is invoked once per available task frontier rather than per generated token or per candidate tool. CAP prefetches routing only when the next frontier is already known, such as a queued user request or a bundled sub-task. For turns whose tool needs depend on the current model response or tool observation, CAP defers routing until the dependency is resolved or falls back to the full tool prompt.

Strategy 3 History Pruner: Controlling Monotonic Context Growth. While Tool Pruning reduces the constant intercept, it cannot prevent the monotonic growth of action traces and observations. As interaction history accumulates, the prompt suffix expands continuously, eventually dominating context length and degrading system efficiency. History Pruner bounds this growth using a delayed, structure-aware compaction strategy that reduces historical redundancy while preserving logical continuity.

Delayed Triggering. For prompt lengths $P_t < L_{threshold}$, CAP keeps the history append-only to maintain prefix-cache stability. Once $P_t \geq L_{threshold}$, a one-shot restructuring pass is triggered. This avoids frequent modifications to the stable prefix and maximizes cache reuse during early turns. The implementation uses deterministic text processing and lexical similarity rather than another SLM, avoiding an additional model on the pruning path.

Structure-Aware Retention. CAP constructs a lightweight relevance reference from the original user request, recent actions, and recent observations. Older observations are ranked against this reference using lexical similarity, while the most recent assistant-observation pairs are always preserved verbatim. Older interaction traces are folded into a compact summary that keeps the tool invocation trace, critical action arguments, JSON keys, guard messages, and high-scoring observations. This design compresses low-value details while keeping structural anchors available for later turns.

Cache-Friendly Restoration. After compaction, the optimized history is frozen into a new stable prefix. CAP intentionally absorbs a single cache-disruptive event at t_{prune} to permanently lower the prefill slope of all subsequent turns, avoiding continuous cache churn.

5.3 End-to-End Synergy

CAP's three components target complementary dimensions of context redundancy. Prompt Builder reduces invocation *frequency* by merging fragmented interactions. Tool Selector shrinks the *constant width* of the prompt by filtering unused tool schemas. History Pruner bounds the *dynamic length* of accumulated context through delayed compaction. These mechanisms operate orthogonally and therefore compose naturally. By jointly optimizing across these dimensions, CAP systematically reduces redundant computation while preserving agent correctness and tool-calling fidelity.

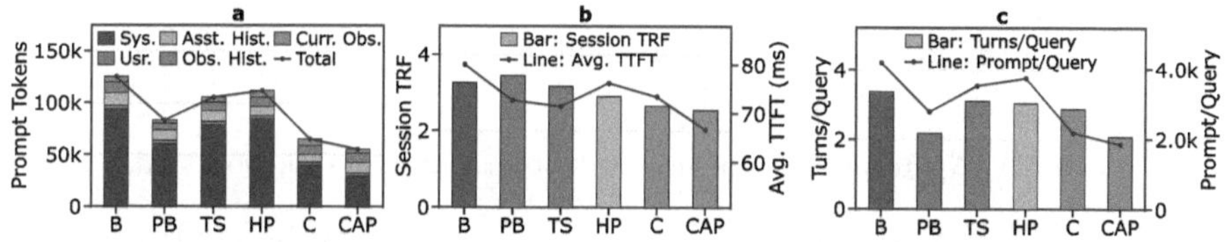

Fig. 4. End-to-end comparison across six configurations on the 30-task workload. (a) Prompt cost and token composition; (b) Session TRF and average TTFT; (c) Turn fragmentation and prompt cost per query.

6 Evaluation

This section evaluates CAP to answer four aspects: (1) effectiveness in reducing structural redundancy, (2) impact on system-level performance (TTFT and throughput), (3) latency hiding of the asynchronous pipeline, and (4) synergy among cross-layer controls.

Setup: Experiments are conducted on an NVIDIA A10 GPU (24GB VRAM) using `vLLM`. The main model is `Qwen2.5-7B-Instruct`, while the auxiliary router uses `Qwen2.5-1.5B-Instruct`. We evaluate 30 tasks from BFCL, which preserve realistic function schemas, multi-turn dependencies, and parallel tool-calling structures. Deterministic mock tools are used to remove external API latency and network jitter while returning schema-consistent observations for the corresponding tool interfaces. This setup isolates runtime prompt construction and serving-side context cost, which are the focus of CAP. Because BFCL does not include request-arrival timestamps, Prompt Builder is evaluated by grouping semantically related and tool-overlapping queries while preserving all agent-tool interaction boundaries. Figure 4 and Table 1 compare six configurations (Baseline, PB, TS, HP, CAP w/o PB, and full CAP) across efficiency, latency, and LLM-as-a-judge quality scores (`Qwen2.5-32B-Instruct`).

Main End-to-End Results. Figure 4 and Table 1 show that full CAP achieves the highest efficiency, reducing total prompt tokens by **55.8%** (from 125,023 to 55,230) and lowering Session TRF from 3.25 to 2.54. This indicates CAP effectively mitigates both absolute cost and cross-turn redundancy amplification.

Intermediate ablations reveal specific contributions: Prompt Builder (PB) alone cuts prompt tokens by **33.5%** and total turns from 101 to 65 by aggregating fragmented requests. Tool Selector (TS) provides a **15.9%** token reduction, while History Pruner (HP) primarily improves the redundancy structure (TRF). Combining TS and HP (CAP w/o PB) reduces tokens by **48.0%**, demonstrating the efficacy of prompt-side controls even without request merging.

These savings translate to improved latency: average TTFT drops by **16.6%** (from 79.9 ms to 66.7 ms). Meanwhile, system throughput remains stable (29.97 vs. 29.36 tok/s), confirming that CAP's gains are concentrated in the prefill phase and context management rather than decoding.

Table 1. Aggregate end-to-end results on the full 30-task workload.

Method	Logical	Turns	Prompt Tokens	Prompt/Query	TRF	Turns/Query	Avg TTFT (ms)	Thr.
Baseline	30	101	125,023	4167.4	3.2518	3.3667	79.9	29.97
Prompt Builder	18	65	83,129	2771.0	3.4413	2.1667	72.6	29.96
Tool Selector	30	93	105,139	3504.6	3.1635	3.1000	71.4	29.46
History Pruner	30	91	111,730	3724.3	2.8980	3.0333	76.1	29.90
CAP w/o PB	30	86	64,983	2166.1	2.6491	2.8667	73.4	29.23
CAP	18	62	55,230	1841.0	2.5411	2.0667	66.7	29.36

Where the Savings Come From. Panel (a) of Fig. 4 shows that the largest absolute savings come from the static system-and-tools portion of the prompt. Baseline spends 93,829 tokens on system content alone, whereas CAP reduces that number to 29,752, a **68.3%** reduction. This directly supports the characterization in Sect. 4: schema-heavy constant prefixes are a dominant source of structural redundancy.

The component breakdown elucidates these distinct behaviors: Prompt Builder (PB) primarily minimizes turn frequency, lowering system-token replay to 60,385. Tool Selector (TS) directly targets the constant prefix, reducing system tokens to 78,655 while maintaining workload structure. History Pruner (HP) shows moderate impact here as few tasks reach deep history regimes. By synergizing TS and HP, CAP w/o PB reduces system tokens to 39,907 and slashes redundant tokens from 86,576 to 40,453. Finally, full CAP achieves the minimum prompt cost by combining prefix reduction with lower interaction frequency.

Panel (c) further clarifies the role of Prompt Builder. Prompt Builder alone reduces turns per query from 3.37 to 2.17, while full CAP lowers this value to 2.07. At the same time, prompt cost per query drops from 4167.4 in the Baseline to 2771.0 with Prompt Builder alone, 2166.1 with CAP w/o Prompt Builder, and 1841.0 with full CAP. These trends indicate that Prompt Builder and the two prompt-side pruning modules are complementary: one reduces how often prompts are rebuilt, while the others reduce how much repeated content each rebuilt prompt contains.

Efficiency–Quality Trade-off. Efficiency improvements are only useful if they do not substantially degrade task outcomes. Table 2 reports the bundle-aware task-quality evaluation used for the current figure data. Baseline obtains an overall score of 6.17. Prompt Builder alone drops slightly to 6.00, indicating that aggressive request merging by itself may sacrifice some task fidelity. However, once the full CAP pipeline is enabled, the overall score recovers to 6.10, which is close to both Baseline (6.17) and CAP w/o Prompt Builder (6.13).

This comparison is important for interpreting the efficiency results above. Prompt Builder is highly effective in reducing turns and prompt replay, but using it alone introduces a quality trade-off. Full CAP compensates for that loss by pairing request merging with more selective prompt construction, thereby retaining most of the quality level while delivering the strongest efficiency gains. The small quality differences should be interpreted as behavior preservation rather than a guaranteed quality gain. In several long-chain cases, pruning removes repeated low-progress traces and makes the retained state more focused.

Engine-Level Optimization Ablation. One may hypothesize that engine-level scheduling alone could mitigate the observed redundancy. To examine this, we evaluated four configurations combining Prefix Caching and Chunked Prefill (without CAP). Across all settings (both enabled, both disabled, or individually enabled), the Session TRF clustered tightly between 4.78 and 4.82 (averaging 4.80). This indicates minimal impact from engine-level features alone.

This limitation arises because prefix caching requires stable leading prefixes, whereas agent prompts continuously change as observations are appended and tool selections vary. Furthermore, chunked prefill improves scheduling fairness but does not reduce the underlying prompt-side computation. This ablation

Table 2. Bundle-aware quality evaluation across the six configurations.

Method	Accuracy	Completeness	Relevance	Reasoning	Conciseness	Overall
Baseline	3.47	3.13	3.97	2.57	4.60	6.17
Prompt Builder	2.87	2.60	3.57	2.10	4.23	6.00
Tool Selector	3.47	3.13	4.07	2.57	4.73	6.07
History Pruner	3.57	3.20	4.07	2.57	4.63	6.23
CAP w/o PB	3.57	3.17	4.10	2.70	4.67	6.13
CAP	3.47	3.23	4.13	2.67	4.53	6.10

therefore reinforces our central claim: engine-level optimizations are useful complements, but they cannot substitute for runtime-level context management.

7 Related Work

Prompt Compression: NLP-centric compression techniques, such as LLMLingua [5] and Selective Context [7], utilize information-theoretic approaches to remove low-information tokens. While effective for generic text, they are fundamentally incompatible with agent runtimes. Aggressive token-level compression destroys the strict structural integrity (e.g., JSON schemas, control delimiters) required for correct tool invocation. Furthermore, executing these analyzers sequentially introduces a latency overhead on the critical path that often negates the prefill savings.

LLM Serving Systems: Engines like vLLM [6] and SGLang [18] optimize hardware utilization and request scheduling. Additionally, StreamingLLM [16] addresses the KV cache expansion problem via attention sinks for infinite length streams, though it does not explicitly target the structural redundancy inherent in agent-specific runtimes.

8 Conclusion

CAP reduces structural context redundancy in multi-turn LLM agent execution through cross-layer runtime optimization. By coordinating Prompt Builder, Tool Selector, and History Pruner, CAP minimizes redundant prompt construction, filters unused tool schemas, and bounds context growth while preserving semantic continuity. Experiments on BFCL with vLLM show that CAP reduces total processed prompt tokens by 55.8% and lowers average TTFT by 16.6% without sacrificing throughput or correctness. These results demonstrate that cross-layer redundancy control is an effective and practical approach for improving the efficiency of LLM agent serving systems.

Acknowledgments. This work was supported in part by the National Natural Science Foundation of China (NSFC) under Grant No. 62402346.

Artificial Intelligence Tools. The technical solution and experimental design presented in this paper were independently completed by the authors. AI tools were used solely for language polishing and formatting optimization, and did not participate in the development of the research ideas or core content.

Disclosure of Interests. The authors have no competing interests to declare that are relevant to the content of this article.

References

1. Chase, H.: Langchain (2022). https://github.com/langchain-ai/langchain. Accessed 20 May 2024
2. Dao, T.: Flashattention-2: Faster attention with better parallelism and work partitioning. arXiv preprint arXiv:2307.08691 (2023)
3. Gim, I., Chen, G., Lee, S.S., Sarda, N., Khandelwal, A., Zhong, L.: Prompt cache: modular attention reuse for low-latency inference. In: Proceedings of Machine Learning and Systems, vol. 6, pp. 325–338 (2024)
4. Han, T., Wang, Z., Fang, C., Zhao, S., Ma, S., Chen, Z.: Token-budget-aware LLM reasoning. In: Findings of the Association for Computational Linguistics: ACL 2025, pp. 24842–24855 (2025)
5. Jiang, H., Wu, Q., Lin, C.Y., Yang, Y., Qiu, L.: Llmlingua: compressing prompts for accelerated inference of large language models. In: Proceedings of the 2023 Conference on Empirical Methods in Natural Language Processing, pp. 13358–13376 (2023)
6. Kwon, W., et al.: Efficient memory management for large language model serving with pagedattention. In: Proceedings of the 29th Symposium on Operating Systems Principles (SOSP), pp. 611–626. ACM (2023)
7. Li, Y., Dong, B., Guerin, F., Lin, C.: Compressing context to enhance inference efficiency of large language models. In: Proceedings of the 2023 Conference on Empirical Methods in Natural Language Processing, pp. 6342–6353 (2023)
8. Naveed, H., et al.: A comprehensive overview of large language models. ACM Trans. Intell. Syst. Technol. **16**(5), 1–72 (2025)
9. Patil, S.G., Zhang, T., Wang, X., Gonzalez, J.E.: Gorilla: large language model connected with massive apis. Adv. Neural. Inf. Process. Syst. **37**, 126544–126565 (2024)
10. Pope, R., et al.: Efficiently scaling transformer inference. In: Proceedings of Machine Learning and Systems (MLSys), vol. 5, pp. 1–14 (2023)
11. Schick, T., et al.: Toolformer: language models can teach themselves to use tools. Adv. Neural. Inf. Process. Syst. **36**, 68539–68551 (2023)
12. Shen, Y., Song, K., Tan, X., Li, D., Lu, W., Zhuang, Y.: Hugginggpt: solving AI tasks with chatgpt and its friends in hugging face. Adv. Neural. Inf. Process. Syst. **36**, 38154–38180 (2023)
13. Shinn, N., Cassano, F., Gopinath, A., Narasimhan, K., Yao, S.: Reflexion: language agents with verbal reinforcement learning. Adv. Neural. Inf. Process. Syst. **36**, 8634–8652 (2023)

14. Wei, J., et al.: Chain-of-thought prompting elicits reasoning in large language models. Adv. Neural. Inf. Process. Syst. **35**, 24824–24837 (2022)
15. Wu, Q., et al.: Autogen: enabling next-gen LLM applications via multi-agent conversations. In: First Conference on Language Modeling (2024)
16. Xiao, G., Tian, Y., Chen, B., Han, S., Lewis, M.: Efficient streaming language models with attention sinks. In: International Conference on Learning Representations (ICLR) (2024)
17. Yao, S., et al.: React: synergizing reasoning and acting in language models. In: International Conference on Learning Representations (ICLR) (2023)
18. Zheng, L., et al.: Sglang: efficient execution of structured language model programs. Adv. Neural. Inf. Process. Syst. **37**, 62557–62583 (2024)

Do Not Let Sandboxes Sit Idle: Cross-Agent Sandbox Re-allocation for LLM Agents

Yiming Li, Yichi Chen, Laiping Zhao(✉), and Wenyu Qu

Tianjin Key Lab. of Advanced Networking, Tianjin University, Tianjin, China
{l_ym,chenyichi,laiping,wenyu.qu}@tju.edu.cn

Abstract. Agent workflows typically rely on exclusive sandbox allocation for resource management. However, prolonged waiting for large language model invocations leads to resource inefficiency. To address this issue, prior work has explored spatial sharing via overcommit and temporal sharing by reusing sandboxes across requests within the same agent. Nevertheless, these approaches achieve limited improvements due to resource contention and sparse invocation patterns.

To overcome these limitations, we propose re-allocating idle sandboxes across agents to enable efficient resource sharing. We present `aShare`, an agent system that decouples computation from communication to enable idle resource re-allocation. It combines offline agent partitioning with online latency-aware scheduling to optimize resource efficiency. Experimental results demonstrate that `aShare` reduces resource consumption by 35.9%–92.9% compared to state-of-the-art systems.

Keywords: Agent workflow · Resource management · Re-allocation

1 Introduction

Agentic workflows have become a dominant paradigm in modern AI systems, evolving from simple prompt–response loops into flexible, graph-based execution frameworks [1,2]. In these workflows, nodes represent LLM inferences or external tool invocations, while edges capture control flow and data dependencies. This paradigm underpins state-of-the-art autonomous services, enabling multi-step reasoning and interaction with external environments.

To provide performance guarantees and isolation, existing platforms adopt exclusive provisioning, executing each agent in a dedicated sandbox with isolated CPU, memory, and storage [3,4]. However, unlike traditional workflows (Fig. 1), LLM inference dominates end-to-end latency, e.g., >97% of response time [5]. As a result, sandboxes remain idle for most lifetime while waiting for LLM responses, leading to extremely low resource utilization (e.g., 1.96% in Fig. 2).

Y. Li and Y. Chen—Both authors contributed equally to this research.

L. Eeckhout et al. (Eds.): APPT 2026, LNCS 16693, pp. 189–202, 2027.
https://doi.org/10.1007/978-981-92-4805-6_13

To improve resource efficiency, prior work explores two approaches: (1) *Overcommit*, which co-locates multiple sandboxes on shared physical resources for spatial sharing [6,7]; and (2) *Reuse*, which decomposes applications into fine-grained functions to enable temporal sharing across requests within the same application [8,9].

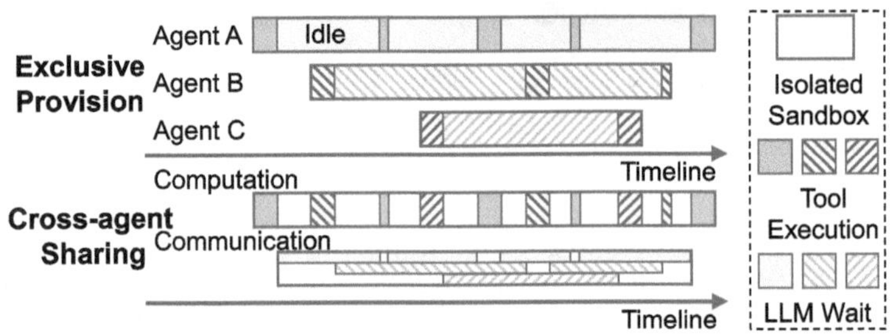

Fig. 1. Schematic overview of agent workflow management.

Applying these techniques to agent workflows only partially mitigates inefficiency due to prolonged LLM-induced idle periods. (1) *Spatial sharing struggles to guarantee SLOs.* The high variability of LLM inference undermines profiling-based *overcommit*, and co-locating sandboxes introduces non-negligible interference. For example, 9.8% latency increase with 10 sandboxes (Fig. 4a), despite >97% I/O wait. (2) *Temporal sharing has limited applicability. Reuse* is effective only for frequently invoked workflows, whereas most workloads are sparse (e.g., 80% in Azure Durable Functions [9]). As a result, existing approaches fail to achieve both high resource efficiency and SLO guarantees for agent workflows.

To address these limitations, we propose *cross-agent sandbox sharing* (Fig. 1), which decouples tool execution and LLM invocation into computation and communication sandboxes, respectively. Compute-intensive tool nodes adopt temporal sharing across agents with exclusive execution to avoid interference, while I/O-bound LLM invocations enable spatial sharing within communication sandboxes to maximize efficiency under low compute contention.

Enabling cross-agent sandbox sharing introduces two challenges. (1) *Sharing efficiency*: Heterogeneous dependencies across agents make dynamic installation costly. We address this by prebuilding sandbox images with required dependencies and preloading expensive libraries, allowing only lightweight code updates at runtime. (2) *Resource efficiency*: Dependency conflicts and heterogeneous SLOs complicate co-location and scheduling. We partition agents offline to resolve conflicts and apply earliest-deadline-first scheduling at runtime to minimize sandbox usage while meeting latency SLOs.

We present `aShare`, a novel cross-agent sandbox sharing system designed to mitigate resource inefficiency caused by waiting for LLM inference. `aShare` decouples agent workflow execution, enabling temporal sharing of computation sandboxes across agents and spatial sharing of communication sandboxes. This design achieves high resource efficiency while preserving end-to-end latency guarantees for agent workflows.

Our contributions are as follows:

- We analyze the resource inefficiency of existing workflow execution models, including *exclusivity*, *overcommit* and *reuse*.
- We propose **aShare**, a cross-agent sandbox sharing solution that achieves high resource efficiency while preserving latency SLOs.
- Experimental results on diverse workloads demonstrate that implementing **aShare** can reduce resource consumption by 35.9%–92.9% and increase cost efficiency by up to 66.5× compared with state-of-the-art.

2 Background and Motivation

2.1 Agent Workflow

LLM-based agents are increasingly implemented as structured workflows, where execution is modeled as a directed graph with computation (tool) nodes and LLM communication nodes. While this abstraction is explicit in modern frameworks, production systems still execute the entire workflow within a single sandbox for isolation [3], reserving resources throughout execution even during prolonged LLM waiting periods.

Next, we illustrate this inefficiency using a MapReduce-style summarization agent [10]. It performs document splitting, parallel LLM summarization, aggregation, and iterative refinement. In our experiments, the agent spent 1.22 s on computation (5 tool nodes) but 42.79 s on communication (4 LLM nodes, 23 calls). When executed within a single sandbox, these long LLM waits lead to extended idle resource allocation.

2.2 Observations

We evaluate resource efficiency using the *Summarization* agent on three systems: (1) *Base*, which employs exclusive sandboxes (1 vCPU, 2,GB memory); (2) *OWL* [6], which adopts *overcommit*; and (3) *StepConf* [8], which enables *reuse*. All sandboxes are pre-warmed, and detailed configurations are provided in Sect. 5.1.

To eliminate variability from LLM outputs and backend performance, we use a simulation-based replay approach. We first record real LLM outputs and execution times, and then replay them via a simulated inference backend, ensuring reproducible and fair comparisons.

Observation I: $\underline{Resourceinefficiency}$: *The exclusive provision suffers from prolonged I/O wait, leading to* $< 2\%$ *usage of allocated resources.*

Figure 2 illustrates the time series of CPU utilization when a single sandbox exclusively occupies the physical resources. It can be observed that CPU utilization reaches its peaks only during the execution of tool nodes, while it rapidly

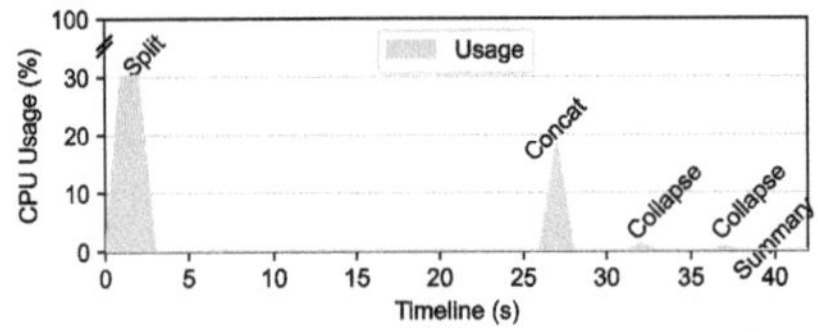

Fig. 2. Timeline of CPU utilization.

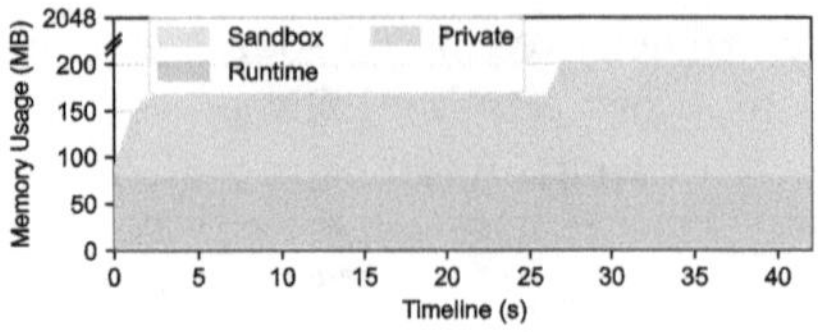

Fig. 3. Timeline of Memory usage.

drops to nearly zero during each LLM invocation. Out of the 41.9 s end-to-end latency, node execution accounts for only 2.91%, whereas I/O waiting for LLM responses dominate the critical path. More critically, the peak CPU utilization of tool nodes is merely 30.3%, resulting in an overall utilization of only 1.96% of the allocated CPU time slices throughout the agent's execution.

This exclusive provision also leads to significant memory resource waste. While waiting for LLM responses, the sandbox must keep the runtime environment, dependency libraries, and workflow state resident in memory. However, as shown in the time series of sandbox memory usage in Fig. 3, the actual memory consumption of the sandbox (peaking at 202 MB) is far below the allocated capacity (i.e., 2 GB), and the agent's private state occupies only about 122 MB. Consequently, 91.4% of the memory resources remain idle throughout the execution. Although the gap between allocated and usage memory is an inherent characteristic of exclusive resource allocation, the prolonged I/O wait further exacerbates this inefficiency.

Observation II: *Limitedimprovement: Overcommit results in competition for hardware resources among sandboxes, leading to performance degradation and limitation of over-provisioning degree.*

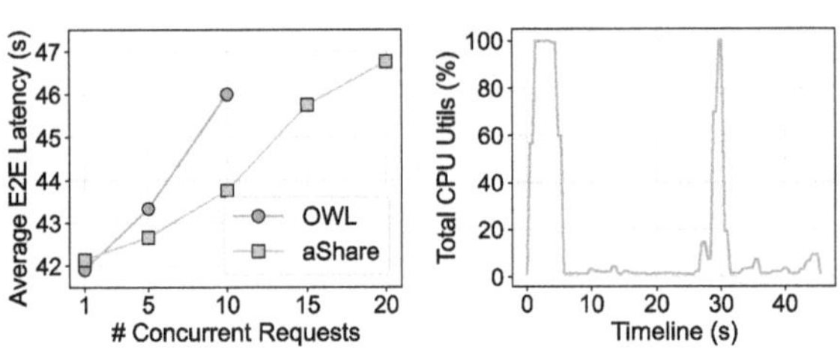

Fig. 4. Performance analysis of *Summarization* under *overcommit*. (a) The performance under various workloads. (b) The timeline of total CPU utilization under 10 co-located sandboxes.

We evaluate the impact of co-locating multiple sandboxes on a single-sandbox resource budget (1 vCPU, 2 GB), as shown in Fig. 4a. Due to CPU contention, latency increases with the number of co-located sandboxes. For example, co-locating 10 sandboxes incurs a 4 s (9.8%) latency increase over exclusive execution, and is 2.2 s slower than `aShare`. Moreover, memory constraints limit co-location to at most 10 sandboxes, preventing *OWL* from sustaining 20 QPS even under relaxed SLOs.

Figure 4b shows CPU utilization with 10 co-located sandboxes. Although peak utilization can reach 100%, most time is still spent waiting for LLM responses, resulting in only 15.9% effective CPU utilization.

Observation III: *Limitedapplicability*: *Reuse is unsuitable for scenarios with sparse invocations, which is common in practice.*

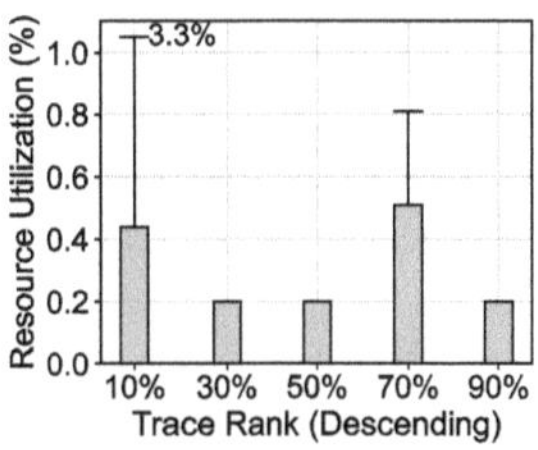

Fig. 5. Average and maximum resource utilization under various ranks of Azure traces.

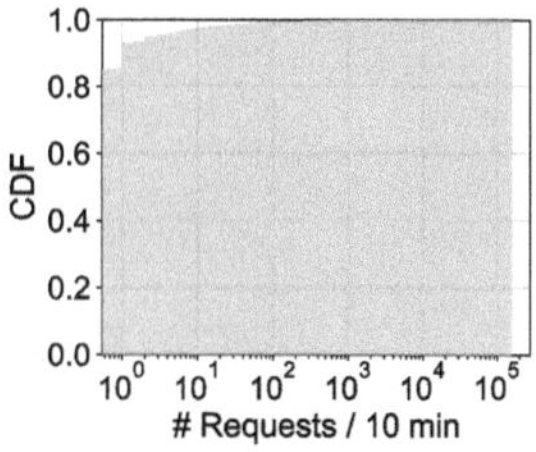

Fig. 6. The distribution of number of requests per 10 min in Azure traces.

To evaluate *reuse*, we analyze Azure Functions traces [11] and measure sandbox utilization in *StepConf* (Fig. 5). With a 10-minute keep-alive, even the top 10% most frequently invoked workloads achieve only 0.44% average utilization (maximum 3.3%), and drop to 0.2% when no reuse occurs—primarily due to sparse invocations [9].

Analyzing 46,412 functions from the Azure day01 trace (Fig. 6), 95% of 10-minute intervals contain at most one request. Although a few functions are highly active, 53.8% of sandboxes are never reused, and 76.5% have reuse counts ≤ 1. This indicates that intra-application sandbox reuse is largely ineffective in practice.

2.3 Implications

Exclusive provisioning combined with LLM-dominated execution leads to low resource utilization **(Observation I)**. While *overcommit* improves spatial sharing, it fails to eliminate prolonged idleness **(Observation II)**. *Reuse* enables temporal sharing within an agent, but sparse invocations limit its effectiveness **(Observation III)**. Consequently, a more effective execution model is needed.

Our goal is to improve efficiency via cross-agent sandbox sharing. This requires (1) forming effective sharing partitions, (2) scheduling requests to minimize idleness while meeting latency constraints, and (3) enabling fast environment switching for efficient reuse across agents.

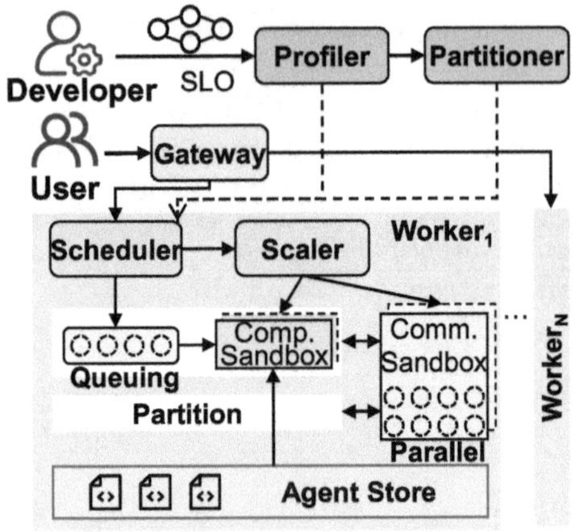

Fig. 7. The overall architecture of `aShare`.

3 Design

3.1 Overview

The basic idea of `aShare` is that the resource inefficiency can be significantly reduced by re-allocating idle sandboxes across agents. Figure 7 illustrates its architecture. The *Profiler* collects per-node execution times to guide scheduling, while the *Partitioner* groups agents by dependencies to define sharing scopes. Upon request arrival, the *Gateway* dispatches it to a worker, where the *Scheduler* selects a suitable computation sandbox under latency SLO and invokes the *Scaler* if needed. The sandbox then loads agent code from the *Agent Store*, and execution proceeds across computation and communication sandboxes until completion.

To reduce cross-agent switching overhead (**Challenge 1**), `aShare` preloads heavyweight dependencies during sandbox initialization, which are identified by the *Profiler*. And a host-mounted directory stores agent code for sandbox, enabling lightweight switching via direct file transfer from the *Agent Store*, avoiding redundant compression and copying.

To maximize sharing efficiency (**Challenge 2**), `aShare` combines offline and online scheduling to minimize sandbox usage. The *Partitioner* first groups agents into minimal partitions based on dependency conflicts, and the *Scheduler* then applies an SLO-aware algorithm to assign requests using the fewest sandboxes.

3.2 Execution Model

Similar to existing orchestrators such as *LangGraph* [1], `aShare` models agent execution as a directed graph, where nodes are defined via APIs with their type and function, and edges specify control and data dependencies. Unlike conventional designs, `aShare` explicitly distinguishes between computation (tool) nodes and communication (LLM) nodes. In particular, LLM nodes return invocation payloads instead of performing blocking calls, enabling subsequent decoupling of execution. `aShare` maintains the complete workflow state in the *Scheduler*, allowing each request to resume execution at any node across different sandboxes.

Based on this abstraction, `aShare` decouples workflows into two types of sandboxes: computation sandboxes for tool execution and communication sandboxes for LLM invocations. Computation sandboxes execute nodes sequentially using the current workflow state and hand off LLM invocation payloads when needed. Communication sandboxes process these payloads, issue LLM calls, and return results for further computation. This separation avoids blocking execution within a single sandbox.

By decoupling computation and communication, `aShare` enables idle resources to be dynamically re-allocated across agents. Computation sandboxes are shared across agents in a time-multiplexed manner to avoid interference, while communication sandboxes exploit parallelism across multiple LLM requests to improve utilization. Combined with stateful execution and dynamic scheduling, this design allows workflows to migrate across sandboxes, supporting efficient cross-agent sharing and significantly reducing resource idleness.

`aShare` enforces isolation across agents through a multi-layered design. In computation sandboxes, the runtime environment is reset before proceeding each request, and user code is executed in a fresh process, preventing residual memory state or cross-request leakage. In communication sandboxes, no user code is executed, and only validated LLM invocation payloads are accepted, with strict input checking to prevent code injection or unauthorized execution.

3.3 Partitioner

Agents may rely on different library versions (e.g., *langchain* 0.3.27 vs. 1.0.0), leading to compatibility conflicts. Therefore, sandbox sharing is restricted to agents without dependency conflicts. The *Partitioner* groups agents into the minimum number of conflict-free partitions to maximize sharing opportunities.

Conflict Graph of Dependency: *Partitioner* first models sharing constraints among agents using a conflict graph $G = (V, E)$, where each vertex corresponds to an agent, and an edge between two vertices indicates that the corresponding agents have dependency conflicts and therefore cannot share the same sandbox. Denoting the dependency of agent i as $D_i = \{(p, v)\}$, with package p and version v. Two agents conflict if they require incompatible versions of any package:

$$(i, j) \in E \iff \exists p : (p, v_i) \in D_i \wedge (p, v_j) \in D_j \wedge v_i \neq v_j.$$

When a dependency does not specify a version, *Partitioner* resolves it to the latest version before conflict detection, ensuring all dependencies are comparable.

Algorithm 1: Core-First Partitioning

Input: Conflict Graph $G = (V, E)$, Threshold δ

Output: Agent Partition P

1 $H \leftarrow G$, $score(v) \leftarrow 0$, $\forall v \in V$;
2 **while** $V(H) \neq \emptyset$ **do**
3     $v \leftarrow \arg\min_{u \in V(H)} \deg_H(u)$;
4     $score[v] \leftarrow \deg_H(v)$; `// compute core number`
5     $H \leftarrow$ remove v and all incident edges from H;
6 $C \leftarrow \{v \in V \mid score(v) \geq \delta\}, R \leftarrow V \setminus C$ `// core set & remaining vertices`
7 $\phi(v) \leftarrow null$, $\forall v \in V; K \leftarrow 0$ `// coloring map & number of colors`
8 **foreach** $v \in C$ *in non-increasing order of* $score(v)$ **do**
9     $\phi(v) \leftarrow$ the smallest feasible color in $\{1, \ldots, K\}$;
10   **if** $\phi(v) = null$ **then**
11         $K \leftarrow K + 1$, $\phi(v) \leftarrow K$;
12 **while** *there exists* $v \in R$ *with* $\phi(v) = null$ **do**
13     $v \leftarrow$ select the uncolored vertex with maximum saturation degree;
14     $\phi(v) \leftarrow$ the smallest feasible color in $\{1, \ldots, K\}$;
15   **if** $\phi(v) = null$ **then**
16         $K \leftarrow K + 1$, $\phi(v) \leftarrow K$;
17 $P_k \leftarrow \{v \in V \mid \phi(v) = k\}$, $\forall k \in \{1, \ldots, K\}; P \leftarrow \{P_1, \ldots, P_K\}$;
18 **return** P;

Core-First Partitioning: The *Partitioner* adopts a heuristic based on the DSatur graph coloring algorithm [12], prioritizing high-conflict agents to stabilize partitioning. It first computes a *core number* [13] by iteratively removing the vertex with the minimum degree and recording its degree at removal (Lines 2–5), and selects high-score vertices as the *core set* (Line 6). It then assigns agents in descending score order, placing each into an existing conflict-free partition or creating a new one if necessary (Lines 8–11).

Next, the *Partitioner* applies the DSatur algorithm to the remaining agents, iteratively selecting the uncolored vertex with the highest saturation degree (Line 13) and assigning the smallest available color not used by its neighbors (Line 14). This process continues until all vertices are colored, yielding the final agent partitions (Line 17).

3.4 Scheduler

Given the partitioning results, the *Scheduler* aims to minimize sandbox usage while meeting latency SLOs. Due to differing execution characteristics, it adopts distinct strategies: for CPU-intensive computation sandboxes, it uses Earliest Deadline First (EDF) scheduling with queued, time-shared execution; for I/O-intensive communication sandboxes, it enables parallel execution based on the sandbox's concurrency limit.

Algorithm 2: SLO-Aware Sandbox Scheduling via EDF

Input: Request queue Q, Current time t, Execution time C, Deadline D, Arriving request τ_{new}

1 **for** $s \leftarrow 1$ **to** m **do** `// first-fit`
2     $Q_s \leftarrow Q_s \cup \{\tau_{\text{new}}\}$ `// tentative queuing`
3   **if** EDFCheck(Q_s, t) **then**
4   **return** s `// schedule to sandbox s`
5     $Q_s \leftarrow Q_s \setminus \{\tau_{\text{new}}\}$ `// rollback`
6 $Q \leftarrow Q \cup \{Q_{s+1}\}, Q_{s+1} \leftarrow \{\tau_{\text{new}}\}$ `// scaling a new sandbox`
7 **Function** EDFCheck(Q, t):
8   Sort Q by nondecreasing deadlines;
9     $S \leftarrow 0$ `// cumulative queuing time`
10   **for** $i \leftarrow 1$ **to** k **do**
11   **if** $t + S + C_i > D_i$ **then**
12   **return false**`// EDF infeasible`
13         $S \leftarrow S + C_i$;
14   **return true**;

The scheduling strategy for computation sandboxes is shown in Algorithm 2. The *Scheduler* adopts a first-fit policy, attempting to insert each request into existing sandbox queues (Lines 1–2). It then applies EDF ordering to verify SLO feasibility (Lines 7–14). If satisfied, the request is admitted (Lines 3–4); otherwise, it evaluates the next sandbox. If none meet the SLO, a new sandbox is created via the *Scaler* (Line 6).

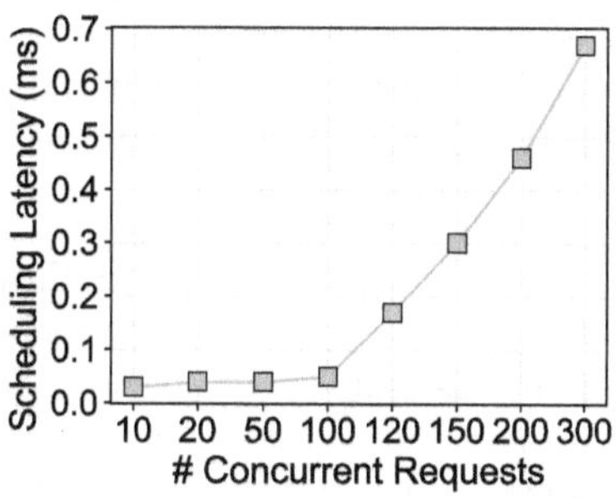

Fig. 8. Scheduling latency of event loop under various concurrent requests.

For I/O-bound communication sandboxes, `aShare` sets a parallelism limit to balance concurrency and scheduling overhead. As shown in Fig. 8, scheduling latency increases sharply beyond a parallelism of 100. Thus, the maximum parallelism is set to 100. The *Scheduler* assigns requests using a first-fit policy across available communication sandboxes.

4 Implementation

We implement `aShare` on Docker using Python 3.12. All components expose their functionality as web services built with *FastAPI* [14].

For intra-node communication, we use Unix Domain Sockets (UDS) instead of TCP to reduce latency. The *Scaler* and *Agent Store* bind to UDS endpoints at startup, while the *Scheduler* connects via *aiohttp* [15]. Additionally, the *Scheduler* exposes a dedicated socket for sandbox interaction. Each sandbox mounts this socket at startup and registers with the *Scheduler* to establish communication.

To ease adoption, `aShare` provides an interface that converts blocking LLM calls into transferable payloads, avoiding manual refactoring. Built on *LangChain*, we introduce *get_payload* as a drop-in replacement for *invoke*, enabling payload extraction for models, chains, and tools via native APIs without modifying the framework.

5 Evaluation

5.1 Methodology

Experimental Setup: We evaluate `aShare` on a 12-node cluster running Ubuntu 22.04. Each node is equipped with 128 CPU cores (Intel Xeon Gold 6338 @ 2.00 GHz) and 256 GB of memory. And these nodes are connected via 25 Gbps, full-bisection bandwidth Ethernet.

Benchmarks: We evaluate `aShare` and the comparison systems using three benchmarks. *Summarization* [10] is a MapReduce-style document summarization agent. *SQL* [16] is a database question-answering agent that queries a local database based on user inputs. *TravelPlanner* [17] is a task-oriented agent that produces travel itineraries, including flights, accommodations, and dining options. These three agents exhibit substantial differences in the frequency and latency characteristics of tool invocations and LLM invocations.

Comparison Systems: We compare `aShare` with *Base*, *OWL*, and *StepConf*. Specifically, *Base* allocates a dedicated sandbox for each request. *OWL* achieves spatial sharing by determining the number of co-located sandboxes on the same physical resource based on given latency SLO. *StepConf* derives per-node sub-SLO from latency requirements and enables temporal sharing among requests within the same agent. Note that, we also decompose the workflows in *StepConf* into communication and computation nodes to enable sandbox sharing for a fair comparison.

5.2 Overall Performance

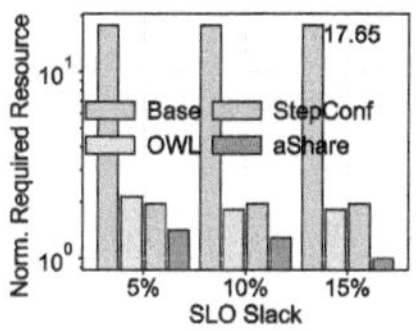

Fig. 9. Comparison of resource.

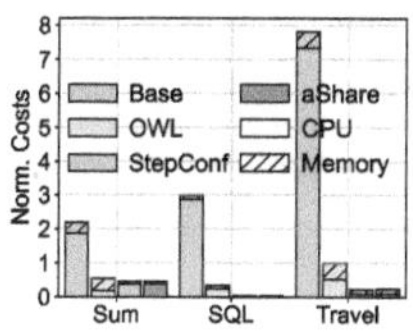

Fig. 10. Comparison of overall cost.

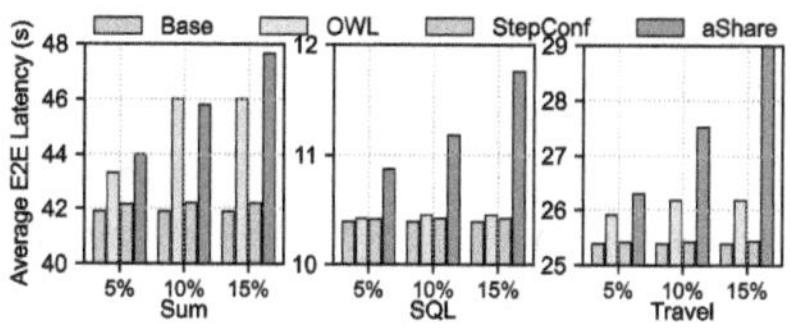

Fig. 11. Comparison of overall latency under Poisson trace.

Resource Consumption: We first evaluate benchmarks using generated Poisson workloads. Specifically, we set the SLOs by adding 5%, 10%, and 15% slack to the baseline latency under the exclusive configuration. Figure 9 illustrates the resource consumption required by each system to sustain the workload. The results show that `aShare` consistently achieves the highest resource efficiency, and its advantage becomes more pronounced as the latency constraints are relaxed. Overall, `aShare` reduces resource consumption by an average of 92.9%, 35.9%, and 36.8% compared to *Base*, *OWL*, and *StepConf*, respectively.

Overall Latency: Figure 11 presents the overall latency under Poisson workloads. The results show that `aShare` effectively exploits SLO slack to improve resource efficiency compared to other systems. Although *OWL* and *StepConf* retain considerable SLO slack, their resource-sharing efficiency remains limited due to physical resource constraints and the sparsity of invocation patterns.

Cost Efficiency: Figure 10 reports the resource cost of different systems under AgentCore [3] pricing model. By decoupling workflows into tool and LLM nodes, `aShare` eliminates redundant CPU and memory charges, achieving 4.8–66.5× and 1.2–7.7× cost improvements over *Base* and *OWL*, respectively. Note that, compared to *StepConf*, which also adopts a decoupled design, `aShare` incurs slightly higher costs due to additional dependency loading and code reloading overhead. However, the increase is ranging from only 1.9–5.6%.

5.3 Overhead and Scalability

Performance Breakdown: Figure 12 illustrates the contribution of individual components to overall latency. Preloading dependencies, replacing TCP with UDS, and EDF scheduling reduce latency by 5.49 s, 0.18 s, and 1.38 s, respectively.

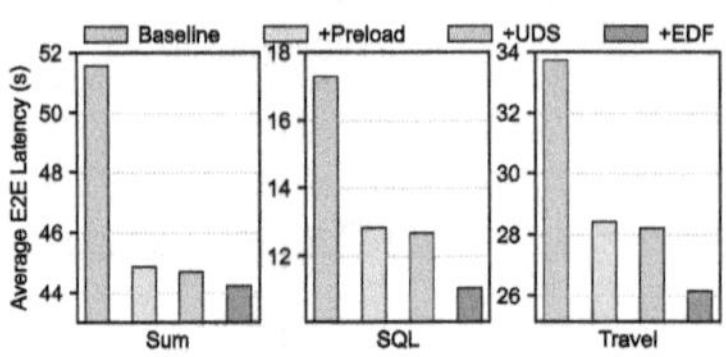

Fig. 12. Performance contribution of different components.

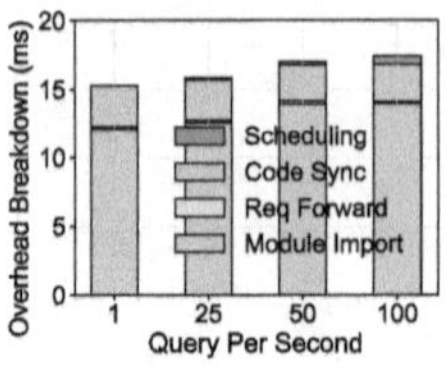

Fig. 13. Overhead breakdown.

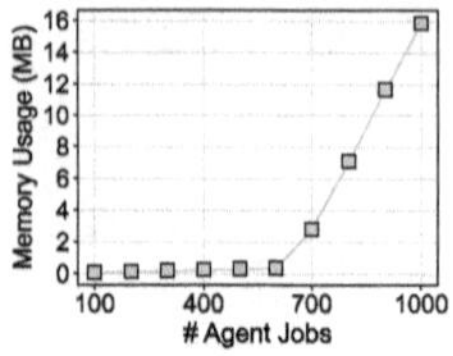

Fig. 14. Overhead of caching state.

Performance Breakdown: Figure 13 presents the overhead introduced by different stages. The overheads of scheduling, code synchronization, and request forwarding are minimal, at 0.25ms, 2.82ms, and 0.17ms, respectively. In contrast, dependency import incurs overhead of 13.13ms, primarily because each request involves spawning a new process and loading partial modules. As agents typically include LLM invocations on the order of seconds, these overheads are negligible in practice.

State Caching: Figure 14 shows the memory overhead of caching execution states for *Summarization*. The average state size per request is 4.8KB. Even with 1000 concurrent requests, the total memory consumption is only 15.8MB, indicating that the state storage overhead is negligible in practice.

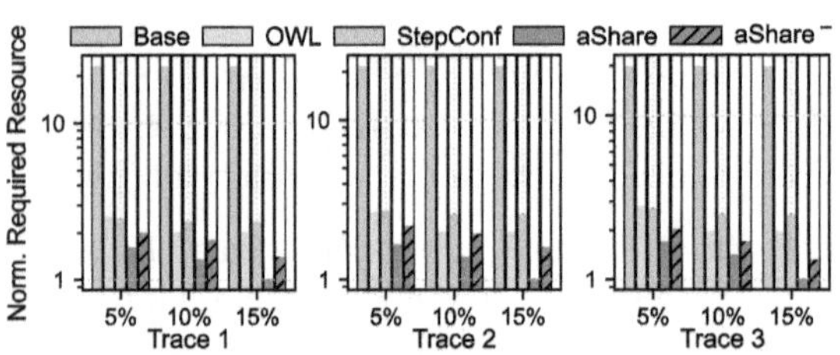

Fig. 15. Resource consumption with Azure trace.

Scalability: We further evaluate `aShare` at a larger scale. Specifically, we collect dependency information from 72 applications drawn from open-source benchmarks such as AgentBench [18] and FunctionBench [19], and map the original three agents onto these benchmarks to construct a large-scale deployment. Then, we adopt an Azure production workload [11] to evaluate resource consumption, with results shown in Fig. 15.

As the deployment scale increases, `aShare` is able to more effectively share idle sandboxes across agents, thereby achieving higher resource efficiency. Overall, `aShare` reduces resource consumption by an average of 93.7%, 40.1%, and 46.9% compared to *Base*, *OWL*, and *StepConf*, respectively. Even when restricting the number of agents per partition to at most five (i.e., $\texttt{aShare}^{-}$), it still achieves resource savings of 91.7%, 20.8%, and 30.2% relative to these baselines.

6 Related Work

Allocating a dedicated sandbox for each request remains the predominant design in current agent systems [3,4]. *TrEnv-X* [5] mitigates memory redundancy under exclusive allocation through cross-sandbox memory sharing. To address low CPU utilization, *OWL* [6] and *Gsight* [7] co-locate multiple sandboxes on the same set of cores. However, since agents spend most execution time waiting for LLM responses, such spatial sharing approaches provide limited improvements in overall resource efficiency. Alternatively, *StepConf* [8] and *Aquatope* [20] leverage SLO-aware scheduling and dynamic resource provisioning to enable temporal resource sharing. Nevertheless, in practice, most applications exhibit sparse invocation patterns, making it difficult to effectively share resources across requests within the same application.

7 Conclusions

This paper presents `aShare`, an agent system that re-allocates idle sandboxes to enable cross-agent resource sharing. It makes two key contributions: (1) Resource efficiency: `aShare` mitigates resource inefficiency caused by prolonged waiting during LLM invocations through cross-agent sandbox sharing. (2) Cost efficiency: `aShare` decouples computation from communication, thereby eliminating redundant resource billing.

Acknowledgments. This work is supported by the National Key Research and Development Program of China under Grant No.2024YFB4505204, the National Natural Science Foundation of China under Grant 62372322, 62432015, and Tianjin Science and Technology Plan Project 24ZXKJGX00060.

The technical solution and experimental design presented in this paper were independently completed by the authors. AI tools were used solely for language polishing and formatting optimization, and did not participate in the development of the research ideas or core content.

References

1. LangChain Inc: LangGraph: Agent Orchestration Framework for Reliable AI Agents (2026). https://www.langchain.com/langgraph
2. LangGenius, Inc: Dify: Leading Agentic Workflow Builder (2026). https://dify.ai/
3. Amazon Web Services, Inc: Amazon Bedrock AgentCore - Accelerate agents to production with composable services that work with any framework, any model (2026). https://aws.amazon.com/bedrock/agentcore/
4. FoundryLabs, Inc: E2B: Open-source infrastructure for AI apps (2026). https://e2b.dev/
5. Huang, J., Ma, T., Liu, Z., et al.: Trenv: transparently share serverless execution environments across different functions and nodes (2025). https://arxiv.org/abs/2509.09525

6. Tian, H., Li, S., Wang, A., et al.: Owl: performance-aware scheduling for resource-efficient function-as-a-service cloud. In: Proceedings of the 13th Symposium on Cloud Computing, SoCC '22, pp. 78–93. Association for Computing Machinery, New York (2022). https://doi.org/10.1145/3542929.3563470
7. Zhao, L., Yang, Y., Li, Y.: Understanding, predicting and scheduling serverless workloads under partial interference. In: Proceedings of the International Conference for High Performance Computing, Networking, Storage and Analysis, SC '21. Association for Computing Machinery, New York (2021). https://doi.org/10.1145/3458817.3476215
8. Wen, Z., Wang, Y., Liu, F.: Stepconf: slo-aware dynamic resource configuration for serverless function workflows. In: IEEE INFOCOM 2022 - IEEE Conference on Computer Communications, pp. 1868–1877 (2022). https://doi.org/10.1109/INFOCOM48880.2022.9796962
9. Mahgoub, A., Yi, E.B., Shankar, K., et al.: ORION and the three rights: sizing, bundling, and prewarming for serverless DAGs. In: 16th USENIX Symposium on Operating Systems Design and Implementation (OSDI 22), pp. 303–320. USENIX Association, Carlsbad (2022)
10. LangChain, Inc: Summarization agent (2024). https://github.com/langchain-ai/langchain/blob/v0.1.17rc1/docs/docs/use_cases/summarization.ipynb
11. Shahrad, M., Fonseca, R., Goiri, I.: Serverless in the wild: characterizing and optimizing the serverless workload at a large cloud provider. In: 2020 USENIX Annual Technical Conference (USENIX ATC 20), pp. 205–218. USENIX Association (2020)
12. Brélaz, D.: New methods to color the vertices of a graph. Commun. ACM **22**(4), 251–256 (1979)
13. Seidman, S.B.: Network structure and minimum degree. Social Netw. **5**(3), 269–287 (1983)
14. Ramírez, S.: Fastapi is a modern, fast (high-performance), web framework for building apis with python based on standard python type hints (2026). https://fastapi.tiangolo.com/
15. aiohttp contributors: aiohttp: Asynchronous http client/server for asyncio and python (2026). https://docs.aiohttp.org/
16. LangChain, Inc: Build a sql agent - docs by langchain (2026). https://docs.langchain.com/oss/python/langchain/sql-agent
17. Xie, J., Zhang, K., Chen, J., et al.: Travelplanner: a benchmark for real-world planning with language agents. In: Proceedings of the 41st International Conference on Machine Learning. ICML 2024. JMLR.org (2024)
18. Liu, X., Yu, H., Zhang, H., et al.: Agentbench: evaluating LLMs as agents. In: The Twelfth International Conference on Learning Representations, ICLR 2024, Vienna, Austria, 7–11 May 2024. OpenReview.net (2024)
19. Kim, J., Lee, K.: Functionbench: a suite of workloads for serverless cloud function service. In: IEEE 12th International Conference on Cloud Computing (CLOUD), pp. 502–504 (2019)
20. Zhou, Z., Zhang, Y., Delimitrou, C.: Aquatope: QoS-and-uncertainty-aware resource management for multi-stage serverless workflows. In: Proceedings of the 28th ACM International Conference on Architectural Support for Programming Languages and Operating Systems, ASPLOS 2023, vol. 1, p. 1–14. Association for Computing Machinery, New York (2022)

CGR: A Budget-Aware Closed-Loop Framework for Efficient Knowledge Graph Question Answering

Yapeng Li[1], Hu Zhang[1,2(✉)], Jibin Wang[1,2], Jing Chen[1,2], and Lijuan Xu[1,2]

[1] Key Laboratory of Computing Power Network and Information Security, Ministry of Education, Shandong Computer Science Center (National Supercomputer Center in Jinan), Qilu University of Technology (Shandong Academy of Sciences), Jinan 250013, Shandong, China
zhanghu@sdas.org
[2] Shandong Provincial Key Laboratory of Computing Power Internet and Service Computing, Shandong Fundamental Research Center for Computer Science, Jinan 250013, Shandong, China

Abstract. Large Language Models (LLMs) have shown strong performance in knowledge-intensive question answering, yet practical deployment on complex Knowledge Graph Question Answering (KGQA) tasks remains challenging. Existing KG-augmented methods often face a trade-off between cost and robustness: interactive search requires frequent LLM calls and incurs high token cost and latency, while rigid retrieval pipelines are vulnerable to early retrieval errors and provide little support for correction. To address this problem, we propose Cognitive Graph Reasoning (CGR), a budget-aware closed-loop framework for efficient KGQA. CGR consists of a query initialization module, System 1, a High-Density Evidence Interface, and System 2. System 1 combines lightweight neural graph search, dynamic pruning, and multi-source collaboration to efficiently construct relevant evidence paths. The High-Density Evidence Interface compresses these paths into compact contexts, and System 2 triggers feedback retrieval when the current evidence is insufficient, mitigating the error propagation problem of single-pass pipelines. Experiments on WebQSP, CWQ, and GrailQA show that CGR maintains or improves accuracy while reducing token consumption by up to 92.9% and lowering end-to-end latency by 4–6×. These results suggest that CGR is a practical KGQA solution for resource-constrained settings.

Keywords: Knowledge Graphs · Large Language Models · Natural Language Processing · Retrieval-Augmented Generation

1 Introduction

Large Language Models (LLMs) have advanced significantly across a wide range of tasks [4,15,21], but they still face clear limitations in complex multi-hop reasoning [13,32]. In such settings, LLMs often suffer from outdated knowledge [22],

L. Eeckhout et al. (Eds.): APPT 2026, LNCS 16693, pp. 203–218, 2027.
https://doi.org/10.1007/978-981-92-4805-6_14

factual hallucinations, and limited verifiability. Structured Knowledge Graphs (KGs) [19,28] provide traceable and verifiable evidence, making KG–LLM integration an important direction for improving reasoning reliability.

However, existing fusion methods still face practical challenges. Interactive search methods such as ToG [25] are flexible, but their step-by-step reliance on LLMs often leads to high computational cost and latency, as illustrated in Fig. 1(c). In contrast, serial architectures (Fig. 1(b)) follow a fixed feed-forward pipeline, where missing key evidence in retrieval can cause irreversible "error propagation" [34] in downstream reasoning, with little support for dynamic correction. Moreover, without explicit budget control, reflective retrieval-augmented reasoning [14,17,24] may trigger excessive retries and further increase computation overhead. Therefore, we ask: *How can we build a KG-augmented LLM reasoning system that balances cost, robustness, and error correction?*

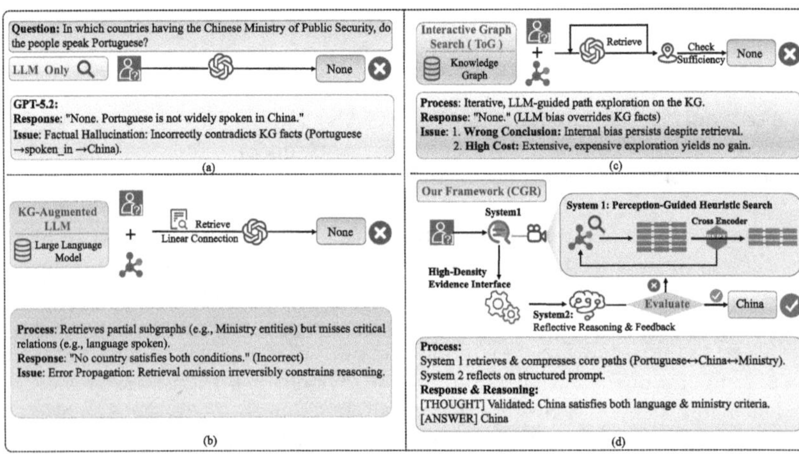

Fig. 1. Comparison of existing KGQA paradigms and CGR. (a) LLM Only. (b) Linear RAG. (c) Interactive Search (ToG). (d) CGR.

To describe the different roles of retrieval and reasoning in complex KGQA more clearly, we draw inspiration from the "Dual-Process Theory" in cognitive science [12] and use its terminology to denote the two major stages of our framework as System 1 and System 2. Specifically, Cognitive Graph Reasoning (CGR) (Fig. 1(d)) organizes the high-throughput graph retrieval stage as System 1 and the on-demand reasoning and verification stage as System 2. In KGQA, this separation fits the task structure well: large-scale knowledge graph traversal is better handled by a high-throughput retrieval module, while answering complex queries depends more on downstream evidence integration and logical verification.

Unlike existing methods that require expensive LLMs to participate deeply in low-level graph traversal (Fig. 1(c)), CGR decouples high-frequency but lightweight graph search from low-frequency but critical reasoning decisions. Concretely, System 1 (Fast Retrieval) performs query-aware path expansion, pruning, and evidence construction, while System 2 (Reflective Reasoning) performs answer generation and sufficiency checking based on compressed evidence, and triggers further retrieval only when needed. This design concentrates additional computation on the samples that truly require complex reasoning, leading to a better balance between effectiveness and cost in complex KGQA.

We frame CGR primarily as a system-level architectural contribution that integrates existing techniques into a unified closed-loop design for cost-controlled KGQA. The main contributions of this paper are as follows:

- **Closed-Loop KGQA Framework:** We present CGR, a budget-aware closed-loop framework for complex KGQA. CGR assigns high-throughput graph retrieval to System 1 and reserves on-demand reasoning and verification for System 2, reducing unnecessary LLM usage.
- **Key Mechanisms:** In System 1, CGR combines lightweight neural graph search, dynamic pruning, and multi-source collaboration to efficiently construct multi-hop evidence paths. It further introduces a High-Density Evidence Interface to compress redundant paths and a Reflection-Driven Feedback mechanism to trigger re-retrieval when evidence is insufficient, mitigating the error propagation problem of single-pass pipelines.
- **Empirical Results:** Experiments on WebQSP, CWQ, and GrailQA show that CGR maintains or improves accuracy on complex queries while reducing token consumption by up to 92.9% and lowering inference latency by 4–6$\times$, demonstrating strong practical utility in resource-constrained settings.

2 Related Work

KG-Augmented Retrieval and Reasoning. Recent work has extensively explored integrating Knowledge Graphs (KGs) with Large Language Models (LLMs) for knowledge-intensive tasks [16,20,35]. Most methods follow a retrieval-generation paradigm, where KGs serve as external knowledge sources. A central challenge is how to maintain sufficient evidence coverage without incurring excessive reasoning cost.

LLM-guided search methods, such as ToG [25], treat the LLM as an agent for step-by-step graph exploration. While flexible and interpretable, they incur high cost and latency due to repeated LLM involvement. Expansion-based methods such as ReKnoS [29] enlarge the search space through "Super-Relations," but still require expensive relation scoring and provide limited support for correction. Serial pipelines such as StructGPT [11] and tool-augmented approaches [23] improve single-pass efficiency, but retrieval omissions can directly propagate to downstream reasoning and hurt robustness.

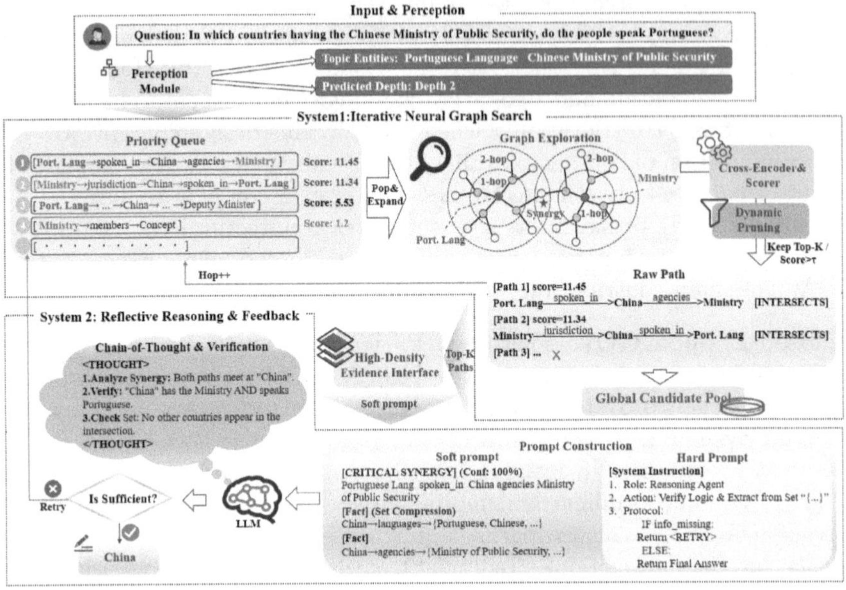

Fig. 2. Overview of CGR. System 1 performs iterative neural graph search with dynamic pruning, and System 2 performs answer generation with feedback-driven correction. A High-Density Evidence Interface compresses graph paths into token-efficient prompts. The red dashed line denotes the <RETRY>-triggered feedback loop. (Color figure online)

Reasoning, Self-correction, and Knowledge Injection. Reflection-based reasoning methods aim to improve reliability. Chain-of-Thought (CoT) [30] increases reasoning transparency, but its reliance on parametric knowledge often leads to factual hallucination. In KG reasoning, PoG [6] introduces backtracking and multi-round correction, but each correction requires additional global search, resulting in high computational overhead.

Another related line studies how to inject structured KG evidence into LLMs [7,9,31]. Traditional linearization methods [27] often produce redundant contexts, while dynamic prompting methods such as KAPING [2] and Light-PROF [1] usually treat prompt construction as a separate post-processing step. As a result, they provide limited support for jointly optimizing retrieval, compression, and downstream reasoning in multi-hop settings.

Summary and Baselines. Existing KG-augmented reasoning methods typically trade off flexibility, robustness, and cost. Interactive approaches such as ToG and PoG are flexible but expensive, whereas serial and expansion-based methods such as StructGPT and ReKnoS often lack effective feedback or robustness. Therefore, we use ToG, PoG, and ReKnoS as our primary baselines. These methods are representative training-free frameworks from different design paradigms, allowing us to focus on the practical impact of reasoning system design rather than model-specific fine-tuning gains.

3 CGR Framework

3.1 Overall Framework

CGR draws inspiration from the terminology of the Dual-Process paradigm [12] and uses System 1 and System 2 to denote the two major stages of the framework. We model the knowledge base as a multi-relational heterogeneous graph $\mathcal{G} = (\mathcal{V}, \mathcal{R}, \mathcal{E})$.

As shown in Fig. 2, CGR organizes KGQA as a budget-aware closed-loop process rather than a static linear retrieval pipeline. The framework comprises four modules described below.

3.2 Perception Module

The Perception module aligns the search scope with the difficulty of the query by initializing the key navigation parameters for retrieval.

Entity Anchoring: Given a query q, the module identifies the topic entity set $E_{topic} = \{e_i\}_{i=1}^{m}$ as the starting points for graph traversal. We adopt a hybrid extraction strategy: the module primarily uses the Named Entity Recognition (NER) capability of spaCy [10], and falls back to Regex-based rule matching when the neural parser is unavailable.

Complexity-Aware Depth Prediction: The module also predicts the search depth K according to the complexity of the query. In our framework, K is adaptively assigned to either a baseline depth ($K = 2$) or an extended depth ($K = 3$), allowing the retrieval stage to avoid unnecessary expansion on simple queries while preserving coverage for more complex multi-hop questions.

The baseline $K = 2$ suffices for most queries; $K = 3$ is triggered only when the question contains deep-chain keywords such as `grandmother`, `grandfather`, `ancestor`, `timeline`, or `chronology`.

3.3 System 1: Iterative Neural Graph Search

Given the initialized topic entities E_{topic} and the predicted search depth K, System 1 performs budget-aware iterative graph exploration. Unlike discrete text retrieval, it searches directly over the topological structure of the knowledge graph and progressively constructs a task-specific evidence subgraph.

Concretely, System 1 maintains a frontier initialized by the topic entities and repeatedly applies an "expand-score-prune" loop. Candidate paths are expanded along graph connectivity, ranked by a priority queue, and evaluated with a Cross-Encoder for fine-grained semantic relevance. Low-relevance branches are pruned online to control the search space and avoid combinatorial explosion. Under the constraints of the search budget and predicted depth, System 1 returns a set of Top-K evidence paths for downstream reasoning.

Neural Search Strategy. In System 1, we maintain a Priority Queue in which each element represents a path p:

$$p = [e_0, r_1, e_1, \ldots, r_t, e_t] \quad (1)$$

where e_t is the current tail node and r_t is the corresponding relation. The priority of a path is determined by a neural scoring function $s(q, p)$, which uses a Cross-Encoder to batch-evaluate the relevance between the path and the query q.

To avoid combinatorial explosion from long-tail degree distributions, we adopt a relation-first strategy: candidate relations from the current node are scored and ranked before path expansion, with only top-ranked paths expanded. An adaptive per-relation cap (`rel_cap`) and dynamic threshold pruning further control cost.

Dynamic Pruning: Max-δ with Top-K Guarantee. To further control the search space, we use a dynamic pruning mechanism. We first compute the maximum score among the current candidate paths and then define a dynamic threshold:

$$\tau = \max_i(s_i) - \Delta \quad (2)$$

where s_i is the score of a candidate path and Δ is a relaxation term adjusted according to task complexity. A path is retained only if its score is greater than τ or if it is ranked within the top K.

In our experiments, we set $\Delta = 8.0$ for single-entity tasks and $\Delta = 5.0$ for multi-entity tasks, with `rel_cap` = 30 vs. 15 and beam width 50 vs. 30, respectively.

Evidence Synergy and Aggregation. For multi-anchor tasks, we identify joint evidence by detecting intersections between search frontiers. When paths from different anchors meet at the same node, they are merged into a synergy path marked with `[INTERSECTS]` and assigned higher priority. To reduce pseudo-intersection noise, we filter out nodes belonging to a predefined blocklist of high-degree Freebase type concepts (e.g., "City", "Year", "Country", "Person") that appear across diverse domains and provide no discriminative semantic evidence for specific queries; nodes with purely numeric names or fewer than two characters are filtered under the same principle.

We further apply CVT-aware pruning: paths terminating at Freebase Compound Value Type nodes (identifiers prefixed with `m.` or `g.`) are retained with a relaxed threshold (`keep_k` = 20 for multi-entity CVT paths vs. 8 for non-CVT paths; single-entity tasks use 20 uniformly) to avoid prematurely truncating paths whose answer lies one hop beyond the intermediate node.

To improve coverage and diversity, we maintain a global candidate pool P_{pool}. After search, the pool undergoes deduplication (highest-score instance retained), ranking by descending score, and per-relation quota control: we set `MAX_PER_REL` $= 30$ for single-entity and 3 for multi-entity, with a global cap of 60 paths; synergy paths marked with `[INTERSECTS]` bypass the quota.

This process allows System 1 to preserve more relevant and diverse evidence paths under a fixed context budget.

3.4 High-Density Evidence Interface

The High-Density Evidence Interface connects System 1 and System 2. Although the candidate paths produced by System 1 contain rich structural information, their symbolic form is not directly suitable for LLM reasoning. The interface therefore linearizes and compresses these structured paths into a compact context, preserving key evidence while controlling token cost.

Let the output of System 1 be a set of candidate paths with relevance scores:

$$P = (p_i, s_i)_{i=1}^{M}. \tag{3}$$

The interface converts them into a context $C = f(P)$ under a context budget constraint. Specifically, only the Top-L compressed entries are retained to match the effective context window of the downstream LLM. This encourages the interface to maximize information density per token while avoiding context overflow.

To reduce redundancy, paths sharing the same prefix are merged into set-based representations. Intersecting paths are preserved separately with explicit labels such as `[CRITICAL SYNERGY]`. The final compressed context is defined as

$$C = \text{Top-}L(\text{Compress}(P)). \tag{4}$$

The compressed token cost of this procedure can be characterized as follows. For M paths sharing a depth-k prefix with distinct tails, $T_{\text{comp}} \approx k + M$ versus $T_{\text{raw}} \approx M(k+1)$, yielding a best-case compression ratio $\rho \approx 1/(k+1)$ (the actual ratio is lower due to partial prefix overlap and synergy paths that cannot be merged). This compression is *answer-preserving*: the set notation $\{x_1, \ldots, x_n\}$ is semantically equivalent to flat enumeration under the explicit instructions provided to System 2, and the `[CRITICAL SYNERGY]` label ensures that intersecting paths survive prefix merging.

The resulting `soft_prompt` is then passed to System 2 as the evidence context for downstream reasoning.

3.5 System 2: Reflective Reasoning and Feedback

System 2 takes this compressed context C and generates the final answer. We formulate the model input as

$$x = [\text{Instruction}; C; q], \quad y = \text{LLM}(x), \tag{5}$$

Algorithm 1. Reflective Reasoning and Feedback Loop

Input: query q, initial paths $\mathcal{P}_{raw}$, max retries $R_{\max}$
Parameters: search depth K, beam width $\mathcal{B}$
Output: final answer y

$r \leftarrow 0$, $\mathcal{P} \leftarrow \mathcal{P}_{raw}$
while $r \leq R_{\max}$ **do**
  $C \leftarrow$ HighDensityInterface($\mathcal{P}$)
  $prompt \leftarrow$ [Instruction; C; q]
  $y \leftarrow$ LLM($prompt$)
  if `<RETRY>` $\notin y$ **and** y is sufficient **then**
    return y
  else if $r < R_{\max}$ **then**
    $r \leftarrow r + 1$
    $K \leftarrow \min(K + 1, K_{\max})$
    $\mathcal{P} \leftarrow$ System1Search($q, K, \mathcal{B}$)
  else
    return "Unable to answer"
  end if
end while

where `Instruction` constrains the model to prioritize evidence-based answering and output the special token `<RETRY>` only when the current evidence is insufficient or irrelevant.

To mitigate the irrecoverable retrieval omission problem in static pipelines, System 2 performs sufficiency checking after generation. If the output contains `<RETRY>` or negative signals such as "unable to answer" or "no information," the current evidence is treated as insufficient and re-retrieval is triggered. The gating function is defined as

$$g(y) = \mathbb{I}(\langle \text{RETRY} \rangle \in y \vee y \in \mathcal{U}), \tag{6}$$

where $\mathcal{U}$ denotes the set of negative responses.

When $g(y) = 1$, System 2 triggers feedback-driven re-retrieval by updating the retrieval budget and re-running System 1, for example by increasing the search depth K or the beam width $\mathcal{B}$. The new evidence is then used for another round of reasoning. To control the overall cost, the number of retries is capped at R, which guarantees

$$N_{LLM} \leq 1 + R. \tag{7}$$

This closed loop enables CGR to perform error correction through "re-retrieve and re-reason" when evidence is insufficient, while keeping invocation cost bounded. The detailed procedure is given in Algorithm 1.

The prompt (see released code) instructs the LLM to output `[THOUGHT]` followed by `[ANSWER]`, with explicit guidance that compressed set notation $\{A, B, C\}$ represents entities sharing the same relation; a few-shot example is selected dynamically based on whether the task involves single or multiple topic entities. The negative response set U in Eq. (6) includes patterns such as `"i don't know"` and `"no information"` (case-insensitive).

4 Experiments

4.1 Datasets and Metrics

We evaluate CGR on three mainstream KGQA benchmarks built on Freebase [5]: WebQSP [33], CWQ [26], and GrailQA [8]. These datasets cover basic relational reasoning, complex multi-hop questions, and generalization to unseen query structures, respectively.

Because training-free methods can be costly at benchmark scale, we adopt a deterministic protocol with a fixed random seed and evaluate each method on 1,000 test instances per benchmark. This provides a practical balance between evaluation coverage and cost, while enabling consistent comparison of answer quality, LLM usage, and latency under the same budget.

We justify this sample size as follows. With $n = 1{,}000$, the maximum standard error of Hits@1 is 1.58% (binomial, $p = 0.5$), yielding a 95% CI half-width of 3.1%. All CGR–baseline gaps in Table 1 exceed this threshold (e.g., +7.6 pp on CWQ), confirming $p < 0.05$ significance. CGR ranks first on all six dataset–backbone settings, indicating that the observed advantage is systematic rather than an artifact of sampling. We report Hits@1 for accuracy, together with three efficiency metrics: average token consumption (Avg.Tokens), average API calls (Avg.Calls), and end-to-end latency (Latency).

4.2 Baselines

We compare CGR with three representative training-free KGQA baselines to evaluate different reasoning paradigms in a plug-and-play setting:

- **ToG (Think-on-Graph)** [25]: a representative LLM-guided interactive graph search method. It offers flexibility and interpretability, but incurs high reasoning cost due to repeated LLM interaction.
- **PoG (Plan-on-Graph)** [6]: a representative agentic planning method with feedback-based correction. It improves answer quality through multi-round search and revision, but typically requires more LLM calls.
- **ReKnoS (Reasoning with Super-Relations)** [29]: a representative search-space expansion method. It broadens retrieval scope through super-relations, providing a useful comparison against CGR's feedback-based handling of retrieval gaps.

These baselines represent three different design choices—interactive search, agentic planning, and search-space expansion—and allow us to compare CGR from both accuracy and cost perspectives.

4.3 Experimental Setup

Fairness Control. To focus the comparison on the reasoning framework itself and reduce variance from entity linking, all graph-based methods (ToG, PoG, ReKnoS, and CGR) use the annotated topic entities provided by the datasets as Freebase retrieval anchors. In addition, all methods use the same answer normalization and evaluation scripts to ensure a consistent scoring protocol.

All baselines are evaluated using their public code releases, with the LLM backbone and decoding parameters aligned to match CGR's settings (`max_length` 4096, temperature 0.3).

System 1 uses `cross-encoder/ms-marco-MiniLM-L-6-v2` (used off-the-shelf without fine-tuning) on a single NVIDIA A100 (40GB) GPU with batch size 32. Key hyperparameters are: $R = 2$, adaptive $K \in \{2, 3\}$, beam width 50 (single) or 30 (multi), $\Delta = 8.0$ (single) or 5.0 (multi), `rel_cap` $= 30$ (single) or 15 (multi), pool cap 60, and interface budget $L = 20$. All latency measurements are end-to-end—including SPARQL execution, Cross-Encoder scoring, graph traversal, prompt construction, and LLM inference—measured under identical hardware with sequential execution. We release the full source code at https://github.com/ICALab-nsccjn/CGR-Cognitive-Graph-Reasoning.

Models and Hardware Environment. To evaluate CGR under different deployment conditions, we conduct experiments with both a cloud-based large model and a locally deployed smaller model, and report accuracy, LLM usage, and latency under a unified hardware setting.

Table 1. Performance and efficiency comparison under different backbones.

Dataset	Method	DeepSeek-V3.1				Qwen2.5-7B-Instruct			
		H@1	Tokens	Calls	Time	H@1	Tokens	Calls	Time
CWQ	PoG	68.7	23669	34.86	61.12	52.8	9528	15.10	20.87
	ToG	60.3	12955	16.30	85.69	49.0	8969	14.24	31.53
	ReKnoS	62.8	6439	3.93	33.61	43.2	3687	3.92	18.20
	CGR	**76.3**	**1677**	**1.49**	**15.12**	**68.7**	**1314**	**1.30**	**5.83**
WebQSP	PoG	86.4	12226	17.97	36.33	70.0	5033	7.75	5.53
	ToG	80.8	9705	12.96	59.19	75.0	8960	11.65	23.30
	ReKnoS	77.2	7286	3.97	40.49	59.2	4062	3.97	20.70
	CGR	**86.4**	**1491**	**1.21**	**11.90**	**81.1**	**1196**	**1.06**	**4.36**
GrailQA	PoG	78.0	7714	11.59	26.79	72.5	4594	7.98	4.86
	ToG	71.0	6465	9.03	44.97	59.8	6104	8.38	17.17
	ReKnoS	81.7	5141	3.93	21.57	57.1	3011	3.93	13.67
	CGR	**87.1**	**1229**	**1.09**	**7.10**	**82.2**	**1143**	**1.10**	**2.71**

- **Cloud-based LLM (DeepSeek-V3.1 API)** [18]: used as the high-performance reasoning backbone. Since the main LLM inference is handled in the cloud, the local A100 GPU only hosts the lightweight System 1 Cross-Encoder (approximately 33M parameters).

- **Local Small Model (Qwen2.5-7B-Instruct)** [3]: used to represent local or resource-constrained deployment scenarios. This model is deployed on a single NVIDIA A100 (40GB) GPU. To ensure fair comparison in the local setting, we use sequential evaluation so that each baseline has exclusive access to GPU resources during runtime.

We implement CGR as a lightweight prototype of around 2,000 lines of code.

4.4 Main Results

Comprehensive Performance Comparison. Table 1 reports the results of different methods on the three Freebase benchmarks using the DeepSeek-V3.1 backbone.

Accuracy. CGR achieves the best performance on all three datasets. On the most challenging CWQ benchmark, CGR reaches a Hits@1 of 76.3%, outperforming PoG (68.7%) and ReKnoS (62.8%). This suggests that CGR can preserve more useful evidence and support downstream reasoning more reliably in complex multi-hop settings. On GrailQA, CGR also achieves 87.1%, substantially higher than ToG (71.0%), indicating strong performance on unseen query structures.

Efficiency and Cost. On CWQ, CGR uses 1,677 tokens vs. PoG's 23,669—demonstrating the Interface's compression effect—and 15.12 s latency vs. ToG's 85.69 s, reflecting the efficiency of neural graph search over repeated LLM interaction. CGR averages 1.49 LLM calls vs. PoG's 34.86; on WebQSP and GrailQA the call count is near 1, indicating that feedback is triggered only for hard cases.

Across typical CGR runs, LLM inference dominates end-to-end latency; SPARQL query execution over the local Virtuoso endpoint is the secondary component, while Cross-Encoder scoring (batch size 32, ~33M parameters) and prompt construction contribute a minor fraction. A detailed latency decomposition and characterization under concurrent request loads remain as engineering extensions.

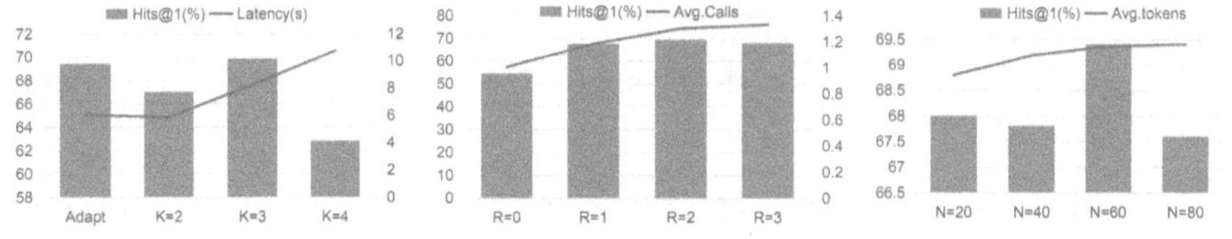

(a) Search depth K (b) Max retries R (c) Pool size N

Fig. 3. Sensitivity analysis of CGR with respect to search depth K, retry limit R, and candidate pool size N.

Generalization Verification on Local Models. Table 1 reports the results in the local setting with Qwen2.5-7B-Instruct. Compared with frameworks that rely more heavily on repeated large-model interaction, CGR maintains strong performance under the local small-model setting. For example, on CWQ, the accuracy of PoG drops to 52.8%, while CGR still achieves 68.7%. In terms of efficiency, CGR uses about 1,300 tokens on average, whereas other baselines typically require 5,000–9,000 tokens. CGR also maintains low latency, for example 2.71 s on GrailQA. Overall, these results suggest that CGR is better suited to resource-constrained and local deployment scenarios.

4.5 Sensitivity Analysis

To examine the effect of key hyperparameters in CGR, we conduct a sensitivity analysis on 500 randomly sampled CWQ instances using Qwen2.5-7B-Instruct as the backbone. The absolute latency values differ slightly from those in Table 1 because this analysis uses sequential execution for more stable measurement, but the overall trends remain consistent.

Search Depth (K). We study $K \in \{2, 3, 4\}$ (excluding $K = 1$ because Freebase CVT structures require at least two hops). As shown in Fig. 3(a), fixing $K = 2$ yields 67.0% accuracy (5.83 s); $K = 3$ improves to 69.8% but raises latency to 8.21 s; $K = 4$ degrades to 62.8% due to noise. The adaptive $K \in \{2, 3\}$ achieves the best balance: 69.4% and 6.03 s.

Max Retries (R). Figure 3(b) shows that one retry recovers most of the gain (54.4% $\rightarrow$ 67.4%), $R = 2$ further improves to 69.4%, and $R = 3$ yields diminishing returns (67.8%). We therefore use $R = 2$.

Candidate Pool Size (N). Figure 3(c) shows accuracy peaks at $N = 60$ (69.4%); expanding to $N = 80$ drops to 67.6% while token cost remains similar, indicating that excess candidates introduce noise.

4.6 Ablation Study

To analyze the impact of CGR's key components on performance and efficiency, we conduct an ablation study on the most challenging CWQ benchmark. Since ablation requires multiple runs of different variants, we randomly sample 500 instances from the CWQ test set as the evaluation subset. All experiments are conducted on the locally deployed Qwen2.5-7B-Instruct. The results are summarized in Table 2.

- **w/o Neural Graph Search (Replace with BFS):** We remove the neural scoring and dynamic pruning mechanisms in System 1 and replace them with parameter-free BFS that uniformly expands neighboring nodes.
  Analysis: Accuracy drops from 69.4% to 34.4%, showing that indiscriminate expansion is insufficient for obtaining useful evidence on a graph as large as Freebase. Neural scoring and pruning are therefore important for controlling search direction.

- **w/o High-Density Interface (Remove Compression):** We remove the evidence compression module and no longer construct set-based representations. Instead, the Top-K paths returned by System 1 are linearized and passed directly to System 2.
  Analysis: Compared with the linear-input variant, the full CGR reduces token usage substantially (1,333 vs 2,054) while maintaining comparable accuracy. This suggests that the High-Density Evidence Interface does more than shorten the context: it also reduces redundant evidence and improves the efficiency of evidence representation.
- **w/o Reflective Feedback (Remove Feedback):** We disable the feedback loop in System 2, so the model answers only from the initial retrieval result and can no longer trigger `<RETRY>` for re-retrieval.
  Analysis: The average number of calls drops to 1.0, but accuracy falls back to 54.4%. This indicates that, for complex multi-hop questions, the feedback mechanism helps recover from insufficient initial evidence and reduces error accumulation in single-pass pipelines.

Error Analysis. Removing feedback ($R = 0$) reduces accuracy from 69.4% to 54.4%, indicating that approximately 15 pp of errors in a single-pass setting can be recovered through re-retrieval with expanded depth and beam width. Replacing neural search with BFS causes a far larger drop (to 34.4%), confirming that unguided expansion on Freebase-scale graphs is the dominant failure source. The residual error rate under full CGR (30.6%) reflects cases where the correct answer lies beyond the maximum exploration budget or where the LLM produces a confident but incorrect answer from sufficient evidence—a limitation of the decoupled architecture.

Budget Modeling. The current framework controls cost through discrete parameters (K, beam width, R, candidate pool cap) rather than through an explicit optimization objective over a token or latency budget. Formalizing the accuracy–cost trade-off as a constrained optimization and deriving a principled budget allocation policy across the System 1/System 2 boundary remain as future work.

Table 2. Ablation study on CWQ (500 samples).

Variant	Hits@1 (%)	Tokens	Calls
CGR (Full)	**69.4**	**1333**	**1.30**
w/o Neural Search	34.4	1811	1.99
w/o Interface	69.2	2054	1.28
w/o Feedback	54.4	937	1.00

5 Conclusion

This paper presents Cognitive Graph Reasoning (CGR), a budget-aware closed-loop framework for complex KGQA. By assigning high-throughput graph retrieval to System 1 and reserving on-demand reasoning and feedback for System 2, CGR improves the balance between answer quality, LLM usage, and latency. Experimental results show that the High-Density Evidence Interface reduces context overhead, and that CGR lowers token consumption by up to 92.9% and latency by 4–6× compared with interactive baselines. Overall, CGR provides a practical solution for efficient KGQA in resource-constrained settings. CGR still depends on the initial recall of System 1, and future work will explore multimodal extension and budget optimization.

Acknowledgments. This work was supported in part by the National Key R&D Program of China (2024YFB2906605); in part by the Pilot Project for Integrated Innovation of Science, Education, and Industry of Qilu University of Technology (Shandong Academy of Sciences) (2024ZDZX08); and in part by the "20 Articles" Project for Universities in Jinan (202534093).

Disclosure of Interests. The authors have no competing interests to declare that are relevant to the content of this article.

AI Usage Statement.. Artificial intelligence tools, if used, were used only for language organization and figure/table polishing, and did not participate in the generation of the core ideas or technical content.

References

1. Ao, T., et al.: Lightprof: a lightweight reasoning framework for large language model on knowledge graph. In: AAAI, pp. 23424–23432 (2025)
2. Baek, J., Aji, A.F., Saffari, A.: Knowledge-augmented language model prompting for zero-shot knowledge graph question answering. In: NLRSE, pp, 78–106 (2023)
3. Bai, J., et al.: Qwen technical report. arXiv preprint arXiv:2309.16609 (2023)
4. Besta, M., et al.: Graph of thoughts: solving elaborate problems with large language models. In: AAAI, pp. 17682–17690 (2024)
5. Bollacker, K., Evans, C., Paritosh, P., Sturge, T., Taylor, J.: Freebase: a collaboratively created graph database for structuring human knowledge. In: SIGMOD, pp. 1247–1250 (2008)
6. Chen, L., Tong, P., Jin, Z., Sun, Y., Ye, J., Xiong, H.: Plan-on-graph: self-correcting adaptive planning of large language model on knowledge graphs. In: NeurIPS, pp, 37665–37691 (2024)
7. Cheng, D., et al.: Uprise: universal prompt retrieval for improving zero-shot evaluation. In: EMNLP, pp. 12318–12337 (2023)
8. Gu, Y., et al.: Beyond IID: three levels of generalization for question answering on knowledge bases. In: WWW, pp. 3477–3488 (2021)

9. He, X., et al.: G-retriever: retrieval-augmented generation for textual graph understanding and question answering. In: NeurIPS, pp. 132876–132907 (2024)
10. Honnibal, M., Johnson, M.: An improved non-monotonic transition system for dependency parsing. In: EMNLP, pp. 1373–1378 (2015)
11. Jiang, J., Zhou, K., Dong, Z., Ye, K., Zhao, X., Wen, J.R.: Structgpt: a general framework for large language model to reason over structured data. In: EMNLP, pp. 9237–9251 (2023)
12. Kahneman, D.: Thinking, Fast and Slow. Macmillan (2011)
13. Khot, T., et al.: Decomposed prompting: a modular approach for solving complex tasks. In: ICLR (2023)
14. Lewis, P., et al.: Retrieval-augmented generation for knowledge-intensive nlp tasks. In: NeurIPS, pp. 9459–9474 (2020)
15. Li, X., Zhou, Y., Dou, Z.: Unigen: a unified generative framework for retrieval and question answering with large language models. In: AAAI, pp. 8688–8696 (2024)
16. Li, X., et al.: Chain-of-knowledge: grounding large language models via dynamic knowledge adapting over heterogeneous sources. In: ICLR, pp. 9565–9587 (2024)
17. Lin, S.C., et al.: How to train your dragon: diverse augmentation towards generalizable dense retrieval. In: Findings of ACL: EMNLP, pp. 6385–6400 (2023)
18. Liu, A., et al.: Deepseek-v3 technical report. arXiv preprint arXiv:2412.19437 (2024)
19. Luo, L., Ju, J., Xiong, B., Li, Y.F., Haffari, G., Pan, S.: Chatrule: mining logical rules with large language models for knowledge graph reasoning. In: PAKDD, pp. 314–325 (2025)
20. Luo, L., Li, Y.F., Haffari, G., Pan, S.: Reasoning on graphs: faithful and interpretable large language model reasoning. In: ICLR, pp. 14400–14423 (2024)
21. Pan, S., Luo, L., Wang, Y., Chen, C., Wang, J., Wu, X.: Unifying large language models and knowledge graphs: a roadmap. IEEE Trans. Knowl. Data Eng. **7**, 3580–3599 (2024)
22. Petroni, F., Ret al.: Language models as knowledge bases? In: EMNLP-IJCNLP, pp. 2463–2473 (2019)
23. Schick, T., et al.: Toolformer: language models can teach themselves to use tools. NeurIPS **36**, 68539–68551 (2023)
24. Shi, W., et al.: Replug: retrieval-augmented black-box language models. In: NAACL-HLT, pp. 8371–8384 (2024)
25. Sun, J., et al.: Think-on-graph: deep and responsible reasoning of large language model on knowledge graph. In: ICLR, pp. 3868–3898 (2024)
26. Talmor, A., Berant, J.: The web as a knowledge-base for answering complex questions. In: NAACL-HLT, pp. 641–651 (2018)
27. Wang, Q., et al.: Paperrobot: incremental draft generation of scientific ideas. In: ACL, pp. 1980–1991 (2019)
28. Wang, S., Sui, Y., Wang, C., Xiong, H.: Unleashing the power of knowledge graph for recommendation via invariant learning. In: WWW, pp. 3745–3755 (2024)
29. Wang, S., Lin, J., Guo, X., Shun, J., Li, J., Zhu, Y.: Reasoning of large language models over knowledge graphs with super-relations. In: ICLR, pp. 4208–4226 (2025)
30. Wei, J., et al.: Chain-of-thought prompting elicits reasoning in large language models. In: NeurIPS, pp, 24824–24837 (2022)
31. Wen, Y., Wang, Z., Sun, J.: Mindmap: knowledge graph prompting sparks deep reasoning in large language models. In: ACL, pp. 10370–10388 (2024)
32. Xiong, W., Hoang, T., Wang, W.Y.: Deeppath: a reinforcement learning method for knowledge graph reasoning. In: EMNLP, pp, 564–573 (2017)

33. Yih, W.T., Richardson, M., Meek, C., Chang, M.W., Suh, J.: The value of semantic parse labeling for knowledge base question answering. In: ACL, pp. 201–206 (2016)
34. Yoran, O., Wolfson, T., Ram, O., Berant, J.: Making retrieval-augmented language models robust to irrelevant context. In: ICLR, pp. 29862–29883 (2024)
35. Zhang, H., et al.: Poolingformer: long document modeling with pooling attention. In: ICML, pp. 12437–12446 (2021)

AI Design Automation

SysVCoder: An LLM-Driven Framework for Systematic Generation of System-Level Design

Jian Zuo[1], Junzhe Liu[1], Xianyong Wang[1], Chen Liang[1], Navya Goli[2], Umamaheswara Rao Tida[2], Zhenge Jia[1(✉)], Zhaoyan Shen[1], and Mengying Zhao[1]

[1] School of Computer Science and Technology, Shandong University, Qingdao, China
{202320822,junzheliu,wangxianyong,chenliang123}@mail.sdu.edu.cn,
{zhengejia,shenzhaoyan,zhaomengying}@sdu.edu.cn

[2] Department of Electrical and Computer Engineering, North Dakota State University, Fargo, USA
{navya.goli,umamaheswara.tida}@ndsu.edu

Abstract. Recent advances in large language models (LLMs) have demonstrated strong potential in generating hardware designs using hardware description languages (HDLs) such as Verilog. However, existing LLM-based frameworks struggle to accurately capture the complexity of real-world architectural designs, particularly for large-scale systems with hierarchical, multi-level module instantiations. To address this issue, we present SysVCoder, an LLM-driven framework that enhances both the generation quality and efficiency of system-level design in Verilog. SysVCoder introduces a two-stage generation pipeline that leverages an intermediate representation to enable a more structured and accurate translation from natural language specifications to complex multi-module designs. Furthermore, we incorporate a rule-based alignment mechanism and a domain-specific retrieval-augmented generation strategy (DS-RAG) to enhance functional correctness by grounding LLM outputs in domain knowledge. We also present SysVDB, a comprehensive dataset comprising 60 system-level hardware designs along with their corresponding verification testbenches. Experimental results demonstrate that SysVCoder outperforms state-of-the-art frameworks such as CodeV and VeriGen by 30.7% and 38.3% in terms of functional correctness under the same base LLM. Notably, SysVCoder achieves performance comparable to NVIDIA's GPT-4-based VerilogCoder while using only a 7B-parameter model, reducing token consumption by 7.6× and synthesis latency by 37.5×. Both SysVCoder and SysVDB are made public at https://gitee.com/sdu-aes-lab/sysvcoder/.

1 Introduction

Large language models (LLMs) have shown strong potential in accelerating agile hardware design tasks. Among these tasks, one of the most promising directions

L. Eeckhout et al. (Eds.): APPT 2026, LNCS 16693, pp. 221–237, 2027.
https://doi.org/10.1007/978-981-92-4805-6_15

is the automatic synthesis of hardware designs from natural language instructions [4,10]. LLMs are used to directly translate functional descriptions written in natural language into hardware description language (HDL), such as Verilog or VHDL [11,26]. Despite the remarkable progress of LLMs in generating high-level programming languages [7,23], HDL imposes far more stringent requirements on logical structure [4], making it difficult for LLMs to effectively learn and reason about the hardware description of the circuit design. Moreover, the availability of high-quality HDL datasets is considerably more limited than high-level languages, and the lack of standardized benchmark implementations further restricts the ability to evaluate LLM-driven HDL generation frameworks [4,26].

To address these issues, datasets and benchmarks such as VerilogEval [9], RTLLM [11], and MG-Verilog [25] are introduced to address the scarcity of training data and enrich the diversity of available Verilog code. Building on these datasets, existing explorations to improve LLM performance in HDL code generation can be categorized into three perspectives: *prompt engineering (PE), domain-specific fine-tuning (DSFT)*, and *agent-based generation (AG)*. Prompt engineering aims to enhance code generation quality by modifying the phrasing and structure of prompts without altering the model's parameters [1,11,18]. Domain-specific fine-tuning takes a more direct approach by continuing model training on Verilog datasets, with strategies ranging from full model fine-tuning [3,16] to domain-adaptive pre-training [8,10,12,26]. Agent-based generation leverages multiple specialized AI agents (based on full-parameter LLMs such as GPT-4) to synthesize HDL code. Representative works such as VerilogCoder [5] and MAGE [27] construct different AI agents specialized in task planning, code synthesis, and syntax checking to collaboratively generate syntactically and functionally correct Verilog code.

Despite efforts to enable effective LLM-based Verilog code generation, three key challenges impede the adoption of LLM in practical EDA design flow: 1) Existing frameworks are typically learned and evaluated on benchmarks composed of isolated, single-module Verilog designs, which fail to capture the complexity of real-world, system-level design involving hundreds of lines of code and multi-level instantiations; 2) Current generation workflows generally translate natural language descriptions directly into Verilog code, reducing the overall interpretability, adjustability, and transparency of the generation process; 3) Extensive state-of-the-art (SOTA) frameworks rely heavily on powerful but proprietary LLMs like GPT-4, while open-source and affordable models tailored for practical system-level design generation frameworks still lag significantly in performance.

To address these challenges, we propose SysVCoder, an LLM-driven framework to enable accurate and systematic generation of system-level, multi-hierarchical hardware designs. Specifically, we propose a two-stage generation pipeline that bridges the gap between simple natural language inputs and system-level design through a novel intermediate representation named General Intermediate Representation (GIR). Unlike abstract syntax tree (AST)-like formats, GIR distills designs into fundamental hardware design variables annotated with concise one-sentence comments on module functionality and streamlined logic structures. In the first stage of generation (i.e., translating natural language descriptions to GIR), we propose an automated augmentation mechanism that generates high-quality, diverse description-GIR training pairs, and a GIR-specific instruction tuning method to strengthen the model's understanding of system-level design structures. In the second stage of generation (i.e., translating GIR to system-level design), we introduce a rule-based alignment method that converts GIR into implementation details to enhance the LLM's understanding on structured intermediate representations. Additionally, we integrate a domain-specific retrieval-augmented generation (DS-RAG) module, leveraging the GIR's embedded comments to retrieve relevant single-module implementations for better generation quality. Experimental results demonstrate that SysVCoder outperforms existing SOTA frameworks VeriCoder [19] and VeriGen [17] by 31.6% and 38.3% in terms of functional correctness on system-level design benchmarks. Remarkably, it achieves comparable function correctness with a parameter count of only 7B to the SOTA agent-based generation framework VerilogCoder [5] (with GPT-4 as base model), with 7.6× fewer tokens consumed and 37.5× less generation latency. Our contributions are summarized as follows:

- We propose SysVCoder, a LLM-driven framework for system-level, real-world hardware design generation.
- We introduce a two-stage generation pipeline based on GIR, which improves the LLM's synthesis capability on system-level design and enhances the transparency of the synthesis process.
- Experimental results show that SysVCoder outperforms SOTA frameworks across various benchmarks in terms of functional correctness and practical performance.
- SysVCoder framework and SysVDB are made open-sourced, including the data generation pipeline, training datasets, testbenches, and fine-tuned model weights, to facilitate future research and reproducibility.

2 Background and Motivation

Current research efforts toward effective LLM-based HDL generation generally focus on two key areas: high-quality dataset preparation and post-training techniques (such as fine-tuning and instruction tuning) to enhance the model's understanding and generation capabilities.

2.1 Datasets for Verilog Synthesis

Several efforts have been made to construct high-quality Verilog design datasets along with corresponding testbenches to evaluate functional and syntactic correctness. For instance, the authors of [16] collect Verilog code from open-source GitHub projects to create a large-scale dataset for LLM training. VerilogEval [9], released by NVIDIA Research, offers a comprehensive evaluation suite comprising 156 problems sourced from HDLBits [22], accompanied by a benchmarking framework for automated functional verification. RTLLM [11] also contributes a benchmark of 29 RTL designs paired with natural language descriptions and their respective testbenches.

Despite these advances, most datasets and benchmarks focus on evaluating LLM performance on isolated, standalone Verilog modules. This narrow scope fails to reflect the complexity and scale of real-world hardware design scenarios, which often involve extensive Verilog codebases with multi-level instantiations and interdependent modules. These limitations underscore the need for more comprehensive and realistic benchmarks that assess LLMs in the context of large-scale, system-level Verilog design tasks.

2.2 LLM-Based Hardware Design Synthesis Framework

Prior works in LLM-driven Verilog synthesis focus on improving generation quality can be summarized in three categories: 1) Prompt Engineering (PE) improves the quality of LLM's synthesized code by adjusting the descriptions and structures of prompts. This approach does not involve altering model parameters, making it efficient and low-cost. The attempts in PE include introducing a prompt template for more efficient hardware design [1], developing a self-planning prompt engineering approach [11], embedding compiler error messages into prompts as multi-loop synthesis feedback [18], etc.; 2) Domain-Specific Fine-Tuning (DSFT) focuses on conducting further training on the pre-trained LLM using the Verilog dataset to obtain better performances. For instance, [16] uses full-parameter fine-tuning on LLMs using data collected from GitHub while ChipNeMo [8] developed by NVIDIA deploys a domain adaptive pre-training approach with their private data. CodeV [26], VeriThoughts [24], VeriCoder [19], RTLCoder [10], and AutoVCoder [4] improve LLM capability by invoking various parameter-efficient fine-tuning strategies; 3) Agent-based generation leverages multiple specialized AI agents to synthesize HDL code [5,27]. VerilogCoder [5] proposed by NVIDIA constructs AI agents specialized in task planning, code synthesis, and syntax checking to collaboratively generate syntactically and functionally correct Verilog code.

Despite these advances, existing frameworks fall short when it comes to generating real-world, system-level Verilog designs, which often span hundreds of lines of code and involve multi-level module instantiations. Moreover, when presented with simple natural language descriptions of functional requirements in practice, the existing framework (even with the full-parameter LLMs such as GPT-4) struggles to generate correct and complete Verilog code. This highlights the pressing need for a more capable LLM-based framework that can reliably generate functionally correct Verilog designs from concise natural language inputs.

3 System-Level Hardware Design Generation Framework

The system overview of SysVCoder is shown in Fig. 1. SysVCoder adopts a two-stage generation approach, which leverages the proposed General Intermediate Representation (GIR) to break down the synthesis process, making it more manageable and transparent. The GIR and the two-stage synthesis approach will be illustrated in the following sections.

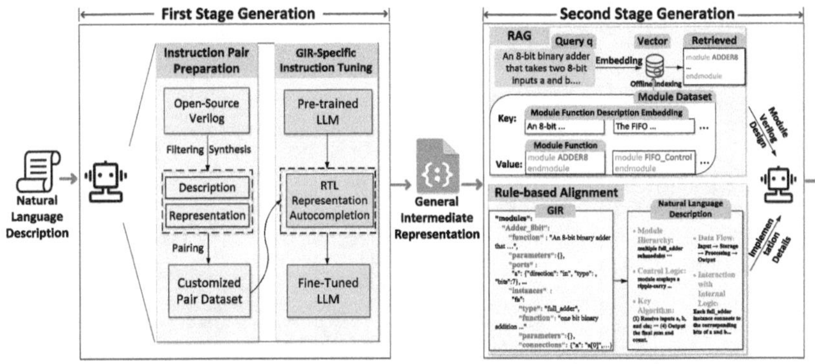

Fig. 1. An overview of SysVCoder framework: (a) First stage generation from natural language description to intermediate representation, including the instruction pair preparation and GIR-specific instruction tuning approaches to enable the LLM to understand the natural language description and translate it into a structural representation; (b) Second stage generation from GIR to system-level hardware design, including retrain-free RAG and rule-based alignment approaches to enrich the input prompt to improve the LLM capability.

3.1 General Intermediate Representation

The General Intermediate Representation (GIR) introduced in this study serves as a critical abstraction layer designed to automate hardware design by bridging the gap between natural language descriptions and the system-level Verilog design. In the existing Verilog generation frameworks, LLMs are generally expected to infer hardware constructs (i.e., ports, instances, and signal connections) from unstructured text [4,10] or structured but verbose instructions [25,26]. It often leads to syntactic errors or functional inaccuracies due to a lack of explicit structural guidance. Tailored specifically for LLMs, the GIR transforms unstructured, rough descriptions of the demanded function into a standardized, semantically rich format that is both human-readable and machine-processable.

As illustrated in Fig. 2, the GIR is structured in a hierarchical, JSON-like format that encapsulates the essential components of a hardware module, including fields such as `"modules"`, `"parameters"`, `"ports"`, `"instances"`, and

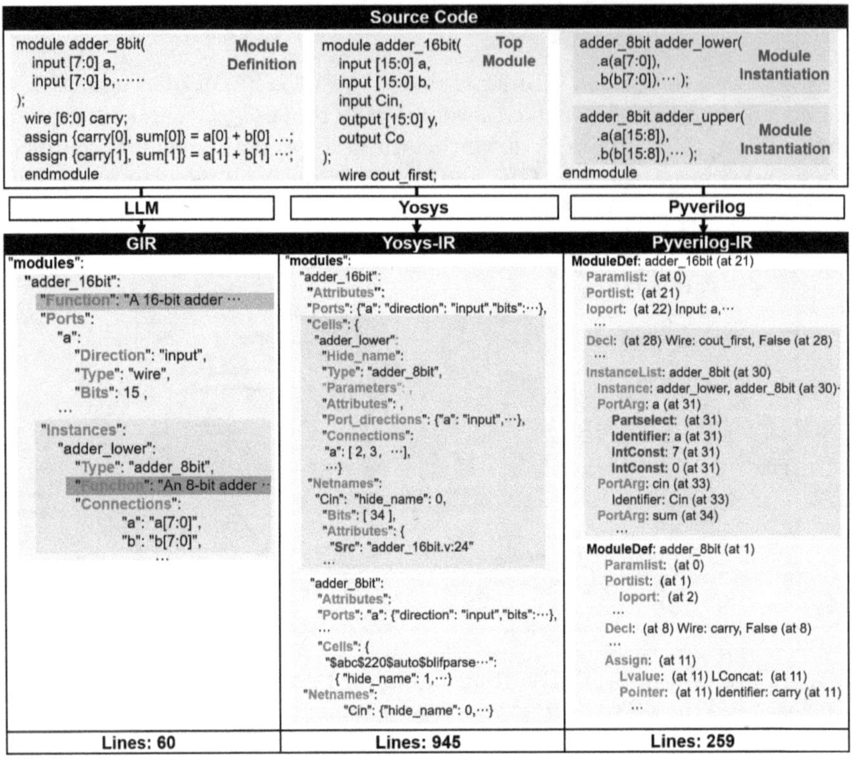

Fig. 2. Intermediate representation of `adder_16bit` design by GIR, Yosys and Pyverilog. It turns out GIR achieves a more concise representation to describe the design.

`"connections"`. Each field is carefully defined to capture the architectural and functional semantics of hardware designs. To ensure interoperability and rigorous analysis, the complete GIR schema is formally parameterized as a tuple $\mathcal{S}_{\text{GIR}} = \langle \mathcal{M}, \mathcal{R}, \mathcal{P}, \mathcal{I}, \mathcal{C} \rangle$. Specifically, `modules` ($\mathcal{M}$) acts as the root container defining the hierarchy and namespace scope for all local logic. Within this scope, `parameters` ($\mathcal{R}$) defines elaboration-time configuration constants for generic hardware templates, while `ports` ($\mathcal{P}$) delineates the module's I/O boundaries by explicitly specifying signal names, widths, and directions. For structural composition, `instances` ($\mathcal{I}$) tracks child module instantiations and their corresponding scope bindings. Finally, `connections` ($\mathcal{C}$) formalizes the netlist topology by mapping signal propagation from drivers to loads; this graph-based representation is critical for tracing dependency chains and identifying propagation paths of differential characteristics. Consequently, this normalized schema guarantees architectural fidelity while facilitating seamless automated parsing and algorithmic processing.

The conciseness of GIR is illustrated in Fig. 2, which compares its parsing of the `adder_16bit` module with the intermediate representations (IR) generated via Yosys [21] and Pyverilog [13]. As shown in Fig. 2, existing IR designs remain closely tied to Verilog syntax. To extract meaningful semantics from Pyverilog's AST, it requires significant post-processing since the output is difficult for LLMs to utilize directly. It lacks semantic information and is heavily dependent on strict Verilog compliance, making it unsuitable for incomplete or iterative design workflows. In contrast, GIR provides a concise, only 60-line representation that captures both the hierarchical structure and functional intent of the module. On the other hand, compared to a purely natural-language specification, the GIR introduces a highly interpretable and deterministic structure. While a natural-language description merely conveys functional intent, the GIR translates these implicit requirements into explicit structural boundaries. This semantic scaffolding allows LLMs to map text to hardware components without losing the flexibility of high-level abstractions. It abstracts away low-level syntax in favor of modular, semantically meaningful fields that are easily populated and understood by LLMs. This structure enables generation through guided template completion rather than reverse engineering from verbose and syntax-bound outputs. Furthermore, the IR supports incremental refinement, allowing developers to gradually complete the design in a flexible and interpretable manner. Its JSON-like format aligns naturally with LLM tokenization strategies, facilitating seamless integration without the adaptation overhead.

3.2 First Stage Generation

In the first stage of generation shown in Fig. 1, the goal is to enable the LLM to interpret a concise natural language description of a hardware design and translate it into GIR. To achieve this, we propose a GIR-specific instruction tuning method to teach the LLM domain-specific knowledge for accurately performing the translation.

We first collect 30k high-quality Verilog implementations from public datasets and open source projects. We then construct description-GIR pairs by leveraging Iverilog [20] and commercial LLMs to generate natural language descriptions covering key module attributes such as name, function, parameters, and the intermediate representations that conform to the proposed GIR formatting rule. All GIR and the descriptions are manually rectified to avoid hallucination errors (R1.1, 2.3).

Based on the prepared instruction pairs, we proposed a GIR-specific instruction tuning method to inject structured knowledge into LLMs. The method leverages the instruction samples to guide the model to generate detailed GIR representations from descriptive inputs. The underlying learning mechanism of LLMs follows an auto-regressive paradigm. Let $\boldsymbol{z} = z_1, z_2, \ldots, z_T$ represent a training sequence comprising both an instruction and its response. An LLM parameterized by $\boldsymbol{\phi}$ estimates the probability of the entire sequence by factorizing it via the chain rule of probability [12]:

$$p_\phi(z) = \prod_{t=1}^{T} p_\phi(z_t | z_{j<t}). \tag{1}$$

During fine-tuning, particularly with Low-Rank Adaptation (LoRA), the LLM is optimized to minimize the expected negative log-likelihood (or equivalently, cross-entropy loss) across a dataset $\mathcal{D} = \boldsymbol{z}^{(1)}, \ldots, \boldsymbol{z}^{(N)}$. The training objective is formalized as:

$$\mathcal{J}(\phi) = -\frac{1}{N}\frac{1}{T}\sum_{n=1}^{N}\sum_{t=1}^{T} \log p_{\phi}(z_t^i | z_{j<t}^i). \tag{2}$$

By integrating GIR as an intermediate representation of generation, we mitigate the synthesis difficulty imposed by the concise description against the complexity of system-level Verilog design. The GIR serves as both a scaffold and a semantic guide, enabling more accurate and syntactically valid Verilog generation.

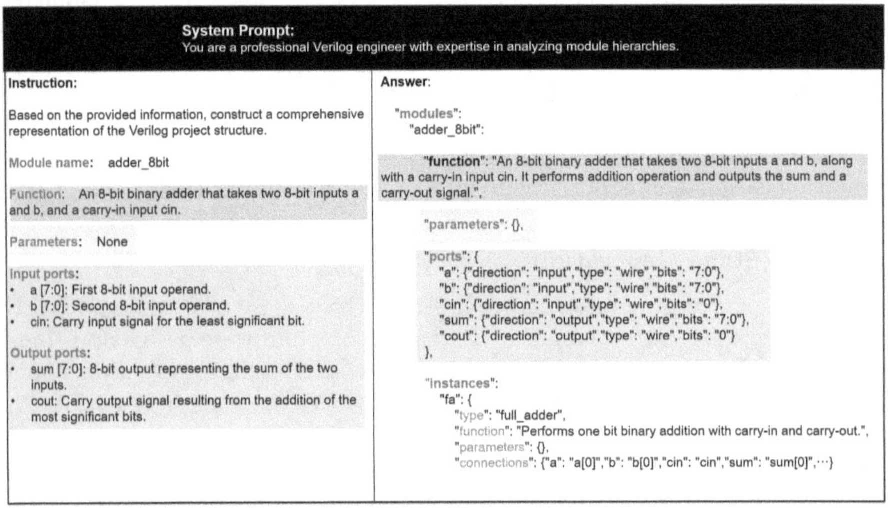

Fig. 3. A case study to illustrate the instruction tuning process. This example demonstrates how the LLM is guided to understand the natural language description of hardware functionality and generate its corresponding GIR.

3.3 Second Stage Generation

In the second stage of generation, as shown in Fig. 1, the objective is to enable an LLM to generate system-level Verilog designs from GIR. Rather than relying on computationally expensive and time-consuming retraining on the retrieval model, we introduce a domain-specific Retrieval-Augmented Generation (DS-RAG) approach that combines rule-based alignment and a retraining-free retrieval to enhance prompt content to improve code generation performance.

Rule-Based Alignment. We first develop a rule-based natural language conversion mechanism that translates structured GIR data into rich, human-readable descriptions to enrich the quality of prompt input to the LLM. As shown in Fig. 3, the translated descriptions are utilized as part of the input prompt as detailed guidance to the LLM's generation process. This framework operates across three abstraction layers. At the top layer, the module definition captures the essential structure of the hardware design. The port description layer encodes individual port attributes. At the lowest layer, instantiation logic captures the hierarchical relationships and connectivity among modules. To automate this conversion, we define a syntactic rule set that enables translation from GIR to structured natural language descriptions. The core transformation rules are as follows:

- **Module Declaration Rule**: Parses ir_data['modules'] into "<module_name> module defined with <parameter_count> parameters, <input_count> input ports, and <output_count> output ports."
- **Port Mapping Rule**: Generates for ir_data['modules'][ports] the description "Port <n> is of <direction> type, with bit-width <width>, synchronized to the <clock_domain> clock domain."
- **Instantiation Description Rule**: Converts ir_data['modules']['instances'] into "Instantiates <count> submodules, where <submodule_name> implements <function_description>, connected to the parent module via <interface_name>."

The semantic descriptions generated through multi-stage translation are fed into an LLM to guide the production of implementation details covering the following aspects:

- **Architecture Decomposition**: Include a module hierarchy matrix, a key submodule function mapping table, and storage configuration parameters.
- **Control Logic**: Define a state machine with <state_count>, timing control based on <synchronous/asynchronous> reset mechanisms, and finite state machine encoding for processing steps.
- **Data Path**: Define a signal flow architecture from input buffers to pipeline registers, computational units, and output latches, incorporating an <n>-stage pipeline design with a bit-width conversion strategy named <strategy_name>.

Retraining-Free Retrieval. RAG retrieves relevant data from a database and integrates it into the prompt, enabling an LLM to generate accurate and contextually appropriate code. Prior approaches such as ChipNeMo [8] and AutoV-Coder [4] achieve this by retraining the retriever model to improve the quality of retrieval. However, preparing the required fine-tuning datasets and executing the retraining process is labor-intensive and computationally demanding.

To overcome this challenge, we propose a retraining-free retrieval mechanism that uses structured information in the GIR. By leveraging natural language descriptions instead of Verilog code, we can effectively use a general embedding and retriever model without retraining the LLM. As shown in Fig. 1, we create a high-quality, single-module retrieval codebase from over 12,500 open-source Verilog and SystemVerilog projects. The code is revised using regular expressions to remove single-line comments, multi-line annotations, and conditional compilation directives. Independent modules with clear input/output interfaces are extracted, and their semantic function descriptions are converted into semantic vectors using a pre-trained embedding model. These are indexed with code fingerprints as <code_fingerprint, semantic_vector>.

During retrieval, the GIR-derived functional description is embedded using the same pre-trained model. A coarse-grained retrieval phase selects the top ten candidates by calculating cosine similarity between query and database vectors. A fine-grained re-ranking stage uses a pre-trained NLP Cross-Encoder [15] with the input format `[CLS] Query [SEP] Document [SEP]` to assess query-document pairs, improving relevance accuracy. Notably, the RAG mechanism retrieves contextually relevant individual modules to assist the generation, though discrepancies may exist between these retrieved source sub-modules and the actual target requirements. To reconcile these variations, the GIR leverages its structural `instance` metadata to enforce cross-module consistency, thereby guaranteeing the architectural correctness of multi-module connections and systemic interactions. This RAG mechanism efficiently identifies contextually relevant code, boosting the LLM's ability to generate high-quality Verilog code without retriever retraining.

Table 1. Metadata of SysVDB.

Benchmark	Dataset Size	Avg. Lines	Avg. Hierarchies
VerilogEval-Human [9]	156	22	1
Problem-Set-VeriGen [17]	17	23	1
RTLLM [11]	50	54	1.22
SysVDB	60	215	1.96

4 Experiments

4.1 Experimental Setup

Dataset Preparation: We construct an open-source dataset named *SysVDB*, which is used to evaluate the capabilities of LLMs in generating system-level, real-world Verilog designs. As shown in Table 1 and Table 2, SysVDB comprises 60 meticulously crafted Verilog designs, ranging from 7 different design domains. To mitigate potential test-contamination concerns, we performe a de-duplication procedure between the 30K training corpus and the SysVDB benchmark. Specifically, all training samples are compared against SysVDB designs at three levels: (1) lexical similarity of functional descriptions; (2) structural similarity of the generated GIR representations; (3) RTL-level similarity based on module hierarchy and behavioral signatures. Any sample exhibiting high similarity under any criterion is removed from the training set. Furthermore, GIR-description embedding analysis reveal that although several SysVDB tasks belong to commonly studied hardware categories (e.g., FIFO, UART, SPI, I2C, DMA, Cache, and FFT), their implementations, specifications, and module organizations differ substantially from the training samples. We emphasize that SysVDB is intentionally constructed from manually curated system-level designs emphasizing complex inter-module interactions rather than isolated IP blocks, thereby reducing benchmark memorization risk. Nevertheless, as with all evaluations based on open-source hardware designs, we cannot completely exclude the possibility that some concepts or implementation patterns appeared in the pretraining corpora of foundation models such as Qwen2.5 or DeepSeek. Importantly, all compared methods are built upon the same underlying foundation models and are evaluated on the same benchmark. Therefore, the substantial performance gains achieved by ComplexVCoder are attributable to the proposed GIR-based intermediate representation and two-stage generation framework rather than privileged access to benchmark-specific training data.

Each case in the SysVDB represents a realistic circuit design involving intricate inter-module interactions and structural hierarchies. In addition, each case is provided with a testbench and a comprehensive end-to-end pipeline to evaluate functional and syntactic correctness of the generated Verilog code. The evaluation employs line coverage as the primary metric. Beyond basic functional verification, the testbench incorporates corner cases, exceptional inputs, and signal integrity checks to ensure a robust and comprehensive assessment. A design is officially designated as "passed" only after successfully satisfying all verification checkpoints.

We further detail the cross-module interactions in SysVDB. Unlike existing benchmarks composed of isolated modules, SysVDB requires multi-module reasoning in three ways. First, it uses hierarchical parameter propagation, where a parent module overrides parameters to define the data widths and functions of its submodules during compilation. Second, it includes complex inter-module netlist topologies with multi-level dependency graphs; for example, signals in our security designs must pass through multiple hierarchy levels to connect with top-level control logic. Finally, submodules are connected via state-dependent protocols, such as multi-cycle handshakes, meaning an LLM must reason about joint timing behaviors across module boundaries rather than processing components individually. This structural density ensures that SysVDB functions as a system-level hardware benchmark. To further assess the generalization ability of the SysVCoder framework, Problem-Set-VeriGen [17] is included to further evaluate SysVCoder's generalization.

Baseline: We evaluate the generation performances of SysVCoder against the following three categories of baselines: 1) Commercial LLMs: we invoke general-purpose LLMs including *GPT-4*, *Deepseek-V3*, and *GPT-3.5* to conduct Verilog generation; 2) Domain-specific LLMs: we invoke SOTA domain-specific Verilog

Table 2. Module Types and Design Domain of SysVDB.

Design Domain	Module Types	Verification Approach
Bus & Interconnect	AHB Master, APB Mux, DMA Controller	Verify AMBA protocol compliance, burst transfers, multi-master contention, error injection, and randomized corner cases
Arithmetic Units	ALU, Multiplier, FFT	Check functional accuracy against golden models, boundary values, signed/unsigned operations, overflow, and formal equivalence
Memory & Storage	Cache, FIFO Memory, SDRAM Controller	Cover read/write consistency, cache hit/miss, clock domain timing, ECC, state machine transitions, and flag coverage
Signal Processing	CIC Filter, Audio DAC, I2S Interface	Validate signal response, protocol alignment, sample rate variations, noise injection, and reference model comparison
Communication	SPI Interface, UART, I2C Interface	Verify protocol transactions, error handling, arbitration, and edge cases with randomized packets
CPU & Control	Simple CPU, Interrupt Controller	Check instruction decoding, interrupt/exception handling, control flow, software co-simulation, and cycle-accurate timing
Miscellaneous	Combination Lock, SIPO Shift Register, DAC	Validate state transitions, output conversions, functional paths, and behavior under valid/invalid inputs using directed and random tests

generation frameworks based on open-source LLMs, including *codeV* [26], *RTL-Coder* [10], *ChipGPT* [1], *VeriGen* [17], *MG-Verilog* [25], *VeriThoughts* [24], and *VeriCoder* [19]; 3) Agent-based frameworks: we invoke multi-agent Verilog generation frameworks *HiVeGen* [14], *VerilogCoder* [5] by NIVIDIA and *MAGE* [27] for comparison. We adopt the widely used pass@k [2] metric to evaluate Verilog code generation, which measures the probability that at least one out of k generated code samples successfully passes validation. This metric can be calculated as:

$$\text{pass@}k = \mathbb{E}\left[1 - \frac{\binom{n-c}{k}}{\binom{n}{k}}\right], \tag{3}$$

where n is the total number of test attempts for the task, and c is the number of correct code generations for the task.

Implementation Details: We adopt different LLMs as the base models in SysVCoder, including commercial LLMs (i.e., Deepseek-V3, GPT-4), and open-source LLMs with smaller scale (i.e., Qwen2.5-7B, Qwen2.5-14B). We use Iverilog [20] and Pyverilog [13] to check the syntactic correctness of the generated Verilog solutions. If the design is syntactically correct, we proceed by running the corresponding test bench from the benchmark suite and comparing the output of the generated solution against the golden reference to verify its functional correctness. During the instruction tuning process, we apply LoRA [6]

Table 3. Generation performances of SysVCoder and SOTA frameworks over different benchmarks.

Type	Model	Param	SysVDB		VeriGen	
			pass@1	pass@5	pass@1	pass@5
Commercial	Deepseek-V3	671B	33.3	51.6	76.5	88.2
	GPT-3.5	175B	26.6	45.0	58.8	64.7
	GPT-4	1.8T	35.0	51.6	76.5	88.2
DS-LLMs	CodeV [26]	7B	11.6	16.6	52.9	70.6
	RTLCoder [10]	6.7B	5.0	6.6	47.1	70.6
	ChipGPT [1]	7B	8.3	11.6	47.1	64.7
	VeriGen [17]	16B	3.3	8.3	41.1	58.8
	MG-Verilog [25]	7B	3.3	5.0	41.1	52.9
	VeriCoder [19]	14B	8.3	15.0	29.4	47.1
	VeriThoughts [24]	7B	10.0	18.3	58.8	70.6
Agent	HiVeGen (GPT-4) [14]	1.8T	36.6	48.3	88.2	94.1
	VerilogCoder(GPT4) [5]	1.8T	45.0	60.0	94.1	100.0
	MAGE (GPT-4) [27]	1.8T	46.6	63.3	100.0	100.0
Ours	SysVCoder (Deepseek)	671B	43.3	61.6	94.1	100.0
	SysVCoder (GPT-4)	1.8T	43.3	65.0	94.1	100.0
	SysVCoder (Qwen2.5)	14B	40.0	63.3	64.7	76.4
	SysVCoder (Qwen2.5)	7B	41.6	58.3	64.7	70.6

to enhance efficiency while preserving model performance. The learning rate γ is set to 2×10^{-4}, and the models are trained for 3 epochs. Experiments are conducted using eight NVIDIA 4090 GPUs. The implementations of SysVCoder and SysVDB are made public at https://gitee.com/sdu-aes-lab/sysvcoder/.

4.2 Experimental Results

We first evaluate SysVCoder's generation performance (in terms of pass@1 and pass@5) on system-level Verilog designs of SysVDB against baseline approaches. As shown in Table 3, SysVCoder substantially outperforms all existing generation frameworks with domain-specific LLMs. As shown in Table 3, SysVCoder with base LLM Qwen2.5-7B surpasses CodeV by over 30% on pass@1 and 40% on pass@5 with the LLM of a comparable scale. Moreover, SysVCoder with a 7B-LLM outperforms the VeriGen framework, which is based on a larger 16B-CodeGen LLM, by 38.3% and 50.0% in terms of pass@1 and pass@5 respectively. When compared with HiVeGen, the framework specifically designed for hierarchical Verilog generation based on GPT-4, SysVCoder with Qwen2.5-7B achieves 5% and 10% increase in terms of pass@1 and pass@5. Most existing Verilog generation frameworks conduct their training on isolated single-module Verilog examples, which limits their ability to handle system-level hardware designs in

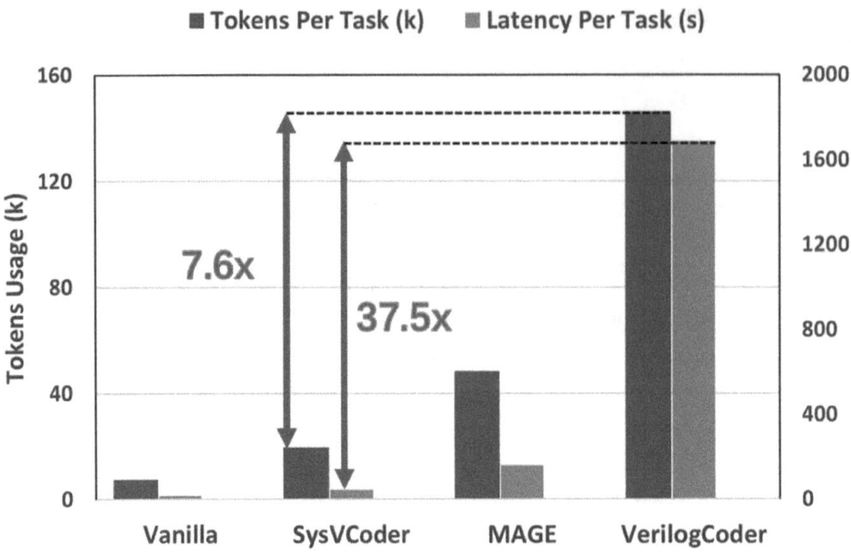

Fig. 4. Comparison of average generation latency and tokens consumed by SysVCoder and agent-based approaches.

real-world scenarios. These performances underscore SysVCoder's capability to effectively guide LLMs in understanding and generating complex circuit logic.

Notably, when compared with SOTA agent-based frameworks VerilogCover devised by NVIDIA, SysVCoder(QWen2.7-7B) achieves comparable performances, with only a 3.33% drop in pass@1 and 1.65% drop in pass@5, as shown in Table 3. In addition, as illustrated in Fig. 4, SysVCoder consumes 7.6× fewer tokens and generates 37.5× faster than VerilogCoder, which requires an iterative generation process with multiple full-scale LLM agents. Remarkably, SysVCoder delivers comparable performance through a streamlined two-stage generation process, effectively obviating the need for a syntax-failure retry loop. This highlights that SysVCoder can significantly reduce the resource demand to enable lightweight LLMs to efficiently produce high-quality, system-level Verilog code, offering a scalable and practical solution for real-world hardware design automation.

To further assess the generalization capability of SysVCoder, we evaluate its performance of syntax and functional correctness on the public dataset Problem-Set-VeriGen [17]. As shown in Table 3, SysVCoder(Qwen2.5-14B) achieves a pass@5 of 76.4%, the highest among all frameworks based on small-scale LLMs, while SysVCoder(Deepseek) achieves perfect generation performances as the other baseline approaches based on GPT-4 or Deepseek-v3. These results demonstrate the strength of SysVCoder in enabling LLMs to more effectively capture the intrinsic characteristics of Verilog design, ultimately leading to higher-quality and more functionally accurate code generation.

4.3 Ablation Study

Table 4 presents the results of an ablation study evaluating the contribution of the key optimizations of SysVCoder. These optimizations include general intermediate representation (GIR), instruction tuning for GIR generation (IT), rule-based alignment (RBA), and retraining-free retrieval-augmented generation (RAG). The study is conducted across SysVDB benchmark dataset. For comparison, we also include a vanilla baseline, where the LLM directly generates Verilog code without any enhancements.

As shown in Table 4, SysVCoder consistently delivers the best performance across all base LLMs, indicating the effectiveness of the proposed optimizations. The performance drop of *SysVCoder w/o GIR* indicates the important role of the intermediate representation as the bridge to enable an accurate translation from concise natural language description to system-level hardware design. The performance gap between SysVCoder and *SysVCoder w/o IT* indicates the critical role of structural guidance through instruction tuning. Notably, the zero-shot Qwen-7B baseline employing only GIR scaffolding as a prompt template fails to achieve significant performance gains, underscoring the limitations of relying solely on prompt engineering without instruction tuning. In addition, removing the rule-based alignment (*SysVCoder w/o RBA*) in the second-stage generation of SysVCoder results in significant performance drops. This highlights the importance of enriching prompts with structured, semantically aligned content. Similarly, removing RAG (*SysVCoder w/o RAG*) leads to moderate but consistent declines in performance, underscoring the benefit of including high-quality, standard Verilog module references in pormpt during generation.

Table 4. Generation performances under different scheme settings on SysVDB.

Method	Qwen-7B		Qwen-14B		GPT-4		Deepseek	
	pass@1	pass@5	pass@1	pass@5	pass@1	pass@5	pass@1	pass@5
Vanilla	13.3	20.0	18.3	22.6	35.0	51.6	33.3	51.6
SysVCoder	**41.6**	**58.3**	**40.0**	**63.3**	**41.6**	**60.0**	**43.3**	**61.6**
SysVC w/o GIR	15.2	30.0	31.6	48.3	28.3	51.6	30.0	53.3
SysVC w/o IT	23.3	33.3	26.0	38.3	-	-	-	-
SysVC w/o RBA	28.3	45.0	31.6	55.0	35.0	53.3	38.3	50.0
SysVC w/o RAG	26.6	43.3	30.0	51.6	33.3	55.0	35.0	56.6

5 Conclusion

In this paper, we propose an LLM-driven framework, SysVCoder, for systematic generation of system-level hardware design. SysVCoder aims to generate real-world Verilog designs via the proposed two-stage generation mechanism, leveraging an intermediate representation to enable a more accurate and structured transition from natural language descriptions to intricate Verilog code. We also introduce SysVDB, a comprehensive dataset of 60 system-level Verilog designs with corresponding verification benchmarks derived from real-world implementations. Experimental results show that SysVCoder outperforms SOTA Verilog generation frameworks and enables the small-scale LLM (i.e., Qwen-7B) to achieve comparable performances against agent-based frameworks with much less token consumption and generation latency.

Acknowledgments. This study is supported in part by the National Natural Science Foundation of China (Grant No.62502279) and Young Talent of Lifting Engineering for Science and Technology in Shandong, China (Grant No. SDAST2024QTA078).

The technical solution and experimental design presented in this paper were independently completed by the authors. AI tools were used solely for language polishing and formatting optimization, and did not participate in the development of the research ideas or core content.

References

1. Chang, K., et al.: ChipGPT: how far are we from natural language hardware design. arXiv preprint arXiv:2305.14019 (2023)
2. Chen, M., et al.: Evaluating large language models trained on code (2021). arXiv preprint arXiv:2107.03374
3. Dehaerne, E., Dey, B., Halder, S., De Gendt, S.: A deep learning framework for verilog autocompletion towards design and verification automation (2023). arXiv preprint arXiv:2304.13840
4. Gao, M., et al.: AutoVCoder: a systematic framework for automated Verilog code generation using LLMs. In: 2024 IEEE 42nd International Conference on Computer Design (ICCD), pp. 162–169. IEEE (2024)
5. Ho, C.T., Ren, H., Khailany, B.: VerilogCoder: autonomous Verilog coding agents with graph-based planning and abstract syntax tree (AST)-based waveform tracing tool. In: Proceedings of the AAAI Conference on Artificial Intelligence, vol. 39, pp. 300–307 (2025)
6. Hu, E.J., et al.: LoRA: low-rank adaptation of large language models. In: ICLR, vol. 1, no. 2, p. 3 (2022)
7. Liu, F., et al.: Exploring and evaluating hallucinations in LLM-powered code generation. arXiv preprint arXiv:2404.00971 (2024)
8. Liu, M., et al.: ChipNeMo: domain-adapted LLMs for chip design (2023). arXiv preprint arXiv:2311.00176
9. Liu, M., Pinckney, N., Khailany, B., Ren, H.: VerilogEval: evaluating large language models for Verilog code generation. In: 2023 IEEE/ACM International Conference on Computer Aided Design (ICCAD), pp. 1–8. IEEE (2023)
10. Liu, S., et al.: RTLCoder: fully open-source and efficient LLM-assisted RTL code generation technique. IEEE Trans. Comput.-Aided Des. Integr. Circuits Syst. (2024)
11. Lu, Y., Liu, S., Zhang, Q., Xie, Z.: RTLLM: an open-source benchmark for design RTL generation with large language model. In: 2024 29th Asia and South Pacific Design Automation Conference (ASP-DAC), pp. 722–727. IEEE (2024)

12. Pei, Z., Zhen, H., Yuan, M., Huang, Y., Yu, B.: BetterV: controlled Verilog generation with discriminative guidance. In: International Conference on Machine Learning, pp. 40145–40153. PMLR (2024)
13. Takamaeda-Yamazaki, S.: Pyverilog: a Python-based hardware design processing toolkit for Verilog HDL. In: Sano, K., Soudris, D., Hübner, M., Diniz, P.C. (eds.) ARC 2015. LNCS, vol. 9040, pp. 451–460. Springer, Cham (2015). https://doi.org/10.1007/978-3-319-16214-0_42
14. Tang, J., et al.: HiVeGen-hierarchical LLM-based Verilog generation for scalable chip design. In: 2025 IEEE International Conference on LLM-Aided Design (ICLAD), pp. 30–36. IEEE (2025)
15. sentence-transformers Team: all-MiniLM-L6-v2 (2024). https://huggingface.co/sentence-transformers/all-MiniLM-L6-v2
16. Thakur, S., et al.: Benchmarking large language models for automated Verilog RTL code generation. In: 2023 Design, Automation & Test in Europe Conference & Exhibition (DATE). pp. 1–6. IEEE (2023)
17. Thakur, S., et al.: VeriGen: a large language model for Verilog code generation. ACM Trans. Des. Autom. Electron. Syst. **29**(3), 1–31 (2024)
18. Thakur, S., Blocklove, J., Pearce, H., Tan, B., Garg, S., Karri, R.: AutoChip: automating HDL generation using LLM feedback (2023). arXiv preprint arXiv:2311.04887
19. Wei, A., et al.: VeriCoder: enhancing LLM-based RTL code generation through functional correctness validation (2025). arXiv preprint arXiv:2504.15659
20. Williams, S., Baxter, M.: Icarus Verilog: open-source Verilog more than a year later. Linux J. **2002**(99), 3 (2002)
21. Wolf, C., Glaser, J., Kepler, J.: Yosys: a free Verilog synthesis suite. In: Proceedings of the 21st Austrian Workshop on Microelectronics (Austrochip), p. 97 (2013)
22. Wong, H.: HDLBits — Verilog Practice (2024). https://hdlbits.01xz.net/wiki/Main_Page
23. Yang, Z., et al.: Exploring and unleashing the power of large language models in automated code translation. Proc. ACM Softw. Eng. **1**(FSE), 1585–1608 (2024)
24. Yubeaton, P., et al.: VeriThoughts: enabling automated Verilog code generation using reasoning and formal verification (2025). arXiv preprint arXiv:2505.20302
25. Zhang, Y., Yu, Z., Fu, Y., Wan, C., Lin, Y.C.: MG-Verilog: multi-grained dataset towards enhanced LLM-assisted Verilog generation. In: 2024 IEEE LLM Aided Design Workshop (LAD), pp. 1–5. IEEE (2024)
26. Zhao, Y., et al.: CodeV: empowering LLMs for Verilog generation through multi-level summarization. arXiv preprint arXiv:2407.10424 (2024)
27. Zhao, Y., Zhang, H., Huang, H., Yu, Z., Zhao, J.: MAGE: a multi-agent engine for automated RTL code generation. arXiv preprint arXiv:2412.07822 (2024)

TensorAgent: Multi-agent Framework for Automated Tensor Core Code Generation

Bingjie Liu, Zhongchun Zheng, and Xianwei Zhang(✉)

School of Computer Science and Engineering, Sun Yat-sen University, Guangzhou, China
{liubj8,zhengzhch3}@mail2.sysu.edu.cn, zhangxw79@mail.sysu.edu.cn

Abstract. WMMA (Warp Matrix Multiply-Accumulate) is the CUDA warp-level interface for matrix multiply-accumulate on Tensor Cores, making it a central building block of high-throughput deep learning training and inference. In practice, developing WMMA kernels remains difficult because API-level correctness, fragment memory and layout constraints, and runtime numerical behavior under precision-specific rules must be satisfied jointly. LLM-based CUDA kernel generation has progressed quickly, yet existing methods offer limited support for structured, failure-aware repair across development stages and thus leave much of the potential of LLMs for WMMA-focused Tensor Core programming unrealized. We present TensorAgent, a multi-agent framework that separates planning, synthesis, and execution diagnosis and connects them with hierarchical feedback as an explicit repair policy. That feedback is directed at failures arising during algorithm design, compilation, and execution. We evaluate on 15 WMMA benchmarks spanning six data-type settings and two kernel-complexity tiers and report execution time relative to expert-written baselines. Relative to direct prompting, TensorAgent improves run pass@1 by up to 43.2% points and reaches 99.0% run pass@1 on simple kernels.

Keywords: Multi-agent systems · Code generation · Tensor Core · CUDA · Large language models

1 Introduction

The rapid scaling of deep learning has driven extraordinary demand for GPU compute. Training and inference throughput hinges on a few compute-intensive operators—matrix multiply, attention, convolution, and element-wise fusions—whose efficiency dictates end-to-end performance. On modern NVIDIA GPUs, Tensor Cores provide the primary dense-arithmetic throughput for these operators.

The standard warp-level programming interface for Tensor Cores is WMMA (warp matrix multiply-accumulate) [1]. WMMA coordinates 32 threads within

L. Eeckhout et al. (Eds.): APPT 2026, LNCS 16693, pp. 238–252, 2027.
https://doi.org/10.1007/978-981-92-4805-6_16

a warp to load, compute, and store matrix fragments across multiple precision formats (FP16, BF16, TF32, FP64, INT8). Despite its central role, writing correct WMMA kernels remains difficult: developers must simultaneously satisfy API-level constraints (fragment types, supported operations), memory and layout rules, and runtime numerical correctness. The resulting error space is layered: a kernel may compile yet violate layout constraints at runtime, or pass layout checks yet produce numerically wrong results.

Large language models trained on code generate high-quality programs from natural language [2–4], and LLM-based GPU kernel generation is advancing rapidly [5,6]. However, recent benchmarks reveal a persistent gap between compilation success and functional correctness [6]: code that compiles is far from code that runs correctly. Pass@1 is the fraction of independent trials in which the first generated sample meets a correctness criterion; we report compile pass@1 and run pass@1 separately. Figure 1 summarizes this setting: the left panel shows that direct prompting is largely feed-forward with no explicit error feedback from later stages, while the right panel shows the substantial compile–run gap that results. Existing approaches provide limited support for structured, failure-aware repair across algorithm design, compilation, and runtime, leaving the potential of LLMs for WMMA-oriented Tensor Core programming underused. Multi-agent coding systems show that explicit roles and feedback loops improve complex synthesis [7–10], yet their task-generic decompositions do not match the layered error structure of Tensor Core development. We therefore propose TensorAgent, a multi-agent framework in which each agent aligns with a distinct constraint layer—planning, code synthesis, and execution diagnosis—linked by hierarchical feedback that routes each failure to the lowest level capable of resolving it.

Our contributions are threefold. First, we propose TensorAgent, a multi-agent framework that maps planning, code generation, and execution diagnosis onto the WMMA failure stratification (algorithm design, compilation, and runtime) and links them with hierarchical feedback that routes each failure to the lowest layer able to resolve it before escalating. Second, we construct a benchmark of 15 WMMA kernel tasks in simple and complex layers, spanning BF16, FP16, FP64, INT8, TF32, and mixed-precision workloads. Third, we evaluate three LLMs with 100 trials per kernel per method (9,000 runs): TensorAgent consistently improves compile and run pass@1 over direct prompting, and we report the same metrics under CudaForge [11], a state-of-the-art agentic CUDA workflow with hardware feedback, as a workflow-level reference (Sect. 5.3). We additionally report execution time relative to expert baselines (Sect. 5.4) and practical-cost statistics—repair iterations, plan-escalation rate, and wall-clock time (Sect. 5.6).

2 Related Work

LLM Code Generation and Iterative Prompting. Large language models trained on code achieve strong results on standard benchmarks, from Codex [2] to open models such as StarCoder and Code Llama [3,4]. Reasoning-oriented methods such as chain-of-thought [12], self-debugging [13], and flow engineering [14] improve correctness by introducing intermediate structure. Most evaluations, however, focus on algorithmic benchmarks where correctness is test-driven and platform details are abstracted away. Tensor Core kernel generation differs: validity depends on low-level API rules and hardware runtime behavior that standard benchmarks rarely capture.

Multi-agent Coding Systems. Prior multi-agent coding systems (AgentCoder [7], MapCoder [8], CodeAgent [9], CODESIM [10]) demonstrate that role decomposition and iterative collaboration improve complex coding outcomes. These systems are nevertheless largely task-generic and are typically evaluated on repository-level or algorithmic tasks; they do not explicitly model the compile–run failure stratification of Tensor Core development. Our setting requires a domain-specific decomposition in which each role aligns with a distinct constraint layer: algorithmic design, API-correct synthesis, and runtime verification.

GPU Kernel Stacks and Tensor Core Programming. CUDA Agent [15] scales agentic CUDA generation with reinforcement learning, emphasizing training infrastructure rather than lightweight inference-time escalation across design, compilation, and runtime. CudaForge [11] represents the state of the art among *agentic* CUDA workflows, integrating hardware feedback for iterative optimization. We adopt CudaForge as the primary workflow reference on the same WMMA template tasks, so each model is evaluated under both single-shot prompting and a hardware-feedback pipeline. CudaForge emphasizes hardware-guided optimization loops, whereas TensorAgent emphasizes robust WMMA synthesis from fixed templates by localizing failures hierarchically across algorithm design, compilation, and runtime. Broader surveys [16,17] identify specialization and feedback as central mechanisms in LLM multi-agent systems; we apply these mechanisms to WMMA-oriented Tensor Core generation and evaluate them through kernel-level compile and run outcomes.

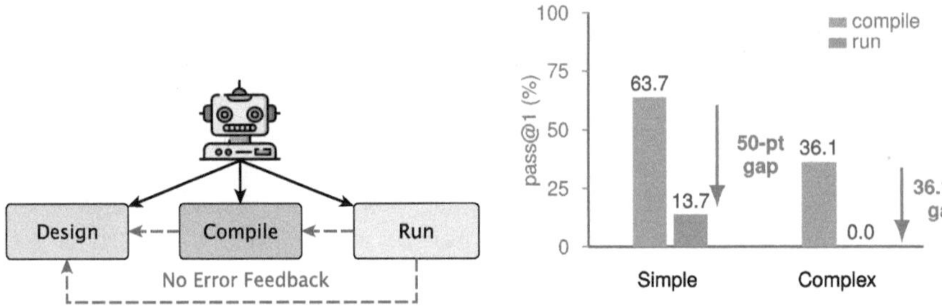

Fig. 1. Direct prompting lacks error feedback from compilation and execution stages (**left**), resulting in low run pass@1 despite moderate compile success (**right**).

3 Motivation

Preliminary baseline experiments on our WMMA benchmark (direct single-shot prompting; details in Sect. 5.3) reveal two patterns, previewed in Fig. 1, that directly motivate the architectural design choices in TensorAgent.

Observation 1: Compile Success Does Not Imply Runtime Correctness. Under direct prompting, the compile-to-run gap is large. For example, DeepSeek-v3.2 compiles 63.7% of simple-layer trials yet only 13.7% run correctly—a 50-point gap; on complex kernels, it compiles 36.1% but achieves 0% runtime success (Table 4). The pattern holds across models: many WMMA faults (layout mismatches, synchronization errors, precision-dependent accumulation bugs) pass `nvcc` yet surface only at execution. This gap, documented also in broader GPU benchmarks [6], shows that any effective workflow must include explicit runtime verification rather than treating compilation as a sufficient correctness signal.

Observation 2: Failures Span Algorithm, API, and Runtime Levels. Baseline failures distribute across three levels: algorithm-design errors (wrong tiling or layout), API misuse caught by the compiler (incorrect API calls), and runtime-only faults (synchronization races, numerical accumulation errors). A single undifferentiated feedback channel mixes these signals, increasing cognitive load [18] and leading to repeated surface-level patches that never address the underlying design flaw.

Together, these observations motivate a multi-agent framework that aligns each agent with a distinct failure level—algorithm design, code synthesis, and execution diagnosis—and connects them through hierarchical feedback so that each error is routed to the agent best positioned to resolve it with minimal cross-stage interference.

4 Framework Design

4.1 Overview

Given a CUDA source file whose kernel body has been replaced by a placeholder, TensorAgent produces a correct kernel implementation through the coordinated action of three specialized agents (Fig. 2). PlanAgent analyzes the template and emits a structured plan fixing algorithm-level decisions before any code is written. GenAgent converts the plan into compilable CUDA and iteratively repairs compiler errors through a local self-feedback loop with `nvcc`. ExecAgent runs the compiled binary on the target GPU, and when execution fails, produces a structured diagnostic routed to GenAgent or escalated to PlanAgent depending on fault severity.

The key design principle is hierarchical feedback: each error is first handled at the lowest layer capable of resolving it, and escalation occurs only when local repair is insufficient.

The remainder of this section describes the feedback mechanism (Sect. 4.2) and then each agent in detail (Sects. 4.3–4.5).

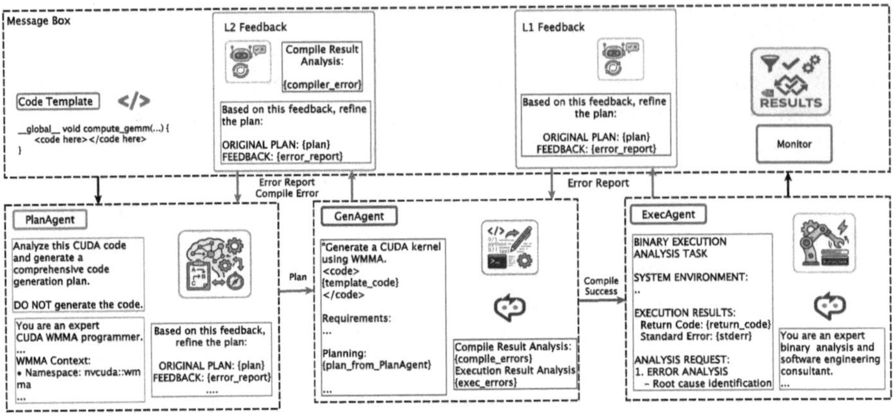

Fig. 2. Overview of TensorAgent. Arrows indicate feedback flow. GenAgent maintains a local compile-feedback loop; execution failures are diagnosed by ExecAgent and routed back to GenAgent. Unresolved errors escalate to PlanAgent for plan revision.

4.2 Hierarchical Feedback

TensorAgent is organized around *hierarchical feedback* (Sect. 3), which routes each error to the lowest layer capable of resolving it before escalating to higher layers (Fig. 2). Because compile success does not guarantee runtime correctness, the feedback loop does not stop at `nvcc` success; execution outcomes are fed back into the workflow so that runtime-only faults receive targeted repair. Because WMMA failures span algorithm, API, and runtime levels, feedback is structured into three corresponding layers rather than a single undifferentiated loop. At the compile level, diagnostics from `nvcc` are fed back to GenAgent, which re-invokes the LLM to fix syntax errors, type mismatches, and API misuse in a local self-correction loop bounded at k iterations. At the runtime level, ExecAgent launches the compiled binary and, on failure, produces a structured diagnostic (root cause, error class, repair suggestions) that is returned to GenAgent for code-level repair. If code-level repair does not resolve the issue, the diagnostic escalates to PlanAgent for plan-level revision, so that deeper design errors (wrong tiling strategy, incorrect layout) are corrected at the layer where they originate. Agents communicate via typed messages routed by an asynchronous message bus with per-task tracing; a central *TaskMonitor* tracks compile/run status and signals completion. This hierarchical feedback design is the core mechanism behind TensorAgent: it closes the compile–run gap with explicit execution checks, and resolves mixed failure modes through layer-specific repair rather than conflating them in a single loop.

4.3 Planning Agent

PlanAgent occupies the top layer of the hierarchical feedback chain: it converts an underspecified CUDA template into a structured implementation plan that constrains downstream synthesis and reduces the algorithm-design errors identified in Sect. 3.

Domain-Specific Context and Plan Structure. The system prompt front-loads WMMA API and hardware constraints (supported fragment types, precision formats, standard tile sizes, and memory layouts) so that the plan references concrete API elements rather than generic pseudo-instructions. PLANAGENT analyzes the surrounding host code (launch dimensions, data types, stride conventions) and produces a plan of at most five actionable steps.

Feedback-Driven Revision. When plan-level escalation is triggered (Sect. 4.2), PLANAGENT receives the structured diagnostic from EXECAGENT and revises the plan accordingly. A per-task counter bounds iterations at k attempts.

4.4 Generation Agent

GENAGENT occupies the middle layer of the hierarchical feedback chain: it converts the plan into compilable CUDA and absorbs compiler-visible defects through a local feedback loop before any escalation occurs.

Constrained Code Synthesis. GENAGENT receives the plan, the original template, and any prior error feedback. Its system prompt encodes coding-level constraints (Tensor Core usage patterns, fragment loading/storing conventions, memory coalescing rules, synchronization requirements, and data-type handling) that complement the plan with code-level best practices. The LLM returns only the kernel code, delimited by triple backticks for automated extraction.

Compiler Self-feedback Loop. After splicing the generated code into the template, GENAGENT invokes `nvcc`. On failure, compiler diagnostics are appended to the prompt and the LLM is re-invoked, forming the compile-level feedback loop described in Sect. 4.2. This local loop resolves frequent compile-time faults (syntax errors, type mismatches, API misuse) without engaging the full pipeline. If the loop exhausts its k-iteration budget, the failure escalates to PLANAGENT for plan revision.

4.5 Execution Agent

EXECAGENT occupies the final layer of the hierarchical feedback chain, closing the compile–run gap identified in Sect. 3 by validating post-compile correctness and producing the structured diagnostics.

Structured Failure Diagnosis. EXECAGENT launches the compiled binary on the target GPU; exit status zero signals success under the task's bundled checks. On a non-zero return code, EXECAGENT invokes its LLM backend with execution context (stderr, return code, CUDA and driver versions, and the original requirements) to produce a structured report: (i) failure-mode identification, (ii) root-cause attribution to a constraint layer (algorithm design, API usage, or runtime behavior), and (iii) repair suggestions.

Escalation Policy. The diagnostic is first sent to GenAgent for code-level repair (runtime-level feedback). If regeneration fails, the failure escalates to PlanAgent for plan revision (plan-level escalation). Shallow defects (e.g., a missing synchronization call) are thus contained at the generation layer, while deeper algorithmic problems (e.g., an incorrect tiling strategy) reach the planning layer. Escalation is not uniform across models: plan-level escalation is triggered for 66.7–98.9% of Claude Sonnet-4.6 and DeepSeek-v3.2 trials but only 2–3% of GPT-5.3-codex-high trials (Sect. 5.6, Table 6), showing that the diagnosis-and-escalation path is exercised exactly when the model cannot solve the kernel in one shot.

5 Experimental Evaluation

We assess generation with compile pass@1 and run pass@1, and compare execution time against expert baselines for successful trials. Correctness tables list three settings per model (direct prompting, TensorAgent, and CudaForge), enabling comparison against both a single-shot baseline and a state-of-the-art agentic workflow.

5.1 Benchmark Design

Task Formulation. Each task is a CUDA source file from the NVIDIA `cuda-samples` repository [19] in which the kernel body has been replaced by a placeholder. Host-side boilerplate—data allocation, memory transfers, result verification, and launch configuration—is left intact, so the LLM receives the full surrounding context and must produce only the kernel that fills the placeholder. This formulation isolates kernel logic while providing type signatures, matrix dimensions, and memory layouts that constrain a valid solution. By design, it tests the warp-level WMMA logic where the compile–run gap is most acute, but it does not exercise host integration or end-to-end performance tuning.

We assemble 15 WMMA kernel tasks from these templates, covering BF16, FP16, FP64, INT8, TF32, and mixed-precision operations in two complexity layers. The simple layer (S1–S6) contains six WMMA GEMM kernels that use core WMMA APIs. The complex layer (C1–C9) contains nine kernels that add asynchronous memory copies, cooperative-group synchronization, and optimized compute patterns (Table 1).

5.2 Experimental Setup

Models. We evaluate three LLMs: Claude Sonnet-4.6 (Anthropic), DeepSeek-v3.2 (DeepSeek), and GPT-5.3-codex-high (OpenAI). All models are accessed via API with identical prompts and temperature settings (0.1 for planning, 0.5 for generation, 0.2 for execution analysis).

Table 1. Kernel code mapping used throughout the paper: **left**, simple layer S1–S6; **right**, complex layer C1–C9; numeric order within each layer.

Simple (S1–S6)		Complex (C1–C9)	
K.	Source program	K.	Source program
S1	wmma_gemm_a_col_major_b_col_major	C1	cudaTensorCoreGemm_compute_gemm
S2	cudaTensorCoreGemm_simple_wmma_gemm	C2	dmmaTensorCoreGemm_compute_dgemm
S3	dmmaTensorCoreGemm_simple_wmma_gemm	C3	dmmaTensorCoreGemm_compute_dgemm_async_copy
S4	immaTensorCoreGemm_simple_wmma_gemm_imma	C4	dmmaTensorCoreGemm_compute_dgemm_cg_async_copy
S5	bf16TensorCoreGemm_simple_wmma_bf16gemm	C5	immaTensorCoreGemm_compute_gemm_imma
S6	tf32TensorCoreGemm_simple_wmma_tf32gemm	C6	bf16TensorCoreGemm_compute_bf16gemm
		C7	bf16TensorCoreGemm_compute_bf16gemm_async_copy
		C8	tf32TensorCoreGemm_compute_tf32gemm
		C9	tf32TensorCoreGemm_compute_tf32gemm_async_copy

Baselines. The baseline uses single-pass direct prompting: each model receives the template without planning or feedback, using the same prompt structure as GENAGENT but without the plan, compiler feedback, or execution verification. We include CudaForge [11] as a workflow-level reference, reporting TensorAgent alongside Direct and CudaForge for comparison against both a single-shot baseline and a state-of-the-art agentic workflow.

Evaluation Protocol. Following standard pass@k evaluation [2,7–9,20,21], we report compile pass@1 (compiles without errors) and run pass@1 (compiles and executes correctly) over 100 independent trials per kernel per model per method on NVIDIA A100 GPUs (CUDA 12.3).

Performance Protocol. For trials that pass runtime checks, we measure kernel execution time and compare against the expert reference kernel from the CUDA samples [19], compiled with the same matrix dimensions and launch configuration. Speedup is the expert execution time divided by the generated-kernel time; ratios above one indicate faster generated code.

5.3 Correctness Comparison

Overview. We foreground run pass@1 as the stricter final objective because it requires compilation and correct execution; on this metric TensorAgent achieves higher pass@1 than CudaForge for Claude Sonnet-4.6 (43.2% vs. 19.5% on the simple layer; 12.6% vs. 0.4% on the complex layer) and for DeepSeek-v3.2 on the simple layer (56.8% vs. 28.5%), while all three workflows tie at 0.0% run pass@1 for DeepSeek-v3.2 on the complex layer (Table 4). Although CudaForge attains higher compile pass@1 in several settings, many of its generated kernels still fail runtime checks (Tables 2–3): its hardware-guided optimization loop drives builds to succeed without closing runtime-numerics faults that determine run pass@1. TensorAgent's advantage is therefore largest for capable-but-not-saturated models (Claude Sonnet-4.6 and DeepSeek-v3.2 on simple kernels), precisely where compilation success is an unreliable proxy for correctness. For GPT-5.3-codex-high, which already saturates, mean run pass@1 under TensorAgent is essentially the same as under CudaForge (within one to two percentage points on each layer); and when the model lacks the required WMMA fundamentals (DeepSeek-v3.2 on the complex layer), all three workflows tie at 0% because feedback cannot supply knowledge the model does not have.

Table 2. Simple kernel results (S1–S6). Compile (C) and Run (R) pass@1 (%) over 100 trials per kernel. Within each model block, the best run pass@1 per kernel (among the three workflows) is in **bold**. Ties share bold. (In all tables, Claude = Claude Sonnet-4.6, Deepseek = DeepSeek-v3.2, GPT = GPT-5.3-codex-high. Each model appears with three rows: Baseline (single-pass prompting), TensorAgent (our framework), and CudaForge (state-of-the-art agentic CUDA workflow).)

	S1		S2		S3		S4		S5		S6	
	C	R	C	R	C	R	C	R	C	R	C	R
Claude / Baseline	19	3	25	4	13	12	20	9	45	15	3	0
Claude / TensorAgent	64	**46**	67	**47**	39	**38**	47	**31**	65	**42**	61	**55**
Claude / CudaForge	52	29	100	16	98	19	98	5	99	41	97	7
Deepseek / Baseline	32	4	71	19	73	16	58	16	81	23	67	4
Deepseek / TensorAgent	100	**72**	97	**73**	98	**44**	99	**60**	100	**47**	100	**45**
Deepseek / CudaForge	90	14	99	17	98	37	98	23	97	39	91	41
GPT / Baseline	76	76	80	80	49	48	50	49	81	79	86	81
GPT / TensorAgent	98	98	100	**100**	99	99	98	98	100	**100**	99	99
GPT / CudaForge	100	**100**	100	**100**	100	**100**	100	**100**	100	**100**	100	**100**

Simple Kernels. Table 2 compares Baseline, CudaForge, and TensorAgent on six simple kernels. Relative to Baseline, TensorAgent raises average compile pass@1 by 28.8–36.4 points and run pass@1 by 30.3–43.2 points. The run gain is larger because one-shot generation often yields code that compiles yet fails at runtime; execution-stage diagnosis closes this gap. For Claude Sonnet-4.6 and DeepSeek-v3.2, the mean run pass@1 on S1–S6 under TensorAgent exceeds that under CudaForge by 23.7 and 28.3 points, respectively. For GPT-5.3-codex-high, compile and run pass@1 are both near saturation under the agentic workflows, with only a small spread between TensorAgent and CudaForge (Table 2).

Complex Kernels. Table 3 lists per-kernel results on C1–C9; Table 4 averages them per layer. For compile pass@1, TensorAgent exceeds baseline by 30.3 % and 40.1 % for Claude Sonnet-4.6 and DeepSeek-v3.2, respectively, and also improves over Direct for GPT-5.3-codex-high (Table 3). For run pass@1, DeepSeek-v3.2 averages 0% under baseline, TensorAgent, and CudaForge. Claude Sonnet-4.6 averages 0.6% (baseline), 12.6% (TensorAgent), and 0.4% (CudaForge). For

Table 3. Complex kernel results (C1–C9). Compile (C) and Run (R) pass@1 (%) over 100 trials. Within each model block, the best run pass@1 per kernel (among the three workflows) is in **bold**. Ties share bold. There is no highlight when all three run values are 0.

	C1		C2		C3		C4		C5		C6		C7		C8		C9	
	C	R	C	R	C	R	C	R	C	R	C	R	C	R	C	R	C	R
Claude / Baseline	42	1	36	0	32	1	25	1	59	1	53	0	43	0	7	1	7	0
Claude / TensorAgent	85	**6**	73	**14**	58	**17**	52	**17**	80	**19**	90	**7**	60	**13**	37	**10**	42	**10**
Claude / CudaForge	99	1	98	0	97	0	97	1	98	0	96	0	97	2	96	0	96	0
Deepseek / Baseline	57	0	60	0	12	0	13	0	60	0	57	0	14	0	38	0	14	0
Deepseek / TensorAgent	98	0	93	0	44	0	68	0	97	0	88	0	52	0	87	0	59	0
Deepseek / CudaForge	92	0	84	0	41	0	52	0	88	0	78	0	43	0	82	0	39	0
GPT / Baseline	95	84	70	53	61	59	62	58	48	46	85	69	84	83	84	79	82	78
GPT / TensorAgent	99	97	99	98	100	98	100	**100**	95	93	99	99	100	**100**	98	98	99	99
GPT / CudaForge	100	**100**	100	**100**	100	**100**	100	**100**	100	**100**	100	**100**	100	**100**	100	**100**	100	**100**

GPT-5.3-codex-high, mean run pass@1 is high under both agentic workflows and differs little between TensorAgent and CudaForge; per-kernel values are in Table 3.

Per-kernel run pass@1 is plotted in Fig. 3; Tables 2 and 3 report compile and run pass@1 for each kernel.

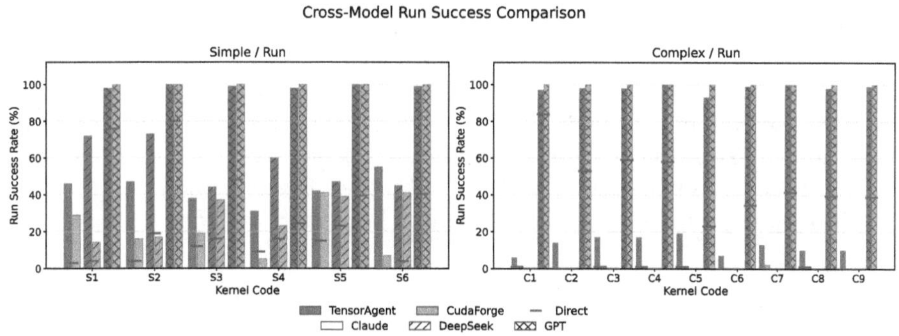

Fig. 3. Per-kernel run pass@1 (%) for each model and workflow (Direct, TensorAgent, CudaForge) on the simple and complex layers.

5.4 Performance Evaluation

Figure 4 plots per-kernel average and maximum speedup relative to expert baselines.

On simple kernels, average speedup stays close to 1.0×. DeepSeek-v3.2 achieves the highest single-kernel speedup on S5 (avg 1.23×, max 1.52×), followed by Claude Sonnet-4.6 on S3 (avg 1.15×, max 1.45×). Most remaining

Table 4. Summary of average compile and run pass@1 (%) across all kernels per layer. Columns are Direct prompting, TensorAgent, and CudaForge (SOTA workflow). Within each row, the best run pass@1 among the three workflows is in **bold** (no highlight when all three tie at 0%).

		Compile pass@1 (%)			Run pass@1 (%)		
Layer	Model	Baseline	TensorAgent	CudaForge	Baseline	TensorAgent	CudaForge
Simple	Claude	20.8	57.2	90.7	7.2	**43.2**	19.5
	Deepseek	63.7	99.0	95.5	13.7	**56.8**	28.5
	GPT	70.3	99.0	100.0	68.8	99.0	**100.0**
Complex	Claude	33.8	64.1	97.1	0.6	**12.6**	0.4
	Deepseek	36.1	76.2	66.6	0.0	0.0	0.0
	GPT	74.6	98.8	100.0	67.7	98.0	**100.0**

kernels fall within 0.87–1.06×, indicating that correctly generated simple kernels approach expert-level execution time.

On complex kernels, performance drops: most bars fall below 1.0×. Only TF32 kernels sustain competitive speedup—GPT-5.3-codex-high reaches avg 1.12× on C8 (max 1.83×) and Claude Sonnet-4.6 avg 1.06× on C9 (max 1.48×)—while others average 0.59–0.96×. Asynchronous pipelines and cooperative-group orchestration remain difficult for current generation loops to realize efficiently.

Across both layers, high run pass@1 does not by itself mean that generated kernels match expert wall-clock time. In this work we target the compile–run gap, so a runtime-correct kernel is the immediate goal, and performance tuning builds naturally on top of it. Because TensorAgent returns a runtime-correct kernel, it provides a solid starting point for such tuning: the kernel can be handed to an autotuner. A natural next step is to couple performance signals into the agent loop, so that the same hierarchical feedback also drives latency reduction on asynchronous-pipeline and cooperative-group kernels (Sect. 5.7).

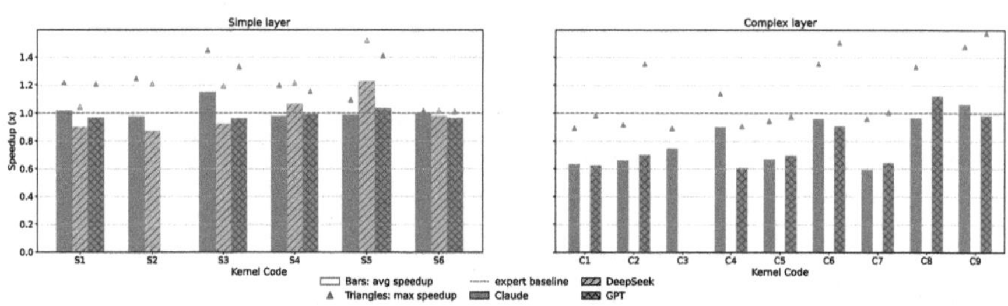

Fig. 4. Per-experiment speedup relative to the expert baseline (> 1 is faster). *Left:* simple layer; *right:* complex layer. Bar height is average speedup; triangles mark max speedup per kernel. Colors and hatches distinguish models (shared legend). The dashed red line is the 1.0× expert baseline.

5.5 Ablation Study

We ablate on S1 (`wmma_gemm_a_col_major_b_col_major`, 100 trials). Table 5 compares GenAgent alone, PlanAgent +GenAgent, and the full pipeline. The Gen-only row shows high compile pass@1 but very low run pass@1, consistent with the compile–run gap discussed in Sect. 3: many WMMA faults—wrong fragment layouts, missing barriers, or check failures—do not appear in `nvcc` output. Adding PlanAgent raises run pass@1 to 40% because the structured plan commits to tile shape, WMMA steps, and layout or synchronization requirements before synthesis, so GenAgent follows a coherent algorithm instead of one-shot guessing from the template. Including ExecAgent brings run pass@1 to 67%: execution on the target GPU is the only reliable signal for several failure modes, and structured diagnostics let the workflow iterate on those runtime-only errors rather than stopping at a successful build.

Table 5. Ablation study on `wmma_gemm_a_col_major_b_col_major` (S1, 100 trials). Rows add agents from Gen-only to the full pipeline. Best run pass@1 in **bold**.

Configuration	Agents	Compile (%)	Run (%)
Gen only	GenAgent	90	2
Plan + Gen	PlanAgent + GenAgent	98	40
Full pipeline	PlanAgent + GenAgent + ExecAgent	100	**67**

5.6 Efficiency and Practical Cost

Table 6 reports practical-cost statistics: the mean number of LLM calls per trial, the mean number of GenAgent (compile-repair) calls per trial, the fraction of trials that trigger plan-level escalation, and the mean end-to-end wall-clock time. Direct prompting issues exactly one LLM call per trial by construction. Iteration count scales with task difficulty and inversely with model competence, while absolute wall-clock is set by the backend. For GPT-5.3-codex-high, which usually succeeds on the first attempt, TensorAgent averages only 2.5 calls per trial and escalates the plan in 2–3% of trials, so its overhead over direct prompting is small. For Claude Sonnet-4.6 and DeepSeek-v3.2, which need substantial repair, the framework averages 9.9–13.5 calls per trial and escalates in 66.7–98.9% of trials. On the complex layer the agent loop runs to nearly the same budget for both models (13.3 vs 13.5 calls; the plan-revision cap saturates on ~90% of trials in both), yet mean wall-clock differs by 2.8× (402 s for Claude Sonnet-4.6 vs 1,143 s for DeepSeek-v3.2); the gap reflects per-call latency on the underlying API (~ 30 s vs ~85 s) rather than additional repair work.

Table 6. Practical cost of TensorAgent, averaged over all logged trials per layer. **Calls**: mean LLM calls per trial (Direct = 1). **Repair**: mean GenAgent compile-repair calls per trial. **Escal.**: fraction of trials triggering plan-level escalation. **Wall**: mean end-to-end wall-clock time per trial (includes compilation, execution, and API latency).

Model	Layer	Calls	Repair	Escal. (%)	Wall (s)
Claude	Simple	9.9	7.2	79.0	173
	Complex	13.3	9.5	94.9	402
Deepseek	Simple	10.4	5.5	66.7	386
	Complex	13.5	8.3	98.9	1143
GPT	Simple	2.5	1.5	3.0	178
	Complex	2.5	1.4	2.0	279

5.7 Future Work

TensorAgent opens several promising directions for extending hierarchical-feedback agents to broader Tensor Core programming. First, we plan to move beyond the warp-level WMMA setting toward end-to-end kernel development: lifting the fixed host code, opening up free data-layout and tiling choices, and integrating host–device boundaries so that the same layered diagnosis can guide production-scale kernel workflows. Second, we will extend the framework from the compile–run gap to performance tuning by coupling latency and occupancy signals into the agent loop, so that hierarchical feedback drives not only correctness but also wall-clock speedup, naturally connecting TensorAgent with autotuners. Third, we see strong potential in combining TensorAgent with complementary repair mechanisms such as constraint-aware decoding, symbolic verification, and reinforcement-based repair, which can further sharpen each layer of the feedback hierarchy. Finally, our cross-model study suggests a model-adaptive variant: calibrating the granularity and aggressiveness of feedback to the underlying LLM's capability, so that capable-but-not-saturated models, saturated models, and models lacking WMMA fundamentals can each be served by an appropriately tuned agent loop.

6 Conclusion

We presented TensorAgent, a multi-agent framework for WMMA Tensor Core code generation that aligns planning, synthesis, and execution diagnosis with the layered failure structure of WMMA programming and links them through hierarchical feedback that repairs failures at the layer where they originate. Across 15 benchmarks, six data-type settings, two complexity tiers, three LLMs, and 9,000 trials, TensorAgent improves compile and run pass@1 over direct prompting and outperforms the agentic CudaForge [11] baseline on run pass@1 for capable-but-not-saturated models, while remaining inexpensive when the model already succeeds (Sect. 5.6). As discussed in Sect. 5.7, coupling performance signals into the agent loop and extending beyond WMMA-centric templates are the main directions ahead, broadening hierarchical feedback from correctness to end-to-end Tensor Core performance.

Acknowledgment. We thank the anonymous reviewers for their constructive and insightful feedback. This work was supported in part by the National Natural Science Foundation of China (NSFC) under grant 62472462 and fund GBA NCTI-ISDC[2026]048.

AI Use Statement. The technical solution and experimental design presented in this paper were independently completed by the authors. AI tools were used solely for language polishing and formatting optimization, and did not participate in the development of the research ideas or core content.

References

1. NVIDIA Corporation: CUDA C++ programming guide: Warp matrix functions (2024). https://docs.nvidia.com/cuda/cuda-c-programming-guide/index.html
2. Chen, M., Tworek, J., Jun, H., et al.: Evaluating large language models trained on code (2021). https://arxiv.org/abs/2107.03374
3. Li, R., et al.: StarCoder: may the source be with you! (2023). https://arxiv.org/abs/2305.06161
4. Rozière, B., et al.: Code Llama: open foundation models for code (2024). https://arxiv.org/abs/2308.12950
5. Ouyang, A., et al.: KernelBench: can LLMs write efficient GPU kernels? (2025). https://arxiv.org/abs/2502.10517
6. Zhu, J., et al.: CUDABench: benchmarking LLMs for Text-to-CUDA generation (2026). https://arxiv.org/abs/2603.02236
7. Huang, D., Zhang, J.M., Luck, M., Bu, Q., Qing, Y., Cui, H.: AgentCoder: multi-agent-based code generation with iterative testing and optimisation (2024). https://arxiv.org/abs/2312.13010
8. Islam, M.A., Ali, M.E., Parvez, M.R.: MapCoder: multi-agent code generation for competitive problem solving. In: Proceedings of the 62nd Annual Meeting of the Association for Computational Linguistics (Volume 1: Long Papers). Association for Computational Linguistics, August 2024. https://aclanthology.org/2024.acl-long.269/
9. Zhang, K., Li, J., Li, G., Shi, X., Jin, Z.: CodeAgent: enhancing code generation with tool-integrated agent systems for real-world repo-level coding challenges. In: Proceedings of the 62nd Annual Meeting of the Association for Computational Linguistics (Volume 1: Long Papers). Association for Computational Linguistics, August 2024. https://aclanthology.org/2024.acl-long.737/
10. Islam, M.A., Ali, M.E., Parvez, M.R.: CodeSim: multi-agent code generation and problem solving through simulation-driven planning and debugging. In: Findings of the Association for Computational Linguistics: NAACL 2025. Association for Computational Linguistics, April 2025. https://aclanthology.org/2025.findings-naacl.285/

11. Zhang, Z., Wang, R., Li, S., Luo, Y., Hong, M., Ding, C.: CudaForge: an agent framework with hardware feedback for CUDA kernel optimization (2025). https://arxiv.org/abs/2511.01884
12. Wei, J., et al.: Chain-of-thought prompting elicits reasoning in large language models (2023). https://arxiv.org/abs/2201.11903
13. Chen, X., Lin, M., Schärli, N., Zhou, D.: Teaching large language models to self-debug (2023). https://arxiv.org/abs/2304.05128
14. Ridnik, T., Kredo, D., Friedman, I.: Code generation with AlphaCodium: from prompt engineering to flow engineering (2024). https://arxiv.org/abs/2401.08500
15. Dai, W., et al.: CUDA agent: large-scale agentic RL for high-performance CUDA kernel generation (2026). https://arxiv.org/abs/2602.24286
16. Guo, T., et al.: Large language model based multi-agents: a survey of progress and challenges (2024). https://arxiv.org/abs/2402.01680
17. Tran, K.T., Dao, D., Nguyen, M.D., Pham, Q.V., O'Sullivan, B., Nguyen, H.D.: Multi-agent collaboration mechanisms: a survey of LLMs (2025). https://arxiv.org/abs/2501.06322
18. Adapala, S.T.R.: Cognitive load limits in large language models: benchmarking multi-hop reasoning (2025). https://arxiv.org/abs/2509.19517
19. NVIDIA Corporation: CUDA samples (2024). https://github.com/NVIDIA/cuda-samples
20. Austin, J., et al.: Program synthesis with large language models (2021). https://arxiv.org/abs/2108.07732
21. Li, Y., Choi, D., Chung, J., Kushman, N., Schrittwieser, J., et al.: Competition-level code generation with AlphaCode. Science **378**(6624), 1092–1097 (2022). https://doi.org/10.1126/science.abq1158

CUTE-XS: Bottleneck Analysis and Collaborative Optimization for Integrating CUTE Into XiangShan

Junyu Yue[1,2], Chongxi Wang[1,2(✉)], Jinpeng Ye[1,2], Jianan Xie[1,2], Ziyang Liu[1,2], Wenqing Li[1,2], Chao Yang[3], Longbing Zhang[1,2], Fuxin Zhang[1,2], and Jian Wang[1,2]

[1] State Key Lab of Processors, Institute of Computing Technology, Chinese Academy of Sciences, Beijing, China
{yuejunyu25s,wangchongxi,yejinpeng21s,xiejianan25s,liwenqing, lbzhang,fxzhang,jw}@ict.ac.cn

[2] University of Chinese Academy of Sciences, Beijing, China
liuziyang20a@mails.ucas.ac.cn

[3] State Grid Liaoning Electric Power Supply Co., Ltd., Shenyang, China

Abstract. CPUs remain an important deployment platform for AI inference, especially in general-purpose, edge, and locally deployed systems. In a CPU SoC that integrates a tensor coprocessor, even when dense tensor kernels are offloaded to specialized hardware, end-to-end execution still depends on the host CPU for control, synchronization, cache-coherent data access, and CPU-side epilogue processing. The key problem is therefore not only accelerator throughput, but also which system-level bottlenecks emerge after integration.

This paper presents a low-intrusion integration of CUTE, an open-source tensor coprocessor for dense tensor computation, into XiangShan Kunminghu. The design reuses the existing CSR control path, coherent cache hierarchy, and CPU-side DCache write path, without introducing a separate accelerator memory subsystem. Using cycle-level RTL simulation, hardware counters, and trace analysis, we show that end-to-end performance is limited primarily by CPU-side write-path pressure, CoupledL2 slice imbalance, and insufficient overlap between tensor-engine execution and CPU-side epilogue processing.

To mitigate these bottlenecks, we reuse the existing store buffer (SBuffer) for buffered writes, apply reversible L2 slice hashing, and introduce software double buffering (SoftPipe). Across kernels extracted from ResNet50, BERT, and LLaMA inference paths, the optimized integration achieves geometric-mean speedups of 82.2×, 117.4×, and 96.1× over an OpenBLAS RVV baseline. Relative to the CUTE baseline, the same optimizations raise the corresponding speedups from 48.8× to 82.2×, from 43.3× to 117.4×, and from 44.6× to 96.1× on ResNet50, BERT, and the baseline-comparable LLaMA subset, respectively. These gains indicate that write-path decoupling, slice-level load balance, and overlap between tensor-engine execution and CPU-side epilogue processing are central design concerns for a CPU-integrated tensor coprocessor.

L. Eeckhout et al. (Eds.): APPT 2026, LNCS 16693, pp. 253–266, 2027.
https://doi.org/10.1007/978-981-92-4805-6_17

Keywords: XiangShan · RISC-V SoC · tensor coprocessor · tightly coupled accelerator · bottleneck analysis

1 Introduction

CPUs remain an important deployment platform for AI inference, especially in general-purpose, edge, and locally deployed systems. Although specialized tensor hardware can accelerate dense kernels substantially, end-to-end execution in a CPU SoC still depends on the surrounding control, synchronization, cache-coherent data access, and CPU-side epilogue processing paths. As a result, the practical value of a CPU-integrated tensor coprocessor is determined not only by the coprocessor's peak throughput, but also by how well it is integrated into the host system.

Open-source hardware makes this question timely. XiangShan provides a realistic open out-of-order RISC-V platform with a coherent cache hierarchy, and CUTE provides an open asynchronous tensor coprocessor [9,12,17,19]. Together they let us study not another tensor engine, but what happens when an existing tensor coprocessor is integrated into a coherent CPU SoC.

Prior work has studied CPU-side matrix and tensor support such as Intel AMX, Arm SME, and IBM MMA, as well as integrated tensor acceleration through systems such as Gemmini and CUTE [3,6,7,9,18]. Prior work has also shown that shared-cache behavior and slice-aware placement can materially affect performance in distributed LLCs [5,8,13,14]. In contrast, we ask which post-integration bottlenecks dominate end-to-end performance in a coherent CPU SoC, and which low-intrusion remedies matter most.

To answer that question, we integrate CUTE into XiangShan Kunminghu by reusing the CSR control path, coherent cache hierarchy, and CPU-side DCache write path, without introducing a separate accelerator memory subsystem [4,11]. CUTE is added mainly as a new module subtree, while modifications to existing XiangShan and CoupledL2 Chisel code are limited to 297 lines in total. This low-intrusion methodology keeps the study focused on practical post-integration constraints rather than artifacts of a custom accelerator subsystem.

Using cycle-level RTL simulation, hardware counters, and trace analysis on this integrated platform, we identify three first-order bottlenecks. First, CUTE output stores contend with the CPU-side write path and create substantial write-path pressure. Second, bursty miss traffic can concentrate on individual CoupledL2 slices and reduce effective parallelism. Third, end-to-end throughput is reduced when tensor-engine execution and CPU-side epilogue processing are insufficiently overlapped. These limits arise after integration and are not captured by evaluating the tensor engine in isolation.

We therefore apply three targeted optimizations: SBuffer reuse, reversible L2 slice hashing, and software double buffering (SoftPipe). Across convolution and Transformer kernels extracted from real inference paths, the optimized design reaches 82.2×, 117.4×, and 96.1× speedup over the RVV baseline on ResNet50, BERT, and baseline-comparable LLaMA kernels, respectively, while improving the corresponding CUTE-baseline speedups from 48.8×, 43.3×, and 44.6×. These gains show that post-integration SoC bottlenecks, not tensor-engine throughput alone, define end-to-end efficiency, and that write-path decoupling, slice-level load balance, and overlap between tensor-engine execution and CPU-side epilogue processing are central design concerns for a CPU-integrated tensor coprocessor.

Our main contributions are as follows.

1. We present a low-intrusion integration of CUTE into XiangShan Kunminghu that reuses the existing CSR control path, coherent cache hierarchy, and CPU-side DCache write path without adding a separate accelerator memory subsystem; only 297 lines of existing XiangShan/CoupledL2 Chisel code are modified.
2. We analyze the post-integration bottlenecks using cycle-level RTL simulation, hardware counters, and trace analysis, and identify CPU-side write-path pressure, CoupledL2 slice imbalance, and limited overlap between tensor-engine execution and CPU-side epilogue processing as the dominant end-to-end constraints.
3. We propose three targeted optimizations—SBuffer reuse, reversible L2 slice hashing, and SoftPipe—and show that they substantially improve performance beyond the CUTE baseline on kernels extracted from ResNet50, BERT, and LLaMA inference paths.

2 Background

2.1 XiangShan SoC Overview

XiangShan is an open high-performance RISC-V processor project [12,17,19]. We target the Kunminghu generation, whose platform follows an `XSCore + CoupledL2` organization [11,12]: out-of-order CPU cores with private L1 caches, a shared CoupledL2, and a TileLink-based coherent interconnect. This matters because CUTE is integrated as a tightly coupled coprocessor that reuses the same coherent cache path and write-buffering structures, rather than a standalone accelerator with a private memory path [4,16].

2.2 CoupledL2 Organization

CoupledL2 in Kunminghu is a shared non-blocking cache organized as four slices. Requests are routed by low-order address bits above the 64 B block offset, and each slice has its own miss-handling path with a finite *MSHRCtl* budget for outstanding cache-line operations [13,14]. In the default implementation, each slice contains 16 MSHR entries, of which 15 are normally available for new upstream accesses.

This structure is central to our study because CUTE shares the same CoupledL2 slices as CPU traffic. As a result, accelerator performance depends not only on cache bandwidth, but also on slice-level load balance and available

Table 1. Chisel code changes introduced by the XiangShan–CUTE integration.

Category	Baseline LOC	Delta LOC
Existing XiangShan code	116,728	+229
Existing CoupledL2 code	18,740	+68
New CUTE subtree	0	+20,836
Existing-code total	135,468	+297

miss concurrency. Under regular tensor streams, low-order slice selection can over-concentrate requests on a subset of slices rather than distributing them evenly, so both the mapping policy and the per-slice MSHR capacity determine how much bursty accelerator traffic CoupledL2 can absorb before backpressure reaches CUTE.

2.3 CUTE Tensor Coprocessor

CUTE is an open-source tensor coprocessor for dense tensor computation [9]. It exposes a tensor-execution block, a memory interface, and a command interface for software launch and synchronization [9]. We treat it as an existing accelerator block and focus on the post-integration system path rather than on the internal tensor-engine design.

3 Integrating CUTE Into XiangShan: Bottlenecks and Optimizations

3.1 Design Goals

Our integration follows three goals: low intrusion to the baseline CPU microarchitecture, maximum reuse of existing SoC structures, and a software interface that remains natural to XiangShan programs. Here, low intrusion means avoiding a separate accelerator memory subsystem, preserving XiangShan's baseline coherence protocol, and avoiding a trap-heavy launch path. This fits both XiangShan's SoC organization and CUTE's own split between the compute-centric `CUTETile` and the `Cute2TL` memory path. As summarized in Table 1, CUTE is added primarily as a new module subtree, while modifications to existing XiangShan and CoupledL2 Chisel code are limited to 297 lines in total. This keeps the study focused on practical post-integration constraints rather than artifacts of a custom accelerator subsystem.

3.2 CSR-Based Control Interface

We adopt a CSR-based control interface for CUTE. The CPU configures the accelerator through `tcmd`, `trs1`, `trs2`, and `tresp`: software writes command and operand information into these CSRs, triggers execution, and later observes completion through the response state. Compared with a heavier MMIO- or trap-oriented path, this better matches CUTE's asynchronous submit-and-run model, reuses XiangShan's existing CSR framework, and avoids trap-heavy launch overhead for fine-grained tensor kernels.

3.3 Data Path Integration

The CUTE data path is integrated by reusing XiangShan's coherent cache hierarchy rather than introducing a separate accelerator memory subsystem. Inputs are fetched through CoupledL2 and TileLink, while CUTE outputs are issued into the CPU-side DCache write path; in short, the design is "L2-read, L1-write".

Software observes completion once the final store microtask has injected all output writes into the coherent CPU-side cache path, rather than when those writes reach lower cache levels or main memory. It synchronizes by polling the completion state (`InstFIFO_Finish`) before consuming the output buffer. After this point, outputs are accessed through the normal coherent load path; a conservative `fence` may still be inserted if stronger ordering with surrounding CPU memory operations is required.

At the SoC-construction level, the CSR-side control path connects directly to `CUTETile`, while the TileLink-side memory path goes through `Cute2TL` inside XiangShan's Diplomacy-based framework [1,2,4,19]. We intentionally avoid a separate non-coherent scratchpad or result buffer, so output writes reuse the existing SBuffer/L1D/cache-coherence machinery; replay, same-block conflicts, and ownership transitions are therefore handled by the baseline protocol rather than by an accelerator-private coherence mechanism. This choice favors producer-consumer locality: CPU-side epilogue stages often consume CUTE outputs immediately, so keeping them in the nearest coherent CPU-visible domain avoids an extra refill.

Figure 1 summarizes the resulting XiangShan–CUTE integration path.

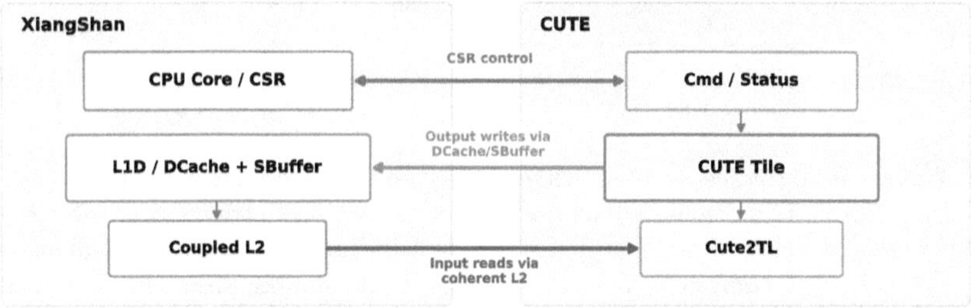

Fig. 1. Compact overview of XiangShan–CUTE integration. CUTE is integrated through three reused SoC paths: a CSR-based control path for command submission and status polling, a coherent CoupledL2 read path for input fetches via Cute2TL, and a DCache/SBuffer-based coherent write path for output stores. No separate accelerator-side memory subsystem is introduced.

3.4 Baseline System Performance and Bottleneck Analysis

The CUTE baseline is functionally correct, but its achieved utilization remains below expectation and the runtime still shows substantial memory-related stall behavior. This indicates that the dominant limits lie not in the tensor engine itself, but in the surrounding SoC path, especially the coherent write path, CoupledL2 behavior, and the interaction between tensor-engine execution and CPU-side epilogue processing.

Profiling Methodology. We therefore analyze the integrated system using cycle-level RTL simulation, hardware performance counters, and trace analysis on representative GEMM and convolution kernels. Following the general spirit of top-down bottleneck localization [20], we relate end-to-end runtime to replay, queue occupancy, outstanding misses, and slice-level utilization to identify the dominant post-integration bottlenecks.

Write-Path Bottleneck. The first major bottleneck appears on the CPU-side DCache write path. In the baseline design, CUTE-generated output writes are directly injected into the same admission path used by CPU stores, without an accelerator-specific buffering stage in front. Under tensor workloads, bursty output traffic can saturate this shared path, creating write-buffer pressure, replay behavior, and backpressure toward the accelerator.

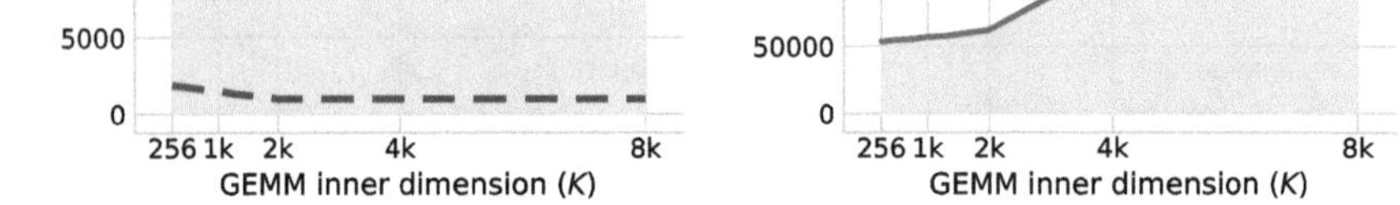

Fig. 2. Baseline-only trace-derived evidence for the CPU-side DCache write-path bottleneck in GEMM. Left: cycles spent draining outstanding output stores after the last tensor-engine execution phase completes; the dashed line marks an empirical sustained write-service bound computed from the writes that remain after the last compute phase, assuming one 64 B cache-line write every four cycles plus a fixed 2-cycle drain tail. Right: cycles stalled while admitting writes into the CPU-side DCache write path. Under the same 1024 output writes per run, the baseline shows a substantial post-compute store-drain tail together with large write-admission stalls.

To confirm that this is a root-cause bottleneck, Fig. 2 reports two baseline-only metrics that would remain small if write handling were not on the critical path: the post-compute store-drain tail after the last tensor-engine execution phase, and the cycles stalled while admitting writes into the CPU-side DCache write path. Across 32 GEMM traces with $K = 256 \ldots 8192$ and the same 1024 output writes per run, the baseline spends 13.3k–24.8k cycles in post-compute drain tail, with 14.7k cycles on average, and 53.5k–281.1k cycles stalled while admitting writes, with 126.8k cycles on average. The dashed line in the left panel is an empirical sustained write-service bound, $T_{\text{ref}}(K) = 4 \cdot N_{\text{remain}}(K) + 2$, rather than a peak-port bandwidth bound: the 4-cycle service term comes from the sustained drain rate observed in trace, and the final 2 cycles capture the fixed drain/bookkeeping tail. Even against this bound, the observed tail remains very large: the reference is only 1.0k–1.9k cycles, whereas the measured tail is 13.3k–24.8k cycles, or about 13× higher across the sweep. The effect is especially severe at small K, where the fixed drain tail consumes a large fraction of runtime, while substantial admission stalls persist throughout the sweep. We therefore attribute a substantial part of the baseline penalty to CPU-side write-path backpressure rather than to arithmetic throughput alone.

CoupledL2 Slice Imbalance and Limited Miss Concurrency. The second bottleneck is slice-local concentration in CoupledL2. In the baseline design, the target slice is selected by the two low-order address bits immediately above the 64 B cache-line offset. With four slices, any regular tensor stream whose stride is an integer multiple of 256 B can keep those slice-select bits unchanged across adjacent accesses, so GEMM-style row or tile walks can repeatedly route bursts to one slice rather than distributing them across all four. This lowers effective parallelism and can temporarily exhaust that slice's MSHR window before refill responses return. The resulting slice-local backpressure stalls new misses even when other slices remain underutilized.

Trace-level inspection suggests that concentrated cold-miss bursts can transiently exhaust one slice's MSHR budget before the earliest refill returns from lower levels. However, as we show later, this effect is largely mitigated once slice hashing disperses regular streams across slices. We therefore treat MSHR tuning as a supporting parameter study rather than a primary optimization target.

Tensor-Execution/Epilogue-Processing Serialization. Finally, insufficient overlap between tensor-engine execution and CPU-side epilogue processing can become another end-to-end bottleneck after integration. We quantify this effect most clearly in the baseline convolution pipeline, where tensor execution and CPU-side epilogue work are largely serialized: the CPU waits for accelerator output before beginning epilogue processing, and the accelerator in turn does not fully overlap with subsequent work. This lack of pipelining leaves additional performance opportunity beyond the purely hardware-side bottlenecks.

3.5 Collaborative Optimizations

Reusing SBuffer for Buffered Writes. The evidence in Fig. 2 points to a specific baseline failure mode: CUTE outputs are produced quickly, but they must still be admitted through a CPU-oriented direct-injection path. We therefore avoid adding a new accelerator-private write queue. Instead, as illustrated in Fig. 3, we reuse the existing SBuffer to buffer and merge CUTE-generated writes before they re-enter the existing DCache MainPipe/WB path. This keeps the integration lightweight and changes the write path from direct injection to buffered admission.

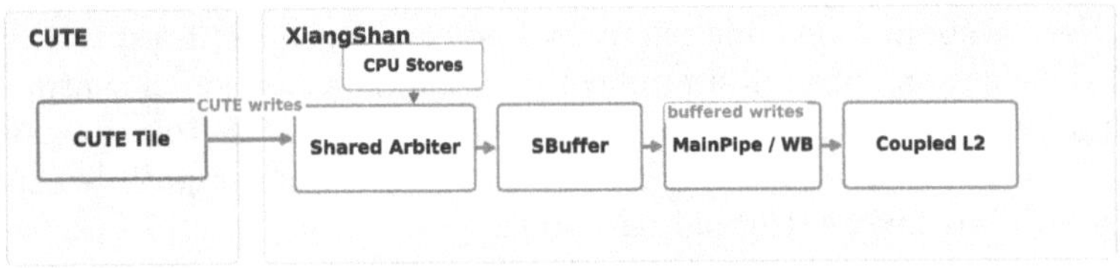

Fig. 3. Zoom-in of the reused CPU-side buffered write path for CUTE outputs. CUTE output writes are admitted through the shared arbiter, absorbed by the existing SBuffer, and then forwarded into the normal DCache MainPipe/WB writeback path, which continues along the coherent path to CoupledL2.

This directly targets the symptoms in Fig. 2: once CUTE writes are absorbed by the SBuffer, the accelerator is much less likely to stall behind immediate write admission and downstream write draining. As shown later in the ablation study, it is the most important write-side optimization.

L2 Slice Hashing. As discussed above, the baseline slice routing can concentrate regular tensor streams on one CoupledL2 slice and create transient hot-slice backpressure when miss bursts arrive together.

Following the general pseudo-random interleaving idea of Rau [15], we introduce a lightweight reversible XOR-based slice hash, illustrated in Fig. 4. The 64 B block offset $A[5:0]$ is kept unchanged, while the two-bit slice index is recomputed from an XOR fold over $A[19:6]$:

$$\text{slice}' = A[7:6] \oplus A[9:8] \oplus A[11:10] \oplus A[13:12] \oplus A[15:14] \oplus A[17:16] \oplus A[19:18].$$

This transformation is interposed around `l1_xbar` through lightweight TileLink adapter nodes rather than by changing the internal crossbar decode logic. We hash A/C-channel addresses before they enter `l1_xbar`, and we restore the canonical full address when leaving the slice-local view: on the L2 → L3 path for A/C and on the L2 → core path for B/D. Because the same XOR transform is applied again during restoration, the mapping is reversible and the coherence-visible block-address view remains unchanged outside the slice-local routing path.

Fig. 4. Effect of L2 slice hashing on a regular 256 B-stride request stream. Left: under the baseline routing, the slice index is determined by $A[7:6]$, so adjacent accesses keep the same slice-select bits and repeatedly target one CoupledL2 slice. Right: after XOR-folded hashing over $A[19:6]$, the same requests are redistributed across the four slices. The original full address is restored outside the slice-local routing view, so only the slice-selection decision changes.

In other words, only the slice-selection decision is changed. Streams that would otherwise keep stressing one slice are redistributed across the four slices, while the original software-visible address semantics are preserved. This keeps the intervention lightweight and avoids changing the software memory model. As shown later in evaluation, the gain is most visible at larger K, where long sequential streams would otherwise keep stressing a limited subset of slices.

SoftPipe. To eliminate unnecessary serialization between tensor-engine execution and CPU-side epilogue processing, we introduce SoftPipe. A ping-pong buffer pair lets CUTE write into one buffer while the CPU consumes the other for epilogue processing, reducing idle cycles without changing the hardware interface. As shown later in Fig. 5(b), this schedule-level overlap contributes substantially to end-to-end performance.

Variable Hardware Parameters

L2 MSHR Count. Guided by the trace-level observation above, we also evaluate a modest increase in the per-slice L2 MSHR count from 16 to 20 as a sensitivity study. It improves burst tolerance in the non-hashed baseline, but contributes little once slice hashing is enabled. This does not contradict the earlier trace-level observation; it indicates that hot-slice concentration, rather than raw MSHR count, is the dominant issue in the optimized design. We therefore interpret extra MSHRs as burst-tolerance margin rather than a primary source of end-to-end speedup.

4 Evaluation

4.1 Experimental Setup

Experiments are conducted on XiangShan Kunminghu with the integrated CUTE tensor coprocessor using Verilator-based cycle-level RTL simulation. All results are reported in simulated cycles. Table 2 summarizes the SoC and CUTE settings that matter most to the earlier write-path, slice-routing, and MSHR analyses. Unless otherwise stated, these settings are shared by all reported experiments.

Table 2. Key SoC and CUTE configuration of the XiangShan–CUTE platform.

Item	Setting
SoC platform	XiangShan Kunminghu (`DefaultConfig`), single-core, integrated CUTE
CoupledL2	4 slices, 64 B cache lines
Per-slice L2 MSHR	16 (baseline)
CUTE datapath	LLC/vector 256-bit; memory 64-bit
CUTE tiles/spads	`TM/TN/TK = 64/64/2`, `MM/MN = 4/4`; A/B/C = 4/4/16 KiB, 4 banks each

We evaluate kernels extracted from real inference traces in the OpenCUTE `cutetest` suite [10], rather than synthetic microbenchmarks. The workload set covers ResNet50 convolutions, BERT matrix multiplications, and LLaMA matrix multiplications. All workloads use batch-1 inference settings. For the Transformer workloads, both BERT and LLaMA use sequence length 128. The LLaMA scores and attention cases are evaluated on head0 only. We use four names throughout this section: the OpenBLAS RVV baseline, the CUTE baseline, *CUTE + HWOpt*, and *SoftPipe*, where SoftPipe denotes software double buffering and may be combined with either hardware configuration. The ablation study uses GEMM with fixed $M = N = 128$ and varying K from 256 to 8192.

4.2 Main Results Across Workloads

Figure 5 highlights the main result of the paper. Both *SoftPipe* and *CUTE + HWOpt* materially improve the CUTE baseline, and their benefits are complementary rather than redundant. *SoftPipe* contributes more strongly on convolution, while hardware-side optimization still adds visible gains on top of it, with *CUTE + HWOpt + SoftPipe* delivering the best overall ResNet50 performance. This matches the bottleneck analysis: convolution throughput is limited by both

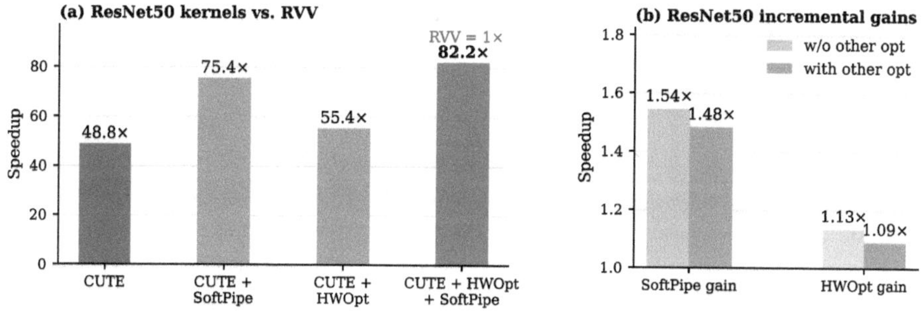

Fig. 5. ResNet50 convolution results on the evaluated kernel set. (a) Absolute geometric-mean speedup over the *RVV baseline*. (b) Two groups of incremental gains, *SoftPipe gain* and *HWOpt gain*, each measured under two contexts: with and without the other optimization already enabled.

write-path pressure and insufficient overlap between tensor-engine execution and CPU-side epilogue processing.

Figure 6 shows that the same post-integration bottlenecks and remedies generalize beyond convolution to both BERT and LLaMA workloads. On the BERT kernels, optimization substantially raises both speedup and CUTE utilization. On the LLaMA kernels, both the baseline-comparable kernels in Fig. 6(b) and the larger FFN-heavy cases in Fig. 6(c) improve. The gains are strongest on the attention kernels, while the FFN-heavy cases still improve consistently. These results indicate that the same system bottlenecks matter not only for baseline-comparable kernels but also for the larger Transformer kernels that are most relevant to deployment.

4.3 Ablation Study

Unless otherwise stated, *Full* denotes the integrated XiangShan–CUTE platform in Table 2 with SBuffer reuse, slice hashing, and 20 MSHRs per CoupledL2 slice; each ablated variant disables only the named change. We compare this fully optimized design against ablated variants for SBuffer reuse, L2 slice hashing, and per-slice MSHR tuning.

Figure 7(a) and (b) show a clear ordering among the four configurations: *w/o SBuffer* causes the largest regression, *w/o Slice Hash* causes a smaller but still consistent slowdown, and *w/ Fewer L2 MSHRs* remains very close to *Full*. The behavior of *w/o SBuffer* also explains why its utilization rises with K: when K is small, fixed launch, drain, and write-admission stalls occupy a large fraction of the execution window, whereas larger K values amortize these short blocking intervals with a longer steady-state compute phase.

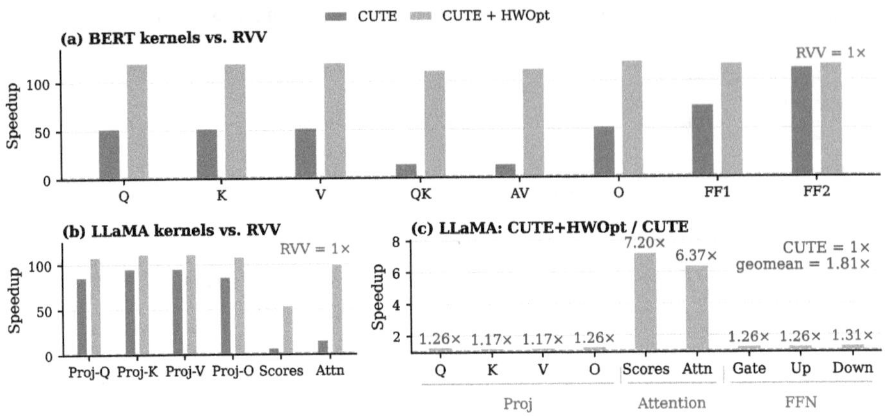

Fig. 6. Transformer generalization results. (a) BERT kernels versus the *RVV baseline*. (b) LLaMA baseline-comparable kernels versus the *RVV baseline*. (c) Optimization gain of *CUTE + HWOpt* over the *CUTE baseline* across all measured LLaMA kernels, grouped into projection, attention, and FFN workloads, including FFN cases whose vector-only baselines are infeasible because of simulation cost.

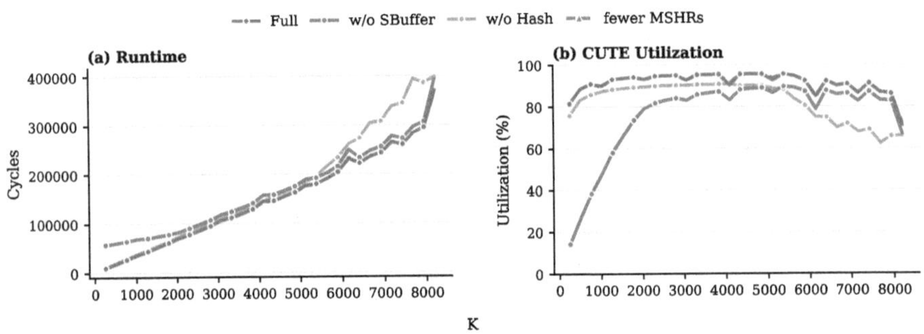

Fig. 7. GEMM ablation results for fixed $M = N = 128$ and varying K: (a) runtime and (b) CUTE utilization. Removing SBuffer causes the largest regression, removing slice hashing causes a smaller but consistent slowdown, and reducing the number of L2 MSHRs has negligible impact.

The ablation summary confirms the same ordering. Relative to *w/o SBuffer*, *Full* achieves 1.26× geometric-mean speedup; the gain over *w/o Slice Hash* is 1.11×; and the gap to *w/ Fewer L2 MSHRs* is essentially 1.00×. Utilization follows the same ordering, with gains of 15.0% points, 8.6% points, and less than 0.1% points, respectively. This confirms that hot-slice concentration, not raw MSHR count, is the dominant L2-side issue once hashing is enabled.

5 Conclusion

This paper presents a practical path for integrating an open-source tensor coprocessor into XiangShan as an asynchronous tightly coupled CPU-integrated tensor coprocessor. Once functional integration is complete, the dominant limits to performance come mainly from SoC-level bottlenecks rather than from the tensor engine itself.

Three design insights stand out. First, write-path decoupling has the largest performance impact, making SBuffer reuse the most important write-side optimization. Second, load balance across CoupledL2 slices matters more than modest increases in raw miss-level parallelism: slice hashing yields larger gains than limited MSHR expansion, while extra MSHRs mainly improve burst tolerance. Third, overlapping tensor-engine execution with CPU-side epilogue processing is essential for end-to-end throughput, especially for convolution-oriented kernels. By combining SBuffer reuse, L2 slice hashing, SoftPipe, and modest supporting parameter retuning, we substantially improve the efficiency of the integrated accelerator while preserving a low-intrusion integration style. The integration remains small-touch: CUTE is added mainly as a new module subtree, while only 297 lines of existing XiangShan/CoupledL2 Chisel code are modified.

Overall, tightly coupled accelerator integration requires more than attaching the accelerator: it also requires co-optimizing the instruction/control path, the data path, and the software pipeline after integration. The same principles should generalize beyond XiangShan and CUTE to other CPU-centric tightly coupled accelerators.

Acknowledgments. This work was supported by the National Key Research and Development Program of China (Grant No. 2022YFB3105100).

Disclosure of Interests. The authors have no competing interests to declare that are relevant to the content of this article.

AI Use Statement. The technical solution and experimental design presented in this paper were independently completed by the authors. AI tools were used solely for language polishing and formatting optimization, and did not participate in the development of the research ideas or core content.

References

1. Asanovic, K., Avizienis, R., Bachrach, J.: The Rocket Chip generator. Technical report, UCB/EECS-2016-17, EECS Department, University of California, Berkeley (2016)
2. Bachrach, J., Vo, H., Richards, B.: Chisel: constructing hardware in a Scala embedded language. In: Proceedings of the 49th Annual Design Automation Conference, pp. 1216–1225 (2012)
3. de Carvalho, J.P., Moreira, J.E., Amaral, J.N.: Compiling for the IBM matrix engine for enterprise workloads. IEEE Micro **42**(5), 34–40 (2022)
4. Cook, H., Terpstra, W., Lee, Y.: Diplomatic design patterns: a TileLink case study. In: Workshop on Computer Architecture Research with RISC-V (2017)
5. Farshin, A., Roozbeh, A., Maguire Jr., G.Q., Kostić, D.: Make the most out of last-level cache in Intel processors. In: Proceedings of the Fourteenth EuroSys Conference 2019, pp. 1–17 (2019)

6. Genc, H., Kim, S., Amid, A.: Gemmini: enabling systematic deep-learning architecture evaluation via full-stack integration. In: Proceedings of the 58th Annual Design Automation Conference (2021)
7. Kim, H., Ye, G., Wang, N., Yazdanbakhsh, A., Kim, N.S.: Exploiting Intel advanced matrix extensions (AMX) for large language model inference. IEEE Comput. Archit. Lett. **23**(1), 117–120 (2024)
8. Maurice, C., Le Scouarnec, N., Neumann, C., Heen, O., Francillon, A.: Reverse engineering intel last-level cache complex addressing using performance counters. In: Bos, H., Monrose, F., Blanc, G. (eds.) RAID 2015. LNCS, vol. 9404, pp. 48–65. Springer, Cham (2015). https://doi.org/10.1007/978-3-319-26362-5_3
9. OpenCUTE Contributors: CUTE. Repository (2026). https://github.com/OpenCUTE/CUTE
10. OpenCUTE Contributors: cutetest. Repository (2026). https://github.com/OpenCUTE/cutetest
11. OpenXiangShan Project: XiangShan design documentation. Documentation (2024). https://github.com/OpenXiangShan/XiangShan-Design-Doc
12. OpenXiangShan Project: XiangShan repository. Repository (2024). https://github.com/OpenXiangShan/XiangShan
13. Qureshi, M.K., Lynch, D.N., Mutlu, O., Patt, Y.N.: A case for MLP-aware cache replacement. In: Proceedings of the 33rd Annual International Symposium on Computer Architecture, pp. 167–178 (2006)
14. Qureshi, M.K., Patt, Y.N.: Utility-based cache partitioning: a low-overhead, high-performance, runtime mechanism to partition shared caches. In: 39th Annual IEEE/ACM International Symposium on Microarchitecture, pp. 423–432 (2006)
15. Rau, B.R.: Pseudo-randomly interleaved memory. In: Proceedings of the 18th Annual International Symposium on Computer Architecture, pp. 74–83 (1991)
16. RISC-V International: The RISC-V instruction set manual, volume I: Unprivileged ISA, document version 20191213. Specification (2019). https://riscv.org/technical/specifications/
17. Wang, K., Chen, J., Xu, Y.: XiangShan: an open-source project for high-performance RISC-V processors meeting industrial-grade standards. In: 2024 IEEE Hot Chips 36 Symposium, pp. 1–25 (2024)
18. Wilkinson, F., McIntosh-Smith, S.: An initial evaluation of Arm's scalable matrix extension. In: 2022 IEEE/ACM International Workshop on Performance Modeling, Benchmarking and Simulation of High Performance Computer Systems, pp. 135–140 (2022)
19. Xu, Y., Yu, Z., Tang, D.: Towards developing high-performance RISC-V processors using agile methodology. In: 2022 55th IEEE/ACM International Symposium on Microarchitecture, pp. 1178–1199 (2022)
20. Yasin, A.: A top-down method for performance analysis and counters architecture. In: IEEE International Symposium on Performance Analysis of Systems and Software, pp. 35–44 (2014)

Scalable Computing

C^{3}FT: Computation-Centric Checkpointing for Distributed Large Model Training

Yonghua Huang[1], Baodong Wu[2], Shigang Li[1(✉)], Jiahao Ding[1], Rongtian Fu[1], Qingping Li[2], Boxun Li[2], Zhenhua Zhu[3], and Yu Wang[3]

[1] Beijing University of Posts and Telecommunications, Beijing, China
shigangli.cs@gmail.com
[2] Infinigence-AI, Beijing, China
[3] Tsinghua University, Beijing, China

Abstract. With the continuous growth of deep learning model sizes, their training processes face significant challenges in fault tolerance efficiency. Existing solutions, however, struggle to deliver both low communication overhead and effective fault tolerance. This paper presents C^{3}FT, a ***C***omputation-***C***entric ***C***heckpointing scheme for efficient ***F***ault ***T***olerance of distributed large model training. Specifically, C^{3}FT utilizes the CPU resources to update the optimizer states, and then uses the optimizer states on CPU as the checkpoints. Therefore, updating the optimizer states (including the model parameters) automatically updates the checkpoints on CPU, which also avoids the costly communication overhead in existing fault tolerance solutions. Overall, C^{3}FT achieves the high efficiency of fault tolerance and communication simultaneously. Evaluation results show that when training a 70B model on 32 A100 GPUs (4 nodes × 8 cards), C^{3}FT improves the training throughput by 1.69× compared to Gemini (the SOTA solution with in-CPU-memory checkpointing).

Keywords: Fault tolerance · Distributed training · Large models

1 Introduction

The recent development of artificial intelligence is mainly due to the advancements in deep learning, whose models have grown rapidly in scale [5,9,22]. Models with trillions of parameters can require terabytes of memory just to store weights, making distributed training across many machines necessary to provision resources and accelerate training [8,12,23]. However, as the number of GPUs in the system increases, the incidence of hardware failures also increases [14,25]. A single GPU failure can stall or crash an entire system run, wasting substantial compute resources [11]. For example, the OPT-175B training reported

Y. Huang and B. Wu—These authors contributed equally to this work.

L. Eeckhout et al. (Eds.): APPT 2026, LNCS 16693, pp. 269–281, 2027.
https://doi.org/10.1007/978-981-92-4805-6_18

roughly 178,000 GPU hours were wasted due to failures [27]. As the system scale increases, the malfunction could slow down the training speed by up to 43% [14].

To ensure stable training of large-scale models, fault-tolerant technologies have emerged to enhance efficiency and reliability. The checkpoint mechanism [18] is a widely adopted fault tolerance method used to back up model parameters and optimizer state. When a failure occurs, the model training can be restored from the saved checkpoints. However, checkpointing is time-consuming, leading to increased total training time [4,18]. To improve efficiency, many works have optimized checkpointing. Checkfreq [18] accelerates checkpoint saving by using CPU snapshots, and Gemini [24] backs up checkpoints on CPU memory to enable faster recovery. However, these works cannot achieve efficiency in fault tolerance and communication simultaneously. Gemini requires additional bandwidth to back up CPU checkpoints, and Checkfreq has to load the checkpoint from remote storage when resuming the training process.

Table 1. Comparison across different solutions of distributed training in terms of communication efficiency and fault tolerance.

Method	Fault tolerance	Communication efficiency
ZeRO3 [20]	✗	✗
Gemini [24]	✓	✗
C^{3}FT (ours)	✓	✓

Therefore, we propose a ***C***omputation-***C***entric ***C***heckpointing scheme for efficient ***F***ault ***T***olerance (named as C^{3}FT) of distributed large model training. C^{3}FT is efficient in both fault tolerance and communication, as illustrated in Table 1. In terms of the fault tolerance, C^{3}FT uses the CPU resources to update the optimizer states (including the model parameters), and then uses the optimizer states on CPU as the checkpoints, which are used to resume the training when failures happen. Consequently, updating the optimizer states automatically updates the checkpoints on CPU, which significantly reduces the checkpointing overhead. To hide the computational overhead of updating the optimizer states on the CPU, the C^{3}FT employs a pipelined optimizer module to overlap the CPU and GPU computation.

In terms of the communication cost, C^{3}FT only requires an Allreduce operation to accumulate the local gradients across all GPUs to obtain the global gradients. After that, the global gradients are passed to CPU to update the optimizer states (including the model parameters). During the forward and backward computation, C^{3}FT fetches the model parameters from CPU memory. Therefore, the communication cost of C^{3}FT between GPU cards is the same as that in the original data parallelism, and is even lower than that in ZeRO3 [20]. Overall, C^{3}FT can achieve high fault tolerance efficiency and high communication efficiency simultaneously.

C^{3}FT targets static and synchronous training with fixed computing resources, following common industrial practices [1,5,7]. Elastic training and asynchronous training [15,17,26] are beyond the scope of this paper.

2 Background and Related Work

2.1 Parallel Techniques and Optimizations

Parallel techniques are crucial in large-scale training, allowing computation to be distributed across multiple devices when a model cannot fit on a single device. Common approaches include data parallelism, pipeline parallelism, and tensor parallelism. Data parallelism maintains complete model replicas with different input data, simplifying the implementation but introducing memory redundancy. Pipeline parallelism divides the model layers into pipeline stages across devices for pipelined execution, reducing communication but incurring pipeline bubbles. Tensor parallelism partitions the model along tensor dimensions, but it requires frequent tensor aggregation and causes higher communication cost.

To reduce memory redundancy in data parallelism, ZeRO [20] proposes to partition the optimizer states and the model parameters such that each device holds only a portion of them. Specifically, ZeRO1 partitions the optimizer; ZeRO2 partitions both the optimizer and gradients. ZeRO3 partitions the parameters, gradients, and optimizer, completely eliminating the redundancy in data parallelism. However, it requires all-gather operations to reconstruct the complete parameters, which increases the communication volume by 50% compared to the original data parallelism. To reduce GPU memory overhead, ZeRO-Offload [22] offloads the optimizer to CPU memory and updates it on the CPU. To further hide the time cost of optimizer updates, ZeRO-Offload also proposes the delayed parameter update (DPU) strategy, which delays the optimizer update by one step and uses the forward and backward propagation of the next iteration to hide the cost.

2.2 Checkpoint Technology and Fault Tolerance Efficiency

Checkpointing is a widely used mechanism for fault tolerance during model training. A checkpoint stores the model parameters and the optimizer states, and can be directly loaded to resume the training process when a failure occurs. However, checkpointing usually introduces significant overhead. Additionally, the recovery and rollback time will increase the total training time.

Existing works focus on improving fault tolerance efficiency by reducing checkpointing time, recovery time, or communication overhead. CheckFreq [18] uses CPU memory snapshots as the cache to reduce time of saving the checkpoint to remote storage, however CheckFreq does not support CPU checkpointing and only the checkpoint in remote storage can be used to recover the training. Gemini [24] stores checkpoints in CPU memory, which is implemented based on ZeRO3 [20]. Gemini backs up the CPU checkpoint through inter-node communication to increase the probability of successful recovery from CPU memory. However,

Gemini incurs high communication cost, which may affect the training speed. For the fault tolerance of mixture-of-expert models, MoC-System [3] stores only partial experts each time to reduce checkpoint size and further shortens checkpointing time, but the stored experts may not be in the same version.

2.3 Limitations of Existing Solutions

All the aforementioned works have made significant progress in large-scale model training, but they still face two key challenges: extra communication overhead and inefficient fault tolerance. To address these limitations, we propose C^{3}FT to achieve low communication overhead and high fault tolerance efficiency simultaneously.

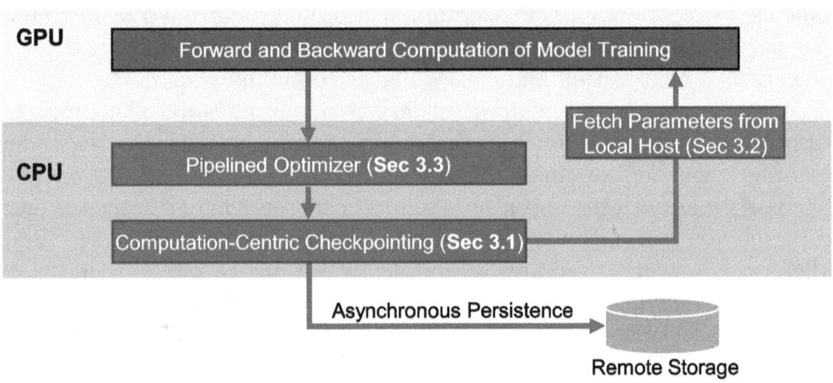

Fig. 1. The architecture of C^{3}FT.

3 The Technical Scheme of C^{3}FT

The architecture of C^{3}FT is illustrated in Fig. 1. C^{3}FT comprises three components: a low-cost checkpointing mechanism called computation-centric checkpointing (Sect. 3.1), which achieves high-efficiency checkpointing (i.e., checkpointing without communication overhead); to minimize the inter-node communication cost, model parameters are fetched from local host to GPUs (Sect. 3.2) to conduct forward and backward computation; the pipelined optimizer strategy (Sect. 3.3) to further reduce the overhead of the computation-centric checkpointing. C^{3}FT uses the optimizer states updated on CPU as the checkpoints. If a failure occurs, C^{3}FT recovers the training using the most recent checkpoint stored in the CPU memory, or in the remote storage if no CPU checkpoint is available.

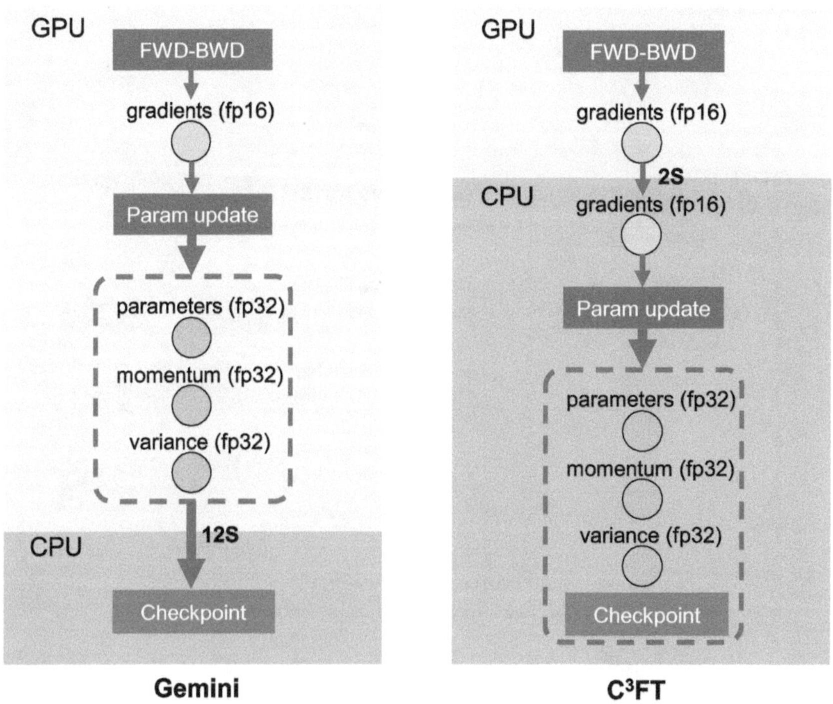

Fig. 2. Dataflows of CPU checkpoints for different schemes. S represents the model size (i.e., total number of parameters). Gemini transfers a checkpoint with $12S$ bytes from GPU to CPU. C^3FT only transfers the gradients with $2S$ bytes from GPU to CPU and updates the optimizer states in CPU memory, generating a CPU checkpoint.

3.1 Computation-Centric Checkpointing on CPU

The computation-centric checkpointing of C^3FT is shown in the right part of Fig. 2. Specifically, C^3FT utilizes the GPU resources to conduct the computation of forward and backward propagation. After that, the gradients (fp16) are offloaded from GPU memory to CPU memory. The optimizer states, including the parameters (fp32), momentum (fp32), and variance (fp32), are updated on CPU using the gradients. Then, C^3FT uses the optimizer states on CPU as the checkpoints. Essentially, the CPU checkpoints of C^3FT are constructed and maintained by the computation on CPU. We use S to represent the total number of model parameters. In the computation-centric checkpointing strategy, C^3FT only transfers the gradients with $2S$ bytes from GPU to CPU through PCIe. As the optimizer states are updated on CPU, the CPU checkpoints of C^3FT are also updated. In Sect. 3.3, we will discuss how to hide the CPU computational overhead of the computation-centric checkpointing.

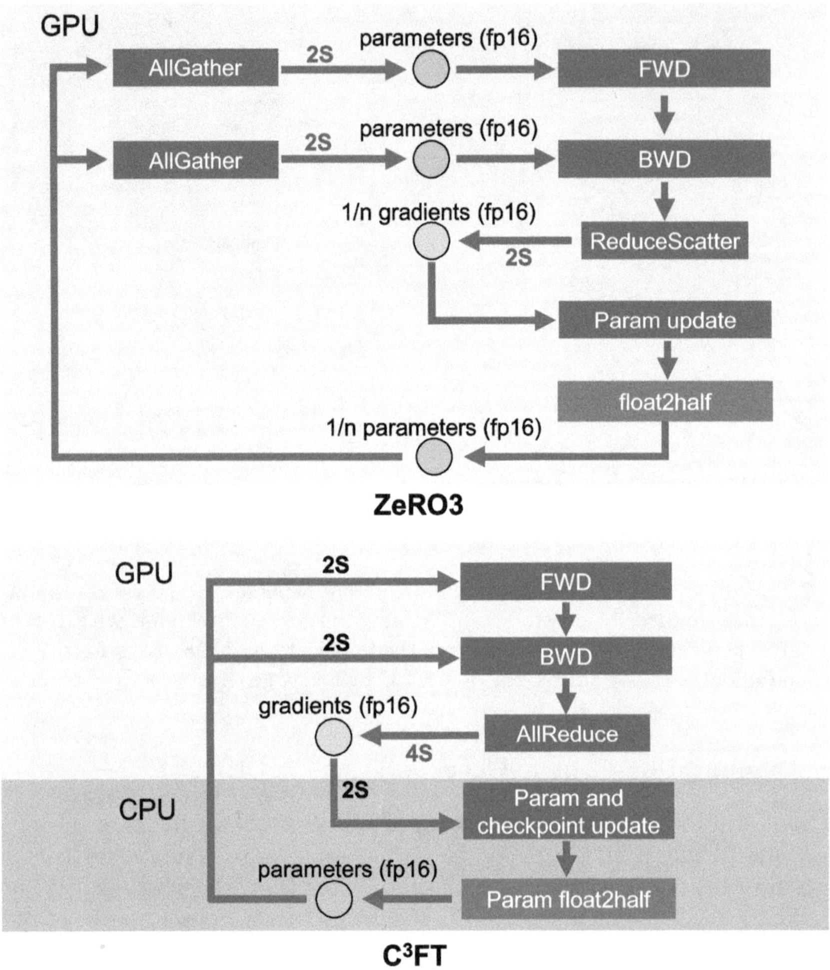

Fig. 3. Dataflows in different methods, where n represents the number of processes for data parallelism. ZeRO3 uses AllGather to fetch the complete model parameters from all GPUs during both forward and backward propagation. C^3FT fetches the complete model parameters on CPU memory via PCIe during both forward and backward propagation.

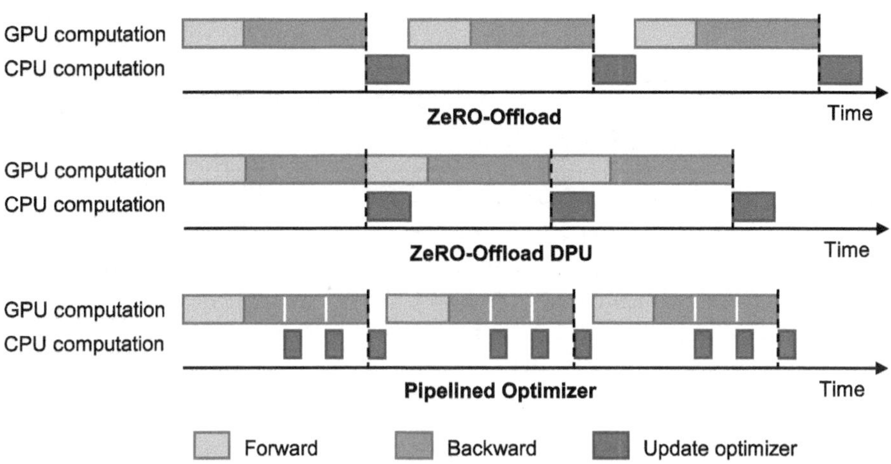

Fig. 4. The process of updating the optimizer states in different methods.

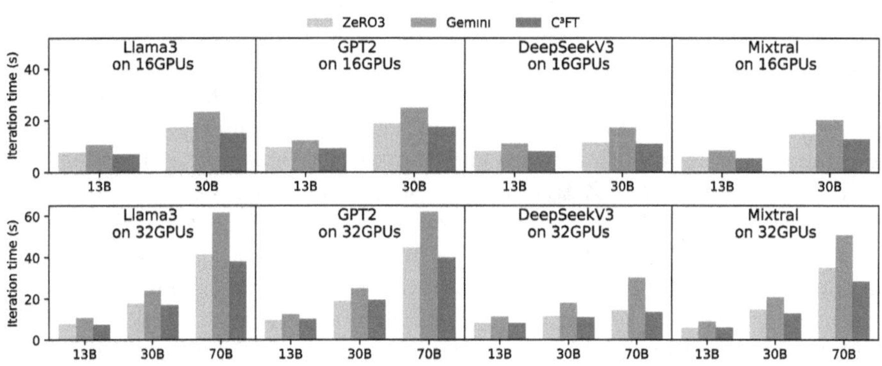

Fig. 5. The runtime of each iteration for different methods at various scales.

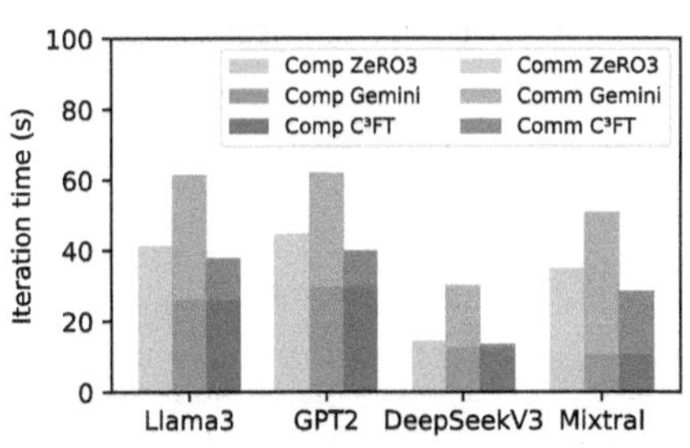

Fig. 6. GPU computation time and the unhidden communication time of the 70B models for different methods on 32 GPUs.

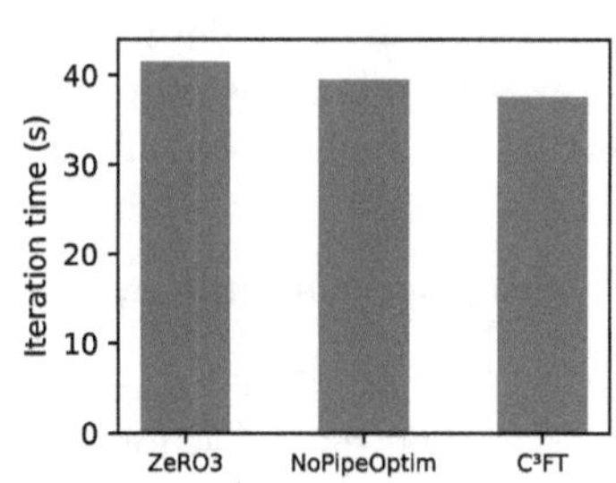

Fig. 7. Ablation study for C^3FT using the Llama3 70B model on 32 GPUs.

In Gemini, the optimizer states are computed and updated on GPUs as shown in the left part of Fig. 2. After that, the optimizer states (with the size of $12S$ bytes) are offloaded from GPU memory to CPU memory. Then, the optimizer states on CPU serve as the CPU checkpoints. Overall, Gemini has to transfer the optimizer states with $12S$ bytes from GPU to CPU, which brings a high pressure to PCIe. Even if the computation can be used to overlap the transmission of CPU checkpoints, the high PCIe overhead may still impact training performance [28]. Furthermore, to back up the CPU checkpoints, Gemini relies on extra inter-node communication operations, which brings high communication cost. In contrast, the PCIe transmission overhead C^3FT is only 1/6 of Gemini, and the computation-centric checkpointing strategy does not incur any communication overhead to back up the CPU checkpoints.

3.2 Fetch Model Parameters from Local Host

ZeRO3 eliminates the memory redundancy of data parallelism, but introduces additional communication overhead compared to the traditional data parallelism. The dataflow of ZeRO3 is shown in the upper part of Fig. 3. When the parallel degree of data parallelism is n, only $1/n$ of the model parameters are stored on each GPU in ZeRO3. However, both forward and backward propagation require complete model parameters for computation. Therefore, in ZeRO3, AllGather communication is conducted to collect the complete model parameters from all GPUs in both forward and backward propagation. The inter-GPU communication volume of ZeRO3 is $1.5\times$ of the traditional data parallelism.

We notice that PCIe bandwidth is usually higher than inter-GPU communication bandwidth. Therefore, C^3FT fully utilizes the PCIe bandwidth to fetch the complete model parameters from local host (i.e., CPU memory) in both forward and backward propagation, which significantly reduces the inter-GPU communication overhead, as shown in the lower part of Fig. 3. Specifically, C^3FT is built up on the traditional data parallelism. After finishing the computation of local gradients, AllReduce communication is conducted to get the global gradients, which are then offloaded to CPU to update the parameters and checkpoints. The fp16 version of model parameters are transferred to GPU through PCIe in both forward and backward propagation. Overall, the inter-GPU communication volume of C^3FT is equivalent to the traditional data parallelism.

3.3 Pipelined Optimizer

Updating the optimizer states on the CPU incurs significant computational overhead. As shown in Fig. 4, for ZeRO-Offload, the optimizer states must be fully updated before proceeding to the next training iteration. ZeRO-Offload also proposes DPU [22], which overlaps the CPU optimizer computation of the current iteration with the forward-backward propagation of the next iteration. However, the asynchronous computation of the CPU optimizer in ZeRO-Offload DPU does not mathematically guarantee training convergence.

Therefore, we propose the pipelined optimizer for C^3FT, an efficient method for synchronously updating the optimizer, as shown in Fig. 4. When performing the backward propagation of losses, the gradients are divided into chunks and the gradient computation is scheduled on the GPUs in chunks. Once the computation of a gradient chunk is finished on GPUs, C^3FT immediately transfers the gradient chunk to CPU memory. Since the optimizer update depends solely on gradients, the corresponding optimizer states are updated on CPU once receiving a gradient chunk. Each chunk (except for the last one) of optimizer update on CPU overlaps with the backward propagation on GPU, allowing C^3FT to hide most of the computational overhead on CPU.

In the practical training process of large models, gradients may contain non-numeric (NaN) or infinite (INF) values, in which case the current optimizer update needs to be skipped. Besides, the gradient norm must be computed using all gradients for gradient clipping. When the gradient norm exceeds a preset range, gradient clipping is triggered. At this point, the optimizer is updated use the clipped gradients. This means that the optimizer update should wait for all gradients to be generated. We adopt a post-inspection strategy: Before the updating a chunk of optimizer in the pipeline, C^3FT checks whether a gradient chunk contains NaN/INF values. If such values exist, skip all the optimizer updates in this training iteration. By default, we assume the gradient clipping is not triggered. After the backward propagation finishes, we check gradient clipping. If gradient clipping is triggered, we roll back the checkpoint to the version of the previous iteration using a double-buffer strategy.

4 Evaluations

4.1 Experimental Setup

We implemented C^3FT based on DeepSpeed [21]. We evaluate C^3FT using Llama3 [6], GPT2 [19], DeepSeek-V3 [13], and Mixtral [10] with different model sizes. The training dataset is OpenWebText Corpus [2]. We conduct the experiments on a GPU cluster with 4 computing nodes which are connected by a 400Gbps infiniband network. Each computing node haves 8 NVIDIA A100 (80GB) GPUs. We use ZeRO3 and Gemini as baselines. Mixed precision training [16] is used for all the schemes. ZeRO3 does not support checkpointing. Gemini saves CPU checkpoints at each training iteration, and backs up CPU checkpoints between nodes. Only data parallelism is used for all the schemes. The local batch size on each GPU is 2 and the sequence length is set to 4,096.

4.2 Training Efficiency

We test the runtime of each training iteration for ZeRO3, Gemini, and C^3FT using different models. The tests are conducted on 16 GPUs and 32 GPUs, respectively. Figure 5 shows the results for the runtime of each training iteration. We can see that C^3FT outperforms both ZeRO3 and Gemini in all cases. Note that C^3FT (with checkpointing) even consistently slightly outperforms ZeRO3 (without support for checkpointing) since C^{3}FT has lower communication overhead than ZeRO3. Furthermore, as the model size increases, the gap between Gemini and C^{3}FT widens. For Llama3 70B on 32 GPUs, C^{3}FT improves the training throughput by 1.62× compared to Gemini; for Mixtral 70B on 32 GPUs, C^{3}FT improves the training throughput by 1.69× compared to Gemini. In summary, C^{3}FT accelerates the training while updating the CPU checkpoints, which demonstrates the effectiveness of the technical scheme of C^{3}FT. Moreover, the training iteration time of C^{3}FT remains nearly constant across different training scales for the same model, which demonstrates the strong parallel scalability of C^{3}FT.

4.3 Performance Breakdown for Computation and Communication

Figure 6 shows the percentage of GPU computation time and unhidden communication time in a training iteration for the 70B models on 32 GPUs. We can see that the dense models, such as Llama3, spend more computation time, while sparse MoE models, such as DeepSeek-V3, spend less computation time. Meanwhile, for the sparse MoE models, only the activated experts need to perform computations and update their parameters. DeepSeekV3, with a larger number of experts, has less unhidden communication time compared to Mixtral with fewer experts.

The results in Fig. 6 indicate that the gap between Gemini and C^{3}FT mainly originates from the unhidden communication time. The computation time is almost the same across different schemes, but the unhidden communication time varies significantly. Gemini even has more unhidden communication than ZeRO3 due to the overhead of transmitting checkpoints between nodes. C^{3}FT has less unhidden communication than both ZeRO3 and Gemini due to the computation-centric checkpointing strategy (no communication overhead for checkpointing) and consistently fetching model parameters from local host (the communication cost is as low as the traditional data parallelism).

4.4 The Effectiveness of Fetching Parameters from Local Host and Pipelined Optimizer

In this section, we evaluate the effectiveness of the strategies in C^{3}FT. The ablation study results using the Llama3 70B model on 32 GPUs are shown in Fig. 7, in which the evaluated schemes are defined as follows:

- ZeRO3: Serving as the baseline without support for checkpointing.
- NoPipeOptim: Removing the pipelined optimizer from C^{3}FT, but with fetching parameters from local host and the computation-centric checkpointing.
- C^{3}FT: The whole technical scheme C^{3}FT including all the strategies.

From the results in Fig. 7, we can see that NoPipeOptim has slightly lower iteration time compared to ZeRO3, demonstrating that fetching parameters from local host and the computation-centric checkpointing effectively minimize the inter-GPU communication overhead, which is 50% lower than ZeRO3. Compared to NoPipeOptim, C³FT further reduces the iteration time by 5.3%, demonstrating that the pipelined optimizer effectively hide the computational overhead on CPU.

5 Conclusion and Future Work

This paper proposes C³FT, a computation-centric checkpointing for the fault tolerance of distributed large model training. C³FT achieves the low communication overhead and the high-efficiency checkpointing simultaneously. Extensive experiments conducted on an A100 GPU cluster demonstrate the performance advantages of C³FT. For training a 70B model on 32 GPUs, C³FT improves the training throughput by up to 1.69× compared to Gemini, the SOTA fault tolerance solution with in-CPU-memory checkpointing. Although the implementation of C³FT is based on data parallelism, it can be easily fused with other parallel dimensions, such as tensor parallelism and pipeline parallelism, to form a fault-tolerant hybrid parallelism scheme for distributed large model training.

Acknowledgments. This project was supported by the National Science and Technology Major Project (2023ZD0120502), the National Natural Science Foundation of China under Grant No. 62372055, School-Enterprise Cooperation Project of Beijing University of Posts and Telecommunications under Grant No. A2024038, and the Fundamental Research Funds for the Central Universities.

Artificial intelligence tools, if used, were used only for language organization and figure/table polishing, and did not participate in the generation of the core ideas or technical content.

Disclosure of Interests. The authors have no competing interests to declare that are relevant to the content of this article.

References

1. Bloom chronicles (2022). https://github.com/bigscience-workshop/bigscience/blob/master/train/tr11-176B-ml/chronicles.md
2. Aaron Gokaslan, Vanya Cohen, E.P., Tellex, S.: Openwebtext corpus (2019). http://Skylion007.github.io/OpenWebTextCorpus
3. Cai, W., Qin, L., Huang, J.: Moc-system: efficient fault tolerance for sparse mixture-of-experts model training. In: Proceedings of the 30th ACM International Conference on Architectural Support for Programming Languages and Operating Systems, vol. 2, pp. 655–671. Association for Computing Machinery (2025)
4. Chen, M., Hua, Y., Bai, R., Huang, J.: A cost-efficient failure-tolerant scheme for distributed DNN training. In: 2023 IEEE 41st International Conference on Computer Design, pp. 150–157. IEEE (2023)
5. Chowdhery, A., et al.: Palm: Scaling language modeling with pathways. J. Mach. Learn. Res. **24**(240), 1–113 (2023)
6. Dubey, A., et al.: The llama 3 herd of models. arXiv e prints pp. arXiv–2407 (2024)

7. Eisenman, A., et al.: {Check-N-Run}: a checkpointing system for training deep learning recommendation models. In: 19th USENIX Symposium on Networked Systems Design and Implementation (NSDI 22), pp. 929–943 (2022)
8. Huang, Y., et al.: Gpipe: efficient training of giant neural networks using pipeline parallelism. Adv. Neural Inf. Process. Syst. **32** (2019)
9. Jia, X., et al.: Whale: efficient giant model training over heterogeneous {GPUs}. In: 2022 USENIX Annual Technical Conference (USENIX ATC 22), pp. 673–688 (2022)
10. Jiang, A.Q., et al.: Mixtral of experts. arXiv preprint arXiv:2401.04088 (2024)
11. Kokolis, A., et al.: Revisiting reliability in large-scale machine learning research clusters. In: 2025 IEEE International Symposium on High Performance Computer Architecture (HPCA), pp. 1259–1274. IEEE (2025)
12. Li, S., Xue, F., Baranwal, C., Li, Y., You, Y.: Sequence parallelism: long sequence training from system perspective. arXiv preprint arXiv:2105.13120 (2021)
13. Liu, A., et al.: Deepseek-v3 technical report. arXiv:2412.19437 arXiv preprint (2024)
14. Maeng, K., et al.: Understanding and improving failure tolerant training for deep learning recommendation with partial recovery. Proc. Mach. Learn. Syst. **3**, 637–651 (2021)
15. Mai, L., Li, G., Wagenländer, M., Fertakis, K., Brabete, A.O., Pietzuch, P.: {KungFu}: making training in distributed machine learning adaptive. In: 14th USENIX Symposium on Operating Systems Design and Implementation, pp. 937–954 (2020)
16. Micikevicius, P., et al.: Mixed precision training. arXiv:1710.03740 arXiv preprint (2017)
17. Mnih, V., et al.: Asynchronous methods for deep reinforcement learning. In: International Conference on Machine Learning, pp. 1928–1937 (2016)
18. Mohan, J., Phanishayee, A., Chidambaram, V.: {CheckFreq}: frequent,{Fine-Grained}{DNN} checkpointing. In: 19th USENIX Conference on File and Storage Technologies, pp. 203–216 (2021)
19. Radford, A., Wu, J., Child, R., Luan, D., Amodei, D., Sutskever, I., et al.: Language models are unsupervised multitask learners. OpenAI blog **1**(8), 9 (2019)
20. Rajbhandari, S., Rasley, J., Ruwase, O., He, Y.: Zero: memory optimizations toward training trillion parameter models. In: SC20: International Conference for High Performance Computing, Networking, Storage and Analysis, pp. 1–16 (2020)
21. Rasley, J., Rajbhandari, S., Ruwase, O., He, Y.: Deepspeed: system optimizations enable training deep learning models with over 100 billion parameters. In: Proceedings of the 26th ACM SIGKDD International Conference on Knowledge Discovery & Data Mining, pp. 3505–3506 (2020)
22. Ren, J., et al.: {Zero-offload}: democratizing {billion-scale} model training. In: 2021 USENIX Annual Technical Conference (USENIX ATC 21), pp. 551–564 (2021)
23. Shoeybi, M., Patwary, M., Puri, R., LeGresley, P., Casper, J., Catanzaro, B.: Megatron-LM: training multi-billion parameter language models using model parallelism. arXiv preprint arXiv:1909.08053 (2019)
24. Wang, Z., et al.: Gemini: fast failure recovery in distributed training with in-memory checkpoints. In: Proceedings of the 29th Symposium on Operating Systems Principles, pp. 364–381 (2023)
25. Weng, Q., et al.: {MLaaS} in the wild: workload analysis and scheduling in {Large-Scale} heterogeneous {GPU} clusters. In: 19th USENIX Symposium on Networked Systems Design and Implementation (NSDI 22), pp. 945–960 (2022)

26. Zhang, S., Zhang, C., You, Z., Zheng, R., Xu, B.: Asynchronous stochastic gradient descent for DNN training. In: 2013 IEEE International Conference on Acoustics, Speech and Signal Processing. pp. 6660–6663. IEEE (2013)
27. Zhang, S., et al.: Opt: open pre-trained transformer language models. arXiv preprint arXiv:2205.01068 (2022)
28. Zhong, Y., Sheng, G., Liu, J., Yuan, J., Wu, C.: Swift: expedited failure recovery for large-scale DNN training. In: Proceedings of the 28th ACM SIGPLAN Annual Symposium on Principles and Practice of Parallel Programming, pp. 447–449 (2023)

FlexUSFL: A Scalable and Memory-Efficient U-Shaped Split Federated Learning Framework for Large Language Model Fine-Tuning

Zihan Liu[1], Yizhen Wang[1], Rui Wang[1,2](✉), Youhui Bai[3], and Sai Wu[1]

[1] Zhejiang University, Zhejiang, China
rwang21@zju.edu.com
[2] Innovation and Management Center, School of Software Technology (Ningbo), Zhejiang University, Zhejiang, China
[3] University of Science and Technology of China, Anhui, China

Abstract. Fine-tuning large language models (LLMs) using split federated learning (SFL) enables task-specific optimization across distributed clients while addressing privacy and scalability challenges. U-shaped split federated learning (USFL) further enhances SFL by retaining sensitive labels on clients and computing loss locally, mitigating label leakage risks. However, existing USFL approaches, USFL-V1 and USFL-V2, face critical limitations: USFL-V1 imposes high storage overhead due to per-client trunk models, while USFL-V2 suffers from synchronization delays that degrade training efficiency. This paper proposes FlexUSFL, a novel USFL framework tailored for LLM fine-tuning. By introducing delayed synchronization with gradient accumulation and dynamic activation recomputation, FlexUSFL minimizes memory usage and server idle time while preserving data privacy by processing both inputs and outputs locally on clients. Extensive experiments across diverse datasets and models demonstrate that FlexUSFL outperforms USFL-V1 and USFL-V2, achieving superior scalability and efficiency for split federated LLM fine-tuning. Our code is available at https://github.com/nazhilanbi/FlexUSFL.

Keywords: Large language model · split learning · federated learning

1 Introduction

Large language model fine-tuning (LLM-FT) [13,19] adapts pre-trained modelst specific tasks. However, as model sizes grow and public datasets are exhausted, fine-tuning private LLMs faces significant challenges of resource bottlenecks [9] and privacy leakage risks [41]. Emerging split learning (SL) [38] technique addresses these issues by dividing models and distributing model segments across resource-constrained local clients and cloud servers, enabling collaborative training without exposing raw data [3,22,35]. Split federated learning (SFL) [37] further enhances this paradigm by enabling parallel computation across multiple

L. Eeckhout et al. (Eds.): APPT 2026, LNCS 16693, pp. 282–297, 2027.
https://doi.org/10.1007/978-981-92-4805-6_19

clients, effectively overcoming the computational inefficiencies introduced by the serial training process in single-client SL.

Current SFL approaches [5,40], primarily designed for conventional machine learning tasks, divide models into two segments: a client-side model (with few layers) and a server-side model (hosting most layers). Clients process private data locally using their client models and transmit smashed intermediate data to a central server for completing the server-side model training, thereby avoiding direct exposure of raw input data. However, in LLM scenarios, attackers may still reconstruct the inputs from output labels due to LLMs' auto-regressive nature, posing significant privacy risks [4]. U-shaped split learning (USL) [26,30,34] addresses this vulnerability by splitting the model into three parts: head, trunk, and tail models. When integrated with federated learning as U-shaped split federated learning (USFL) [36,44], it maintains both input and output processing on clients through head and tail models, while only sharing intermediate trunk-processed features with the server. This architecture substantially reduces privacy exposure compared to standard SFL.

Despite its potential, current USFL implementations face critical resource efficiency challenges. The baseline approach (USFL-V1) [44] maintains a dedicated replica of the server-side trunk model for each client, updated independently with periodic synchronization. This design imposes storage requirements that grow linearly with the client count, becoming increasingly impractical as LLM model sizes grow [15]. Inspired by recent SFL works aimed at reducing redundant model replicas [15,16,37], a shared global trunk model updated sequentially by all clients (USFL-V2) reduces server memory demand. However, the introduction of client-side tail models creates a synchronization bottleneck: the server must wait for the current client to complete both forward and backward passes through its tail model before processing the next client's request. This synchronous blocking ensures consistent weights during processing a same batch but causes severe server idle time, significantly degrading training efficiency compared to USFL-V1. Thus, a key scalability trade-off emerges: USFL-V1 struggles with prohibitive storage overhead on the server, while USFL-V2 suffers from excessive training latency due to synchronization delays.

To overcome these challenges, we propose FlexUSFL, a Flexible U-Shaped Split Federated Learning framework designed to simultaneously address storage overhead and training efficiency issues in LLM-FT. FlexUSFL presents two core innovations: (1) *delayed synchronization with gradient accumulation*, which eliminates server idle time by removing server synchronization barriers; and (2) *dynamic activation management*, which intelligently reduces storage for activations awaiting backward passes from concurrent clients. Through the synergistic optimization of server trunk model storage and updating, FlexUSFL achieves superior scalability, delivering training time efficiency on par with USFL-V1 and memory efficiency equivalent to USFL-V2. Our key contributions include:

- We systematically characterize the bottlenecks of USFL-V1 and USFL-V2 for LLM fine-tuning, identifying the rigid trade-off between memory costs and synchronization latency.

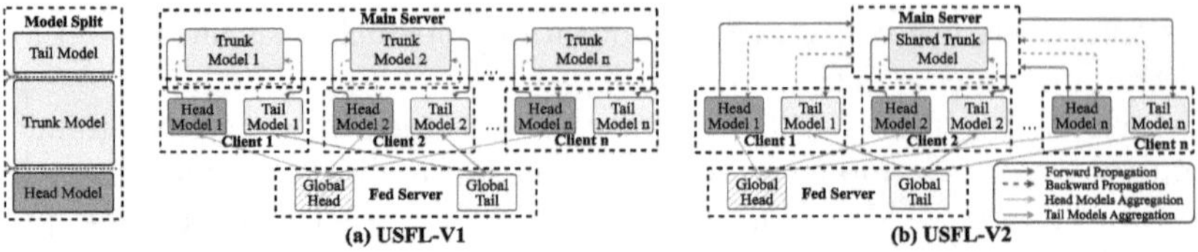

Fig. 1. Illustration of USFL framework, showcasing its two variants: USFL-V1 (left) and USFL-V2 (right).

- We introduce FlexUSFL, a novel USFL framework tailored for efficient LLM fine-tuning. By integrating *delayed synchronization with gradient accumulation*, it optimizes resource utilization while striking a careful balance between memory efficiency and computational overhead, without compromising model convergence.
- To further reduce server memory overhead from client activations, we introduce a *dynamic activation management strategy* that selectively discards and recomputes activations based on memory constraints
- We implement FlexUSFL, and conduct extensive experiments on diverse datasets and models, demonstrating that FlexUSFL achieves superior scalability and efficiency compared to USFL-V1 and USFL-V2, validating its effectiveness for USFL based LLM fine-tuning.

2 Background and Related Works

2.1 Fine-Tuning of LLMs

Fine-tuning (FT) is the standard for adapting LLMs to downstream tasks [13, 19]. Supervised fine-tuning further refines performance, particularly in natural language generation, by optimizing models against labeled outputs [32]. However, even with parameter-efficient methods like LoRA [17] and prefix tuning [20], the computational burden remains prohibitive for resource-constrained users, often necessitating expensive multi-GPU setups [9]. This creates a steep barrier for small-to-medium enterprises (SMEs) and underfunded research teams. While cloud platforms offer scalability, privacy concerns regarding sensitive data often deter organizations from uploading data, necessitating local training solutions [41]. Thus, enabling local LLM-FT on limited hardware (e.g., single GPUs or small clusters) is a critical challenge.

2.2 Split Learning and Split Federated Learning

Split learning (SL) [12,14,35,38,39] addresses the resource constraints and privacy preservation through a partitioned model architecture. By offloading the majority of the model to the server, SL relieves the computational pressure on resource-constrained clients, while processing raw data locally prevents direct server access to inputs. U-shaped split learning (USL) [26,30,34] enhances privacy by sandwiching a server-side trunk between client-side head and tail models. This structure creates a closed loop that isolates the server from both inputs and outputs, serving high-privacy needs in healthcare and finance [43]. Split federated learning (SFL) [15,37,40] combines SL's privacy benefits with federated learning's (FL) [27] parallel training capabilities. By enabling simultaneous processing across multiple clients while maintaining the split architecture, SFL overcomes SL's inherent sequential training limitations, achieving both scalability and privacy preservation.

2.3 Split-Based LLM-FT

To address the prohibitive computational demands of LLM fine-tuning for resource-constrained organizations, split-based approaches [5,22,35,45] leverage SFL. This enables efficient and privacy-preserving adaptation through model partitioning. However, autoregressive LLM training generates labels by shifting inputs, inherently exposing sensitive data and preventing server-side loss computation [4,25]. To mitigate label leakage, U-shaped split federated learning (USFL) [36,44,46] combines USL with SFL, enabling clients to compute loss locally without sharing sensitive labels, making it ideal for privacy-sensitive LLM fine-tuning. However, due to its unique computational workflow, this architecture faces a rigid trade-off between storage scalability and computational latency in multi-client scenarios, as detailed in Sect. 3. While recent SFL advancements optimize communication and latency via scheduling and merging strategies [10,21,28], they remain ill-suited for USFL-based LLM fine-tuning. Existing methods fail to address prohibitive server memory pressure from massive concurrency, computational bottlenecks in U-shaped workflows, and label leakage risks in autoregressive training.

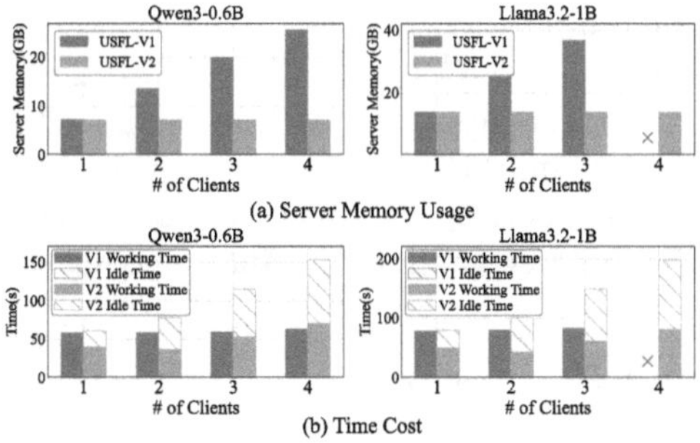

Fig. 2. "Server GPU memory usage and time cost of USFL-V1 and USFL-V2 on GSM8K. "×" indicates that the server ran out of memory at that configuration.

3 Motivation

Figure 1 shows the USFL-based LLM-FT workflow, splitting the LLM into private client-side head/tail models and a server-side trunk model. Building upon the SFL paradigm [37], USFL offers two variants: USFL-V1 employs client-specific replicas for independent processing, while USFL-V2 utilizes a single shared trunk updated sequentially. However, both face significant resource inefficiencies.

USFL-V1 Incurs High Storage Overhead Scaling Linearly With Client Count. USFL-V1 maintains a separate server-side trunk model replica for each client. During training, the server independently executes forward and backward passes from concurrent clients using these replicas. Once all server-side partitions complete training, their parameters are aggregated to update the global trunk model (Fig. 1(a)). While this design enables independent client training without interference, allowing the server to process activations and gradients immediately upon receiving them from a client, it introduces a critical drawback: server storage costs grow linearly with the number of clients. As shown in Fig. 2(a), training LLaMA3.2-1B consumes 13.8 GB for a single client but surges to 37.0 GB for 3 clients, failing with OOM errors at 4 clients. This linear memory dependency renders USFL-V1 impractical for high-concurrency scenarios.

USFL-V2 Suffers from Severe Synchronization Bottlenecks. In contrast to USFL-V1 which maintains dedicated trunk replicas, USFL-V2 employs a single shared server-side trunk updated in a strictly serialized manner. While this design ensures constant memory complexity and eliminates the linear growth, it introduces a severe synchronization bottleneck. To maintain gradient consistency, the server must block after each trunk forward pass, idling until the current client completes its tail computation and updates the trunk parameters before processing the next request. Crucially, naive pipelining (i.e., processing the next client immediately) is rendered infeasible by gradient staleness, as subsequent clients would compute gradients based on obsolete trunk parameters before prior updates are applied. Consequently, USFL-V2 prioritizes algorithmic consistency over system throughput, resulting in significant server idle time and GPU resource wastage. Figure 2(b) confirms that USFL-V2's training latency increases sharply; for instance, Qwen3-0.6B training time nearly triples from 60.6 s (1 client) to 153.0 s (4 clients), significantly lagging behind USFL-V1.

4 The Proposed Framework

To simultaneously minimize prohibitive storage and excessive latency while maintaining scalability across large client populations, we present FlexUSFL, a scalable USFL-based LLM-FT framework illustrated in Fig. 3. The architecture splits the LLM into lightweight head/tail models stored locally on multiple clients, and a shared trunk model on the main server to ensure memory scalability. To optimize GPU resources, FlexUSFL introduces two key innovations:

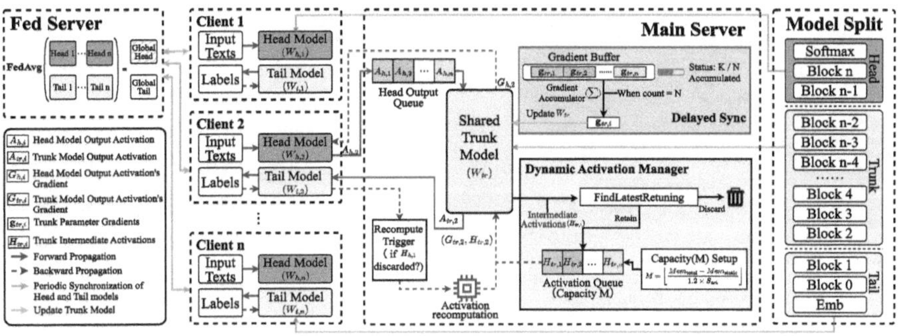

Fig. 3. Overview of the FlexUSFL architecture. The framework splits the LLM into client-side head and tail models and a single shared server-side trunk model. The server employs Delayed Synchronization to process requests continuously without idle waiting, and Dynamic Activation Management to intelligently discard or recompute intermediate activations based on real-time memory availability, ensuring scalability across multiple concurrent clients.

(1) *delayed sync with gradient accumulation* to eliminate server idle time, and (2) *dynamic activation management* to intelligently balance memory usage via selective recomputation.

4.1 Delayed Sync with Gradient Accumulation

While USFL-V1 maintains separate trunk models for parallel processing, USFL-V2's shared trunk model creates sequential dependencies and server idle time during client computations. FlexUSFL overcomes this synchronization bottleneck through delayed synchronization with gradient accumulation. During each training round, clients perform local forward and backward passes on their head and tail models, computing gradients for the shared trunk model. Instead of updating the trunk model immediately upon receiving each client's gradients, the server accumulates gradients from multiple clients within a synchronization window. After aggregating gradients from all participating clients for the current batch, the server performs a single update to the shared trunk model. This deferred update strategy merges the best of both approaches: USFL-V2's memory efficiency and USFL-V1's computational throughput. By enabling continuous execution of server-side forward and backward passes from multiple clients, it minimizes server idle time and accelerates training while maintaining low memory overhead. Formally, FlexUSFL updates the shared trunk model parameters w_{tr} using the aggregated gradients averaged across N clients ($\frac{1}{N}\sum_{i=1}^{N}\nabla_{w_{tr}}L_i$), while the head ($w_{h,i}$) and tail ($w_{t,i}$) parameters are updated independently by each client i using their local gradients. To better visualize the training process across USFL variants, Fig. 4 compares the timeline of a single training round for USFL-V1, USFL-V2, and FlexUSFL. While USFL-V1 achieves the fastest training, with high memory overhead, and USFL-V2 suffers from synchronization

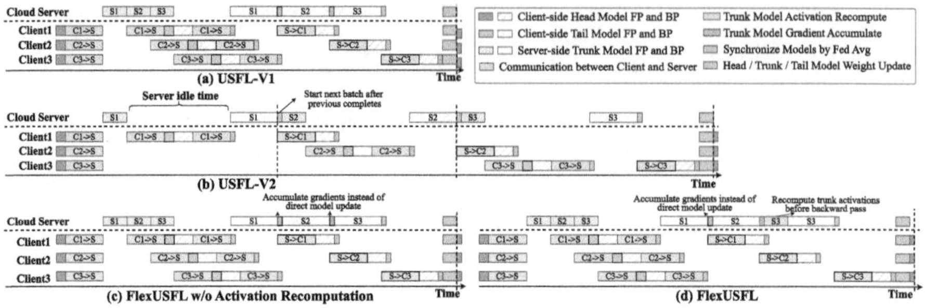

Fig. 4. Examples of timelines for one round with three clients when using different USFL frameworks.

delays, FlexUSFL strikes an optimal balance: each client independently updates its head and tail parameters using local gradients, while the trunk model parameters are updated once per synchronization cycle with aggregated gradients computed after backward propagation across all clients' batch data. This design reduces per-round training time to USFL-V1 levels while maintaining USFL-V2's memory efficiency. By minimizing server idle time through delayed synchronization and optimizing update frequency, FlexUSFL enhances both computational efficiency and convergence stability.

Consistency and Fairness. FlexUSFL guarantees zero gradient staleness despite its asynchronous execution flow. By adopting an *intra-iteration asynchronous, inter-iteration synchronous* paradigm [10], our framework ensures that all clients within a training iteration compute gradients based on the same trunk model version. The server defers the parameter update until gradients from all N clients are fully accumulated. Thus, gradients remain consistent with the current model parameters, and no stale updates are introduced. Furthermore, since each server update aggregates exactly one batch from every client, it ensures uniform contribution from all participants. This guarantees fairness by preventing faster clients from dominating the optimization path, thereby maintaining an unbiased gradient estimate. Crucially, this accumulation strategy renders the optimization of the shared trunk parameters mathematically equivalent to synchronous SGD with an effective global batch size of $N \times B$ (where B is the local batch size), thereby strictly preserving the convergence properties of centralized training.

4.2 Dynamic Activation Management

Although the aforementioned methods reduce the time overhead of maintaining a single trunk model, they introduce a new challenge: high memory overhead from storing activations of multiple concurrent clients. Conversely, performing full recomputation for all clients would incur significant computation latency. To address this, FlexUSFL introduces a dynamic activation checkpointing mechanism that adapts to the server's memory capacity. Specifically, during the initial warm-up phase, the server performs runtime profiling to measure the precise

Table 1. Total cost and Memory Usage analysis of the Four USFL approaches for one round. Underlined terms highlight the specific differences in the time cost analysis across methods

Method	Total time for τ batches and aggregation	Server Peak Memory Usage
USFL-V1	$((T_{tr}^f + T_{tr}^b) \cdot N + \underline{T_{idle}} + 2 \cdot T_{comm} + T_h^f + T_h^b) \cdot \tau + T_{Fed}$	$N \cdot (W+O+A)$
USFL-V2	$((T_t^f + T_t^b) \cdot N + \underline{(T_{tr}^f + T_{tr}^b + 2 \cdot T_{comm}) \cdot N} + 2 \cdot T_{comm} + T_h^f + T_h^b) \cdot \tau + T_{Fed}$	$W + O + A$
FlexUSFL w/o AR	$((T_{tr}^f + T_{tr}^b) \cdot N + \underline{T_{idle}} + 2 \cdot T_{comm} + T_h^f + T_h^b) \cdot \tau + T_{Fed}$	$W + O + N \cdot A$
FlexUSFL	$((T_{tr}^f + T_{tr}^b) \cdot N + \underline{(N - M) \cdot T_{tr}^f + T_{idle}} + 2 \cdot T_{comm} + T_h^f + T_h^b) \cdot \tau + T_{Fed}$	$W + O + M \cdot A \quad (M \in [1, N])$

memory footprint of a single trunk activation. We then calculate the maximum storage capacity strictly reserving a safety headroom of 1.2× the size of a single activation. This margin compensates for memory fragmentation overhead in caching allocators [11], necessitating such additional buffering to prevent OOM errors [24]. When the memory limit is reached, instead of defaulting to discarding the current activation, the system compares the current activation against the candidate with the furthest estimated arrival time in the stored queue, and discards whichever is expected to return its gradient last. This decision is supported by an adaptive timing module that continuously updates the estimated round-trip latency of each client based on real-time feedback throughout the training process. Formally, for a batch size of B across N clients, the activation memory footprint is reduced from $O(N \cdot B \cdot A)$ to $O(M \cdot B \cdot A)$, where A is the per-sample activation size and $M \leq N$ is the number of activations retained according to available server GPU memory. Unlike offloading strategies (e.g., to CPU or disk) that introduce I/O latency and require scalable auxiliary storage for each client, our approach relies solely on server GPU resources, making it particularly practical for SFL servers deployed on rented cloud instances.

Interleaved Task Scheduling. To efficiently orchestrate server-side computational workflows, including forward propagation, backward gradient calculation, and conditional activation recomputation, FlexUSFL employs an event-driven scheduler. Specifically, the scheduler enforces a latency-aware eviction policy that dynamically discards cached activations with the latest estimated return times to strictly bound memory usage. Concurrently, it maintains a strict delayed synchronization barrier, updating the shared trunk parameters only after all gradients are accumulated to guarantee global consistency and fairness. Unlike rigid schedules (e.g., F-then-B [18] or 1F1B [29]) that suffer from pipeline bubbles due to client heterogeneity, our scheduler dynamically interleaves these requests to saturate the pipeline. Regarding execution ordering, strict priority is given to resolving blocking data dependencies: evicted activations are immediately recomputed during the backward phase to prevent stalls, ensuring scalable and correct training.

4.3 Performance Analysis

Time Cost Analysis. We conduct a time cost analysis under homogeneous settings with N clients performing τ local iterations per round. We define T_{comm} as the latency for a single transmission (activation or gradient). Computation time is denoted as T_m^d, where $m \in \{h, tr, t\}$ represents the model segment and $d \in \{f, b\}$ denotes the forward or backward pass. T_{Fed} represents the global aggregation overhead. In USFL-V2, the server incurs an initial latency of $T_h^f + T_{comm}$ to receive the first activation. Subsequently, it processes N clients sequentially. During each client's processing, the server blocks between trunk forward and backward passes to await the tail model computation, leading to a total duration of $N \cdot (T_{tr}^f + T_{tr}^b + 2T_{comm} + T_t^f + T_t^b)$. Note that the head model computation is masked by the server's execution and is thus excluded from the serial term. The iteration concludes with the last client's backward propagation $(T_{comm} + T_h^b)$. Finally, after τ iterations, the aggregation phase takes T_{fed}. In contrast, for USFL-V1 and FlexUSFL w/o AR, the total training latency is constrained by the server's processing throughput. While maintaining the same initialization $(T_h^f + T_{comm})$ and teardown $(T_{comm} + T_h^b)$ latencies as USFL-V2, the core execution operates as a saturated pipeline. This phase consumes $N \cdot (T_{tr}^f + T_{tr}^b) + T_{idle}$, where T_{idle} represents potential idle time. As the number of clients increases, the continuous influx of tasks fully saturates the server, rendering T_{idle} negligible. For FlexUSFL, recomputation adds $(N - M) \cdot T_{tr}^f$ to the server-side computation. As shown in Table 1, FlexUSFL matches the computational efficiency of USFL-V1 using a single shared trunk, significantly outperforming USFL-V2 in training speed. Even in the worst-case scenario $(M \ll N)$, given that the backward pass typically costs twice the forward pass $(T_{tr}^b \approx 2T_{tr}^f)$, the recomputation incurs a limited overhead (computationally capped at $\approx 33\%$), ensuring scalability without prohibitive latency.

Memory Usage Analysis. We also compare the memory usage of USFL frameworks, where W, O, and A denote the memory footprints of the trunk parameters, optimizer states, and single-client activations, respectively. Additionally, M represents the maximum number of activation copies retained by the server. The comparative results are presented in Table 1. FlexUSFL achieves computational efficiency comparable to USFL-V1 by sharing a single trunk model, while maintaining a minimal memory footprint similar to USFL-V2. Unlike FlexUSFL (w/o AR), which scales linearly by storing activations for all concurrent clients, FlexUSFL dynamically retains only up to M activations based on available memory and recomputes the remainder, thereby fully utilizing available memory to maximize computational efficiency.

Privacy Analysis. FlexUSFL operates under the standard honest-but-curious threat server: the server observes intermediate activations and gradients but never accesses raw inputs or labels [4,33]. We emphasize that retaining or recomputing activations does not expand the privacy attack surface, as these activations are inherently visible to the server during forward passes; our method merely adjusts their lifecycle in memory. Furthermore, FlexUSFL is fully compatible with privacy-enhancing technologies such as Differential Privacy [1], Secure Aggregation [2], and DualGuard [25], enabling deployment in scenarios demanding stringent privacy guarantees.

5 Experiment

5.1 Experiment Setup

System Setup. Our experiments are conducted on a server equipped with eight NVIDIA A6000 GPUs, each with 48 GB of HBM memory. One GPU is designated as the server, hosting the trunk model, while the remaining seven GPUs simulate multiple clients, each managing local head and tail models. To ensure standardized communication conditions, the bandwidth between the server and clients is fixed at 230 Mbps through simulation, similar to existing works [10,23].

Models and Datasets. We choose three representative open-source large language models, i.e., Qwen3-0.6b [42], LLaMA3.2-1b [8], and Qwen3-1.7b [42]. We perform experiments on three datasets. Each dataset corresponds to a different natural language generation (NLG) task, including structured data text generation (E2E [31]), mathematical reasoning (GSM8k [7]), and dialogue summary generation (Dialogsum [6]).

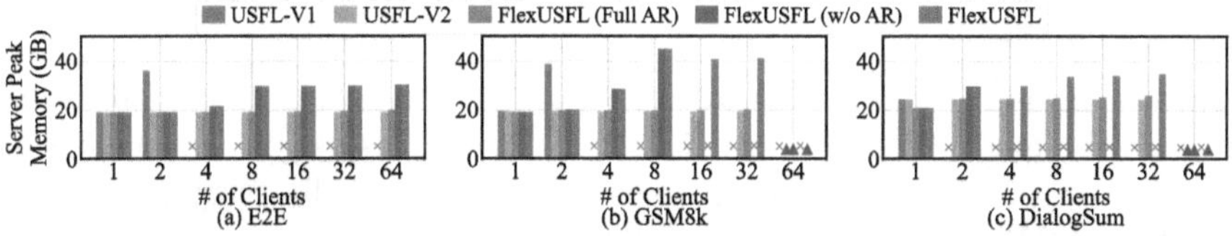

Fig. 5. Server GPU memory usage. "×" denotes server-side GPU OOM, and "△" indicates that our testbed could not simulate an excessive number of clients due to client-side GPU OOM.

Experimental Setup. For all models, we adopt a consistent partitioning scheme: the head and tail models, each consisting of two Transformer layers, are deployed on the client side, while the remaining layers are assigned to the main server as the trunk model. Maximum sequence lengths are 128 for E2E, 256 for GSM8K, and 512 for DialogSum. Each client performs 20 local iterations per communication round, followed by global aggregation of the head and tail models. Unless otherwise stated, we employ AdamW on both the client and server models with an initial learning rate of 5×10^{-5} and a local batch size of 4.

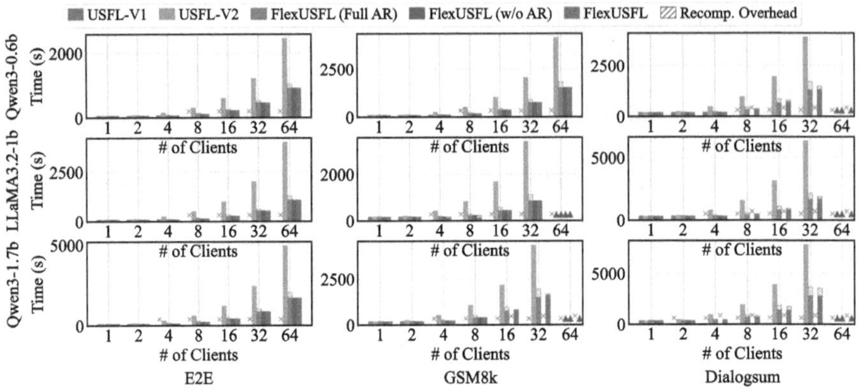

Fig. 6. Total time of five communication rounds (each round consisting of 20 local iterations for each client.

5.2 Results and Analysis

We evaluate the scalability of USFL architectures by assessing server memory consumption and time costs across three datasets. Experiments are conducted on three models with the number of clients varying from 1 to 64, with all results averaged over three runs. We compare the baselines (USFL-V1 and USFL-V2) against three variants of our proposed framework: (1) FlexUSFL (Full AR), which enforces exhaustive activation recomputation; (2) FlexUSFL (w/o AR), which disables recomputation entirely; and (3) FlexUSFL, which employs Dynamic Activation Management to adaptively balance memory and computation.

Memory consumption evaluation. Figure 5 illustrates the memory consumption for fine-tuning Qwen3-1.7 across three datasets. As the client count increases, USFL-V1 exhibits linear memory growth, rapidly triggering Out-Of-Memory (OOM) errors (e.g., at 4 clients for E2E and GSM8K, and at 2 clients for DialogSum). While FlexUSFL (w/o AR) mitigates parameter overhead via a single shared trunk, it remains susceptible to linear growth due to concurrent activation storage. Consequently, it triggers OOM at 16 clients for GSM8K and at 4 clients for DialogSum, as longer sequence lengths significantly amplify the activation footprint. In contrast, FlexUSFL (Full AR) maintains a stable, low footprint comparable to USFL-V2. By eliminating concurrent activation storage via recomputation, it effectively decouples memory usage from the client scale. Finally, FlexUSFL adopts Dynamic Activation Management to fully utilize the available server memory resources. Unlike FlexUSFL (Full AR) which minimizes memory usage aggressively, FlexUSFL deliberately retains activations up to a calculated safety threshold. Consequently, while it exhibits a higher memory footprint than the Full AR variant, it strictly enforces an upper bound to guarantee OOM-free execution under all client scales.

Table 2. Downstream task performance comparison (ROUGE-L-F1) of LLaMA3.2-1B on three datasets across varying client numbers ($N \in \{2, 16\}$)

Method	E2E		GSM8k		DialogSum	
	Clients = 2	Clients = 16	Clients = 2	Clients = 16	Clients = 2	Clients = 16
USFL-V1	0.7941	OOM	0.7163	OOM	0.6218	OOM
USFL-V2	0.7812	0.7866	0.7275	0.7066	0.6327	0.6001
FlexUSFL	0.7829	0.7839	0.7270	0.7012	0.6385	0.6061

Time Cost Evaluation. Figure 6 illustrates the training latency, with the dashed regions specifically denoting the recomputation overhead. USFL-V2 shows a sharp, near-linear increase due to synchronization bottlenecks; for instance, on LLaMA3.2-1B (Dialogsum, 5 rounds, 20 batches/round), its duration rises from 340.48 s (1 client) to 6335.39 s (32 clients). Notably, while USFL-V1 achieves low latency, it is severely constrained by OOM errors on a 48 GB GPU. Conversely, FlexUSFL demonstrates superior efficiency, increasing only from 330.98 s to 1883.82 s under the same conditions, thanks to delayed synchronization and gradient accumulation. Furthermore, while FlexUSFL (Full AR) maximizes memory savings, the computational overhead of exhaustive activation recomputation incurs a noticeable latency penalty (e.g., taking 2171.62 s at 32 clients, including 529.95 s of recomputation). Conversely, FlexUSFL completes the same task in 1883.82 s by dynamically limiting the recomputation overhead to just 207.69 s, proving the optimal efficiency of our dynamic activation policy.

Downstream Task Performance. We use ROUGE-L (F1) across all datasets to evaluate the generation quality. Table 2 presents the performance of LLaMA3.2-1B under 2-client and 16-client settings. while USFL-V1 fails with OOM errors beyond 2 clients, FlexUSFL achieves comparable generation quality to baselines, confirming that our optimizations (delayed synchronization and dynamic activation management) do not compromise learning capability.

Performance Under System Heterogeneity. To evaluate the performance of FlexUSFL under varying degrees of client heterogeneity, we constructed three client clusters by employing the delay simulation methodology from [10]. The detailed configurations are listed in Table 3. In this table, the values represent the Overall Lag Ratio relative to the baseline performance. Specifically, a ratio of 1.0 denotes the standard processing time without extra delay, while other values indicate the delay multiplier (e.g., a ratio of 2.0 implies that the client requires twice the baseline time to complete an iteration). By injecting delays based on these ratios, we simulate scenarios ranging from homogeneous environments to severe heterogeneity where stragglers exhibit 10× latency. To ensure a comprehensive evaluation, we compare FlexUSFL against adapted state-of-the-art methods tailored for heterogeneous environments: (1) MergeSFL, which migrates the Feature Merging and Batch Size Regulation mechanisms from [21] to the standard USFL architecture; and (2) FlexUSFL (SF), a straggler-aware

Table 3. Heterogeneous client cluster configurations, following the setup in [10].

Cluster ID	Heterogeneity Level	Overall Lag Ratio
Cluster 0	Mild Heterogeneity	1.0 : 1.2 : 1.4 : 1.6
Cluster 1	Moderate Heterogeneity	1.0 : 2.0 : 3.0 : 4.0
Cluster 2	Severe Heterogeneity	1.0 : 1.0 : 2.0 : 10.0

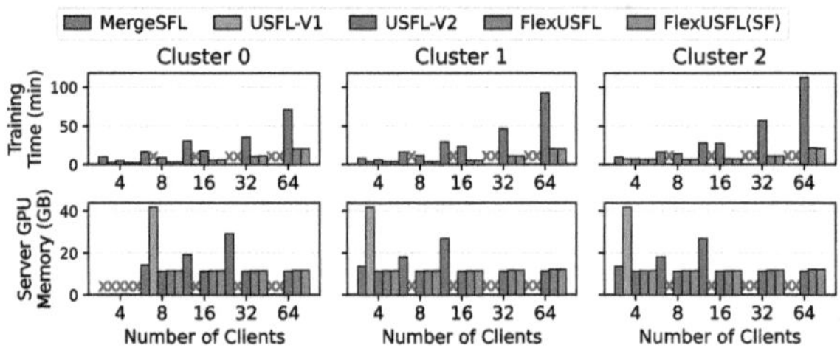

Fig. 7. Training time and server GPU memory overhead across varying heterogeneity levels. "×" indicates server OOM.

FlexUSFL variant that incorporates the "Straggler-First" scheduling strategy proposed in PipeSFL [10] into our dynamic framework to mitigate the impact of stragglers on global training time. Figure 7 presents the comparative results. FlexUSFL demonstrates superior overall efficiency: it maintains a consistently low server-side footprint comparable to USFL-V2, effectively resolving the OOM failures of USFL-V1, while simultaneously achieving significant speedups over the USFL-V2. Furthermore, MergeSFL's feature merging strategy aggregates client batches into a single large batch, significantly inflating peak memory usage and triggering OOM failures at scale (e.g., ≥ 32 clients). Regarding time efficiency, the "Straggler-First" strategy yields negligible gains. This is because USFL performance is dictated by server-side computation saturation; with the server pipeline already operating at full capacity, reordering client submissions offers limited scope for latency reduction.

6 Conclusion

This paper presents FlexUSFL, a novel U-shaped split federated learning framework that enhances scalability and efficiency for large language model fine-tuning. By integrating gradient accumulation with delayed synchronization, and dynamic activation management, FlexUSFL significantly reduces server memory overhead and training latency compared to existing USFL approaches. Experiments across diverse datasets and models confirm its superior performance.

Acknowledgments. This research is supported by the Fundamental and Interdisciplinary Disciplines Breakthrough Plan of the Ministry of Education of China (No.JYB2025XDXM103), Ningbo Natural Science Foundation (No.2025J033), Ningbo

Key Research and Development Program (No.2025Z190), the Young Scientists Fund of the National Natural Science Foundation of China (No.62502438). The author gratefully acknowledges the support of Zhejiang University Education Foundation Qizhen Scholar Foundation.

Note on AI Use. The technical solution and experimental design presented in this paper were independently completed by the authors. AI tools were used solely for language polishing and formatting optimization, and did not participate in the development of the research ideas or core content.

References

1. Abadi, M., et al.: Deep learning with differential privacy. In: Proceedings of the ACM SIGSAC Conference on Computer And Communications Security, pp. 308–318 (2016)
2. Bonawitz, K., et al.: Practical secure aggregation for privacy-preserving machine learning. In: proceedings of the 2017 ACM SIGSAC Conference on Computer and Communications Security, pp. 1175–1191 (2017)
3. Cao, L., Zhu, Y., Gong, W.: Sfprompt: communication-efficient split federated fine-tuning for large pre-trained models over resource-limited devices. arXiv:2407.17533 arXiv preprint (2024)
4. Chen, G., et al.: Unveiling the vulnerability of private fine-tuning in split-based frameworks for large language models: a bidirectionally enhanced attack. In: Proceedings of the ACM SIGSAC Conference on Computer and Communications Security, pp. 2904–2918 (2024)
5. Chen, X., Li, L., Ji, F., Wu, W.: Memory-efficient split federated learning for LLM fine-tuning on heterogeneous mobile devices. arXiv:2506.02940 (2025)
6. Chen, Y., Liu, Y., Chen, L., Zhang, Y.: Dialogsum: a real-life scenario dialogue summarization dataset. arXiv preprint arXiv:2105.06762 (2021)
7. Cobbe, K., et al.: Training verifiers to solve math word problems. arXiv:2110.14168 arXiv preprint (2021)
8. Dubey, A., et al.: The llama 3 herd of models. arXiv e-prints pp. arXiv–2407 (2024)
9. Feng, Y., Wang, Q., Xie, M., Shu, J.: From Bert to Chatgpt: challenges and technical development of storage systems for large model training. J. Comput. Res. Dev. **61**(4), 809–23 (2024)
10. Gao, Y., Hu, B., Mashhadi, M.B., Wang, W., Bennis, M.: Pipesfl: a fine-grained parallelization framework for split federated learning on heterogeneous clients. IEEE Trans. Mob. Comput. (2024)
11. Guo, C., et al.: Gmlake: efficient and transparent GPU memory defragmentation for large-scale DNN training with virtual memory stitching. In: Proceedings of the 29th ACM International Conference on Architectural Support for Programming Languages and Operating Systems, vol. 2, pp. 450–466 (2024)
12. Gupta, O., Raskar, R.: Distributed learning of deep neural network over multiple agents. J. Netw. Comput. Appl. **116**, 1–8 (2018)
13. Gururangan, S., et al.: Don't stop pretraining: adapt language models to domains and tasks. arXiv:2004.10964 arXiv preprint (2020)
14. Han, D.J., Bhatti, H.I., Lee, J., Moon, J.: Accelerating federated learning with split learning on locally generated losses. In: ICML 2021 Workshop on Federated Learning for User Privacy and Data Confidentiality. ICML Board (2021)

15. He, Q., et al.: Hourglass: enabling efficient split federated learning with data parallelism. In: Proceedings of the Twentieth European Conference on Computer Systems, pp. 1317–1333 (2025)
16. Hu, C., Li, B.: Menos: split fine-tuning large language models with efficient GPU memory sharing. In: Proceedings of the 25th International Middleware Conference, pp. 185–198 (2024)
17. Hu, E.J., et al.: Lora: low-rank adaptation of large language models. ICLR **1**(2), 3 (2022)
18. Huang, Y., et al.: Gpipe: efficient training of giant neural networks using pipeline parallelism. Adv. Neural Inf. Process. Syst. **32** (2019)
19. Lee, J., et al.: Biobert: a pre-trained biomedical language representation model for biomedical text mining. Bioinformatics **36**(4), 1234–1240 (2020)
20. Li, X.L., Liang, P.: Prefix-tuning: optimizing continuous prompts for generation. arXiv preprint arXiv:2101.00190 (2021)
21. Liao, Y., Xu, Y., Xu, H., Wang, L., Yao, Z., Qiao, C.: Mergesfl: split federated learning with feature merging and batch size regulation. In: 2024 IEEE 40th International Conference on Data Engineering (ICDE), pp. 2054–2067. IEEE (2024)
22. Lin, Z., et al.: Splitlora: a split parameter-efficient fine-tuning framework for large language models. arXiv preprint arXiv:2407.00952 (2024)
23. Lin, Z., Qu, G., Wei, W., Chen, X., Leung, K.K.: Adaptsfl: adaptive split federated learning in resource-constrained edge networks. arXiv:2403.13101 (2024)
24. Liu, G., et al.: ACESO: efficient parallel DNN training through iterative bottleneck alleviation. In: Proceedings of the European Conference on Computer Systems, pp. 163–181 (2024)
25. Liu, Z., Wang, Y., Wang, R., Wu, S.: Dualguard: a parameter space transformation approach for bidirectional defense in split-based LLM fine-tuning. In: Proceedings of the 63rd Annual Meeting of the Association for Computational Linguistics (Volume 1: Long Papers), pp. 17065–17080 (2025)
26. Lyu, S., Lin, Z., Qu, G., Chen, X., Huang, X., Li, P.: Optimal resource allocation for u-shaped parallel split learning. In: 2023 IEEE Globecom Workshops (GC Wkshps), pp. 197–202. IEEE (2023)
27. McMahan, B., Moore, E., Ramage, D., Hampson, S., y Arcas, B.A.: Communication-efficient learning of deep networks from decentralized data. In: Artificial Intelligence and Statistics, pp. 1273–1282. PMLR (2017)
28. Nair, S., Lin, M., Ju, P., Talebi, A., Bentley, E.S., Liu, J.: FSL-sage: accelerating federated split learning via smashed activation gradient estimation. In: Forty-second International Conference on Machine Learning (2025)
29. Narayanan, D., et al.: Pipedream: generalized pipeline parallelism for DNN training. In: Proceedings of the 27th ACM Symposium on Operating Systems Principles, pp. 1–15 (2019)
30. Nguyen, K., Khan, T., Michalas, A.: Split without a leak: Reducing privacy leakage in split learning. In: International Conference on Security and Privacy in Communication Systems, pp. 321–344. Springer (2023)
31. Novikova, J., Dušek, O., Rieser, V.: The e2e dataset: new challenges for end-to-end generation. arXiv:1706.09254 arXiv preprint (2017)
32. Ouyang, L., et al.: Training language models to follow instructions with human feedback. Adv. Neural. Inf. Process. Syst. **35**, 27730–27744 (2022)
33. Paverd, A., Martin, A., Brown, I.: Modelling and automatically analysing privacy properties for honest-but-curious adversaries. Tech. Rep (2014)

34. Poirot, M.G., Vepakomma, P., Chang, K., Kalpathy-Cramer, J., Gupta, R., Raskar, R.: Split learning for collaborative deep learning in healthcare. arXiv:1912.12115 arXiv preprint (2019)
35. Shen, X., et al.: A split-and-privatize framework for large language model fine-tuning. arXiv preprint arXiv:2312.15603 (2023)
36. Sun, X., Yang, T., Han, C., Lee, G.C., Sun, S.: An efficient and privacy-enhanced u-shaped split federated learning method for distributed multi-client systems. In: 2025 IEEE International Conference on Communications Workshops (ICC Workshops), pp. 1432–1437. IEEE (2025)
37. Thapa, C., Arachchige, P.C.M., Camtepe, S., Sun, L.: Splitfed: when federated learning meets split learning. In: Proceedings of the AAAI Conference on Artificial Intelligence, vol. 36, pp. 8485–8493 (2022)
38. Vepakomma, P., Gupta, O., Swedish, T., Raskar, R.: Split learning for health: Distributed deep learning without sharing raw patient data. arXiv:1812.00564 arXiv preprint (2018)
39. Wang, Y., Lin, Y., Zeng, X., Zhang, G.: Privatelora for efficient privacy preserving LLM. arXiv:2311.14030 arXiv preprint (2023)
40. Xia, Z., et al.: Multisfl: towards accurate split federated learning via multi-model aggregation and knowledge replay. In: Proceedings of the AAAI Conference on Artificial Intelligence, vol. 39, pp. 914–922 (2025)
41. Yan, B., et al.: On protecting the data privacy of large language models (LLMs): a survey. arXiv:2403.05156 arXiv preprint (2024)
42. Yang, A., et al.: Qwen3 technical report. arXiv preprint arXiv:2505.09388 (2025)
43. Yang, Z., et al.: Robust split federated learning for u-shaped medical image networks. arXiv:2212.06378 arXiv preprint (2022)
44. Zhang, S., Zhao, Z., Liu, D., Cao, Y., Tang, H., You, S.: Edge-assisted u-shaped split federated learning with privacy-preserving for internet of things. Expert Syst. Appl. **262**, 125494 (2025)
45. Zhao, K., Yang, Z., Huang, C., Chen, X., Zhang, Z.: FEDSLLM: federated split learning for large language models over communication networks. In: 2024 International Conference on Ubiquitous Communication (Ucom), pp. 438–443. IEEE (2024)
46. Zhao, Z., Liu, D., Cao, Y., Chen, T., Zhang, S., Tang, H.: U-shaped split federated learning: an efficient cross-device learning framework with enhanced privacy-preserving. In: 2023 9th International Conference on Computer and Communications (ICCC), pp. 2182–2186. IEEE (2023)

SAW3D: A Performance-Portable Solver for Compressible Turbulence at the $\mathcal{O}(10^{10})$-Cell Scale on Heterogeneous Supercomputers

Siyue Chen, Junshi Chen, Yang Zhao, Yunchi Deng, Yi Zhang, Hong An(✉), and Juchun Ding

University of Science and Technology of China, Hefei, China
{daffodils7,yang_zhao,dyc20030501,yi_zhang}@mail.ustc.edu.cn,
{cjuns,han,djc}@ustc.edu.cn

Abstract. Compressible turbulent mixing is a fundamental phenomenon in high-energy-density systems, including hypersonic propulsion, inertial confinement fusion, and astrophysical flows, where accurate simulation demands simultaneous resolution of strong shocks, material interfaces, and fine-scale turbulent structures. We present SAW3D, a performance-portable solver for large-scale compressible turbulent mixing on heterogeneous supercomputers. SAW3D migrates performance-critical kernels to portable C++ with Kokkos, enabling single-source deployment across HIP, CUDA, and OpenMP backends. It introduces direction-wise shared-memory tiling to confine halo padding to one dimension under on-chip memory constraints, and a device-resident execution pipeline that fuses operators to eliminate redundant host–device transfers between Runge–Kutta sub-steps. To scale to large clusters, SAW3D adopts a three-dimensional Cartesian decomposition with staged face-wise halo exchange and asynchronous computation–communication overlap, reducing inter-node overhead on the critical path. Experiments demonstrate 48×–101× speedup over the CPU baseline, with strong-scaling efficiency above 80% and weak-scaling efficiency exceeding 95% up to $\mathcal{O}(10^{10})$ grid cells on 2,048 DCUs, completing each time step in 6.0 s.

Keywords: Heterogeneous computing · Performance portability · Stencil optimization · Domain decomposition

1 Introduction

Compressible turbulent mixing is a fundamental phenomenon in high-energy-density systems, including hypersonic propulsion, inertial confinement fusion, and astrophysical flows [29,30]. These flows encompass shock structures with Mach numbers reaching tens to hundreds, coupled with turbulent fluctuations spanning more than ten orders of magnitude in Reynolds number [9,22], posing severe challenges to both subgrid-scale closure models and shock-capturing schemes for the compressible Navier–Stokes equations.

L. Eeckhout et al. (Eds.): APPT 2026, LNCS 16693, pp. 298–310, 2027.
https://doi.org/10.1007/978-981-92-4805-6_20

Accurate simulation requires simultaneously resolving strong shocks, material interfaces, and fine-scale turbulent structures. High-order schemes such as WENO and WCNS [11,16] face an inherent accuracy–stability trade-off under strong shock–turbulence interactions [4,17,24]. More critically, conventional CFD solvers designed for homogeneous CPU clusters expose significant bottlenecks on GPU-based heterogeneous nodes: frequent host–device synchronization suppresses GPU occupancy, and stencil kernels fail to exploit on-chip shared memory without explicit tiling, resulting in poor portability, low memory efficiency, and limited scalability [5].

Frontier platforms such as **Dongfang** provide the necessary computational horsepower, yet realized utilization typically falls below 10% of peak without targeted optimization. Closing this gap raises three interrelated challenges. First, fragmented backends (HIP, CUDA, OpenMP) make single-backend solvers non-portable across heterogeneous architectures. Second, wide memory-bound stencils combined with frequent host–device synchronization severely suppress GPU occupancy and on-chip data reuse. Third, one-dimensional decomposition causes $\mathcal{O}(N^2)$ halo scaling, while naïve three-dimensional decomposition introduces diagonal exchanges that sit on the critical communication path.

To address these challenges, this paper presents **SAW3D**, a performance-portable solver for compressible turbulent mixing on heterogeneous supercomputers, with the following contributions.

- We develop SAW3D on Kokkos to achieve zero-modification deployment across OpenMP, HIP, and CUDA backends, delivering 48×–101× end-to-end speedup over the single-core CPU baseline across NVIDIA and DCU platforms, and strong scaling to 2,048 DCUs on the Dongfang cluster.
- We optimize single-node stencil kernel efficiency and GPU execution continuity through direction-wise shared-memory tiling and a device-resident operator fusion pipeline, targeting the stencil-dominated operators that account for approximately 70% of per-step runtime.
- We design a scalable communication strategy that keeps inter-node overhead off the critical execution path at the $\mathcal{O}(10^{10})$-cell scale, combining three-dimensional Cartesian decomposition, staged face-wise halo exchange, and asynchronous computation–communication overlap.

2 Background

2.1 Numerical Methods

High-fidelity simulation of compressible turbulent mixing requires solving the three-dimensional multicomponent compressible Navier–Stokes equations [1,9], with inviscid, viscous, and diffusive fluxes all evaluated at every Runge–Kutta sub-step. SAW3D discretizes inviscid fluxes via WCNS [31], which adaptively balances dissipation near discontinuities with high-order accuracy in smooth regions. Each spatial direction employs a six-point $[-2, +3]$ stencil, yielding 108 global-memory reads per grid point with no inter-direction reuse. Viscous and diffusive fluxes use central finite differences; time advancement uses a third-order TVD Runge–Kutta scheme [25] with three sub-steps per physical time step. These characteristics—a wide memory-bound stencil and three operator invocations per step—directly motivate the optimizations of Sect. 3.

2.2 The Dongfang Supercomputing Platform

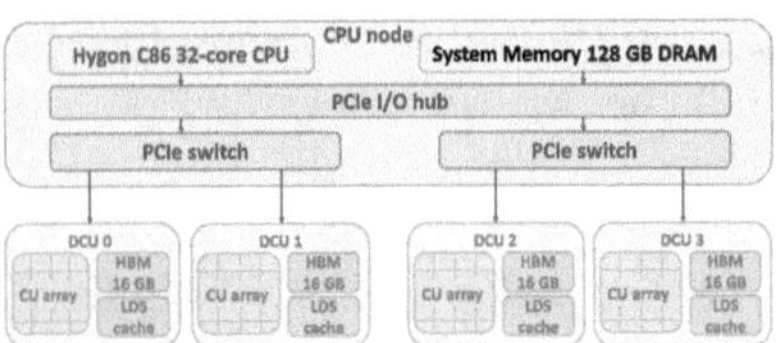

Fig. 1. Architecture of a single Dongfang compute node.

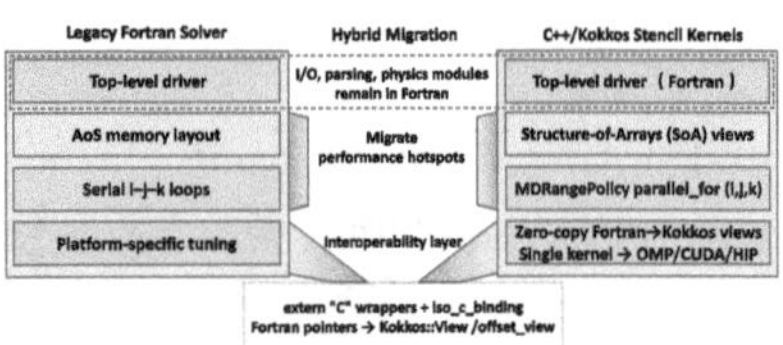

Fig. 2. Hybrid Fortran+Kokkos migration strategy.

The Dongfang supercomputer [28] comprises approximately 7,100 CPU+DCU nodes interconnected via 200 Gb/s HDR InfiniBand, yielding 200 PFLOPS peak throughput. As illustrated in Fig. 1, each node pairs a Hygon C86 7185 processor with four HYGON D160A1 DCU accelerators via PCIe. The DCU shares the same architectural class as AMD GPUs, uses HIP as its programming interface, and delivers 7 TFLOPS double-precision performance with 1,600 GB/s memory bandwidth.

2.3 Related Work

High-order CFD solvers have been successfully ported to GPUs: STREAmS [2] and URANOS [8] demonstrated scalable multi-GPU DNS performance, and HyPar [18] scaled to 1024^3 grids on 1,024 V100 GPUs. However, all are tied to CUDA and cannot be directly migrated to AMD or DCU hardware, as architectural differences require kernel-level tuning amounting to redevelopment [7,26].

Performance-portable models address this gap: studies of Kokkos, OpenMP, and HIP [3,6,10] confirm cross-backend deployment, and solvers such as Neko [15] and OpenSBLI [23] demonstrate practical value. Nevertheless, high-order stencil kernels still require manual shared-memory tuning [14,27], and sub-step operator fusion remains largely unaddressed [13,20].

At large process counts, one-dimensional slab decompositions produce $\mathcal{O}(N^2)$ halo scaling [21]; 3D Cartesian decompositions reduce this to $\mathcal{O}(N^{4/3})$ but naively increase neighbors to 26 [2,18]. MPI–GPU overlap is well established [12,21] but typically applied only within one-dimensional layouts.

No prior work has simultaneously closed all three gaps: CUDA-specific solvers sacrifice portability, portable frameworks leave stencil efficiency to the developer,

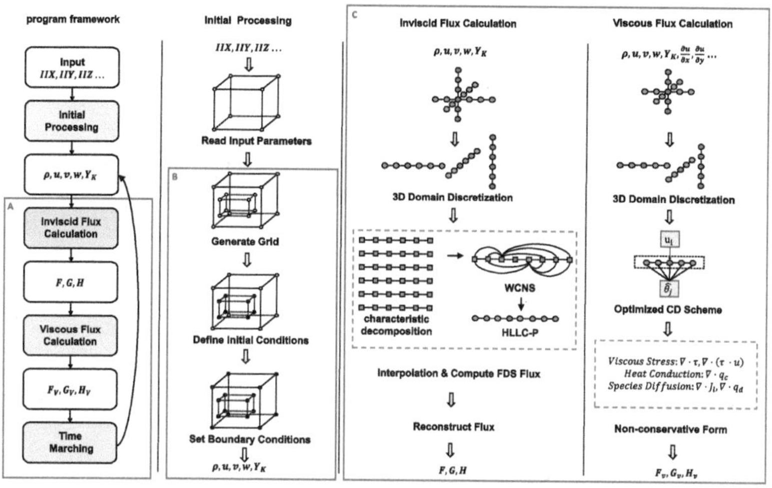

Fig. 3. High-level workflow of SAW3D and major optimization targets: (A) time-marching loop with Kokkos-migrated stencil kernels, (B) 3D domain decomposition for scalable halo exchange, and (C) detailed computation graphs for inviscid and viscous flux operators targeted by shared-memory tiling and direction-wise restructuring. Here ρ, u, v, w denote density and velocity components, Y_k the species mass fraction, F, G, H the inviscid fluxes, and F_v, G_v, H_v the viscous fluxes in the x-, y-, z-directions, respectively.

and scalable 3D decomposition has not been integrated with wide-stencil multi-component CFD at the $\mathcal{O}(10^{10})$-cell scale. SAW3D addresses all three in a single framework.

3 Optimization Methodology

3.1 Kokkos-Based Portable Kernel Migration

SAW3D follows the time-marching workflow in Fig. 3. Each physical time step comprises three TVD-RK3 sub-steps, each invoking inviscid and viscous flux evaluation before updating the conserved state. Profiling confirms that stencil-dominated operators account for approximately 70% of per-step wall-clock time: the WCNS operator evaluates fluxes independently in each direction, reloading overlapping stencil data from global memory with no inter-direction reuse, yielding bandwidth-bound execution on both CPUs and GPUs.

To achieve portability across hardware platforms, SAW3D retains the validated Fortran physics layer unchanged, refactoring only the six performance-critical stencil kernels into portable C++ via Kokkos [19]. As shown in Fig. 2, migrated kernels adopt a structure-of-arrays (SoA) layout to maximize coalesced bandwidth utilization. Execution parallelism is exposed through `MDRangePolicy`, mapping the (i, j, k) iteration space onto thread teams tuned per backend to saturate hardware occupancy. Interoperability with the Fortran

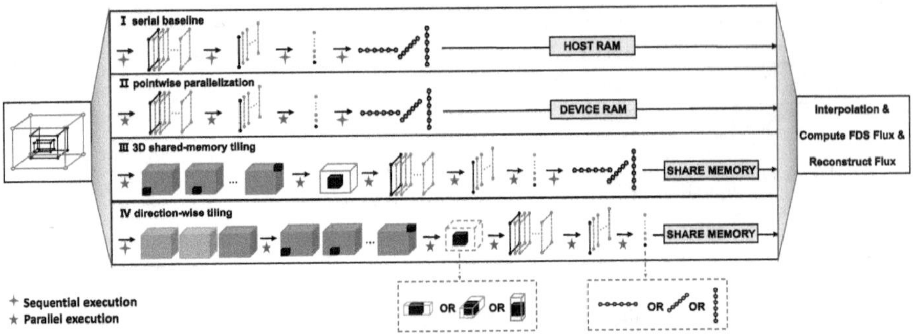

Fig. 4. Four-stage evolution of stencil flux computation: (I) serial baseline, (II) `MDRangePolicy` parallelization, (III) 3D shared-memory tiling constrained by per-block capacity, and (IV) direction-wise tiling enlarging the effective tile by 4.7× under identical hardware constraints.

control layer uses C-compatible wrappers with `DualView` synchronization outside all performance-critical loops.

3.2 Reducing Memory Traffic via Hierarchical Tiling and Device-Resident Execution

Direction-Wise Stencil Tiling. With a portable execution substrate established, we turn to the dominant per-node cost: global memory traffic in stencil kernels. The WCNS $[-2, +3]$ stencil yields 108 global-memory reads per grid point across three directions with no inter-direction reuse. We address this through four design stages (Fig. 4).

Stage I: Serial Baseline. Each grid point independently loads its full six-point stencil neighborhood from global memory with no data sharing between neighboring points. Arithmetic intensity remains far below the Roofline ridge point, leaving the kernel entirely bandwidth-bound. This stage serves as the performance baseline for all subsequent optimizations.

Stage II: `MDRangePolicy` Parallelization. Replacing the serial loop nest with Kokkos `MDRangePolicy` distributes grid points across GPU threads, achieving thread-level parallelism without code restructuring. However, the memory access pattern remains unchanged: neighboring threads still repeatedly fetch overlapping stencil footprints from global memory, leaving the kernel bandwidth-bound. The performance gain over Stage I is attributable solely to increased parallelism, not improved memory efficiency.

Stage III: 3D Shared-Memory Tiling. Thread teams cooperatively load stencil halos into shared memory, enabling intra-tile reuse across all three spatial directions simultaneously. However, supporting x-, y-, and z-direction stencils within a single kernel requires maintaining halo regions in all three dimensions, inflating the scratch-memory footprint to $\mathcal{O}((\texttt{tile} + 5)^3)$. With 48 bytes per point, the 64 KB shared-memory limit of the DCU constrains the tile to at most 216 active points—severely limiting SM occupancy and leaving a large fraction of compute units idle.

Stage IV: Direction-Wise Tiling. We observe that the three spatial directions in WCNS flux evaluation are mutually independent: the x-flux depends only on x-direction neighbors, and likewise for y and z. This structure enables decomposing the monolithic stencil kernel into three dedicated directional kernels, each responsible for a single flux direction.

Within each directional kernel, halo padding is required along only one dimension, reducing the scratch-memory footprint from $\mathcal{O}((\texttt{tile} + 5)^3)$ to $\mathcal{O}((\texttt{tile}_d + 5) \cdot \texttt{tile}_\perp^2)$, where $\texttt{tile}_d$ is the tile extent along the active direction and $\texttt{tile}_\perp$ is the tile extent in the two transverse directions. Under the same 64 KB constraint with $\texttt{tile}_\perp = 8$, the active tile grows to $16 \times 8 \times 8 = 1{,}024$ points—a 4.7× increase over Stage III. The larger tile directly translates to higher shared-memory reuse: stencil neighbors loaded once by the thread team are reused across all threads within the tile, substantially reducing redundant global-memory traffic.

Critically, the three serial kernel launches introduced by this decomposition incur no idle cycles at production mesh sizes. Each directional kernel fully saturates DCU compute units independently, so the sequential launch overhead is negligible. The end-to-end performance gain over Stage III originates entirely from the increased shared-memory reuse enabled by the reduced per-direction halo footprint, not from additional parallelism.

Device-Resident Execution Pipeline. Direction-wise tiling eliminates redundant traffic within kernels; a complementary overhead operates between them. In the original Fortran control flow, every Runge–Kutta operator synchronizes tensors host-to-device on entry and device-to-host on exit, accumulating 110 redundant transfers per sub-step and suppressing sustained GPU utilization.

We adopt a device-resident model: intermediate tensors never leave the device between operators. A single upload at sub-step entry transfers halo fields; the complete operator chain executes as a fused on-device sequence; the conserved state is downloaded once at sub-step exit for MPI exchange. This eliminates 50.9% of all synchronization events. Two compounding benefits follow: L2-resident tile data written by one directional kernel are reused by the next, extending temporal locality across kernel boundaries; and continuous on-device execution sustains a bandwidth-limited regime throughout each sub-step.

3.3 Reducing Communication Cost via Cartesian Decomposition and Asynchronous Overlap

Three-Dimensional Domain Decomposition. The optimizations above maximize per-node kernel throughput, but inter-node communication cost grows

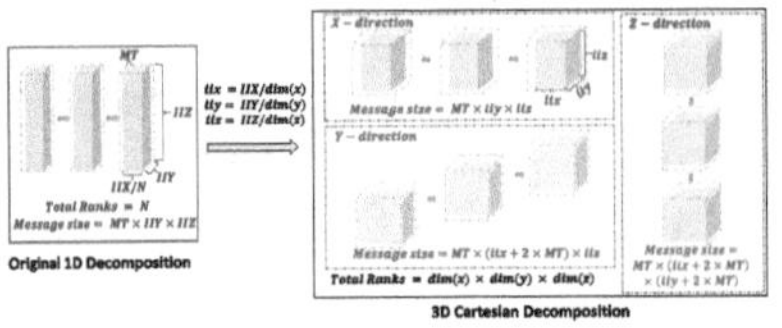

Fig. 5. One-dimensional slab decomposition (left) versus the proposed three-dimensional Cartesian decomposition (right).

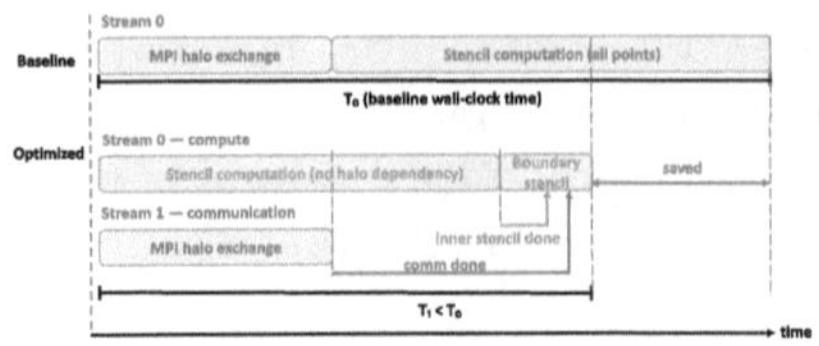

Fig. 6. Execution timeline for the baseline schedule (top) and the proposed overlap strategy (bottom).

independently and can dominate wall-clock time at large process counts. The original one-dimensional slab decomposition produces $\mathcal{O}(N^2)$ halo-to-interior scaling along a single congested axis. We replace it with a $P_x \times P_y \times P_z$ Cartesian decomposition (Fig. 5), reducing per-process halo volume to $\mathcal{O}(N^{4/3})$ with each rank communicating exclusively with six face-adjacent neighbors.

A naïve 3D decomposition requires diagonal exchanges increasing neighbors to 26. We avoid this with a staged face-wise scheme exchanging ghost layers sequentially in x, y, z: after the x-exchange, y-direction send buffers automatically contain the x-ghost data needed for edge cells; the z-exchange populates corners by the same mechanism—all without explicit diagonal messages.

Computation–Communication Overlap. The 3D decomposition reduces communication volume; we further remove it from the critical path. WCNS interpolation depends on ghost data only at a thin boundary shell; interior points—whose stencil footprint lies entirely within the local subdomain—carry no such dependency. This static partition, computed once at initialization, enables a three-phase schedule (Fig. 6): launch the interior kernel immediately; overlap the staged halo exchange concurrently; dispatch six boundary-shell kernels once both complete, with ordering enforced via `Kokkos::fence`.

The fraction of interpolation work hidden behind communication is

$$\eta_{\text{overlap}} = \frac{(N_x - MT)(N_y - MT)(N_z - MT)}{(N_x + 4)(N_y + 4)(N_z + 4)}, \tag{1}$$

where N_x, N_y, N_z are the per-process interior subdomain extents. The denominator counts the total number of points at which an interpolated value must be produced: besides the N interior points, the two outer layers on each side (the $[-2, +2]$ neighbourhood consumed by the subsequent flux computation) must also be interpolated, giving $N + 4$ per direction. In the numerator, $MT = 5$ is the WCNS $[-2, +3]$ stencil span minus one: producing the interpolated value at a single point requires its six-point $[-2, +3]$ neighbourhood, so the five layers nearest each subdomain boundary depend on communicated ghost data and are excluded from the overlappable interior phase. Hence η_{overlap} is the ratio of communication-independent interior points to the total set of points requiring interpolation, with concrete values reported in Sect. 4.4.

4 Performance Evaluation

4.1 Experimental Platforms and Setup

We evaluate SAW3D on three heterogeneous platforms: (i) an NVIDIA A100 node, (ii) an NVIDIA P40 node, and (iii) the Dongfang DCU node equipped with HYGON D160A1 accelerators. Table 1 summarizes the hardware configuration and software toolchain on each system. The A100 and P40 nodes share the same host CPU model, isolating GPU architectural differences from host-side variation.

Table 1. Hardware and software configuration.

	NVIDIA P40	NVIDIA A100 PCIe	HYGON DCU D160A1
Host CPU	Intel Xeon Platinum 8358		Hygon C86 7185
Memory (GiB)	24	40	16
Peak FP64 (TFLOPS)	0.37	9.7	7.0
Peak BW (GB/s)	346	1555	1600
Compiler	CUDA 12.2	CUDA 12.4	ROCm 4.3
Profiler	Nsight Compute		rocprof

Table 2. Pointwise CPU–GPU error norms across all CPU-feasible grid sizes.

Norm	ρ	u	v	w	p	Y_k
L_2	$< 10^{-12}$	$< 10^{-12}$	$< 10^{-12}$	$< 10^{-12}$	$< 10^{-12}$	$< 10^{-12}$
L_∞	$< 10^{-12}$	$< 10^{-12}$	$< 10^{-12}$	$< 10^{-12}$	$< 10^{-12}$	$< 10^{-12}$

4.2 End-to-End Performance

We evaluate end-to-end solver performance on a single GPU using a $160 \times 64 \times 64$ double-precision grid. Each run consists of 10 warm-up steps followed by 100 timed iterations; all simulation data remain device-resident to exclude PCIe and driver overhead. Three implementation stages are compared: the CPU baseline (original Fortran solver, single core), the initial GPU port (Kokkos migration with `MDRangePolicy` parallelism only, prior to any shared-memory or pipeline optimization), and the fully optimized version incorporating all techniques of Sect. 3. The $160 \times 64 \times 64$ grid is used here to isolate per-kernel optimization effects; large-scale multi-GPU results are reported in Sect. 4.3.

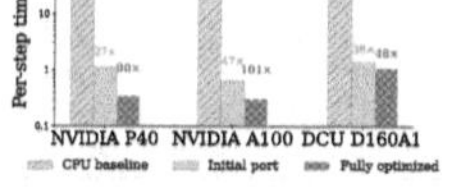

Fig. 7. Per-step wall-clock time on three platforms ($160 \times 64 \times 64$ grid, single GPU).

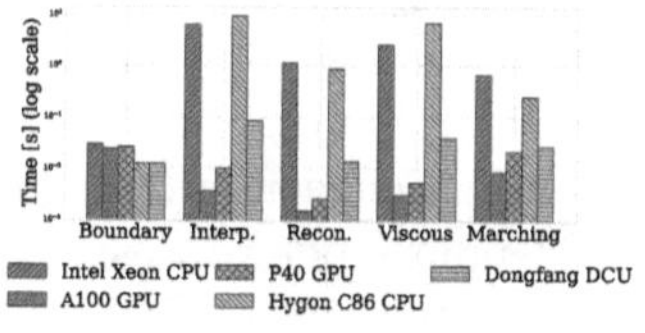

Fig. 8. Kernel-level timing breakdown on three platforms ($160 \times 64 \times 64$ grid, single GPU, fully optimized).

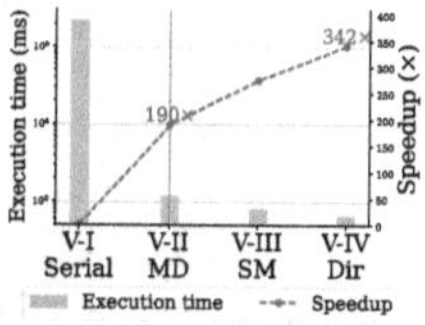

Fig. 9. Interpolation kernel performance across optimization stages on the DCU platform ($344 \times 152 \times 152$ grid).

Figure 7 reports per-step wall-clock time and speedup across the three implementation stages on all three platforms. The initial GPU port delivers 27–47×

speedup over the CPU baseline via `MDRangePolicy` parallelism; the fully optimized version achieves a further 2–3× improvement, confirming that shared-memory tiling, device-resident execution, and communication restructuring must be applied jointly to approach hardware performance ceilings. The A100 achieves the highest absolute speedup (101×), while the DCU reaches 48× relative to its own CPU baseline, with the lower ratio partly attributable to the HIP/ROCm software stack maturity gap relative to CUDA (see Table 1).

Figure 8 decomposes the fully optimized per-step runtime across all three platforms. Stencil-dominated kernels dominate runtime and benefit most from shared-memory tiling; `Boundary_condition` shows limited single-GPU variation as its gains manifest only under MPI traffic.

4.3 Scalability

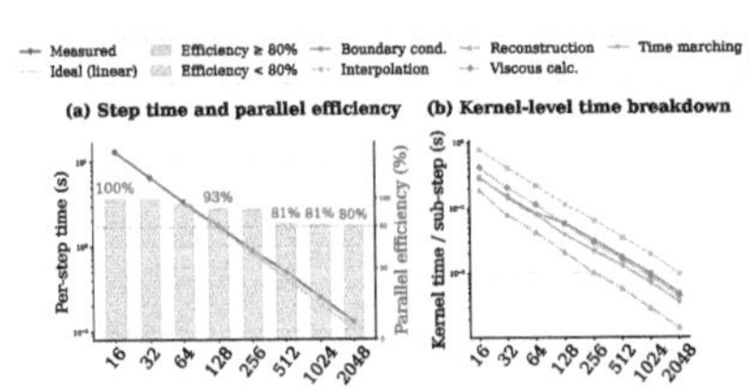

Fig. 10. Strong scaling (864 × 384 × 384, 16–2,048 DCUs): **(a)** per-step time and parallel efficiency; **(b)** kernel time per sub-step.

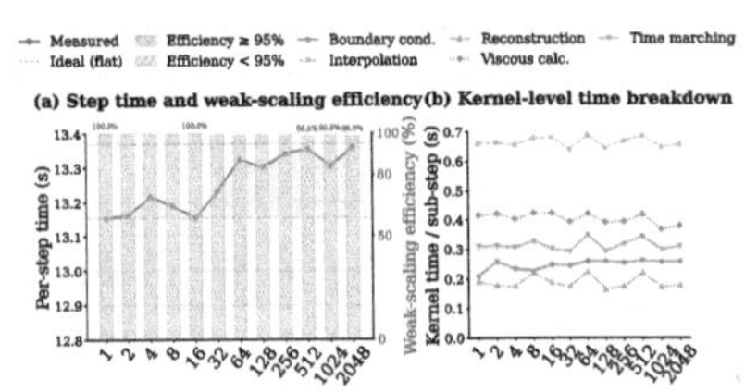

Fig. 11. Weak scaling (8×10^6 points per process, 1–2,048 DCUs): **(a)** per-step time and weak-scaling efficiency; **(b)** kernel time per sub-step.

Strong-scaling efficiency is defined relative to the 16-DCU configuration: $E(P) = T(16)/T(P) \cdot 16/P$. As shown in Fig. 10(a), efficiency remains above 96% up to 64 DCUs and degrades to 80% at 2,048 DCUs; the steeper drop between 256 and 512 DCUs reflects subdomains becoming too small to saturate DCU compute units. All five kernels scale consistently (Fig. 10(b)).

As shown in Fig. 11, weak-scaling efficiency $E_{\text{weak}}(P) = T(16)/T(P) \times 100\%$ with workload fixed at 8×10^6 points per process: per-step time increases by only 4.6% from 13.15 s to 13.76 s across 16 to 2,048 DCUs (Fig. 11(a)), while all kernels remain flat (Fig. 11(b)).

Table 3. Kernel timing for a single RK sub-step, $\mathcal{O}(10^{10})$-cell scale (3,840 × 1,728 × 1,728, 2,048 DCUs).

Kernel	Time (s)	Frac. (%)
Boundary cond.	0.178	16.8
Interpolation	0.426	40.2
Reconstr. flux	0.087	8.2
Viscous calc.	0.222	20.9
Time marching	0.147	13.9
Total	1.059	100

Table 4. Combined interpolation + boundary time with/without overlap (DCU, 8×10^6 points per process).

Procs	Baseline (s)	Overlap (s)	Red.
16	1.08	0.85	21.3%
32	1.06	0.84	20.8%
64	1.11	0.83	25.2%
128	1.19	0.89	25.2%
256	1.11	0.84	24.3%
512	1.17	0.87	25.6%
1024	1.12	0.85	24.1%

On the full 2,048-DCU partition, the 3,840 × 1,728 × 1,728 mesh completes each step in 6.0 s, with `Boundary_condition` accounting for only 16.8% of sub-step time (Table 3), confirming inter-node overhead stays off the critical path at $\mathcal{O}(10^{10})$ cells.

4.4 Optimization Breakdown

Stencil Kernel Optimization (Version I–IV). Figure 9 reports interpolation kernel time across four stages (344 × 152 × 152, DCU). Version II (`MDRangePolicy`) reduces execution time by over two orders of magnitude. Versions III and IV further reduce global-memory traffic and increase SM occupancy via shared-memory and direction-wise tiling.

Device-resident Execution Pipeline. Table 5 shows 44–47% per-step reduction across all platforms. Near-identical ratios confirm the overhead originates from synchronization latency, consistent with the 50.9% reduction in sync events (Sect. 3.2).

Table 5. Per-step time before/after device-resident pipeline (160×64×64, single accelerator).

Platform	Sync. (s)	Dev.-res. (s)	Red.
P40	1.143	0.612	46.5%
A100	0.657	0.346	47.3%
DCU	1.800	1.000	44.4%

Table 6. Communication time before/after 3D decomposition (DCU platform).

Processes	Grid	1D (s)	3D (s)	Red.
16	864 × 384 × 384	0.482	0.286	40.7%
32	864 × 384 × 384	0.392	0.154	60.8%
64	864 × 384 × 384	0.286	0.082	71.3%
64	1296 × 576 × 576	1.831	0.236	87.1%

3D Cartesian Domain Decomposition. Table 6 shows communication time reduction growing from 40.7% at 16 processes to 71.3% at 64 processes on the 864 × 384 × 384 grid, and reaching 87.1% on the larger 1296 × 576 × 576 grid at 64 processes.

Computation–Communication Overlap. The overlap strategy reduces combined `interpolation` + `boundary_condition` time by 20–26% consistently across 16 to 1,024 processes (Table 4), fully hiding halo exchange behind interior interpolation. Because the weak-scaling workload fixes each rank at $\approx 8 \times 10^6$ points, the per-rank subdomain size is essentially invariant, so Eq. 1 yields a nearly constant overlappable fraction η_{overlap} in the range 86.5%–87.3% across 16 to 1,024 processes (e.g. 87.3% for the $4 \times 2 \times 2$ decomposition at 16 processes, $216 \times 192 \times 192$ per rank). This confirms that roughly seven-eighths of the interpolation work resides in the overlappable interior, consistent with the measured time reductions above.

4.5 Numerical Verification

All flow variables are initialized with a deterministic field generator and advanced one complete time step on both CPU and GPU implementations. All variables agree within double-precision round-off (10^{-13}–10^{-12} in L_2 and L_∞, Table 2). Extended runs of 1,000 steps confirm errors remain bounded and do not accumulate, validating the Kokkos kernel layer and Fortran–C++ interoperability layer.

5 Conclusion

SAW3D addresses three interrelated challenges for high-fidelity compressible turbulence on heterogeneous supercomputers: cross-backend portability, per-node stencil memory efficiency, and large-scale communication scalability. Direction-wise shared-memory tiling enlarges the effective tile by 4.7×; a device-resident pipeline eliminates 50.9% of synchronization events; and three-dimensional Cartesian decomposition with staged halo exchange and asynchronous overlap reduces boundary communication by up to 87%. Together, these yield 48×–101× end-to-end speedup over the CPU baseline and sustain above 80% strong-scaling efficiency at 2,048 DCUs on a $\mathcal{O}(10^{10})$-cell mesh.

Future work will explore adaptive load balancing, further overlap of global MPI reductions with stencil computation, and extension to additional backends.

Acknowledgments. The authors would like to thank their colleagues at the Advanced Computer Systems Architecture (ACSA) Laboratory, University of Science and Technology of China, for valuable discussions and support. The numerical experiments were performed on the Dongfang supercomputer (also known as the ORISE supercomputing platform), whose computational resources are gratefully acknowledged.

Disclosure of Interests. The authors have no competing interests to declare that are relevant to the content of this article.

Use of AI Tools. The technical solution and experimental design presented in this paper were independently completed by the authors. AI tools were used solely for language polishing and formatting optimization, and did not participate in the development of the research ideas or core content.

References

1. Abgrall, R., Karni, S.: Computations of compressible multifluids. J. Comput. Phys. **169**(2), 594–623 (2001). https://doi.org/10.1006/jcph.2000.6685
2. Bernardini, M., Modesti, D., Salvadore, F., Pirozzoli, S.: STREAmS: a high-fidelity accelerated solver for direct numerical simulation of compressible turbulent flows. Comput. Phys. Commun. **263**, 107906 (2021). https://doi.org/10.1016/j.cpc.2021.107906
3. Briand, L., Jourdren, H., Pérache, M.: Julia versus C++ Kokkos for performance portable crtesian CFD solvers on heterogeneous architectures. Int. J. High Perform. Comput. Appl. **39**(4) (2025). https://doi.org/10.1177/10943420251341179
4. Chapelier, J.B., et al.: Comparison of high-order numerical methodologies for the simulation of the supersonic Taylor-Green vortex flow. Phys. Fluids **36**(5), 055146 (2024). https://doi.org/10.1063/5.0206359
5. Chen, C.H., Donzis, D.A.: Shock-turbulence interactions at high turbulence intensities. J. Fluid Mech. **870**, 813–847 (2019). https://doi.org/10.1017/jfm.2019.248
6. Dai, Z., Deng, L., Che, Y., Li, M., Zhang, J., Wang, Y.: Evaluating performance portability of five shared-memory programming models using a high-order unstructured CFD solver. J. Parallel Distributed Comput. **187**, 104831 (2024). https://doi.org/10.1016/j.jpdc.2023.104831
7. Davis, J.H., et al.: Taking GPU programming models to task for performance portability. In: Proceedings of the 39th ACM International Conference on Supercomputing (ICS '25) (2025). https://doi.org/10.1145/3721145.3730423
8. De Vanna, F., et al.: URANOS: a GPU accelerated Navier-Stokes solver for compressible wall-bounded flows. Comput. Phys. Commun. **287**, 108717 (2023). https://doi.org/10.1016/j.cpc.2023.108717
9. Dimonte, G., et al.: A comparative study of the turbulent Rayleigh-Taylor instability using high-resolution three-dimensional numerical simulations: the Alpha-Group collaboration. Phys. Fluids **16**(5), 1668–1693 (2004). https://doi.org/10.1063/1.1688328
10. Eichstädt, J., Vymazal, M., Moxey, D., Peiró, J.: A comparison of the shared-memory parallel programming models OpenMP, OpenACC and Kokkos in the context of implicit solvers for high-order FEM. Comput. Phys. Commun. **255**, 107245 (2020). https://doi.org/10.1016/j.cpc.2020.107245
11. Fu, L.: Review of the high-order TENO schemes for compressible gas dynamics and turbulence. Archives Comput. Methods Eng. **30**, 2493–2526 (2023). https://doi.org/10.1007/s11831-022-09877-7
12. Ghioldi, F., Piscaglia, F.: A hybrid CPU-GPU paradigm to accelerate reactive CFD simulations. Int. J. Numer. Meth. Fluids **96**(8), 1461–1488 (2024). https://doi.org/10.1002/fld.5297
13. Gysi, T., Grosser, T., Hoefler, T.: MODESTO: data-centric analytic optimization of complex stencil programs on heterogeneous architectures. In: Proceedings of the 29th ACM International Conference on Supercomputing (ICS '15), pp. 177–186 (2015). https://doi.org/10.1145/2751205.2751223
14. Howard, M., et al.: Towards performance portability in a compressible CFD code. In: 23rd AIAA Computational Fluid Dynamics Conference. No. AIAA 2017-4407 (2017). https://doi.org/10.2514/6.2017-4407
15. Jansson, N., Karp, M., Podobas, A., Markidis, S., Schlatter, P.: Neko: a modern, portable, and scalable framework for high-fidelity computational fluid dynamics. arXiv preprint arXiv:2107.01243 (2021). https://arxiv.org/abs/2107.01243

16. Jiang, G.S., Shu, C.W.: Efficient implementation of weighted ENO schemes. J. Comput. Phys. **126**(1), 202–228 (1996). https://doi.org/10.1006/jcph.1996.0130
17. Johnsen, E., et al.: Assessment of high-resolution methods for numerical simulations of compressible turbulence with shock waves. J. Comput. Phys. **229**(4), 1213–1237 (2010). https://doi.org/10.1016/j.jcp.2009.10.028
18. Kim, Y., Ghosh, D., Constantinescu, E.M., Balakrishnan, R.: GPU-accelerated DNS of compressible turbulent flows. Comput. Fluids **251**, 105744 (2023). https://doi.org/10.1016/j.compfluid.2022.105744
19. Kokkos Development Team: Kokkos (2023). https://github.com/kokkos/kokkos. Accessed 31 Mar 2023
20. Kronawitter, S., Lengauer, C.: Polyhedral search space exploration in the ExaStencils code generator. ACM Trans. Architect. Code Optimiz. **15**(4), 40:1–40:25 (2018). https://doi.org/10.1145/3274653
21. Lai, J., Yu, H., Tian, Z., Li, H.: Hybrid MPI and CUDA parallelization for CFD applications on multi-GPU HPC clusters. Sci. Program. **2020**, 8862123 (2020). https://doi.org/10.1155/2020/8862123
22. Livescu, D.: Turbulence with large thermal and compositional density variations. Annu. Rev. Fluid Mech. **52**, 309–341 (2020). https://doi.org/10.1146/annurev-fluid-010719-060114
23. Mudalige, G.R., Reguly, I., Jammy, S.P., Jacobs, C.T., Giles, M.B., Sandham, N.D.: Large-scale performance of a DSL-based multi-block structured-mesh application for direct numerical simulation. J. Parallel Distributed Comput. **131**, 130–146 (2019)
24. Pirozzoli, S.: Numerical methods for high-speed flows. Annu. Rev. Fluid Mech. **43**, 163–194 (2011). https://doi.org/10.1146/annurev-fluid-122109-160718
25. Shu, C.W., Osher, S.: Efficient implementation of essentially non-oscillatory shock-capturing schemes. J. Comput. Phys. **77**(2), 439–471 (1988). https://doi.org/10.1016/0021-9991(88)90177-5
26. Stone, C.P., Walden, A., Zubair, M., Nielsen, E.J.: Accelerating unstructured-grid CFD algorithms on NVIDIA and AMD GPUs. In: Proceedings of the 11th Workshop on Irregular Applications: Architectures and Algorithms (IA3), held in conjunction with SC21 (2021). https://doi.org/10.1109/IA354616.2021.00010
27. Sun, Q., Liu, Y., Yang, H., Jiang, Z., Luan, Z., Qian, D.: Adaptive auto-tuning framework for global exploration of stencil optimization on GPUs. IEEE Trans. Parallel Distrib. Syst. **35**(1), 20–33 (2024). https://doi.org/10.1109/TPDS.2023.3325630
28. Wei, J.: A performance-portable kilometer-scale global ocean model on ORISE and new sunway heterogeneous supercomputers. In: Proceedings of the International Conference for High Performance Computing, Networking, Storage and Analysis (SC) (2024). https://doi.org/10.1109/SC41406.2024.00009
29. Zhou, Y.: Rayleigh–Taylor and Richtmyer–Meshkov instability induced flow, turbulence, and mixing. I. Physics Reports **720–722**, 1–136 (2017). https://doi.org/10.1016/j.physrep.2017.07.005
30. Zhou, Y., et al.: Turbulent mixing and transition criteria of flows induced by hydrodynamic instabilities. Phys. Plasmas **26**(8), 080901 (2019). https://doi.org/10.1063/1.5088745
31. Zhou, Z., Ding, J., Huang, S., Luo, X.: A new type of weighted compact nonlinear scheme with minimum dispersion and adaptive dissipation for compressible flows. Comput. Fluids **262**, 105934 (2023). https://doi.org/10.1016/j.compfluid.2023.105934

AI Accelerators

BitFly: A Low-Bit Mixed-Precision Acceleration Framework for Edge RISC-V Vector Processors

Zixuan Zeng[1,2], Chen Zhang[3], Zhe Liu[3], and Peng Li[1,2](✉)

[1] Institute of Software, Chinese Academy of Sciences, Beijing, China
[2] University of Chinese Academy of Sciences, Beijing, China
lipeng@iscas.ac.cn
[3] Shanghai Jiao Tong University, Shanghai, China

Abstract. Low-bit quantization is increasingly important for edge large language model (LLM) inference, but reduced model storage does not automatically yield proportional runtime speedup on processors without native support for low-bit mixed-precision general matrix multiplication (LBMP-GEMM). This limitation is especially acute on RISC-V Vector Extension (RVV) processors, where low-bit operands still traverse higher-precision vector datapaths and incur substantial packing, sequencing, and partial-sum overheads. We present BitFly, an RVV-compatible hardware-software co-design. BitFly integrates a lane-local bit-plane mixed-precision unit (BMPU) built around a 1-bit primitive, a context-banked accumulation store, and a lightweight instruction interface with offline-searched, shape-specific execution configurations, enabling efficient LBMP-GEMM computation. Cycle-accurate evaluation shows up to a 35.7× prefill speedup in llama2.c over RVV baselines across W1A8, W2A8, and W4A8 on models ranging from 15M to 3B parameters. Relative to the synthesized baseline accelerator, BitFly improves peak throughput by 27.3× with 28.2% additional area, while increasing area and energy efficiency by 21.4× and 14.3×, respectively.

Keywords: Edge LLM Inference · Low-Bit Mixed-Precision GEMM · RISC-V Vector Processors

1 Introduction

Large Language Models (LLMs) are emerging as an important workload for edge intelligence, where inference must simultaneously satisfy stringent latency, privacy, and power constraints [17,31]. This trend is driving deployment from cloud-centric infrastructures toward resource-constrained embedded platforms [1,23]. On RVV embedded processors, inference kernels are carried primarily through software-visible vector paths rather than a dedicated programmable matrix engine. Under such constraints, quantization is indispensable for the feasibility of deployment. However, reductions in model size do not, by themselves, translate into proportional improvements in runtime performance.

L. Eeckhout et al. (Eds.): APPT 2026, LNCS 16693, pp. 313–329, 2027.
https://doi.org/10.1007/978-981-92-4805-6_21

A more fundamental source of this gap lies in the fact that quantized low-bit mixed-precision general matrix multiplication (LBMP-GEMM) does not naturally map onto the organization of baseline RVV processors. Low-bit operands continue to traverse higher-precision vector datapaths, and the nominal arithmetic advantage of quantization is substantially offset by packing, conversion, sequencing, and partial-sum management overheads [26]. The limitation is therefore not explained adequately by arithmetic density alone. Rather, it reflects a structural mismatch between the computational requirements of LBMP-GEMM and the baseline RVV substrate, which does not directly provide the operand organization, accumulation locality, or result-materialization behavior required by low-bit mixed-precision computation.

This mismatch is particularly restrictive in edge-oriented RVV deployment. Inference in this setting is typically latency-sensitive and low-batch under tight area and power budgets, while matrix multiplication continues to dominate execution time. At the same time, INT8 activations and low-bit weights differ substantially in packing granularity, reuse behavior, and accumulation requirements [14,15]. Consequently, efficient support for LBMP-GEMM cannot be obtained simply by attaching a denser arithmetic primitive to an otherwise unchanged vector pipeline. An effective design must instead satisfy three conditions simultaneously: it must consume heterogeneous operands efficiently under lane-local, banked vector register file organization; it must retain intermediate reduction state close to compute rather than repeatedly materializing partial sums through the vector register file; and it must preserve compatibility with the RVV control model without introducing a heavyweight detached accelerator.

To address this architectural gap, we propose BitFly, an RVV-compatible hardware-software co-design methodology for LBMP-GEMM, which supports W1A8, W2A8, and W4A8 mixed-precision computation, where WpA8 denotes p-bit weights and 8-bit activations. Rather than treating low-bit support as an isolated arithmetic extension, BitFly organizes it as a native low-bit execution flow spanning a VRF-backed operand scratchpad, a lane-local bit-plane compute fabric, a context-banked accumulation store, and a deferred result-export path under a lightweight instruction protocol with offline-selected mappings. On the baseline processor, cycle-accurate evaluation shows that BitFly achieves geometric-mean kernel speedups of 77.8×, 54.5×, and 29.0× for W1A8, W2A8, and W4A8, respectively, and up to 35.7× framework-level prefill speedup in llama2.c [2]. Post-synthesis analysis shows a 27.3× peak low-bit compute-throughput increase at 28.2% additional area, indicating that efficient low-bit mixed-precision computation in RVV depends jointly on operand residency, accumulation locality, and execution control.

Our key contributions are summarized as follows. **(1)** We identify and formalize three RVV constraints for efficient LBMP-GEMM execution: lane-local and VRF-banked operand organization, long-lived accumulation state, and strict control-path integration. These constraints explain why low-bit quantization does not automatically translate into proportional runtime speedup on RVV processors. **(2)** We propose BitFly as an RVV-compatible co-design for LBMP-GEMM. BitFly enables efficient low-bit execution through a VRF-backed operand scratchpad, a lane-local bit-plane compute fabric, a context-banked accumulation store, and a deferred result-export datapath with a minimal instruction interface. **(3)** We implement and evaluate BitFly across kernel-level, layer-level, and framework-level workloads as well as synthesis analysis. The results show that BitFly can substantially improve low-bit computational throughput and hardware efficiency with moderate hardware overhead.

2 Background

Low-Bit Quantized LLMs. Low-bit quantization is increasingly attractive for edge LLM deployment because it reduces both parameter storage and memory traffic [15]. As precision drops below 4 bits, model quality becomes more sensitive to outliers and value imbalance, motivating mixed-precision formulations that preserve critical values using higher precision while quantizing the dominant weights more aggressively [16,24,29]. Recent BitNet-style models and edge-oriented runtimes suggest that such sub-4-bit regimes, including binary-dominant weight formats, are evolving from primarily algorithmic explorations into plausible deployment targets [27,28]. Compression-quality trade-offs alone do not determine realized performance. Practical speedup still depends on whether the processor can execute low-bit mixed-precision operations without repeatedly incurring unpacking, conversion, and auxiliary control overheads [26].

Microarchitecture for Low-Bit Mixed-Precision Inference. These execution-side constraints make RVV a useful target for study. RVV preserves a general-purpose vector programming model while exposing customization opportunities at both the ISA and dataflow levels. Prior RVV-oriented designs have explored packed or asymmetric arithmetic support, hybrid scheduling, and remapping low-bit operations onto wider datapaths [3,9,25]. More broadly, open RISC-V platforms such as Gemmini, Snitch, and Spatz illustrate a wider design space of customized compute backends [6,12,30]. Nevertheless, support for low-bit mixed-precision execution under conventional vector-register-file (VRF) organization and operand-layout constraints remains limited, especially when execution must remain compatible with RVV control logic.

3 Motivation

On RVV processors, low-bit compression does not automatically translate into proportional throughput improvement. For LBMP-GEMM, lowering weight precision reduces storage costs, but the speedup still depends on whether packed low-bit weights and INT8 activations can traverse without incurring substantial reshuffling or serialization overhead. The RVV accelerator is not organized around the accumulation, data-layout, and control requirements of

Table 1. An example throughput comparison in the llama.cpp framework [13].

Model	Quantization Method	Size (MiB)	Compression Ratio	Phase	Throughput (token/s)	Speedup	Acceleration Density
Qwen3 0.6B	BF16	1136.64	–	Prefill	932.78	–	–
				Decode	43.83	–	–
	IQ1_S	199.02	5.71×	Prefill	655.35	0.70×	0.12
				Decode	78.73	1.80×	0.32
	IQ2_XXS	217.55	5.22×	Prefill	634.78	0.68×	0.13
				Decode	72.89	1.66×	0.32
	IQ3_XXS	263.34	4.32×	Prefill	570.66	0.61×	0.14
				Decode	64.41	1.47×	0.34

LBMP-GEMM. Consequently, expressing such execution through standard vector instructions increases the instruction count, synchronization costs, and data movement overhead.

Table 1 makes this realization gap explicit through measurements collected from llama.cpp. The observed pattern is informative: although quantization yields substantial compression in model storage, the corresponding throughput improvement remains smaller than the compression ratio. This discrepancy indicates that software implementations of low-bit computation preserve much of the memory-footprint reduction, while converting only a limited portion of that reduction into realized runtime acceleration, owing to the repeated unpacking, reformatting, and accumulation of low-bit operands within higher-precision computation. To quantify the extent to which compression is translated into realized speedup, the following metric is introduced: $\eta = \frac{\text{Observed Speedup}}{\text{Compression Ratio}}$.

An ideal implementation would yield $\eta \rightarrow 1$, indicating that compression is converted almost fully into runtime improvement. However, Table 1 shows that η remains well below 1 across representative quantized settings. This observation indicates that the bottleneck lies in the execution substrate rather than the quantization quality. Although lower-bit weights reduce the number of bytes moved, a substantial fraction of the potential speedup is still lost to unpacking, control, and synchronization overheads. This shortfall motivates BitFly.

4 BitFly Framework

4.1 Microarchitecture Design

BitFly targets LBMP-GEMM on RVV accelerators. Its goal is to embed native low-bit execution into the RVV lane organization. BitFly keeps the RVV frontend and vector substrate, attaches one tightly coupled bit-plane mixed-precision unit (BMPU) per lane, and derives higher weight precision by reusing a native 1-bit primitive across bit planes. This section introduces the RVV constraints, the lane microarchitecture, and the accumulation and export methods.

RVV Constraints. Efficient support for LBMP-GEMM on an RVV accelerator is governed by three constraints. First, **operand organization** is lane-local and VRF-banked. Each lane stores only a slice of a vector register, so operands with different precisions cannot be rearranged freely at execution time without additional movement, replication, or bank conflicts. Second, **accumulation state** is long-lived. LBMP-GEMM does not produce a final output from a single vector operation; instead, intermediate sums can be preserved across reduction steps and bit-plane composition steps, making repeated VRF round-trips expensive. Third, **control integration** must remain in the RVV issue/retire datapaths. Low-bit support must fit within the existing decode, issue, and retire logic.

These constraints define BitFly's design target. An effective RVV solution must consume heterogeneous operands with a low lane-local access cost, keep intermediate sums near computation until reduction completes, and expose execution progress through the standard RVV control path. BitFly addresses this target with a lane-local bit-plane compute fabric, a VRF-backed operand scratchpad for staged operand residency, a context-banked accumulation store for partial sums, and a deferred result-export path for finalized outputs. Figure 1 shows the physical-slot organization rather than a fixed activation/weight role assignment. Section 4.2 explains software tiling, grouping, and instruction sequencing.

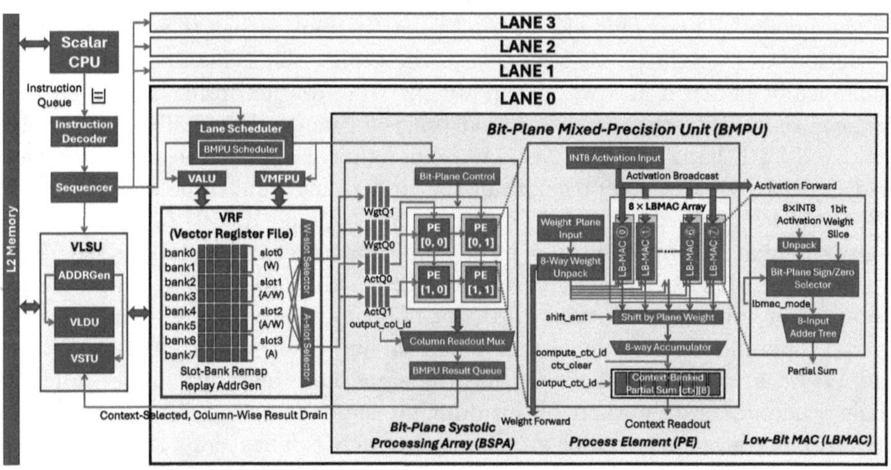

Fig. 1. BitFly extends the RVV lane backend with a lane-local BMPU, a VRF-backed resident-operand scratchpad, and a context-banked accumulation store; finalized outputs are drained through a deferred export path.

Lane Microarchitecture. The lane-local BMPU is organized hierarchically from low-bit MAC units (LBMACs), to processing elements (PEs), to a bit-plane systolic processing array (BSPA). This hierarchy is described bottom-up.

LBMAC. LBMAC is the primitive compute unit. It consumes one 8-element activation group and one 8×1 weight slice and produces the dot product for one weight column of one bit plane. For each activation element, the weight bit selects pass, negate, or suppress under the active mode, after which an adder tree reduces the eight selected values. LBMAC therefore realizes the per-plane mixed-precision operation directly, without introducing a general low-bit multiplier.

PE. PE is the first aggregation level above the 1-bit primitive. Each PE instantiates eight LBMACs and processes one complete 8×8 weight tile per cycle. The activation group is broadcast to all LBMACs, while column-wise slicing delivers one 8×1 weight slice to each unit. As a result, one PE performs a tile-level GEMV between one 1×8 INT8 activation group and one 8×8 1-bit weight tile and produces an 8-element output fragment. A local plane scheduler derives the active LBMAC mode and shift alignment from the precision mode and wavefront position, enabling W1A8, W2A8, and W4A8 to share the same PE structure. The output fragment is accumulated into context-indexed local registers, making the PE both the first output-stationary stage and the first level at which multi-plane partial results are merged across the accumulation dimension.

BSPA. BSPA is the lane-level spatial fabric that composes PE-local updates into GEMM progress. Each lane has a 2×2 BSPA served by four resident operand slots in the VRF-backed scratch and by two activation queues and two weight queues. These four slots form a shared pool rather than a fixed two-activation/two-weight partition: for each tile group, the sequencer assigns them dynamically between activation and weight windows according to the current (g_m, g_n) reuse pattern, tile shape, and precision mode. Physically, slot s maps to a fixed VRF bank pair $(2s, 2s + 1)$; the dynamic assignment changes the payload carried by each slot rather than the underlying bank topology. Together, LBMACs, PEs, and the BSPA form one tightly coupled BMPU per lane. BitFly reuses the existing frontend and most lane infrastructure, including the VRF, lane pipeline, dispatcher/sequencer, and VLSU, while specializing only the lane backend for low-bit execution. BMP-specific modifications are therefore confined to operand delivery, local accumulation, and result export. W1A8, W2A8, and W4A8 are all derived by reusing the same lane hierarchy under different plane schedules, rather than by introducing separate arithmetic backends. At the processor level, activations are partitioned across lanes along the row dimension, while the same weight tile is broadcast to all lanes. Under the default four-lane configuration, this yields a processor-wide minimum block of 8×16, formed by four lane-local 2×16 blocks sharing one weight tile.

Context-Banked Accumulation and Deferred Result Export. BitFly retains partial sums in context-banked local state rather than materializing them through the VRF after each update. Under an execution configuration, one software tile is decomposed into lane-local micro-blocks indexed by $(m_{\text{blk}}, n_{\text{blk}})$, and this micro-block index is mapped to a BSPA context id. The selected context id determines the PE-local accumulation bank updated by the compute wavefront, so the same bank is reused across all later iterations along the reduction dimension and across all required bit-plane composition steps for that micro-block. A bank is cleared only when a new reduction epoch begins. The context-banked accumulation store is an effective accumulation unit and is the key mechanism that allows BitFly to keep reduction state on chip.

Result export is handled by a separate context/column readout datapath. Once accumulation for a context completes, the BMPU supplies an output-context id and an output-column id to the BSPA. The BSPA then reads the selected column for that context while returning all BSPA rows in parallel. The returned values are packed into 64-bit lane words and pushed into the result queue for deferred store-out. This context-banked accumulation combined with context/column-selective drain is architecturally distinct from a conventional RVV realization: accumulation placement is governed by local reduction state, whereas result materialization follows a later deterministic drain order. This decoupling removes repeated VRF read-modify-write traffic for intermediate sums and keeps the lane backend compact despite wider accumulated outputs.

4.2 LBMP-GEMM Mapping and Execution

The execution of LBMP-GEMM on BitFly is determined in two stages. Offline, BitFly selects an efficient tile configuration and operand reuse group configuration subject to BMPU alignment, buffer-capacity, and bank-capacity constraints. At runtime, the kernel uses the selected configuration to traverse tile groups, accumulate along the reduction dimension, and export finalized outputs.

BitFly maps LBMP-GEMM at three levels. First, the matrices are partitioned into software tiles of size (m_t, n_t, k_t), with the corresponding tile counts (m_b, n_b, k_b). Second, neighboring output tiles are grouped by (g_m, g_n): g_m reuses one weight tile across adjacent M-direction output tiles, whereas g_n reuses one activation tile across adjacent N-direction output tiles. Third, each software tile is executed as a sequence of processor-wide micro-block updates. For a full tile, (B_m, B_n, B_k) denote the update counts along the M, N, and K dimensions. Since only the boundary tile in the K direction may reduce the required reduction depth, the full-tile count B_k is distinguished from the boundary-tile count B_k^{eff}, which is determined by the aligned effective depth k_{eff} of the final K tile.

Offline search first determines whether a tile/group configuration is legal. Tile sizes must match PE granularity, so m_t is searched in steps of 8 and n_t in steps of 16. Once (g_m, g_n) is chosen, the grouped outputs retained on chip during grouped reuse must fit within the local accumulation budget:

$$m_t n_t g \cdot 16\,\text{bit} \le C_{buf}, \qquad g = g_m g_n. \tag{1}$$

The left-hand side is the 16-bit storage space required to hold one grouped $(g_m \times g_n)$ output region before the group is drained. Candidates that underfill this budget remain legal, they are ranked later by computational latency. In addition, k_t must satisfy the bank capacity constraints:

$$m_t k_t \cdot 8\,\text{bit} \le N_{row} \cdot W_{bank} \cdot D_{bank}, \qquad n_t k_t \cdot p_{weight} \le N_{col} \cdot W_{bank} \cdot D_{bank}. \tag{2}$$

Here, N_{row} and N_{col} denote the lane-local BSPA row and column counts, W_{bank} and D_{bank} denote the bank width and depth. Meanwhile, C_{buf} is the grouped-output buffer budget for one mapped tile group. All legal grouped mappings also satisfy $g = g_m g_n \leq 8$. For full tiles in the definition, $k_{\text{exec}} = k_t$, only the boundary K tile replaces k_t with the aligned effective depth k_{eff} at runtime.

Legal candidates are ranked by an event-driven timing model that matches the computation method: one load channel, one compute channel, and a four-slot resident-operand schedule that overlaps grouped reuse with operand staging. For a full-tile candidate, the numbers of processor-wide updates per software tile are

$$B_m = \left\lceil \frac{m_t}{N_{\text{lane}} \cdot N_{row}} \right\rceil, \qquad B_n = \left\lceil \frac{n_t}{N_{col} \cdot 8} \right\rceil, \qquad B_k = \left\lceil \frac{k_t}{8} \right\rceil, \tag{3}$$

For one processor-wide update, the BSPA wavefront latency and the resulting compute latency of one software tile are given by

$$T_{BSPA} = (N_{row} - 1) + B_k\, p_{weight} + N_{col}, \qquad T_{comp} = B_m B_n\, T_{BSPA}, \tag{4}$$

where $p_{weight} \in \{1, 2, 4\}$ denotes the number of weight planes in the different mixed-precision modes. Memory latency is jointly determined by 8-bit activation transfer and p_{weight}-bit weight transfer under the precision mode. BitFly then evaluates how much of this transfer time can be hidden both within one grouped-reuse epoch and across consecutive groups, and selects configurations by latency.

Runtime execution is orchestrated by four instructions. They encode the selected tile/group configuration, stage operands, trigger computation, and drain results. Table 2 summarizes the instruction definitions. Given a configuration $(m_t, n_t, k_t, g_m, g_n, \text{prec})$, execution follows the three-stage schedule.

Table 2. Semantics of the BitFly custom instructions.

Instr.	Assembly form	Function
`BMPCFG`	`bmpcfg prec, k_exec, m_t, n_t, g_m, g_n`	Programs the selected execution configuration.
`BMPLE`	`bmple imm(rs1), a|w`	Loads one activation or weight tile into a resident slot.
`BMPMM`	`bmpmm`	Launches one resident activation-weight tile pair.
`BMPSE`	`bmpse imm(rs1)`	Drains one completed context/column pair.

Stage I: Group Traversal and Execution Plan Generation. We first traverse the grouped software-tile coordinates implied by the tile counts (m_b, n_b, k_b). For each group origin, the runtime derives the boundary-clipped group extents (mg_len and ng_len). The plan module then specializes the configuration to this concrete group under the four-slot resident budget: it assigns resident slots to activation and weight windows, derives the corresponding window counts, selects the serpentine window walk (row_snake) when beneficial, and chooses the preferred reuse direction (reuse_a). Stage I therefore produces one group-local resident-window traversal strategy. Figure 2.

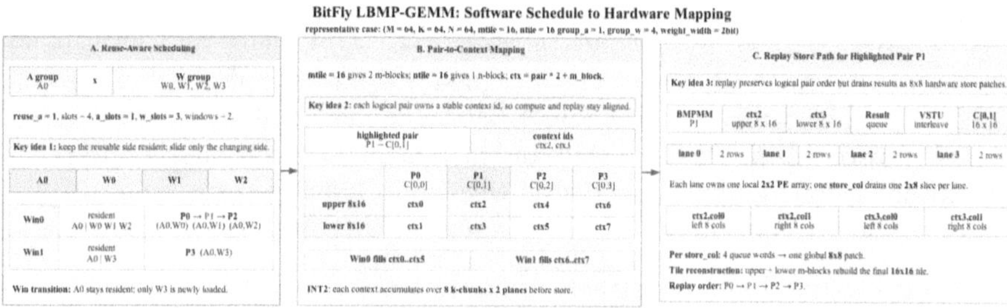

Fig. 2. Runtime execution schedule of LBMP-GEMM on BitFly.

Stage II: Accumulation Across Grouped Tiles. Stage II follows the Stage I schedule while advancing along the K dimension. For each K tile, the runtime forms the depth k_{exec}, equal to k_t for full tiles and to the aligned k_{eff} for the boundary tile. It then walks the activation and weight windows, emits `BMPCFG` for the current window, reloads only the operand whose window has changed via `BMPLE`, and issues `BMPMM` over resident activation-weight pairs in the plan-selected order. The plan is selected once for the current group and then reused for every K tile. This is the key effect of the plan in Fig. 2: it decides which operand remains resident across neighboring pair launches, thereby extending reuse in the VRF-backed operand scratchpad while partial sums stay live in the context-banked accumulation store. For all non-boundary tiles, the corresponding accumulation counts are (B_m, B_n, B_k); only the final K tile may be shorter, in which case its executed update count becomes $B_k^{\text{eff}} = \left\lceil \frac{k_{\text{eff}}}{8} \right\rceil$.

Let $g = (m_g, n_g)$ denote the origin of the current output-tile group, and let $o = (a_i, w_i)$ denote the offset of one output tile within that group. Thus, (g, o) identifies the output tile at $(m_g + a_i,\ n_g + w_i)$. The contribution from the k_i-th tile along the K dimension to this output tile is

$$\Delta \mathbf{C}_{g,o}^{(k_i)} = \sum_{\mu=0}^{B_m-1} \sum_{\nu=0}^{B_n-1} \Delta \mathbf{C}_{g,o,\mu,\nu}^{(k_i)}, \qquad \mathbf{C}_{g,o}^{(k_i+1)} = \mathbf{C}_{g,o}^{(k_i)} + \Delta \mathbf{C}_{g,o}^{(k_i)}. \tag{5}$$

Here, k_i indexes the current tile along the K dimension, $\mathbf{C}_{g,o}$ denotes the accumulated state of output tile (g, o), and $\Delta \mathbf{C}_{g,o,\mu,\nu}^{(k_i)}$ denotes the processor-wide update generated at local micro-block coordinate (μ, ν) for that K tile.

For p_{weight}-bit weights, BitFly decomposes each weight tile into bit planes and reuses the same 1-bit datapath across planes. Let $\mathbf{W}^{(b)}$ denote the b-th bit plane, and let α_b denote the coefficient assigned to the plane b:

$$\mathbf{W} = \sum_{b=0}^{p_{weight}-1} \alpha_b \, \mathbf{W}^{(b)}, \qquad \Delta\mathbf{C}^{(k_i)}_{g,o,\mu,\nu} = \sum_{b=0}^{p_{weight}-1} \alpha_b \, \Delta\mathbf{C}^{(k_i)}_{g,o,\mu,\nu,b}. \tag{6}$$

Here, $\Delta\mathbf{C}^{(k_i)}_{g,o,\mu,\nu,b}$ is the 1-bit partial result from bit plane b for local micro-block (μ, ν) of output tile (g, o). For unsigned magnitude composition, $\alpha_b = 2^b$; for signed or mixed modes, the active LBMAC mode supplies the effective sign or zero behavior during PE-level shift and merge. These equations describe Stage II: hardware accumulates across (μ, ν, b) within one `BMPMM` stream, while software advances k_i and retains grouped partial sums until the tile group completes.

Stage III: Deterministic Export. After the last K tile has been accumulated, Stage III exports finalized outputs through `BMPSE`. It follows the same window sequence and pair order fixed in Stage I, reissues `BMPCFG` with the final aligned K setting, derives the destination address $cptr = \mathrm{addr}_C(\cdot)$ for each completed output pair, and replaces `BMPMM` with `BMPSE`. Stage III is therefore the export phase of the same group-local schedule: finalized outputs are drained in the Stage I order, and the store path preserves that issue order.

4.3 Roofline Analysis

We further project legal configurations under an architecture-aware roofline that fixes the precision-specific BMPU compute roof and varies only tile/group configurations. Each point in Fig. 3 corresponds to one legal candidate for the representative shape, evaluated under the buffer constraints above and the same event-driven load/compute/drain model used in offline search. In this space, (m_t, n_t) control how much computation is amortized over one staged activation/weight residency interval, while (g_m, g_n) control how far that staged residency can be reused across neighboring output tiles before drain. Varying (g_m, g_n) therefore changes reuse, resident-slot behavior, and exposed drain overhead.

Points farther to the right achieve higher reuse, whereas points higher on the plot convert more of the fixed compute headroom into sustained throughput. In particular, larger (m_t, n_t) increase the amount of work extracted from each staged operand fill, whereas larger (g_m, g_n) further improve operational intensity when the accumulation store can retain grouped partial sums long enough to suppress intermediate drains. For the shape $(128, 2048, 8192)$, the best configurations are $(m_t, n_t, k_t, g_m, g_n) = (8, 128, 64, 1, 1)$ for W1A8 and $(8, 16, 128, 2, 4)$ for both W2A8 and W4A8. The following evaluation uses the best legal configurations searched by this same execution model and constraint set.

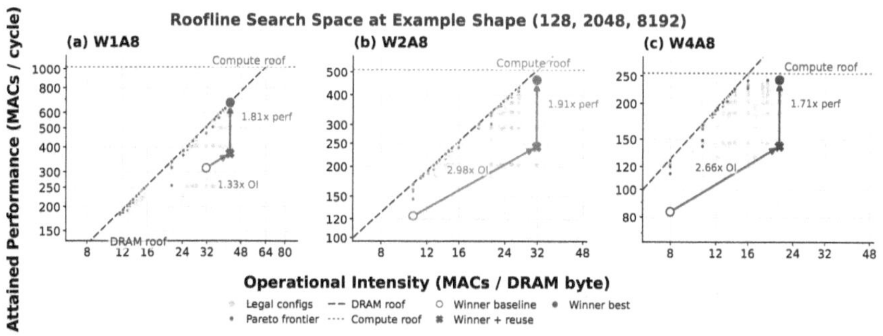

Fig. 3. Architecture-aware roofline. Each subplot shows the legal design space for the representative shape (128,2048,8192); filled points mark the Pareto frontier.

5 Evaluation

We use Ara as the baseline platform, a 64-bit RISC-V vector accelerator compatible with RVV 1.0 [5,19,21]. All experiments use the default Ara configuration with $N_{\mathrm{LANE}}=4$ and VLEN=4096. Cycle-level results are obtained from Verilator v5.012 and QuestaSim v2024.1, with identical memory-system assumptions for BitFly and the RVV baseline. Both implementations use the same quantized model format and arithmetic semantics. The RVV baseline executes low-bit linear layers by vectorized unpack followed by W8A8 GEMM, whereas BitFly executes the same layers directly on its native low-bit datapath.

We evaluate BitFly at three levels. The kernel-level suite covers 18 GEMM shapes sampled from square, small-M, and projection-dominated regimes. The layer-level suite covers the seven dominant projections in one transformer block, across ten edge-oriented quantized LLM workloads spanning the Gemma, SmolLM2, Qwen2.5, Replit-Code, TinyLlama, OPT, and StableLM families. We sample block 0 because these transformer blocks repeat the same projection shapes within each model. At the framework level, we integrate BitFly into llama2.c and evaluate W1A8, W2A8, and W4A8 prefill execution on TinyStories-15M, TinyStories-42M, TinyStories-110M, Llama-3.2-1B, and Llama-3.2-3B with sequence lengths $L \in \{32, 64, 128, 256\}$ [2]. For each quantized linear layer, BitFly uses a pre-searched offline configuration $(m_t, n_t, k_t, g_m, g_n)$. The search is performed once per layer shape offline and cached as a configuration table; runtime execution only performs configuration lookup. The search is therefore excluded from the reported runtime. We report geometric means for kernel speedups across heterogeneous shape instances and arithmetic means for the layer-level and framework-level suites, where each workload instance is treated as an equally weighted evaluation point (Fig. 4).

5.1 Performance Evaluation

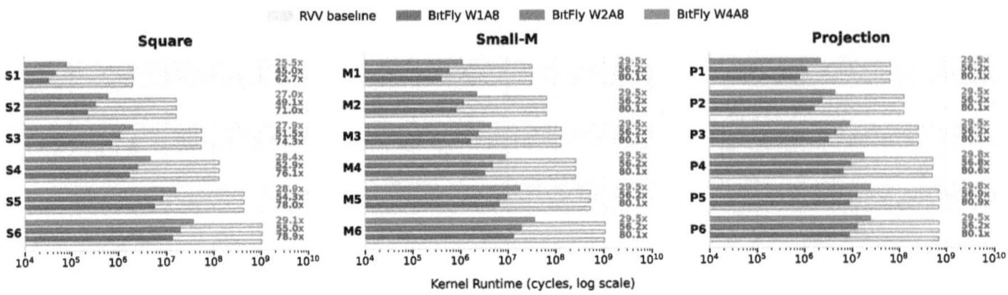

Fig. 4. Kernel-level speedup of BitFly over the RVV baseline on 18 representative GEMM shapes spanning square, small-M, and projection-dominated regimes. Speedup is reported as RVV kernel cycles over BitFly kernel cycles.

Kernel-Level. For all three precision modes, the RVV reference is the post-unpack W8A8 GEMM on the same (M, N, K) shape. This is because the evaluated RVV baseline supports integer execution only down to 8-bit granularity, so W1A8, W2A8, and W4A8 must first be unpacked into 8-bit operands before GEMM execution. Kernel cycles include the compute body together with in-kernel load/store, address generation, and loop control. BitFly achieves geometric-mean speedups of 77.8×, 54.5×, and 29.0× for W1A8, W2A8, and W4A8, respectively. Square matrices are the least favorable cases, with speedups of 62.7×–78.9×, 45.0×–55.0×, and 25.5×–29.1×, while projection-dominated and small-M shapes are slightly higher on average (Fig. 5).

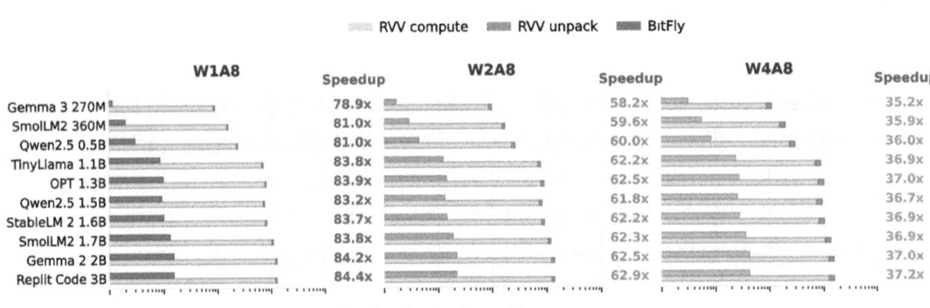

Fig. 5. Layer-level evaluation across ten LLM workloads. Each point aggregates the seven dominant linear layers from one transformer block for one model and one precision; the RVV baseline performs vectorized unpack followed by W8A8 GEMM, whereas BitFly executes the same layers directly in low precision.

Layer-Level. Unlike the kernel-level result, this comparison measures layer-level execution and includes the RVV unpack overhead that precedes the W8A8 GEMM. This difference in accounting explains why the gains at the layer-level can exceed the gains at the kernel-level. Using arithmetic means across the ten workloads, BitFly reduces the layer runtime by 82.8×, 61.4×, and 36.6× for W1A8, W2A8, and W4A8, respectively. The performance among different workloads remains narrow, at 78.8× – 84.4×, 58.1× – 62.8×, and 35.2× – 37.2×, consistent with a stable advantage across different LLM layer shapes (Fig. 6).

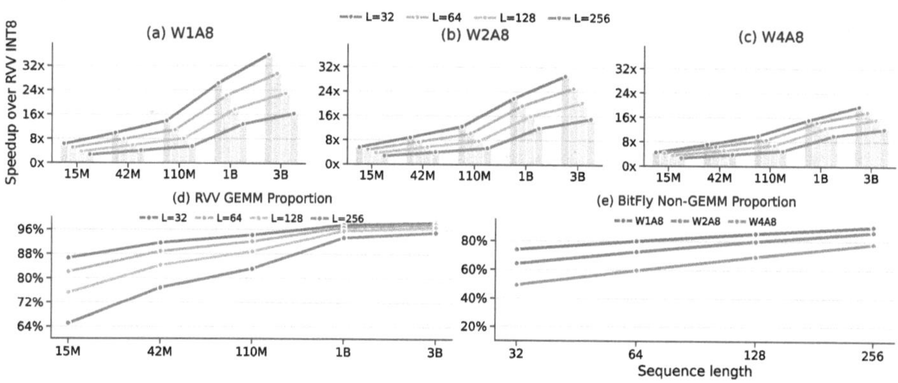

Fig. 6. Prefill speedup of llama2.c over the baseline [2]. The lower-left panel reports the GEMM proportion of total RVV prefill cycles. The lower-right panel reports the non-GEMM proportion of total BitFly prefill cycles.

Framework-Level. The RVV and BitFly variants execute the same computation graph and differ only in the backend used for quantized linear layers. In all configurations, the speedup remains ordered as W1A8 > W2A8 > W4A8. The maximum speedup reaches 35.7× on the 3B model at L=32, and the arithmetic means over all model-size and sequence-length pairs are 13.4×, 11.8×, and 9.2× for W1A8, W2A8, and W4A8, respectively. The lower panels explain the scaling trends: the GEMM proportion of RVV prefill cycles increases with model size, whereas the non-GEMM proportion of BitFly prefill cycles increases with sequence length. Together, these trends are consistent with BitFly delivering larger gains when GEMM dominates the workload and smaller prefill gains as non-GEMM operators absorb a larger fraction of the critical path.

5.2 Synthesis Results

BitFly and Ara were synthesized in Synopsys Design Compiler (T-2022.03-SP2) using the TSMC 28 nm PDK [5,19,21]. Relative to Ara, BitFly increases peak throughput by 27.3× with 28.2% additional area. This translates into 21.4× higher area efficiency and 14.3× higher energy efficiency. As summarized

Table 3. Comparison with prior RISC-V AI accelerators.

Metric	BitFly (Ours)	Ibex† [3,8]	MixGEMM-v2 [9]	XPULPNN [10]	Marcellus [7]	SPEED [25]	DORY [4]	DARKSIDE [11]	Dustin [18]	Yun [20]	Vega [22]
Tech. (nm)	28 (22)	7 (22)	22	22	22	28 (22)	65 (22)	65 (22)	65 (22)	65 (22)	22
Arch. (-)	RV64+ Decoupled	RV32	RV64	8×RV32	RV32+ Decoupled	RV64+ Decoupled	8×RV32	8×RV32	16×RV32	RV64+ Decoupled	10×RV32
Freq. (MHz)	851 (1083)	14.75 (79.61)	1200	400	420	1050 (1337)	260 (767)	290 (855.5)	205 (604.75)	280 (826)	450
Area (mm²)	1.13 (0.69)	0.038 (0.375)	0.03	0.086	0.46	1.20 (0.740)	-	12.00 (1.38)	10.00 (1.15)	6.00 (0.69)	12.00
Peak Perf. (GOPS)	**1742.84 (2217.99)**	0.85 (0.27)	29.0	47.9	569	737.9 (937.1)	4.2 (12.4)	65 (172.3)	58 (171.1)	22.9 (67.5)	15.6
Area Eff. (GOPS/mm²)	**1542.33 (3214.47)**	22.37 (0.72)	1580	557	1236	614.6 (1266.4)	-	5.4 (124.5)	5.8 (149)	3.8 (97.5)	1.3
Energy Eff. (GOPS/W)	**3125.80 (3977.99)**	1470 (468.15)	1335	1100	5370	1383.4 (1757)	15.9 (47)	835 (2463.25)	1152 (3398)	100.5 (296.5)	614
Benchmark	LLM & GEMM	CNN	CNN	CNN	CNN	CNN	CNN	CNN	CNN	GEMM	CNN

Note: All metrics are reported at their original technology. Values in parentheses project non-22 nm designs to the 22 nm using standard scaling laws: area $\propto L^2$, frequency $\propto 1/L$, and power unchanged due to non-scaled supply voltage (V_{dd}).
† Ibex extended with specialized MAC FUs for mixed-precision workloads.

in Table 3, under 22 nm normalization BitFly achieves 2.22 TOPS peak throughput, 3214.47 GOPS/mm² area efficiency, and 3977.99 GOPS/W energy efficiency. Among the other state-of-the-art accelerators, BitFly provides the highest peak throughput and area efficiency while remaining competitive in energy efficiency, demonstrating its hardware efficiency for edge LLM inference.

6 Conclusion

BitFly shows that the central challenge of LBMP-GEMM on RVV is not merely how to execute fewer-bit arithmetic, but how to organize operand delivery, reduction state, and execution control so that low-bit computation remains native throughout the full execution flow. We summarize three takeaways.

Takeaway 1: Low-bit mixed-precision execution on RVV is constrained primarily by asymmetric operand delivery rather than by arithmetic density alone. Flexible on-chip tiling and grouped reuse are necessary to amortize operand staging overhead, reduce data latency, and mitigate pipeline stalls.

Takeaway 2: Partial-sum residency is an essential architectural requirement for LBMP-GEMM. By retaining intermediate results in a programmable context-banked accumulation store across software execution rounds, BitFly absorbs the long-lived and irregular reduction workload of low-bit mixed-precision computation and decouples accumulation from final result export.

Takeaway 3: Practical RVV integration should preserve the original RVV control pipeline while reorganizing the VRF into a VRF-backed operand scratchpad. Window-based scheduling and serpentine traversal then realize low-overhead, shape-adaptive operand reuse without introducing a detached execution path.

Statement. Artificial intelligence tools, if used, were used only for language organization and figure/table polishing, and did not participate in the generation of the core ideas or technical content.

Acknowledgments. We sincerely thank the anonymous reviewers for their valuable suggestions that improved this paper. This work is supported by the National Natural Science Foundation of China (NSFC) under Grant 62502305, and the Natural Science Foundation of Shanghai (NSFS) under Grant 25ZR1402275.

References

1. Abadade, Y., Temouden, A., Bamoumen, H., Benamar, N., Chtouki, Y., Hafid, A.S.: A comprehensive survey on tinyml. IEEE Access **11**, 96892–96922 (2023). https://doi.org/10.1109/ACCESS.2023.3294111
2. Andrej Karpathy: Karpathy/llama2.c: Inference Llama 2 in one file of pure C. GitHub repository (2025). https://github.com/karpathy/llama2.c
3. Armeniakos, G., Maras, A., Xydis, S., Soudris, D.: Mixed-precision Neural Networks on RISC-V Cores: ISA extensions for Multi-Pumped Soft SIMD Operations **10**(1145/3676536), 3676840 (2024)
4. Burrello, A., Garofalo, A., Bruschi, N., Tagliavini, G., Rossi, D., Conti, F.: Dory: automatic end-to-end deployment of real-world DNNs on low-cost IoT MCUs. IEEE Trans. Comput. **70**(8), 1253–1268 (2021). https://doi.org/10.1109/TC.2021.3066883
5. Cavalcante, M., Schuiki, F., Zaruba, F., Schaffner, M., Benini, L.: Ara: a 1-GHz+ scalable and energy-efficient RISC-V vector processor with multiprecision floating-point support in 22-nm FD-SOI. IEEE Trans. Very Large Scale Integration (VLSI) Syst. **28**(2), 530–543 (2020). https://doi.org/10.1109/TVLSI.2019.2950087
6. Cavalcante, M., Wüthrich, D., Perotti, M., Riedel, S., Benini, L.: Spatz: a compact vector processing unit for high-performance and energy-efficient shared-L1 clusters. In: Proceedings of the 41st IEEE/ACM International Conference on Computer-Aided Design, pp. 1–9 (2022). https://doi.org/10.1145/3508352.3549367
7. Conti, F., et al.: Marsellus: a heterogeneous RISC-v AI-Iot end-node soc with 2–8 b DNN acceleration and 30%-boost adaptive body biasing. IEEE J. Solid-State Circuits **59**(1), 128–142 (2024). https://doi.org/10.1109/JSSC.2023.3318301
8. Davide Schiavone, P., et al.: Slow and steady wins the race? a comparison of ultra-low-power RISC-v cores for internet-of-things applications. In: 2017 27th International Symposium on Power and Timing Modeling, Optimization and Simulation (PATMOS), pp. 1–8 (2017). https://doi.org/10.1109/PATMOS.2017.8106976
9. Fornt, J., et al.: Mix-GEMM: extending RISC-V CPUs for energy-efficient mixed-precision DNN inference using binary segmentation. IEEE Trans. Comput. **74**(2), 582–596 (2025). https://doi.org/10.1109/TC.2024.3500369
10. Garofalo, A., Tagliavini, G., Conti, F., Benini, L., Rossi, D.: XPULPNN: enabling energy efficient and flexible inference of quantized neural networks on RISC-v based IoT end nodes. IEEE Trans. Emerg. Top. Comput. **9**(3), 1489–1505 (2021). https://doi.org/10.1109/TETC.2021.3072337
11. Garofalo, A., et al.: DARKSIDE: a heterogeneous RISC-V compute cluster for extreme-edge on-chip DNN inference and training. IEEE Open J. Solid-State Circuits Soc. **2**, 231–243 (2022). https://doi.org/10.1109/OJSSCS.2022.3210082

12. Genc, H., et al.: Gemmini: enabling systematic deep-learning architecture evaluation via full-stack integration (2021). https://doi.org/10.48550/arXiv.1911.09925
13. ggml-org: ggml-org/llama.cpp. GitHub repository (2025). https://github.com/ggml-org/llama.cpp
14. Gholami, A., Kim, S., Dong, Z., Yao, Z., Mahoney, M.W., Keutzer, K.: A survey of quantization methods for efficient neural network inference (2021). https://arxiv.org/abs/2103.13630
15. Gong, R., et al.: A survey of low-bit large language models: basics, systems, and algorithms (2024). https://doi.org/10.48550/arXiv.2409.16694
16. Ma, L., Sun, M., Shen, Z.: FBI-LLM: scaling up fully binarized LLMs from scratch via autoregressive distillation (2024). https://doi.org/10.48550/arXiv.2407.07093
17. Minaee, S., et al.: Large language models: a survey (2025).https://arxiv.org/abs/2402.06196
18. Ottavi, G., et al.: Dustin: a 16-cores parallel ultra-low-power cluster with 2b-to-32b fully flexible bit-precision and vector lockstep execution mode. IEEE Trans. Circuits Syst. I Regul. Pap. **70**(6), 2450–2463 (2023). https://doi.org/10.1109/TCSI.2023.3254810
19. Perotti, M., Cavalcante, M., Andri, R., Cavigelli, L., Benini, L.: Ara2: exploring single- and multi-core vector processing with an efficient RVV 1.0 compliant open-source processor. IEEE Trans. Comput. **73**(7), 1822–1836 (2024). https://doi.org/10.1109/TC.2024.3388896
20. Perotti, M., Cavalcante, M., Ottaviano, A., Liu, J., Benini, L.: Yun: an open-source, 64-Bit RISC-V-based vector processor with multi-precision integer and floating-point support in 65-nm CMOS. IEEE Trans. Circuits Syst. II Express Briefs **70**(10), 3732–3736 (2023). https://doi.org/10.1109/TCSII.2023.3292579
21. Perotti, M., Cavalcante, M., Wistoff, N., Andri, R., Cavigelli, L., Benini, L.: A new ARA for vector computing: an open source highly efficient RISC-V v 1.0 vector processor design. In: 2022 IEEE 33rd International Conference on Application-specific Systems, Architectures and Processors (ASAP), pp. 43–51 (2022). https://doi.org/10.1109/ASAP54787.2022.00017
22. Rossi, D., et al.: Vega: a ten-core soc for IoT endnodes with DNN acceleration and cognitive wake-up from MRAM-based state-retentive sleep mode. IEEE J. Solid-State Circuits **57**(1), 127–139 (2022). https://doi.org/10.1109/JSSC.2021.3114881
23. Sai, S., Prasad, M., Dashore, G., Chamola, V., Sikdar, B.: On-device generative AI: the need, architectures, and challenges. IEEE Consumer Electron. Magazine **14**(4), 21–32 (2025). https://doi.org/10.1109/MCE.2024.3518761
24. Shang, Y., Yuan, Z., Wu, Q., Dong, Z.: Pb-LLM: partially binarized large language models (2023). https://arxiv.org/abs/2310.00034
25. Wang, C., Fang, C., Wu, X., Wang, Z., Lin, J.: SPEED: a scalable RISC-V vector processor enabling efficient multi-precision DNN inference. IEEE Trans. Very Large Scale Integration (VLSI) Syst. **33**(1), 207–220 (2025). https://doi.org/10.1109/TVLSI.2024.3466224
26. Wang, H., et al.: Bitnet: scaling 1-bit transformers for large language models (2023). https://arxiv.org/abs/2310.11453
27. Wang, H., Ma, S., Wei, F.: BitNet v2: native 4-bit activations with Hadamard transformation for 1-bit LLMs (2025). https://doi.org/10.48550/arXiv.2504.18415
28. Wang, J., et al.: Bitnet.cpp: Efficient Edge Inference for Ternary LLMs (2025). https://doi.org/10.48550/arXiv.2502.11880
29. Xu, Y., et al.: OneBit: towards extremely low-bit large language models (2024). https://doi.org/10.48550/arXiv.2402.11295

30. Zaruba, F., Schuiki, F., Hoefler, T., Benini, L.: Snitch: a tiny pseudo dual-issue processor for area and energy efficient execution of floating-point intensive workloads. IEEE Trans. Comput. **70**(11), 1845–1860 (2021). https://doi.org/10.1109/TC.2020.3027900
31. Zheng, Y., Chen, Y., Qian, B., Shi, X., Shu, Y., Chen, J.: A review on edge large language models: design, execution, and applications (2025). https://arxiv.org/abs/2410.11845

Fold-FP4: Folding for Energy Efficient FP4 Matrix Multiplication

Qiyan Fang[1,2], Yifan Wang[1], Yongwei Zhao[2,3](✉), Yi Chen[1,2], and Zetao Guo[1]

[1] University of Science and Technology of China, Hefei, China
[2] State Key Laboratory of Processors, Institute of Computing Technology, Chinese Academy of Sciences, Suzhou, China
[3] University of Chinese Academy of Sciences, Beijing, China
zhaoyongwei@ict.ac.cn

Abstract. FP4 is a format for low-bit neural network inference. Existing FP4 hardware fails to exploit the redundancy in the FP4(E2M1) multiplication, 256 operand pairs collapse to only 37 distinct products. However, normal and subnormal values obey different encoding rules, which break the regularity of the multiplication and require separate hardware handling. We therefore recode each nonzero operand into a linearized form. We propose FOLD-FP4 for FP4 matrix multiplication, the architecture reformulates MAC computation into four steps: recoding, exponent selection, weighted counting, and conversion. Compared with an FP4MAC baseline, FOLD-FP4 achieves about 1.6x higher array level energy efficiency.

Keywords: Large Language Models Accelerator · Low-bit Matrix Multiplication · Floating-point Computing

1 Introduction

The rapid scaling of large neural networks has increased the compute and memory demands of inference, making efficient deployment a central challenge for modern AI systems [8,17]. As a result, low-bit quantization has become an important direction for reducing memory footprint and accelerating large-model inference [17]. Among ultra-low-precision formats, FP4 has received increasing attention in recent hardware and system support. Compared to integer quantization, floating-point schemes offer greater flexibility, better accommodating long-tail or bell-shaped distributions at extremely low bit widths. [13]. Recent hardware support from NVIDIA Blackwell and the AMD Instinct MI350 series further suggests that FP4-class formats are moving toward practical deployment [1,15].

Existing designs still inherit overhead from generic floating-point MAC, including decode logic, numerical processing, and normalization circuitry. FP4 operand combinations map to the same product value, yet existing designs still

L. Eeckhout et al. (Eds.): APPT 2026, LNCS 16693, pp. 330–342, 2027.
https://doi.org/10.1007/978-981-92-4805-6_22

process them as independent multiplications. For FP4 (E2M1), the multiplication of two 4-bit operands contains $16 \times 16 = 256$ input combinations, but these combinations correspond to only 37 distinct product values, yielding a product redundancy of 85.5%. This observation suggests that existing FP4 designs do not exploit the redundancy in the multiplication.

Conventional hardware cannot exploit the FP4 multiplication redundancy, since mapping from FP4 encodings to real values is piecewise. Normal and subnormal numbers follow different encoding rules, which break the regularity of the multiplication and require separate hardware handling. This leads to the central question of this work: can a lightweight and regular representation transform explicitly convert the numerical equivalence in the FP4 multiplication into a linearly composable form for hardware computation?

Based on the observation, the key to eliminating redundant multiplications lies in establishing a linearized input representation. We propose a fold recoding method for FP4 multiplication, it applies a lightweight transform to map FP4 operands into a linearized encoding. Leveraging this recoding, We propose FOLD-FP4 for FP4 matrix multiplication, the architecture reformulates MAC computation into four steps: recoding, exponent selection, weighted counting, and conversion. Experimental results show that, compared with an FP4MAC baseline, FOLD-FP4 achieves approximately 1.6× higher array-level energy efficiency.

The main contributions of this work are summarized as follows:

- We analyze FP4(E2M1) multiplication and show that its 256 operand pairs collapse to only 37 distinct product values, revealing substantial structural redundancy that is not exploited by existing FP4 compute units.
- We propose a fold recoding method that transforms FP4 operands into a linearized encoding, enabling the hidden equivalence in FP4 multiplication to be utilized in hardware.
- Based on this formulation, we develop an efficient FP4 matrix multiplication architecture. Experimental results show that FOLD-FP4 achieves 1.6× higher array-level energy efficiency than an FP4MAC baseline.

2 Motivation

Due to its limited dynamic range, INT4 quantization often relies on algorithm compensation to alleviate the mismatch between fixed quantization intervals and data distributions with large dynamic variation [12,17]. In contrast, FP4 provides stronger dynamic representation under the same bit-width budget. We highlight two observations: conventional FP4 multiplication obscures substantial reuse opportunities, and wide accumulation remains the dominant cost.

2.1 Pairwise FP4 Multiplication Obscures Redundancy

Existing FP4 hardware fails to exploit the numerical redundancy inherent in the multiplication, as it treats each operand pair as a distinct computation.

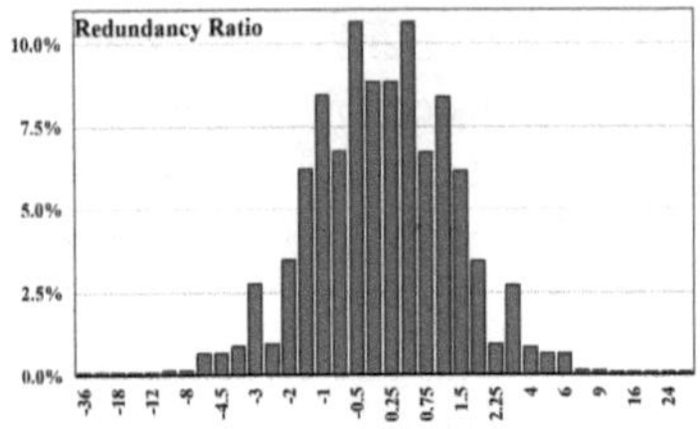

Fig. 1. Distribution of nonzero FP4 multiplication values in LLaMA-7B.

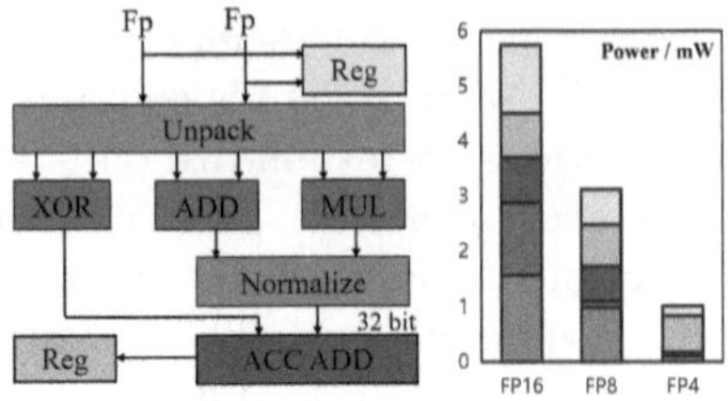

Fig. 2. Power breakdown on a minimalist FP MAC-based systolic array processing element.

While the multiplication of two FP4 operands yields 256 combinations, the 196 nonzero pairs map to only 36 unique product values, representing a theoretical redundancy of 81.6%. Different encoded operand pairs can map to the same product value. However, conventional pairwise multiplication flows still process them independently, leading to redundant execution of numerically equivalent operations.

In practical LLM inference, this redundancy is further amplified by workload distribution. As demonstrated by our analysis of LLaMA-7B on the WikiText dataset, real-world workloads do not uniformly traverse the theoretical FP4 multiplication; instead, they cluster around a narrow set of frequent products. As shown in Fig. 1, over 95% of nonzero products fall within the range $[-3, 3]$. This concentration means the active multiplication during GEMM is significantly smaller than the full theoretical range. This phenomenon is consistent with prior observations that low-bit computation often exhibits substantial arithmetic redundancy. For example, Stripes exploits bit-level serial structure and Cambricon-C leverages primitive-level regularity [4,10], but neither targets FP4 multiplication.

2.2 Wide Accumulation as a Bottleneck to Low-Bit Efficiency

The input bit width determines the size of the multiplier, whereas accumulation precision is usually determined by dynamic-range and numerical-stability requirements rather than by the input format itself. As a result, existing FP4 MAC accumulate partial sums in a high precision format.

As shown in Fig. 2, when precision is reduced from FP16 to FP8 and FP4, the power contribution of the multiplier decreases rapidly, while the contribution of the accumulation path formed by the wide adder and result registers continues to rise. For FP4, this path accounts for 71.9% of total PE power. This trend indicates that reducing operand precision alone does not proportionally reduce the cost of accumulation updates.

When precision reaches FP4, the main dynamic overhead of a PE no longer comes from product generation itself, but from updating wide accumulation state every cycle. This observation suggests that improving FP4 efficiency requires more than simplifying the multiplier; it also requires reducing the activity and update cost of the wide accumulation. Existing FP4 hardware efforts, such as hardware support for microscaling data types, still largely optimize around FP4 MAC or scale execution [5]. These proposals are hard to achieve net improvements on FP4.

2.3 Representation for Efficient FP4 Compute

These observation motivates the need for a lightweight and regular representation transform. By mapping raw FP4 into a linearized encoding, equivalence in the numerical domain can be expressed in hardware. On top of this representation, pairwise FP4 multiplication can be reorganized into four steps: recoding, exponent selection, weighted counting, and conversion. The next section presents the proposed Fold-FP4 recoding method.

3 FOLD-FP4 Formulation

FOLD-FP4 linearizes FP4 values with different original representations through recoding, and thereby redefines FP4 MAC computation. In the following, we first introduce the recoding rule and then describe how it leads to the overall matrix multiplication flow.

3.1 FOLD-FP4 Recoding

The numerical interpretation of FP4(E2M1) is piecewise, normal and subnormal values follow different encoding rules. To address this issue, we recode each nonzero FP4 operand into a linearized encoding

$$x = (-1)^s \cdot p \cdot 2^E, \qquad p \in \{0.5,\, 0.75\}, \tag{1}$$

where s is the sign bit, p is a primitive coefficient, and E is the exponent. Under this representation, both normal and subnormal nonzero FP4 values are mapped into the same arithmetic form.

Given two recoded FP4 operands a and b, their multiplication can be written as

$$ab = (-1)^{s_a \oplus s_b}\,(p_a p_b)\,2^{E_a+E_b}. \tag{2}$$

Since $p_a, p_b \in \{0.5, 0.75\}$, the primitive product $p_a p_b$ can only take three values, $p_a p_b \in \{0.25,\, 0.375,\, 0.5625\}$. Therefore, each nonzero FP4 multiplication can be decomposed into three components: sign, primitive category, and exponent position. This formulation provides the basis for reorganizing FP4 MAC into linearized representation in the next subsection.

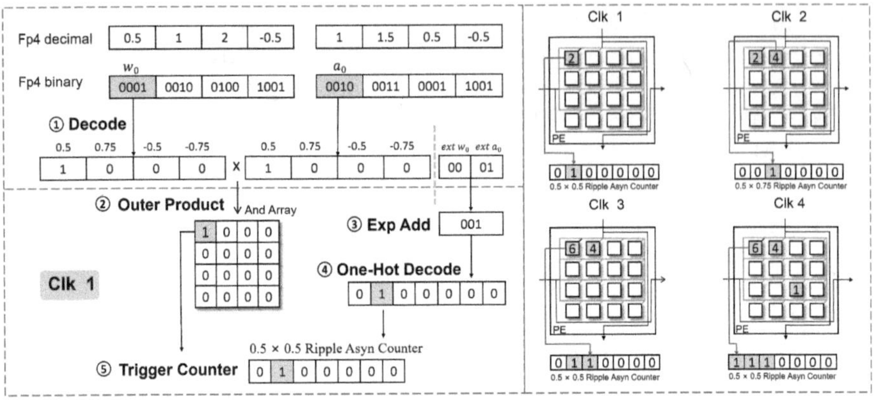

Fig. 3. FOLD-FP4 execution in one PE. Left panel illustrates the computation flow of one FP4 multiplication within a single cycle. The right panel shows the work flow of the vector multiply vector in one PE.

3.2 FOLD-FP4 Matrix Multiplication Flow

In the previous subsection, we introduced the FOLD-FP4 recoding rule. We now illustrate the computation flow of FOLD-FP4 matrix multiplication using an example. As shown in Fig. 3, a weight sequence $\mathbf{w} = [0.5, 1, 2, -0.5]$ and an activation sequence $\mathbf{a} = [1, 1.5, 0.5, -0.5]$ are streamed into the array, with one FP4 operand pair processed in each cycle.

For each input pair, the system first recodes the original FP4 encodings into primitive coefficients and exponent fields. The left side of Fig. 3 illustrates this procedure using the first multiplication $(w_0, a_0) = (0.5, 1)$ as an example. After Decode, both 0.5 and 1 are mapped to the primitive coefficient 0.5, which activates a valid entry at position $(0, 0)$ in the AND array. Their exponents are taken from the original middle two bits of the FP4 encodings, and their sum is further decoded into the one-hot value 010000. Together, the primitive location and the exponent one-hot code determine the update of the corresponding weighted counter.

The right side of Fig. 3 shows the state evolution in the following cycles. As the input stream proceeds, different FP4 operand pairs are mapped to their corresponding primitive categories and exponent positions. Contributions mapped to the same category and the same position are merged during accumulation.

After the entire MAC has been processed, the conversion stage combines the accumulated results from all categories and positions to reconstruct the final output. The hardware architecture that implements this computation flow is described in the next section.

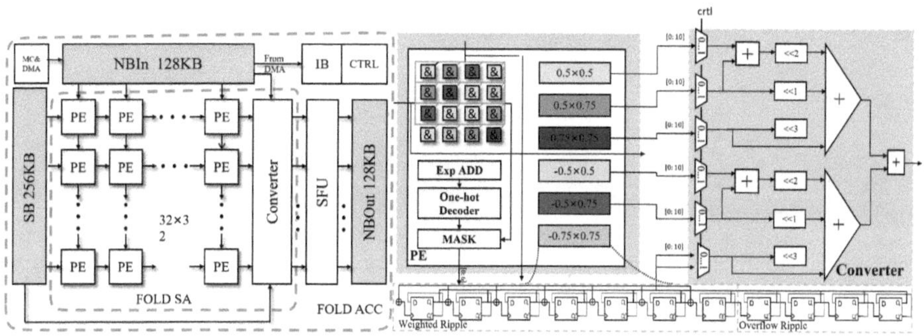

Fig. 4. Overall architecture of FOLD-FP4.

4 FOLD Architecture

4.1 Architecture Overview

Figure 4 illustrates the overall architecture of FOLD-FP4. The main compute unit is a 32×32 output stationary systolic array, referred to as FOLD SA, which is designed for the proposed computation flow. To support FOLD-FP4, raw FP4 activations and weights are decoded at the array boundary before entering the PE array, and the accumulated internal states are converted to final numerical results by a Converter at the output.

For system level evaluation, we further build a complete accelerator architecture, referred to as FOLD ACC. FOLD ACC adopts a classic three buffer accelerator organization derived from DianNao [3]. Besides FOLD SA, the output path also includes an SFU for result processing. This organization preserves the regular structure of the systolic array while keeping the additional support logic outside the PE core.

4.2 Decode

The Decode module preprocesses FP4 inputs before they enter FOLD SA. For each FP4, it produces two outputs, a one hot selection signal that indicates the primitive coefficient category, and the corresponding exponent information. Since this mapping is predefined, the module can be implemented using lightweight combinational logic.

By placing Decode at the array boundary, FOLD-FP4 converts raw FP4 inputs into the internal representation required by the proposed computation flow before they reach the PE array. This organization avoids replicating the same input decoding logic inside every PE.

4.3 PE Design

The PE is the key microarchitectural component in FOLD-FP4. As shown in Fig. 5, each PE receives decoded signals and converts the current FP4 operand

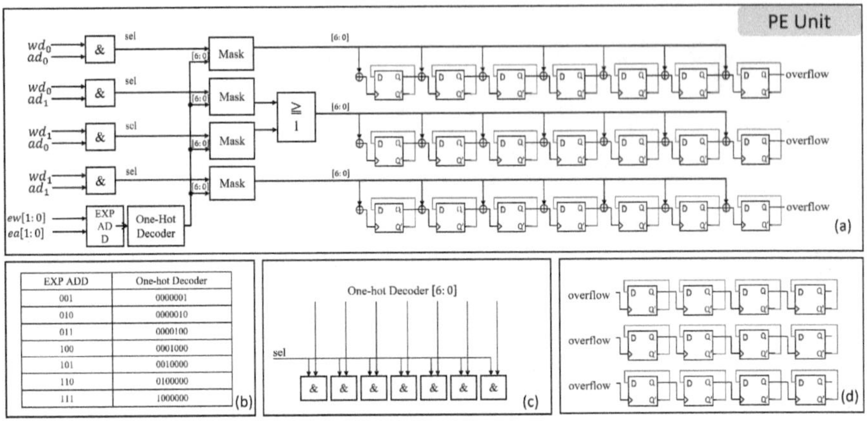

Fig. 5. Microarchitecture of the FOLD-FP4 processing element. For clarity, only the positive primitive multiplication are shown.

pair into an update to the local accumulation state. The computation is decomposed into primitive product category selection and exponent position update. The main components are an AND array, exponent handling logic, weighted ripple asynchronous counters, and overflow counters.

AND Array. The AND array determines the primitive category of the current input pair by combining the decoded signals. Two paths correspond to the same primitive category and are merged into one update request.

Exponent Handling. The exponent path determines where the current contribution is accumulated. The exponents are first added and then decoded into a one hot position selection vector. This vector is broadcast to all primitive product paths and combined with the primitive category signal to generate the weighted update request.

Weighted Ripple Asynchronous Counter. Local accumulation is performed by three weighted ripple asynchronous counter chains, each corresponding to one primitive category. When a valid request is written, ripple carry propagates automatically toward higher positions through cascaded flip flops. To support correct counter updates when the DFF output and the exponent one-hot signal are simultaneously asserted, each cycle is divided into an update phase and a reset phase, allowing the falling edge of the XOR output to be transformed into a valid rising-edge trigger. Because at most one exponent position is updated in each cycle, the resulting design preserves low dynamic power consumption.

Overflow Counter. When carry propagation exceeds the most significant position of the main counter chain, the overflow is recorded by a separate overflow counter. At the end of accumulation, the states of the main counter chains and the overflow counter are forwarded to the Converter for final numerical reconstruction.

4.4 Converter

After all multiply-accumulate operations for the current output block are completed, control signals are asserted to read out the counter outputs. Converter are then mapped back to numerical contributions through fixed shift operations and a small number of adders. Partial sums from different primitive product categories are accumulated separately and combined at the output to produce the final result, which is then forwarded to the downstream units.

5 Evaluation

5.1 Experimental Setup

Hardware Configuration. All designs are implemented in Verilog RTL and synthesized under the FreePDK 45 nm technology node using Synopsys Design Compiler. Power is estimated by PrimeTime PX with gate level VCD activity. On chip SRAM buffers are modeled with CACTI 7 [2]. Cycle level evaluation is conducted on a unified accelerator template built on ANT [6]. The template adopts a 32×32 output stationary systolic array, a 128 KB input buffer, a 256 KB weight buffer, and a 128 KB output buffer.

Baselines. We compare FOLD-FP4 with FP4MAC, Cam.FP4, and LUT-FP4. FP4MAC serves as the conventional baseline, each PE performs FP4 multiplication and accumulation. To ensure a fair comparison, all baselines are evaluated under the same accelerator template and matched compute capability.

Adaptation of Prior Designs. Cam.FP4 is adapted from Cambricon-C [4] the mantissa multiplication produces only four possible outcomes, the CAM can be simplified to an R32 organization by further merging these outcomes under exponent information. LUT-FP4 is adapted from LUT Tensor Core [14]. It maps the sign and mantissa pattern of each operand pair to a compact LUT index and restores the final numerical scale through exponent guided shift operations.

5.2 Hardware Evaluation

In this section, we evaluate the hardware cost of FOLD-FP4 at both the PE and accelerator levels. We first report the overall hardware characteristics of FOLD ACC, and then compare the PE-level cost of different computation methods.

Overall Hardware Characteristics. Table 1 reports the hardware characteristics of FOLD ACC. The complete FOLD ACC occupies an area of 11.07 mm^2 and consumes 3641.28 mW power. For the baselines, FP4MAC, LUT-FP4, and Cam-FP4 occupy 12.83 mm^2, 11.98 mm^2, and 18.99 mm^2, respectively, with power consumption of 4575.04 mW, 4346.69 mW, and 4192.07 mW. These results show that FOLD-FP4 achieves the lowest overall area and power among all compared designs.

Table 1. Hardware characteristics of FOLD ACC.

Module	Area (mm^2)	(%)	Power (mW)	(%)
FOLD ACC	11.07	100.00	3641.28	100.00
FOLD SA	1.80	16.28	372.85	10.24
PE Array	1.79	16.17	368.95	10.13
Decode	0.002	0.01	0.23	0.01
Converter	0.011	0.10	3.68	0.10
SFU	1.06	9.57	483.87	13.29
NBIn	1.95	17.61	1173.33	32.22
SB	1.10	9.93	605.85	16.64
NBOut	2.63	23.75	742.60	20.39
Ctrl	0.11	0.99	50.05	1.37
IB	0.36	3.25	25.28	0.69
MC	0.23	2.08	83.00	2.28
PHY	1.83	16.53	104.45	2.87

The overhead of the additional support logic is negligible. In particular, Decode and Converter together account for only 0.013 mm^2 area and 3.91 mW power.

PE-level Hardware Characteristics. To validate the proposed design, we reproduce three baselines and list the PE-level hardware characteristics in Table 2. Under the same target clock, FOLD-FP4 PE achieves approximately 3.54×, 2.92×, and 2.50× energy savings over FP4-MAC, LUT-FP4, and Cam-FP4, respectively. The advantage of FOLD-FP4 mainly comes from two aspects. First, it removes the wide adder-based accumulation path in conventional FP4 computation, which is one of the dominant contributors to PE power. Second, it adopts a weight counter organization that reduces the number of counters, thereby further reducing both area and switching activity.

Table 2. PE hardware characteristics performing of different designs.

Item	FP4-MAC	LUT-FP4	Cam-FP4	FOLD-FP4
Area (μm^2)	3476.11	2653.00	9498.16	1748.14
Power (mW)	1.276	1.053	0.902	0.360

5.3 GEMM Kernel-Level Evaluation

In this section, we compare the kernel-level energy efficiency of different designs on matrix multiplication. Figure 6 shows the GOPS/J results and the corresponding normalized energy breakdowns under different matrix dimensions.

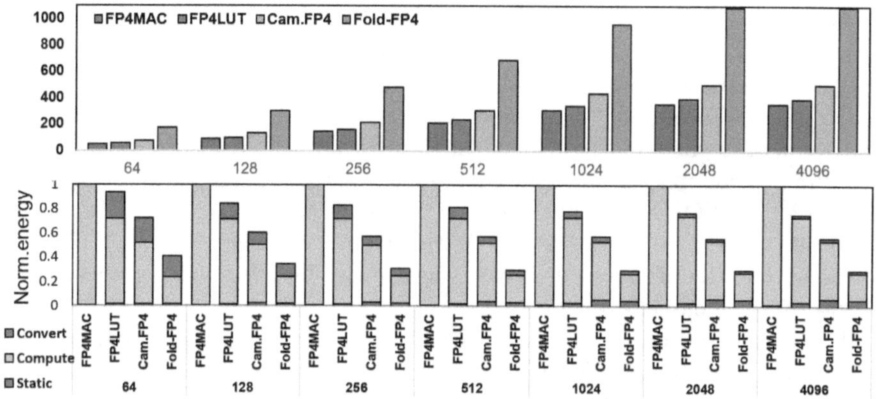

Fig. 6. Energy breakdown and energy efficiency across different matrix dimensions.

FOLD-FP4 achieves the highest energy efficiency across all tested matrix dimensions. From 64 to 4096, FOLD-FP4 improves GOPS/J by approximately 3.30×, 3.10×, and 2.30× over FP4-MAC, LUT-FP4, and Cam-FP4 on average, respectively. For 64 matrix dimensions, the converter contributes to the energy cost. As the matrix dimension grows to 512 and 1024, the computational advantage of the FOLD systolic array becomes more pronounced due to its smaller number of counters and lower compute power. At 4096 dimensions, the energy savings from computation are overshadowed by kernel level overheads.

Since the original LUT Tensor Core targets a GPU-oriented execution model rather than a systolic-array template, the LUT-FP4 baseline in this work is implemented as a LUT-based FP4 design with the same compute capability under the same accelerator configuration.

5.4 Model End-to-End Evaluation

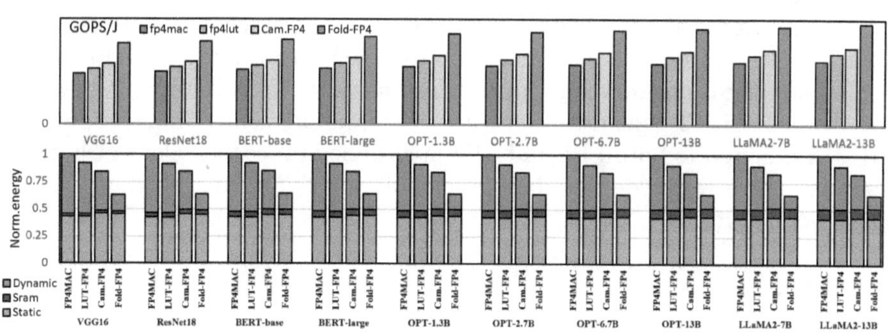

Fig. 7. Energy breakdown and energy efficiency across different workloads.

We further evaluate the proposed design on real-model workloads. Figure 7 shows the system level GOPS/J and the corresponding normalized energy breakdowns on CNNs, Transformers, and LLMs.

FOLD-FP4 achieves the highest GOPS/J on all evaluated models. The improvement is particularly evident on transformer and LLM workloads, where high dimensional matrix multiplication dominates execution. In the observed on LLaMA2-13B, FOLD-FP4 improves GOPS/J by approximately 1.57×, 1.39×, and 1.30× over FP4MAC, FP4LUT, and Cam.FP4, respectively. This result indicates that the proposed design advantage can be effectively preserved after integration into model execution.

The end-to-end improvement of FOLD-FP4 is smaller than its PE-level and kernel-level advantage, which is expected for two reasons. First, the buffer and DRAM components are largely shared across different designs, so they do not scale down with the local compute datapath. Second, once the computation energy is substantially reduced, the static component becomes relatively more significant in the total system energy. Therefore, the gain of FOLD-FP4 at the full-model level remains stable, while its upper bound is increasingly constrained by memory and static overheads rather than by the PE computation itself.

6 Related Work

Prior low-bit accelerators have already explored different forms of redundancy reduction, aiming to avoid treating every multiplication as an independent arithmetic operation. UCNN exploits weight repetition to reuse sub-computations, Carat further exposes value-level parallelism by reformulating multiplication into accumulation, and Cambricon-C introduces primitivization for 4-bit matrix units to explicitly exploit repetition in the multiplication [4,7,16]. Another line of work reduces redundant arithmetic through bit-serial or lookup-based execution. For example, Stripes scales computation with effective precision through bit-serial processing, while LUT Tensor Core replaces part of low-bit mpGEMM with table lookups and table reuse [10,14]. These efforts suggest that low-bit computation can be made more efficient once regularity in the numerical domain is exposed to hardware.

Recent work has also begun to support FP4-oriented formats and hardware. Efficient Precision-Scalable Hardware for Microscaling (MX) Processing in Robotics Learning develops arithmetic support for MX formats, M2XFP improves low-bit FP4 quantization with metadata-augmented microscaling, and DHFP-PE supports both FP8 and FP4 in a unified processing element [5,9,11]. However, these works do not directly exploit the redundancy within the FP4 multiplication itself.

7 Conclusion

We propose FOLD-FP4, an FP4 matrix multiplication architecture based on folded accumulation. We further design the corresponding systolic-array microarchitecture and complete accelerator. Experimental results show that FOLD-FP4 achieves up to 3.30×, 3.10×, and 2.30× GOPS/J improvement over FP4MAC, FP4LUT, and Cam.FP4, respectively, across matrix-level evaluation. For the complete accelerator, FOLD-FP4 also delivers the best overall efficiency on DNN workloads, with the best case reaching 1.57×, 1.39×, and 1.30× improvement, respectively.

Acknowledgments. This work is partially supported by the National Key R&D Program of China (Grant No. 2024YFB4505501), Strategic Priority Research Program of the Chinese Academy of Sciences (Grants No. XDB0660300, XDB0660301, XDB0660302), CAS Project for Young Scientists in Basic Research (YSBR-029), and Youth Innovation Promotion Association CAS.

Disclosure of Interests. The authors have no competing interests to declare that are relevant to the content of this article.

Use of Artificial Intelligence Tools. Artificial intelligence tools, if used, were used only for language organization and figure/table polishing, and did not participate in the generation of the core ideas or technical content.

References

1. AMD: AMD Instinct MI350 Series GPUs. AMD Official Product Page (2025)
2. Balasubramonian, R., Kahng, A.B., Muralimanohar, N., Shafiee, A., Srinivas, V.: CACTI 7: new tools for interconnect exploration in innovative off-chip memories. ACM Trans. Archit. Code Optim. **14**(2), 14:1–14:25 (2017). https://doi.org/10.1145/3085572
3. Chen, T., Du, Z., Sun, N., Wang, J., Wu, C., Chen, Y., et al.: DianNao: a small-footprint high-throughput accelerator for ubiquitous machine-learning. In: Proceedings of the 19th International Conference on Architectural Support for Programming Languages and Operating Systems, pp. 269–284 (2014). https://doi.org/10.1145/2541940.2541967
4. Chen, Y., Zhao, Y., Hao, Y., Wen, Y., Dai, Y., Li, X., et al.: Cambricon-c: efficient 4-bit matrix unit via primitivization. In: Proceedings of the 2024 57th IEEE/ACM International Symposium on Microarchitecture, pp. 538–550 (2024). https://doi.org/10.1109/MICRO61859.2024.00047
5. Cuyckens, S., Yi, X., Murthy, N.S., Fang, C., Verhelst, M.: Efficient precision-scalable hardware for microscaling (MX) processing in robotics learning. arXiv preprint arXiv:2505.22404 (2025)
6. Guo, C., Zhang, C., Leng, J., Liu, Z., Yang, F., Liu, Y., et al.: ANT: exploiting adaptive numerical data type for low-bit deep neural network quantization. In: Proceedings of the 55th IEEE/ACM International Symposium on Microarchitecture, pp. 1414–1433 (2022). https://doi.org/10.1109/MICRO56248.2022.00097
7. Hegde, K., Yu, J., Agrawal, R., Yan, M., Pellauer, M., Fletcher, C.W.: UCNN: exploiting computational reuse in deep neural networks via weight repetition. In: Proceedings of the 2018 ACM/IEEE 45th Annual International Symposium on Computer Architecture, pp. 674–687 (2018). https://doi.org/10.1109/ISCA.2018.00062
8. Hoffmann, J.: Training compute-optimal large language models. arXiv preprint arXiv:2203.15556 (2022)

9. Hu, W., et al.: M2XFP: a metadata-augmented microscaling data format for efficient low-bit quantization. In: Proceedings of the 31st ACM International Conference on Architectural Support for Programming Languages and Operating Systems (2026). https://doi.org/10.1145/3779212.3790185
10. Judd, P., Albericio, J., Hetherington, T.H., Aamodt, T.M., Moshovos, A.: Stripes: Bit-serial deep neural network computing. In: Proceedings of the 2016 49th Annual IEEE/ACM International Symposium on Microarchitecture, pp. 1–12 (2016). https://doi.org/10.1109/MICRO.2016.7783722
11. Kumar, S., Sharma, V.P., Neema, V., Vishvakarma, S.K.: DHFP-PE: dual-precision hybrid floating point processing element for ai acceleration. arXiv preprint arXiv:2604.04507 (2026). https://doi.org/10.48550/arXiv.2604.04507
12. Lin, J., Tang, J., Tang, H., Yang, S., Chen, W.M., Wang, W.C., et al.: AWQ: activation-aware weight quantization for LLM compression and acceleration. In: Proceedings of Machine Learning and Systems (2024)
13. Liu, S.y., Liu, Z., Huang, X., Dong, P., Cheng, K.T.: LLM-FP4: 4-bit floating-point quantized transformers. In: Proceedings of the 2023 Conference on Empirical Methods in Natural Language Processing (2023)
14. Mo, Z., Wang, L., Wei, J., Zeng, Z., Cao, S., Ma, L., et al.: LUT tensor core: a software-hardware co-design for LUT-based low-bit LLM inference. In: Proceedings of the 52nd Annual International Symposium on Computer Architecture, pp. 514–528 (2025). https://doi.org/10.1145/3695053.3731057
15. NVIDIA: NVIDIA TensorRT unlocks fp4 image generation for NVIDIA blackwell geforce RTX 50 series GPUs. NVIDIA Technical Blog (2025)
16. Pan, Z., San Miguel, J., Wu, D.: Carat: unlocking value-level parallelism for multiplier-free GEMMs. In: Proceedings of the 29th ACM International Conference on Architectural Support for Programming Languages and Operating Systems, vol. 2, pp. 167–184 (2024). https://doi.org/10.1145/3620665.3640364
17. Xiao, G., Lin, J., Seznec, M., Wu, H., Demouth, J., Han, S.: SmoothQuant: accurate and efficient post-training quantization for large language models. In: Proceedings of the 40th International Conference on Machine Learning (2023)

Helios: Scalable Multi-accelerator FPGA Architecture for Efficient Inference of Transformer-Based Models

Yanwei Wang[1(✉)], Jun Liu[2], Wei Huang[2], Qun Li[3], Tianle Mai[3], and Keqiu Li[1]

[1] School of New Media and Communication, Tianjin University, Tianjin, China
{ywwang,keqiu}@tju.edu.cn

[2] Shandong Mass Information Technology Research Institute, Jinan, China

[3] School of Information and Communication Engineering, Beijing University of Posts and Communications, Beijing, China

Abstract. The rapid scaling of Transformer-based Models, such as Large Language Models (LLMs) and Vision Transformer (ViT), has led to increasing demands on computational throughput, memory capacity, and system scalability during inference. While FPGA-based accelerators offer advantages in energy efficiency and programmability, existing designs predominantly rely on low-precision quantization and are often restricted to single-device deployments, limiting both numerical generality and scalability. In this paper, we propose **Helios**, a scalable FPGA architecture for efficient inference of transformer-based models. Helios features an FP16-oriented end-to-end execution core that supports both linear and nonlinear operators through specialized hardware units and multi-granularity scheduling, enabling accurate and efficient execution without aggressive quantization. To address scalability challenges, **Helios** further introduces a distributed multi-accelerator architecture with a high-bandwidth interconnect, supporting both pipeline and tensor parallelism across FPGA devices. Experimental results demonstrate our FP16-oriented accelerator architecture achieves performance comparable to state-of-the-art INT8-based designs, with almost no loss in accuracy. Under the dual-accelerator configuration, **Helios** achieves a 1.88× speedup on Vision Transformer (ViT) and a 1.69× speedup during the decoding stage of the Qwen2-0.5B model. Moreover, for ViT, the proposed architecture delivers up to 1.98× faster inference performance for the SOTA single-accelerator.

Keywords: Multi-Accelerator FPGA Architecture · Transformer Inference · FP16 Precision

1 Introduction

Transformer architectures have become the foundation of modern artificial intelligence, powering a wide range of applications from computer vision to large language models (LLMs) [20]. As model sizes continue to grow, inference workloads

L. Eeckhout et al. (Eds.): APPT 2026, LNCS 16693, pp. 343–358, 2027.
https://doi.org/10.1007/978-981-92-4805-6_23

increasingly demand high computational throughput, large memory capacity, and efficient data movement. Conventional CPU and GPU platforms, while powerful, face challenges in energy efficiency and scalability when serving large-scale Transformer models.

One of the promising hardware platforms, Field-Programmable Gate Arrays (FPGAs) have been shown its potential to accelerate transformer model inference due to their energy efficiency and reconfigurability, which offers high adaptability to the fast-changing nature of AI models. Even with the potential of the FPGA-based acceleratores, Transformer models are highly difficult to scale effectively in the process of inference. The main obstacles are the following:

1) Low-precision Formats: Lots of hardware available today is capable of producing quantized low-precision formats. Even though quantization may be effective in certain workloads, it is not always successful particularly in complex nonlinear computations. Nonlinear operations that are hardware friendly are normally optimized using look-up tables or radix substitution, although this is a far more challenging task when floating-point formats like FP16 are considered.

2) Scalability: Current FPGA accelerators have been typically programmed with single-device configurations and are not easily scaled to multi-FPGA systems [8]. The high bandwidth and low latency required for effective communication between multiple FPGA devices often lead to bottlenecks in multi-accelerator systems [6].

In this paper, a scalable FPGA architecture for efficient inference of transformer-based model named **Helios** is proposed. It employs an FP16-oriented execution core that separates matrix-intensive and nonlinear computations into specialized hardware units in combination with multi-granularity operator scheduling to improve resource utilization. Furthermore, Helios supports multi-accelerators architecture with high-bandwidth interconnect. And it enables both pipeline parallelism and tensor parallelism across multiple FPGA accelerators to improve inference performance.

We evaluate Helios on representative workloads, including Vision Transformers (ViT) and Qwen2 LLM. Experimental results show that Helios achieves both efficient single-device execution and strong scalability across multiple accelerators.

The main contributions of this paper are as follows:

- **A Unified Single-to-Multi-FPGA Execution Paradigm for Transformers.** We propose a holistic FPGA architecture that bridges efficient single-device execution and scalable multi-accelerator deployment through a unified abstraction. Unlike prior works that focus on either kernel-level optimization or isolated multi-FPGA systems, Helios enables seamless mapping of Transformer workloads across devices with consistent execution semantics.
- **An FP16-Centric Design Eliminating the Need for Aggressive Quantization.** We present an end-to-end FP16-oriented architecture with dedicated support for nonlinear and normalization operators, addressing a

key limitation of prior FPGA accelerators that rely on low-precision quantization. Our design demonstrates that high-precision inference can achieve performance comparable to INT8-based approaches while preserving model accuracy.

- **A Communication-Aware Multi-Accelerator Architecture for Transformer Parallelism.** We design a distributed FPGA system with high-bandwidth interconnect and explicitly support both pipeline and tensor parallelism. By co-designing computation partitioning and inter-device communication, Helios minimizes communication overhead and enables efficient scaling across multiple accelerators.
- **End-to-End Evaluation on Representative Vision and Language Models.** We implement Helios on real FPGA platforms and evaluate it using both encoder-based (ViT) and decoder-based (Qwen2) models. Results show that Helios achieves competitive single-device performance and up to 1.96× speedup with multi-accelerator scaling, validating both efficiency and scalability.

2 Background

2.1 Related Works

Most existing works [2,7,15,21] primarily focus on accelerating large language models (LLMs) on a single FPGA device. A subset of these studies targets the acceleration of key Transformer components, such as the attention mechanism and feed-forward neural networks (FFNs), which are dominated by operations including GEMM, linear transformations, and softmax. Several works [12,22] propose specialized hardware architectures tailored to the attention and FFN modules. Compared to generic GEMM-based acceleration, these designs achieve higher efficiency by exploiting operation-level characteristics and data-flow patterns. Nonlinear operations, particularly the softmax function, is challenging due to exponential and normalization computations. To address this issue, [22]

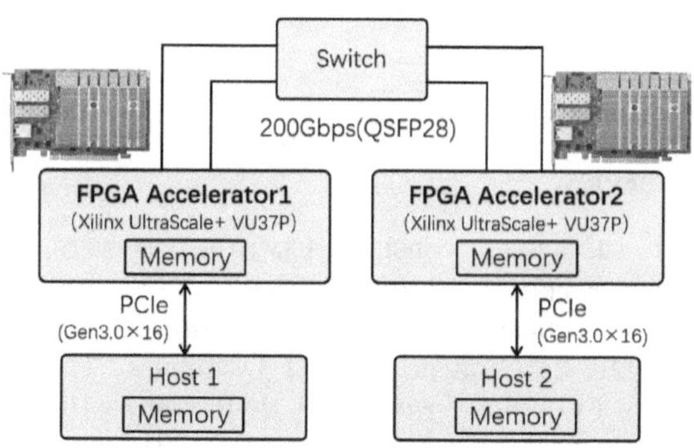

Fig. 1. The System Overview.

proposes a hardware-friendly modification of the softmax function by replacing the natural exponential with base-2 exponentiation under integer constraints. [9] reformulates the exponential using a logarithmic transformation to avoid retraining. Although these works simplified hardware implementation, they restrict input data types and may not generalize well across different Transformer models.

There are a few works focused on multi-FPGA acceleration. Zheng et al. [24] propose LoopLynx, a scalable dataflow architecture that improves FPGA utilization through a hybrid spatial–temporal execution model. Ma et al. [13] present a heterogeneous multi-FPGA system with a compute-dedicated architecture, leveraging FPGA-specific resources to achieve high peak performance for distributed LLM inference. However, their methods are designed for LLMs containing decoder-only transformer architectures which are not suitable for encoder-only Transformer models such as Vision Transformer(ViT).

2.2 Transformer Workloads and Inference Characteristics

There are two kinds of transformer-based models with different structure, including Encoder-dominant models such as ViT and decoder-only models such as LLM. So transformer workloads have distinct architectural patterns and inference behaviors. For encoder-style models, the inference process is dominated by dense matrix computations, which has relatively regular execution patterns and predictable data dependencies. Therefore, performance is primarily limited by compute throughput and memory bandwidth. For decoder-only LLMs, its inference process is more complex which consists of two distinct stages: prefill and decoding. The prefill stage is similar to that in encoder-model, while the decoding stage processes tokens sequentially, introducing strong latency sensitivity. As a result, efficient execution requires not only high-throughput matrix computation but also fine-grained scheduling of nonlinear and control-dependent operations.

The above differences impose distinct requirements on hardware design. High-throughput execution favors large-scale parallelism and data reuse, while low-latency decoding requires flexible scheduling. Furthermore, scaling to large models needs parallel execution across multiple devices, introducing additional challenges in efficient inter-device cooperation.

3 Helios Architecture

3.1 System Overview

As shown in Fig. 1, the system consists of two host servers, two Xilinx UltraScale+ VU37P FPGA accelerators, and a high-speed switch supporting 200 Gbps QSFP28 interfaces. Each host serves as a control and preprocessing node, maintaining model weights, task queues, and I/O buffers. The hosts connect to their corresponding FPGA accelerators via PCIe Gen3×16 [4]. Each FPGA is equipped with on-board memory (HBM or DDR4) to store partitioned model weights, intermediate activations, and temporary data. The accelerators are interconnected through dual 100 Gbps QSFP28 links, forming a 200 Gbps low-latency communication channel for exchanging intermediate inference data. All computations use FP16, which is sufficient to meet inference precision requirements for both linear and nonlinear operators.

3.2 Accelerator Architecture

Helios adopts a modular accelerator architecture designed for efficient execution of transformer-based model inference. The architecture separates matrix-dominant computations from nonlinear and vector-oriented operations, enabling specialized hardware pipelines for each computation class while maintaining a unified execution model.

As illustrated in Fig. 2(Left), the accelerator consists of two main components: target-related modules and target-independent modules. The target-related modules include the memory controller, PCIe controller, and network interface controller (NIC), which interact with the host system and off-chip memory. These modules encapsulate platform-specific logic, allowing the core accelerator design to remain portable across different FPGA platforms. The target-independent modules implement the core computation and data movement infrastructure, including the matrix multiplication unit (MMU), special function unit (SFU), on-chip network (NoC), register file, instruction cache, and dedicated data transformation modules.

The accelerator follows a decoupled compute architecture in which the MMU handles matrix-intensive operations while the SFU executes nonlinear and element-wise functions. This separation allows each unit to be optimized for its computational characteristics while enabling flexible scheduling through a unified instruction interface.

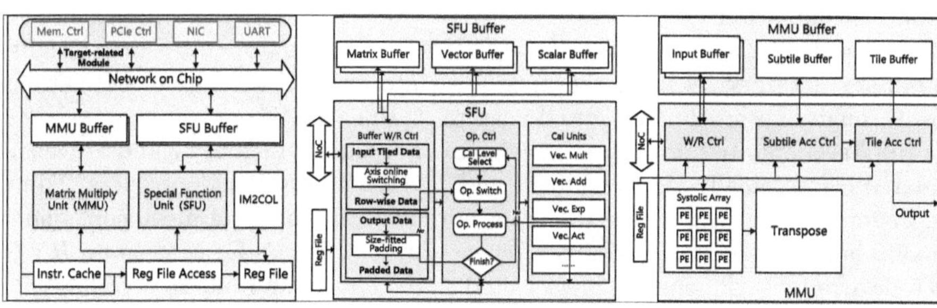

Fig. 2. The Accelerator Architecture.

3.3 Memory Architecture

Following the unit-level decomposition in Sect. 3.2, the linear units and nonlinear units are physically implemented with dedicated computation and memory organizations, referred to as MMU and SFU in the following description. As shown in the Fig. 2, the MMU and SFU in this hardware accelerator share a high degree of consistency in their memory architecture design. Generally, both fetch data from off-chip memory via an NoC and temporarily store the data in their respective dedicated high-speed on-chip caches (MMU Buffer and SFU Buffer, respectively) [1]. To minimize memory access latency, both types of caches employ a double buffering design (as shown by the stacked cache boxes in the figure) [17]. This mechanism allows the computation unit to process the current data block while the read/write controller (W/R Ctrl or Buffer W/R Ctrl) prefetches the next data block to be processed or writes back the result of the previous step in the background. This achieves deep overlap between computation and communication (memory access), significantly improving the overall system throughput. On-chip buffer capacities are configured as follows: the Instruction Cache is 48 KB; the MMU Buffer and SFU Buffer sizes are each set to $S^2 \times C$, where S is the systolic array dimension and C is an integer coefficient constrained by hardware platform resources ($C = 128$ in this work, yielding $64^2 \times 128 = 512$ KB for the 64×64 configuration).

Addressing the two distinct computational scenarios of the two units, this memory architecture emphasizes different aspects in its implementation, fully leveraging its customization advantages:

MMU: Within the MMU unit, tailored to the data flow characteristics of Generalized Multiplication (GEMM), its cache is finely divided into an input buffer, a subtile buffer, and a tile buffer [19]. This hierarchical storage architecture is highly compatible with the MMU's internal systolic array and two-stage accumulation logic. During computation, the partial sum calculated by the systolic array is first locally accumulated in the subtile buffer under the scheduling of the subtile accumulation controller (Subtile Acc Ctrl); subsequently, a larger-scale global accumulation is completed in the tile buffer through the tile accumulation controller (Tile Acc Ctrl). The MMU systolic array operates in a weight-stationary dataflow: weights are preloaded into the PE array, and activations flow through in a pipelined, skewed pattern, with each PE performing one FP16 multiply-accumulate per cycle. Partial sums propagate diagonally and are accumulated hierarchically via the Subtile and Tile Accumulation Controllers. Tiling parameters are statically determined to minimize off-chip data movement under on-chip buffer capacity constraints: for an $M \times K \times K \times N$ GEMM on an $R \times C$ systolic array, tile dimensions are selected as the largest sub-blocks fitting within the MMU Buffer, Input Buffer, Subtile Buffer, and Tile Buffer capacities.

SFU: Within the SFU unit, its primary task is to execute complex nonlinear functions such as Softmax and LayerNorm, as well as basic arithmetic operations. Since these operations often involve a mix of matrix, vector, and scalar computations, the SFU buffer is specifically divided into matrix buffers, vector buffers, and scalar buffers to accommodate parallel data access at multiple granularities [23]. More importantly, the SFU's buffer read/write controller (Buffer W/R Ctrl) is endowed with stronger data reorganization capabilities, supporting online axis switching and size-fitted padding. This means that the storage module can dynamically convert input-tiered data into computationally friendly row-wise data during the memory access phase before sending it to the computation unit. This memory architecture design, strongly correlated with data dimensions, not only eliminates additional data alignment and transport overhead but also provides extremely high memory access flexibility and efficiency for various backend vector computation units (such as Vec. Mult, Vec. Exp, etc.).

3.4 High-Bandwidth Interconnect

Helios enforces execution determinism at the hardware level through compiler support, which employs absolute physical addressing and fixed-latency on-chip SRAMs (GMEM). The high bandwidth module is shown in Fig. 3. Both accelerators operate as master devices in a peer-to-peer communication model. During remote memory access, the receiving accelerator issues a read DMA request and stalls until the interconnect delivers the data [5], while the sending accelerator concurrently executes a write DMA to directly push results into the remote GMEM, DDR, or HBM. This direct memory access model eliminates intermediate synchronization barriers, ensuring fully deterministic scheduling and execution across the system.

Decoupled Network Module and Frame Processing: The interconnect module leverages a highly decoupled software-hardware design to bridge the internal execution core with external physical links. The transmission pipeline is managed through specialized FIFO queues and frame processors.

Transmit Path: To enable non-blocking execution, the on-chip DMA controller firstly separates transmission metadata (e.g., destination IDs and payload sizes) from payload data, and then uses independent asynchronous queues to buffer them. The payload is then encapsulated with appropriate headers, synchronized across clock domains, and dispatched to the physical interface.

Receive Path: Incoming data is first buffered asynchronously at the physical interface. Upon successful verification, network headers are stripped, and the payload is transferred across clock domains directly into the accelerator's memory hierarchy for immediate processing, without software involvement.

Topology Adaptability and Interface Compatibility: Internally, the NET module interfaces via standard AXI-Stream (AXIS), completely decoupling the network protocol stack from the core computing engine to facilitate future protocol iterations. Externally, the architecture supports diverse physical media, including Ethernet (ETH) and Direct Attach Copper (DAC), allowing for scalable deployments spanning optical interconnects and copper cabling. When deployed in a direct point-to-point topology without intermediate switches, the network module can drop the standard MAC frame header. Instead, it utilizes a lightweight, custom header composed solely of a Board ID, data length, and addressing information to minimize overhead and maximize effective bandwidth. This streamlined, direct connection is highly advantageous for measuring accurate link latency and ensuring deterministic data delivery across the multi-accelerator fabric.

Interconnection Module Data Transmission Flow: In the interconnection module, the sender employs a stream-based processing mechanism that separates descriptors from data, as shown in Fig. 3:

Transmit-Side Data Flow: At the transmit side, the DMA controller writes the transmission metadata, such as the destination board ID and data length, into the descriptor FIFO (desc_afifo), while the payload data is stored in the data FIFO (axi_afifo). The transmit frame module (Tframe) reads the descriptor information, queries the routing table to obtain the destination MAC address, and fetches payload data from axi_afifo. It then adds the frame header to form a complete packet. Finally, the packet passes through axi_reg for clock-domain crossing and is sent to the external ETH/DAC interface.

Receive-Side Data Flow: At the receive side, incoming data from the ETH/DAC interface is first buffered in axi_afifo. The receive frame module (Rframe) reads the descriptor information from desc_afifo, obtains the local and remote MAC addresses from the routing table, and verifies the frame header. If the verification succeeds, the header is removed and the payload is forwarded across the clock domain to the local accelerator for further processing; otherwise, the frame is discarded.

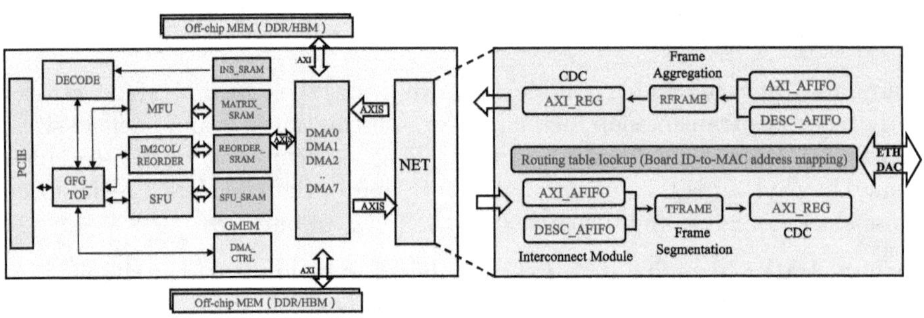

Fig. 3. The Interconnection Module.

4 Helios Execution Model

4.1 Multi-granularity Operators

The architectural difference in transformer primarily manifests at two distinct levels: block-level and layer-level. With the rise of multimodal models, encoder-only or decoder-only structures are increasingly shifting toward an encoder-decoder structure. The decoder is similar to the encoder, except for masked self-attention. In this paper, both are supported.

For linear operations (i.e.,GEMM), the key of multi-granularity operation is to split large matrix multiplications into small ones while maximizing the utilization of computing units. For non-linear operations, the key is the variation of layer-level computing operations within a block across different models. Taking layer normalization of ViT and Qwen2 as an example, shown in Eq. (1) and (2). μ_i is the average value of row $\boldsymbol{x}_i$. γ_j is the scale factor and β_j is the shift factor. n is the number of elements in row$\boldsymbol{x}_i$. So, the LN_{ViT} and LN_{Qwen2} operations are decomposed into specific hardware computational steps, as illustrated in Fig. 4a. We further define function-level and arithmetic-level hardware operators using layer normalization as the example. It is obvious that the calculation steps for layer normalization in Qwen2 constitute a subset of those in ViT. Function-level operators, executed via hardcoded data paths in FPGA, achieve lower latency. Meanwhile, arithmetic-level operators provide the fundamental hardware support required to adapt to novel function-level operations.

Each Transformer Operation can be decomposed into a sequence of operators at two granularity levels: function-level for well-known computations with pre-optimized hardware datapaths (e.g., LayerNorm, Softmax) and arithmetic-level for custom operations composed from primitive instructions (Vec.Mult, Vec.Exp etc.). The resulting operator sequence is translated into a fixed stream of LD $\rightarrow$ CAL $\rightarrow$ SYNC instruction groups, with LOOP wrappers for repeated block structures; a SYNC barrier is placed after each CAL that produces data consumed by a subsequent operator, ensuring deterministic, deadlock-free execution. For tensor-parallel workloads, GEMM weight matrices are partitioned along the column dimension into equal-sized slices—one per accelerator—so that each device performs the same number of MAC operations per input token, achieving load balance by construction. For pipeline-parallel workloads, layers are partitioned sequentially across accelerators, with double-buffered LD/ST at pipeline boundaries so that downstream devices begin computation on layer $l+1$ activations while upstream devices process the next input at layer l, hiding inter-device transfer latency.

4.2 Instruction Set Architecture

We adopt an instruction set paradigm based on computational flow decoupling: operator-specific implementation logic is decoupled from instruction control flow, neural network models are converted into a standardized intermediate representation, and a custom parser decomposes computational tasks into operations matching the hardware computing units, after which computing core interfaces are invoked to generate instructions—realizing end-to-end mapping from algorithms to hardware instructions.

As shown in Fig. 4b, the instruction set consists of three types of instructions: data access (`LD/ST`), computation (`CAL`), control (`LOOP`, `SYNC`), and debugging (`DEBUG`). `LD/ST` instructions copy data to specified buffers or off-chip memory via NoC, which may be accompanied by operations such as IM2COL [18]. `CAL` instructions launch MMU or SFU for computation. Combined with `SYNC` instructions and double buffers, they achieve the overlap between computation and

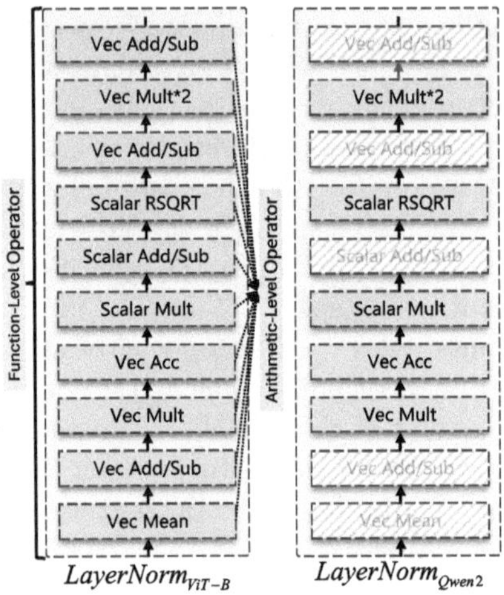

(a) The example of function-level operators and arithmetic-level operators

Ins. Type	Fuction
LD/ST	Handle data communication between buffers and off-chip memory
SYNC	Enable overlaping between CAL and LD/ST
CAL	Launch MMU/SFU for calculating tasks
LOOP	Enable loopping for block-wise computation
DEBUG	Assist in monitoring instruction execution (print register or string)

(b) ISA details

Fig. 4. The two-level operators and ISA details.

communication. To reduce the number of instructions, `LOOP` instructions can execute instructions cyclically according to the block structure of the model.

$$LN_{ViT}(x_{i,j}) = \frac{x_{i,j} - \mu_i}{\sqrt{\frac{\sum_{j=1}^{n}(x_{i,j}-\mu_i)^2}{n} + \epsilon}} \odot \gamma_j + \beta_j \tag{1}$$

$$LN_{Qwen2}(x_{i,j}) = \frac{x_{i,j}}{\sqrt{\frac{\sum_{j=1}^{n} x_{i,j}^2}{n} + \epsilon}} \odot \gamma_j \tag{2}$$

5 Experimental Setup

5.1 FPGA Implementation

The hardware environment used for the evaluation is shown in Fig. 5. The target platform consists of two Inspur F37X FPGA boards (with Xilinx VU37P), where each board is equipped with 3 DDR4 memories, totaling 24 GB in capacity per device. The HBM is not used in this work. The size of SA is 32×32 or 64×64 due to the limitation of FPGA resource. Based on post-implementation resource utilization, the estimated board-level power consumption is approximately 32.15 W for 32 × 32 SA and 45.62 W for 64 × 64 SA per accelerator, as reported by Vivado.

Baseline. We select some other FPGA-based accelerators targeting ViT-B or DeiT-base, because the number of parameters and structures of ViT-B and DeiT-base are almost the same. In addition to focusing on throughput, we also list some other key information, such as programming languages and data format. The

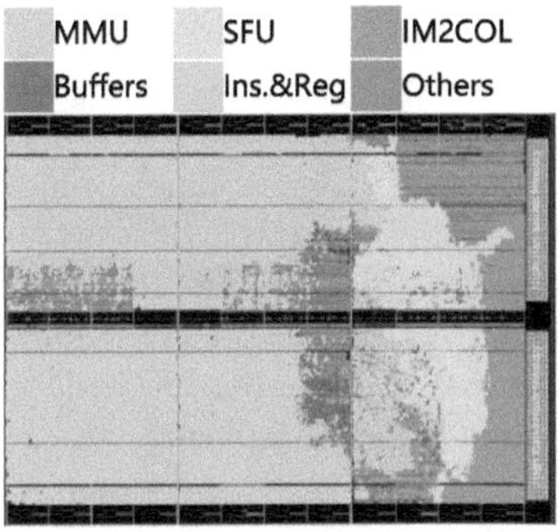

(a) FPGA implementation

Module	LUT/k	FF/k	BRAM	URAM	DSP
Available	1303	2607	2016	960	9024
MMU	547	522	0	0	4096
SFU	95	81	82	0	171
Buffers	3	8	33	130	0
IM2COL	75	62	0	0	33
Others	40	42	44	0	0
Total	760	715	159	130	4310

(b) FPGA resource utilization

Fig. 5. The implementation layout of Helios and FPGA resources utilization for different modules.

data format, in particular, plays a critical role in determining the accelerator's throughput by affecting both FPGA resource consumption and computational efficiency. As for the Qwen2 model, we focus on presenting our experimental findings regarding decoder blocks, without direct comparison to existing literature, to provide key differences in computational efficiency between the decoder and encoder on SA.

6 Experimental

6.1 Evaluation of ViT

Before evaluating the scalability of the multi-accelerator system, we first assess the inference performance of a single-accelerator architecture and compare it with existing solutions to establish its efficiency and reliability as a foundation for distributed deployment.

Table 1. ViT evaluating results compared with other works

	Helios Config.1 (32*32)	Helios Config.2 (64*64)	Ref.[15]	Ref.[16]	Ref.[11]	Ref.[10]	Ref.[14]
Model Name	ViT-B		ViT-B	DeiT-base	ViT-B	DeiT-base	ViT-B
Params. Count/M	86		86	86	86	86	86
FPGA	Xilinx VU37P		Xilinx Zynq ZC7020	Xilinx ZCU102	Xilinx VU37P	Xilinx ZCU102	Xilinx Alveo U200
Clock Freq./MHz	250		150	150	400	150	300
Language	Verilog		–	HLS	–	HLS	HLS
Data Format (W/A)	FP16/FP16		INT8/INT8	INT1/INT8	INT8/FP16	INT8/INT8	–
Latency/ms	102.09	29.51	363.64	40.32	31.09	38.61	48.44
Throughout/GOPS	344.0	1190.1	96.6	861.2	1129.6	899.6	725.0

Table 1 summarizes the comparison between the proposed Helios and prior accelerators achieving end-to-end model acceleration. Latency is reported for two systolic array (SA) configurations: 32×32 and 64×64. Work [15], targeting edge applications with a lightweight FPGA, reports a latency of 363.64 ms. By deploying similar models (DeiT-base) with low-precision quantization, [10,16] achieve 40 ms latency, corresponding to approximately 40% and 133% of our Config.1 and Config.2, respectively. Similarly, [14] reaches 47.45% and 163.15% of the latency of Config.1 and Config.2. Notably, [11] operates on a similar hardware platform; by leveraging INT8-based GEMM, it achieves 4× higher GOPS and attains latency comparable to our Config.2. By aligning the number of low-level FMA units, our floating-point design achieves performance comparable to—or exceeding—finely optimized low-precision implementations. For fair performance comparison with related works, we adopt giga operations per second (GOPS) as the unified accelerator throughput metric, eliminating confounding effects from disparate benchmark models. As shown in Table 1, Helios achieves the highest throughput under Config.2 compared to other SOTAs. Furthermore, precision ablation on the ViT-B model (Table 2) shows that FP16 delivers accuracy comparable to FP32 without noticeable degradation. The +1.04% Top-1 difference falls within the normal run-to-run variance of ImageNet evaluation, which is commonly observed due to floating-point non-associativity across different precision and evaluation runs.

6.2 Interconnection Bandwidth Test Between Two Accelerators:

This design is based on the Inspur F37X card, which has two 100G optical ports. Therefore, the accelerator currently supports two external interconnect interfaces, totaling 200Gbps. The accelerator supports the load/store command, which, via DMA, can directly read/write data from the remote accelerator's DDR/SRAM. The single-channel bandwidth test results are as follows when connected directly with copper cable: The two channels can work independently and transmit different data simultaneously.

Table 2. Precision ablation experiments of the ViT-B model

Implementations	Data Type	Top-1 Accuracy	Top-5 Accuracy
Baseline	FP32	84.53%	97.29%
Helios	FP16	85.57%	97.33%

6.3 Dual-Accelerator Deployment of the Google ViT Model

The ViT model has a total of 12 layers [3]. With a matrix multiplication clock frequency of 250 MHz and a nonlinear unit clock frequency of 250 MHz, the single-card deployment time is 29.51 ms. When deployed collaboratively on two boards, board 0 handles layers 1–6, and board 1 handles layers7-12. Under the same clock frequency configuration, the computation time is 15.644 ms. The data transfer size between the two boards is 256*768*2B, and the communication time is 0.046 ms. Therefore, the dual-card deployment time is 15.69 ms.

To evaluate the acceleration performance, the speedup is calculated. The single-accelerator configuration achieves a throughput of 33.88 FPS (calculated as 1000 ms/29.51 ms per image). With dual-accelerator partitioning, the throughput increases significantly to 63.73FPS (1000 ms/15.69 ms per image). Consequently, the dual-accelerator deployment yields an overall speedup of 1.88x (63.73/33.88)compared to the baseline (Table 3).

Table 3. Data transmission performance test results

Data size/KB	Sender clock cycle	Sender time/us	bandwidth/GB
2	393	1.572	1.213326102
4	407	1.628	2.343180139
256	5871	23.484	10.39604092
1024	22712	90.848	10.7494111
4096	90224	360.896	10.82375532
262144	5726634	22906.536	10.91391557

6.4 Dual-Accelerator Deployment of the Qwen2-0.5B Model

The Qwen2-0.5B model comprises a total of 24 layers. When operating at a clock frequency of 250 MHz for matrix multiplication (GEMM) operations and 250 MHz for non-linear units, the per-token inference latency during the decoding stage is 32.37 ms on a single device. For the collaborative dual-accelerator deployment, we employ a tensor parallelism strategy to partition all GEMM workloads. Specifically, Accelerator 0 executes the first half of the matrix computations, while Accelerator 1 processes the remaining half. Maintaining the identical clock frequency configuration, the pure computation time is reduced to 18.78 ms. Factoring in a total inter-board data communication latency of 0.43 ms, the overall decoding stage latency for the dual-accelerator deployment is effectively 19.21 ms per token.

To evaluate the acceleration performance, we calculate the speedup based on the inference throughput (tokens per second). Prior to partitioning, the single-device throughput is 30.89 tokens/s (calculated as 1000 ms/32.37 ms). After applying the dual-accelerator partitioning, the throughput significantly increases to 52.06 tokens/s (1000 ms/19.21 ms). Consequently, the distributed deployment achieves an overall speedup of 1.69x (52.06/30.89).

6.5 Discussion: Scalability and Generalization

While our prototype is limited to two VU37P boards, we estimate Helios's behavior at larger scales by extrapolating from measured per-layer latency (2.46 ms for ViT-B) and per-boundary communication latency (0.046 ms for 384 KB activations over the 200 Gbps link). For pipeline-parallel ViT workloads, communication overhead remains below 3% at N = 8 devices because only layer-boundary activations traverse the interconnect. For tensor-parallel Qwen2 decoding, communication cost grows with N; extrapolation suggests communication begins to dominate at N = 4–6 devices for Qwen2-0.5B, while larger models (e.g., Qwen2-7B, hidden dimension 3584) push this crossover further out due to higher computation-per-byte-communicated ratio. Beyond the two evaluated models, Helios's multi-granularity operator abstraction generalizes without hardware changes: larger decoder-only models scale via the same tensor-parallelism strategy; encoder-decoder architectures (e.g., T5) are supported by combining pipeline parallelism for the encoder with tensor parallelism for the decoder; and emerging operators such as SwiGLU and RMSNorm decompose directly into existing MMU and SFU arithmetic-level instructions. These estimates are derived from measured two-board data; multi-board validation at $N \geq 4$ is planned as immediate future work.

The current prototype uses DDR4 (19.2 GB/s per channel); migrating to the VU37P's integrated HBM provides approximately 460 GB/s aggregate bandwidth, a 24× improvement that would directly reduce the weight-loading latency in memory-bandwidth-bound decoding. This is particularly impactful for larger models (e.g., Qwen2-7B) where weight volume far exceeds on-chip buffer capacity, making off-chip bandwidth the dominant bottleneck. The memory controller abstraction (Sect. 3.1) decouples the compute core from memory technology, requiring only a memory controller IP swap and re-synthesis—no other architectural changes.

7 Conclusion

In this paper, we propose Helios, a scalable FPGA architecture that enables efficient Transformer inference via an FP16-oriented execution core with specialized operators and multi-granularity scheduling, jointly optimizing computation partitioning and inter-device communication to achieve high efficiency without aggressive quantization. The experimental results show that the proposed FP16-oriented accelerator achieves performance comparable to state-of-the-art INT8 designs with negligible accuracy loss. In a dual-accelerator setup, Helios delivers substantial gains, achieving a 1.88× speedup on Vision Transformer (ViT) and a 1.69× improvement during the decoding stage of Qwen2-0.5B. Moreover, for ViT workloads, it achieves up to a 1.98× speedup over leading single-accelerator solutions, demonstrating strong efficiency and scalability.

References

1. Bjerregaard, T., Mahadevan, S.: A survey of research and practices of network-on-chip. ACM Computing Surveys (CSUR) **38**(1), 1–es (2006)

2. Chen, Y., Li, T., Chen, X., et al.: High-frequency systolic array-based transformer accelerator on field programmable gate arrays. Electronics **12**(4), 822 (2023)
3. Dosovitskiy, A., Beyer, L., Kolesnikov, A., et al.: An image is worth 16x16 words: Transformers for image recognition at scale. In: International Conference on Learning Representations (ICLR) (2021), https://arxiv.org/abs/2010.11929
4. Firestone, D., Putnam, A., Mundkur, S., Chiou, D., et al.: Azure accelerated networking:{SmartNICs} in the public cloud. In: 15th USENIX Symposium on Networked Systems Design and Implementation (NSDI 18). pp. 51–66 (2018)
5. Gouk, D., Lee, S., Kwon, M., Jung, M.: Direct access, high-performance memory disaggregation with directcxl. In: USENIX Annual Technical Conference, pp. 287–294. (2022)
6. Hong, H., Choi, D., Kim, N., Lee, H., et al.: Survey of convolutional neural network accelerators on field-programmable gate array platforms: architectures and optimization techniques. J. Real-Time Image Proc. **21**(3), 64 (2024)
7. Lai, Y.H., Rong, H., Zheng, S., et al.: Susy: a programming model for productive construction of high-performance systolic arrays on fpgas. In: Proceedings of the 39th International Conference on Computer-Aided Design. Association for Computing Machinery, New York, NY, USA (2020). https://doi.org/10.1145/3400302.3415644
8. Li, S., Tao, Y., Tang, E., Xie, T., Chen, R.: A survey of field programmable gate array (fpga)-based graph convolutional neural network accelerators: challenges and opportunities. PeerJ Computer Science **8**, e1166 (2022)
9. Li, T., Zhang, F., Xie, G., Fan, X., et al.: A high speed reconfigurable architecture for softmax and gelu in vision transformer. Electron. Lett. **59**(5), e12751 (2023)
10. Li, Z., Sun, M., Lu, A., et al.: Auto-vit-acc: An fpga-aware automatic acceleration framework for vision transformer with mixed-scheme quantization. In: 2022 32nd International Conference on Field-Programmable Logic and Applications (FPL). pp. 109–116 (2022). https://doi.org/10.1109/FPL57034.2022.00027
11. Li Tianyang, Zhang Fan, W.S.C.W.C.L.: Fpga-based unified accelerator for convolutional neural network and vision transformer. Journal of Electronics & Information Technology **46**(6), 2663–2672 (2024)
12. Lu, S., Wang, M., Liang, S., Lin, J., Wang, Z.: Hardware accelerator for multi-head attention and position-wise feed-forward in the transformer. In: 2020 IEEE 33rd International System-on-Chip Conference (SOCC). pp. 84–89 (2020). https://doi.org/10.1109/SOCC49529.2020.9524802
13. Ma, W., Yang, X., Zeng, S., Liu, T., et al.: Cd-llm: A heterogeneous multi-fpga system for batched decoding of 70b+ llms using a compute-dedicated architecture. ACM Trans. Reconfigurable Technol. Syst. **19**(1) (Mar 2026). https://doi.org/10.1145/3771288
14. Marino, K., Zhang, P., Prasanna, V.K.: ME-ViT: A Single-Load Memory-Efficient FPGA Accelerator for Vision Transformers . In: 30th International Conference on High Performance Computing, Data, and Analytics (HiPC). pp. 213–223. IEEE Computer Society, Los Alamitos, CA, USA (2023). https://doi.org/10.1109/HiPC58850.2023.00039
15. Nag, S., Datta, G., Kundu, S., Chandrachoodan, N., Beerel, P.A.: Vita: A vision transformer inference accelerator for edge applications. In: 2023 IEEE International Symposium on Circuits and Systems (ISCAS). pp. 1–5 (2023). https://doi.org/10.1109/ISCAS46773.2023.10181988
16. Sun, M., Ma, H., Kang, G., Jiang, Y., Chen, T., Ma, X., Wang, Z., Wang, Y.: Vaqf: Fully automatic software-hardware co-design framework for low-bit vision transformer (2022), https://arxiv.org/abs/2201.06618

17. Tan, X., Shen, X.W., et al.: A non-stop double buffering mechanism for dataflow architecture. J. Comput. Sci. Technol. **33**(1), 145–157 (2018)
18. Trusov, A.V., Limonova, E.E., Nikolaev, D.P., Arlazarov, V.V.: p-im2col: Simple yet efficient convolution algorithm with flexibly controlled memory overhead. IEEE Access **9**, 168162–168184 (2021)
19. Vasudevan, A., Anderson, A., Gregg, D.: Parallel multi channel convolution using general matrix multiplication. In: 28th international conference on application-specific systems, architectures and processors (ASAP), pp. 19–24. IEEE (2017)
20. Vaswani, A., Shazeer, N., Parmar, N.: Attention is all you need. In: Advances in Neural Information Processing Systems, vol. 30, pp. 5998–6008. Curran Associates, Inc (2017)
21. Wang, J., Guo, L., Cong, J.: Autosa: A polyhedral compiler for high-performance systolic arrays on fpga. In: The 2021 ACM/SIGDA International Symposium on Field-Programmable Gate Arrays, pp. 93–104. (2021)
22. Ye, W., Zhou, X., Zhou, J., Chen, C., Li, K.: Accelerating attention mechanism on fpgas based on efficient reconfigurable systolic array. ACM Transactions on Embedded Computing Systems **22**(6), 1–22 (2023)
23. Zhang, W., Peng, X., Wu, H., et al.: Design guidelines of rram based neural-processing-unit: A joint device-circuit-algorithm analysis. In: Proceedings of the 56th Annual Design Automation Conference 2019. pp. 1–6 (2019)
24. Zheng, J., Chen, G.: Looplynx: A scalable dataflow architecture for efficient llm inference (2025), https://arxiv.org/abs/2504.09561

A Hierarchical Adaptive Posit-CIM Architecture for Edge Transformer Inference

Xuchang Liu, Chang Liu, Jun Wang, and Li Shen(✉)

College of Computer Science and Technology, National University of Defense Technology, Changsha, China
{liuxuchang,liuchang,wangjun24,lishen}@nudt.edu.cn

Abstract. Edge Transformer inference requires high fidelity under strict energy constraints, where data movement dominates cost. Compute-in-Memory (CIM) mitigates the memory wall, but floating-point CIM is costly and fixed low-bit formats lack precision. Posit arithmetic offers a compelling low-bit alternative. However, existing Posit-CIM designs remain input-generic and fail to exploit Transformer dataflow heterogeneity. We present TAP-CIM, a hierarchical adaptive Transformer-aware Posit-CIM architecture that maps dataflow semantics to hardware optimizations. By leveraging sign priors, token contribution, and sparsity, TAP-CIM eliminates redundant operations across decoding, in-array execution, and reduction. Experimental results demonstrate that TAP-CIM preserves inference accuracy while reducing energy consumption by 8.27% over PD-CIM and up to 32.7% over FP16-CIM, achieving 9.21% and 38.49% higher energy efficiency, respectively.

Keywords: Transformer inference · Posit · Compute-in-Memory

1 Introduction

Transformers have been widely adopted in natural language processing (NLP), computer vision, and multimodal tasks, emerging as the core model for modern intelligent computing systems [1–3,5]. For edge deployment, however, Transformer inference faces a critical dilemma: it demands high numerical fidelity to maintain model performance, yet operates under stringent energy constraints. The root cause lies in intensive parameter access, activation movement, and matrix computation [4], which dominate energy consumption and create severe data migration pressure–making high-accuracy, high-efficiency edge Transformer inference a pivotal challenge for intelligent chip design.

Compute-in-Memory (CIM) is a promising solution to alleviate the memory and power walls, as it executes multiply-accumulate (MAC) and reduction operations inside or near memory arrays, thereby minimizing costly data movement [11,12]. Nevertheless, existing low-bit optimization methods (e.g., FP8,

L. Eeckhout et al. (Eds.): APPT 2026, LNCS 16693, pp. 359–371, 2027.
https://doi.org/10.1007/978-981-92-4805-6_24

INT8 quantization) fail to balance dynamic range and local precision for Transformers, whose activations are sensitive to small perturbations and concentrated near zero [6,19,20]. This makes low-bit numerical formats that align with Transformer data distributions critical for edge CIM design.

The Posit number system addresses this gap by employing dynamic encoding of regime, exponent, and fraction, enabling flexible dynamic range and fine-grained local precision under limited bit widths [9]. Its inherent distribution characteristics are well-matched to Softmax outputs, normalized values, and intermediate activations in Transformers, making Posit a compelling low-bit alternative for high-fidelity edge Transformer inference.

Despite Posit's advantages, its benefits do not directly translate into system-level gains for edge Transformer inference. The fundamental limitation is the mismatch between generic Posit-CIM execution and Transformer-specific dataflow. Existing designs rely on a unified execution path and fail to exploit key dataflow characteristics, including sign priors, skewed token contribution, and reduction sparsity. This leads to substantial redundancy across decoding, in-array computation, and reduction, limiting the achievable energy efficiency of Posit-CIM.

To address these critical challenges, this paper proposes TAP-CIM, a hierarchical adaptive Transformer-aware Posit-CIM architecture that maps Transformer dataflow semantics to hardware optimizations. By explicitly integrating sign priors, token contribution, and sparsity into hardware control, TAP-CIM eliminates redundant operations across the entire pipeline. The main contributions of this work are as follows:

- We propose TAP-CIM, a hierarchical adaptive Transformer-aware Posit-CIM architecture that exploits Transformer dataflow heterogeneity across decoding, in-array execution, and reduction.
- We design a Sign-Aware Bypass Regime Processing Unit (SA-BRPU) that leverages operator-specific data characteristics to bypass redundant decoding logic, reducing frontend overhead.
- We present a Token-Aware Cascaded Precision (TACP) mechanism that grades execution paths by token contribution to improve array efficiency while preserving fidelity.
- We develop a Sparse-Aware Gated Adder Tree (SAAT) that disables non-contributive reduction paths to reduce energy via multi-source sparsity.

2 Background and Motivation

2.1 Operator and Dataflow in Transformer Inference

The attention weight matrix in self-attention is formulated as

$$A = \mathrm{Softmax}\left(\frac{QK^T}{\sqrt{d_h}}\right), \quad 0 \leq A_{i,j} \leq 1, \quad \sum_j A_{i,j} = 1, \tag{1}$$

where Q and K denote query and key matrices, and d_h is the head hidden dimension. The attention weights in the Score×V path form a normalized probability distribution. Exploiting such semantics can reduce critical-path overhead without accuracy loss [15].

Attention weights exhibit concentrated and long-tailed distributions. For the i-th query vector $A_i = \{a_{i,1}, a_{i,2}, \ldots, a_{i,S}\}$, let $\bar{A}_i$ be its descending sorted version. The cumulative contribution is

$$C_i(k) = \sum_{j=1}^{k} \bar{a}_{i,j}. \tag{2}$$

In practical inference of ViT and BERT, attention weights follow a pattern of a few dominant tokens and numerous long-tailed ones. As shown in Fig. 1, a small number of top tokens provide most of the contribution. Uniform bit-width and resource allocation lead to inefficient execution, dominated by low-contribution MAC operations.

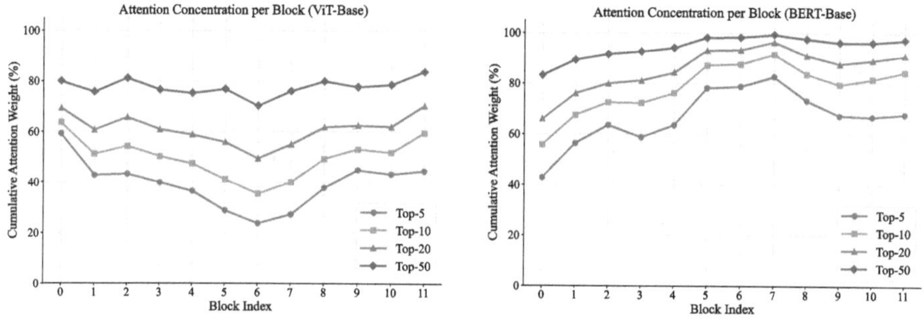

(a) ViT-B/16 (b) BERT-base

Fig. 1. Attention distribution characteristics in Transformer inference.

In Posit-based Score×V computation, array outputs are fed into the backend adder tree as partial sums. Sparsity in these partial sums stems from bypass decisions and zero values. Additionally, Posit reduction requires exponent alignment, which may lead to non-overlapping effective bit ranges. Uniformly enabling full adders causes redundant switching and extra dynamic power.

2.2 Posit-CIM Challenges for Transformer Inference

Existing high-precision and mixed-precision CIM macros have demonstrated feasible high-fidelity edge neural network inference [16–18]. Dedicated datapaths and organizations further improve efficiency [7,8,21,22]. MINOTAUR [13] shows the potential of Posit for edge Transformers, while PD-CIM [10] and AdaP-CIM [14] reduce overheads for generic Posit datapaths. However, existing optimizations focus on general Posit designs rather than Transformer-specific features.

As shown in Fig. 2, Posit is a dynamically encoded format composed of sign, regime, exponent and fraction, denoted as Posit(n, es) [9]. It adaptively balances dynamic range and local precision via variable regime length, making Posit$\langle 8, 1\rangle$ suitable for edge Transformer inference.

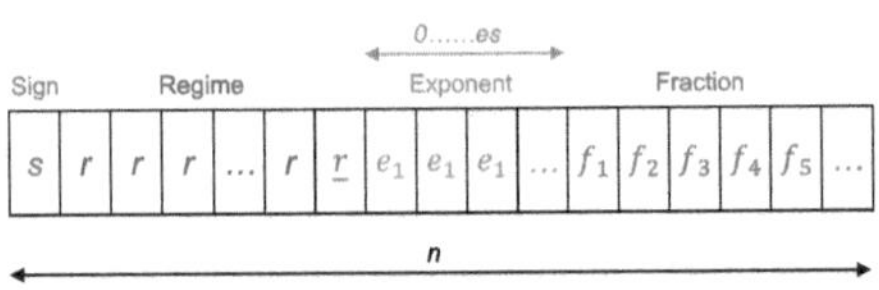

Fig. 2. Posit numerical format.

Nevertheless, dynamic encoding introduces hardware overhead, and the unified execution architecture has an inherent mismatch with Transformer dataflow. Regime decoding depends on leading 0/1 detection and boundary parsing, while dynamic fraction width complicates array mapping and backend alignment [10,14].

Furthermore, existing Posit-CIM architectures do not explicitly exploit the sign, contribution, and reduction patterns of Transformer dataflow, leading to notable redundancy. Studies indicate that layers and operators vary in sensitivity to quantization error [12], and leveraging Softmax semantics enhances efficiency [15]. Optimizing only generic Posit datapaths is insufficient to achieve both high accuracy and hardware efficiency in Transformer inference.

3 TAP-CIM: Hierarchical Adaptive Posit-CIM Architecture

3.1 Overall Architecture and Data Path

As shown in Fig. 3, this paper proposes TAP-CIM, a hierarchical adaptive Transformer-aware Posit-CIM architecture for edge Transformer inference, which designs differentiated execution mechanisms based on the sign priors, contribution distribution, and reduction sparsity inherent in Transformer dataflow.

The TAP-CIM system generates mode identifiers according to operator types and input tensors, which are embedded into the dataflow. In the frontend decoding stage, the SA-BRPU dynamically switches execution modes based on data sign priors. In the array execution stage, the TACP classifies computations into three types (full execution, controlled truncation, direct bypass) based on attention weight contribution via the token mode function, enabling differentiated precision and resource scheduling. In the backend reduction stage, the SAAT dynamically selects among full addition, logical OR, and bypass transmission paths according to input states via gating functions.

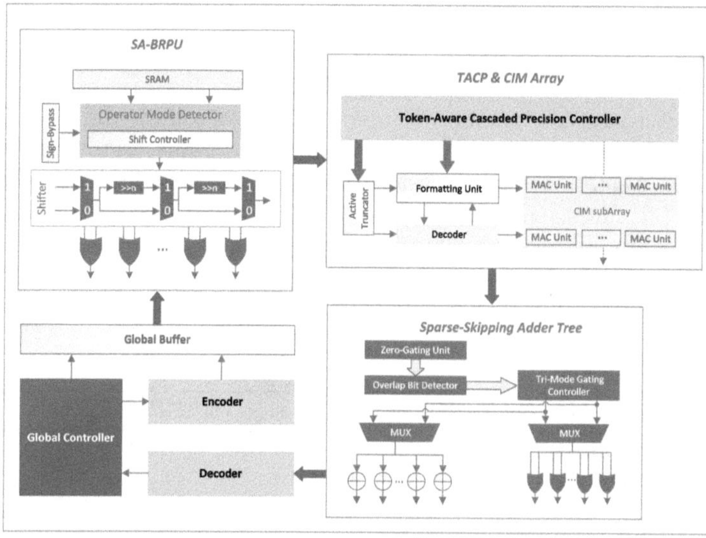

Fig. 3. Overall architecture of TAP-CIM.

3.2 SA-BRPU: Sign-Aware Bypass Regime Processing Unit

Traditional Posit decoders execute a universal pipeline of sign judgment, extension, two's complement conversion, Regime parsing and shift control, which is redundant for Transformer's Score×V path. Attention weights here are strictly non-negative Softmax outputs, so sign-related logic for negative numbers is semantically irrelevant but incurs unnecessary switching and power overhead.

To address this, the SA-BRPU integrates operator mode recognition into the frontend control layer. For Softmax-derived inputs ($x \in S_{softmax}$), the system enables an unsigned bypass mode ($m_{sign} = 0$), disabling sign detection, extension and negative compensation logic while retaining only essential Regime/shift operations. For other generic Posit inputs ($m_{sign} = 1$), the full decoding pipeline is preserved. Unlike approximate decoding, SA-BRPU achieves lossless decoding–its correctness is guaranteed by operator definition rather than input distribution–conditionally pruning redundant decoder logic without numerical error and translating Softmax's non-negativity prior into frontend decoding efficiency gains.

3.3 Token-Aware Cascaded Precision (TACP)

Token-Aware Cascaded Precision (TACP) leverages the contribution distribution of attention weights to dynamically allocate computing precision and hardware resources for different tokens, reducing redundant computations from low-contribution tokens and improving SRAM-CIM array energy efficiency. Existing array reuse mechanisms such as CPCS [10] rely on natural data distribution to utilize idle units, leading to unstable gains across layers and heads. In contrast,

TACP actively classifies token execution modes, converting the non-uniformity of attention distribution into controllable array resource scheduling and enabling adaptive matching between precision and resources.

TACP uses a controller module to map token categories to different execution paths in the CIM array. The array stores bit-sliced value vectors column-wise, and attention weights are broadcast to the array to generate partial products with stored bit slices, which are then locally accumulated into partial sums. Based on the cumulative contribution function $C_i(k)$, TACP classifies tokens into three modes—Full, Half, and Bypass—using thresholds τ_F and τ_B. The overall scheme is given in Alg. 1.

Algorithm 1: Token-Aware Cascaded Precision (TACP)

```
Input: Attention vector a_i, value vectors V, thresholds τ_F, τ_B
Output: Output vector o_i, mode map φ
Sort a_i to obtain π;
Compute cumulative contribution C_i(k);
o_i ← 0;
for k = 1 to N do
    j ← π(k);
    if C_i(k) ≤ τ_F then
        φ(a_{i,j}) ← Full;
        o_i ← o_i + a_{i,j} v_j;
    else
        if C_i(k) ≤ τ_B then
            φ(a_{i,j}) ← Half;
            o_i ← o_i + ã_{i,j} v_j;
        else
            φ(a_{i,j}) ← Bypass;
```

Full mode retains full Posit bit-width and the standard datapath for high-contribution tokens. Weight decoding and alignment are followed by full-precision MAC and accumulation, guaranteeing numerical fidelity while consuming full array resources.

Half mode applies controlled mantissa truncation to free idle bit slices, which are reorganized into dense computing units for parallel MAC operations, thus enhancing array utilization while reducing effective bit-width [10]. This idle-slice reuse enables dual-bit parallel MAC in the CIM array, which we quantify as dual-bit MAC utilization in later experiments.

Bypass mode skips Score×V MAC for low-contribution long-tailed tokens directly, halts weight broadcasting, and generates structured zero-value labels propagated to the backend reduction. Gating logic identifies these labels and bypasses corresponding addition paths to eliminate useless computations and switching power.

At the conservative operating point with $\tau_F = 85\%$ and $\tau_B = 98\%$, approximately 37.1% of tokens are in Full mode, 41.6% in Half mode, and 21.3% in Bypass mode. TACP translates token contribution differences into array-level dynamic strategies: preserving precision for high-contribution tokens, enhancing reuse for medium tokens, and reducing redundancy for low tokens. By deeply aligning array scheduling with attention statistics, TACP reduces redundant energy consumption and significantly improves effective array utilization.

3.4 SAAT: Sparse-Aware Gated Adder Tree

SAAT (Sparse-Aware Gated Adder Tree) is designed to improve the utilization of multi-source sparsity in the backend reduction stage. For Posit partial sums, exponent alignment is required before adder tree execution. If the valid bit ranges of two aligned operands do not overlap, the full adder path can be replaced by lightweight OR logic. Moreover, structured zeros from TACP Bypass and natural zeros in intermediate results create significant gating optimization opportunities.

To this end, the proposed SAAT evaluates three types of input characteristics for each partial sum pair P_L, P_R: structured zeros from TACP Bypass, non-overlapping valid bits after alignment, and natural data zeros. It dynamically selects full addition, OR, or bypass paths based on input states, with the decision logic defined as:

$$g(P_L, P_R) = \begin{cases} \text{BYPASS}, & P_L = 0 \text{ or } P_R = 0, \\ \text{OR}, & \text{Overlap}(P_L, P_R) = 0, \\ \text{ADD}, & \text{otherwise}, \end{cases} \tag{3}$$

where $\text{Overlap}(P_L, P_R)$ indicates whether the aligned valid bits of P_L and P_R overlap. SAAT avoids uniformly feeding all inputs into full adders, instead dynamically selecting the optimal reduction path based on input states, converting multi-source sparsity into gating gains and reducing unnecessary logic switching and power consumption.

4 Experimental Setup and Results

4.1 Methodology, Baselines and Metrics

To evaluate the effectiveness of our proposed TAP-CIM architecture, we develop a cycle-accurate simulator to model its execution behavior and performance. We conduct experiments from three aspects: threshold sensitivity analysis of TACP, ablation study of SA-BRPU, TACP and SAAT, and comprehensive comparison with multiple baselines. Experiments are conducted on representative Transformer models including ViT-B/16, DeiT-S/16, Swin-T, BERT-base, MobileBERT and RoBERTa-base, with ImageNet-1K for vision and WikiText-2 for NLP tasks. Hardware evaluation is based on 28 nm CMOS with 16 KB SRAM-CIM and 28 KB global SRAM.

4.2 TACP Thresholding with Attention Statistics

Statistics on ViT-B/16 show that approximately 25% of tokens contribute nearly 80% of the cumulative attention weight, exhibiting a highly concentrated distribution with a long tail. This observation aligns with the inherent sparsity and contribution concentration of attention mechanisms, indicating that only a small subset of tokens dominates final model outputs while the majority provide marginal contributions.

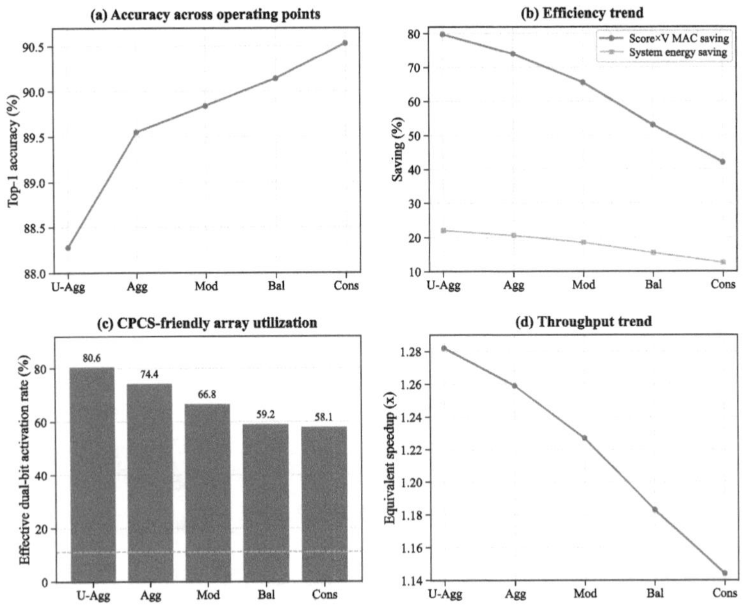

Fig. 4. System-level performance and energy efficiency of TACP under different scheduling policies.

As illustrated in Fig. 4(a)(b), increasing the Full/Bypass thresholds gradually recovers accuracy, while slightly reducing MAC and energy savings. Even at the Conservative point, the dual-bit MAC utilization reaches 58.1%, far exceeding the natural baseline (11%), leading to 1.14×–1.28× throughput speedup (Fig. 4(d)).

As listed in Table 1, aggressive configurations achieve high MAC reduction but large accuracy drops. The Conservative configuration achieves the best trade-off with only 0.10% Top-1 accuracy loss, 42.11% MAC reduction, and 12.57% system energy saving. This configuration is used in all subsequent experiments.

4.3 Mechanism-Level Analysis

After determining the Conservative operating point, we decompose the gains of our design and compare with PD-CIM [10] as shown in Fig. 5. SA-BRPU exploits

Table 1. Performance under different TACP thresholds

Config	Full/Bypass	Top-1 Acc (%)	Acc Drop	MAC Red.	Energy Red.
Ultra-Aggressive	50/80	88.28	-2.34%	79.82%	22.02%
Aggressive	60/85	89.55	-1.07%	74.02%	20.57%
Moderate	70/90	89.84	-0.78%	65.55%	18.49%
Balanced	80/95	90.14	-0.49%	53.09%	15.45%
Conservative	**85/98**	**90.53**	**-0.10%**	**42.11%**	**12.57%**

the non-negative property of Softmax outputs to bypass sign and complement logic, improving the decode saving from 20.04% to 40.00%. TACP reduces effective computation in the Score×V stage and improves dual-bit MAC utilization.

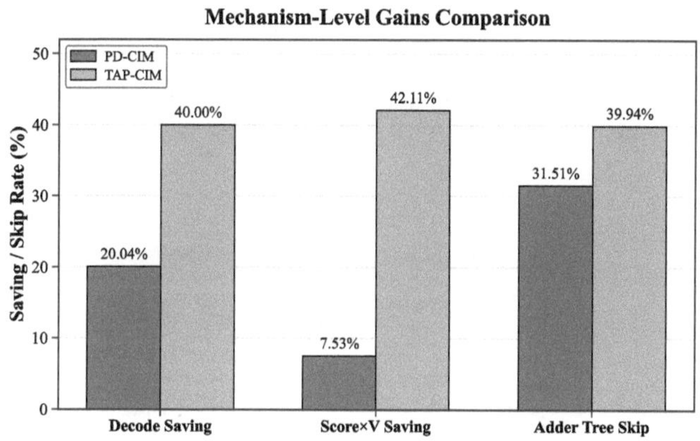

Fig. 5. Gain breakdown of the three key mechanisms.

Under the Conservative configuration, 21.3% tokens are bypassed and 41.6% are truncated to 2-bit mantissa, increasing dual-bit MAC utilization from 11.12% to 58.14% and achieving 42.11% MAC reduction. SAAT achieves 39.94% adder-tree skipping in the backend reduction by leveraging structured zeros from TACP. The proposed mechanisms introduce 7.09% area overhead from control logics, which is moderate for supporting attention-aware dynamic execution.

4.4 Comprehensive Comparison with Baselines

We evaluate our design against Plain Posit8, PD-CIM [10], and FP16-CIM under unified settings. Plain Posit8 uses Posit$\langle 8, 1\rangle$ with fixed datapath to isolate format overhead. PD-CIM represents the state-of-the-art general Posit-CIM design, and FP16-CIM serves as the high-precision baseline.

As shown in Fig. 6, our design achieves the lowest single-inference energy consumption across all models. It reduces single-inference energy by 8.27% on

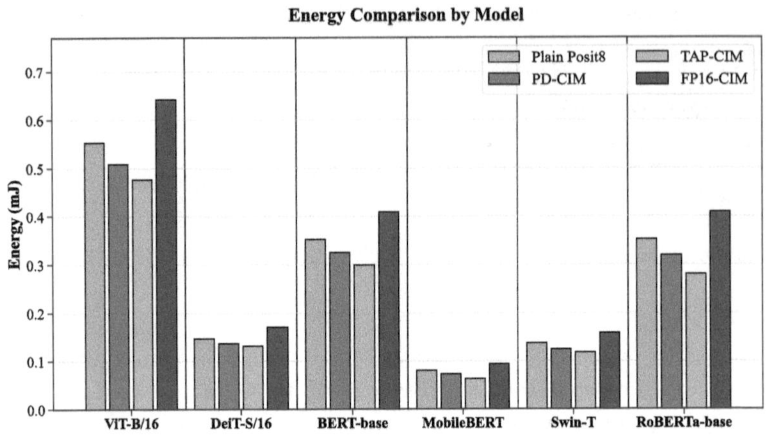

Fig. 6. Cross-model inference energy consumption.

average over PD-CIM and by up to 32.7% over FP16-CIM, indicating that format advantages must be coupled with Transformer-aware optimization to realize system-level efficiency gains.

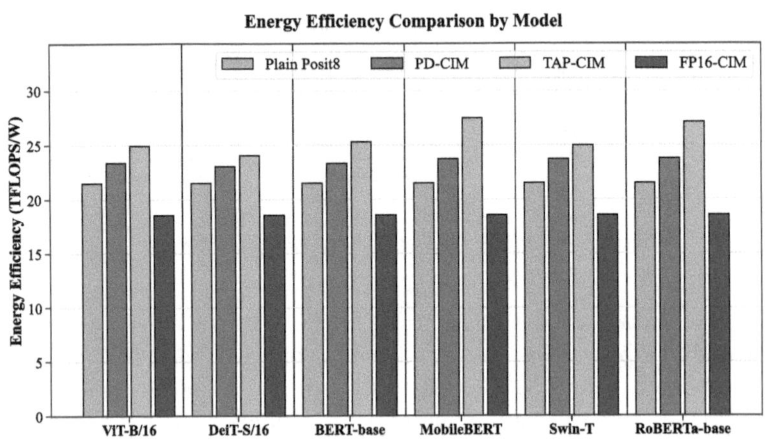

Fig. 7. Cross-model energy efficiency.

Our design reaches 25.62 TFLOPS/W on average as shown in Fig. 7, outperforming PD-CIM, Plain Posit8, and FP16-CIM by 9.21%, 19.27%, and 38.49% respectively. The benefits generalize consistently across vision and language Transformers.

As illustrated in Fig. 8, Score$\times$V, Adder and Decode contribute 45.6%–66.6%, 10.9%–46.0%, and 8.4%–26.9% of total energy savings, respectively. All three modules achieve synchronized energy reduction in ViT-B/16, indicating that the

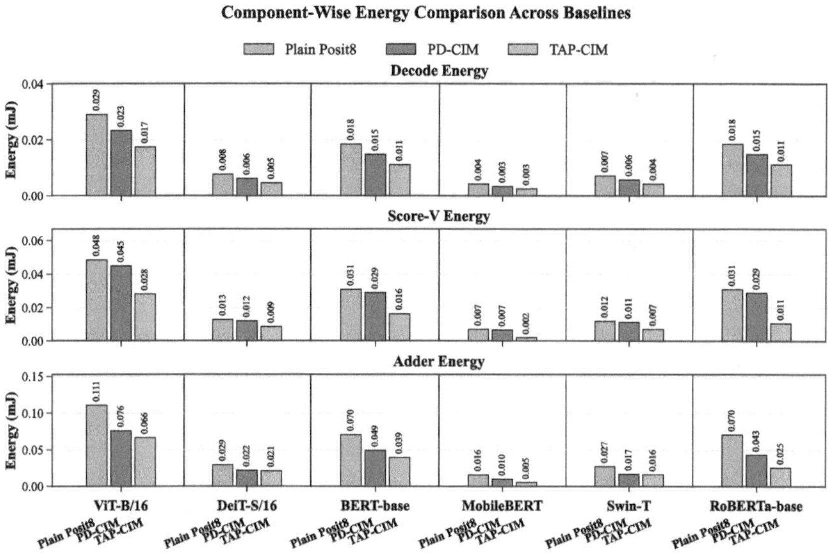

Fig. 8. Energy breakdown per module across models.

hierarchical design delivers consistent and stackable gains. Overall, TAP-CIM effectively reduces redundant operations while preserving accuracy, achieving a better trade-off among energy, efficiency and area.

5 Conclusion

This paper presents TAP-CIM, a hierarchical adaptive Transformer-aware Posit-CIM architecture for edge Transformer inference. TAP-CIM addresses the mismatch between generic Posit-CIM execution and Transformer-specific dataflow by exploiting sign priors, token contribution, and reduction sparsity across frontend decoding, in-array execution, and backend reduction. Built on SA-BRPU, TACP, and SAAT, TAP-CIM eliminates redundant operations while preserving inference accuracy. Experimental results show consistent energy-efficiency gains across both vision and language Transformer models, demonstrating the effectiveness of Transformer-aware Posit-CIM co-design.

Acknowledgments. This work is supported by the National Natural Science Foundation of China (No. 62472436).

Statement of AI Usage. Artificial intelligence tools, if used, were used only for language organization and figure/table polishing, and did not participate in the generation of the core ideas or technical content.

References

1. Vaswani, A., Shazeer, N., Parmar, N.: Attention is all you need. In: Advances in Neural Information Processing Systems, vol. 30, pp. 5998–6008 (2017)
2. Dosovitskiy, A., Beyer, L., Kolesnikov, A., et al.: An image is worth 16×16 words: transformers for image recognition at scale. In: International Conference on Learning Representations (2021)
3. OpenAI: GPT-4 technical report. arXiv:2303.08774 (2023)
4. Peebles, W., Xie, S.: Scalable diffusion models with transformers. In: Proceedings of the IEEE/CVF International Conference on Computer Vision, pp. 4195–4205 (2023)
5. Rombach, R., Blattmann, A., Lorenz, D.: High-resolution image synthesis with latent diffusion models. In: Proceedings of the IEEE/CVF Conference on Computer Vision and Pattern Recognition, pp. 10684–10695 (2022)
6. Micikevicius, P., Narang, S., Alben, J.: FP8 formats for deep learning (2022). arXiv:2209.05433
7. Yue, J., He, C., Wang, Z., et al.: A 28 nm 16.9–300 TOPS/W computing-in-memory processor supporting floating-point NN inference/training with intensive-CIM sparse-digital architecture. In: IEEE International Solid-State Circuits Conference, pp. 1–3 (2023)
8. Yao, S., Shen, L.: ImprLM: an improved logarithmic multiplier design approach via iterative linear-compensation and modified dynamic segment. In: International Conference on Computer Design, pp. 66–69 (2023)
9. Gustafson, J.L., Yonemoto, I.T.: Beating floating point at its own game: posit arithmetic. Supercomput. Front. Innov. **4**(2), 71–86 (2017)
10. Wang, Y., Yang, X., Qin, Y.: an energy-efficient posit compute-in-memory macro for high-accuracy AI applications. IEEE J. Solid-State Circuits (2025)
11. Tambe, T., Garg, S., Prakash, A.: A 12 nm 18.1 TFLOPs/W sparse transformer processor with entropy-based early exit, mixed-precision predication and fine-grained power management. In: IEEE International Solid-State Circuits Conference (2023)
12. Yu, J., Prabhu, K., Urman, Y.: 8-bit transformer inference and fine-tuning for edge accelerators. In: Proceedings of the 29th ACM International Conference on Architectural Support for Programming Languages and Operating Systems, pp. 5–21 (2024)
13. Prabhu, K., Radway, R.M., Yu, J., et al.: MINOTAUR: a posit-based 0.42–0.50-TOPS/W edge transformer inference and training accelerator. IEEE J. Solid-State Circuits (2025)
14. He, J., Tu, F., Cheng, K.T.: AdaP-CIM: compute-in-memory based neural network accelerator using adaptive posit. In: Design, Automation and Test in Europe Conference, pp. 1–2 (2024)
15. Stevens, J.R., Venkatesan, R., Dai, S.: SofterMax: hardware/software co-design of an efficient Softmax for transformers. In: Proceedings of the 58th ACM/IEEE Design Automation Conference, pp. 469–474 (2021)
16. Wu, P.C., Su, J.W., Hong, L.Y., et al.: A 22 nm 832Kb hybrid-domain floating-point SRAM in-memory-compute macro with 16.2–70.2 TFLOPS/W for high-accuracy AI-edge devices. In: IEEE International Solid-State Circuits Conference, pp. 126–128 (2023)
17. Wu, P.C., Su, J.W., Hong, L.Y., et al.: A floating-point 6T SRAM in-memory-compute macro using hybrid-domain structure for advanced AI edge chips. IEEE J. Solid-State Circuits **59**(1), 196–207 (2024)

18. Guo, A., Xi, C., Dong, F.: A 28-nm 64-kb 31.6-TFLOPS/W digital-domain floating-point-computing-unit and double-Bit 6T-SRAM computing-in-memory macro for floating-point CNNs. IEEE J. Solid-State Circuits **59**(9), 3032–3044 (2024)
19. Dettmers, T., Lewis, M., Belkada, Y., et al.: LLM.int8(): 8-bit matrix multiplication for transformers at scale. In: Advances in Neural Information Processing Systems, vol. 35, pp. 4496–4509 (2022)
20. Frantar, E., Ashkboos, S., Hoefler, T.: GPTQ: accurate post-training quantization for generative pre-trained transformers (2022). arXiv:2210.17323
21. Zhang, D., Shen, L., Lu, K.: Eliminate data divergence in SpMV via processor and memory co-computing framework. IEEE Trans. Comput. (2025)
22. Tu, F., Wang, Y., Wu, Z.: A 28nm 29.2 TFLOPS/W BF16 and 36.5 TOPS/W INT8 reconfigurable digital CIM processor with unified FP/INT pipeline and bitwise in-memory booth multiplication for cloud deep learning acceleration. In: IEEE International Solid-State Circuits Conference, pp. 1–3 (2022)

Kernel Acceleration

DOA: Dataflow Optimization for Attention on Multi-core DSPs with Three-Level Memory Hierarchy

Shengwei Li, Zhiquan Lai(✉), Shuai Xu, Shun Ouyang, Han Xiao, Zhaoning Zhang, Menghan Jia, Huayou Su, and Dongsheng Li

National Key Laboratory of Parallel and Distributed Computing, College of Computer Science and Technology, Changsha, China
zqlai@nudt.edu.cn

Abstract. Attention has become a major performance and memory bottleneck in transformer-based models. Existing implementations either materialize large intermediate tensors and incur high memory traffic, or rely on GPU-oriented execution assumptions built around a two-level on-chip/off-chip memory organization, which do not directly fit architectures with a three-level memory hierarchy. This mismatch makes efficient attention execution challenging on multi-core DSPs, which are becoming increasingly valuable for AI and HPC systems. In this paper, we present DOA, a dataflow optimization method for attention on multi-core DSPs. First, DOA designs a *hierarchical attention dataflow* to reorganize attention around the DSP three-level memory hierarchy and cross-core coordination, so that attention can be executed without materializing large intermediates while keeping cross-core coordination lightweight. Second, DOA incorporates *DSP-oriented optimizations*, including *adaptive value parallelization* and *broadcast-efficient operators*, to reduce the remaining coordination overhead and unnecessary off-chip traffic. Experiments show that on attention workloads with sequence lengths up to 8K, DOA improves kernel performance over FlashAttention-2 by up to 1.69× and reduces off-chip traffic by up to 2.53×.

Keywords: Attention kernel · Dataflow optimization · Multi-core DSPs

1 Introduction

Large language models (LLMs) are increasingly used in demanding generation and reasoning workloads [3,17,20,33], including long-document understanding, code completion, and multi-turn reasoning [9,10,29]. Supporting longer contexts has therefore become an important trend in both training [11,14,18,19] and inference [32,35]. In this regime, attention becomes one of the most expensive components because both the score tensor and the normalized softmax tensor scale quadratically with the sequence length. For example, increasing the sequence

L. Eeckhout et al. (Eds.): APPT 2026, LNCS 16693, pp. 375–389, 2027.
https://doi.org/10.1007/978-981-92-4805-6_25

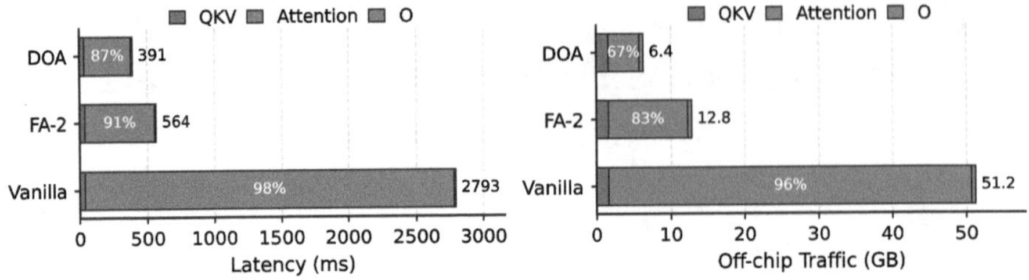

(a) Runtime breakdown. (b) Off-chip traffic breakdown.

Fig. 1. Overhead breakdown of a Transformer layer on multi-core DSPs. At sequence length 4K, attention dominates the runtime and off-chip traffic in the vanilla unfused implementation and FlashAttention-2 (FA-2).

length from 2K to 8K enlarges the score matrix by 16×; even for a single head, storing it in FP16 requires about 8 MB at 2K and about 128 MB at 8K. As a result, long-context attention is constrained not only by arithmetic cost, but also by memory capacity and data movement [12,16,22,25].

Recent work addresses this bottleneck by rethinking attention from a dataflow perspective. Instead of materializing the full score matrix and normalized softmax matrix in off-chip memory, FlashAttention and its successors process attention block by block, maintain online softmax statistics across blocks, and fuse operations to keep intermediate states on chip [4,5,7,27]. This design substantially reduces off-chip traffic and has been widely adopted for attention on GPUs [35]. However, its efficiency relies on GPU-oriented execution assumptions and a two-level on-chip/off-chip memory organization.

Meanwhile, DSP-based accelerators are becoming increasingly important in heterogeneous HPC and AI systems because of their power and energy efficiency [8,36,38]. Unlike GPU-oriented attention execution that usually targets a two-level on-chip/off-chip hierarchy, modern multi-core DSPs are organized around a software-managed three-level memory hierarchy, including per-core local memory, global shared memory (GSM), and off-chip DDR. Data movement between memory levels is explicit and must be coordinated carefully. As shown in Fig. 1, attention remains the dominant component of both runtime and off-chip traffic on multi-core DSPs even after fusion. In this setting, attention is no longer a straightforward adaptation of GPU kernels. Thus the core question of this paper is: *how should attention dataflow be reorganized around the DSP three-level memory hierarchy and multi-core coordination?*

Optimizing attention on multi-core DSPs introduces several challenges. First, designing the attention dataflow is challenging. To reduce data movement across the three-level memory hierarchy, computation partitioning, data placement, and cross-level data movement must be co-designed so that intermediate data and states can be reused efficiently. Second, the rest of the bandwidth-sensitive operations, such as the value-side computation and binary operations, contributes considerable overhead. These executions can become expensive on DSPs if they introduce excessive coordination or unnecessary off-chip traffic. Therefore, a holistic solution must optimize both the attention dataflow and the remaining architecture-specific overheads around it.

To address these issues, we present **DOA**, a **D**ataflow **O**ptimization method for **A**ttention on multi-core DSPs with a three-level memory hierarchy. DOA first introduces *hierarchical attention dataflow*, which rebuilds the attention dataflow around the three-level memory hierarchy. Query blocks are reused through shared memory, while key and value blocks are streamed so that score computation, online softmax state aggregation, and output accumulation can be coordinated across cores. On top of this dataflow, DOA further applies *DSP-oriented optimizations*. Specifically, *adaptive value parallelization* dynamically selects different execution modes for the value computation according to workload scale, while *broadcast-efficient operators* eliminate unnecessary tensor expansion in binary operations.

The contributions of this paper are summarized as follows:

- We identify the limitations of GPU-oriented attention dataflow on multi-core DSPs with a three-level memory hierarchy. To the best of our knowledge, we present the first comprehensive optimization of attention on this architecture.
- We propose *hierarchical attention dataflow*, which co-designs softmax-state maintenance, cross-core aggregation, and output accumulation to reduce IO across the three-level memory hierarchy.
- We introduce *adaptive value parallelization* and *broadcast-efficient operators* to reduce coordination overhead in value computation and off-chip data traffic in broadcast-heavy binary operations.
- We implement DOA on a multi-core DSP platform and integrate it with PyTorch. Experiments show that DOA improves kernel performance over the vanilla implementation and FlashAttention-2 by up to 6.68× and 1.69×, respectively.

2 Preliminaries

2.1 Attention and Online Softmax

Given query, key, and value matrices $\mathbf{Q}, \mathbf{K}, \mathbf{V} \in \mathbb{R}^{N \times d}$, attention [1,24,30] computes:

$$\mathbf{S} = \mathbf{Q}\mathbf{K}^{\top}, \qquad \mathbf{P} = \text{softmax}(\mathbf{S}), \qquad \mathbf{O} = \mathbf{P}\mathbf{V},$$

where $\mathbf{O} \in \mathbb{R}^{N \times d}$ is the output.

Default framework implementations typically materialize both the score matrix $\mathbf{S}$ and the normalized attention matrix $\mathbf{P}$ before forming $\mathbf{O}$ [31]. Since both $\mathbf{S}$ and $\mathbf{P}$ have size $N \times N$, the intermediate memory footprint and tensor movement grow quadratically with the sequence length N. Data movement therefore becomes a central cost in attention [6,28].

Block-wise exact attention avoids this materialization by processing keys and values block by block and maintaining only row-wise running softmax states

[4,5]. After processing the t-th block, let $m^{(t)}$, $\ell^{(t)}$, and $o^{(t)}$ denote the running row-wise maximum, the running normalization term, and the partially accumulated output, respectively. For the current block, let $\tilde{m}^{(t)}$ and $\tilde{\ell}^{(t)}$ denote the local row-wise maximum and the local exponential sum. The online softmax update is $m^{(t)} = \max(m^{(t-1)}, \tilde{m}^{(t)})$, $\ell^{(t)} = e^{m^{(t-1)}-m^{(t)}}\ell^{(t-1)} + e^{\tilde{m}^{(t)}-m^{(t)}}\tilde{\ell}^{(t)}$. The output $o^{(t)}$ can be updated in the same manner by rescaling the previous partial result and accumulating the contribution of the current block. In this way, attention can be computed without materializing either $\mathbf{S}$ or $\mathbf{P}$.

2.2 Multi-core DSP with Three-Level Memory Hierarchy

We use FT-M7032 as the target platform in this work, as it is a representative multi-core DSP with a software-managed three-level memory hierarchy. As shown in Fig. 2, FT-M7032 consists of four DSP clusters with an ARMv8 CPU. Each cluster is connected to an 8 GB DDR module and contains 8 DSP cores and a 6 MB global shared memory (GSM). The GSM is private to each cluster and is shared among DSP cores. Within each DSP core, the on-chip memory further includes a 768 KB array memory (AM). Since clusters operate independently, we focus on attention execution within a single cluster in the following sections. On multi-core DSPs, DDR, GSM, and AM are managed explicitly by software, and data transfers across memory levels are carried out through DMA. This hierarchical organization provides high on-chip bandwidth and flexible data placement, while making data movement a central factor in kernel design.

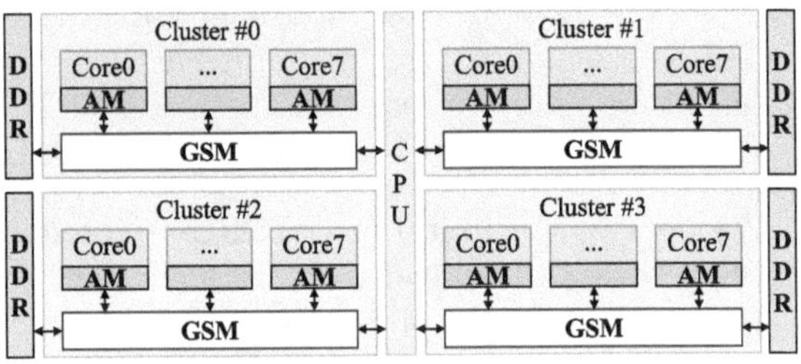

Fig. 2. FT-M7032 cluster architecture and software-managed three-level memory hierarchy. Each cluster contains 8 DSP cores, a shared GSM, and per-core AM.

3 Motivation and Opportunity

Attention is Highly Bandwidth-Sensitive. Attention is inherently bandwidth-sensitive, and this issue becomes more pronounced on architectures with a three-level memory hierarchy. Compared with GPU-oriented attention execution, which is usually organized around a two-level SRAM/HBM hierarchy [4,5,36], multi-core DSPs expose a three-level hierarchy consisting of per-core AM, GSM, and off-chip DDR, and the off-chip DDR bandwidth is much lower than the HBM bandwidth in the two-level hierarchy. In this setting, attention contributes disproportionately to both runtime and off-chip traffic on this platform (Fig. 1). This makes attention execution the primary optimization target.

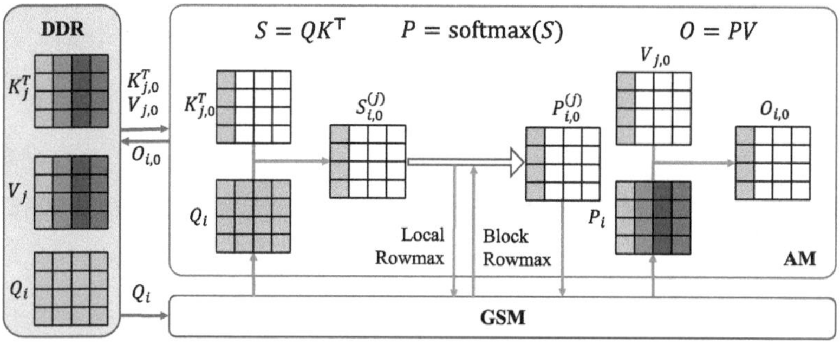

Fig. 3. Hierarchical attention dataflow within one DSP core. A query block is shared through GSM, and key and value blocks are streamed through AM, reducing off-chip traffic with lightweight cross-core coordination.

Opportunities in Three-Level Memory Hierarchy. The three-level memory hierarchy also creates optimization opportunities. Its software-managed shared-memory level allows selected data to remain on chip, turning data reuse into an explicit design choice [8]. It also provides a natural coordination layer across cores, so cross-core state exchange and staged data movement can be organized explicitly in the execution flow. Moreover, bandwidth-sensitive operators can also benefit from this hierarchy by avoiding large data transfers through the low-bandwidth outer-memory level. Together, these motivate that attention dataflow and bandwidth-sensitive operators should be organized around the hierarchy.

4 Hierarchical Attention Dataflow

Figure 3 illustrates the hierarchical attention dataflow of DOA within one DSP cluster. For each query block $\mathbf{Q}_i$, $\mathbf{Q}_i$ is shared through GSM, while the corresponding key and value blocks are streamed into per-core AM, and the online softmax state is maintained through cross-core row-wise aggregation. The full score matrix and softmax matrix are never materialized in DDR.

Query Reuse and KV Streaming. We process one query row block $\mathbf{Q}_i$ at a time and iterate over the corresponding key and value blocks $\mathbf{K}_j$ and $\mathbf{V}_j$. This organization matches the hierarchy of multi-core DSPs. $\mathbf{Q}_i$ can stay in GSM across the full block loop, while $\mathbf{K}_j$ and $\mathbf{V}_j$ are streamed into AM and consumed block by block. On GPU-style architectures, reducing row-wise max and sum across groups at every score-block update is expensive. The running row-wise softmax state is therefore usually maintained within a local execution group, and it is more natural to partition $\mathbf{Q}$ and reload the corresponding key and value blocks for each block update. This difference also changes the data movement pattern. If $\mathbf{Q}$ is partitioned, then processing one row tile over N iterations requires one transfer for $\mathbf{Q}$ and N transfers each for $\mathbf{K}$ and $\mathbf{V}$, for a

Algorithm 1. DOA forward pass

Require: Matrices $\mathbf{Q}, \mathbf{K}, \mathbf{V} \in \mathbb{R}^{N \times d}$ in DDR, block sizes B_c, B_r, number of cores N_c.

Divide $\mathbf{Q}$ into $T_r = \left\lceil \frac{N}{B_r} \right\rceil$ blocks $\mathbf{Q}_1, \ldots, \mathbf{Q}_{T_r}$ of size $B_r \times d$, and divide $\mathbf{K}, \mathbf{V}$ into $T_c = \left\lceil \frac{N}{B_c} \right\rceil$ blocks $\mathbf{K}_1, \ldots, \mathbf{K}_{T_c}$ and $\mathbf{V}_1, \ldots, \mathbf{V}_{T_c}$ of size $B_c \times d$.
Divide the output $\mathbf{O} \in \mathbb{R}^{N \times d}$ into T_r blocks $\mathbf{O}_1, \ldots, \mathbf{O}_{T_r}$ of size $B_r \times d$, and divide ℓ and m into T_r blocks $\ell_1, \ldots, \ell_{T_r}$ and $m_1, \ldots, m_{T_r}$ of size B_r.
for $1 \leq i \leq T_r$ **do**
  Load $\mathbf{Q}_i$ from DDR to GSM.
  Initialize $\mathbf{o}_i^{(0)} = \mathbf{0} \in \mathbb{R}^{B_r \times d}$, $\ell_i^{(0)} = \mathbf{0} \in \mathbb{R}^{B_r}$, and $m_i^{(0)} = -\infty \in \mathbb{R}^{B_r}$.
  for $1 \leq j \leq T_c$ **do**
    for each core k in parallel, $1 \leq k \leq N_c$ **do**
      Load $\mathbf{K}_{j,k}$ from DDR to AM.
      Compute $\mathbf{S}_{i,k}^{(j)} = \mathbf{Q}_i \mathbf{K}_{j,k}^T$ in AM.
      Compute row-max $m_{i,k}^{(j)} = \mathrm{rowmax}(\mathbf{S}_{i,k}^{(j)})$, and write $m_{i,k}^{(j)}$ to GSM.
      Aggregate in GSM and compute $m_i^{(j)} = \max(m_i^{(j-1)}, \max_{k=1}^{N_c} m_{i,k}^{(j)}) \in \mathbb{R}^{B_r}$.
      Compute $\widetilde{\mathbf{P}}_{i,k}^{(j)} = \exp(\mathbf{S}_{i,k}^{(j)} - m_i^{(j)})$.
      Compute row-sum $\ell_{i,k}^{(j)} = \mathrm{rowsum}(\widetilde{\mathbf{P}}_{i,k}^{(j)}) \in \mathbb{R}^{B_r}$, and write $\ell_{i,k}^{(j)}$ to GSM.
      Aggregate in GSM and compute $\widetilde{\ell}_i^{(j)} = \sum_{k=1}^{N_c} \ell_{i,k}^{(j)} \in \mathbb{R}^{B_r}$, and update $\ell_i^{(j)} = e^{m_i^{(j-1)} - m_i^{(j)}} \ell_i^{(j-1)} + \widetilde{\ell}_i^{(j)}$.
    end for
    // $\widetilde{\mathbf{P}}_i^{(j)} \mathbf{V}_j$ is scheduled by the adaptive value parallelization in Section 5.1.
    Load the required partition(s) of $\mathbf{V}_j$ from DDR to AM.
    Compute $\mathbf{o}_i^{(j)} = \mathrm{diag}(e^{m_i^{(j-1)} - m_i^{(j)}}) \mathbf{o}_i^{(j-1)} + \widetilde{\mathbf{P}}_i^{(j)} \mathbf{V}_j$.
  end for
  Compute $\mathbf{O}_i = \mathrm{diag}(\ell_i^{(T_c)})^{-1} \mathbf{o}_i^{(T_c)}$.
  Write $\mathbf{O}_i$, $\ell_i^{(T_c)}$, and $m_i^{(T_c)}$ to DDR.
end for

total of $2N+1$ transfers. If $\mathbf{Q}_i$ is reused across the KV-block loop, the movement becomes N transfers for $\mathbf{Q}$ and one transfer each for $\mathbf{K}$ and $\mathbf{V}$, for a total of $N+2$. The score partitions ($\mathbf{S}_i^{(j)}$) are therefore generated and consumed on chip, without being written back to DDR.

Cross-Core Online Softmax. For each block update, each core loads its assigned partition of $\mathbf{K}_j$ into AM and computes the corresponding local score partition with the shared $\mathbf{Q}_i$. From this local score partition, it derives the row-wise max and sum states and writes them to GSM. These row-wise states are then aggregated through GSM to update the global row-wise state for the current block, so that the exponentiated scores can proceed without moving score partitions across cores. This works well on multi-core DSPs because GSM is designed for fast sharing within the cluster. Only row-wise softmax states are communicated across cores, while the score partitions remain in the AMs that produced them. As a result, cross-core coordination stays lightweight and online softmax can still be maintained across the distributed score computation.

On-Chip Output Accumulation. Once the row-wise softmax state has been updated, the required partition(s) of the current value block are loaded and the output accumulator is updated on chip through the current value-side computation ($\widetilde{\mathbf{P}}_i^{(j)}\mathbf{V}_j$). The final normalization is deferred until all KV blocks have been processed. This keeps the intermediate softmax-related state on chip and avoids materializing normalized softmax blocks in DDR. This organization also fits the following value-side computation. After the row-wise softmax state has been aggregated in GSM, we can continue with the current value block and update the on-chip accumulator directly, instead of organizing the computation around materialized softmax blocks. The corresponding value-side optimization is described in Sect. 5.1.

Algorithm 1 presents the forward pass of DOA. The backward pass follows the same hierarchical organization. Due to space constraints, we omit its algorithmic details. It reuses the same block schedule, exchanges compact row-wise softmax states across cores, and keeps intermediate results on chip as much as possible. Overall, we organize attention on multi-core DSPs around query sharing, GSM aggregation, and on-chip accumulation.

5 DSP-Oriented Optimizations

After reorganizing the attention dataflow around the three-level memory hierarchy and cross-core coordination, two costs remain visible on multi-core DSPs. One is the value-side computation in $\widetilde{\mathbf{P}}\mathbf{V}$. The other is the tail of broadcast-heavy elementwise operators in the softmax and output-update path. We optimize them with adaptive value parallelization and broadcast-efficient operators.

5.1 Adaptive Value Parallelization

The value-side computation in DOA does not use a fixed parallelization strategy. Instead, DOA selects the partitioning strategy according to the output width of $\widetilde{\mathbf{P}}_i^{(j)}\mathbf{V}_j$. This is possible because the value-side path does not need to maintain shared states across cores, and partitioned output can be written back directly after local accumulation. When the output width is small, a naive column-wise partition leaves many cores underutilized because each core receives only a narrow slice of work. When the output width becomes larger, however, always forcing all cores to collaborate on the same columns introduces repeated merge steps and pushes reduction overhead onto the critical path. A single execution pattern therefore performs well only in a limited range.

We switch among three execution patterns according to the output width d, the number of cores N_c, and the per-core compute width w_c, where w_c is a hardware constant determined by the core design (96 in FT-M7032):

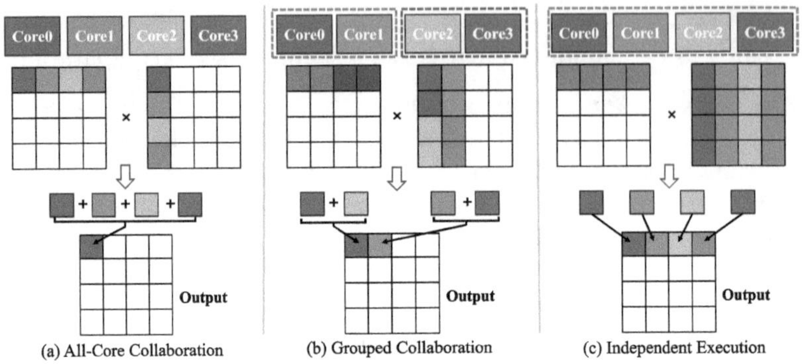

Fig. 4. Adaptive value parallelization. DOA switches among all-core, grouped, and independent execution according to the output width of the current value-side computation, to ensure overall DSP core utilization.

- **All-core collaboration.** When $d \leq w_c$, all cores collaboratively compute the same output-column range and merge their partial sums once. This is useful when the tile is too small to keep the cluster busy with disjoint column assignments. In this regime, the extra merge cost is small, while the gain in core utilization is substantial.
- **Grouped collaboration.** When $w_c < d \leq N_c w_c$, the cores are partitioned into several groups. Each group computes a subset of output columns collaboratively and merges results within the group. It reduces merge traffic compared with full-cluster collaboration, while still avoiding the poor utilization of fully independent execution.
- **Independent execution.** When $d > N_c w_c$, each core processes disjoint output columns independently. At this point, the tile already provides enough work per core, so exposing more collaboration brings little benefit. Avoiding repeated merge steps becomes more important.

Figure 4 illustrates the three execution patterns. At runtime, DOA selects among them according to the output width of $\widetilde{\mathbf{P}}_i^{(j)}\mathbf{V}_j$. This avoids both always partitioning columns independently and always forcing cluster-wide collaboration, and reduces the cost of the value-side computation.

5.2 Broadcast-Efficient Operators

After the score path is compressed, another visible cost comes from binary operators with scalar or vector operands. In the attention pipeline, such operators appear in row-wise rescaling and normalization (Algorithm 1 Lines 12, 17, and 19). A naive implementation first expands a scalar or row vector into a full matrix operand and then applies the binary operation elementwise. For example, the row-wise factors in the update of $\mathbf{o}_i^{(j)}$ or the final normalization can be broadcast into a $B_r \times d$ matrix before multiplication or division. On multi-core

DSPs, this is wasteful because the expanded tensor carries no new information, yet still consumes on-chip capacity and data movement bandwidth.

We avoid this overhead with broadcast-efficient operators. Instead of materializing the broadcasted operand, we keep the scalar or vector compact in on-chip memory and apply the broadcast on the fly with assembly instructions during the elementwise update. This removes redundant tensor expansion and reduces both memory traffic and operator overhead. Although each operator is simple, these costs still accumulate and remain worth optimizing.

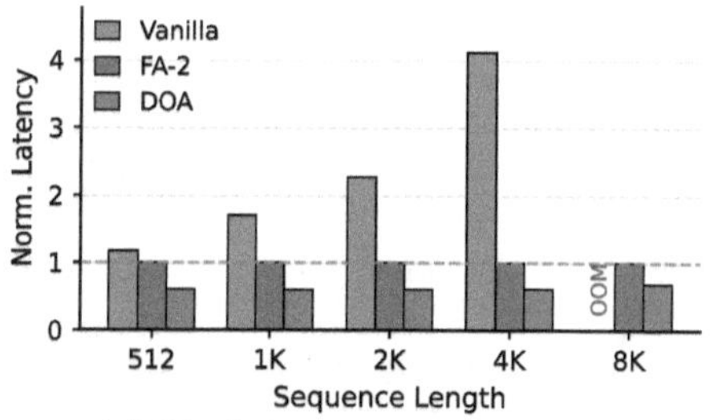

(a) Head size 64, 1.45×–1.69×.

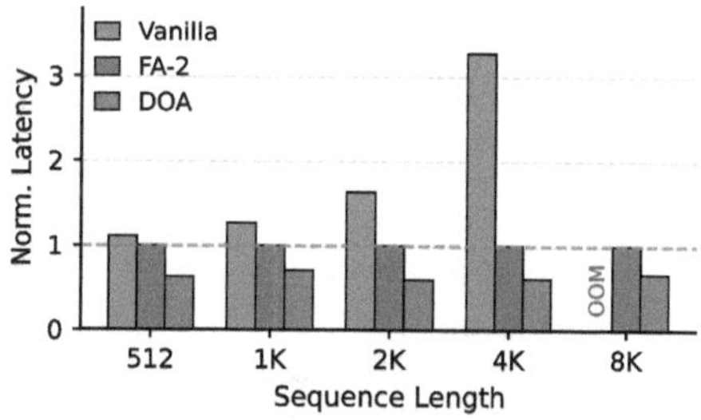

(b) Head size 128, 1.42×–1.68×.

Fig. 5. Kernel latency normalized to FA-2 at different sequence lengths and head sizes. The numbers are the speedups of DOA over FA-2.

6 Experiments

6.1 Implementation

We implement DOA as an attention operator on PyTorch [21]. The implementation contains about 1.2K lines of C++, 2.6K lines of C, and 6.1K lines of DSP assembly. The C++ layer exposes DOA as a PyTorch operator and handles runtime-facing integration. The C layer implements tiling, DMA orchestration, and cluster-level scheduling. The assembly layer covers the performance-critical inner kernels and low-level data movement path. Users can invoke DOA directly through the PyTorch interface with a single operator call.

6.2 Experimental Setup

We evaluate all methods on FT-M7032. Unless otherwise specified, all experiments use the representative Transformer layer as the default workload, with batch size 2, hidden size 1024, 16 attention heads, and sequence length 4096. DOA is an exact attention method that does not affect model convergence, so we focus only on performance. The reported numbers are averaged over 50 iterations. We compare against the following baselines:

- **Vanilla Attention (Vanilla)**: The default unfused implementation from Sect. 2.1, which materializes intermediate score-related tensors.

Table 1. Off-chip traffic (GB) at different sequence lengths.

Method	512	1K	2K	4K	8K
Vanilla	0.34	1.58	8.28	49.06	-
FA-2	0.17	0.67	2.67	10.67	42.67
DOA	0.07	0.27	1.06	4.23	16.84

Table 2. Peak memory footprint (GB) at different sequence lengths.

Method	512	1K	2K	4K	8K
Vanilla	1.39	2.15	4.22	11.42	OOM
FA-2	1.31	1.78	2.77	4.78	8.97
DOA	1.31	1.78	2.76	4.75	8.91

- **FlashAttention-2 (FA-2)**: We reimplement the FlashAttention-2 dataflow on FT-M7032 using block-wise exact attention and online softmax, used here as the strongest local fused reference.

To ensure a fair comparison, all methods use the same numerical precision, tile sizes, number of DSP cores, and performance-critical assembly kernels. Both implementations use DMA-based data movement and overlap data transfer with computation through double buffering. Therefore, the comparison primarily reflects the difference in attention dataflow and data reuse, rather than differences in low-level kernel implementation.

6.3 Kernel Performance

Figure 5 reports the latency of the full attention kernel, normalized to FA-2, for two representative head sizes with sequence lengths ranging from 512 to 8K. DOA maintains a clear advantage over FA-2 across all measured sequence lengths for both head sizes. The gain is stable, which indicates that the hierarchical dataflow remains effective as the KV-block loop becomes longer. Vanilla degrades much more quickly and eventually becomes infeasible because its temporary tensors grow with the full attention matrix. For head size 64, DOA improves kernel performance over FA-2 by 1.45×–1.69×. For head size 128, the gain is 1.42×–1.68×. The gap to Vanilla is much larger: DOA is already 1.93×–6.68× faster for head size 64 and 1.78×–5.39× faster for head size 128, before Vanilla runs out of memory at 8K sequence length.

Off-Chip Traffic and Peak Memory. Tables 1 and 2 show that DOA substantially cuts off-chip traffic relative to both baselines while keeping peak memory close to FA-2 and far below Vanilla. This confirms that the kernel-speed advantage of DOA comes from reducing data movement rather than from trading off extra temporary-storage cost.

6.4 Transformer Layer Performance

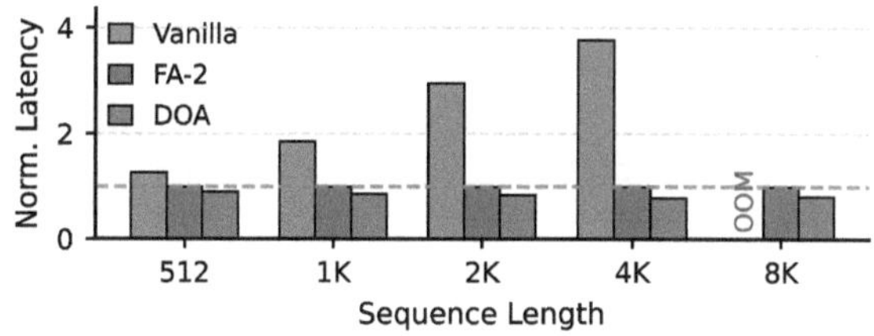

Fig. 6. Transformer layer latency normalized to FA-2. DOA reduces Transformer layer latency over FA-2 by 1.11×–1.28×.

Figure 6 reports normalized Transformer layer latency after the attention kernel is integrated with QKV projection, output projection, and FFN. The layer performance gain is smaller than the isolated kernel gain because the surrounding operators are unchanged. Even so, DOA remains consistently faster than FA-2 across the measured sequence lengths. Across sequence lengths from 512 to 8K, DOA improves Transformer layer performance over FA-2 by 1.11×–1.28×. Compared with Vanilla, the gap reaches 4.8× at 4K before Vanilla runs out of memory at 8K.

6.5 Scalability

Figure 7 evaluates scalability by varying model hidden size from 1K to 8K while fixing the sequence length at 2K and the head size at 128. As the hidden size grows, the latency of both FA-2 and DOA increases steadily, but DOA consistently remains faster. Across the evaluated range, DOA achieves 1.60×–1.75× speedup over FA-2. This result shows that DOA maintains stable scalability as hidden size grows. Due to the memory limit of the current DSP platform, we cannot evaluate even larger models here, but we expect the same trend to continue on future DSP platforms with larger memory capacity.

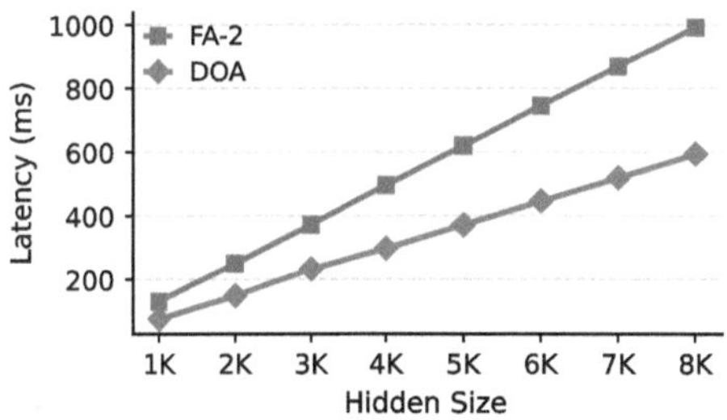

Fig. 7. Scalability of attention w.r.t. hidden size at sequence length 2K and head size 128. DOA achieves consistent speedup over FA-2 of 1.60×–1.75×.

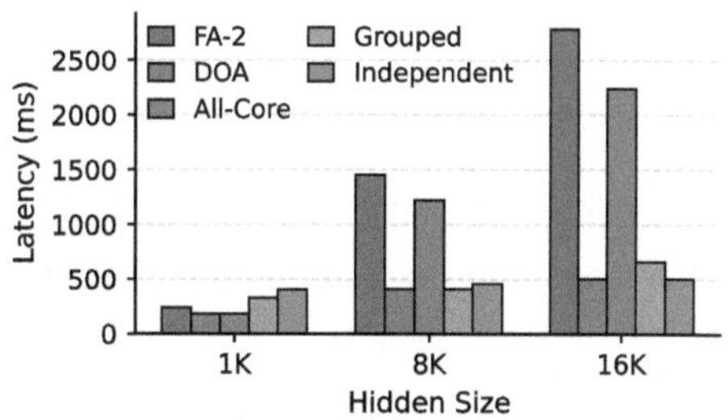

Fig. 8. The effect of adaptive value parallelization. Different hidden sizes favor different execution modes, and DOA adapts to the best mode for each size.

6.6 Ablation Study

Adaptive Value Parallelization. Figure 8 isolates the value-side computation and compares the fixed execution modes under different hidden sizes. The best execution mode changes with hidden size. All-core collaboration is best at hidden size 1K and provides 1.31× speedup over FA-2, grouped collaboration is best at hidden size 8K with 3.59× speedup, and independent execution is best at hidden size 16K with 5.51× speedup. This shows that a single static mode is suboptimal for the value-side computation. By switching among these modes, DOA consistently matches the fastest choice.

Broadcast-Efficient Operators. Figure 9 isolates binary operators and compares a naive implementation on DSP against broadcast-efficient operators of DOA. DOA is consistently faster, achieving 1.50×–1.56× speedup for Tensor-Vector and 1.85×–1.96× speedup for Vector-Tensor. Although each operator is simple, such elementwise operations are invoked frequently in Transformer model execution. These savings therefore remain worthwhile.

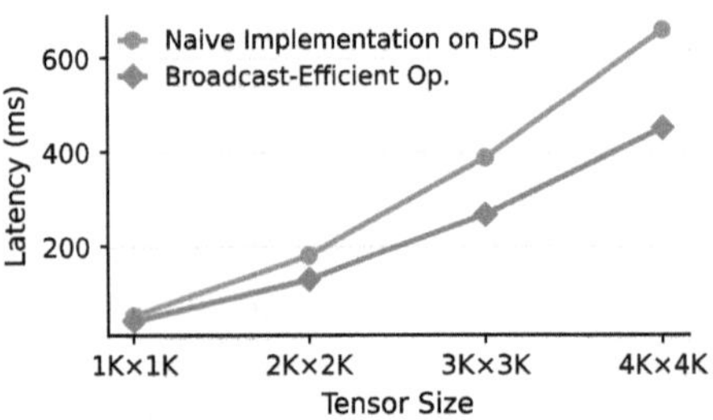

(a) Tensor-Vector.

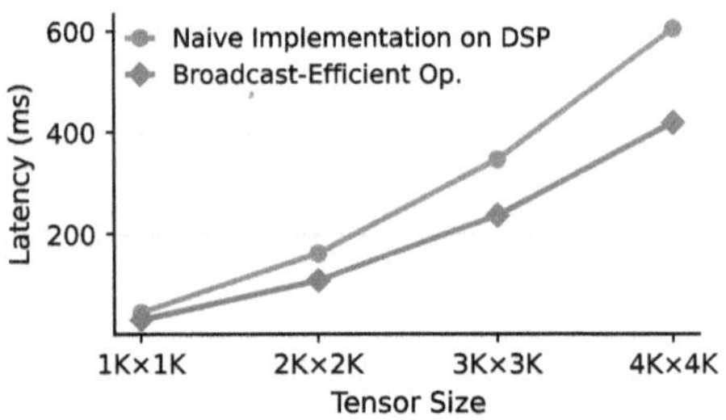

(b) Vector-Tensor.

Fig. 9. The performance of binary operators on different tensor sizes. The broadcast-efficient operators of DOA can provide speedups of 1.50×–1.96×.

7 Related Work

7.1 Attention Acceleration

Recent work on attention acceleration has shown that dataflow plays a central role in kernel performance. FlashAttention-style methods [4,5,7,27,35] avoid materializing the full score matrix by combining block-wise execution with online softmax, and later designs improve efficiency through better work partitioning, fused attention generation, and serving-oriented attention engines. Other attention-oriented work redesigns attention execution flow or prunes weak attention computation [13,23,26,37]. These methods show that attention performance depends strongly on dataflow and memory organization. However, they are mainly designed for GPUs or accelerator-oriented platforms that differ from multi-core DSPs with software-managed three-level hierarchical memory.

7.2 Long-Context LLM System Optimization

Supporting longer sequences has become an important trend in LLM development. Prior efforts can improve the sequence capacity of LLM systems through context-parallel execution [32], sequence parallelism [11,15], long-sequence training optimizations [2,34], and efficient long-context inference systems [26,35]. These studies highlight the importance of long-context LLM optimization, while DOA is orthogonal to them.

7.3 DSP Software Stacks and Kernel Libraries

Recent efforts have improved the programmability of modern multi-core DSP platforms by providing optimized GEMM kernels, batched matrix multiplication support, and efficient kernel libraries for Transformer-scale workloads [8,36,38]. These systems provide the operator-level foundation needed to run Transformer workloads on DSPs, but they do not determine how attention should be organized and fused. In this sense, DOA complements existing DSP kernel libraries by extending optimization from individual operators to the full attention.

8 Conclusion

This paper presented DOA, a dataflow optimization framework for attention on multi-core DSPs with a three-level memory hierarchy. DOA proposes hierarchical attention dataflow, which reorganizes attention around query reuse, cross-core row-wise aggregation, and on-chip accumulation. DOA further introduces adaptive value parallelization and broadcast-efficient operators to reduce coordination overhead in the value-side computation and eliminate unnecessary data movement in binary operators. On FT-M7032 multi-core DSPs, DOA improves kernel performance over FA-2 by 1.45×–1.69× for head size 64 and 1.42×–1.68× for head size 128, while also reducing Transformer layer latency by up to 1.28×. We hope this work can inspire more optimization designs on architectures with three-level memory hierarchies.

Acknowledgments. This work is sponsored in part by the National Natural Science Foundation of China under Grant No. 62421002, and Fundamental and Interdisciplinary Disciplines Breakthrough Plan of the Ministry of Education of China (No.JYB2025XDXM202). The technical solution and experimental design presented in this paper were independently completed by the authors. AI tools were used solely for language polishing and formatting optimization, and did not participate in the development of the research ideas or core content.

References

1. Ainslie, J., Lee-Thorp, J., de Jong, M., Zemlyanskiy, Y., Lebron, F., Sanghai, S.: GQA: training generalized multi-query transformer models from multi-head checkpoints. In: Proceedings of the 2023 Conference on Empirical Methods in Natural Language Processing, pp. 4895–4901 (2023)

2. Chen, Q., Li, S., Gao, W., Sun, P., Wen, Y., Zhang, T.: SPPO: efficient long-sequence LLM training via adaptive sequence pipeline parallel offloading (2025). arXiv:2503.10377 arXiv preprint
3. Chowdhery, A., et al.: PaLM: scaling language modeling with pathways. J. Mach. Learn. Res. **24**(240), 1–113 (2023)
4. Dao, T.: FlashAttention-2: faster attention with better parallelism and work partitioning (2023). arXiv:2307.08691 arXiv preprint
5. Dao, T., Fu, D., Ermon, S., Rudra, A., Ré, C.: FlashAttention: fast and memory-efficient exact attention with io-awareness. In: Advances in Neural Information Processing Systems, vol. 35, pp. 16344–16359 (2022)
6. Ding, W., Tang, X., Kandemir, M., Zhang, Y., Kultursay, E.: Optimizing off-chip accesses in multicores. In: Proceedings of the 36th ACM SIGPLAN Conference on Programming Language Design and Implementation, pp. 131–142 (2015)
7. Dong, J., Feng, B., Guessous, D., Liang, Y., He, H.: FlexAttention: a programming model for generating fused attention variants. Proc. Mach. Learn. Syst. **7** (2025)
8. Fang, J., et al.: MTGEMM: an efficient GEMM library for modern multi-core DSPs. IEEE Trans. Parallel Distrib. Syst. (2026)
9. GitHub: Github copilot. https://copilot.github.com/ (2022)
10. Guo, D., et al.: DeepSeek-R1 incentivizes reasoning in LLMs through reinforcement learning. Nature **645**(8081), 633–638 (2025)
11. Jacobs, S.A., et al.: System optimizations for enabling training of extreme long sequence transformer models. In: Proceedings of the 43rd ACM Symposium on Principles of Distributed Computing. pp. 121–130 (2024)
12. Jain, P., et al.: CheckMate: breaking the memory wall with optimal tensor rematerialization. In: Proceedings of Machine Learning and Systems, vol. 2, pp. 497–511 (2020)
13. Kao, S.C., Subramanian, S., Agrawal, G., Yazdanbakhsh, A., Krishna, T.: FLAT: an optimized dataflow for mitigating attention bottlenecks. In: Proceedings of the 28th ACM International Conference on Architectural Support for Programming Languages and Operating Systems, vol. 2, pp. 295–310 (2023)
14. Lai, Z., et al.: Merak: an efficient distributed DNN training framework with automated 3D parallelism for giant foundation models. IEEE Trans. Parallel Distrib. Syst. **34**(5), 1466–1478 (2023)
15. Li, S., Xue, F., Baranwal, C., Li, Y., You, Y.: Sequence Parallelism: long sequence training from system perspective. In: Proceedings of the 61st Annual Meeting of the Association for Computational Linguistics, (vol. 1: Long Papers), pp. 2391–2404 (2023)
16. Li, Y., Phanishayee, A., Murray, D., Tarnawski, J., Kim, N.S.: Harmony: overcoming the hurdles of GPU memory capacity to train massive DNN models on commodity servers. Proc. VLDB Endow. **15**(11), 2747–2760 (2022)
17. Liu, A., et al.: DeepSeek-V3 technical report (2024). arXiv:2412.19437 arXiv preprint
18. Liu, W., et al.: AutoPipe-H: a heterogeneity-aware data-paralleled pipeline approach on commodity GPU servers. IEEE Trans. Comput. **74**(4), 1196–1209 (2024)
19. Narayanan, D., et al.: Efficient large-scale language model training on GPU clusters using Megatron-LM. In: Proceedings of the International Conference for High Performance Computing, Networking, Storage and Analysis, pp. 1–15 (2021)
20. OpenAI: GPT-4 technical report. https://openai.com/research/gpt-4 (2024)
21. Paszke, A., et al.: PYTorch: an imperative style, high-performance deep learning library. In: Advances in Neural Information Processing Systems, vol. 32 (2019)

22. Peng, X., et al.: Capuchin: tensor-based GPU memory management for deep learning. In: Proceedings of the Twenty-Fifth International Conference on Architectural Support for Programming Languages and Operating Systems, pp. 891–905 (2020)
23. Qu, Z., Liu, L., Tu, F., Chen, Z., Ding, Y., Xie, Y.: DOTA: detect and omit weak attentions for scalable transformer acceleration. In: Proceedings of the 27th ACM International Conference on Architectural Support for Programming Languages and Operating Systems, pp. 14–26 (2022)
24. Raffel, C., et al.: Exploring the limits of transfer learning with a unified text-to-text transformer. J. Mach. Learn. Res. **21**(140), 1–67 (2020)
25. Rajbhandari, S., Ruwase, O., Rasley, J., Smith, S., He, Y.: Zero-infinity: breaking the GPU memory wall for extreme scale deep learning. In: Proceedings of the International Conference for High Performance Computing, Networking, Storage and Analysis, pp. 1–14 (2021)
26. Sanovar, R., Bharadwaj, S., St Amant, R., Rühle, V., Rajmohan, S.: LeanAttention: hardware-aware scalable attention mechanism for the decode-phase of transformers. Proc. Mach. Learn. Syst. **7** (2025)
27. Shah, J., Bikshandi, G., Zhang, Y., Thakkar, V., Ramani, P., Dao, T.: FlashAttention-3: fast and accurate attention with asynchrony and low-precision. In: Advances in Neural Information Processing Systems, vol. 37, pp. 68658–68685 (2024)
28. Tang, Y., et al.: Delta: Memory-efficient training via dynamic fine-grained recomputation and swapping. ACM Trans. Archit. Code Optimiz. **21**(4), 1–25 (2024)
29. Team, G., et al.: Gemini: a family of highly capable multimodal models (2023). arXiv:2312.11805 arXiv preprint
30. Vaswani, A., et al.: Attention is all you need. In: Advances in Neural Information Processing Systems, vol. 30 (2017)
31. Wolf, T., et al.: Transformers: state-of-the-art natural language processing. In: Proceedings of the 2020 Conference on Empirical Methods in Natural Language Processing: System Demonstrations, pp. 38–45 (2020)
32. Yang, A., et al.: Context parallelism for scalable million-token inference. In: Eighth Conference on Machine Learning and Systems (2025)
33. Yang, A., et al.: Qwen3 technical report. arXiv preprint arXiv:2505.09388 (2025)
34. Yao, J., Jacobs, S.A., Tanaka, M., Ruwase, O., Subramoni, H., Panda, D.K.: Training ultra long context language model with fully pipelined distributed transformer. Proc. Mach. Learn. Syst. **7** (2025)
35. Ye, Z., et al.: FlashInfer: efficient and customizable attention engine for LLM inference serving. Proc. Mach. Learn. Syst. **7** (2025)
36. Yu, K., et al.: Optimizing general matrix multiplications on modern multi-core DSPs. In: 2024 IEEE International Parallel and Distributed Processing Symposium (IPDPS), pp. 964–975. IEEE (2024)
37. Zhou, Z., Liu, J., Gu, Z., Sun, G.: EnerGON: toward efficient acceleration of transformers using dynamic sparse attention. IEEE Trans. Comput. Aided Des. Integr. Circuits Syst. **42**(1), 136–149 (2022)
38. Zuo, X., Xiao, C., Wang, Q., Shi, C.: Optimizing batched small matrix multiplication on multi-core DSP architecture. In: 2024 IEEE International Symposium on Parallel and Distributed Processing with Applications (ISPA), pp. 426–435. IEEE (2024)

ARROW: Adaptive Row Reorganization for Warp-Balanced SpMV

Yuxiang Zhang, Jianhua Gao(✉), and Weixing Ji(✉)

Beijing Normal University, Beijing, China
zyx@mail.bnu.edu.cn, {gaojh,jwx}@bnu.edu.cn

Abstract. The performance of sparse matrix-vector multiplication (SpMV) is limited by irregular sparsity patterns, indirect memory accesses, and workload imbalance. In this paper, we propose ARROW, a Tensor Core-based optimization method for SpMV, which reorganizes sparse matrices into dense blocks suitable for Tensor Core execution by reordering rows, forming row groups, and extracting local dense blocks. We also design a warp-level execution workflow and further incorporate efficient result extraction, double buffering, and vectorized memory access to reduce data movement and memory access overhead. To address ultra-long rows and workload imbalance, ARROW introduces a dedicated kernel and a group-level workload redistribution strategy to improve parallel efficiency. Experimental results on large-scale real-world sparse matrices show that ARROW achieves geometric mean speedups of 1.78×, 1.10×, and 3.22× over cuSPARSE, DASP, and Spaden on A100, respectively. On RTX 3090, ARROW achieves geometric mean speedups of 1.57×, 1.06×, and 3.58× over cuSPARSE, DASP, and Spaden, respectively.

Keywords: Sparse matrix-vector multiplication · Tensor Cores · GPU · Load balancing

1 Introduction

Sparse matrix-vector multiplication (SpMV) is widely used in scientific and engineering applications and often dominates the runtime of iterative methods [12]. However, its low arithmetic intensity and irregular memory access patterns make it difficult to achieve high performance on modern hardware.

Conventional GPU implementations of SpMV mainly rely on CUDA Cores and CSR-like sparse formats. Their performance is often limited by memory bandwidth, indirect memory accesses, and load imbalance caused by irregular row lengths. Recent GPU architectures provide new opportunities to revisit this

J. Gao and W. Ji—Equal contribution.

L. Eeckhout et al. (Eds.): APPT 2026, LNCS 16693, pp. 390–403, 2027.
https://doi.org/10.1007/978-981-92-4805-6_26

problem. Since Volta, Tensor Cores have offered much higher matrix multiply-accumulate throughput than CUDA Cores, and Ampere further extended this capability [25,26]. On NVIDIA A100, for example, the theoretical peak FP16 throughput reaches 312 TFLOPS with Tensor Cores, compared with 78 TFLOPS with CUDA Cores. However, Tensor Cores favor regular dense fragments and warp-synchronous execution, whereas SpMV is sparse and irregular. Directly mapping SpMV onto Tensor Cores, therefore, introduces padding and extra accumulation overhead. Recent methods such as DASP [21] and Spaden [5] show the potential of Tensor Core-based SpMV. However, highly irregular matrices remain difficult because large variations in row length still cause padding, load imbalance, and extra fragment-handling overhead.

To address these issues, we propose ARROW, an adaptive row reorganization method for warp-balanced Tensor Core-based SpMV. ARROW reorganizes the input matrix into local dense tiles, executes them with a warp-level execution pipeline, and further improves efficiency through double buffering and vectorized memory access. For highly irregular matrices, it also introduces dedicated handling for ultra-long rows and group-level workload redistribution for lightweight row groups. Overall, ARROW provides a unified framework for Tensor Core-based SpMV on highly irregular sparse matrices.

The main contributions of this paper are as follows.

- We develop a warp-level execution pipeline that exploits Tensor Core hardware characteristics and register layout. The pipeline integrates register-aware fragment organization, direct result extraction, double buffering, and vectorized memory access to reduce data movement and improve execution efficiency.
- We propose two complementary load-balancing mechanisms for highly irregular matrices: a dedicated kernel for ultra-long rows and a group-level workload redistribution strategy for lightweight row groups. These mechanisms improve hardware utilization and extend the effectiveness of Tensor Core-based SpMV on highly irregular sparsity patterns.

2 Background

To improve SpMV with Tensor Cores, it is necessary to understand how Tensor Core fragments are organized at the hardware level. Recent NVIDIA GPUs provide Tensor Cores for warp-level matrix multiply-accumulate operations [25,26]. Although these operations are exposed through the WMMA interface, the underlying fragment register layout is unknown at that level. Prior work has shown that Tensor Core inputs can also be organized directly according to the mapping between fragment registers and warp lanes, and has used this mapping to load a matrix fragment at the register level [5]. Although this mapping is not publicly documented and may vary across architectures and MMA shapes, it provides useful background for the register-aware method design used in ARROW. Figure 1 shows the register-to-thread mapping for FP16 $16 \times 16 \times 16$ MMA on

Ampere. This layout is an architectural property rather than a contribution of ARROW, but it provides the necessary background for the method described in the next section.

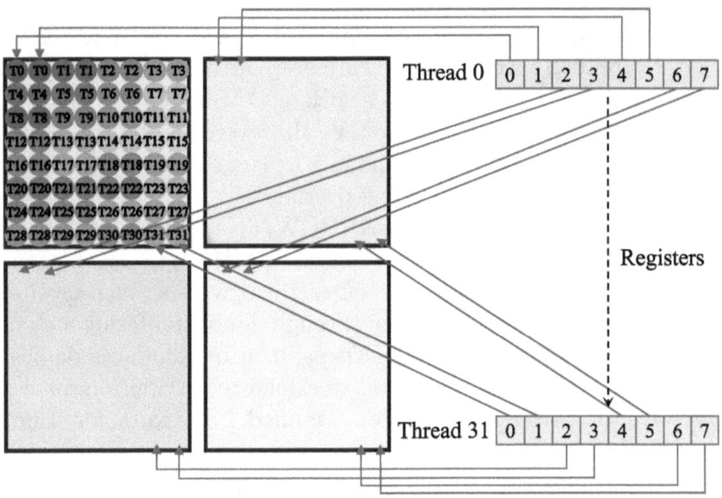

Fig. 1. Register-to-thread mapping of Tensor Core fragments for FP16 16 × 16 × 16 MMA on Ampere.

3 Design

3.1 Overview

Tensor Core-based SpMV faces a mismatch between dense hardware execution and sparse computation. Tensor Cores operate on fixed-size dense fragments, whereas SpMV has irregular row lengths, indirect accesses, and vector outputs. Directly mapping sparse rows to MMA fragments, therefore, introduces substantial padding.

ARROW begins with a preprocessing step that reorganizes the input matrix into local dense tiles for Tensor Core execution, as shown in Fig. 2. It converts the matrix to CSR, sorts rows by nonzero count, groups them into batches of MMA_M rows, and scans each group with a window of size MMA_K to extract nonempty $MMA\_M \times MMA\_K$ tiles. The extracted tile values and starting columns are stored in `tcVal` and `tcColIdx`, and `rowIndices` records the row mapping for output write-back. Based on this layout, ARROW combines register-aware Tensor Core execution with load balancing for highly irregular matrices.

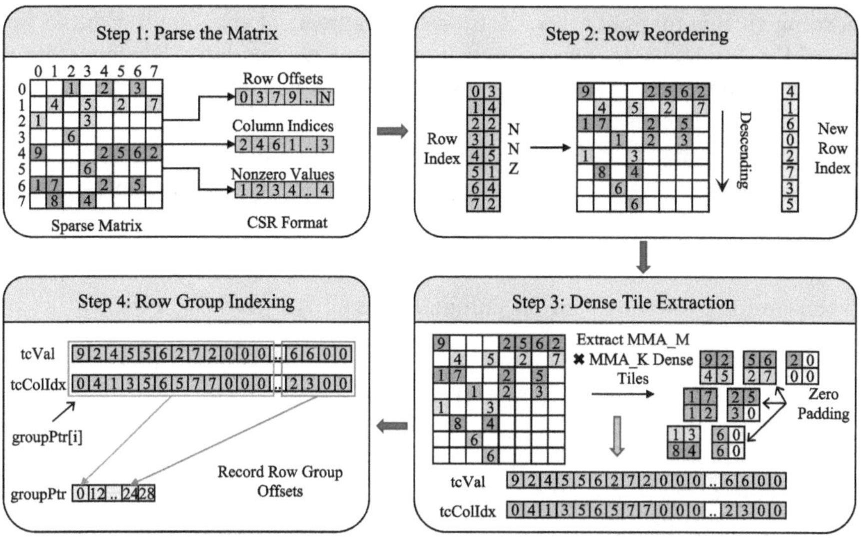

Fig. 2. Construction of the Tensor Core-oriented sparse layout in ARROW.

3.2 Register-Aware Tensor Core Execution

ARROW uses a warp-level Tensor Core SpMV pipeline for FP16 $16 \times 16 \times 16$ MMA. This pipeline exploits Tensor Core hardware characteristics and register layout through register-aware fragment organization, direct efficient result extraction, double buffering, and vectorized memory access.

As discussed in Sect. 2, ARROW loads matrix tiles directly into the register layout of the left-hand MMA fragment according to the mapping between fragment registers and warp lanes. Based on `tcColIdx`, the kernel gathers the corresponding segment of the input vector and reorganizes it into the right-hand fragment. In this way, the extracted sparse tiles and their associated vector segments are directly mapped to the two MMA operands.

More importantly, ARROW aligns data placement with the complete fragment layout used in Tensor Core computation. In contrast, methods that directly load matrix elements into registers may use only part of the fragment register space, which can leave hardware resources underutilized [5]. By organizing data and computation around the full fragment layout, ARROW reduces this underutilization and improves Tensor Core efficiency.

After each MMA operation, ARROW extracts only the results that contribute to the final SpMV output. A single MMA produces a full 16×16 output fragment, whereas SpMV requires one accumulated scalar for each output row. Under the fragment layout shown in Sect. 2, only a small subset of accumulator results corresponds to the final outputs of SpMV. For a warp lane indexed by *laneId*, the candidate row and column positions are given by

$$i = laneId \gg 2, \qquad j = (laneId \bmod 4) \ll 1. \tag{1}$$

According to this mapping, the useful results appear at diagonally related positions of the fragment and are stored in different accumulator locations for the upper and lower halves. The useful results in the upper half of the fragment are accumulated as

$$Y_{\text{out}}[i] \leftarrow Y_{\text{out}}[i] + \begin{cases} C_{\text{frag}}[0], & \text{if } i = j, \\ C_{\text{frag}}[1], & \text{if } i = j+1, \\ 0, & \text{otherwise,} \end{cases} \tag{2}$$

and those in the lower half are accumulated as

$$Y_{\text{out}}[MMA\_M/2+i] \leftarrow Y_{\text{out}}[MMA\_M/2+i] + \begin{cases} C_{\text{frag}}[6], & \text{if } i = j, \\ C_{\text{frag}}[7], & \text{if } i = j+1, \\ 0, & \text{otherwise.} \end{cases} \tag{3}$$

Here, $C_{\text{frag}}[0]$, $C_{\text{frag}}[1]$, $C_{\text{frag}}[6]$, and $C_{\text{frag}}[7]$ are the accumulator entries aligned with valid SpMV outputs. This avoids writing irrelevant MMA outputs to global memory.

To reduce memory latency, ARROW uses two register buffers within a warp. One buffer feeds the current MMA operation, while the next tile and vector segment are prefetched into the other. ARROW also uses 128-bit vectorized loads for matrix tiles and vector fragments whenever alignment permits.

3.3 Adaptive Load Balancing for Irregular Matrices

Even with this preprocessing and register-aware Tensor Core execution, highly irregular matrices can still suffer from load imbalance. In ARROW, the main sources are ultra-long rows and lightweight row groups. Ultra-long rows increase padding and create a few heavy tasks, while lightweight row groups contain too few tiles to utilize a thread block efficiently. As a result, thread blocks are not utilized evenly, and the overhead of block scheduling and synchronization becomes more significant. Figure 3 illustrates the load-balancing strategy.

ARROW uses two dedicated mechanisms. During preprocessing, rows whose nonzero counts exceed `LONG_ROW_THRESHOLD` are removed from the standard row-group path and processed by a separate kernel. Each long row is split into multiple dense tiles, and the partial products are reduced to produce the final output value. Since ultra-long rows are locally denser, this strategy introduces relatively little padding while preventing a few heavy rows from dominating the main kernel.

For the remaining rows, ARROW merges consecutive lightweight row groups until the cumulative tile count reaches `MIN_TILES_PER_BLOCK`. The merged groups are indexed by `block_group_begin`, while warp-level assignments are recorded in `warp_tile_begin`, `warp_tile_nums`, and `warp_tile_group_idx`. One thread block can then process multiple lightweight groups, which improves occupancy and reduces inefficiency from small workloads. Algorithm 1 summarizes the resulting kernel. It should be noted that this pseudocode focuses

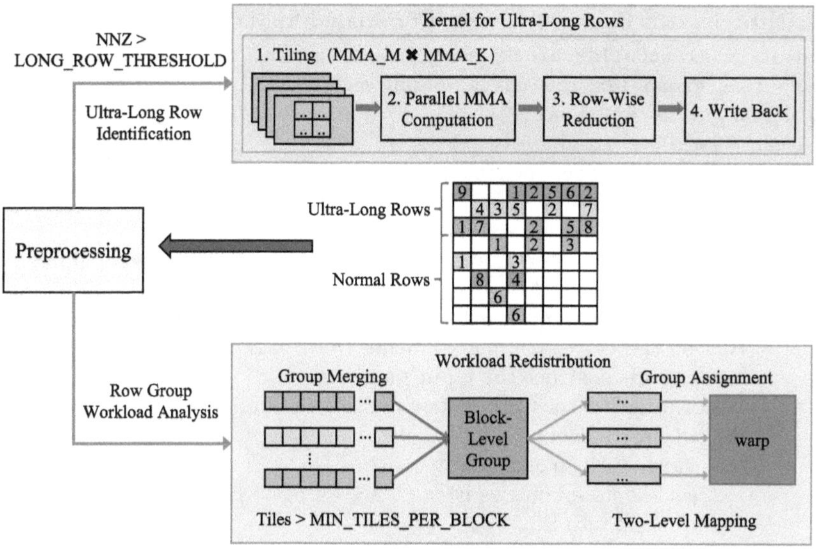

Fig. 3. Adaptive load-balancing strategy in ARROW: dedicated handling for ultra-long rows and block-level redistribution for lightweight row groups.

on the high-level execution and scheduling flow of the proposed load-balanced SpMV kernel, and omits several low-level implementation optimizations for clarity, including double buffering and vectorized memory access used in the actual GPU implementation.

These two mechanisms are designed around local tile extraction and warp-level Tensor Core execution. Dedicated handling of ultra-long rows removes dominant heavy tasks from the main path, while group-level redistribution improves thread block utilization for lightweight row groups.

4 Experimental Evaluation

4.1 Experimental Setup

We evaluate ARROW on two NVIDIA Ampere GPUs: an A100 with 40 GB memory and a GeForce RTX 3090 with 24 GB memory. These platforms represent a data-center GPU and a high-end consumer GPU. Both systems use Ubuntu 22.04, CUDA 12.0, NVIDIA driver 535.274.02, and GCC 11.4.0.

We compare ARROW with cuSPARSE, DASP and Spaden on 2800 sparse matrices from the SuiteSparse Matrix Collection [7]. We further select 14 representative matrices for case studies on ARROW's preprocessing, register-aware Tensor Core execution, and load-balancing mechanisms. Their metadata is listed in Table 1.

In all experiments, the parameters are fixed at `LONG_ROW_THRESHOLD` = 8192 and `MIN_TILES_PER_BLOCK` = 16. We use GFLOPS and relative speedup to compare ARROW with other methods.

Algorithm 1 Load-Balanced Tensor Core-based SpMV

Input: `tcVal`, `tcColIdx`, `block_group_begin`, `warp_tile_begin`, `warp_tile_nums`, `warp_tile_group_idx`, `rowIndices`, input vector `valX`, valid rows `validRows`
Output: output vector `valY`
for each block-level group b **do**
  $[g_s, g_e) \leftarrow$ (`block_group_begin`$[b]$, `block_group_begin`$[b+1]$)
  Initialize shared-memory accumulation buffers $\mathbf{S}[g_s, g_e)$
  for each warp w in the thread block **do**
    Determine the tile interval of w from `warp_tile_begin` and `warp_tile_nums`
    for each assigned tile t **do**
      Load dense tile t and construct the Tensor Core input matrix A_t
      Gather the corresponding elements from `valX` according to the column indices and construct the input matrix B_t
      Perform the Tensor Core matrix multiply-accumulate operation and obtain the output fragment C_t
      $u \leftarrow$ `warp_tile_group_idx`$[t]$
      Extract the useful entries from C_t according to Eqs. (2) and (3), and accumulate them into $\mathbf{S}[u - g_s]$
    end for
  end for
  Reduce the partial sums stored in $\mathbf{S}$ for each row group
  for $u = 0$ **to** $g_e - g_s - 1$ **do**
    for $r = 0$ **to** $MMA\_M - 1$ **do**
      if $MMA\_M \times (g_s + u) + r <$ `validRows` **then**
        $row \leftarrow$ `rowIndices`$[MMA\_M \times (g_s + u) + r]$
        `valY`$[row] \leftarrow \mathbf{S}[u][r]$
      end if
    end for
  end for
end for

4.2 Overall Performance

ARROW consistently outperforms all baseline methods across the evaluation dataset. For methods with multiple implementation variants, including ARROW and DASP, the reported results correspond to the best-performing variant on each platform. On A100, it surpasses cuSPARSE, the CUDA Core baseline, on 2266 matrices, achieving a geometric mean speedup of 1.78×. Compared with DASP, a Tensor Core baseline, ARROW delivers a geometric mean speedup of 1.10× and performs better on 2013 matrices. In comparison with Spaden, ARROW achieves a geometric mean speedup of 3.22× and outperforms it on 2551 matrices.

On RTX 3090, ARROW outperforms cuSPARSE on 2095 matrices with a geometric mean speedup of 1.57×. Relative to DASP, it achieves a geometric mean speedup of 1.06× and performs better on 1871 matrices. Compared with Spaden, ARROW attains a geometric mean speedup of 3.58× and outperforms it on 2498 matrices.

Table 1. Metadata of the 14 representative matrices

Matrix	Dimension	Nonzeros	Matrix	Dimension	Nonzeros
airfoil_2d	14 K × 14 K	259 K	F1	343 K × 343 K	26.8 M
bibd_20_10	184 K × 184 K	8.3 M	Ga41As41H72	268 K × 268 K	18.4 M
cage11	39 K × 39 K	559 K	Goodwin_040	17 K × 17 K	561 K
circuit5M	5.5 M × 5.5 M	59.5 M	k1_san	67 K × 67 K	559 K
crankseg_2	63 K × 63 K	14.1 M	mycielskian16	49 K × 49 K	33.3 M
denormal	89 K × 89 K	1.1 M	n4c6-b11	132 K × 132 K	830 K
dielFilterV3real	1.1 M × 1.1 M	89.3 M	rgg_n_2_16_s0	65 K × 65 K	684 K

The differences in the numbers of winning matrices mainly reflect the varying performance characteristics of different baseline methods and GPU architectures. Overall, these results demonstrate that ARROW consistently improves upon both conventional CUDA Core-based SpMV implementations and recent Tensor Core-based approaches across a wide range of sparse matrices.

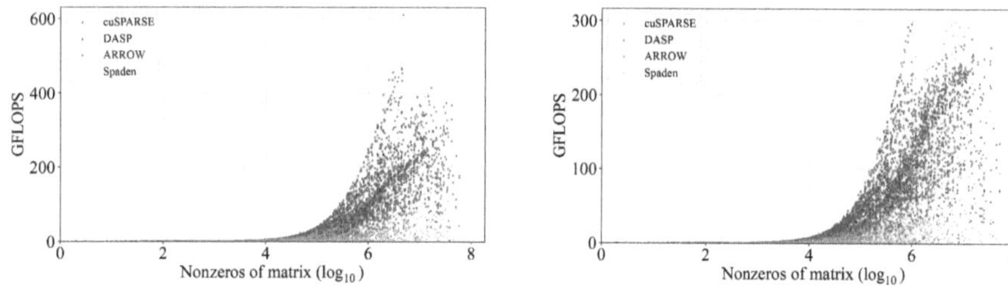

(a) GFLOPS on A100 (b) GFLOPS on RTX 3090

Fig. 4. GFLOPS comparison of cuSPARSE, DASP, Spaden and ARROW on 2800 sparse matrices.

Figure 4 shows the GFLOPS achieved for different matrix sizes. On both GPUs, the highest performance of ARROW remains above that of cuSPARSE and DASP over most of the observed range. Throughput generally increases with matrix size because larger matrices provide more parallel work and reduce the relative impact of kernel launch overhead. ARROW maintains its advantage across a wide range of matrix sizes and sparsity patterns, indicating that the benefit is not limited to a narrow set of inputs.

However, GFLOPS does not directly show how common these improvements are, so Fig. 5 evaluates the benefit of migrating SpMV computation from conventional CUDA Cores to Tensor Cores by comparing ARROW with cuSPARSE. In Fig. 5, the speedup over cuSPARSE is mainly distributed between 1× and 3×, indicating stable improvements for a large portion of the dataset. A few matrices achieve much larger speedups, which suggests that ARROW is particularly

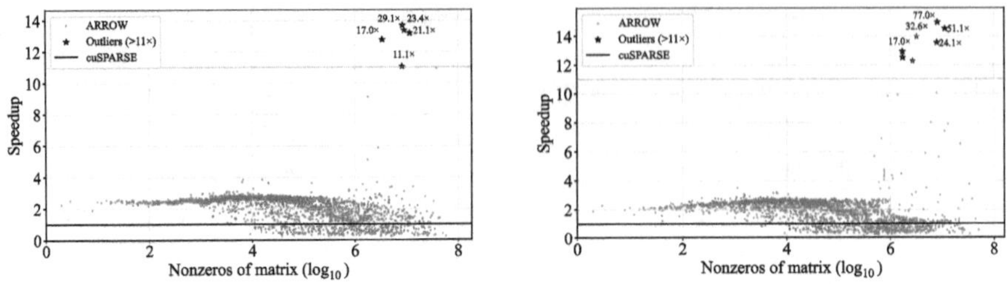

(a) Speedup on A100 (b) Speedup on RTX 3090

Fig. 5. Speedup comparison of ARROW over cuSPARSE on 2800 sparse matrices.

effective for certain sparsity structures. For example, `bibd_20_10` reaches 29.1× on A100 and 77.0× on RTX 3090.

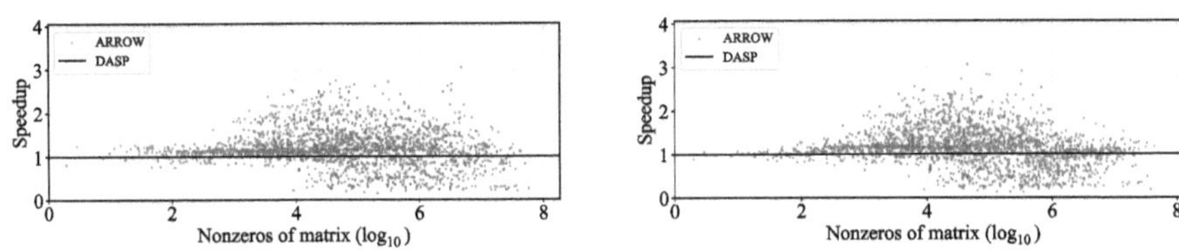

(a) Speedup on A100 (b) Speedup on RTX 3090

Fig. 6. Speedup comparison of ARROW over DASP on 2800 sparse matrices.

Figure 6 presents the speedup distribution relative to DASP. While both DASP and Spaden are Tensor Core-based baselines, DASP achieves stronger overall performance on the large-scale matrix collection presented earlier and therefore serves as the primary representative baseline for a detailed comparison. Since both ARROW and DASP utilize Tensor Cores, this comparison more directly reflects the contribution of ARROW's preprocessing strategy, register-aware Tensor Core execution, and load-balanced scheduling.

As shown in the figure, the overall speedups are smaller than those observed against cuSPARSE, yet most matrices still achieve speedups above 1×, with the upper range reaching approximately 3× on both GPUs. Although DASP outperforms ARROW on a small subset of matrices, the overall distribution indicates that ARROW provides more effective acceleration for irregular sparse matrices across the dataset.

4.3 Representative Matrix Analysis

The representative matrix study helps explain the source of the overall improvements and the contribution of the proposed load-balancing mechanisms. Figures 7 and 8 compare six implementations on 14 representative matrices: cuSPARSE, DASP_V1, DASP_V2, ARROW_V1, ARROW_V2 and Spaden.

DASP_V1 and DASP_V2 correspond to the two variants reported in the original work, where DASP_V2 extends DASP_V1 with additional cache-oriented optimizations. For ARROW, ARROW_V1 consists of the proposed preprocessing and register-aware Tensor Core execution, while ARROW_V2 further incorporates the load-balancing mechanisms.

ARROW_V1 already achieves the best or near-best performance on a substantial number of matrices. Representative examples on A100 include `airfoil_2d`, `dielFilterV3real`, `F1`, `Ga41As41H72`, `Goodwin_040`, and many others. Similar behavior is observed on RTX 3090, where ARROW_V1 remains highly competitive on matrices such as `airfoil_2d`, `dielFilterV3real`, `F1`, and `Goodwin_040`. These results indicate that the core design of ARROW is already highly effective for a broad class of sparse matrices.

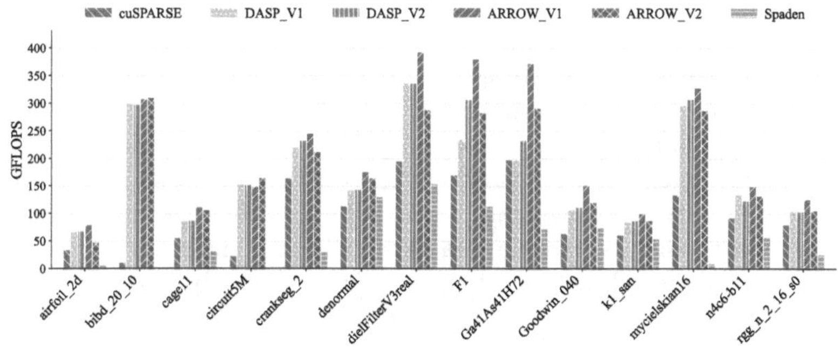

Fig. 7. GFLOPS comparison of different methods on representative matrices on A100.

This behavior can be attributed to the fact that their sparsity patterns naturally match ARROW's row reordering and local tile extraction mechanisms. As a result, the preprocessing stage can effectively expose fine-grained dense structures for Tensor Core execution, while the register-aware execution strategy further improves data reuse and reduces execution overhead. Consequently, most of the performance benefits are already realized in ARROW_V1, making additional optimizations contribute only marginal gains on these matrices.

In contrast, the advantages of ARROW_V2 become more apparent on matrices with highly irregular sparsity patterns. Representative examples include `bibd_20_10`, `circuit5M`, and several other matrices on A100, where large variations in row lengths and tile counts introduce substantial workload imbalance. Under such conditions, the execution time is often dominated by a small number of thread blocks assigned disproportionately large workloads, limiting overall parallel efficiency. ARROW_V2 mitigates this issue through its load-balancing mechanism, resulting in noticeably higher performance on these matrices.

A similar trend is observed on RTX 3090 and is even more evident for matrices such as `crankseg_2`, `k1_san`, `mycielskian16`, and `n4c6-b11`. These matrices exhibit stronger workload imbalance, making them particularly sensitive to

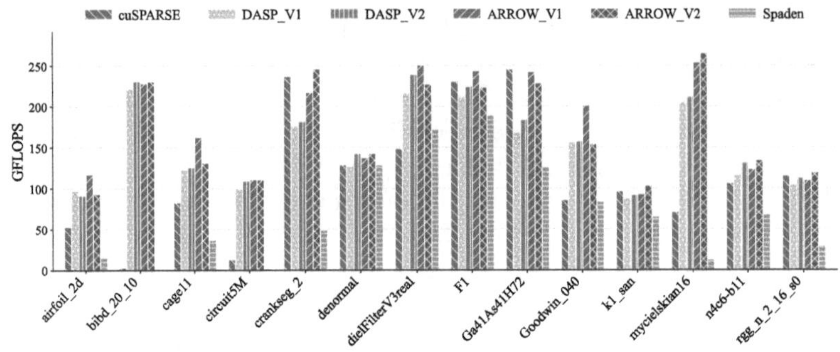

Fig. 8. GFLOPS comparison of different methods on representative matrices on RTX 3090.

scheduling efficiency. By redistributing work more evenly across thread blocks, ARROW_V2 is able to improve resource utilization and alleviate performance bottlenecks caused by extreme sparsity irregularity.

Overall, the results highlight the complementary nature of the two ARROW variants. While ARROW_V1 is sufficient to exploit most optimization opportunities on structurally favorable matrices, ARROW_V2 extends the applicability of the framework to highly irregular matrices by improving workload distribution and execution balance. Together, they provide consistently strong performance across a diverse range of sparse matrix structures.

5 Related Work

GPU SpMV has been extensively studied from multiple perspectives, including workload mapping, load balancing, sparse-format design, and data representation [10,12]. Representative approaches include row-based kernels, merge-based strategies, and format-aware designs, which improve performance through more efficient workload distribution and memory access patterns. These methods improve performance mainly by changing the way nonzeros are assigned to threads and by improving memory access behavior. Representative formats such as HYB, SELL-C-σ, CSR5, AMF-CSR, and CSR2 improve memory behavior and parallel efficiency on irregular matrices [2,4,6,11,13,16,20,23,24]. Mixed precision methods further reduce storage cost and data movement through precision selection, precision aware decomposition, and block wise control [1,14,18,27,29]. These directions substantially improve CUDA Core-based SpMV, but their performance remains largely limited by memory bandwidth. They also show that SpMV performance depends not only on parallel workload distribution, but also on data representation, memory efficiency, and numerical accuracy.

Beyond manually optimized SpMV implementations, sparse auto-tuning and compiler-based optimization have emerged as another important direction for improving performance across diverse matrices and hardware platforms. Auto-tuning frameworks such as SMAT [17], BestSF [3], and AlphaSparse [8] automatically select sparse formats, implementation parameters, or architecture-aware execution strategies according to matrix characteristics and target platforms. Compiler-based systems, including TACO [15], WACO [28], SRSparse [9], and SpF [19], further improve sparse computation by generating optimized sparse kernels from high-level representations and applying techniques such as sparse kernel specialization, register-level optimization, and architecture-aware code generation. Compared with manually optimized implementations, these approaches improve portability and productivity while adapting sparse computations to diverse matrices and hardware platforms. However, they primarily focus on format selection, code generation, or implementation automation rather than the efficient execution of Tensor-Core-based SpMV kernels on modern GPUs.

Recent studies have explored Tensor Core-based SpMV as an alternative approach to overcoming the memory-bandwidth limitations of conventional CUDA Core-based implementations [5,21,22]. The main challenge in this direction is how to map irregular sparse data to regular MMA fragments while controlling padding overhead and data movement. Existing work in this area involves fragment mapping, sparse layout transformation for MMA computation, and workload adaptation for Tensor Core execution. DASP groups rows and constructs dense tiles for Tensor Core execution [21], while Spaden reduces data movement through register-aware fragment handling and bitmap-based storage [5]. Although both approaches effectively exploit Tensor Cores for SpMV acceleration, their design focuses differ from that of ARROW. DASP primarily emphasizes sparse layout transformation and Tensor Core mapping, whereas ARROW further considers hardware execution characteristics, including register-aware computation and load-balanced scheduling for irregular sparse matrices. Spaden focuses on reducing data movement and storage overhead, while ARROW emphasizes maximizing effective hardware utilization by optimizing Tensor Core execution efficiency and workload balance. Ma et al. [22] study warp fixed and warp balanced Tensor Core SpMV variants in the context of PCG. Building upon these ideas, ARROW targets highly irregular sparse matrices by combining preprocessing, register-aware Tensor Core execution, and load-balanced scheduling within a unified framework.

Overall, existing studies improve SpMV from different perspectives, including workload distribution, sparse-format optimization, automatic tuning, compiler-assisted code generation, and Tensor Core adaptation. However, highly irregular sparse matrices still remain challenging, especially when Tensor Core utilization and load balance must be considered together.

6 Conclusion

This paper presents ARROW, a Tensor Core-based SpMV method for highly irregular sparse matrices. By combining adaptive row reorganization, register-aware Tensor Core execution, and load-balanced execution, ARROW reduces padding, avoids unnecessary output movement, and improves hardware utilization under irregular workloads. Experiments on 2800 SuiteSparse matrices show that ARROW consistently outperforms both cuSPARSE and DASP on A100 and RTX 3090, achieving average speedups of up to 2.03× over cuSPARSE and 1.18× over DASP. Results on representative matrices further show that the dedicated handling of ultra-long rows and the group-level workload redistribution strategy are especially effective for highly irregular sparsity patterns.

Acknowledgments. This work was supported by the National Natural Science Foundation of China under Grant 62372046. The technical solution and experimental design presented in this paper were independently completed by the authors. AI tools were used solely for language polishing and formatting optimization, and did not participate in the development of the research ideas or core content.

References

1. Ahmad, K., Sundar, H., Hall, M.: Data-driven mixed precision sparse matrix-vector multiplication for GPUs. ACM Trans. Archit. Code Optim. **16**(4) (2019)
2. Bell, N., Garland, M.: Efficient sparse matrix-vector multiplication on CUDA, NVIDIA Corporation (2008). NVR-2008-004 NVIDIA Technical Report
3. Benatia, A., Ji, W., Wang, Y., Shi, F.: BestSF: a sparse meta-format for optimizing SpMV on GPU. ACM Trans. Archit. Code Optim. **15**(3) (2018)
4. Bian, H., Huang, J., Dong, R., Liu, L., Wang, X.: CSR2: a new format for SIMD-accelerated SPMV. In: Proceedings of the 2020 IEEE/ACM International Symposium on Cluster, Cloud and Internet Computing, pp. 350–359 (2020)
5. Chen, Y., Yu, J.X.: Bitmap-based sparse matrix-vector multiplication with tensor cores. In: Proceedings of the 53rd International Conference on Parallel Processing, pp. 1135–1144 (2024)
6. Daga, M., Greathouse, J.L.: Structural agnostic SPMV: adapting CSR-adaptive for irregular matrices. In: Proceedings of the 2015 IEEE 22nd International Conference on High Performance Computing, pp. 64–74 (2015)
7. Davis, T.A., Hu, Y.: The university of Florida sparse matrix collection. ACM Trans. Math. Softw. **38**(1) (2011)
8. Du, Z., Li, J., Wang, Y., Li, X., Tan, G., Sun, N.: AlphaSparse: generating high performance SPMV codes directly from sparse matrices. In: SC22: International Conference for High Performance Computing, Networking, Storage and Analysis, pp. 1–15 (2022)
9. Du, Z., Liu, Y., Sun, N., Cui, H., Feng, X., Li, J.: SRSparse: generating codes for high-performance sparse matrix-vector semiring computations. ACM Trans. Archit. Code Optim. **22** (2025)
10. Filippone, S., Cardellini, V., Barbieri, D., Fanfarillo, A.: Sparse matrix-vector multiplication on GPGPUs. ACM Trans. Math. Softw. **43**(4) (2017)
11. Gao, J., Ji, W., Liu, J., Shao, S., Wang, Y., Shi, F.: AMF-CSR: adaptive multi-row folding of CSR for SPMV on GPU. In: Proceedings of the 2021 IEEE 27th International Conference on Parallel and Distributed Systems, pp. 418–425 (2021)
12. Gao, J., Liu, B., Ji, W., Huang, H.: A systematic literature survey of sparse matrix-vector multiplication (2024). arXiv:2404.06047 arXiv preprint
13. Greathouse, J.L., Daga, M.: Efficient sparse matrix-vector multiplication on GPUs using the CSR storage format. In: SC'14: Proceedings of the International Conference for High Performance Computing, Networking, Storage and Analysis, pp. 769–780. IEEE (2014)

14. Isupov, K.: Multiple-precision sparse matrix-vector multiplication on GPUs. J. Comput. Sci. **61**, 101609 (2022)
15. Kjolstad, F., Kamil, S., Chou, S., Lugato, D., Amarasinghe, S.: The tensor algebra compiler. Proc. ACM Program. Lang.**1** (2017)
16. Kreutzer, M., Hager, G., Wellein, G., Fehske, H., Bishop, A.R.: A unified sparse matrix data format for efficient general sparse matrix-vector multiplication on modern processors with wide simd units. SIAM J. Sci. Comput. **36**(5), C401–C423 (2014)
17. Li, J., Tan, G., Chen, M., Sun, N.: SMAT: an input adaptive auto-tuner for sparse matrix-vector multiplication. In: Proceedings of the 34th ACM SIGPLAN Conference on Programming Language Design and Implementation, pp. 117–126 (2013)
18. Liu, J., Wang, Y., Gao, J., Ji, W.: PSPMV: precision-based sparse matrix partition and SPMV optimization. CCF Trans. High Perf. Comput. **6**(6), 549–565 (2024)
19. Liu, J., Zhao, Z., Ding, Z., Brock, B., Rong, H., Zhang, Z.: UniSparse: an intermediate language for general sparse format customization. Proc. ACM Program. Lang **8** (2024)
20. Liu, W., Vinter, B.: CSR5: an efficient storage format for cross-platform sparse matrix-vector multiplication. In: Proceedings of the 29th ACM International Conference on Supercomputing, pp. 339–350 (2015)
21. Lu, Y., Liu, W.: DASP: specific dense matrix multiply-accumulate units accelerated general sparse matrix-vector multiplication. In: Proceedings of the International Conference for High Performance Computing, Networking, Storage and Analysis (2023)
22. Ma, T., Gou, Z., Xu, N., Sun, S.: Efficient multi-GPU implementations of preconditioned conjugate gradient method. Adv. Eng. Softw. **207** (2025)
23. Merrill, D., Garland, M.: Merge-based parallel sparse matrix-vector multiplication. In: SC '16: Proceedings of the International Conference for High Performance Computing, Networking, Storage and Analysis, pp. 678–689 (2016)
24. Monakov, A., Lokhmotov, A., Avetisyan, A.: Automatically tuning sparse matrix-vector multiplication for GPU architectures. In: International Conference on High-Performance Embedded Architectures and Compilers, pp. 111–125. Springer (2010)
25. NVIDIA: Volta Architecture Whitepaper, NVIDIA White Paper (2017)
26. NVIDIA: NVIDIA A100 Tensor Core GPU Architecture, NVIDIA White Paper (2020)
27. Tezcan, E., Torun, T., Koşar, F., Kaya, K., Unat, D.: Mixed and multi-precision SPMV for GPUs with row-wise precision selection. In: 2022 IEEE 34th International Symposium on Computer Architecture and High Performance Computing (SBAC-PAD), pp. 31–40 (2022)
28. Won, J., Mendis, C., Emer, J.S., Amarasinghe, S.: WACO: learning workload-aware co-optimization of the format and schedule of a sparse tensor program. In: Proceedings of the 28th ACM International Conference on Architectural Support for Programming Languages and Operating Systems, vol. 2, pp. 920–934 (2023)
29. Zhao, Z., Zhang, G., Wu, Y., Hong, R., Yang, Y., Fu, Y.: Block-wise dynamic mixed-precision for sparse matrix-vector multiplication on GPUS. J. Supercomput. **80**(10), 13681–13713 (2024)

HieraNTT: A Memory Hierarchy-Aware Data Access Architecture for Efficient Number Theoretic Transform on GPU

Qian Xiong[1], Weiliang Ma[1], Ligang He[2], Yufan Bai[1], Yao Chen[1], Hai Jin[1], and Xuanhua Shi[1(✉)]

[1] Key Laboratory of Services Computing Technology and System, Ministry of Education, Key Laboratory of Cluster and Grid Computing, Hubei Province, National Engineering Research Center for Big Data Technology and System, Huazhong University of Science and Technology, Wuhan, China
{qianxiong,weiliangma,yufanbai,chenyao_cs,hjin,xhshi}@hust.edu.cn
[2] University of Warwick, Coventry, UK
ligang.he@warwick.ac.uk

Abstract. The Number Theoretic Transform (NTT) is a fundamental primitive with increasingly critical applications in privacy-preserving protocols such as Zero Knowledge Proofs (ZKP) and Fully Homomorphic Encryption (FHE). Despite substantial progress in GPU-accelerated NTT, existing designs still suffer from severe memory stalls caused by inefficient data movement across the memory hierarchy. In this paper, we present HieraNTT, a memory hierarchy-aware data access architecture for high-performance NTT on GPUs. Our key contribution is to holistically model and optimize the end-to-end data access, spanning global memory, through the cache hierarchy from L2 cache to L1 cache (shared memory), and finally to registers. First, we introduce a novel memory layout alignment that ensures every memory transaction fully utilizes cache lines, thereby maximizing bandwidth utilization when moving data from global memory to L2 cache. Second, we reorganize the computation order of butterfly operations to fundamentally reshape the shared memory access pattern, significantly reducing bank conflicts and wavefront serialization when transferring data from shared memory to registers. Experimental results show that, for standalone NTT computation, HieraNTT improves performance by up to **77%** for ZKP primes and **49%** for FHE primes. When integrated into full protocols, HieraNTT improves ZKP and FHE workloads by up to **8%** and **24%**, respectively, outperforming state-of-the-art GPU-based systems. While our implementation targets NVIDIA GPUs and ZKP/FHE workloads, it is based on a methodology that aligns the data layout with the minimum transaction granularity of the memory hierarchy, which allows the approach to be readily adapted to other GPU platforms and NTT-intensive applications.

Keywords: Number Theoretic Transform · GPU acceleration

L. Eeckhout et al. (Eds.): APPT 2026, LNCS 16693, pp. 404–419, 2027.
https://doi.org/10.1007/978-981-92-4805-6_27

1 Introduction

The Number Theoretic Transform (NTT) has emerged as a foundational primitive in modern cryptography—serving as the computational backbone for large-scale polynomial operations in protocols such as Zero-Knowledge Proofs (ZKP) [6,10] and Fully Homomorphic Encryption (FHE) [1,2,5]. In practical deployments, NTT often constitutes the main computational bottleneck: our measurements show it accounts for **16%–65%** of the total runtime in ZKP and FHE pipelines (see Table 1). As a result, high-performance NTT implementations are vital for scaling privacy-preserving applications.

Table 1. The proportion of time spent on NTT in modern GPUs

	Protocol	prime width	NTT Scale	Proportion
ZKP	zkSnark [6],Plonky2 [10]	64, 254 $\sim$ 753 bits	$2^{18} \sim 2^{26}$	16% $\sim$ 29%
FHE	BFV [5], TFHE [2], CKKS [1]	30 $\sim$ 60, 64 bits	$2^{12} \sim 2^{17}$	65% $\sim$ 90%

Recent advances have leveraged GPUs to accelerate NTT operations, but our in-depth profiling and analysis reveal that memory subsystem inefficiencies remain the dominant performance limiter. State-of-the-art GPU NTT implementations (*e.g.*, sppark [11], GZKP [8], Phantom [12]) either optimize coalescing for global memory (GMEM) access or reduce bank conflicts in shared memory (SMEM), but never both holistically. Our empirical and analytical studies (see Sect. 3, Table 2, and Fig. 2(a)) demonstrate that this fragmented optimization leads to inherent tradeoffs: attempting to improve global memory bandwidth almost invariably increases SMEM bank conflicts and wavefront serialization, and vice versa. On NVIDIA V100/A100 GPUs, these inefficiencies cause bandwidth utilization to drop as low as **12.5%** (column-strided) or double the memory instruction count (row-coalesced), significantly constraining achievable speedups.

To bridge these limitations, we present **HieraNTT**, a memory hierarchy-aware data access strategy for efficient NTT computation on GPUs. HieraNTT is driven by two core insights: (1) end-to-end memory efficiency must be co-designed across global memory, the cache hierarchy, and registers; (2) aligning data granularity and computation order with the transaction units of each hierarchy layer is essential for minimizing bandwidth waste and instruction overhead.

Our main contributions are as follows:

- **Comprehensive Bottleneck Analysis:** We provide the first empirical and quantitative study, using both hardware profiling and analytical modeling, to expose fundamental inefficiencies in state-of-the-art GPU NTT implementations—demonstrating the memory-bound behavior and uncovered architectural mismatches that prevent existing designs from simultaneously minimizing memory transactions and bank conflicts.

- **End-to-End Hierarchy-Aware Architecture:** We propose HieraNTT, an architecture that tightly co-designs memory layout alignment and transaction policies across all GPU memory layers. Our approach guarantees that every memory instruction fully utilizes cache-line bandwidth and that each layer's transaction granularity is respected, eliminating the tradeoff between GMEM and SMEM efficiency.
- **Flexible and Workload-Adaptive Kernel:** HieraNTT introduces a general, flexible kernel that reorganizes both computation and memory access to avoid bank conflicts and maximize vectorized LD/ST instruction utilization. An automated policy maker models candidate configurations and selects the optimal strategy for any combination of NTT scale and modulus size—ensuring robustness across both ZKP and FHE use cases.
- **Extensive Evaluation and Advanced Results:** Our CUDA implementation on NVIDIA V100 and A100 GPUs achieves up to **77%** improvement in standalone NTT throughput for ZKP prime moduli, and up to **35%** higher bandwidth for FHE primes, compared to the best existing GPU baselines. Integrated end-to-end, HieraNTT accelerates ZKP proof generation by **8%** and the FHE ModUp operation by **24%**.

2 Background

2.1 NTT Computation

NTT is the core primitive for polynomial multiplication in ZKP and FHE (see Table 1). Given a prime modulus q and the primitive Nth root of unity $\omega \in \mathbb{Z}_q$, where N is a power of 2, the transform maps the coefficient array $\mathbf{A} = [A_0, \dots, A_{N-1}]$, $A \in \mathbb{Z}_q$ to the point-value representation: $\boldsymbol{a} = \mathrm{NTT}(\mathbf{A}) = [\sum_{i=0}^{N-1} A_i, \dots, \sum_{i=0}^{N-1} A_i \omega^{(N-1)i}]$. In different application domains, the bit-width of q and the scale N vary (see Table 1). Each **element** A_i is stored as W D-bit words, where D denotes the machine word size. Calculating NTT can be achieved effectively using the Cooley-Tukey algorithm [3]. An N-NTT contains $n = \log_2 N$ iterations. In each iteration s, the algorithm executes $N/2$ independent butterfly operations (see Fig. 1), and the distance (stride) of the two elements involved in each butterfly operation is 2^s.

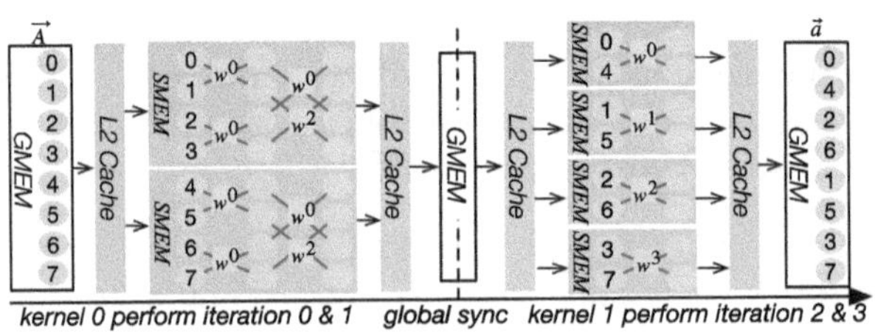

Fig. 1. A 16-point NTT, where ω is 16th root of unity.

2.2 GPU Memory Hierarchy and NTT Access Characteristics

Two Dominant NTT Element Access Patterns. Practical implementations improve locality by grouping several butterfly operations that share common input elements and caching them in SMEM. A reusable set of elements (see Fig. 1, 0,1,2,3 for iterations 0–1) is a **group**. Existing GPU implementations fall into two contrasting access styles, regardless of element layout: **Strided element access** (e.g., [11]). Each warp (contains 32 threads) loads its butterfly operands directly from GMEM using large, non-unit strides; **Coalesced block access** (e.g., [8,12]). Contiguous blocks of elements are fetched from GMEM via coalesced loads, merging physically adjacent portions of multiple groups while preserving group structure in SMEM. This reduces global transactions but introduces severe SMEM bank conflicts. Both patterns optimize only one layer of the hierarchy while degrading another, exposing an end-to-end memory bottleneck.

Two Main Element Layouts. Considering an element composed of W words, the two typical layouts for an array of such elements are [9]: **Row-major layout** [11]. All W words of a single element A_i are stored contiguously; **Column-major layout** [8]. The j-th word of every element is stored contiguously. Both layouts preserve locality along only one dimension of the array while disrupting the other, creating a fundamental tension between per-thread element locality and warp-level coalescing.

Memory Efficiency Metrics. To characterize these bottlenecks, we use three hardware-level metrics [9]: **Memory transactions.** GMEM and SMEM loads are served in fixed-size cache-line units (e.g., 32B at L2, 128B at SMEM/L1). **Vectorized memory instructions.** Nvidia GPUs support wide (128-bit) LD/ST instructions. Using them reduces instruction count but requires memory-aligned layouts. **Bank conflicts.** SMEM is divided into 32 banks with 4-byte bank granularity. When multiple threads in a warp access different addresses mapped to the same bank in the same instruction, bank conflicts occur.

3 Observation and Motivation

To understand why existing GPU-based implementations fail to achieve high memory efficiency and how these inefficiencies arise across different layers of the memory hierarchy, our methodology consists of three complementary steps: (1) **empirically profiling of memory bottlenecks** via roofline and stall reason analysis; (2) developing an **analytical modeling of access patterns and data layouts** to quantify bandwidth utilization, instruction efficiency (3) **comparatively analyzing existing GPU designs.** to validate our analytical model.

3.1 Empirical Profiling of Memory Bottlenecks

Roofline Profile. We profile the fastest publicly available NTT library, sppark [11] and GZKP [8], across a wide spectrum of prime sizes and scales.

Most configurations are predominantly memory-bound, indicating that performance is dominated by constraints in the GMEM subsystem (see Fig. 2(a)). Only 768-bit prime case shifts toward a compute-bound regime.

Finding 1. *NTT performance is memory-bound for nearly all prime moduli.*

Stall-Reason Variability. Our detailed GPU stall profiling on the last kernel (see Fig. 2(b)) reveals that the dominant stall sources shift with both modulus size and scale. For large primes (e.g., 256-bit), performance is primarily limited by GMEM-related stalls, which become more pronounced due to intensified contention in the L2 cache. For small primes (e.g., 64-bit), SMEM stalls also constitute a significant fraction of execution time, indicating overhead caused by SMEM bank conflicts. Collectively, these observations indicate that optimal performance requires optimization across the entire memory hierarchy.

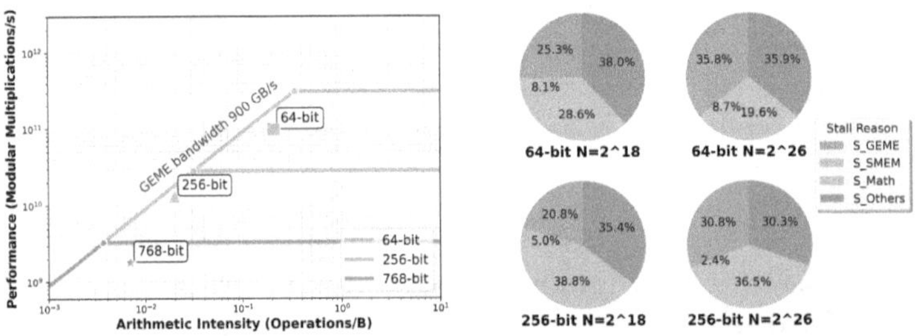

(a) roofline analysis (b) kernel stall analysis

Fig. 2. Performance analysis, (a) Most NTT performance lie on the memory roof. (b) Stall reasons are grouped into GMEM-, SMEM-, math-, and other-related classes.

Finding 2. *The dominant bottleneck shifts across different levels of the memory hierarchy depending on prime modulus and NTT scale, implying that single-layer optimizations are fundamentally insufficient.*

3.2 Analytical Modeling of Access Patterns and Layouts

With the access patterns and element layouts defined in Sect. 2.2, we construct an analytical model that quantifies how their interaction affects bandwidth utilization and instruction efficiency. Unlike classical GPU workloads, NTT calculations must simultaneously navigate (1) the butterfly-induced element stride and (2) the multi-word of each element. This creates four fundamental combinations: *(Row-major, Strided)*, *(Row-major, Coalesced Block)*, *(Column-major, Strided)*, and *(Column-major, Coalesced Block)*.

Bandwidth Utilization Model Each transaction fetches several cache lines, but only a subset of these bytes are *useful* to the requesting warp. We define bandwidth utilization as $\eta_{bw} = \frac{\text{Useful Bytes}}{\text{Total Bytes Transferred}}$. The number of useful bytes depends on whether adjacent threads in a warp access memory addresses that reside in the same cache line. Row-major layouts group the words of the *same* element, while column-major layouts concentrate the *same word index* across *different* elements, producing different patterns of cache line overlap. Strided access's bandwidth utilization is no higher than $\eta_{bw} \leq 50\%$ (see Table 2). In contrast, coalesced block has higher bandwidth efficiency, typically satisfying $\eta_{bw} \geq 50\%$.

Instruction Efficiency. Each thread must ultimately load all W words of an element. We define the instruction efficiency as $\eta_{inst} = \frac{\text{Min. Load Instructions}}{\text{Actual Load Instructions}}$. A row-major layout can achieve Min. Load Instructions $= \lceil \frac{W \cdot \text{word\_size}}{\text{LD/ST instructions wide}} \rceil$. because all W words of that element are stored contiguously. In contrast, a column-major layout forces each thread to issue W separate loads.

Overall Efficiency. $\eta_{total} = \eta_{bw} \times \eta_{inst}$ reflects the combined cost of wasted cache line bytes due to discontinuous accesses and redundant instructions. Table 2 summarizes η_{bw}, η_{inst} and η_{total}.

Finding 3. *Our analytical model is strongly validated by hardware profiling on V100 and A100. Across all prime moduli, existing combinations of layout (row/column) and access pattern (strided/coalesced) exhibit an inherent architectural mismatch, where optimizing instruction efficiency necessarily degrades bandwidth utilization, and vice versa, across the GPU memory hierarchy.*

Table 2. Bandwidth and Instruction Analysis (**Worst case**). Word size is 32-bit; elements are 753/256/64/32-bit.

metrics	Row + Coalesced (%)	Row + Strided (%)	Col + Coalesced (%)	Col + Strided (%)
η_{bw}	50/50/100/100	50/50/25/12.5	100/100/100/100	12.5/12.5/12.5/12.5
η_{inst}	100/100/50/25	100/100/50/25	25/25/50/25	25/25/50/25
η_{total}	50/50/50/25	50/50/12.5/3.1	25/25/50/25	3.1/3.1/6.2/3.1

3.3 Comparative Analysis of Existing GPU Designs

To validate this model in Sect. 3.2, we profile existing implementations that commit to specific access-layout combinations, and record hardware-level metrics.

GMEM Layer. sppark [11] adopts the strided element access approach, combined with a row-major layout. Each thread benefits from vectorized loads within its own element, but the warp rarely shares cache lines. Profiling indicates that a 2^{26}-NTT with 256-bit primes actually generate $9.6 \sim 10.8$ memory transactions per warp per instruction (see Fig. 3). The gap is larger on V100, whose smaller L2 cache evicts partially used cache lines more aggressively than A100. GZKP [8], in contrast, reorganizes elements into column-major layout and applies a coalesced block access. Empirically, this yields only about 2 memory transactions per load instruction. However, the number of load instructions rises significantly. Thus, GZKP shifts overhead from bandwidth waste to instruction inflation.

SMEM Layer. In sppark, the combination of row-major layout with coalesced block access maps many threads onto the same bank, resulting in a consistent 8-way bank conflict per load instruction. In contrast, GZKP adopts a column-major layout with strided element access, causing the conflict degree to vary with the stride. Profiling shows an average of 2.2-way and 2.7-way conflicts per load instruction on A100 and V100, respectively. However, because GZKP issues roughly four times as many load instructions as sppark, the total number of transactions caused by bank conflicts is ultimately higher than that of sppark.

Impact of Cache Size. When comparing GPUs with different L2 cache capacities, the gap in bandwidth utilization and hit rate between the two designs becomes markedly amplified. On A100, whose 40MB L2 cache can retain most of the data reused across warps, the unused portions of cache lines fetched under row-major strided element access persist long enough to be occasionally reused. On V100, however, the 6MB L2 cache cannot accommodate the working set generated by thousands of concurrent warps, causing these partially consumed cache lines to be rapidly evicted; as a result, both the effective bandwidth utilization and the L2 hit rate drop sharply for the same access pattern. In contrast, the coalesced block approach exhibits much weaker sensitivity to cache capacity. Because its large contiguous loads naturally pack full cache lines, the method maintains consistently high hit rates across architectures, consistent with our analytical prediction. However, its per thread instruction count is determined primarily by the column-major layout and therefore remains unchanged across GPU generations regardless of cache size.

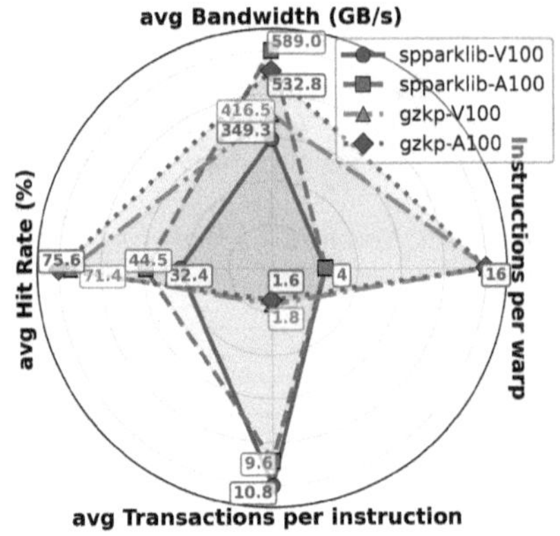

Fig. 3. Comparison of input-loading behavior in different implementations.

Finding 4. *Our analytical model is strongly validated by hardware profiling on V100 and A100. Neither design achieves low instruction cost* and *low transaction cost simultaneously at both GMEM and SMEM, confirming the need for a new access–layout co-design.*

3.4 Motivation for a New Access Architecture

This motivates the need for a fundamentally new approach that: (1) provides uniform access efficiency by achieving coalesced GMEM and SMEM accesses while preserving locality among all words of each element; (2) maintains architectural robustness by delivering high bandwidth utilization across all GPU architectures with varying cache hierarchies; (3) adapts automatically to diverse workloads by adjusting its internal tiling and access structures to accommodate prime sizes and NTT scales common in FHE and ZKP applications.

4 HieraNTT Design

HieraNTT introduces a memory hierarchy-aware data access architecture with four key components, as shown in Fig. 4. First, it incorporates a **memory layout alignment** to minimize memory instructions by ensuring that each thread can fetch elements with the wide LD/ST instructions. Second, HieraNTT establishes a **transaction policy** to minimize memory transactions by ensuring that each L2 and SMEM transaction is immediately useful to a warp. Third, the **flexible kernel** reorganizes butterfly operations to flexibly conform to the established policy. Finally, the policy maker is used to adapt to different prime moduli and GPU architectures.

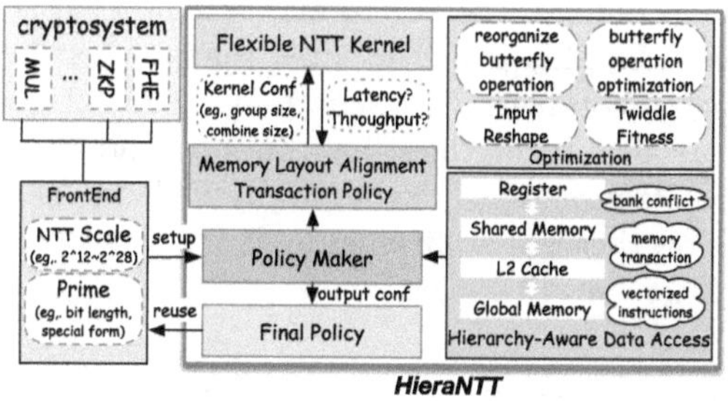

Fig. 4. Overview of HieraNTT.

Although our design targets NVIDIA GPUs and ZKP and FHE workloads, the proposed memory hierarchy-aware data access architecture is not tied to specific cache-line sizes or instruction widths. Instead, it relies on aligning the data layout with the minimum transaction granularity of the memory hierarchy, which allows this approach to be adapted to other GPU architectures, such as AMD GPUs, and to other NTT-intensive workloads, such as lattice-based cryptography, by appropriately adjusting the alignment unit.

4.1 Memory Layout Alignment

HieraNTT uses fixed 128-bit slots as the basic storage unit throughout the memory hierarchy, matching the width of wide LD/ST instructions on NVIDIA GPUs. This unified layout allows data to move between GMEM, L2, and SMEM with vectorized accesses, reducing the instruction count while exposing regular access patterns for the later transaction policy. The mapping from NTT elements to the slots depends on the modulus bit-width l. If $l \geq 128$, one element spans multiple 128-bit slots, so each element is represented as a sequence of aligned blocks. If $l < 128$, each slot packs $m = 128/l$ adjacent elements, so one instruction fetches multiple elements at once. This alignment alone minimizes memory instructions, but it does not guarantee that all fetched cache-line data are consumed immediately; that requirement is enforced by the transaction policy below.

4.2 Transaction Policy

As observed, the transaction granularity of the L2 cache and SMEM differs, a distinction overlooked by previous solutions. In HieraNTT, we treat both layers holistically. The key idea is to ensure that a load instruction issued by a warp can efficiently utilize data at the cache-line granularity of either memory level.

Policy Configuration. We use two key parameters: the group size (gs) and the combine size (cs), which determine how butterfly groups are mapped to a thread block (see Sect. 2) and how many groups are processed together.

L2 Cache Transaction Policy. The key to maximizing transaction efficiency lies in ensuring that $cs \geq 2$. This policy ensures that an instruction from a warp can be merged into 16 complete L2 cache lines. The L2 cache controller can recognize the spatial locality of these instructions and process them with 16 efficient 32B memory transactions, thereby fully utilizing cache line bandwidth and eliminating the overhead of additional memory transactions caused by non-contiguous memory accesses in sppark.

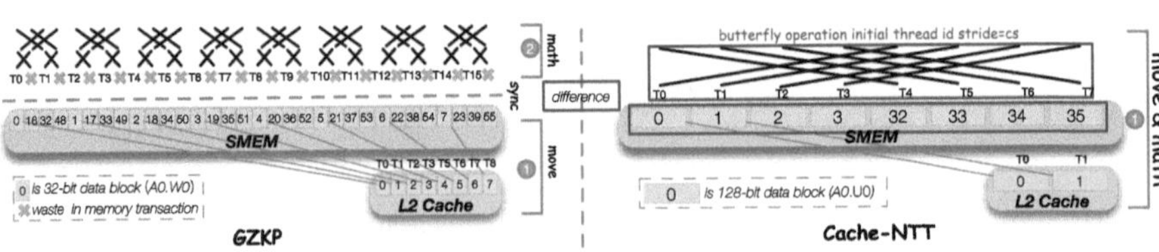

Fig. 5. Different SMEM transaction policies in GZKP and HieraNTT for an $N = 64$ example with iterations 4–5, $gs = 4$, and $cs = 4$.

SMEM Transaction Policy. SMEM requires careful data placement due to its involvement in multiple, tightly coupled butterfly operations, each of which repeatedly accesses SMEM. While ensuring minimal L2 cache memory transactions, adjacent threads access elements from different groups. GZKP [8] maintains data continuity within a group, allowing efficient computation, the data loaded by threads in a warp are typically placed in corresponding groups (see Sect. 2.2 and Fig. 5). However, this approach offers no performance benefit beyond conceptual simplicity. In contrast, our per-thread-block transaction policy, as shown in Eqn 1, addresses this by reorganizing butterfly operations in SMEM to ensure that data accessed by adjacent threads remain contiguous and are fetched through coalesced block accesses.

$$\begin{aligned} SMEM[Ti] &= GMEM[group_{Ti\&(cs-1)}|(Ti/cs) << kernel\_begin\_iteration\_j] \\ SMEM[(gs*cs/2)|Ti] &= GMEM[group_{Ti\&(cs-1)}|(((Ti/cs)|(gs/2)) << kernel\_begin\_iteration\_j)] \end{aligned} \tag{1}$$

As shown on the right of Fig. 5, the threads T0 $\sim$ T3 load the first elements of the first butterfly operation from different groups to SMEM (elements $A_0 \sim A_3$), while T4 $\sim$ T7 load the first operand of the second butterfly operation from different groups (elements $A_{32} \sim A_{35}$). This not only aligns with the L2 cache policy, but also ensures that data in SMEM transactions are fully utilized during computation (all threads read the first elements of butterfly operations simultaneously). Although 4-way bank conflicts per load instruction still persist, the conflict degree is halved compared with sppark under the same load instruction count. Compared with GZKP, HieraNTT reduces the overall bank-conflict-induced overhead mainly because the memory layout alignment in Sect. 4.1 reduces the number of load instructions to one quarter. The remaining key challenge is how to efficiently handle the computation of butterfly operations in mixed groups, because the stride of butterfly operations is related to configuration cs and gs. We address this using the flexible kernel described below.

4.3 Flexible Kernel

The computation of NTT exhibits a highly regular structure. This property makes it possible to use a unified kernel to handle different NTT stages. HieraNTT exploits this structure to reuse the same kernel across scales, moduli, and batch settings rather than specializing kernels for each case.

Reorganized Butterfly Operation. Specifically, a thread block can be viewed as implementing a larger $cs * gs$-NTT in each SMEM, as shown in Fig. 5, starting from iteration $log_2(cs)$ and then performing $log_2(gs)$ iterations. This is significantly different from GZKP and sppark, where the calculation starts at iteration 0. Algorithm 1 not only satisfies the previous memory transaction policy but also ensures that the same kernel can efficiently handle various combinations of NTT groups without modification; only cs and gs need to be adjusted via policy maker. The implementation uses two synchronization primitives in line 6 and 11, respectively, for intra-warp exchange and SMEM exchange.

Support for Arbitrary Prime Modulus. When $l < 128$ bits, our 128-bit aligned layout automatically packs adjacent $m = 128/l$ elements into a single slot. Algorithm 1 can be reused without modification by either treating the input as $A\_slot[N/m]$ or equivalently adjusting the combine size to $cs' = m * cs$, while keeping gs unchanged.

Batched NTT support. A key feature of our architecture is its native support for multiple NTT batch operations. We observe that executing a batch of $2^{\mathbf{batch}}$ 2^n-NTTs, is equivalent to computing a single NTT of scale $2^{batch+n}$, while terminating after the first n iterations. This observation allows our kernel to support batched NTT execution without introducing special-case logic, allowing the same layout, policy, and kernel to be reused for FHE-style batched execution.

Policy Maker and Configuration Selection. The policy maker is responsible for selecting an efficient execution configuration for an NTT problem with a given NTT scale (i.e., N) and modulus (i.e., its bit-width l). Rather than introducing new heuristics, it systematically explores the configuration space exposed by HieraNTT's design. The policy maker operates as an end-to-end process that takes reshaped inputs and GPU hardware constraints (e.g., SMEM size and maximum threads per thread block). It produces an optimal configuration tuple $(kernel0\_gs, kerneli\_gs, kerneli\_cs, kernelj\_gs, kernelj\_cs)$. The parameter $kernel0\_gs$ specifies the group size for the fully contiguous data access in the 0th kernel (see Fig. 1). This kernel covers the initial iterations whose data can be accessed contiguously after the memory layout alignment. The parameter $kerneli\_gs$ is the primary group size for dividing the remaining iterations into regular kernels, and $kernelj\_gs$ is derived as the remainder group size from $(\log_2(N) - \log_2(kernel0\_gs)) \bmod \log_2(kerneli\_gs)$. This allows flexible strategies when the remaining iterations cannot be evenly divided by the regular kernel size, with respective combine sizes $kerneli\_cs$ and $kernelj\_cs$ configured to optimize memory movement in each kernel. These parameters determine how NTT iterations are partitioned into kernels and how butterfly operations are grouped within each kernel. The policy maker explores all valid combinations of the group size (gs) and the combine size (cs) that satisfy the maximum number of threads per thread block, the available SMEM capacity, and the resource usage required by the fused butterfly groups. For each candidate configuration, the execution cost is evaluated by empirical calibration runs. The configuration with the lowest measured runtime is selected as the final policy. By explicitly evaluating the interaction between algorithmic structure and hardware limits, the policy maker enables HieraNTT to adapt its execution strategy to different NTT parameters and GPU architectures while maintaining high occupancy and controlled SMEM usage. Note that HieraNTT needs to explore the configuration space only once. This exploration takes about $0.03 \sim 180$ s to identify the optimal configuration for different scale and prime modulus, which can then be reused for all NTT instances with the same scale and modulus size.

Algorithm 1: Flexible Kernel for NTT calculations in SMEM

Require: input array in GMEM ($A[N]$); group size (gs); combine size (cs); thread id per GPU block (Ti), $Ti \in [0, gs * cs/2)$; data in SMEM ($shm[gs * cs]$)
Ensure: $A[N]$: write back to GMEM
$shm[gs * cs] \leftarrow A[N]$ {with transactions policy}
$inter\_iter \leftarrow \min(log_2(warp\ size), log_2(gs * cs))$
/* $(gs * cs)$-**"NTT" start from iteration** $log_2(cs)$. */
for $iter \leftarrow log_2(cs)$ *to* $inter\_iter$ **do**
  butterfly operation(U, V); exch = select(U, V) {select an element to exchange}
  exch = (__shfl_xor(exch)) {using warp-level shuffle and sync}
  update(U, V) = exch {update U and V based on the exch}
end for
for iter ← inter_iter *to* $log_2(gs)$ **do**
  exch = select(U, V);
  __syncthreads(); shm[Ti] = exch; __syncthreads(); {using block-level sync}
  update(U, V) = $shm[Ti$ xor $((1 << iter) - 1)]$; butterfly operation(U, V);
end for
Write final results back to global memory {with transactions policy}

5 Evaluation

Baseline. We evaluate HieraNTT on NVIDIA Ampere A100 and Volta V100 from three aspects: single-NTT latency, breakdown analysis, and end-to-end protocol performance. Our experiments compare against several state-of-the-art GPU-based implementations, including sppark [11], GZKP [8] and Phantom-fhe [4, 12], as well as a CPU-based implementation, plonky2-lib [10]. For each prime modulus, we select the best-performing existing GPU system (denoted as "BG") as the baseline, together with the best CPU solution ("BC"), especially in cases where a given workload is not supported by any prior GPU solution.

5.1 NTT Performance with ZKP Prime Moduli

We first measured the latency of a single NTT operation on ZKP-related prime moduli (including Goldilocks, BLS12-381, and MNT4753) on NVIDIA V100 and A100 GPUs. As shown in Table 3, HieraNTT consistently outperforms BG.

For BLS12-381, HieraNTT achieves speedups of up to 1.77× on V100 (average 1.31×) and up to 1.34× on A100 (average 1.12×) over BG (sppark). For the Goldilocks prime modulus, HieraNTT achieves speedups of up to 1.51× (1.15× on average) on V100 and up to 1.58× (1.07× on average) on A100. For the MNT4753 prime modulus, BG (GZKP) is already compute-bound in the Roofline analysis. By reducing butterfly overhead, HieraNTT still achieves average speedups of 1.30× on V100 and 1.21× on A100.

Table 3. Latency (ms) of single NTT with ZKP prime moduli achieves up to **1.77**× speedup on V100 and **1.58**× on A100

Scale	Goldilocks [7]				BLS12-381				MNT4753			
	V100		A100		V100		A100		V100		A100	
	BG	Our	BG	Our	BG	Our	BG	Our	BG	Our	BG	Our
2^{14}	0.017	0.014 (1.24 ×)	0.015	0.015 (1.02 ×)	0.036	0.020 (**1.77** ×)	0.026	0.025 (1.03 ×)	0.102	0.082 (1.24 ×)	0.099	0.085 (1.16 ×)
2^{15}	0.019	0.015 (1.25 ×)	0.015	0.015 (1.00×)	0.036	0.026 (1.39 ×)	0.030	0.028 (1.05 ×)	0.144	0.112 (1.28 ×)	0.148	0.120 (1.23 ×)
2^{16}	0.020	0.017 (1.20 ×)	0.017	0.017 (1.00×)	0.057	0.041 (1.39 ×)	0.040	0.040 (1.00 ×)	0.304	0.245 (1.24 ×)	0.268	0.220 (1.22 ×)
2^{17}	0.026	0.020 (1.29 ×)	0.023	0.019 (1.21 ×)	0.087	0.069 (1.26 ×)	0.063	0.058 (1.09 ×)	0.637	0.517 (1.23 ×)	0.449	0.391 (1.15 ×)
2^{18}	0.039	0.026 (1.51 ×)	0.035	0.025 (1.38 ×)	0.170	0.140 (1.22 ×)	0.137	0.102 (1.34 ×)	1.216	0.942 (1.29 ×)	0.867	0.697 (1.24 ×)
2^{19}	0.060	0.049 (1.24 ×)	0.062	0.039 (**1.58** ×)	0.326	0.267 (1.22 ×)	0.221	0.190 (1.16 ×)	2.397	1.826 (1.31 ×)	1.796	1.461 (1.23 ×)
2^{20}	0.113	0.102 (1.11×)	0.077	0.066 (1.16 ×)	0.629	0.495 (1.27 ×)	0.436	0.388 (1.13 ×)	4.967	3.791 (1.31 ×)	3.656	2.946 (1.24 ×)
2^{21}	0.206	0.201 (1.02 ×)	0.138	0.129 (1.07 ×)	1.336	1.000 (1.37 ×)	0.890	0.791 (1.12 ×)	10.577	7.800 (1.36 ×)	7.541	6.133 (1.23 ×)
2^{22}	0.389	0.384 (1.01 ×)	0.266	0.266 (1.00 ×)	2.646	2.113 (1.25 ×)	1.808	1.671 (1.08 ×)	21.701	16.188 (1.34 ×)	15.440	12.800 (1.21 ×)
2^{23}	0.809	0.784 (1.01 ×)	0.543	0.533 (1.02 ×)	5.168	4.376 (1.18 ×)	3.781	3.461 (1.09 ×)	44.483	33.644 (1.32 ×)	32.147	26.696 (1.20 ×)
2^{24}	1.861	1.733 (1.07 ×)	1.061	1.061 (1.00×)	13.127	10.013 (1.31 ×)	7.730	7.600 (1.02 ×)	91.743	70.872 (1.29 ×)	67.122	55.634 (1.21 ×)
2^{25}	3.860	3.652 (1.06 ×)	2.233	2.235 (1.00 ×)	23.698	20.631 (1.15 ×)	16.127	14.645 (1.10×)	191.269	147.025 (1.30 ×)	142.469	116.130 (1.23 ×)
2^{26}	8.909	8.188 (1.08 ×)	4.773	4.792 (1.00×)	53.327	44.074 (1.21×)	38.788	33.508 (1.16×)	416.281	307.650 (1.35 ×)	297.014	240.797 (1.23 ×)

5.2 NTT Performance with FHE Prime Modulus

Table 4 shows the performance of HieraNTT on an A100 GPU using a 60-bit FHE prime modulus and a scale $\in [12, 17]$ [12]. Our optimization consistently reduces latency across all scales, delivering an average speedup of 1.35× over BG. The performance improvements are most significant at smaller scales, as the effective memory bandwidth increases by approximately 40% to 45%.

Table 4. Performance with FHE prime Moduli on GPU A100

Scale	Execution time (μs)		Bandwidth (GB/s)	
	BG	Our	BG	Our
12	14.37	10.31	10.62	14.80
13	15.56	10.75	19.61	28.39
14	16.81	11.25	36.31	54.25
15	17.20	11.88	70.97	102.80
16	16.96	13.50	143.95	180.84
17	18.62	17.56	262.23	278.02

5.3 Breakdown Analysis

We further conduct a breakdown analysis using the BLS12_381 modulus at scale 2^{24} on V100, as shown in Fig. 6. Starting from GZKP and BG (sppark), we incrementally add the key techniques of HieraNTT to isolate their contributions. Specifically, "GZKP+128" applies our 128-bit aligned layout to GZKP, and "GZKP+128+Policy" further adds the transaction policy. As shown in Fig. 6, the 128-bit aligned layout alone ("GZKP+128") reduces latency by 21% over GZKP and by 10% over BG, indicating the importance of reducing memory instructions. Adding the transaction policy ("GZKP+128+Policy") yields a further 8% reduction by alleviating shared-memory bank conflicts. The full HieraNTT, with the flexible kernel and policy maker, brings another 8% reduction and achieves the lowest latency overall.

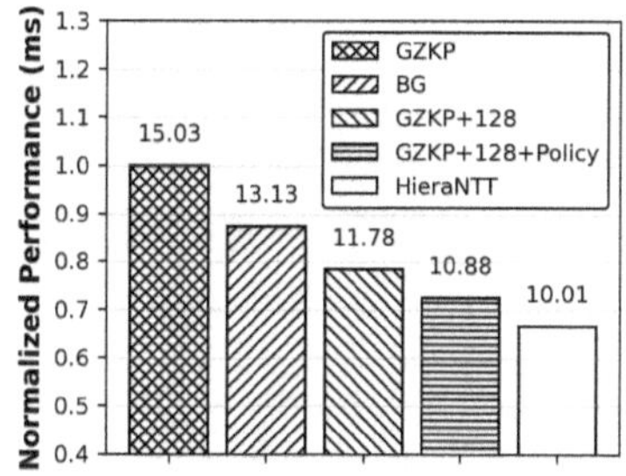

Fig. 6. Breakdown Analysis

In addition, the necessity of our policy maker is demonstrated in Fig. 7, which plots the performance of all valid kernel configurations generated for BLS12-381 prime modulus at 2^{24} scale. Substantial performance variation is observed even among configurations with the same $kerneli\_gs$ value. For instance, when $kerneli\_gs = 5$, the NTT latency varies from approximately 10.38 ms to 23.86 ms, representing a 2.4× difference between the best and worst configurations. These results illustrate that there is no universally optimal configuration and underscore the need for automated configuration search. For each unique combination of prime modulus and scale, the policy maker needs to be run only once. Once the optimal configuration tuple $(kernel0\_gs, kerneli\_gs, kerneli\_cs, kernelj\_gs, kernelj\_cs)$ is obtained, it can be stored and reused for all subsequent NTT calculations with the same scale and prime modulus.

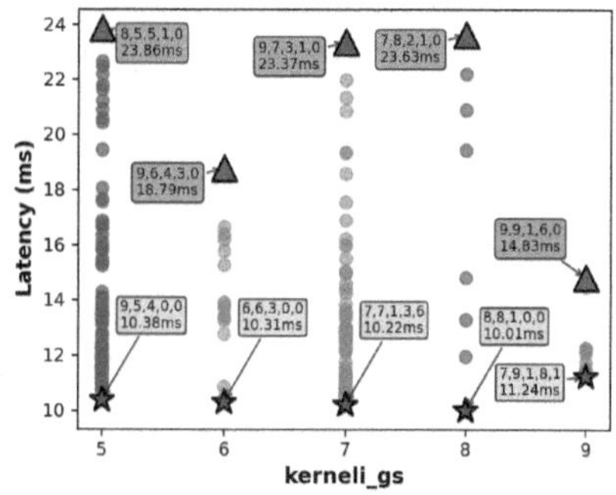

Fig. 7. Performance of different configurations in the policy maker.

5.4 End-to-End Performance of Full Protocols

ZKP protocols. Table 5 presents the end-to-end performance of HieraNTT on representative ZKP protocols; the observed speedups reflect the fraction of total time spent in NTT. For the Fibonacci application implemented with the plonky2 protocol, HieraNTT achieves a 1.08× speedup compared to BC (plonky2-lib [10]). For the Zcash and Auction applications, which are based on the zkSnark protocol, we compare against the state-of-the-art GPU-based framework, GZKP (BG). In these cases, HieraNTT achieves end-to-end speedups of 1.04× and 1.07×, respectively. The larger improvement observed for the Auction application is consistent with its larger NTT operation footprint, where NTT operations account for 29% of the total execution time.

Table 5. ZKP Workload Performance in seconds

Application	Protocol	Prime	NTT	BG/BC	Our
Fibonacci	plonky2	Goldilocks	20%	34	31.49 (1.08×)
Zcash	zkSnark	BLS12_381	16%	0.30	0.29 (1.04×)
Auction	zkSnark	MNT4753	29%	0.52	0.48 (1.07×)

FHE Protocols. We evaluate the performance of HieraNTT in the context of FHE, focusing on the popular CKKS scheme [1]. Table 6 reports the latency of the ModUp operation on an A100 GPU. HieraNTT yields a speedup of 1.24× for a security parameter of $N = 2^{15}$, and 1.13× for $N = 2^{16}$ over the BG (Phantom-fhe [12]). These results demonstrate that the improvements delivered by HieraNTT at the NTT level translate effectively to end-to-end FHE protocol performance.

Table 6. CKKS security parameters and latency in GPU A100.

security parameters						execution time (μs)	
N	|Q|	|QP|	l	k	dnum	BG	Our
15	1,510	2,410	15	15	2	317.2	255.2 (1.24×)
16	2,260	3,160	30	15	3	1084.4	953.2 (1.13×)

6 Conclusion

This paper has presented HieraNTT, an efficient GPU-based architecture for NTT that addresses end-to-end data access bottlenecks through a memory hierarchy-aware approach. By integrating memory layout alignment, a transaction policy for memory hierarchy optimization, and a flexible kernel design, our work systematically minimizes memory transactions and instruction overhead. The key contributions include a unified model for bandwidth and instruction efficiency, which ensures robust performance across varying NTT scales and prime moduli. We evaluate HieraNTT on representative ZKP and FHE workloads. The results show that HieraNTT achieves speedups of up to 1.77× and 1.35× over the best-performing existing solutions for standalone NTT computations. Moreover, the end-to-end performance results for full protocols are consistent with the microbenchmark improvements observed for NTT kernels, scaled by their contribution to overall execution time.

Acknowledgments. This work was supported by the National Key Research and Development Program of China (Grant No. 2023YFB4503200 and 2023YFB4503202), the Major Program (JD) of Hubei Province (No. 2023BAA024), and the Hubei Provincial Natural Science Foundation of China (No. 2026AFA002). We thank Dr. Lutan Zhao, Dr. Bingsheng He, and the anonymous reviewers for their valuable comments.

Disclosure of Interests. The authors have no competing interests to declare that are relevant to the content of this article.

Artificial Intelligence Statement. Artificial intelligence tools, if used, were used only for language organization and figure/table polishing, and did not participate in the generation of the core ideas or technical content.

References

1. Cheon, J.H., Kim, A., Kim, M., Song, Y.: Homomorphic encryption for arithmetic of approximate numbers. In: Proceedings of the Advances in Cryptology, pp. 409–437. Cham (2017)
2. Chillotti, I., Gama, N., Georgieva, M., Izabachène, M.: Faster fully homomorphic encryption: bootstrapping in less than 0.1 seconds. In: Proceedings of the Advances in Cryptology, pp. 3–33. Berlin, Heidelberg (2016)
3. Cooley, J.W., Tukey, J.W.: An algorithm for the machine calculation of complex Fourier series. Math. Comput. **19**, 297–301 (1965)
4. Encryptorion-lab: Phantomfhe: A cuda-accelerated homomorphic encryption library (2025). https://github.com/encryptorion-lab/phantom-fhe/commit/1f4a198443b3af77118e51f53d5b8f332154b875
5. Fan, J., Vercauteren, F.: Somewhat practical fully homomorphic encryption. Cryptology ePrint Archive (2012)
6. Groth, J.: On the size of pairing-based non-interactive arguments. In: Proceedings of the Part II, of the 35th Annual International Conference on Advances in Cryptology, pp. 305–326. Berlin, Heidelberg (2016)
7. Hamburg, M.: Ed448-goldilocks, a new elliptic curve, p. 625 (2015)
8. Ma, W., et al.: GZKP: a GPU accelerated zero-knowledge proof system, pp. 340–353. ASPLOS 2023, New York, NY, USA (2023)
9. Nvidia: GPU Device Memory Guide (2025)
10. PolygonZero: Plonky2: Fast Recursive Arguments With Plonk and Fri (2025). https://github.com/0xPolygonZero/plonky2/commit/5d9da5a65bbcba2c66eb29c035090eb2e9ccb05f
11. Supranational: Zero-Knowledge Template Library (2025). https://github.com/supranational/sppark/commit/9cd5cbd310433665a9e8c26837355cb41ca88b06
12. Yang, H., et al.: Phantom: a CUDA-accelerated word-wise homomorphic encryption library. IEEE Trans. Dependable Secure Comput. **21**(5), 4895–4906 (2024)

Streaming Accelerators

A Configurable Streaming Accelerator for LUT-Based Super-Resolution on FPGA

Xuzhuo Hu, Jianyang Ding, Bowen Jiang, Huachen Zhang, Tianshuo Lu, and Zhilei Chai(✉)

School of Artificial Intelligence and Computer Science, Jiangnan University, Wuxi, China
{xuzhuo,bwjiang,hczhang,tslu}@stu.jiangnan.edu.cn, {jyding,zlchai}@jiangnan.edu.cn

Abstract. Image super-resolution (SR) remains difficult to deploy on resource-constrained FPGA platforms because conventional CNN-based pipelines require heavy computation, large intermediate feature maps, and irregular dataflows. We present a configurable streaming accelerator for lookup-table (LUT)-based SR that targets this system bottleneck directly. The proposed design co-optimizes a LUT-centric SR model, a receptive field-driven streaming dataflow, and a configurable inference kernel so that inference relies only on table lookup, integer addition, and bit-shift operations. In the proposed dataflow, each receptive-field-sized window becomes a compact work unit, which enables window-level parallel processing while avoiding full intermediate feature maps. At the same time, the front, middle, and back LUT stages can be organized as a streamed pipeline, exposing an explicit throughput–resource trade-off through configurable kernel replication. Experimental results show competitive ×2 SR quality with only 28.75 KB model storage. On ZU3EG, the architecture achieves 15 FPS with 128 KB BRAM and scales to 192 FPS with 650 KB BRAM for ×2 FHD inference. These results demonstrate that LUT-oriented model–architecture co-design is effective for building compact and scalable FPGA SR accelerators.

Keywords: streaming accelerator · parallel processing · lookup-table inference · FPGA architecture

1 Introduction

Image super-resolution (SR) reconstructs a high-resolution image from a low-resolution input and is widely used in practical imaging pipelines. Modern CNN-based SR methods achieve strong reconstruction quality, but their deployment on resource-constrained hardware remains difficult because of heavy arithmetic, large intermediate feature maps, and high external memory traffic [25]. From a parallel-processing perspective, SR is also challenging because irregular feature-map movement often dominates the execution cost, limiting efficient streaming and scalable hardware mapping.

L. Eeckhout et al. (Eds.): APPT 2026, LNCS 16693, pp. 423–435, 2027.
https://doi.org/10.1007/978-981-92-4805-6_28

Field-programmable gate arrays (FPGAs) are attractive for SR acceleration because they provide reconfigurable datapaths, customizable precision, and efficient on-chip memory usage [22]. Nevertheless, existing lightweight SR models and hardware-aware implementations still face several practical bottlenecks. Lightweight and quantized SR models reduce theoretical complexity [7,8,19,24], but many designs remain difficult to quantize aggressively and often rely on complex multi-branch structures. Tiling-based SR implementations alleviate memory pressure [3,6,12–14,26], yet they may introduce stitching artifacts and usually require operator-specific scheduling. As a result, deploying SR efficiently on small and mid-range FPGAs remains challenging.

Modern FPGA-based SR methods generally follow a multi-stage optimization flow. A lightweight SR model is first trained in full precision, and is then compressed by quantization, pruning, or related simplification techniques so that weights and intermediate activations can be represented in fixed-point format. After that, operator-level optimization, structural fusion, and tiling are introduced to reduce off-chip traffic and redundant feature-map write-backs, followed by a hardware mapping process that customizes compute modules and dataflow for the target platform. Despite these efforts, three bottlenecks remain prominent in practice: multiplication is still expensive on FPGA even after quantization, large SR feature maps still lead to frequent external memory access, and efficient dataflow design becomes increasingly difficult as the network structure grows more diverse and irregular.

LUT-based SR methods provide an alternative direction by replacing convolutional computation with table lookup and lightweight arithmetic [10,15–17,20]. This paradigm is naturally compatible with FPGA BRAM resources. However, existing LUT-based SR designs still suffer from storage growth, interpolation overhead, and non-uniform inference procedures, which limit their hardware efficiency and make compact parallel pipelines difficult to organize.

To address these issues, we propose a configurable streaming accelerator for LUT-based SR on FPGA. The main idea is to co-design the SR model, dataflow, and inference kernel so that computation is reduced to lookup, addition, and bit-shift operations, while intermediate storage is minimized. The resulting pipeline is organized around a regular local-window-to-output-block mapping that is directly amenable to streaming execution, low-overhead buffering, and scalable kernel replication.

The main contributions are as follows:

- We design an ultra-lightweight LUT-based SR formulation whose inference uses only memory lookup, integer addition, and bit-shift operations, eliminating multiplications and enabling a regular integer-only execution path.
- We introduce a receptive field-driven streaming dataflow that processes only receptive-field-sized windows, substantially reducing intermediate storage and external memory access while naturally supporting window-level parallelism.
- We develop a configurable LUT inference kernel that supports resource-aware throughput scaling through both stage-level streaming and multi-window par-

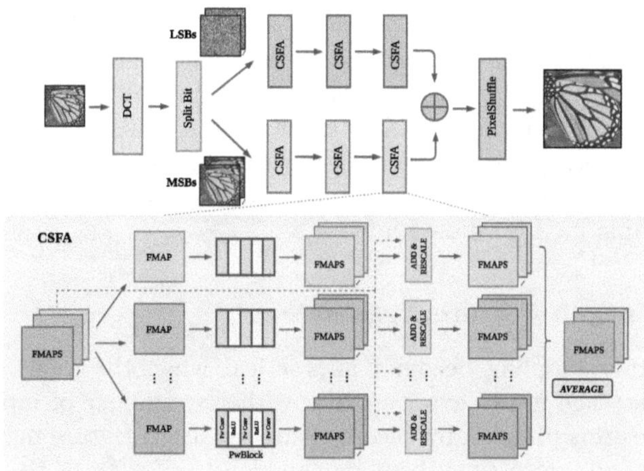

Fig. 1. Overview of the proposed LUT-based SR network.

allel processing with different numbers of instantiated CLIKs, exposing an explicit trade-off between parallelism and hardware cost.

2 Lightweight SR Algorithm with LUTs

2.1 Overview

The proposed SR network is built around a Channel-Split Feature Aggregation (CSFA) strategy, as shown in Fig. 1. The design targets hardware-efficient inference by replacing conventional convolution-heavy processing with a unified LUT-centric computation pattern.

The network first applies Depth-to-Channel Transformation (DCT) to fold spatial neighborhood information into the channel dimension. This converts spatial sampling into channel-wise processing and allows subsequent stages to share a unified inference operator. Bit-plane decomposition is then used to split the input into MSB and LSB branches, reducing the LUT index bit width and therefore the overall storage cost [15]. After that, CSFA performs lightweight channel interaction and aggregation. The final inference graph contains only lookup, addition, and bit-shift operations. To enlarge the effective receptive field without increasing LUT size, we further adopt the rotation-ensemble strategy from SRLUT [10].

2.2 Depth-to-Channel Transformation

DCT transforms local spatial sampling into channel-wise processing. For an input feature map $\mathbf{X}$ and kernel size k, DCT rearranges each $k \times k$ spatial neighborhood into a channel vector:

$$\mathbf{F}^* = \mathrm{DCT}(\mathbf{X}^*, k). \tag{1}$$

Conceptually, DCT can be understood as replacing a spatial convolutional neighborhood with an equivalent channel-domain descriptor: instead of applying multiple spatial operators after local sampling, the sampled pixels inside the local window are flattened and folded into the channel dimension. This transformation preserves the original spatial dependency while removing the need for diverse spatial operators in later stages. As a result, the network becomes more regular and more suitable for LUT-based inference.

2.3 Channel-Split Feature Aggregation

Traditional LUT sampling becomes impractical when the input dimension is high because storage grows exponentially with the number of input variables. CSFA addresses this problem by decomposing the input feature map into single-channel slices and processing them independently. For the i-th slice $\mathbf{X}_i$, the corresponding mapping is

$$\mathbf{R}_i = \mathcal{F}_i(\mathbf{X}_i), \tag{2}$$

where $\mathcal{F}_i$ is a dedicated single-input feature mapper.

The mapped results are then aggregated through a residual branch and quantization-aware training:

$$\mathbf{O}_i = \mathrm{RC}((\mathbf{R}_i + \mathcal{P}(\mathbf{X})) \cdot s)\,, \tag{3}$$

and the final output is

$$\mathbf{Y} = \frac{1}{C_{in}} \sum_{i=1}^{C_{in}} \mathbf{O}_i. \tag{4}$$

This strategy keeps each LUT input low-dimensional while preserving channel interaction, making LUT storage practical for hardware deployment.

2.4 Unified LUT Inference

After sampling, the complete SR pipeline is executed using unified CSFA LUTs. For each input channel, the sampled LUT entry is accumulated into the output vector, followed by a bit-shift normalization. Therefore, all inference stages are reduced to table lookup, integer addition, and bit-shift, without multiplications or divisions. This unified operator is the key to simplifying both the dataflow and the hardware architecture.

3 Dataflow and Hardware Architecture

3.1 Architecture Overview

The proposed hardware architecture is centered on a Configurable LUT Inference Kernel (CLIK), shown in Fig. 2. Each CLIK contains 16 parallel lookup memories mapped to BRAM and a configurable adder tree. Since the SR model is dominated by LUT access, addition, and bit-shift, CLIK becomes the main

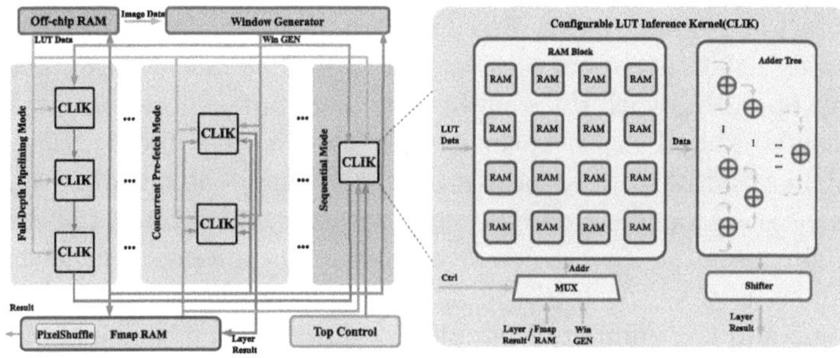

Fig. 2. Overview of the configurable LUT-based FPGA architecture.

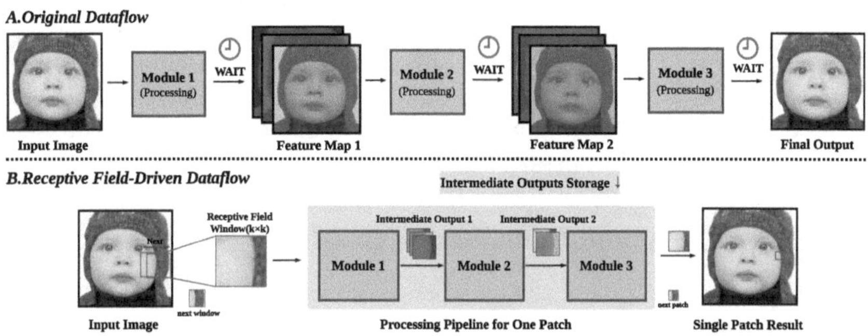

Fig. 3. Conventional SR dataflow versus the proposed receptive field-driven dataflow.

configurable computing unit of the accelerator. The overall RTL design is generated automatically from user-defined configuration parameters, and the CLIK replication factor directly determines the architecture-level throughput.

In addition to the CLIKs, the accelerator includes a window generator, lightweight control logic, and compact on-chip buffers. LUT data is loaded from off-chip memory, while the input image is streamed through the window generator. Since other functional blocks have very low arithmetic cost, changing the number of CLIKs directly controls the main resource–throughput trade-off of the design.

3.2 Receptive Field-Driven Dataflow

In the proposed SR model, spatial dependency is introduced only by the first receptive-field sampling stage, while all subsequent CSFA modules operate in the channel domain. Therefore, the output at position (r, c) depends only on the local receptive-field patch (Fig. 3):

$$\mathbf{Y}_{r,c} = F(\mathbf{X}_{\mathcal{R}(r,c)}). \tag{5}$$

This locality enables a receptive field-driven dataflow that processes receptive-field-sized windows directly instead of full intermediate feature maps. The resulting computation granularity is fixed and uniform, which simplifies scheduling compared with conventional SR accelerators that must coordinate multiple feature-map operators with different spatial footprints. More importantly, once the local neighborhood has been formed by the sliding-window frontend, each receptive-field window can be processed as an independent work unit in the downstream LUT pipeline. Therefore, the dataflow naturally supports window-level parallel processing in addition to conventional pipeline parallelism.

The benefit is that the intrinsic intermediate storage depends only on the receptive field and the number of parallel windows, not on the global image size. If N windows are processed in parallel and the receptive field is 4×4, the first-stage intermediate data contains only 16 N spatial elements. This makes BRAM usage precisely controllable and substantially reduces the need to buffer full feature maps. The buffering requirement is therefore decoupled from the output resolution, allowing the same kernel organization to be reused across different deployment scales. As a result, increasing parallelism does not require buffering larger feature maps; it only requires replicating the compact window-processing path and its associated local state.

3.3 Flexible Tiling and Configurable CLIKs

For very large images, the frontend adopts a sliding-window buffer and a flexible tiling strategy. Large inputs are split into overlapped tiles so that each tile can be processed independently while preserving receptive-field continuity. Because the overlap exactly covers the required receptive field, tiled inference remains mathematically equivalent to full-image inference.

The sliding-window frontend further adopts a pre-store mechanism to reduce off-chip traffic during window extraction. For kernel size k and image width W, k rows are first prefetched into the on-chip buffer, after which the window advances horizontally by shifting in only one new pixel per cycle. When the window moves to the next row, only $k - 1$ additional pixels are required to refresh the buffer. For boundary regions requiring padding, these extra fetches are avoided because padded values are generated on-chip. Although this mechanism already improves bandwidth efficiency, its buffer requirement is still proportional to $k \times W$. Therefore, for very large images, we further partition the image into overlapped tiles with width $W_{\text{tile}} \ll W$. Each tile uses the same sliding-window procedure but requires only $k \times W_{\text{tile}}$ buffer space, while adjacent tiles share exactly a $(k-1)$-pixel overlap to preserve receptive-field continuity.

This flexible tiling strategy changes only the image buffering requirement of the frontend, rather than the intrinsic intermediate feature size of the SR pipeline. Since each inference step still consumes only a receptive-field-sized input window, the intermediate feature footprint remains determined by the receptive field and the processing parallelism rather than by the global image size. Hence, the tile size can be selected according to available BRAM without affecting the numerical correctness of the SR result.

To support different resource budgets, the accelerator provides three basic CLIK execution modes, illustrated in Fig. 4. With one CLIK, inference is seri-

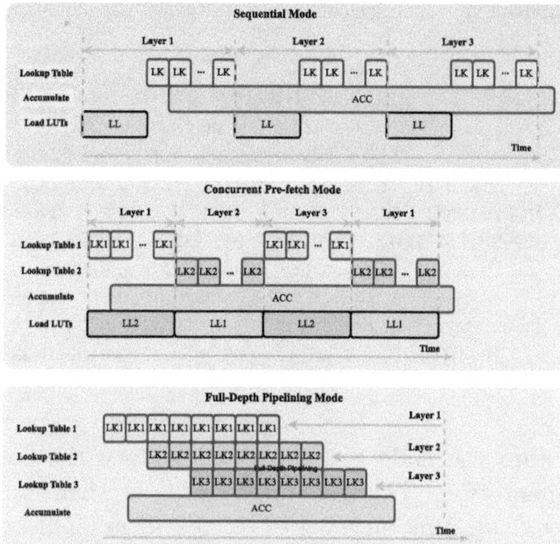

Fig. 4. Execution timing diagrams of different CLIK configurations.

alized to minimize resource cost. In this sequential mode, LUT loading and layer execution are both performed on the same kernel, so each layer must wait until the corresponding LUT is loaded. With two CLIKs, the design enters a concurrent pre-fetch mode in which one CLIK executes the current LUT stage while the other preloads the LUT data for the next stage, effectively hiding part of the loading latency. With three CLIKs, the three LUT stages form a fully pipelined execution path, and all stages can operate concurrently once the LUTs are resident on chip. This three-stage organization corresponds to the natural front, middle, and back LUT processing modules of the network, and therefore provides a direct streaming implementation of the model itself.

When more than three CLIKs are available, the architecture scales by replicating the three-CLIK full pipeline. If the total number of instantiated CLIKs is denoted by N, then N can be decomposed into complete three-stage pipeline groups plus a remainder, allowing the extra kernels to operate in either sequential or pre-fetch mode. In other words, the design scales along two orthogonal axes: streaming across the three LUT stages and parallel replication for multiple windows. This organization gives the accelerator a practical and explicit performance–resource knob, which will be evaluated in the experimental section.

4 Experiments

4.1 Experimental Setup

The proposed dataflow and hardware architecture are encapsulated as a code template. A LUT configuration file together with user-defined architectural

Table 1. Quantitative comparison of SR methods for ×2 super-resolution.

Type	Method	Storage	Mult.	Set5		Set14		Urban100		BSD100	
				PSNR	SSIM	PSNR	SSIM	PSNR	SSIM	PSNR	SSIM
Trad.	bilinear	–	7.4M	32.12	0.9106	29.15	0.8384	25.95	0.8077	28.65	0.8090
	bicubic	–	14.7M	33.63	0.9292	30.23	0.8681	26.86	0.8394	29.53	0.8421
LUT	SRLUT-S [10]	318.5KB	23.3M	35.46	0.9466	31.73	0.8958	28.50	0.8777	30.64	0.8750
	MuLUT-SDY-X2 [16]	1015KB	86.4M	36.65	0.9541	32.49	0.9065	29.31	0.8910	31.23	0.8865
	Ours	**28.75KB**	**0**	36.33	0.9519	32.17	0.9027	28.69	0.8900	31.09	0.8831
NN	SRCNN [4]	224KB	52.7G	36.68	0.9542	32.21	0.9040	29.50	0.8946	31.36	0.8879
	FSRCNN [5]	49KB	6.1G	37.05	0.9560	32.64	0.9088	29.88	0.8957	31.50	0.8908
	VDSR [11]	2.5MB	612.6G	37.53	0.9587	33.03	0.9124	30.76	0.9140	31.90	0.8960
	CARN-M [2]	1004KB	91.2G	37.42	0.9583	33.17	0.9136	31.23	0.9192	31.88	0.8960

parameters is fed into the code generator to produce the corresponding SystemVerilog implementation. The generated RTL is then verified by simulation and synthesized on the target FPGA platform. This workflow enables architecture-level evaluation of changing the number of instantiated CLIKs on resource usage and throughput.

We train the proposed LUT-based SR network on DIV2K [1] using a single NVIDIA RTX 3090 GPU. Random rotation and flipping are used for augmentation. We adopt Adam with $\beta_1 = 0.9$, $\beta_2 = 0.999$, and an initial learning rate of 5×10^{-3}, followed by cosine annealing for 200,000 iterations. The base receptive field is 4×4, which corresponds to an effective 7×7 window under rotation-ensemble inference. All CSFA modules except the last one use 16 input and 16 output channels, while the internal point-wise block maps 1 input channel to 16 output channels with 64 intermediate channels. We use a 6-bit MSB branch and a 2-bit LSB branch, since increasing the MSB beyond 6 bits gives only marginal quality improvement but causes exponential LUT growth, whereas lower MSB precision leads to more obvious quality degradation.

The LUT storage can be computed explicitly from the CSFA configuration. For one CSFA LUT, the storage is

$$S_{\text{CSFA}} = IC \times OC \times 2^{\text{bit}_{in}} \times \text{bit}_{out} \text{ bits}, \quad (6)$$

where IC and OC denote the input and output channel counts, and bit_{in} and bit_{out} are the input and output quantization precisions of the current branch. The total model storage is obtained by summing all CSFA LUTs in the MSB and LSB branches.

All experiments focus on ×2 super-resolution. The trained model is evaluated on Set5, Set14, Urban100 [9], and BSD100 [21] using PSNR and SSIM. For hardware evaluation, RTL is generated by configuring the number of CLIKs and synthesized on a ZU3EG FPGA using Vivado 2022.2.

4.2 SR Algorithm Comparison

Table 1 compares representative interpolation-based, neural, and LUT-based SR methods. Neural baselines achieve the highest absolute reconstruction quality,

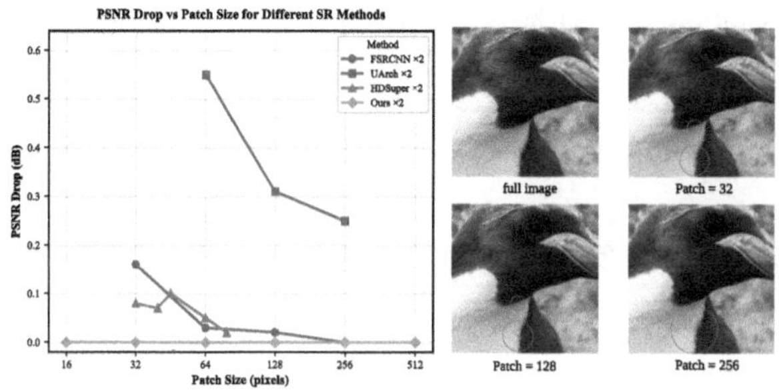

Fig. 5. Patch-based processing comparison. Our method keeps zero PSNR drop once the patch size is no smaller than the receptive field.

but their arithmetic cost is extremely high. LUT-based baselines reduce computation substantially, yet their storage overhead remains non-trivial. Our method preserves competitive reconstruction quality while completely eliminating multiplications and reducing model storage to 28.75 KB, yielding a computation pattern amenable to integer-only streaming execution on FPGA.

4.3 Effectiveness of the Proposed Dataflow

Figure 5 shows that conventional patch-based SR methods may suffer from PSNR degradation and visible stitching artifacts when the patch size is reduced. In contrast, the proposed receptive field-driven dataflow maintains zero PSNR degradation once the patch is at least as large as the receptive field, because tiled processing is mathematically equivalent to full-image inference. This property is desirable for accelerator design, since it allows partitioning for buffering purposes without introducing an additional accuracy penalty from the execution schedule itself.

This dataflow also reduces on-chip memory significantly. Unlike conventional patch- or tile-based accelerators that shrink tile size to fit intermediate feature maps into BRAM, our design keeps the intrinsic intermediate storage independent of the global image partition size. Existing designs such as ADAS, UArch, and HDSuper all rely on reducing the processed block size to control feature-map storage [3,6,26], whereas our pipeline processes only receptive-field-sized windows and forwards partial outputs immediately. Once a local window has been formed, it can be dispatched through the downstream LUT pipeline independently, so the same dataflow also enables straightforward multi-window parallel processing without reintroducing large feature-map buffers.

4.4 FPGA Implementation Results

Table 2 shows that the proposed accelerator achieves a favorable quality–resource trade-off. Ours-CLIK-3 uses only 6,835 LUTs, 8,932 FFs, and 326 KB on-chip

Table 2. Comparison with representative FPGA-based SR accelerators.

Work	HDSuper [26]	UArch [6]	Liu et al. [18]	ERVSR [23]	ADAS [3]	Ours-CLIK-3
Algorithm	CNN-based	U-Net-based	LAPAR-based	RNN-based	ADAS-FH	LUT-based
Tech	XC7VX485T	ZCU111	KV26	XCKU15P	XC7VX485T	ZU3EG
Frequency	200MHz	188MHz	200MHz	160MHz	200MHz	200MHz
Precision (W-A)	16-16	12-12	9-8	12-16	12-12	8-8
PSNR (Set5, X2)	-	-	37.24	36.76	37.08	36.33
LUT	73K	40K	65K	98K	105K	**6835**
FF	53K	50K	143K	57K	123K	**8932**
Memory	496KB	1089KB	4176KB	4842KB	1118KB	**326KB**
DSP	704	1029	1210	1820	1558	**0**
FPS	81(FHD)	72(FHD)	36(FHD) 25(QHD)	76(UHD)	96(UHD)	96(FHD)
Throughput	168	149	74 93	637	799	199

Throughput is reported in Mpixels/s. Resolutions refer to target output resolutions.

Table 3. Architecture variants under different CLIK configurations on ZU3EG.

Variant	CLIK-1	CLIK-2	CLIK-3	CLIK-6
Frequency (MHz)	200	200	200	200
LUT	3525	6964	6835	13620
FF	3628	7106	8932	17663
Memory (KB)	128	239	326	650
DSP	0	0	0	0
FPS (X2, FHD)	15	30	96	192
Throughput (Mpixels/s)	31	62	199	398

memory while completely eliminating DSP usage. Although the compared implementations are reported on different FPGA devices, the result should be interpreted mainly as an architectural trend: by organizing the workload as LUT lookup, lightweight accumulation, and window streaming, the proposed design shifts the implementation burden away from DSP-intensive compute and large intermediate buffers. With three instantiated CLIKs, the design achieves 96 FPS and 199 Mpixels/s for ×2 FHD SR, corresponding to a fully streamed three-stage kernel organization.

The architecture is also scalable. By changing the number of instantiated CLIKs, throughput can be increased without changing the fundamental dataflow. In our implementation, one CLIK sustains 15 FPS for ×2 FHD SR, while six CLIKs scale the throughput to 192 FPS on the same ZU3EG platform through stage-level streaming and additional window-level parallelism.

4.5 Scalability

Table 3 summarizes the resource utilization and runtime performance under different CLIK configurations, where CLIK-1/2/3/6 denote implementations with 1/2/3/6 instantiated CLIKs, respectively. These results directly support the "configurable architecture" claim of this work. With a single CLIK, the design already sustains 15 FPS for ×2 FHD SR while using only 128 KB of on-chip memory. As more CLIKs are instantiated, throughput increases substantially while preserving the same LUT-based computational structure and zero-DSP property. In particular, CLIK-3 corresponds to a fully streamed three-stage kernel, whereas CLIK-6 further exploits multi-window parallelism by replicating this streamed pipeline.

The resource trend is not perfectly linear because the total LUT usage also includes shared control logic and platform-dependent peripheral modules. For example, CLIK-2 consumes slightly more LUTs than CLIK-3, even though CLIK-3 instantiates more CLIKs, because the latter benefits from a more efficient fully pipelined organization. Nevertheless, the overall throughput–resource trend is clear: moderate configurations such as CLIK-3 already provide real-time ×2 FHD performance, while CLIK-6 further doubles the frame rate to 192 FPS at the same operating frequency.

5 Conclusion

We presented a configurable streaming accelerator for LUT-based SR on FPGA. By co-designing a LUT-centric SR model, a receptive field-driven dataflow, and a configurable inference kernel, the proposed framework removes multiplications from inference, greatly reduces intermediate storage, and organizes SR execution as a regular streaming pipeline with explicit parallel scaling through CLIK replication. Experimental results show competitive reconstruction quality with very small model storage, low BRAM usage, and zero DSPs. These results indicate that LUT-oriented model–architecture co-design is a practical direction for resource-constrained SR acceleration on FPGA platforms.

Acknowledgments. This work was supported in part by National Natural Science Foundation of China (61972180) and the Wuxi Science and Technology Development Fund Project (K20241027).

Artificial Intelligence Statement. Artificial intelligence tools, if used, were used only for language organization and figure/table polishing, and did not participate in the generation of the core ideas or technical content.

Disclosure of Interests. The authors have no competing interests to declare that are relevant to the content of this article.

References

1. Agustsson, E., Timofte, R.: Ntire 2017 challenge on single image super-resolution: Dataset and study. In: Proceedings of the IEEE Conference on Computer Vision and Pattern Recognition Workshops, pp. 126–135 (2017)
2. Ahn, N., Kang, B., Sohn, K.A.: Fast, accurate, and lightweight super-resolution with cascading residual network. In: Proceedings of the European Conference on Computer Vision (ECCV), pp. 252–268 (2018)

3. Chang, L., Zhao, X., Zhou, J.: Adas: A high computational utilization dynamic reconfigurable hardware accelerator for super resolution. ACM Trans. Reconfigurable Technol. Syst. **16**(3), 1–22 (2023)
4. Dong, C., Loy, C.C., He, K., Tang, X.: Learning a Deep Convolutional Network for Image Super-Resolution. In: Fleet, D., Pajdla, T., Schiele, B., Tuytelaars, T. (eds.) ECCV 2014. LNCS, vol. 8692, pp. 184–199. Springer, Cham (2014). https://doi.org/10.1007/978-3-319-10593-2_13
5. Dong, C., Loy, C.C., Tang, X.: Accelerating the Super-Resolution Convolutional Neural Network. In: Leibe, B., Matas, J., Sebe, N., Welling, M. (eds.) ECCV 2016. LNCS, vol. 9906, pp. 391–407. Springer, Cham (2016). https://doi.org/10.1007/978-3-319-46475-6_25
6. Duan, X., Chen, Y., Li, M., Rong, Y., Xie, R., Han, J.: Uarch: A super-resolution processor with heterogeneous triple-core architecture for workloads of u-net networks. IEEE Trans. Biomed. Circ. Syst. **17**(3), 633–647 (2023)
7. Gao, D., Zhou, D.: A very lightweight and efficient image super-resolution network. Expert Syst. Appl. **213**, 118898 (2023)
8. Hao, F., Wu, J., Liang, W., Xu, J., Li, P.: Lightweight blueprint residual network for single image super-resolution. Expert Syst. Appl. **250**, 123954 (2024)
9. Huang, J.B., Singh, A., Ahuja, N.: Single image super-resolution from transformed self-exemplars. In: Proceedings of the IEEE Conference on Computer Vision and Pattern Recognition, pp. 5197–5206 (2015)
10. Jo, Y., Kim, S.J.: Practical single-image super-resolution using look-up table. In: Proceedings of the IEEE/CVF Conference on Computer Vision and Pattern Recognition, pp. 691–700 (2021)
11. Kim, J., Lee, J.K., Lee, K.M.: Accurate image super-resolution using very deep convolutional networks. In: Proceedings of the IEEE Conference on Computer Vision and Pattern Recognition, pp. 1646–1654 (2016)
12. Lee, J., Lee, J., Yoo, H.J.: Srnpu: An energy-efficient cnn-based super-resolution processor with tile-based selective super-resolution in mobile devices. IEEE J. Emerg. Selected Top. Circ. Syst. **10**(3), 320–334 (2020)
13. Lee, J., Shin, D., Lee, J., Lee, J., Kang, S., Yoo, H.J.: A full hd 60 fps cnn super resolution processor with selective caching based layer fusion for mobile devices. In: 2019 Symposium on VLSI Circuits, pp. C302–C303. IEEE (2019)
14. Li, G., Liu, Z., Li, F., Cheng, J.: Block convolution: Toward memory-efficient inference of large-scale cnns on fpga. IEEE Trans. Comput. Aided Des. Integr. Circuits Syst. **41**(5), 1436–1447 (2021)
15. Li, H., Guan, J., Rui, L., Ma, S., Gu, L.: Tinylut: Tiny look-up table for efficient image restoration at the edge. Adv. Neural. Inf. Process. Syst. **37**, 85340–85359 (2024)
16. Li, J., Chen, C., Cheng, Z., Xiong, Z.: Toward DNN of LUTs: Learning efficient image restoration with multiple look-up tables. IEEE Trans. Pattern Anal. Mach. Intell. **46**(12), 8284–8301 (2024)
17. Li, Y., Li, J., Xiong, Z.: Look-up table compression for efficient image restoration. In: Proceedings of the IEEE/CVF Conference on Computer Vision and Pattern Recognition, pp. 26016–26025 (2024)
18. Liu, H., et al.: A high-performance accelerator for real-time super-resolution on edge fpgas. ACM Trans. Des. Autom. Electron. Syst. **29**(3), 1–25 (2024)
19. Liu, K., et al.: 2dquant: Low-bit post-training quantization for image super-resolution. Adv. Neural. Inf. Process. Syst. **37**, 71068–71084 (2024)

20. Ma, C., Zhang, J., Zhou, J., Lu, J.: Learning series-parallel lookup tables for efficient image super-resolution. In: Avidan, S., Brostow, G., Cissé, M., Farinella, G.M., Hassner, T. (eds) European Conference on Computer Vision, pp. 305–321. Springer, Cham (2022). https://doi.org/10.1007/978-3-031-19790-1_19
21. Martin, D., Fowlkes, C., Tal, D., Malik, J.: A database of human segmented natural images and its application to evaluating segmentation algorithms and measuring ecological statistics. In: Proceedings Eighth IEEE International Conference on Computer Vision. ICCV, vol. 2, pp. 416–423. IEEE (2001)
22. Mittal, S.: A survey of fpga-based accelerators for convolutional neural networks. Neural Comput. Appl. **32**(4), 1109–1139 (2020)
23. Sun, K., Koch, M., Wang, Z., Jovanovic, S., Rabah, H., Simon, S.: An fpga-based residual recurrent neural network for real-time video super-resolution. IEEE Trans. Circ. Syst. Video Technol. **32**(4), 1739–1750 (2021)
24. Tu, Z., Hu, J., Chen, H., Wang, Y.: Toward accurate post-training quantization for image super resolution. In: Proceedings of the IEEE/CVF Conference on Computer Vision and Pattern Recognition, pp. 5856–5865 (2023)
25. Yang, C.-Y., Ma, C., Yang, M.-H.: Single-Image Super-Resolution: A Benchmark. In: Fleet, D., Pajdla, T., Schiele, B., Tuytelaars, T. (eds.) ECCV 2014. LNCS, vol. 8692, pp. 372–386. Springer, Cham (2014). https://doi.org/10.1007/978-3-319-10593-2_25
26. Zhao, X., Chang, L., Fan, D., Hu, Z., Yue, T., Tu, F., Zhou, J.: HDSuper: High-quality and high computational utilization edge super-resolution accelerator with hardware-algorithm co-design techniques. IEEE Trans. Circuits Syst. I Regul. Pap. **71**(4), 1679–1692 (2024)

TL-Sort: A Fully Pipelined Hardware Architecture for Sorting Without Run-Drain Stalls

Hai Cao, Puguang Liu, Zhang Luo, Yuan Li, Jihang Wang, Xingyun Qi, and Mingche Lai(✉)

National University of Defense Technology, Changsha, China
mingchelai@nudt.edu.cn

Abstract. Merge-based sorting architectures are widely used in FPGA sorting accelerators due to their scalability and high throughput. However, their execution is fundamentally constrained by run-drain stalls, where merge-tree leaves must fully drain their current sorted runs within the same level before admitting new data. This run-level synchronization breaks steady-state pipelined execution and limits sustained throughput under streaming workloads. This paper presents TL-Sort (Triple-Layer Sort), a fully pipelined merge-based sorting architecture that eliminates run-drain stalls. To achieve this, TL-Sort introduces a pipelined virtual tree (PVT) that first explicitly encodes inter-run ordering, thereby eliminating run-level synchronization. Compared with a virtual merge sorter tree, PVT reduces total sorting cycles by up to 2.57× and improves throughput by up to 2.52× with negligible hardware overhead. When sorting 32,768 64-bit records in a multi-pass setting, TL-Sort improves throughput from 0.697 GB/s to 1.474 GB/s compared with a state-of-the-art open-source FPGA sorter.

Keywords: Hardware sorting · Run-drain stalls · FPGA · Merge sorter tree

1 Introduction

Sorting is a fundamental operation in a wide range of data-intensive applications, including databases [1], analytics [2], and scientific computing. It has also become increasingly important in modern AI and machine learning [3], where massive datasets must be efficiently sorted to enable fast downstream processing. This central role has motivated extensive research on high-throughput FPGA-based hardware sorters. Among existing designs [4–11], merge-based architectures have become the dominant approach due to their favorable parallelism and scalability. Despite their widespread adoption, existing merge-based FPGA sorters fail to

H. Cao and P. Liu—These authors contributed equally to this work.

L. Eeckhout et al. (Eds.): APPT 2026, LNCS 16693, pp. 436–449, 2027.
https://doi.org/10.1007/978-981-92-4805-6_29

sustain truly continuous pipelined execution under streaming inputs. This limitation stems from run-level execution behaviors inherent to merge sorter trees, which result in pipeline discontinuities.

A fundamental obstacle in merge-based FPGA sorters is the run-drain stall, a pipeline stall at the leaves of the merge tree during streaming execution. In a conventional merge sorter tree, each leaf receives locally sorted runs at different levels, rather than a globally ordered sequence. The merge tree merges runs within the same level into a globally ordered sequence. To maintain merge correctness, run admission is synchronized across all leaves at the same level, so a new run can only enter once all runs from the current level are fully drained. If records from a subsequent level are admitted prematurely, incorrect ordering occurs. This forces conventional designs to fully drain runs at every leaf, introducing pipeline bubbles and limiting throughput.

Motivated by this execution behavior, we introduce the pipelined virtual tree (PVT), which incorporates our proposed ordering-aware merge mechanism to eliminate run-drain stalls. To fully leverage the performance advantages of PVT, we propose TL-Sort (Triple-Layer Sort), with PVT as core component. TL-Sort is a fully pipelined merge-based sorting architecture, consisting of three stages: 1) a front-end Comparison Counting Sorter (CCS), which generates locally sorted runs from unordered inputs; 2) a middle-tier PVT layer, where these runs are merged without stalls; and 3) a back-end FLiMS-based merge sorter tree (FMST), which performs global merging to produce fully ordered output. By integrating PVT, TL-Sort eliminates run-drain stalls, sustains high throughput under streaming inputs, and achieves up to 100% higher throughput than a state-of-the-art FPGA sorter [7].

In summary, we make the following contributions:

- We formalize the run-drain stall as the key bottleneck limiting pipelined execution in merge-based FPGA sorters, which arises from mandatory run-level synchronization at merge tree leaves.
- We propose PVT—a merge tree architecture enhanced with an ordering-aware merge mechanism. This design eliminates run-drain stalls via explicit inter-run ordering, achieving up to 2.57× cycle reduction and 2.52× throughput improvement over virtual merge sorter trees.
- We present TL-Sort, a fully pipelined sorting architecture integrating PVT, CCS, and FMST stages, which sustains continuous streaming execution and improves throughput by up to 100% compared with state-of-the-art FPGA sorters [7].

2 Pipelined Virtual Tree

2.1 Run-Drain Stalls in Merge Designs

Figure 1 illustrates a 4-leaves merge sorter tree. Each leaf supplies a sequence of sorted runs, which are mutually independent. Each run consists of a single record organized into successive run levels (Level 0, Level 1, etc.). As illustrated in Fig. 1, Level 0 data enters the merge tree at cycle T+1 and is not completely drained until cycle T+5. During cycles T+3 and T+5, even though comparators in Stage 1 of the merge tree are idle, data from Level 1 in the leaves is prohibited from entering. This restriction is necessary to prevent interleaving of data from

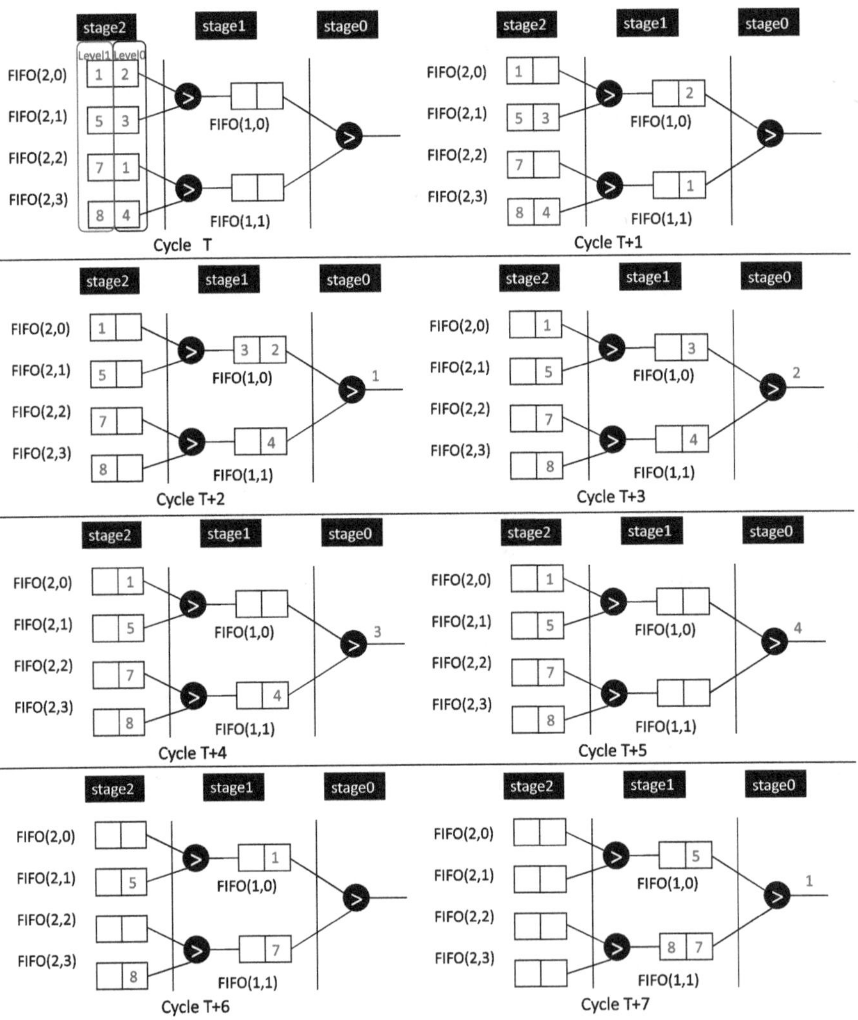

Fig. 1. Illustration of run-drain stalls in a merge sorter tree

different levels, thereby preserving the ordered segments corresponding to each level. Notably, no data is output from the merge tree at cycle T+6. This number of zero-output cycles (bubbles) increases as the depth of the merge tree increases. We refer to this behavior as run-drain stalls. When sorting unordered data using a merge tree, the large number of runs per leaf leads to a sharp increase in bubbles, which limits throughput under streaming workloads.

A representative example of run-drain stalls can be found in the open-source sorter proposed by Kobayashi [7]. This sorter uses a front-end Batcher's odd-even sorting network, followed by virtual merge sorter trees (VMSTs), and a back-end VMS-based merge sorter tree [12]. In this design, the ordered output of each VMST is input into the back-end merge tree. New runs from a higher level can only enter the VMSTs after the current runs from the previous level are fully merged by the back-end tree, creating an input gap at each leaf equal to the combined latency of both stages. This gap introduces recurrent pipeline bubbles and limits throughput.

2.2 Ordering-Aware Merge in the Pipelined Virtual Tree

We propose an ordering-aware merge mechanism to solve the problem of run-drain stalls by introducing explicit run-level ordering, which can be applied to any merge-based sorter. In merge-based sorters, Virtual Merge Sorter Trees (VMST) offer scalability, high throughput, and low resource consumption, making it an ideal foundation for implementing the ordering-aware merge mechanism. Building on this, we propose the Pipelined Virtual Tree (PVT), which integrates the ordering-aware merge approach into the VMST architecture to further enhance throughput by eliminating run-drain stalls.

The structure of PVT is shown in Fig. 2. DIN, which is a set of ordered segments obtained via CCS sorting, is fed into the corresponding leaves according to their sequence numbers. PVT replaces the per-stage compare-and-select (CAS) units in Fig. 1 with a Batcher's odd-even merger (BOEM) [13]. It also introduces a per-stage feedback buffer, implemented as FIFOs and denoted as $FB(i, j)$. At each stage, the BOEM merges two inputs: the feedback sequence from $FB(i, j)$ and the FIFO sequence whose head element is smaller between the two adjacent FIFOs ($FIFO(i, 2j)$ and $FIFO(i, 2j+1)$). The merged output is partitioned into equal halves: the smaller half is forwarded to the next-stage $FIFO(i-1, j)$, while the larger half is written back to the feedback buffer $FB(i, j)$, as shown in Fig. 2. These modifications allow the pipeline to output multiple records per cycle, rather than a single record.

PVT removes run-drain stalls by extending the merge comparison semantics with explicit run-level ordering, as illustrated in Fig. 2. Order tags are assigned to each record within DIN before it is fed into the corresponding leaves. Instead of comparing records solely by key, each record is augmented with a compact 2-bit run-order tag that encodes the relative order of its originating run. Specifically, runs admitted at the same leaf level are assigned an initial tag value of 00. As runs propagate to the next merge level, newly admitted runs are assigned successive tag values in the sequence 01, 10, and 11, after which the assignment wraps

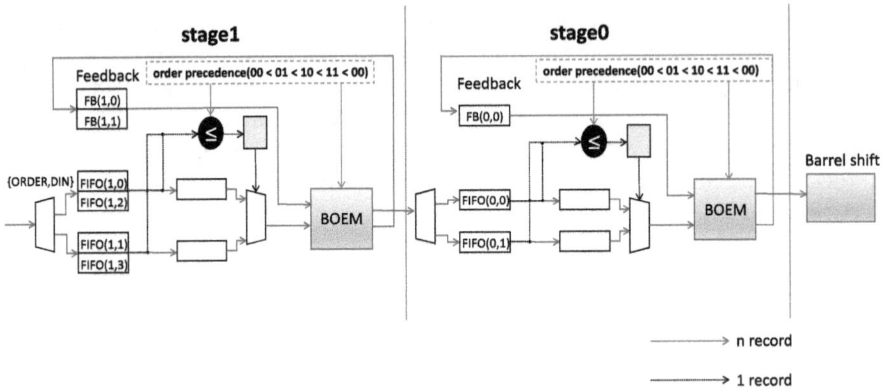

Fig. 2. Pipelined virtual tree.

around to 00. Merge units in PVT perform comparisons on $(key, order)$. The key field preserves the original intra-run merge semantics, while the order field enforces inter-run priority. To support the cyclic reuse of the 2-bit order tags, the comparator is extended with a wrap-around ordering rule, under which 11 is treated as having higher priority than 00. This rule makes the order comparison well-defined across the wrap-around boundary, ensuring a consistent run-level precedence.

The correctness of this cyclic comparison can be intuitively justified as follows. At any moment, the records entering the comparator fall into one of two cases: either all records have the same tag, coming from a single level, or they come from two consecutive levels, in which case only two different tags appear and no others. In the latter case, the two tags are always consecutive in the cyclic sequence $00 < 01 < 10 < 11 < 00$. For records with the same tag, comparing only the key preserves merge correctness. For consecutive tags, the wrap-around rule ensures a well-defined priority even across the $11 \rightarrow 00$ boundary. Therefore, the 2-bit cyclic tag comparison correctly enforces run-level ordering while maintaining global sorting correctness and eliminating run-drain stalls. Note that using only one bit is insufficient to encode the order. With a single bit, the relative priority between $order = 0$ and $order = 1$ may invert across cycles, necessitating more complex control logic to handle these reversals. At least two bits are required to avoid such complexity and enable straightforward ordering.

3 The Architecture of TL-Sort

3.1 TL-Sort Architecture Overview

While the pipelined virtual tree eliminates run-drain stalls within merge sorter trees, a complete streaming sorting engine must also integrate run generation, run admission, and hierarchical merging into a unified pipeline. To this end, we design TL-Sort, a fully pipelined merge-based sorting architecture that leverages PVT to sustain continuous execution across run boundaries.

As shown in Fig. 3, TL-Sort consists of three pipelined stages. A front-end Comparison Counting Sorter (CCS) of width P generates locally sorted runs from unordered inputs, which are admitted into a mid-tier layer of pipelined virtual trees (PVTs), each comprising W leaves. The PVTs output ordered streams to a back-end FLiMS-based merge sorter tree (FMST) with E input ports, which performs global merging of all records. Each input port of the FMST receives the output from a single PVT, so E ports collectively accept the outputs of E PVTs. With deep pipelining and memory round-trip merging, each traversal through the sorter increases the run length by a factor of $W \cdot E$, allowing TL-Sort to maintain high throughput across successive memory passes. Accordingly, the total number of memory passes needed to merge all records can be determined from the growth of the run length. Let N_{pass} denote this number:

$$N_{pass} = \left\lceil \log_{W \cdot E} \frac{N}{P} \right\rceil,$$

where N denotes the total number of input records and is limited by the available external memory capacity.

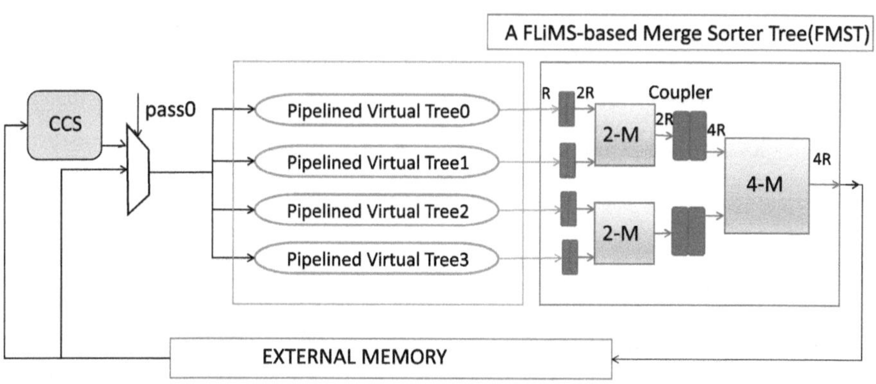

Fig. 3. Architecture of the proposed sorter for P=8, W=4, and E=4.

3.2 Front-End and Back-End Components

The Comparison Counting Sorter (CCS) converts unordered input records into locally sorted blocks based on the comparison counting principle [14], serving as a run generator for downstream merging. As illustrated in Fig. 4, the CCS operates in two stages. In the Comparison stage, all P elements within a block are compared pairwise in parallel, producing for each input element a_i a vector of comparison results $y_i = [C_{i0}, \ldots, C_{iP-1}]$, where C_{ij} denotes the outcome of comparing a_i with a_j. In the Counting stage, the comparison results are summed to obtain a rank $C_i = \sum_{j=0}^{P-1} C_{ij}$, and each record is routed to its output position using a count-indexed multiplexer network. The two stages complete within a single clock cycle, producing a sorted block of P records. In TL-Sort, these blocks constitute the initial runs fed into the PVT layer; in our implementation, we use $P = 8$, as shown in Fig. 4.

At the back end, TL-Sort employs a FLiMS-based merge sorter tree (FMST) to progressively combine ordered streams into larger sorted runs. Merge sorter trees are typically implemented as hierarchical merge structures [4]. As shown in Fig. 3, the FMST in TL-Sort is organized as a multi-way merge hierarchy. In this notation, x-R represents a set of x records, and X-M denotes a merger block that takes two inputs of X records each and produces X sorted records at its output. The Coupler accepts K records per cycle and produces $2K$ records per cycle, effectively aggregating consecutive sets for the next merge stage. In the illustrated configuration, two 2-M blocks feed a 4-M block, producing four sorted records per cycle. All merger blocks are implemented using lightweight 2-way FLiMS units [15]. Compared with earlier MMS- or VMS-based designs [12,16], FLiMS reduces comparator count and pipeline depth, resulting in higher operating frequency and reduced hardware resource usage. Structurally, the FMST remains a conventional merge-based hierarchy. By propagating and interpreting the order tags introduced by PVT, the FMST preserves inter-run ordering across merge stages and supports continuous, fully pipelined operation without requiring run-level draining.

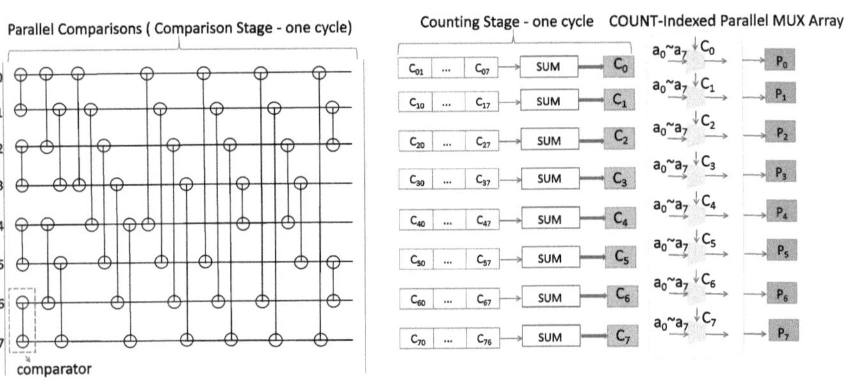

Fig. 4. Comparison counting sorter ($P = 8$).

3.3 Integration of PVT Into the Sorting Pipeline

In TL-Sort, the PVT is placed between CCS and FMST, serving as the interface between run generation and hierarchical merging.

The CCS generates a stream of locally sorted runs that are fed into the leaves of the PVT. By propagating explicit inter-run order information with each record, the PVT allows runs to be admitted independently at different leaves without requiring run-level synchronization. The PVT outputs continuous ordered streams to the back-end merge sorter tree, carrying order tags alongside record values. With inter-run ordering already enforced by the incoming records, the downstream merge hierarchy can directly process records from successive runs without additional control.

3.4 Sorting Procedure

The TL-Sort attains global order through memory round-trips of "read → merge → write". Notably, TL-Sort enables scalable sorting problem size via multi-pass sorting, allowing it to handle larger datasets. For TL-Sort configured with $(P, W, E)=(8, 4, 4)$, 2048 unordered records (as a example) are streamed from external memory to the sorter in groups of eight. In the first pass, the front-end CCS sorts each group of eight records and forwards them to a leaf of a PVT. Each PVT has four leaves and merges four 8-record sorted sequences to produce a 32-record sorted run, which is then fed to a leaf of the FMST. The FMST, also with four leaves, merges four 32-record runs into a 128-record sorted block. Data continuously flow through this hierarchy, producing 16 such 128-record blocks in the first pass. In the second pass, each PVT merges four 128-record runs into a 512-record sorted sequence, which is then merged by the FMST to produce a fully sorted 2048-record sequence. The CCS is used only in the first pass, while subsequent passes rely solely on the PVTs and FMST for hierarchical merging.

4 Evaluation

4.1 Experimental Setup

All designs are implemented in Verilog HDL and synthesized, placed, and routed using Xilinx Vivado 2025.1 targeting a Xilinx `xvu37p-fsvh2892-21-e` FPGA. All experiments use randomly generated input keys. Performance is evaluated using post-implementation results in terms of throughput, total execution cycles, and hardware resource utilization. In this work, resource utilization is reported for lookup tables (LUTs) and flip-flops (FFs), providing a measure of the hardware cost of each design. Throughput is computed as

$$\text{Throughput (GB/s)} = \frac{N \cdot r \cdot f_{\text{MAX}}}{\text{Cycles}},$$

where N is the number of records, r is the record size in bytes, f_{MAX} is the post-implementation clock frequency, and Cycles denotes the total execution cycles. Cycles are measured with a testbench, from the first valid input entering the design to the last valid output being produced.

4.2 Impact of Eliminating Run-Drain Stalls

This experiment compares the proposed PVT with a VMST to study the impact of run-drain stalls. As the number of input runs increases, the two designs exhibit fundamentally different execution behaviors, revealing the effect of run-level draining in conventional merge sorter trees.

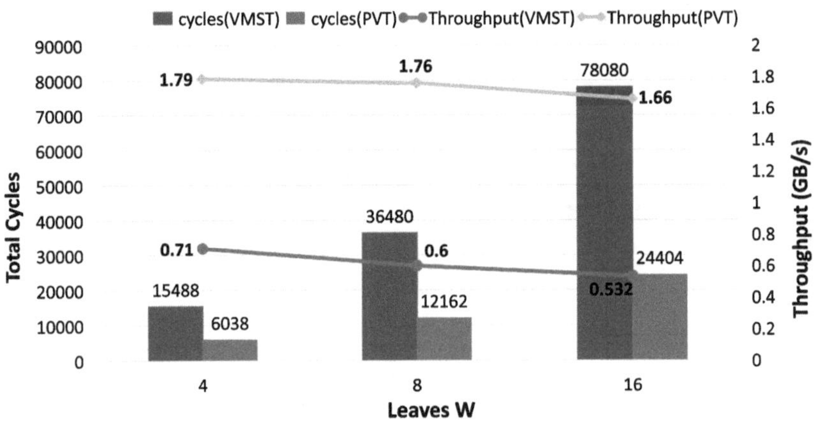

Fig. 5. Comparison between VMST and PVT.

All experiments use 64-bit records with a 32-bit key and a 32-bit value. Each merge tree leaf processes a stream of locally sorted input runs, each containing 8 ordered records, with no ordering enforced across runs. For both PVT and VMST, each leaf handles 64 runs, and three configurations with $W = 4$, $W = 8$ and $W = 16$ leaves are evaluated. Figure 5 compares total execution cycles and effective throughput. In VMST, merge correctness is maintained by enforcing full run draining, so new runs can only be admitted after all corresponding runs are fully merged. With 64 runs per leaf, execution time scales proportionally with the number of runs, i.e., $\text{Cycles}_{\text{VMST}} \approx 64 \cdot \text{Cycles}_{\text{per-run}}$, introducing recurrent pipeline stalls at run boundaries. In contrast, PVT explicitly encodes inter-run ordering and admits new runs as soon as a leaf exhausts its current run, eliminating run-level synchronization across leaves. This enables continuous pipelined execution across run boundaries while preserving global output ordering.

As shown in Fig. 5, by allowing successive runs to overlap across merge stages instead of enforcing full run draining, PVT significantly reduces the total execution cycles. Specifically, total execution cycles are reduced from 15,488 to 6,038 for $W = 4$, from 36,480 to 12,162 for $W = 8$, and from 78,080 to 24,404 for $W = 16$, corresponding to 2.57×, 3.00×, and 3.20× reductions, respectively. This reduction directly translates into higher effective throughput, which improves from 0.71 GB/s to 1.79 GB/s ($W = 4$), from 0.60 GB/s to 1.76 GB/s ($W = 8$), and from 0.53 GB/s to 1.66 GB/s ($W = 16$). Post-implementation frequency and resource utilization are reported in Table 1. PVT reuses the existing merge structure and adds lightweight ordering, maintaining a comparable operating frequency with less than 2% additional LUT and FF overhead across both configurations. These results show that ordering-aware merging incurs negligible structural cost.

Table 1. Resource and Frequency Comparison of VMST and PVT (64-bit)

Design	f_{MAX} [MHz]	LUT(%)	FF(%)
VMST($W = 4$)	675.67	9,417(0.72%)	20,950(0.8%)
PVT($W = 4$)	660.94	9,576(0.73%)	21,047(0.81%)
VMST($W = 8$)	670.24	14,258(1.09%)	28,937(1.11%)
PVT($W = 8$)	655.30	14,508(1.11%)	29,324(1.12%)
VMST($W = 16$)	634.92	19,157(1.47%)	36,934(1.42%)
PVT($W = 16$)	618.42	19,493(1.50%)	37,334(1.43%)

Overall, these results demonstrate that run-drain stalls constitute a dominant performance bottleneck in merge-based designs. By eliminating run-level draining while preserving merge correctness, PVT enables sustained pipeline utilization and delivers substantial throughput improvements with minimal hardware overhead.

4.3 Multi-pass Streaming Comparison

We next evaluate TL-Sort under multi-pass streaming workloads and compare it against a state-of-the-art open-source FPGA sorter [7]. This baseline architecture

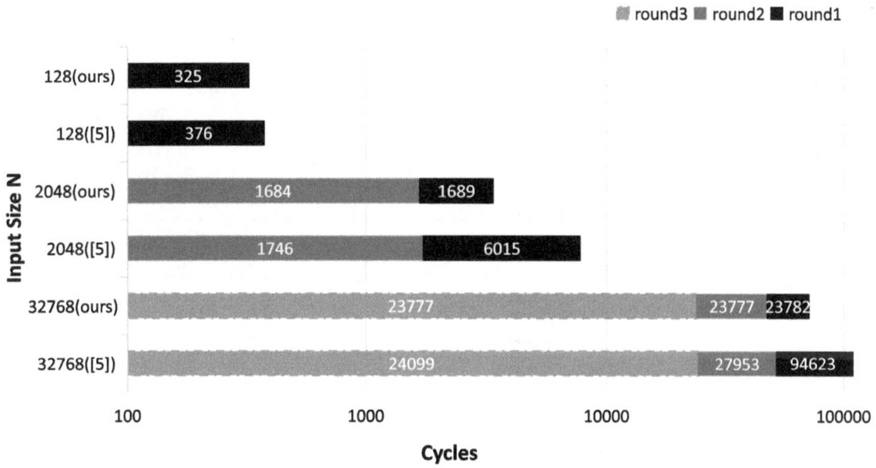

Fig. 6. Execution Cycles Comparison

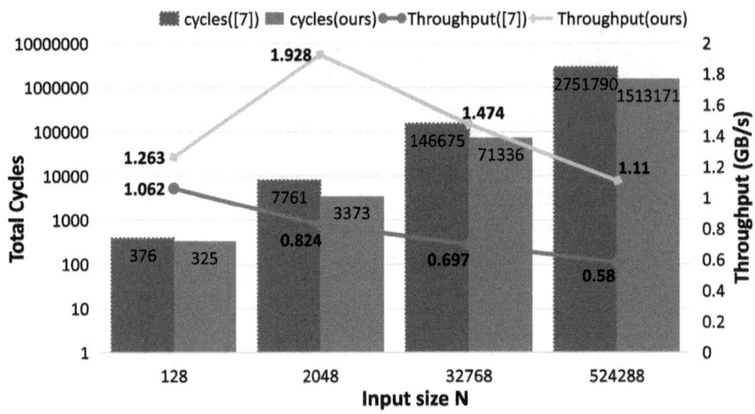

Fig. 7. Multi-pass Throughput Comparison

can likewise be abstracted using the (P, W, E) parameters, and both designs are evaluated under the same configuration $(P, W, E) = (8, 4, 4)$ to ensure a fair comparison.

Under this configuration, TL-Sort uses 28,569 LUTs and 68,269 FFs and operates at 401.12 MHz, while the baseline [7] uses 35,785 LUTs and 94,697 FFs and operates at 390.24 MHz. Figures 6 and 7 illustrate the total sorting cycles and the corresponding throughput for different input sizes, respectively.

For $N = 128$ (single pass), since each leaf only receives a single sorted run and TL-Sort directly produces one final sorted segment of 128 ($P \times W \times E$) elements, the ordering-aware mechanism remains inactive. Consequently, TL-Sort achieves comparable latency to the baseline (325 vs. 376 cycles). For $N = 2048$ (two passes), where ordering-aware mechanism becomes effective, the baseline [7] requires 6,015 and 1,746 cycles in Pass 0 and Pass 1, achieving 0.824 GB/s, whereas TL-Sort completes the two passes in 1,689 and 1,684 cycles, sustaining 1.948 GB/s. When scaling to $N = 32{,}768$ (three passes), the baseline incurs 94,623, 27,953, and 24,099 cycles across Pass 0–2, yielding 0.697 GB/s, while TL-Sort reduces these to 23,782, 23,777, and 23,777 cycles and sustains 1.474 GB/s. For large-scale sorting at $N = 524{,}288$ (four passes, 4 MB), the baseline suffers from severe run-drain stalls, requiring 2,751,790 cycles, whereas TL-Sort maintains stable pipeline execution with similar cycle counts, achieving 1.11 GB/s.

The performance gains primarily stem from eliminating Pass 0 startup stalls. As evidenced by the per-pass cycle counts, the baseline [7] suffers from inflated Pass 0 latency due to run-drain behavior, whereas TL-Sort maintains near-constant pass latency across passes by continuously admitting unsorted inputs into the merge stage.

4.4 Single-Pass Comparison with Prior Sorters

We evaluate TL-Sort under a single-pass setting and compare it with representative FPGA-based sorting architectures using 32-bit records. All records consist of a single 32-bit key and are directly compared without additional payload fields.

The evaluation focuses on small input sizes ((N=256) and (N=512)). To ensure a fair comparison, TL-Sort is configured to operate in a single-pass manner without enabling the proposed order-tag mechanisms. We compare it against two representative FPGA-based sorting architectures that also perform single-pass sorting. The sorter proposed by Papaphilippou [17] combines a linear-insertion sorting stage with a merge sorter tree, operating with (Q=4) parallel input streams. DL-Sort [18] adopts a fully streaming two-layer architecture consisting of a one-way linear-insertion sorter followed by a cyclic bitonic merge network, also using (Q=4) parallel streams.

Table 2. Comparison of FPGA Sorter Implementations (XVU37P, 32-bit)

Design	N	f_{MAX} [MHz]	Cycles	LUT(%)	FF(%)	Throughput [GB/s]	RNT
[17]	256	184.91	180	24,652(1.89%)	31,212(1.20%)	1.05	4.259
DL-Sort		215.84	143	53,558(4.11%)	25,382(0.97%)	1.55	2.894
Ours(8,4,8)		434.22	413	40,501(3.11%)	98,354(3.77%)	1.08	2.667
[17]	512	128.63	356	46,635(3.58%)	59,801(2.29%)	0.74	1.586
DL-Sort		149.57	273	108,631(8.34%)	50,552(1.94%)	1.12	1.031
Ours(8,4,16)		392.46	585	86,374(6.63%)	202,861(7.78%)	1.37	1.591

Table 2 summarizes the post-implementation results. To facilitate performance–area comparison, we use the resource-normalized throughput (RNT), defined as the achieved throughput divided by the normalized LUT count. Formally, RNT is calculated as RNT $= \frac{\text{Throughput}}{\text{LUTs}/10^5}$. At $N = 256$, our TL-Sort reaches 1.08 GB/s, already matching the sorter in [17] (1.05 GB/s).

For a more representative input size ($N = 512$), TL-Sort operates at 392.46 MHz, exceeding both the design in [17] (128.63 MHz) and DL-Sort (149.57 MHz). At this operating point, TL-Sort achieves a throughput of 1.37 GB/s while using 86,374 LUTs, whereas DL-Sort achieves 1.12 GB/s with 108,631 LUTs. As a result, TL-Sort attains the highest resource-normalized throughput (RNT) of 1.591, compared with 1.031 for DL-Sort and 1.586 for [17], indicating the best combined performance–area efficiency among the evaluated designs.

Overall, these results demonstrate that TL-Sort remains competitive under single-pass operation, despite not leveraging PVT's run-overlapping capability. Moreover, at N=512 TL-Sort achieves the best combined performance and resource efficiency among the evaluated designs, with a more balanced utilization of FPGA resources.

5 Conclusion

This paper presents TL-Sort, a fully pipelined merge-based sorting architecture that eliminates run-drain stalls. By incorporating the pipelined virtual tree, TL-Sort enables ordering-aware merging and continuous run admission while maintaining merge correctness. Experimental results show significant reductions in execution cycles and improved sustained throughput with minimal hardware overhead.

Acknowledgments. This work was supported by the National Key Research and Development Program of China (Grant 2023YFB4403400) and by the National University of Defense Technology Research Fund Project (Grant ZK25-09).

Disclosure of Interests. The authors have no competing interests to declare that are relevant to the content of this article.

Artificial Intelligence Statement. Artificial intelligence tools, if used, were used only for language organization and figure/table polishing, and did not participate in the generation of the core ideas or technical content.

References

1. Casper, J., Olukotun, K.: Hardware acceleration of database operations. In: Proceedings of ACM/SIGDA International Symposium on Field-Program. Gate Arrays (FPGA), pp. 151–160 (2014)
2. Dong, B., Byna, S., Wu, K.: SDS-Sort: Scalable Dynamic Skew-aware Parallel Sorting. In: Proceedings of 25th ACM International Symposium on High-Performance Parallel and Distributed Computing (HPDC), pp. 57–68 (2016)
3. Zhu, H., Lo, D., Cheng, L., Govindaraju, R., Ranganathan, P., Erez, M.: Kelp: QoS for accelerated machine learning systems. In: Proceedings of International Symposium on High Performance Computer Architecture (HPCA) (2019)
4. Song, W., Koch, D., Luján, M., Garside, J.: Parallel Hardware Merge Sorter. In: Proceedings of IEEE 24th Annual International Symposium on Field-Programmable Custom Computing Machines (FCCM), pp. 95–102. Washington, DC (2016)
5. Usui, T., Chu, T.V., Kise, K.: A Cost-Effective and Scalable Merge Sorter Tree on FPGAs. In: Proceedings of International Symposium on Computerised Networks (CANDAR), pp. 47–56 (2016)
6. Samardzic, N., Qiao, W., Aggarwal, V., Chang, M.-C.F., Cong, J.: Bonsai: High-Performance Adaptive Merge Tree Sorting. In: Proceedings of ACM/IEEE 47th Annual International Symposium on Computerised Architecture (ISCA), pp. 282–294. Valencia, Spain (2020)
7. Kobayashi, R., Miura, K., Fujita, N., et al.: An Open-Source FPGA Library for Data Sorting. J. Inf. Process. **30**, 766–777 (2022)
8. Jayaraman, S., Zhang, B., Prasanna, V.: Hypersort: High-Performance Parallel Sorting on HBM-Enabled FPGA. In: Proceedings of International Conference on Field-Programmable Technology (FPT), pp. 1–11. Hong Kong, China (2022)

9. Qiao, W., Guo, L., Fang, Z., Chang, M.-C.F., Cong, J.: TopSort: a high-performance two-phase sorting accelerator optimized on HBM-based FPGAs. IEEE Trans. Emerg. Top. Comput. 404–419 (2023)
10. Sun, M., Xie, G., Zhang, F., Guo, W., Fan, X., Chen, L., Du, J.: FPGA-Based Large-Scale Sorting with Optimized Bandwidth Utilization. ACM Trans. Reconfigurable Technol. Syst. (2025)
11. Liu, J., Li, Y., Huang, Z., Chen, C., Chen, R., da Silva, B.: FASE: An FPGA-based accelerator for lightweight sample entropy with Monte Carlo sampling. IEEE Trans. Very Large Scale Integr. (VLSI) Syst. **33**(10), 2883–2896 (2025)
12. Saitoh, M., Kise, K.: Very Massive Hardware Merge Sorter. In: Proceedings of International Conference on Field-Programming Technology (FPT), pp. 86–93 (2018)
13. Batcher, K.E.: Sorting Networks and Their Applications. In: Proceedings of Joint Computing Conference AFIPS, pp. 307–314 (1968)
14. Knuth, D.E.: Sorting and Searching. In: The Art of Computer Programming, vol. 3, 2nd edn. Addison-Wesley, Reading, MA (1998)
15. Papaphilippou, P., Luk, W., Brooks, C.: FLiMS: A Fast Lightweight 2-Way Merger for Sorting. IEEE Trans. Comput. **71**(12), 3215–3226 (2022)
16. Saitoh, M., Elsayed, E.A., Chu, T.V., Mashimo, S., Kise, K.: A High-Performance and Cost-Effective Hardware Merge Sorter Without Feedback Datapath. In: Proceedings of IEEE 26th Annual International Symposium on Field-Programmable Custom Computing Machines (FCCM), pp. 197–204 (2018)
17. Papaphilippou, P., Brooks, C., Luk, W.: An Adaptable High-Throughput FPGA Merge Sorter for Accelerating Database Analytics. In: Proceedings of 30th International Conference on Field-Programmable Logic and Applications(FPL), pp. 65–72 (2020)
18. Oh, H.-W., Park, J., Lee, S.E.: DL-Sort: a hybrid approach to scalable hardware-accelerated fully streaming sorting. IEEE Trans. Circ. Syst. II, Exp. Briefs **71**, 2549–2553 (2024)

Hardware-Accelerated Streaming Graph Processing with Fast Refinement

Jingrui Yuan[1,2], Qinggang Wang[1,2(✉)], Haoran Zhu[1,2], Jin Zhao[1,2], and Xiaofei Liao[1,2]

[1] Huazhong University of Science and Technology (HUST), Wuhan, China
[2] School of Computer Science and Technology, HUST, Wuhan, China
qgwang@hust.edu.cn

Abstract. Existing streaming graph processing solutions typically leverage incremental computation, which relies on an iterative process with two basic phases of *refinement* and *recomputation*, to reduce redundant computations while preserving accuracy. However, these existing efforts still suffer from serious problems of *irregular memory accesses* and *sequential tag propagation* arising in the refinement phase, which severely underutilize many-core processors. To cope with it, we propose **GraphPro**, a hardware-accelerated incremental computation engine that augments many-core processors to enable efficient streaming graph processing. GraphPro is specialized in accelerating the refinement phase and performing the recomputation phase, while the host CPU cores are responsible only for handling graph updates (e.g., edge/vertex additions and deletions). Specifically, GraphPro incorporates two key mechanisms: (1) a *redundancy-aware dependency storage format* that transforms most irregular memory accesses induced by affected vertex identification into sequential accesses while minimizing additional storage overhead, and (2) a *lightweight dependency maintaining scheme* that leverages metadata to reduce maintaining overhead and overlaps dependency maintaining with graph update to further hide latency. Experimental results show that GraphPro achieves speedups of 8.23× ∼17.52× over the state-of-the-art CPU-based system GraphFly and 1.30× ∼1.82× over the best-performing hardware accelerator TDGraph.

1 Introduction

Real-world graphs often evolve continuously over time, commonly referred to as streaming graphs. For example, the Twitter graph experiences up to 6000 tweet-related updates per second. These continuously arriving updates (e.g., edge/vertex additions and deletions) are typically applied to the graph in batches. Streaming graph processing has been widely adopted across a large variety of domains, including social network analysis [10], structural biology [17], financial networks [6], and anomaly detection [18].

Streaming graph processing involves an iterative process comprising two fundamental kernels [5,9,15]: *graph update* and *graph computation*. The former generates a new graph snapshot by applying graph structural mutations

L. Eeckhout et al. (Eds.): APPT 2026, LNCS 16693, pp. 450–463, 2027.
https://doi.org/10.1007/978-981-92-4805-6_30

(i.e., edge/vertex additions and deletions.[1]) to the current graph. Subsequently, graph computation (e.g., graph algorithms or ad-hoc queries) is performed on the latest snapshot to extract useful information. To sustain real-time analysis, existing streaming graph processing systems, such as GraphFly [4] and KickStarter [16], often adopt the technique of incremental computation, which incrementally refines the results calculated before graph mutations rather than recomputing each vertex's state from scratch, thereby reducing redundant computation.

Incremental computation relies on an iterative process with two basic phases [4]: *refinement* and *recomputation*. The *refinement* phase identifies the vertices affected by graph structural mutations by performing the tag propagation and resets their states. In the *recomputation* phase, each reset vertex gathers the states of its incoming neighbors to produce its new state, and then propagates this new state to update its neighbors' states in the latest graph snapshot. Existing studies have proposed many novel techniques to optimize the intrinsic problems of the refinement or recomputation phase, such as utilizing the dependency of intermediate values to reduce the number of affected vertices that need to be processed [8], and a topology-driven incremental execution approach to eliminate redundant computation overhead [20]. However, our investigation reveals that the *refinement* phase is still costly to handle in existing solutions, dominating the overall execution time of incremental computation, due to the following two reasons.

First, in monotonic graph algorithms, the value of a vertex depends on that of a single in-neighbor. Consequently, existing approaches typically store each vertex's state along with the index of its dependent in-neighbor, representing the dependency between the two vertices. In the refinement phase, the destination vertex of a deleted/added edge is first identified as an affected vertex and propagates its index as a tag to all its neighbors. Upon receiving a tag, each vertex determines whether the tag matches the index of its dependent in-neighbor. If so, the vertex is marked as affected, its state is reset, and the above procedure is repeated until no new affected vertices are identified. During this phase, the neighbors and states of affected vertices are read from memory, and the reset states are written back. This incurs serious *irregular memory accesses* because these affected vertices' neighbors and states are typically dispersed very sparsely in the main memory. Besides, the vertex state is often sized of 4 bytes, which is much smaller than a cache line. This causes most vertex states fetched into the *last-level cache* (LLC) are actually not be used, underutilizing the cache and memory bandwidth significantly.

Second, although the tag propagation originated from an affected vertex to all its neighbors along outgoing edges can be parallelized across multiple threads, subsequent propagation steps are constrained by strict data dependencies. Specifically, each successive layer of tags cannot be issued until the corresponding vertices in the preceding layer are formally identified as affected.

[1] Note that we consider only edge updates in this paper since vertex updates can be represented by a series of edge additions and/or deletions [18].

This inter-layer synchronization barrier forces the tag propagation to proceed in a layer-by-layer fashion, severely limiting parallelism and underutilizing the underlying compute resources.

An intuitively feasible approach to eliminating irregular memory accesses and sequential tag propagation is to maintain, for each vertex, a complete set of vertices that directly and transitively depend on it, and to consolidate the storage of this set into a contiguous memory region. This facilitates direct and fast identification of all affected vertices upon a graph mutation and enables sequential memory accesses. Nevertheless, materializing it introduces two key challenges. First, with the continuous growth of the graph size, storing a complete dependency set for each vertex inevitably incurs prohibitive storage cost, which must be carefully controlled. Second, continuous graph structural mutations change the dependencies between vertices dynamically, making it challenging to maintain dependency sets accurately and efficiently.

In this paper, we propose a hardware-accelerated incremental computation engine called **GraphPro**, which augments many-core processors to enable efficient streaming graph processing. Different from existing solutions, GraphPro supports a *fast refinement approach* to transform layer-by-layer tag propagation into direct memory accesses and achieve better access locality in streaming graph processing. Specifically, GraphPro incorporates a redundancy-aware dependency storage format that explicitly represents dependency sets for a few critical vertices in the form of a table, while retaining only a single copy of common non-critical vertices across sets. This design transforms most irregular memory accesses induced by affected vertex identification into sequential accesses, while minimizing redundant storage overhead. GraphPro also features a lightweight dependency maintaining scheme that leverages metadata to mitigate the overhead of maintaining the dependency table and overlaps dependency maintaining with graph update to further hide latency.

This paper makes the following key contributions:

- We investigate the problems of irregular memory accesses and sequential tag propagation arising in the refinement phase of streaming graph processing.
- We propose GraphPro, a hardware-accelerated incremental computation engine that augments many-core processors to enable efficient streaming graph processing.
- GraphPro incorporates two key mechanisms: a redundancy-aware dependency storage format that transforms most irregular memory accesses induced by affected vertex identification into sequential accesses while minimizing storage overhead, and a lightweight dependency maintaining scheme that leverages metadata to reduce maintaining overhead and overlaps dependency maintaining with graph updates to further hide latency.
- We evaluate GraphPro on real-world streaming graph datasets using different graph algorithms, demonstrating that it outperforms the state-of-the-art CPU-based system and hardware accelerator, achieving speedups of $8.23\times \sim 17.52\times$ and $1.30\times \sim 1.82\times$, respectively.

2 Background and Motivation

2.1 Preliminaries

Streaming Graph Processing. Streaming graph processing aims to sustain the latest analytical results while graph updates keep arriving. Specifically, streaming graph processing relies on an iterative process with two basic kernels: *graph update* and *graph computation*. As shown in Fig. 1, graph update involves generating the latest snapshot by applying a batch of graph structural mutations—vertex/ edge additions and deletions—to an existing graph snapshot. Subsequently, graph computation (e.g., graph algorithms or ad-hoc queries) is executed over the latest snapshot to derive analytical results. Without loss of generality, this paper focuses on edge additions and deletions, as vertex updates can be effectively transformed into a series of edge updates.

Incremental Computation. Generally, after applying a batch of graph updates, only a small fraction of vertices become *affected vertices*, whose stale states may lead to incorrect final results [5,15]. Therefore, instead of recomputing the entire graph from scratch, existing streaming graph processing systems often adopt *incremental computation* to identify affected vertices and reset their states, while reusing the states of other vertices to reduce redundant computation and preserve accuracy [1,3].

Incremental computation alternately performs the *refinement* and *recomputation* in each iteration. Refinement performs the tag propagation along the graph topology to identify vertices affected by graph structural mutations and resets their states, while recomputation gathers the states of each affected vertex's incoming neighbors to calculate its new state, and then scatters this calculated state to update its neighbors' states.

Dependencies between vertices are important for identifying affected vertices after applying a batch of graph updates [12]. Specifically, if the state of a vertex v is computed based on the state of a vertex u, then v is said to depend on u [20]. If u is also directly connected to v by an edge, it is referred to as the *parent dependency* of v [4]. Furthermore, these parent dependencies implicitly originated from a root vertex form a dependency tree.

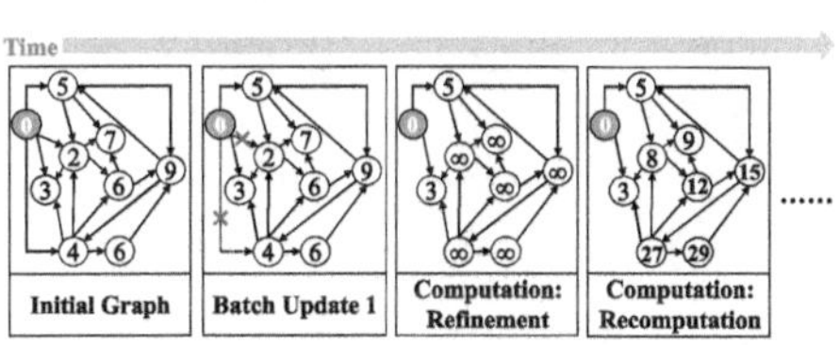

Fig. 1. The basic workflow of streaming graph processing

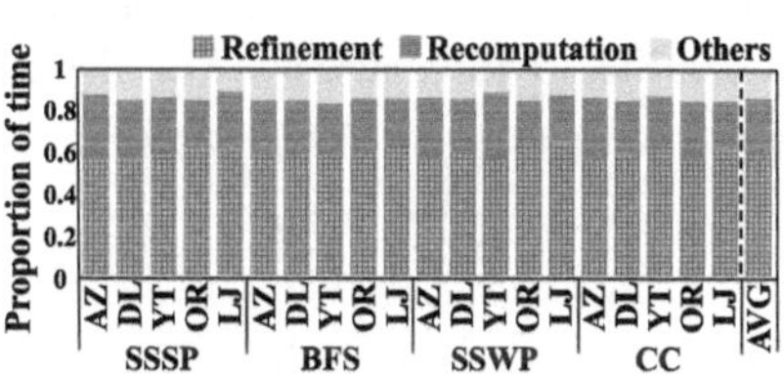

Fig. 2. The execution time breakdown of GraphFly [4]

2.2 Problems of Existing Streaming Processing Solutions

We take the state-of-the-art streaming graph processing system GraphFly [4] as a representative to investigate inefficiencies of existing systems. Figure 2 breaks down the total execution time of GraphFly by benchmarking four graph algorithms on five real-world graph datasets. The datasets can be found in Table 2. We see that only 26.58% of the total time is spent in the *recomputation* phase. Instead, the *refinement* phase is costly to handle, reaching 65.36%, due to two reasons:

Irregular Memory Accesses. Existing solutions typically store each vertex's state along with the index of its parent dependency. In the refinement phase, the streaming graph processing system first identifies the destination vertices of edge additions or deletions as initial root affected vertices. These vertices then propagate their indices as tags to all adjacent neighbors. Upon receiving a tag, the vertex performs a dependency identification: if the tag matches the index of its parent dependency, the vertex is flagged as affected and its state is reset. This process is repeated until no new affected vertices are identified. During this process, the neighbors and states of affected vertices are repeatedly read from memory, and the reset states are written back. This leads to significant irregular memory accesses, as these affected vertices' neighbors and states are typically sparsely distributed in memory.

Consider the graph shown in Fig. 3 as an example. After deleting the edge Ⓐ→Ⓓ, the destination vertex Ⓓ is first identified as the root affected vertex, and its state is reset (I). Subsequently, Ⓓ propagates its index as a tag to its four out-neighbors Ⓒ, Ⓔ, Ⓕ, and Ⓘ. Among them, vertex Ⓔ is flagged as affected because the index of its parent dependency matches the propagated tag (II). The process then continues as Ⓔ propagates its index to its out-neighbor Ⓖ (III). Figure 4 illustrates the storage layout of the graph in Fig. 3, along with the corresponding memory access patterns during the above process. It is clear that vertices are stored sequentially in contiguous physical memory addresses according to their index order, while the access patterns for both vertex states and edges are highly irregular.

Worse still, a vertex state typically occupies 4 bytes, which is much smaller than a standard 64-byte cache line. This size disparity leads to severe over-fetching, where the majority of data brought into the LLC is not used, leading to significant underutilization of both the cache and memory bandwidth.

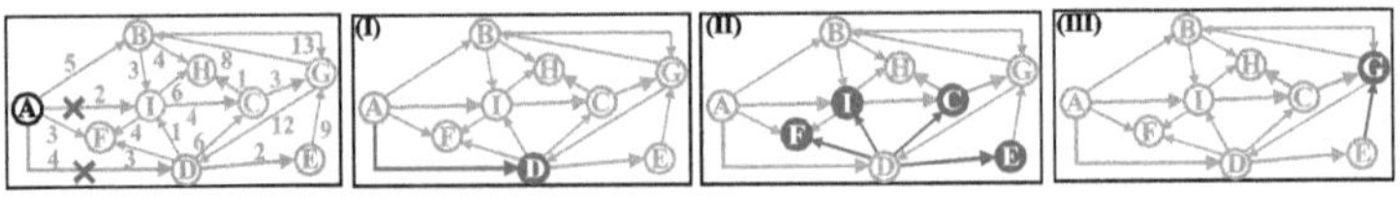

Fig. 3. A simplified example for illustrating the problems of existing efforts

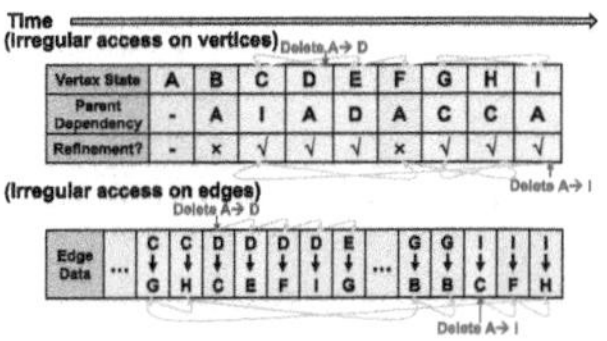

Fig. 4. Illustration of irregular memory accesses in the refinement phase

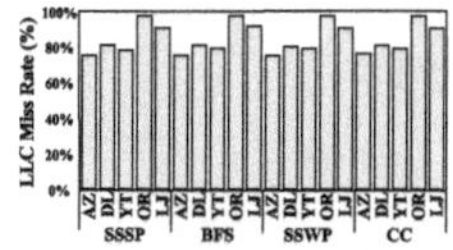

Fig. 5. The LLC miss rate of the refinement phase in GraphFly [4]

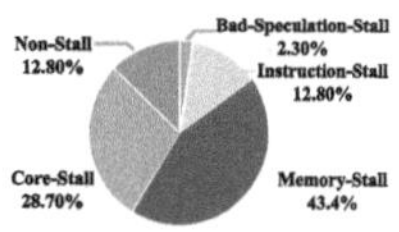

Fig. 6. CPU utilization of the refinement phase in GraphFly [4]

Sequential Tag Propagation. Although the tag propagation from an affected vertex to its neighbors can be parallelized across multiple threads, overall execution is constrained by strict data dependencies. Specifically, each successive layer of tags cannot be issued until the preceding layer of vertices has been identified as the affected ones. This inter-layer synchronization enforces a layer-by-layer execution, effectively serializing propagation along the graph's diameter. Consequently, this bottleneck severely limits parallelism and leads to significant CPU core stalls. Figure 3 shows an example illustrating sequential tag propagation. Ⓓ propagates its index as a tag to its four out-neighbors Ⓒ, Ⓔ, Ⓕ, and Ⓘ. However, the tag propagation from Ⓔ to Ⓖ will not be triggered until Ⓔ is identified as an affected vertex.

Results. We evaluate the LLC miss rate and CPU utilization of GraphFly arising from the two issues above, using four algorithms on five graphs. As depicted in Fig. 5, the irregular memory accesses in GraphFly lead to a prohibitive L3 cache miss rate of 88.51%. Moreover, Fig. 6 reveals that 28.70% of the CPU execution time is consumed by stalls necessitated by sequential tag propagation.

2.3 Overcoming Inefficiencies

The irregular memory accesses and sequential tag propagation arising in the refinement phase primarily stem from identifying affected vertices after applying a batch of graph updates. An intuitive approach to bypass these bottlenecks is to maintain a complete dependency set for each vertex, rather than storing only its parent dependency. The dependency set of a given vertex contains all vertices that directly and transitively depend on it. By storing each dependency set in a contiguous memory region, the process of identifying affected vertices can be transformed into direct and sequential memory accesses.

However, materializing this approach introduces two key challenges. First, as the size of real-world graphs continues to grow, maintaining a complete dependency set for each vertex incurs prohibitive storage overhead, which must be carefully controlled. Moreover, the dependency sets of different vertices often share common vertices, leading to significant storage amplification due to redundancy. Second, dynamic graph updates continuously alter dependencies between

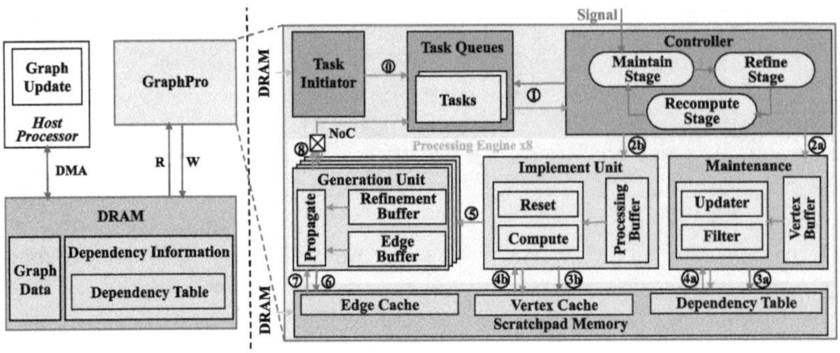

Fig. 7. The overall architecture of GraphPro

vertices, making it challenging to maintain dependency sets in a timely and accurate manner. Furthermore, maintaining these dynamic dependencies can introduce non-trivial runtime overhead, potentially offsetting the benefits of improved access locality.

3 Overview of GraphPro

3.1 Architecture Overview

Figure 7 illustrates the overall architecture of GraphPro. It operates alongside a host processor, with host DRAM storing both graph data and dependency information. GraphPro is specialized in accelerating the refinement phase and performing the recomputation phase, while the host CPU cores are responsible only for handling graph updates (e.g., edge/vertex additions and deletions). The graph data encompasses the edge list and vertex states, while the dependency information is organized as a dependency table consisting of the dependency sets of a few critical vertices and the associated metadata required for subsequent dependency maintenance. GraphPro includes six components, explained below:

Task Initiator. It fetches data from DRAM and orchestrates execution by generating specialized tasks to activate corresponding hardware modules. Specifically, it issues metadata scan tasks to the *Maintenance Unit* to start the dependency maintenance, refinement tasks to the *Implement Unit* for affected vertex identification and state reset, and recomputation tasks to the *Implement Unit* to trigger vertex state recomputation.

Task Queues. The *Task Queues* buffer tasks generated by *Task Initiator* and *Generation Unit*, and dispatch them to the corresponding hardware modules when they become available, thereby enabling pipelined task execution.

Controller. GraphPro further decomposes the execution flow of incremental computation into three stages: *Maintain*, *Refine*, and *Recompute*. The *Controller* acts as a finite state machine that orchestrates switching between these stages.

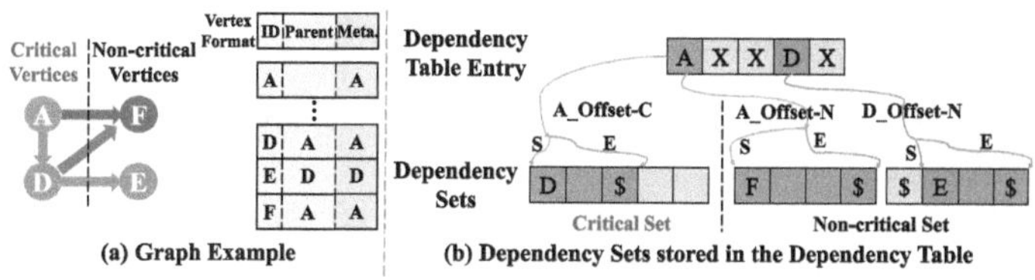

Fig. 8. A simplified example for illustrating the redundancy-aware dependency storage format

Maintenance Unit. It is responsible for updating the dependency table in response to graph topology changes. In the maintain stage, it scans metadata to group vertices based on their associated critical vertices and updates corresponding entries in the dependency table. More details are discussed in Sect. 3.3.

Implement Unit. It is responsible for affected vertex identification and reset, vertex state recomputation, and metadata generation. In the refine stage, the *Implement Unit* treats the destination vertices of added or deleted edges as root affected vertices and determines whether they are critical vertices. If so, it fetches their corresponding dependency sets from DRAM to directly obtain affected vertices. Otherwise, it performs tag propagation along the graph topology to identify affected vertices iteratively. In the recompute stage, the *Implement Unit* updates vertex states using algorithm-specific operators and generates the new metadata for the dependency table.

Generation Unit. The *Generation Unit* generates subsequent tasks based on the information produced by the *Implement Unit.* In the refine stage, it fetches dependency sets from the dependency table or outgoing edges from DRAM to generate subsequent refinement tasks. In the recompute stage, it fetches edges to generate algorithm-specific operator tasks. To facilitate efficient access to the dependency table, the *Generation Unit* incorporates a *Refinement Buffer* that stores the starting addresses and offsets of each critical vertex's dependency set.

Execution Flow. After applying a batch of graph updates, GraphPro first enters the *maintain* stage (⓪ and ①) to update the dependency table by sequentially scanning metadata (2a, 3a, and 4a). It then transitions to the *refine* stage, where the *Task Initiator* issues initial refinement tasks to activate the *Implement Unit* (2b, 3b, 4b, and ⑤). Next, the *Generation Unit* generates subsequent tasks to drive affected vertex identification and state reset (⑥, ⑦, and ⑧). After all affected vertices are identified and reset, GraphPro enters the *recompute* stage, where vertex states are updated in parallel and new metadata is generated. During this stage, the *Implement Unit* performs recomputation and metadata generation, while the *Generation Unit* produces recomputation tasks.

3.2 Redundancy-Aware Dependency Storage

As discussed in Sect. 2.3, maintaining a complete dependency set for each vertex incurs prohibitive storage overhead. Fortunately, we observe that most irregular memory accesses are induced by affected vertex identification and reset root in a small fraction of vertices. Our experimental results, collected from offline trace analysis, show that approximately 78.76%∼89.99% of these memory accesses are contributed by the top 1%∼5% high-degree vertices. This is because vertices tend to depend on high-degree vertices. For monotonic graph algorithms, affected vertices are more likely to depend on high-degree vertices because high-degree vertices participate in more edges and therefore have a higher probability of lying on sequential tag propagation after updates. Therefore, we select the top α high-degree vertices as critical vertices and store their dependency sets in the dependency table, rather than maintaining dependency sets for all vertices. In practice, we set empirically α to be 5%, which seems to be a sweet spot in two dimensions: storage cost and performance. To further reduce storage overhead, GraphPro eliminates redundancy across overlapping dependency sets through a reference-based representation. Specifically, when two dependency sets share common vertices, GraphPro stores references to the corresponding common vertices instead of duplicating the shared portions.

Figure 8(b) illustrates our redundancy-aware dependency storage format. The dependency sets for critical vertices are organized as a dependency table with hash-based indexing for fast access. In this table, each entry records a critical vertex together with the starting addresses and offset of its dependency set. For each critical vertex, its dependency set is partitioned into two subsets: *critical subset* and *non-critical subset*. The critical subset stores the critical vertices within this dependency set, whereas the non-critical subset contains vertices that belong to this dependency set and do not appear in other dependency sets. As shown in Fig. 8(a), A and D are critical vertices, their dependency sets share vertex E, and A is a parent dependency of D. To eliminate redundancy, GraphPro stores D as a referenced critical vertex in the *critical subset* of A and reuses the dependency set of D, thereby avoiding duplicate storage of E. During the *refine* stage, the complete dependency set of a critical vertex is obtained by reading its local dependency set and recursively fetching the dependency sets of referenced critical vertices.

3.3 Lightweight Dependency Maintaining

To maintain the dependency table accurately and efficiently under continuous graph topology mutations, GraphPro introduces an additional metadata field for each vertex to record its *proximal critical vertex*, defined as the critical vertex with the shortest topological distance to the target vertex within the same dependency set. If a vertex has no parent dependency or does not appear in the dependency set of any critical vertex, its *proximal critical vertex* is defined as itself. Consider Fig. 9(a) as an example, where vertices D and I are critical vertices, and the dependency set of I contains vertices C, G, and D, and E. In

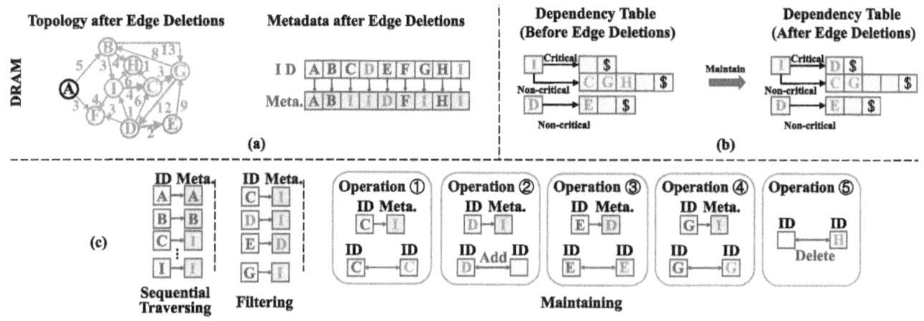

Fig. 9. A simplified example for illustrating lightweight dependency maintaining

this context, I is recorded as the proximal critical vertex of the vertices C, G, and D, while E's proximal critical vertex is D.

The metadata for every vertex is obtained during the *recompute stage* as follows. For a vertex v, let p_v denote its parent dependency and PCV_{p_v} indicates the metadata of p_v. If p_v is a critical vertex, the metadata of the vertex v is set to p_v. Otherwise, we futher determine whether PCV_{p_v} is not equal to p_v. If so, the metadata of the vertex v is set to PCV_{p_v}. If not, it is set to v.

During the *maintain stage*, GraphPro scans each vertex's metadata in parallel and updates the dependency table as follows. For each vertex v, GraphPro first determines whether its metadata PCV_v is different from v. If so, v is inserted into the dependency set of the vertex PCV_v. Otherwise, v does not appear in the dependency table. Instead of traversing the entire graph to reconstruct dependencies after graph updates, GraphPro leverages metadata to quickly capture dependency changes, thereby reducing dependency table maintaining overhead. Besides, our experimental results show that the dependency table maintaining overhead accounts for only 13%∼16% of the execution of the graph update kernel. This provides an opportunity to hide maintaining latency by overlapping the dependency table maintaining with graph updates.

4 Evaluation

4.1 Experimental Setup

GraphPro Settings. We implement GraphPro using a cycle-accurate microarchitecture simulator based on the Structural Simulation Toolkit (SST) [13] and model off-chip memory with DRAMSim2 [14], following prior works [12]. CACTI 7 [2] is used to estimate the area, power, and latency of on-chip buffers. Table 1 summarizes the detailed parameters of our experimental platform.

Benchmarks. Table 2 lists the five real-world graph datasets [7] used in the evaluation. Following prior works [12, 20], we first load 50% of the graph edges to obtain an initial fixed point. The remaining edges are then randomly streamed into model edge additions, while edge deletions are randomly sampled from the initially loaded graph. Edge additions and deletions are mixed in each update batch, with a default batch size of 100K edge updates. We evaluate four graph applications: *Breadth First Search* (BFS), *Single Source Shortest Path* (SSSP), *Single Source Widest Paths* (SSWP), and *Connected Components* (CC).

Table 1. Configurations of GraphPro

	Software Framework	GraphPro
Compute Unit	32× Intel Xeon Gold @2.0 Ghz	8× GraphPro Processor @ 1GHz
On-chip memory	48MB L3 Cache	64MB eDRAM @22nm 1GHz, 0.8ns latency
Off-chip Bandwidth	8× DDR4 25.6GB/s Channel	4× DDR3 17GB/s Channel

Table 2. Real-world graph datasets

Graph	Nodes	Edges	Description
com-Amazon (AZ) [7]	0.3M	0.9M	Amazon product network
com-DBLP (DL) [7]	0.3M	1.0M	DBLP collaboration network
Youtube (YT) [7]	1.1M	2.99M	Youtube online social network
Orkut (OR) [7]	4M	35M	Orkut online social network
LiveJournal (LJ) [7]	3.1M	117M	LiveJournal online social network

Baselines. We compare GraphPro with GraphFly [4], a state-of-the-art CPU-based streaming graph processing system, and two accelerators, JetStream [12] and TDGraph [20]. GraphFly runs on a high-end server whose configuration is listed in Table 1. For fair comparison, all accelerators use the same configuration with 8 processors and 64MB on-chip memory.

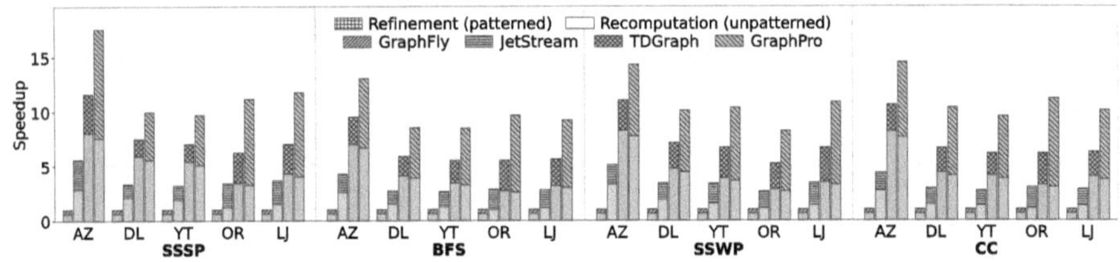

Fig. 10. Performance of GraphPro against GraphFly, JetStream, and TDGraph

4.2 Overall Evaluation

Performance. Figure 10 shows the performance comparison. The height of each bar represents the overall speedup over GraphFly. To better illustrate where the performance improvement comes from, we further break down the overall

Table 3. Area and Power Breakdown of GraphPro Components.

	#	Power (mW)			Area (mm^2)
		Static	Dynamic	Total	
Queue	64	117	23.1	8966.7	195
Scratchpad	8	0.36	1.22	12.7	0.22
NoC		106	6.16	112.38	6.72
Proc.Logic		-	-	1.96	0.73
Total		-	-	9094.02	202.97

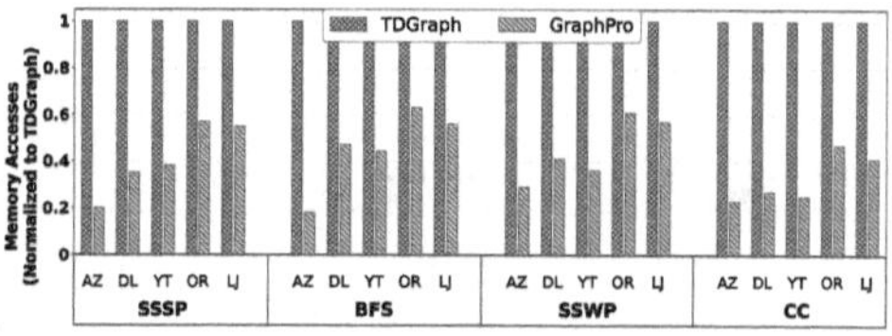

Fig. 11. The number of main memory accesses of GraphPro against TDGraph

speedup according to the two execution phases, i.e., refinement and recomputation. Overall, GraphPro achieves end-to-end speedups of 8.23× ∼17.52× (10.92× on average), 2.81×∼3.73× (3.23× on average), and 1.30×∼1.82× (1.54× on average) over GraphFly [4], JetStream [12], and TDGraph [20], respectively. The performance gain mainly stems from the refinement phase, where irregular memory accesses and sequential tag propagation are transformed into sequential and direct memory accesses. On average, compared to GraphFly, JetStream, and TDGraph, GraphPro reduces the execution time of the refinement phase by 18.15×, 3.86×, and 2.65×, respectively. We further evaluate the recomputation phase to understand whether our dependency maintaining scheme introduces noticeable overhead. Figure 10 shows that GraphPro achieves performance comparable to TDGraph in the recomputation phase, with only a 4.70%∼6.70% slowdown. This is because GraphPro incurs metadata computation and transfer overheads, which are negligible compared to the cost of accessing graph edges during recomputation.

Area and Power Evaluation. We use CACTI 7 [2] to estimate the power and area breakdown of GraphPro, as detailed in Table 3. The queue memory is modeled using 22nm ITRS-HP SRAM logic. The communication network consists of queues and a 16 × 16 NoC [11]. Based on the CACTI 7 configurations and the scaling methodology [19], the total area of GraphPro is about 203 mm^2 with a 28 nm technology.

Main Memory Accesses. Figure 11 compares GraphPro with TDGraph [20]. Compared with TDGraph, GraphPro reduces the total number of main memory accesses by 58.92%, 54.38%, 55.2%, and 67.4% on average for SSSP, BFS, SSWP, and CC, respectively. This reduction stems from GraphPro directly identifying affected vertices via the dependency table, rather than performing dependency-driven graph traversal as in TDGraph.

4.3 Sensitivity Study

Sensitivity to α. Figure 12 plots the execution time of the refinement phase of GraphPro on BFS with different α values. As α increases, the refinement time exhibits a decreasing trend, yet results in a higher storage cost. Meanwhile,

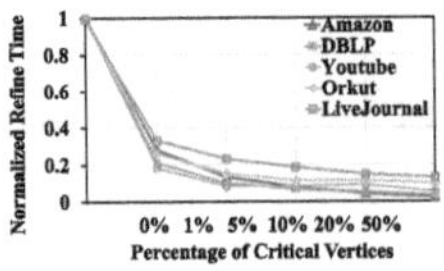

Fig. 12. Impact of the parameter α

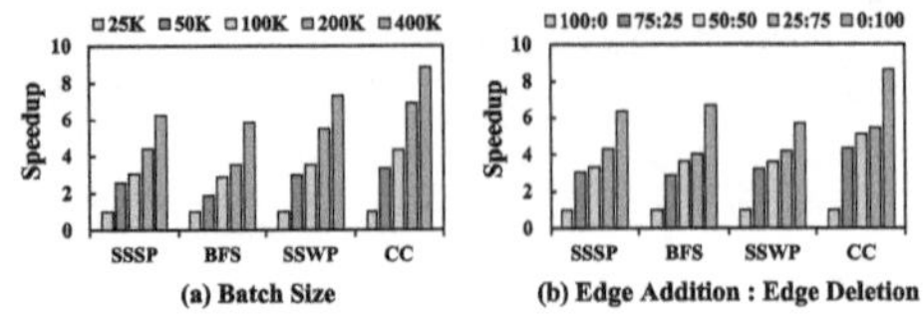

Fig. 13. The impact of (a) batch sizes and (b) batch compositions

the degradation rates of refinement time gradually decrease. Our experimental results show that α=5% achieves a good tradeoff between its benefit and overhead.

Sensitivity to Update Batch Size. Figure 13(a) shows the performance of GraphPro over *LJ* with different batch sizes. GraphPro achieves higher performance as the batch size increases. The reason is simple. Larger batch sizes lead to more affected vertices, making GraphPro's advantages more pronounced.

Sensitivity to Batch Compositions. Figure 13(b) evaluates the performance of GraphPro over *LJ* when the ratio of the number of edge additions to that of edge deletions varies. Since more edge deletions lead to more affected vertices, GraphPro exhibits better performance.

5 Conclusion

This paper proposes a hardware-accelerated incremental computation engine GraphPro to augment the many-core processor for efficient streaming graph processing. GraphPro incorporates two core optimizations: (1) a redundancy-aware dependency storage format that transforms affected vertex identification—associated with irregular memory accesses and sequential tag propagation—into sequential and direct memory accesses while minimizing additional storage overhead, and (2) a lightweight dependency maintaining scheme that leverages metadata to reduce maintaining overhead and overlaps dependency maintaining with graph update to further hide latency. Our evaluation demonstrates that GraphPro outperforms the state-of-the-art streaming graph processing system and hardware accelerators significantly.

Acknowledgments. This work is supported by the Fundamental and Interdisciplinary Disciplines Breakthrough Plan of the Ministry of Education of China (No. JYB2025XDXM103), National Natural Science Foundation of China (No. U25B2023), and Hubei Provincial Natural Science Foundation of China (No. 2026AFA002). The correspondence of this paper should be addressed to Qinggang Wang. Artificial intelligence tools, if used, were used only for language organization and figure/table polishing, and did not participate in the generation of the core ideas or technical content.

References

1. Afarin, M., Gao, C., Rahman, S.: Commongraph: Graph analytics on evolving data. In: Proceedings of ASPLOS, pp. 133–145 (2023)
2. Balasubramonian, R., Kahng, A.B., Muralimanohar, N., et al.: CACTI 7: New tools for interconnect exploration in innovative off-chip memories. ACM TACO (2017) **14**(2), 14:1–14:25 (2017)
3. Bindschaedler, L., Malicevic, J., Lepers, B.: Tesseract: Distributed, general graph pattern mining on evolving graphs. In: Proceedings of EuroSys, pp. 458–473 (2021)
4. Chen, D., Gui, C., Zhang, Y., et al.: Graphfly: Efficient asynchronous streaming graphs processing via dependency-flow. In: Proceedings of SC. pp. 45:1–45:14 (2022)
5. Cheng, R., Hong, J., Kyrola, A.: Kineograph: taking the pulse of a fast-changing and connected world. In: Proceedings of EuroSys, pp. 85–98 (2012)
6. Feng, G., Ma, Z., Li, D.: Risgraph: A real-time streaming system for evolving graphs to support sub-millisecond per-update analysis at millions ops/s. In: Proceedings of SIGMOD, pp. 513–527 (2021)
7. Leskovec, J., Krevl, A.: Snap datasets: Stanford large network dataset collection (2014). http://snap.stanford.edu/data/index.html
8. Mariappan, M., Vora, K.: Graphbolt: Dependency-driven synchronous processing of streaming graphs. In: Proceedings of EuroSys, pp. 25:1–25:16 (2019)
9. Murray, D.G., McSherry, F., Isaacs, R., et al.: Naiad: A timely dataflow system. In: Proceedings of SOSP, pp. 439–455 (2013)
10. Prakash, C., Lee, J., Turner, Y.: Pga: Using graphs to express and automatically reconcile network policies. In: Proceedings of SIGCOMM, pp. 29–42 (2015)
11. Rahman, S., Abu-Ghazaleh, N.B., Gupta, R.: Graphpulse: An event-driven hardware accelerator for asynchronous graph processing. In: Proceedings of MICRO, pp. 908–921 (2020)
12. Rahman, S., Afarin, M., Abu-Ghazaleh, N.B.: Jetstream: Graph analytics on streaming data with event-driven hardware accelerator. In: Proceedings of MICRO, pp. 1091–1105 (2021)
13. Rodrigues, A.F., Hemmert, K.S., Barrett, B.W., et al.: The structural simulation toolkit. PER 2011 **38**(4), 37–42 (2011)
14. Rosenfeld, P., Cooper-Balis, E., Jacob, B.: Dramsim2: A cycle accurate memory system simulator. CAL **10**(1), 16–19 (2011)
15. Shi, X., Cui, B., Shao, Y.: Tornado: A system for real-time iterative analysis over evolving data. In: Proceedings of SIGMOD, pp. 417–430 (2016)
16. Vora, K., Gupta, R., Xu, G.: Kickstarter: Fast and accurate computations on streaming graphs via trimmed approximations. In: Proceedings of ASPLOS, pp. 237–251 (2017)
17. Wang, P., Li, C., Wang, J., et al.: Skywalker: Efficient alias-method-based graph sampling and random walk on gpus. In: Proceedings of PACT, pp. 304–317 (2021)
18. Wang, Q., Zheng, L., Huang, Y.: Grasu: A fast graph update library for fpga-based dynamic graph processing. In: Proceedings of FPGA, pp. 149–159 (2021)
19. Yan, M., Hu, X., Li, S.: Alleviating irregularity in graph analytics acceleration: a hardware/software co-design approach. In: Proceedings of MICRO, pp. 615–628 (2019)
20. Zhao, J., Yang, Y., Zhang, Y.: Tdgraph: a topology-driven accelerator for high-performance streaming graph processing. In: Proceedings of ISCA, pp. 116–129 (2022)

Secure Systems

Pitfall: Uncovering and Exploiting the Store Forwarding Predictor on Intel CPUs

Chang Liu[1], Xin Zhang[2(✉)], Dapeng Ju[1], Yongqiang Lyu[1], and Dongsheng Wang[1]

[1] Tsinghua University, Beijing, China
chang-li17@tsinghua.org.cn, {judapeng,luyq,wds}@tsinghua.edu.cn
[2] Shandong University, Qingdao, China
zhangxin00sdu@gmail.com

Abstract. To bridge the widening gap between CPU execution speed and memory access latency, modern CPUs incorporate a variety of predictors in the memory subsystem to enable high-accuracy data-flow speculation. While these predictors improve performance, they also introduce new security risks.

In this paper, we identify a Store Forwarding Predictor (SFP) in recent Intel desktop and server CPUs. The SFP predicts whether a store can forward its data to a dependent load before the load address becomes available, thereby increasing the parallelism of loads and subsequent data-dependent instructions.

To evaluate the security implications of the SFP, we first reverse-engineer its design, including its state machine, indexing mechanism, and flushing behavior. Based on this analysis, we propose Pitfall, the first side-channel attack exploiting the Intel SFP. Pitfall-v1 exploits SFP mispredictions to trigger in-place transient execution attacks. Pitfall-v2 exploits state sharing across different store-load pairs in the SFP to enable stealthier out-of-place transient execution attacks. Pitfall-v3 leverages SFP state flushing during context switches to detect interrupts, achieving up to 97.6% top-5 accuracy in inferring website visits in Google Chrome. The source code of Pitfall is available at https://github.com/cliu2025/pitfall.

Keywords: Store Forwarding Predictor · Reverse Engineering · CPU Security · Microarchitectural Vulnerability · Side-channel Attack

1 Introduction

To improve performance, modern CPUs employ speculative execution to increase instruction-level parallelism. Beyond the well-known control-flow speculation based on branch predictors, modern CPUs further introduce data-flow speculation in the backend to accelerate memory operations. For example, CPUs from

L. Eeckhout et al. (Eds.): APPT 2026, LNCS 16693, pp. 467–482, 2027.
https://doi.org/10.1007/978-981-92-4805-6_31

Intel, AMD, and Arm deploy Memory Dependence Predictors (MDPs) to predict data dependencies between loads and stores whose addresses are not yet resolved [11–14]. In addition, Apple CPUs introduce a Load Address Predictor (LAP) [8] and a Load Value Predictor (LVP) [7], which predict the load address or value directly when the load address is unavailable.

However, aggressive data-flow speculation also introduces significant security risks. Incorrect speculation in the MDP, LAP, and LVP can be exploited to construct transient execution attacks [7,8,13]. Moreover, the MDP state updates can be used to build cross-domain side-channel attacks [11]. The security implications of these predictors have been widely studied.

Nevertheless, beyond the MDP, LAP, and LVP, modern CPUs may include additional predictors to support more advanced data-flow speculation. For example, Mascot [15] extends the MDP by further predicting whether a store can directly forward its data to a load, effectively combining the function of LVP. In this paper, we refer to such predictors as Store Forwarding Predictors (SFPs).

Existing work on SFPs remains limited. Prior studies only identify their presence on AMD Zen 3 CPUs [13]. For other architectures, whether an SFP is deployed remains unclear. This leads to the following questions:

Is an SFP implemented in CPUs beyond AMD Zen 3? If so, do these SFP designs introduce vulnerabilities?

This paper answers the above questions by identifying and characterizing the SFP on recent Intel CPUs. By constructing microbenchmarks, we identify an SFP, whose design remains undocumented, on seven Intel 11th-generation and later Core CPUs, as well as one Xeon CPU. We further characterize the activation behavior of the SFP and its cross-address state sharing property. We also analyze the security properties of the SFP and find that its state is flushed during context switches, which provides strong inter-process isolation.

Based on these findings, we identify three vulnerabilities in the Intel SFP. First, misprediction of the SFP will cause speculative execution, enabling a new variant of transient execution attacks. Second, the SFP allows out-of-place training within the same process. Third, the flush behavior of the SFP during context switches provides a deterministic signal indicating whether a process has been interrupted, which can be leveraged to build an interrupt side-channel attack [21,23,24].

To exploit these vulnerabilities, we propose Pitfall, the first side-channel attack that exploits the Intel SFP. Pitfall includes three variants: Pitfall-v1, which performs an in-place transient execution attack; Pitfall-v2, which performs an out-of-place transient execution attack; and Pitfall-v3, which implements an interrupt side channel. On P-cores, Pitfall-v1 and Pitfall-v2 achieve near-100% accuracy and a throughput above 2600 Bps. Pitfall-v3 reaches a top-5 accuracy of up to 96.6% in a website fingerprinting attack over 100 webpages. Finally, we discuss possible defenses against Pitfall and evaluate the performance overhead of disabling the SFP, which can be as high as 12.4%.

In summary, this paper makes the following contributions:

- We identify the existence of an SFP on seven Intel CPUs for the first time.

- We conduct an in-depth analysis of the Intel SFP, characterizing its activation conditions, state sharing, and flush behavior during context switches.
- We propose Pitfall, the first side-channel attack that exploits the Intel SFP. We implement three variants of Pitfall and evaluate their performance. We also discuss the defenses and analyze the performance overhead of disabling the SFP.

2 Background and Related Work

2.1 Speculative Execution of Load Instructions

Speculative execution is a common technique used on modern CPUs to improve performance. Some CPUs employ load speculation before the load address is ready, or when there exist preceding stores with unresolved addresses [7,8,12,13]. For example, speculative store forwarding predicts whether a store can directly forward its data to a load when either the store or load address is not ready.

Modern CPUs typically rely on dedicated predictors to support these mechanisms. In particular, the SFP predicts whether speculative store forwarding should be performed [15]. The SFP usually records store-load pairs that access the same address (i.e., they are dependent), and speculatively forwards the store data when the same pair is executed again. As a result, the SFP is typically indexed by the instruction addresses (i.e., Program Counters, PCs) of the store and load. Similar to branch predictors, the SFP maintains a counter to represent prediction confidence, and enables speculative forwarding only after sufficient training [15]. In this paper, we analyze both the indexing and the activation conditions of the SFP on recent Intel CPUs.

2.2 Transient Execution Attacks

Transient execution attacks are a class of side-channel attacks that exploit misspeculation and microarchitectural behaviors. Speculatively executed instructions are not committed, and therefore do not modify architectural state such as registers or memory. However, they leave observable traces in the microarchitectural state. For example, a load executed speculatively may still issue a memory request and bring data into the cache. As a result, a common attack pattern is to trigger misspeculation in victim code, perform out-of-bounds memory accesses using speculative instructions, and use a cache side channel to record the accessed data [2].

Transient execution attacks that rely on misprediction can be categorized into *in-place* and *out-of-place* variants. In an in-place attack, both predictor training and misprediction are triggered using the same instruction at the same address. In contrast, an out-of-place attack allows training and misprediction to occur at different addresses. Out-of-place attacks significantly reduce the number of required victim invocations, which improves stealth and helps bypass defenses based on call frequency or monitoring [3,9]. In this paper, we show that the SFP on Intel CPUs supports both in-place and out-of-place attacks.

3 Characterization and Security Analysis of the Intel SFP

In this section, we first identify the SFP on Intel CPUs in Sect. 3.1. We then characterize the Intel SFP in Sect. 3.2, including its activation conditions and cross-address sharing. We analyze its security implications in Sect. 3.3. All experiments are conducted on the ten Intel CPUs listed in Table 1.

3.1 SFP Identification

```
stld_pc_1:
.rep 30                      ┬
      imul $1, %rsi          │ Delay %rsi
.endr                        ┴
mov $rcx, (%rdi)             ⇨ Store
mov (%rsi), %rax             ⇨ Load
.rep 30                      ┬
      imul $1, %rax          │ Expand timing
.endr                        ┴ difference
ret
```

(a) Microbenchmark

```
int A[9];
for(int i = 0, i < 10000; ++ i)
      stld_pc_2(&A[0], &A[8]);  // Disable MDP
for(int i = 0, i < 100; ++ i)
      stld_pc_1(&A[0], &A[0]);  // Train SFP
for(int i = 0, i < 100; ++ i) {
      size_t t1 = get_time();
      stld_pc_2(&A[0], &A[0]);  // Probe SFP
      size_t t2 = get_time() - t1;
      record_time(t2); }
```

(b) Usage of the microbenchmarks

Fig. 1. Microbenchmarks used for SFP characterization.

We adapt prior microbenchmark designs [13] to enable the analysis of the SFP, as shown in Fig. 1a. To trigger the SFP, we introduce latency in load address generation by inserting 30 multiplication instructions. Since the load address is not ready, the MDP is not activated [11]. In contrast, the store data is ready. Therefore, if the SFP is present, the store data may be forwarded to the load speculatively, allowing the subsequent 30 multiplications to execute earlier. While delaying the store address, as done in [13], can also activate the SFP, it simultaneously triggers the MDP, which greatly complicates the analysis. Therefore, we specifically choose to delay the load address to characterize the SFP.

Depending on whether the SFP prediction is triggered and whether the prediction is correct, the microbenchmark exhibits three possible execution times. First, if the SFP is absent or predicts independence, the load is stalled, leading to a longer execution time T_1. Second, if the SFP predicts dependence and the prediction is correct, forwarding is triggered, resulting in the shortest execution time T_2. Finally, if the SFP predicts dependence but is incorrect, the CPU rolls back and re-executes the load, leading to the longest execution time T_3.

To identify the existence of the SFP, we aim to distinguish between T_1 and T_2. Specifically, we first set the store and load to different addresses and execute the microbenchmark 50 times. We then set the store and load to the same address and execute another 50 runs. If an SFP exists, the first 50 executions train the

SFP toward independence, resulting in execution time T_1. In the following 50 executions, the data dependence causes the SFP to adjust its prediction at some point, leading to a transition in execution time from T_1 to T_2.

To mitigate any potential effects from LVP and LAP in case they exist on the target CPUs, we randomize all load addresses and values, as these predictors could otherwise be triggered during periods of unresolved load addresses.

We conduct the above experiment on ten Intel CPUs, and the results are shown in Fig. 2. The older CPUs such as `i9` and `i10` show no step change in execution time, indicating that the SFP is not present. In contrast, on 11th-generation and later Core and Xeon CPUs, a clear transition in execution time appears after approximately ten executions of dependent store-load pairs. This behavior indicates that the SFP is deployed on these CPUs.

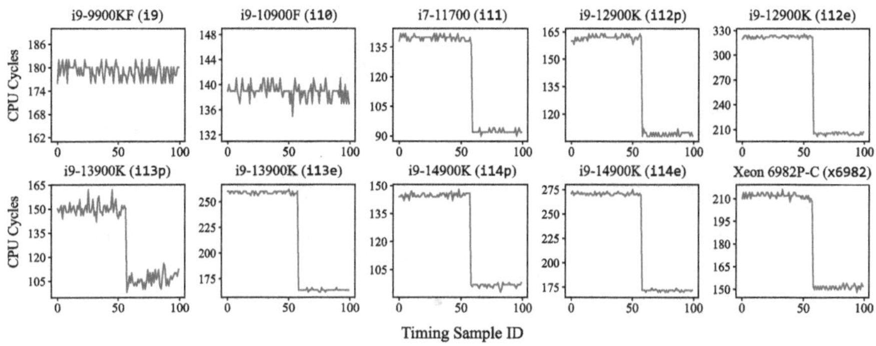

Fig. 2. Existence test of the SFP across ten Intel CPUs.

3.2 SFP Characterization

In Sect. 3.1, we observe that the activation threshold of the SFP is typically below 10 executions. We further validate this observation and find that at most eight executions of dependent store-load pairs are sufficient to activate the SFP. Based on this result, we infer that the Intel SFP uses a 3-bit saturating counter to track prediction confidence. When a dependent store-load pair is observed for the first time, the counter is initialized to zero. Each subsequent dependent execution increments the counter, and once the counter reaches saturation, the predictor outputs a dependence prediction.

We further extend the microbenchmark to study the cross-address sharing of the SFP, as shown in Fig. 1b. We use two microbenchmarks with identical instruction sequences, but vary the PCs of the stores and loads. We then align several least significant bits (LSBs) of the store and load PCs and observe whether the SFP state is shared. We conduct experiments on eight CPUs that deploy an SFP, as shown in Fig. 3. The results indicate that when the 16 LSBs of the load PC are aligned, the SFP prediction is consistently triggered. When the 16 LSBs of the store PC are aligned, the SFP prediction is also consistently triggered on some Efficiency Cores (E-cores). These observations suggest that although the SFP is indexed by both store and load PCs, it only uses their lower bits for indexing. As a result, ensuring that the lower 16 bits of the store and load PCs match is sufficient to make two store-load pairs at different addresses share the same SFP entry on both Performance Cores (P-cores) and E-cores.

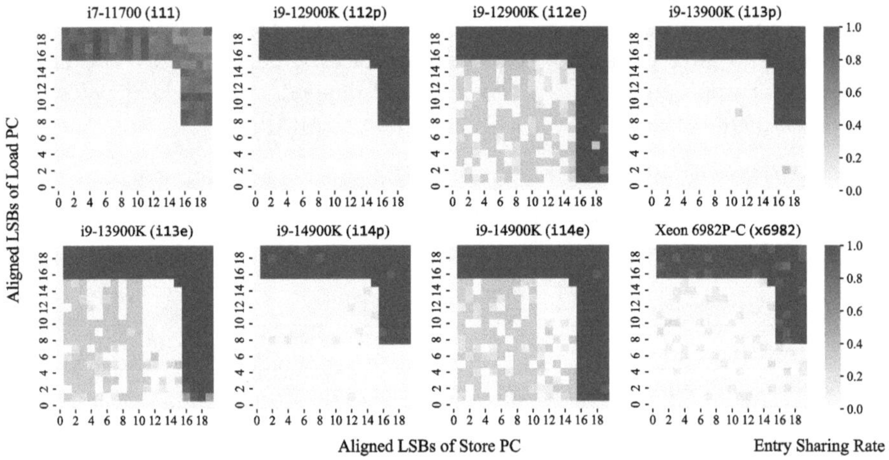

Fig. 3. Indexing test of the SFP across eight Intel CPUs.

3.3 SFP Security Analysis

We finally analyze the isolation of the SFP across different security domains. We first run identical store-load pairs at the same instruction addresses in two processes and observe that the prediction state is not shared, regardless of whether the processes execute on the same core. In particular, when the two processes run on the same core, each context switch resets the SFP state. This result indicates that the Intel SFP is private to each core and enforces inter-process isolation.

To further examine when the SFP state is reset, we trigger a system call after training the SFP and probe its state in kernel space. We observe that the SFP state is already cleared. This suggests that the SFP is flushed during context switches caused by privilege-level transitions. Although this mechanism prevents cross-process training, it also introduces a side effect: a process can infer whether a context switch has occurred by observing changes in the SFP state. This behavior enables an interrupt side-channel attack. In Sect. 4.4, we exploit this mechanism to construct such an attack.

Table 1 summarizes our identification and analysis of the SFP. We identify the SFP on eight recent Intel CPUs and characterize its activation conditions, cross-address sharing, and flush behavior during context switches.

Table 1. Summary of SFP characterization across ten Intel CPUs

Device*		Design Characteristics			Isolation	
CPU	OS	Existence	Store PC**	Load PC	Intra-process	Inter-process
`i9`	ubuntu 22.04	✗	–	–	–	–
`i10`	ubuntu 20.04	✗	–	–	–	–
`i11`	ubuntu 22.04	✔	16	16	✔	✗
`i12e`	ubuntu 22.04	✔	16	16	✔	✗
`i12p`	ubuntu 22.04	✔	16	16	✔	✗
`i13e`	ubuntu 20.04	✔	16	16	✔	✗
`i13p`	ubuntu 20.04	✔	16	16	✔	✗
`i14e`	ubuntu 22.04	✔	16	16	✔	✗
`i14p`	ubuntu 22.04	✔	16	16	✔	✗
`x6982`	ubuntu 24.04	✔	16	16	✔	✗

* `i9`: Intel Core i9-9900KF. `i10`: Intel Core i9-10900F. `i11`: Intel Core i11-11700. `i12e`/`i12p`: Intel Core i9-12900K efficiency/performance cores. `i13e`/`i13p`: Intel Core i9-13900K efficiency/performance cores. `i14e`/`i14p`: Intel Core i9-14900K efficiency/performance cores. `x6982`: Intel Xeon 6982P-C.

** Number of aligned least significant bits of store PC to ensure an SFP entry sharing.

4 Pitfall: Exploiting the Intel SFP to Leak Secrets

In this section, based on the characterization and security analysis of the SFP, we propose Pitfall, the first side-channel attack that exploits the Intel SFP to leak secrets from user space. The workflows of the three variants of Pitfall are shown in Fig. 4. In Sect. 4.2, we present Pitfall-v1, an in-place transient execution attack that exploits the misprediction of the SFP. Next, in Sect. 4.3, we present Pitfall-v2, an out-of-place transient execution attack based on entry sharing of the SFP among different instruction PCs. This method significantly reduces the number of victim function invocations. Finally, in Sect. 4.4, we present Pitfall-v3, which leverages the flush behavior of the SFP during context switches to launch an interrupt side-channel attack.

4.1 Threat Model

In this work, we adopt a common local user-space threat model. We assume that the attacker has user-level privileges, can execute unprivileged code, and uses `rdtsc` for fine-grained timing.

For transient execution attacks, including Pitfall-v1 and Pitfall-v2, we assume the attacker and the victim reside within the same process. This aligns with standard threat models established in prior literature [7,8,13,24], where the attacker cannot directly access secrets protected by sandboxing or similar isolation mechanisms. Under this model, the attacker either possesses the capability to inject malicious code or relies on exploitable gadgets already present in the victim's code. Discovering such gadgets within victim software is an orthogonal research challenge [10,11,16], and thus we defer systematic gadget discovery to future work. By exploiting transient execution, the attacker can speculatively leak data from arbitrary addresses within the victim's domain, enabling cross-domain data leakage in web browsers (e.g., leveraging JIT compilation to exfiltrate data from one webpage to another [7,8,13]).

For Pitfall-v3, we adopt a cross-process/cross-core threat model widely used in prior website fingerprinting works [4,21,24]. Under this model, the attacker and the victim execute in separate processes or even on different cores, and the victim uses a stock, unmodified web browser. The attacker probes the SFP to observe the interrupts triggered by the victim process, and then infers which webpage the victim is accessing.

4.2 Pitfall-V1: In-Place Transient Execution Attack

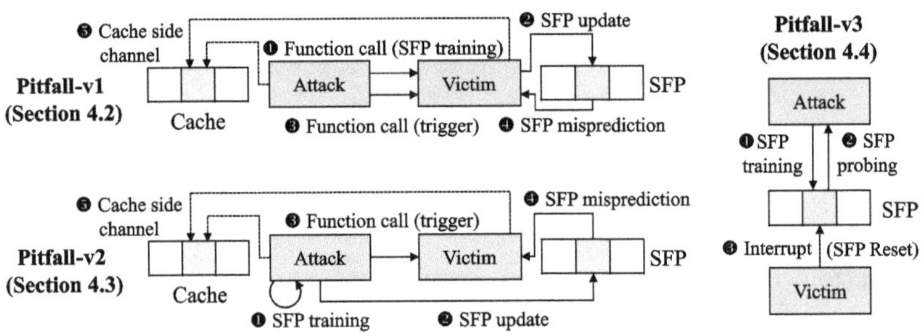

Fig. 4. Attack workflows of Pitfall-v1, Pitfall-v2, and Pitfall-v3.

```c
uint8_t array1[16];
uint64_t array2[256 * 512];
void victim_function(int st_idx, int fwd_val) {
    array2[st_idx * 512] = fwd_val; // store
    uint64_t v = array2[0]; // Load-1
    uint8_t  s = array1[v]; // Load-2
    uint64_t temp;
    temp = array2[s * 512]; // Load-3
    return;
}
```

(a) Victim code in C

```
// rdi: &st_idx, r8: array1, r9: array2
...
mov    (%rdi),%rax
shl    $0xc,%rax
add    %r9,%rax                                    Forwarding
mov    %rsi,(%rax)                // store
mov    (%r9),%rdx                 // Load-1
movzbq (%r8,%rdx,1),%rdx          // Load-2
shl    $0xc,%rdx
mov    (%r9,%rdx,1),%rax          // Load-3
```

(b) Victim code in Assembly

Fig. 5. Victim code in C and Assembly used in Pitfall-v1 and Pitfall-v2.

Pitfall-v1 exploits mispredictions in the SFP to perform a transient execution attack. As shown in Fig. 4, the attacker first calls a victim function in the victim address space (❶). This function contains a store-load pair with address latency. The attacker sets the store and load to the same address and repeatedly executes the victim function to train the SFP toward a dependence prediction (❷). Next, the attacker calls the victim function again (❸), but sets the store and load to different addresses, which triggers a misprediction in the SFP (❹). Under the misprediction, the store wrongly forwards its data to the load. Similar to Spectre-v1, the attacker uses the mispredicted load value to perform an out-of-bounds memory access, which leaks a secret byte from the victim. The attacker then leverages a cache side channel to record and recover the secret byte (❺).

Victim Function. The victim function required in Pitfall-v1 is shown in Fig. 5. The data dependence between the store and load-1 is controlled by `st_idx`. During the training phase, the attacker sets `st_idx` to 0, so the store and load-1 access the same address and are dependent. At the same time, the attacker controls `fwd_val` to ensure that load-1 does not perform an out-of-bounds access. Next, the attacker flushes `st_idx` to introduce latency in store address generation. The attacker repeats the execution eight times to train the SFP to predict dependence and enable speculative forwarding.

During the attack phase, the attacker updates `st_idx` to 10. Under incorrect forwarding by the SFP, `fwd_val` is wrongly forwarded to `v`. The attacker carefully chooses `fwd_val` so that `array1[v]` triggers an out-of-bounds access and retrieves the secret byte `s`. Finally, the attacker uses load-3 to encode `s` into the cache state. In practice, we repeat the attack 100 times to reduce noise. We also introduce an early-stop mechanism. Once the confidence for a leaked byte exceeds a threshold, the attack terminates early.

It is worth noting that delaying either the store or the load can successfully activate the SFP. In Fig. 5, we show the store-delayed variant to provide a clearer illustration of the respective roles played by the three loads during the attack sequence. In a practical attack scenario, delaying the execution of the first load yields an identical effect.

Evaluation. We evaluate the byte recovery accuracy for different leakage lengths on CPUs summarized in Table 1 that support the SFP. The results are illustrated in Fig. 6. On the P-cores such as `i11`, `x6982`, `i12p` and others, the leakage accuracy remains close to 100%.

In contrast, on the E-cores of `i12e`, `i13e`, and `i14e`, the attack only recovers the earliest bytes, typically no more than 10 bytes. This behavior suggests the presence of a watchdog on E-cores: frequent SFP mispredictions temporarily disable the SFP. Further analysis shows that this watchdog is not affected by context switches, but it resets after a certain period. As a result, leaking long secrets on E-cores becomes time-consuming. Therefore, in the following evaluation, we focus only on P-core performance.

We further increase the length and randomness of the secret data and evaluate Pitfall-v1 on P-cores. The results are shown in Table 2. On P-cores, Pitfall-v1 achieves an accuracy above 99%. In addition, due to the early-stop mechanism, the leakage throughput reaches at least 2600 Bps.

4.3 Pitfall-V2: Out-of-Place Transient Execution Attack

Pitfall-v2 improves upon Pitfall-v1 by exploiting the out-of-place SFP training. Frequent calls of the victim function can be detected by hardware performance

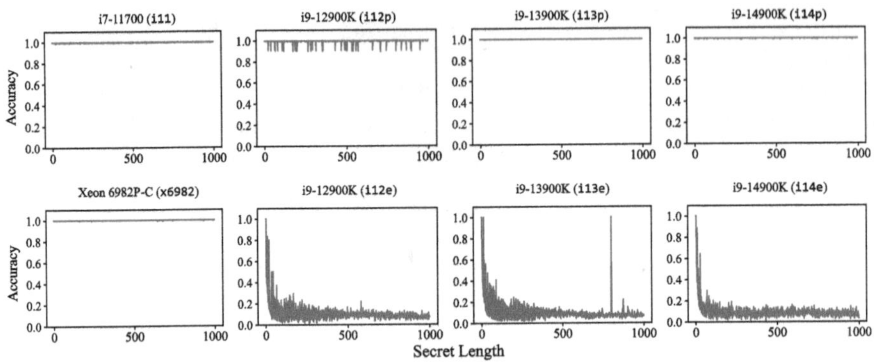

Fig. 6. Accuracy of Pitfall-v1 under different secret lengths.

Table 2. Evaluation of Pitfall-v1 and Pitfall-v2 across five CPUs

CPU	Pitfall-v1			Pitfall-v2		
	Accuracy	Speed/Bps	Function Call*	Accuracy	Speed/Bps	Function Call
`i11`	1.00	6194.82	108.14	1.00	645.77	38.38
`i12p`	1.00	3227.50	93.80	1.00	3596.86	3.25
`i13p`	1.00	3547.86	83.27	1.00	3575.69	3.35
`i14p`	1.00	3513.85	85.35	1.00	3515.25	3.20
`x6982`	1.00	2630.29	82.05	1.00	2591.55	3.14

* Number of victim function calls to leak one byte.

counters or software sampling interfaces [9], which may expose the presence of the attack. To improve stealth, as shown in Fig. 4, Pitfall-v2 replaces the first two steps of the attack. Specifically, it exploits the fact that SFP entries can be shared. The attacker constructs a store-load pair in their own address space that maps to the same SFP entry as the victim (❷), and uses this pair for training (❸). In our implementation, we align the 16 LSBs of the attacker's store and load with the store (line 6) and load (line 7) in Fig. 5b, respectively.

Evaluation. The performance of Pitfall-v2 on P-cores is shown in Table 2. On all P-cores except `i11`, Pitfall-v2 achieves performance comparable to Pitfall-v1, while reducing the number of victim function invocations by more than 20×. On the `i11`, however, Pitfall-v2 shows lower performance. This is because the attacker's training affects the cache state, which increases noise in the cache side channel and prevents the early-stop mechanism from taking effect promptly.

4.4 Pitfall-V3: Website Fingerprinting Attack

In this section, we apply Pitfall-v3 to mount a representative interrupt side-channel attack, i.e., website fingerprinting. Our key insight is that, when accessing a website, distinctive network packets will be sent and received, generating distinctive network interrupts. A co-located attacker can use Pitfall-v3 to capture these temporal patterns and use a machine learning (ML) classifier to associate an observed interrupt trace with the corresponding website, resulting in an ML-based side-channel attack [4,6,22–24].

Attack Design. Pitfall-v3 exploits the following two key properties. First, the SFP state is completely flushed upon context switches. As illustrated in Fig. 7, the attacker deploys an interrupt-probing process that repeatedly executes a loop at fixed intervals (e.g., every 1 s). This loop comprises three sequential phases: *prime*, *wait*, and *probe*. During the *prime* phase, the attacker executes a sufficient number of dependent store-load pairs to fully train a specific entry within the SFP prediction table, saturating its internal counter to 7. In the *wait* phase, the attacker remains quiescent by executing a small sequence of `nops`. Finally, in the *probe* phase, the attacker evaluates the current SFP state. If the SFP prediction table has been flushed, the attacker can reliably infer that an interrupt-induced context switch transpired on the resident core during the preceding *wait* phase.

Second, hardware interrupts in Linux systems are inherently distributed across multiple cores [24]. Consequently, when a browser triggers an interrupt during webpage rendering or complex JavaScript execution, this interrupt may be routed to a core hosting the attacker's interrupt-probing process. In the current attack setup, the probing process is pinned to a single core. While this configuration may omit several cross-core interrupts, experimental results demonstrate that it remains sufficient for robust website fingerprinting. The performance of this side channel can be further improved by deploying concurrent interrupt-probing threads across all available CPU cores.

Our attack consists of an offline phase and an online phase. In the offline phase, the attacker collects interrupt traces generated during website loading and uses them to train a prediction model. In the online phase, the trained model takes a newly observed interrupt trace as input and outputs the most likely website visited. In our evaluation, we directly feed raw Pitfall-v3 traces into a 32-unit LSTM model, following Cook et al. [4]. We perform 10-fold partitioning over the collected traces, reserving one fold for evaluation and splitting the remaining nine folds into a training set and a validation set.

```c
for(int i = 0; i < sample_size; ++ i) {
    while(time_interval_less_than_one_second()) { // sample the number of interrupts within 1s
        sfp_init_to_7(); // Initialize one of the SFP prediction table entries to 7
        wait(); // wait for a few microseconds, during which a context switch may happen
        int sfp_counter_val = sfp_probe(); // Probe the SFP state
        if (sfp_counter_val < 7) { // Detect a flush of SFP state
            number_of_context_switches += 1;
        }
    }
}
```

Fig. 7. C implementation of the Pitfall-v3 attack

Experimental Setup. We evaluate website fingerprinting in both closed-world and open-world settings. In the closed-world case, the attacker is assumed to have prior knowledge of the entire set of websites that the victim may access. The inference task is then to identify which one of 100 candidate websites was visited. Exactly aligned with prior work [4,20], we select the top 100 websites from Alexa [1] and collect 100 interrupt traces for each website. Although the Alexa Top-100 list is no longer maintained, the websites used in our evaluation remain active and accessible. This website set has also been used in recent website fingerprinting studies [5,6,20], making our setup comparable to prior work.

In the open-world case, we augment the monitored set with a single class representing websites outside the top 100. For this purpose, we collect one trace from each of 4000 additional websites drawn from the Alexa Top 1 Million list, excluding the monitored websites. This configuration follows the standard setup used in prior website fingerprinting work [4,17,20]. We acknowledge that the resulting class imbalance may affect aggregate metrics. However, a systematic analysis of this effect is broadly relevant to open-world website fingerprinting and side-channel evaluations, rather than being specific to Pitfall. We therefore leave such an analysis to future work.

Experimental Results. Figure 8 reports confusion matrices of our attack. Each cell indicates the probability that a trace generated by a website on the y-axis is classified as the website on the x-axis. The pronounced diagonal pattern demonstrates the high classification accuracy of our attack. To evaluate end-to-end attack performance, we use top-n accuracy as the evaluation metric, which measures whether the ground-truth website appears among the n candidate websites predicted by the classifier. In the closed-world setting, random guessing over 100 candidate websites yields a top-1 accuracy of only 1%. In contrast, our attack achieves a top-1 accuracy of 78.9% and a top-5 accuracy of 96.6%. In the open-world setting, the attack achieves a top-1 accuracy of 84.5% and a top-5 accuracy of 97.6%. The higher accuracy in the open-world setting is mainly due to the classifier's strong ability to distinguish the non-monitored class from the monitored top-100 websites.

5 Mitigation

The straightforward defense against Pitfall is to disable the SFP. Due to Spectre attacks, Intel introduces Speculative Store Bypass Disable (SSBD) to disable load speculation [13], which also disables the SFP. When SSBD is enabled, the SFP neither performs prediction nor exposes its state through timing. However, enabling SSBD leads to noticeable performance degradation. We evaluate the performance overhead of SSBD on four processors (`i11`, `i12p`, `i13p`, and `i14p`) using SPEC 2017. The results are shown in Table 3. In the `intspeed` benchmark, SSBD introduces an overhead ranging from 6.1% to 12.4%.

Beyond disabling the SFP through SSBD, defenses against Pitfall-v1 and Pitfall-v2 can also rely on detecting and hardening exploitable code patterns. For example, a compiler can identify store-load pairs that may trigger the

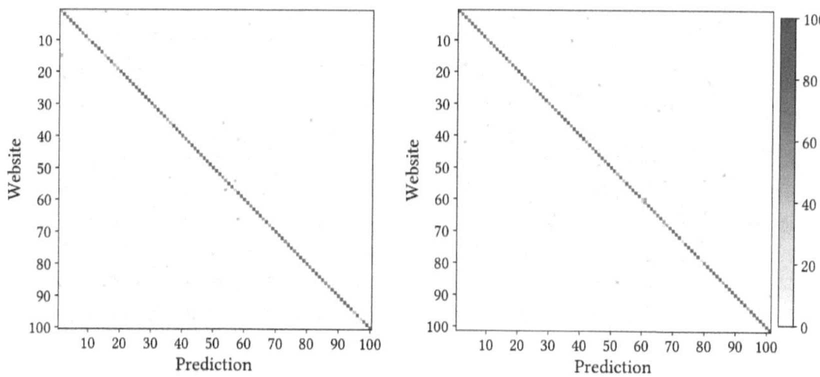

(a) Closed-world Setting (b) Open-world Setting

Fig. 8. Confusion matrices of our website fingerprinting attack using Pitfall-v3.

SFP [10,11] and are potentially exploitable, and then insert fences or enforce explicit data dependencies to prevent speculative execution on those loads. However, such approaches do not mitigate Pitfall-v3, which exploits the flush behavior of the SFP during context switches. To defend against Pitfall-v3, the security design of the SFP must be improved. For example, partitioning or index randomization can be applied to enforce isolation across security domains. These solutions, however, require hardware modifications, making them difficult to deploy immediately.

Table 3. Performance overhead of SSBD on four Intel CPUs

Configuration	`i11`	`i12p`	`i13p`	`i14p`
SSBD Off*	8.26	10.9	11.8	12.9
SSBD On**	7.78	10.1	10.5	11.8
Overhead	6.1%	7.9%	12.4%	9.3%

* Geometric mean score of SPEC **`SPECspeed 2017 Integer`** for SSBD Off configurations.

** Geometric mean score of SPEC **`SPECspeed 2017 Integer`** for SSBD On configurations.

6 Future Work

In this paper, we confirm the existence of the SFP on Intel CPUs for the first time, characterize its functional properties, and demonstrate three distinct variants of exploitation. Beyond these findings, several points around the SFP remain to be explored in future research.

First, a more detailed and finer-grained reverse-engineering of the SFP can be conducted to unveil its structure. Specifically, future work could investigate the total capacity of the SFP prediction table, its associativity, and its index mapping and replacement policies. Characterizing these internal design parameters would provide deeper insights into expanding the SFP attack surface or enhancing the efficiency of existing exploits.

Second, the SFP can be exploited to construct a broader range of practical end-to-end attacks, such as executing cross-domain data leakage within web browsers, and performing transient execution attacks against the Linux kernel. For kernel-level exploitation, static or symbolic analysis techniques need to be employed to systematically search for exploitable gadgets within the kernel space [18]. Furthermore, since the SFP is automatically flushed upon context switches, specialized techniques must be devised to ensure that both the predictor training and the speculative execution phases are contained entirely within the kernel context [19].

Finally, the study of SFPs can be generalized to other CPU architectures, such as AMD and Arm. To achieve this, researchers could build upon the concepts of automated benchmarking frameworks like SSBench [12] to develop a cross-architecture SFP automated analysis tool, which automatically synthesizes microbenchmarks to detect and characterize SFP parameters across diverse hardware platforms.

7 Conclusion

In this work, we identify the presence of the SFP on Intel CPUs for the first time, and analyze its activation conditions, cross-address sharing behavior, and security properties. Based on this analysis, we propose Pitfall, the first side-channel attack that exploits the SFP. Pitfall-v1 and Pitfall-v2 achieve near 100% accuracy with a throughput exceeding 2600 Bps. Pitfall-v3 achieves up to 96.6% top-5 accuracy in a website fingerprinting attack over 100 webpages. Finally, we discuss possible defenses against Pitfall and evaluate the performance overhead of disabling the SFP, which can reach up to 12.4% on some CPUs.

Acknowledgments. This work was supported by the National Natural Science Foundation of China (Grant No. U24A6009). The technical solution and experimental design presented in this paper were independently completed by the authors. AI tools were used solely for language polishing and formatting optimization, and did not participate in the development of the research ideas or core content.

References

1. Alexa: The top 1 million sites on the web (2023). https://www.alexa.com/topsites
2. Canella, C., et al.: A systematic evaluation of transient execution attacks and defenses. In: USENIX Security Symposium, pp. 249–266 (2019)

3. Constable, S., et al.: AEX-Notify: thwarting precise single-stepping attacks through interrupt awareness for intel SGX enclaves. In: USENIX Security Symposium, pp. 4051–4068 (2023)
4. Cook, J., Drean, J., Behrens, J., Yan, M.: There's always a bigger fish: a clarifying analysis of a machine-learning-assisted side-channel attack. In: International Symposium on Computer Architecture (ISCA), pp. 204–217 (2022)
5. Feng, Y., et al.: Fish and chips: on the root causes of co-located website-fingerprinting attacks. IEEE Trans. Dependable Secure Comput. (2025)
6. Feng, Y., et al.: TimeGaps channels: exploiting CPU halted time for fun and profit. In: International Symposium on Computer Architecture (ISCA) (2026)
7. Kim, J., Chuang, J., Genkin, D., Yarom, Y.: FLOP: breaking the apple M3 CPU via false load output predictions. In: USENIX Security Symposium, pp. 2595–2614 (2025)
8. Kim, J., Genkin, D., Yarom, Y.: SLAP: data speculation attacks via load address prediction on apple silicon. In: IEEE Symposium on Security and Privacy (S&P), pp. 3549–3566 (2025)
9. Liu, C., et al.: Thrend: mitigating counting thread-based fine-grained timing on arm and apple CPUs. In: Design Automation Conference (DAC) (2026)
10. Liu, C., Feng, S., Li, Y., Wang, D., Carlson, T.E.: HoBBy: hardening unbalanced branches against control flow attacks on intel SGX and AMD SEV. In: Design Automation Conference (DAC) (2025)
11. Liu, C., et al.: MDPeek: breaking balanced branches in SGX with memory disambiguation unit side channels. In: Architectural Support for Programming Languages and Operating Systems (ASPLOS), pp. 622–638 (2025)
12. Liu, C., et al.: SSBench: automated characterization of memory dependence predictors on modern CPUs. In: International Symposium on Computer Architecture (ISCA) (2026)
13. Liu, C., et al.: Uncovering and exploiting AMD speculative memory access predictors for fun and profit. In: IEEE International Symposium on High-Performance Computer Architecture (HPCA), pp. 31–45 (2024)
14. Liu, C., et al.: SSBleed: non-speculative side-channel attacks via speculative store bypass on Armv9 CPUs. In: IEEE International Symposium on High-Performance Computer Architecture (HPCA) (2026)
15. Mose, K.H., Kim, S.S., Ros, A., Jones, T.M., Mullins, R.D.: Mascot: predicting memory dependencies and opportunities for speculative memory bypassing. In: IEEE International Symposium on High-Performance Computer Architecture (HPCA), pp. 59–71 (2025)
16. Oleksenko, O., Trach, B., Silberstein, M., Fetzer, C.: SpecFuzz: bringing spectre-type vulnerabilities to the surface. In: USENIX Security Symposium, pp. 1481–1498 (2020)
17. Rauscher, F., Gruss, D.: Cross-core interrupt detection: exploiting user and virtualized IPIs. In: ACM SIGSAC Conference on Computer and Communications Security (CCS), pp. 94–108 (2024)
18. Wiebing, S., de Faveri Tron, A., Bos, H., Giuffrida, C.: InSpectre gadget: inspecting the residual attack surface of cross-privilege spectre v2. In: USENIX Security Symposium, pp. 577–594 (2024)
19. Wiebing, S., Giuffrida, C.: Training solo: on the limitations of domain isolation against spectre-v2 attacks. In: IEEE Symposium on Security and Privacy (S&P), pp. 3599–3616 (2025)

20. Zhang, X., et al.: Towards practical interrupt side channel attacks on macOS for apple silicon. In: International Symposium on Computer Architecture (ISCA) (2026)
21. Zhang, X., et al.: Fantastic interrupts and where to find them: exploiting non-movable interrupts on x86. IEEE Transactions on Information Forensics and Security (2025)
22. Zhang, Xet al.: AmpereBleed: exploiting on-chip current sensors for circuit-free attacks on ARM-FPGA SoCs. In: Design Automation Conference (DAC) (2025)
23. Zhang, X., et al.: ThermalScope: a practical interrupt side channel attack based on thermal event interrupts. In: Design Automation Conference (DAC) (2024)
24. Zhang, X., et al.: SegScope: probing fine-grained interrupts via architectural footprints. In: IEEE International Symposium on High-Performance Computer Architecture (HPCA), pp. 424–438 (2024)

InputSnatch: Stealing Input in LLM Services via Cache-Sharing Timing Side-Channel Attacks

Xinyao Zheng[1,2,3], Husheng Han[1], Shangyi Shi[1,2,3], Qiyan Fang[1,3,4], Zidong Du[1,2], Xing Hu[1,2](✉), and Qi Guo[1,2]

[1] State Key Lab of Processors, Institute of Computing Technology, Chinese Academy of Sciences, Beijing, China
{zhengxinyao22s,hanhusheng,shishangyi22s,duzidong,guoqi}@ict.ac.cn, qiyanfang@mail.ustc.edu.cn

[2] University of Chinese Academy of Sciences, Beijing, China
huxing@ict.ac.cn

[3] Cambricon Technologies, Beijing, China

[4] University of Science and Technology of China, Hefei, China

Abstract. Large language model (LLM) services increasingly rely on shared-cache optimizations, including prefix and semantic caching, to amortize expensive prefill computation and response generation across users. We show that this optimization creates a timing side channel: an unprivileged tenant can distinguish cache hits from misses through observable latency and use the signal to reconstruct private user inputs. Unlike prior attacks that require cache-flushing APIs, known prompts, or specific scheduling policies, our threat model assumes only black-box API access in multi-tenant deployments with shared cache state. In this study, we propose a novel timing-based side-channel attack framework consisting of two key components. The input constructor combines machine learning techniques and LLM-based semantic analysis to reduce the vast input search space, while the timing analyzer detects cache hit patterns and iteratively refines input guesses. Our experiments across two widely used cache mechanisms, prefix caching and semantic caching, demonstrate consistently high attack success rates across diverse applications. This work reveals a insight: the very performance optimizations designed to enhance LLM efficiency can inadvertently compromise user privacy, emphasizing the urgent need to balance optimization with security in LLM deployments.

Keywords: Side-channel attacks · LLM Systems · Cache Security

1 Introduction

The proliferation of LLM-based systems in privacy-critical scenarios has catalyzed the development of diverse prompt theft attacks aimed at extracting proprietary system prompts or sensitive user inputs. Existing researches have

L. Eeckhout et al. (Eds.): APPT 2026, LNCS 16693, pp. 483–497, 2027.
https://doi.org/10.1007/978-981-92-4805-6_32

emerged in several forms, including extracting system prompts through adversarial prompting [16,26,38], inverting prompts from embedding vectors [21,28] or model-generated responses [27,36], and recovering input prompts from next-token probability distributions [20], token-length patterns [34], and speculative decoding patterns [4,33].

Although prior studies have demonstrated prompt theft attacks in LLM-based systems, they still face three limitations. (1) **Inability to exactly recover prompts**: response-feature analysis [18,27,36] and embedding-vector inversion [5,28] typically recover only partial semantics, because mapping generated outputs or high-dimensional representations back to the original prompts is inherently lossy. (2) **Limited applicability**: many attacks rely on task-specific methodologies [18,27,36], limiting generalization across broader LLM-based services. (3) **Impractical assumptions**: existing methods often require white-box model access [28] or unlimited queries to retrieve next-token probabilities [20], limiting real-world feasibility.

Beyond algorithmic prompt-theft methods, cache-sharing optimizations introduce an architectural vulnerability. We present InputSnatch, which addresses the above limitations by exploiting hit/miss latency gaps in prefix caching [11,13,37] and semantic caching [3,8,14,19] to test whether probes match cached content (Fig. 1), thereby leaking other users' secret inputs and sensitive personal information. Our method provides a powerful attack vector that overcomes the limitations of existing approaches. (1) **Exact input reconstruction**: Prefix caching enables precise inference due to its exact matching requirements. (2) **Wide applicability**: It generalizes well, given its widespread implementation across mainstream LLM inference backends [10,22] and API providers [1,2,9,12,24]. (3) **Practicality**: The attack requires no privileged access beyond standard API usage.

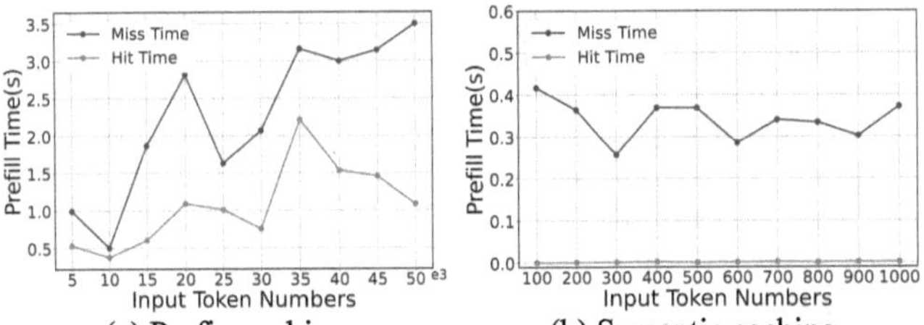

Fig. 1. The prefill time difference between cache hits and misses for varying input token counts using OpenAI API calls with the GPT-4o-mini LLM. (a) Prefix caching deployed by OpenAI. (b) Semantic caching implemented by GPTCache.

Our framework comprises two main components: an *Input Constructor*, which generates candidate inputs to probe cached content, and a *Timing Analyzer*, which detects cache hits through timing analysis. However, this approach faces significant challenges, including the vast search space introduced by large vocabularies [31] and extended context windows [7], alongside practical system constraints like memory capacity, API rate limits, and cache expiration. To overcome these challenges, our framework first profiles target service timing via sampling and noise filtering. It then systematically prunes the massive search space by leveraging semantic relationships from opensource datasets and applying probabilistic ranking to prioritize high-potential inputs.

Our evaluations reveal how routine LLM deployments critically compromise user privacy. Across diverse scenarios, our framework demonstrates efficacy: for prefix caching, it achieves a 100% success rate in extracting exact demographic data and an average 55.5% success rate on free-form disease-history and duration fields. In semantic caching contexts, semantic extraction succeeds across diverse legal domains and reaches up to 70%, underscoring the systemic vulnerability of current optimization mechanisms.

In summary, this paper makes three contributions. First, we formulate cache timing as an oracle for LLM input leakage across both prefix and semantic caching. Second, we design data-driven constructors that rank high-probability probes under realistic memory, TTL, and rate-limit constraints. Third, we validate the attack on representative medical and legal workloads and discuss deployment-level mitigations that balance security and inference efficiency.

2 Attack Hints and Threat Model

2.1 Attack Hints

LLM autoregressive inference proceeds in two phases: *prefill*, which processes the input prompt in parallel to initialize Key-Value (KV) states, and *decoding*, which generates output tokens sequentially. It's imperative to enhance metrics like Time To First Token (TTFT) and Time Per Output Token (TPOT), as latency can be calculated as $Latency = TTFT + (TPOT * N)$, where N represents the number of generated tokens. Since decoding dominates long responses, cloud LLM providers use the KV cache to avoid recomputing all prior attention states at each decoding step. To alleviate the resulting GPU-memory pressure, production systems deploy prefix caching implementations such as vLLM [13,39] to reuse KV states for identical prompt prefixes, and semantic caching systems such as GPTCache [3] to directly retrieve responses for semantically equivalent queries.

Using vLLM and GPTCache as platforms, we analyze the timing characteristics of both mechanisms to pinpoint the optimal attack vector. Empirical analysis (Fig. 2) revealed distinct temporal disparities between prefix cache hits and misses in the prefill and decode phases. We therefore leverage prefill time as our attack vector, enabling early inference termination and significantly accelerating the attack process.

Robustness evaluations across diverse configurations (Fig. 3) confirm a consistent timing separation, allowing our timing analyzer to reliably distinguish caching behaviors regardless of model architecture, hardware, parallelism, or decoding policies.

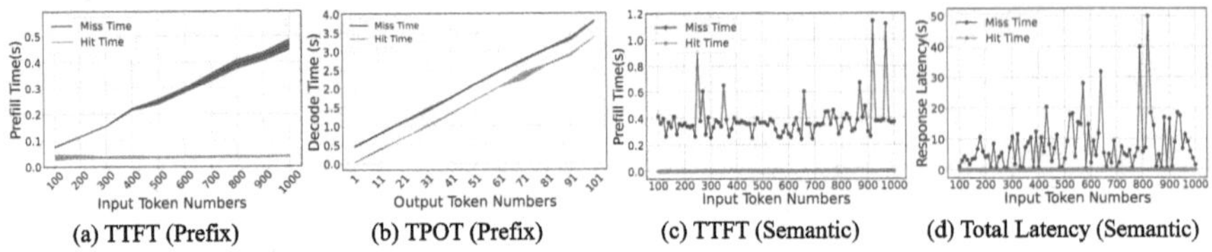

Fig. 2. Latency variations under cache hits vs. misses measured with 500 runs. (a-b) Prefix caching (vLLM on 8×A100): TTFT versus input lengths and TPOT for sequential output tokens. (c-d) Semantic caching (GPTCache with GPT-4o-mini): TTFT and total response latency across varying input lengths.

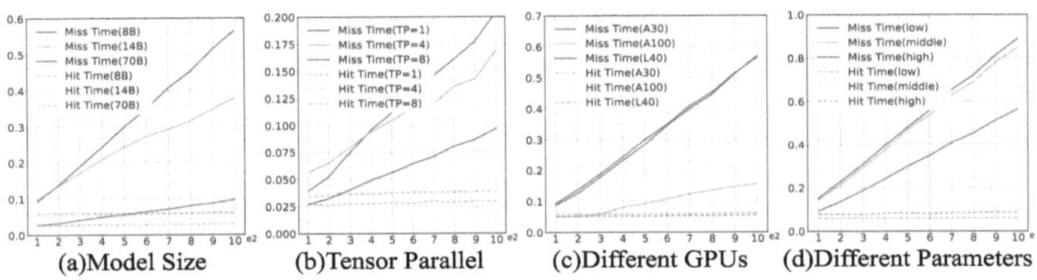

Fig. 3. Prefill time distributions across diverse configurations. (a) varying model scales (8B, 14B, 70B); (b) different tensor parallelism sizes (TP = 1, 4, 8); (c) heterogeneous GPU architectures (A30, A100, L40); and (d) varying sampling diversity (Low, Medium, High).

2.2 Threat Model

Attacker Capability. We target multi-tenant LLM serving infrastructures where computational efficiency is optimized via shared KV cache. Users are co-located on inference nodes, enabling cross-user *prefix* or *semantic* cache sharing. We assume an unprivileged tenant with black-box API access who infers the shared cache state by analyzing the prefill time of attack inputs. The attacker does not know model weights, scheduler internals, hardware placement, or other users' identities, and the communication channel may remain encrypted throughout the attack. The only required observations are request submission time and first-token or response latency. The attacker issues iterative, non-colliding queries within the Time-To-Live (TTL) window to distinguish cache hits from misses, effectively exfiltrating the victim's private context through this architectural side-channel.

Attack Scenario. Caching side-channels broadly threaten diverse deployments, enabling data exfiltration across prompt templates, QA documents, and semantic contexts. We evaluate two high-entropy vectors: prefix caching for static parameterized templates and RAG-based semantic caching. In the prefix-caching setting, the attacker aims to construct inputs that share enough leading tokens with a victim request to trigger block-level cache reuse. In the semantic-caching setting, the objective is not necessarily exact string recovery but finding a semantically equivalent query that reveals the victim's intent or domain-specific private context. These cases demonstrate reliable, timing-based input reconstruction.

3 Attack 1: Prefix Caching

3.1 Attack Scenario

Prompt Engineering Scenario. As prompt engineering significantly enhances LLM capabilities for specific tasks, our attack targets applications using parameterized prompts (e.g., GPT Store [23], GPTforWork [30]). These applications dynamically inject user-provided information into predefined positions within hidden system prompts. This structured integration, designed for personalized generation, creates a precise attack surface for input reconstruction.

Medical Consultation Case Study. We evaluate a system inspired by Zuoshou Doctor [32], where the prompt template enforces a fixed input sequence. Fields vary in entropy: *Age*, *Gender*, and *Chief Complaints* are constrained to distinct choices, whereas *Disease History* and *Lasting Time* accept free-form user-customized text.

3.2 Attack Methodology

Our attack framework (Fig. 4) comprises two key components: an *input constructor* and a *timing analyzer*. In the offline phase, the constructor learns field correlations from open-source datasets, while the analyzer profiles the mapping between response latencies and cache hit ratios. During the online phase, the constructor iteratively generates prompt candidates, and the analyzer measures inference latencies to verify field-level cache hits.

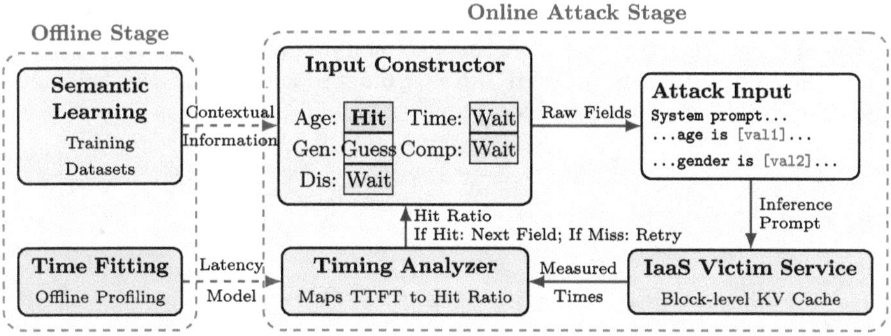

Fig. 4. The attack framework integrates a correlation-driven input constructor to optimize attack prompt generation with a timing analyzer that identifies cache patterns.

Input Constructor. To tackle the vast combinatorial search space, we exploit the block-level KV cache management supported by mainstream inference backend. For example, vLLM allocates and manages KV Cache memory in fixed-size blocks, optimizing memory usage and cache management. This architectural feature enables a *field-by-field* prediction strategy: construct the i-th target field based on previously hit fields. A cache hit allows progression to the next field, whereas a miss triggers an alternative construction to avoid hitting previous attack inputs.

When attacking a single field, exhaustive search of the entire vocabulary is impractical. To improve this, we leverage open-source datasets to identify likely field contents based on context and typical usage patterns. The constructor learns candidate priors from the Chatdoctor [15] dataset. While stealing frequent tokens in public datasets seems to meaning that attacker's information gain would be low, their privacy significance arises from their contextual combinations. Our approach uses these datasets not just for token frequencies but also to learn semantic relationships and field correlations. This allows for a progressive narrowing of the search space: successfully predicting initial fields imposes constraints that make rare, privacy-sensitive tokens more discoverable in subsequent fields. Leveraging these datasets, we optimize the attack to uncover both common and rare sensitive information effectively.

Timing Analyzer. To enable field-by-field prediction, the analyzer maps prefill latencies to block hit ratios (Fig. 5). Based on repeated profiling runs, the y-axis represents prefill times for varying hit counts, while the horizontal gray line denotes the baseline for a complete cache miss. Distinct hit counts typically occupy separate latency intervals (blue), but latencies for different hit counts can overlap across experiments (red), which introduces interference when predicting the hit ratio.

To resolve this, we profile the target service offline to model latency-to-hit relationships and filter anomalies, enabling robust online statistical estimation of hit ratios. Because different input fields typically span multiple blocks and are separated by at least two block lengths, occasional block-level misclassifications can be filtered out. This prevents errors from propagating to the field level, preserving the overall attack success rate.

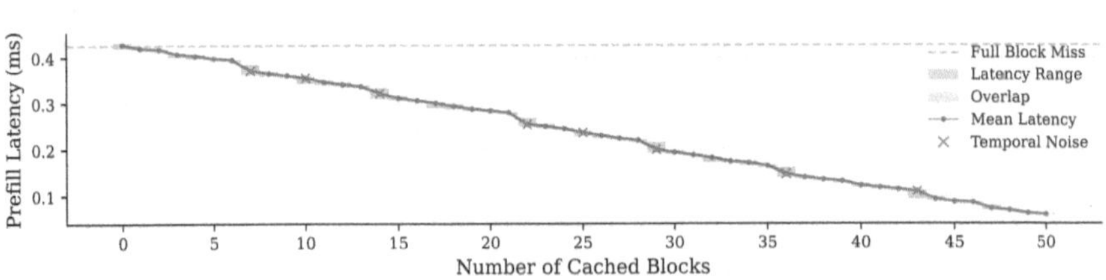

Fig. 5. Relationship between TTFT and hit blocks (800-token, 16 tokens/block).

3.3 Experimental Setup

Datasets. To extract domain-specific vocabulary and inter-field correlations, we processed 110K conversations from the Chatdoctor dataset [15] using GPT-4o, yielding 16,274 structurally standardized Chatdoctor samples. We reserve 200 Chatdoctor samples and 200 GPT-4 generated samples for evaluation to simulate diverse real-world inputs, and use the remaining Chatdoctor records for training. Statistical analysis reveals a highly diverse training set containing **16,074 unique entries**, with the 400 test instances excluded from the training split (**100% novelty ratio**). A representative target entry for successful recovery is illustrated below:

– Recovered Example: `{"Age": "21", "Gender": "Male", "Disease": ["Allergies", "Cough"], "Time": "One day", "Chief Complaint": "What steps should I take to prevent..."}`

Experimental Configuration. We evaluate our attack using vLLM 0.6.2 (prefix caching enabled) in a multi-tenant setting. The cache is shared among n tenants (1 adversary, $n-1$ benign users) issuing requests at a synchronized frequency. We deploy LLaMA-2 70B on an 8×A40 GPU cluster (320GB VRAM) as the inference model. In our **practical** setup, 128GB is reserved for weights, leaving 153GB (~250K tokens) for the KV-cache. Benign requests and attacker probes share this finite budget, so misses can pollute the cache and evict victim entries before the 10-minute TTL expires.

3.4 Evaluation Results

Timing Analyzer Evaluation. We evaluate our analyzer on 800- and 1,600-token prompts using three classifiers (Gradient Boosting, Random Forest, and XGBoost) trained on varying sample sizes (300 and 600) and tested on 1,000 unseen samples (Table 1). The results demonstrate high predictive accuracy with moderate profiling overhead. With 600 profiling queries, GB achieves the highest block-level accuracy, while RF and XGB reach 100% field-level (SR_{Field}) accuracy on 1,600-token prompts. Given this high field-level efficacy, we adopt the 1,600-token configuration and XGB classifier trained on 600 timing samplings for subsequent end-to-end experiments.

End-to-End Attack Evaluation. We evaluate with three input constructor implementations: (1) **Random**: The baseline approach employs random construction based on knowledge learned from datasets; (2) **Fine-tuned LLM**: A LLaMA-3 8B model fine-tuned specifically for high-complexity fields (*Disease History*, *Time*). We use high-temperature sampling ($T = 0.99$) to generate diverse candidate sequences, then filter and rank them before submission as attack attempts; (3) **DistriPredict**: Our probabilistic field predictor learning from datasets.

We primarily measure the **Attack Success Rate (ASR)**, defined as the proportion of successful field recoveries across 400 distinct evaluations. Here, the subscripts for ASR correspond to specific data fields: A, G, D, and T denote

Table 1. Performance of the timing analyzer across different input token lengths.

Sample Sizes	Methods	800 Input Tokens		1600 Input Tokens	
		SR_{Block}	SR_{Field}	SR_{Block}	SR_{Field}
300	GB	81.83%	96.41%	75.84%	100%
	RF	78.76%	95.69%	74.95%	100%
	XGB	72.55%	96.01%	64.06%	100%
600	GB	**86.34%**	**97.25%**	**87.13%**	99.70%
	RF	79.28%	96.21%	84.65%	**100%**
	XGB	81.63%	96.67%	79.31%	**100%**

Age, *Gender*, *Disease History*, and *Lasting Time*, respectively. ASR_{ALL} denotes the cases in which all fields within a single instance are recovered correctly. Additionally, we report the average Attack Attempts (*Attempts*), Memory Consumption ($Memory$), and Time Overhead ($Time$), measured as the number of attempts, token count, and seconds for successful attacks.

Table 2. End-to-end attack under practical configurations across multi-tenants.

Practical configuration with 2 tenants (n=2)							
Methods	$ASR_{A,G}$	ASR_D	ASR_T	ASR_{ALL}	Attempts	Memory	Time
Random	100.00%	47.50%	43.25%	28.50%	442	34139	113
Finetuned LLM	100.00%	8.00%	2.00%	0.00%	39	896	15
DistriPredict	**100.00%**	**57.00%**	**54.00%**	**38.75%**	420	33812	106
Practical configuration with 4 tenants (n=4)							
Methods	$ASR_{A,G}$	ASR_D	ASR_T	ASR_{ALL}	Attempts	Memory	Time
Random	100.00%	45.25%	40.00%	26.50%	329	50660	84
Finetuned LLM	100.00%	6.00%	1.50%	0.00%	25	712	10
DistriPredict	**100.00%**	**51.50%**	**49.25%**	**34.50%**	243	38363	61

As shown in Table 2, DistriPredict achieves the strongest end-to-end performance, reaching an ASR_{ALL} of 38.75% at $n = 2$ and outperforming both baselines. The Fine-tuned LLM performs poorly because high-entropy generation produces many ineffective candidates, quickly exhausting the probing budget and triggering cache eviction. When the number of tenants increases to $n = 4$, all methods decline due to stronger cache contention, but DistriPredict degrades more gracefully because its ranked search avoids many low-value probes.

4 Attack 2: Semantic Caching

4.1 Attack Scenario

Retrieval-Augmented Generation (RAG). While RAG effectively mitigates LLM hallucinations through external knowledge retrieval, its significant computational latency has led to the widespread integration of semantic caching. Figure 6 illustrates this RAG workflow, each user query is embedded, compared with cached query embeddings, and accepted as a cache hit when its similarity exceeds a threshold θ. The service then returns the stored response directly when hit; otherwise, it retrieves external databases, composes an augmented prompt, and invokes the LLM. This conditional path creates a critical timing side-channel: the pronounced latency disparity between cache hits and misses allows adversaries to infer the retrieval state through timing-based observations. We exploit this architectural vulnerability to construct our attack.

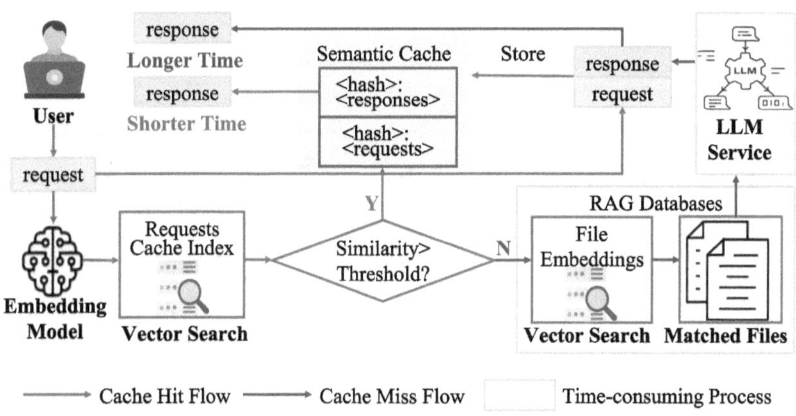

Fig. 6. RAG workflow with semantic caching.

Legal Consultation Case Study. We evaluate our attack within RAG-enhanced legal services, where semantic caching is widely used to manage vast regulatory and case law datasets. In this context, attackers exploit timing side-channels to reconstruct user inputs, including personal statements and litigation strategies. Beyond legal services, this vulnerability poses a systemic threat to financial and governmental RAG deployments, enabling the exfiltration of proprietary intelligence for corporate espionage or downstream social engineering.

4.2 Attack Methodology

Our framework comprises an *input constructor* and a *timing analyzer*, as shown in Fig. 7. Because semantic cache hits bypass expensive retrieval and generation steps, they exhibit a pronounced temporal disparity compared with misses

(Fig. 2). Exploiting this, our timing analyzer achieves 100% hit/miss classification accuracy. Consequently, the primary attack challenge lies in the input constructor, which must efficiently navigate an unbounded, high-dimensional semantic space to craft effective probing queries within strict resource constraints. Unlike prefix caching, where matching depends on exact leading tokens, semantic caching introduces fuzzy boundaries determined by embedding models and similarity thresholds. This makes naive enumeration ineffective: many paraphrases are too far from the target to hit the cache, while overly similar probes may collide with the attacker's own previous attempts.

To systematically conquer this vast search space, the constructor first partitions the semantic landscape by clustering the training dataset D. By calculating the cardinality n_i of each semantic cluster c_i, we model this partitioned space as a weighted search tree T, enabling prioritized exploration. To optimize the search trajectory, the constructor dynamically balances *exploitation* (targeting promising regions near cluster centroids) and *exploration* (probing peripheral boundaries). This dual-focus strategy is mathematically governed by an exploration-exploitation factor α.

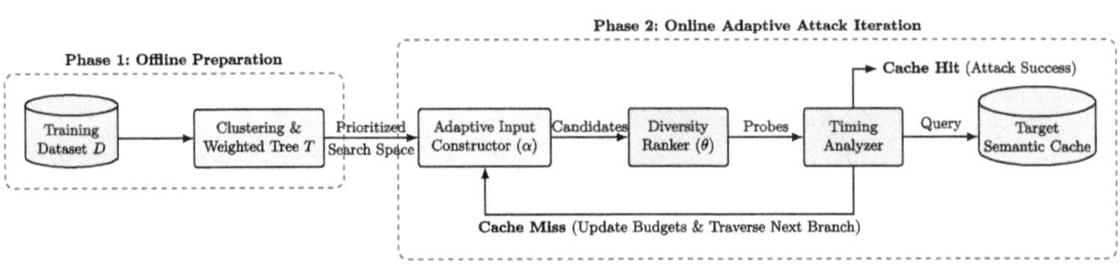

Fig. 7. The offline preparation and online attack iteration of our methodology.

The online attack phase operates as an adaptive feedback loop bounded by practical memory and time termination conditions. During each iteration, the constructor selects a weighted cluster and generates candidate queries around its centroid and peripheral samples, with this exploration-exploitation trade-off modulated by α. To optimize the probing budget, these candidates undergo a diversity-aware ranking mechanism. By enforcing a strict similarity threshold θ against a historical record of *attempted* queries, the ranker ensures each submitted probe is highly representative of the target region yet strictly distinct from prior attempts. The analyzer then evaluates these filtered candidates sequentially. If a cache miss occurs, the consumed memory and time budgets are updated; if all current candidates fail, the search state dynamically traverses to the next optimal branch. This adaptive routing effectively eliminates blind guessing, maximizing attack efficiency before resource exhaustion.

4.3 Experimental Setup and Evaluation

Datasets and Success Criterion. We evaluate our attack on a controlled RAG backend integrated with GPTCache. The constructor is trained on user queries from the CrimeKgAssitant corpus [17] (200K QA pairs across 13 legal domains; details in Table 3); for each legal domain, the test targets are 30 held-out queries excluded from training sets. A successful attack hit requires two conditions: the timing analyzer classifies the probe as a cache hit, and the probe is semantically equivalent to the held-out target under the cache threshold rather than a self-hit on an attempted query. We set this threshold to 0.8. Figure 8 shows the distribution of pairwise similarities within each legal domain; sparse domains have fewer accidental hits and therefore require more precise probes.

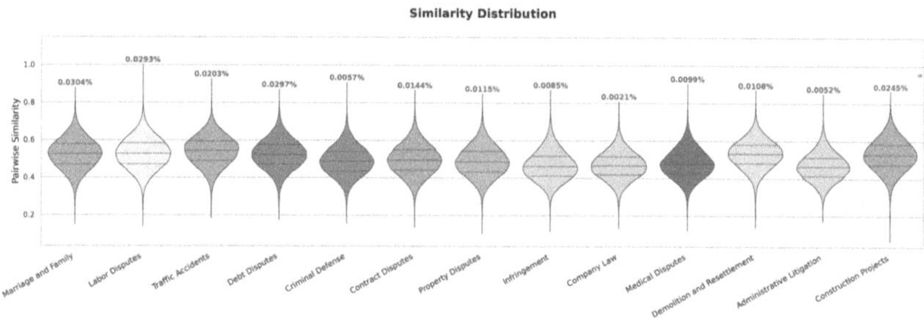

Fig. 8. Intra-domain semantic density analysis.

Input Constructor Evaluation. As shown in Table 3, the constructor navigates semantic boundaries through iterative probing despite the vast search space. Its highest category-level semantic extraction success rate reaches 70%, showing practical reconstruction capability across disparate expression patterns.

To illustrate the practical threat, consider the Labor Disputes domain. The constructor successfully hits the cache for the target "*I want to resign quickly, but the manager disagrees*" using the semantic equivalent "*I want to resign. What if the manager does not approve?*", reliably exposing sensitive user intent. Conversely, our strict evaluation correctly rejects queries that share a broad legal context but differ in nuanced specifics. Ultimately, extracting these semantically equivalent texts shows that adversaries can accurately infer confidential user situations from semantic caches.

5 Discussion and Defenses

5.1 Discussion

While cache side-channels rarely link leaked prompts to specific identities directly, adversaries can weaponize the extracted domain context (e.g., medical conditions, legal disputes) to launch targeted follow-on exploits such as coercion or social engineering. We only measured timing signals on real cloud APIs (Fig. 1); complete input-reconstruction attacks are conducted in controlled vLLM/GPTCache deployments to avoid violating user privacy or provider terms.

Table 3. Systematic evaluation of the input constructor across 13 legal domains from the CrimeKgAssitant dataset. For each **Category**, we report the total training sample **Count**, the average query length and its standard deviation (**Len. Avg.** $\pm$ **Std.**), the attack success rate (**ASR**), and the average number of probes among successful attacks (**Avg. Attempts**).

Category	Count	Len. Avg. $\pm$ Std.	ASR	Avg. Attempts
Marriage and Family	39,857	37.51 $\pm$ 18.49	70.00%	174.19
Labor Disputes	35,541	38.16 $\pm$ 18.05	40.00%	83.58
Traffic Accidents	22,907	38.96 $\pm$ 17.83	36.67%	186.82
Debt Disputes	22,269	37.82 $\pm$ 18.98	70.00%	18.71
Criminal Defense	18,593	35.37 $\pm$ 19.12	26.67%	5.25
Contract Disputes	13,985	39.06 $\pm$ 18.40	23.33%	41.71
Property Disputes	12,227	36.14 $\pm$ 18.38	16.67%	52.80
Infringement	10,739	38.46 $\pm$ 20.68	30.00%	79.67
Company Law	10,211	37.66 $\pm$ 18.34	26.67%	28.00
Medical Disputes	7,359	38.64 $\pm$ 18.65	6.67%	5.00
Demolition and Resettlement	7,131	40.25 $\pm$ 18.22	30.00%	42.00
Administrative Litigation	2,801	35.78 $\pm$ 17.49	10.00%	6.33
Construction Projects	1,629	41.58 $\pm$ 16.27	16.67%	49.20

Our evaluation models cache contention through finite KV-cache budgets and multi-tenant workloads, but it does not fully capture provider-specific eviction policies, admission control, or per-tenant isolation in production clouds. Future work should evaluate these factors in authorized cloud testbeds.

5.2 Potential Defenses

Mitigating timing-based prompt theft requires balancing privacy and performance. Strict user-level cache isolation [6] removes the cross-tenant channel, but reduces cache reuse and throughput. When organization-level sharing is required [24], providers should combine rate limiting [25], anomaly detection for repeated near-duplicate probes, and timing obfuscation such as randomized delays, conservative timing equalization, or reduced streaming granularity. These measures raise the cost of adaptive probing, but must be tuned carefully because aggressive limits and added delays can harm benign workloads and erode the efficiency benefits of caching.

6 Related Work

6.1 LLM Side-Channels and Prompt Theft

Existing research highlights LLM privacy risks through network side channels, such as token-length leakage [34] and speculative decoding patterns [4,33]. Concurrently, prompt theft attacks aim to extract sensitive context via adversarial jailbreaks [16,26,38] or embedding/probability inversion [20,21,28]. However, these inversion and adversarial methods often struggle with partial semantic recovery, narrow scope, or unrealistic white-box assumptions. In contrast, InputSnatch exploits systemic infrastructure flaws in cache sharing to support exact or semantically equivalent reconstruction using unprivileged, black-box API access.

6.2 Comparison with Contemporary Work

Recent concurrent studies [29,35] also explore inference side-channels but operate under highly restrictive assumptions. Song et al. [29] target system prompts via timing channels but rely on unrealistic *flush* APIs to clear caches, small vocabularies, and up to 100 queries per token. Wu et al. [35] exploit response ordering but assume white-box knowledge of service scheduling and local model access, limiting their attack to single-word blanks.

Unlike these constrained approaches, InputSnatch operates in black-box environments without cache-clearing mechanisms. Crucially, our methodology scales to large, structured search spaces to reconstruct complex, multi-phrase user inputs. Furthermore, InputSnatch extends beyond exact prefix matching to exploit semantic cache-sharing architectures, thereby posing a broader threat to highly sensitive user privacy rather than just corporate intellectual property.

7 Conclusions

We identify critical timing side-channel vulnerabilities in LLM inference optimizations, specifically targeting prefix caching and semantic caching mechanisms. We introduce InputSnatch, a framework that exploits variations in prefill timing to leak sensitive user inputs. Our findings demonstrate that while these caching features significantly enhance throughput, they inadvertently create side channels for building unauthorized user profiles and targeted social engineering attacks. We conclude that current LLM architectures prioritize performance at the expense of isolation, highlighting an urgent need for security-first caching protocols that balance computational efficiency with robust information boundary protection.

Acknowledgments. This work is partially supported by the NSF of China (Grants No.62341411, U22A2028), Strategic Priority Research Program of the Chinese Academy of Sciences (Grants No. XDB0660200, XDB0660201, XDB0660202), CAS Project for Young Scientists in Basic Research (YSBR-029), and Youth Innovation Promotion Association CAS.

AI Disclosure. The technical solution and experimental design presented in this paper were independently completed by the authors. AI tools were used solely for language polishing and formatting optimization, and did not participate in the development of the research ideas or core content.

References

1. Anthropic: Prompt caching (beta) (2024). https://docs.anthropic.com/en/docs/build-with-claude/prompt-caching
2. Azure, M.: Tutorial: use azure cache for Redis as a semantic cache (2024). https://learn.microsoft.com/en-us/azure/azure-cache-for-redis/cache-tutorial-semantic-cache
3. Bang, F.: GPTCache: an open-source semantic cache for LLM applications enabling faster answers and cost savings. In: Proceedings of the 3rd Workshop for Natural Language Processing Open Source Software (NLP-OSS 2023), pp. 212–218 (2023)
4. Carlini, N., Nasr, M.: Remote timing attacks on efficient language model inference. arXiv preprint arXiv:2410.17175 (2024)
5. Chen, Y., Lent, H., Bjerva, J.: Text embedding inversion security for multilingual language models. In: Proceedings of the 62nd Annual Meeting of the Association for Computational Linguistics (Volume 1: Long Papers), pp. 7808–7827 (2024)
6. DeepSeek: DeepSeek API introduces context caching on disk, cutting prices by an order of magnitude (2024). https://api-docs.deepseek.com/news/news0802/
7. Ding, Y., et al.: LongRoPE: extending LLM context window beyond 2 million tokens. arXiv preprint arXiv:2402.13753 (2024)
8. Gill, W., Elidrisi, M., Kalapatapu, P., Anwar, A., Gulzar, M.A.: Privacy-aware semantic cache for large language models. arXiv:2403.02694 arXiv preprint (2024)
9. Google: Gemini API: Google AI for Developers (2024). https://ai.google.dev/gemini-api/docs/caching?lang=python
10. Hugging Face: Text Generation Inference: Large language model text generation inference (2022). https://github.com/huggingface/text-generation-inference
11. Juravsky, J., Brown, B., Ehrlich, R., Fu, D.Y., Ré, C., Mirhoseini, A.: Hydragen: high-throughput LLM inference with shared prefixes. arXiv preprint arXiv:2402.05099 (2024)
12. Kanter, S.F.: Improve speed and reduce cost for generative AI workloads with a persistent semantic cache in Amazon MemoryDB (2024). https://aws.amazon.com/cn/blogs/database/improve-speed-and-reduce-cost-for-generative-ai-workloads-with-a-persistent-semantic-cache-in-amazon-memorydb/
13. Kwon, W., et al.: Efficient memory management for large language model serving with pagedattention. In: Proceedings of the 29th Symposium on Operating Systems Principles, pp. 611–626 (2023)
14. Li, J., Xu, C., Wang, F., von Riedemann, I.M., Zhang, C., Liu, J.: SCALM: towards semantic caching for automated chat services with large language models. arXiv preprint arXiv:2406.00025 (2024)
15. Li, Y., Li, Z., Zhang, K., Dan, R., Jiang, S., Zhang, Y.: ChatDoctor: a medical chat model fine-tuned on a large language model meta-AI (LLaMA) using medical domain knowledge. Cureus **15**(6) (2023)
16. Liang, Z., Hu, H., Ye, Q., Xiao, Y., Li, H.: Why are my prompts leaked? Unraveling prompt extraction threats in customized large language models. arXiv preprint arXiv:2408.02416 (2024)
17. Liu, H.: CrimeKgAssitant: crime assistant including crime type prediction and crime consult service based on NLP methods and crime KG (2018). https://github.com/liuhuanyong/CrimeKgAssitant
18. Mahajan, S., Rahman, T., Yi, K.M., Sigal, L.: Prompting hard or hardly prompting: prompt inversion for text-to-image diffusion models. In: 2024 IEEE/CVF Conference on Computer Vision and Pattern Recognition (CVPR), pp. 6808–6817 (2024). https://doi.org/10.1109/CVPR52733.2024.00650

19. Mohandoss, R.: Context-based semantic caching for LLM applications. In: 2024 IEEE Conference on Artificial Intelligence (CAI), pp. 371–376. IEEE (2024)
20. Morris, J.X., Zhao, W., Chiu, J.T., Shmatikov, V., Rush, A.M.: Language model inversion. arXiv preprint arXiv:2311.13647 (2023)
21. Morris, J.X., Kuleshov, V., Shmatikov, V., Rush, A.M.: Text embeddings reveal (almost) as much as text. In: The 2023 Conference on Empirical Methods in Natural Language Processing (2023)
22. NVIDIA Corporation: NVIDIA TensorRT-LLM (2026). https://docs.nvidia.com/tensorrt-llm/index.html
23. OpenAI: Introducing the GPT Store We're launching the GPT Store to help you find (2024). https://chat.openai.com/gpts
24. OpenAI: Prompt caching: Reduce latency and cost with prompt caching (2024). https://platform.openai.com/docs/guides/prompt-caching
25. OpenAI: OpenAI API: Rate limits (2026). https://developers.openai.com/api/docs/guides/rate-limits
26. Perez, F., Ribeiro, I.: Ignore previous prompt: attack techniques for language models. arXiv preprint arXiv:2211.09527 (2022)
27. Shen, X., Qu, Y., Backes, M., Zhang, Y.: Prompt stealing attacks against {Text-to-Image} generation models. In: 33rd USENIX Security Symposium (USENIX Security 24), pp. 5823–5840 (2024)
28. Song, C., Raghunathan, A.: Information leakage in embedding models. In: Proceedings of the 2020 ACM SIGSAC Conference on Computer and Communications Security, pp. 377–390 (2020)
29. Song, L., et al.: The early bird catches the leak: unveiling timing side channels in LLM serving systems. IEEE Trans. Inf. Forensics Secur. **20**, 11431–11446 (2025). https://doi.org/10.1109/TIFS.2025.3622954
30. Talarian: OpenAI GPT prompt generator (2024). https://gptforwork.com/tools/prompt-generator
31. Tao, C., et al.: Scaling laws with vocabulary: larger models deserve larger vocabularies. arXiv preprint arXiv:2407.13623 (2024)
32. Technology, Z.: Zuoshouyisheng open platforms (2024). https://open.zuoshouyisheng.com/
33. Wei, J., Abdulrazzag, A., Zhang, T., Muursepp, A., Saileshwar, G.: When speculation spills secrets: side channels via speculative decoding in LLMs (2025). https://arxiv.org/abs/2411.01076
34. Weiss, R., Ayzenshteyn, D., Amit, G., Mirsky, Y.: What was your prompt? A remote keylogging attack on ai assistants. arXiv preprint arXiv:2403.09751 (2024)
35. Wu, G., et al.: I know what you asked: prompt leakage via kv-cache sharing in multi-tenant LLM serving. In: Proceedings of the 2025 Network and Distributed System Security (NDSS) Symposium, San Diego, CA, USA (2025)
36. Yang, Y., et al.: PRSA: prompt reverse stealing attacks against large language models. arXiv preprint arXiv:2402.19200 (2024)
37. Ye, L., Tao, Z., Huang, Y., Li, Y.: ChunkAttention: efficient self-attention with prefix-aware kv cache and two-phase partition. arXiv preprint arXiv:2402.15220 (2024)
38. Zhang, Y., Carlini, N., Ippolito, D.: Effective prompt extraction from language models. In: First Conference on Language Modeling (2024)
39. Zheng, L., et al.: Efficiently programming large language models using SGLang. arXiv preprint arXiv:2312.07104 (2023)

TArCS: Trusted and Attack-Resilient Clock Source with TEE and RDMA

Yunpeng Xu[1], Yuchen Fan[1], Yu Jin[1], Shuangjie Yao[2], Jia Zhang[3], Teng Ma[3], and Shuwen Deng[1,4](✉)

[1] Tsinghua University, Beijing 100084, People's Republic of China
{xyp24,fanyc22,jiny25}@mails.tsinghua.edu.cn, shuwend@tsinghua.edu.cn
[2] HKUST, Hong Kong 999077, People's Republic of China
joshuay2202@gmail.com
[3] Alibaba Group, Hangzhou 311121, People's Republic of China
qianyue.zj@alibaba-inc.com, stmatengss@163.com
[4] Zhongguancun Laboratory, Beijing 100194, People's Republic of China

Abstract. As confidential computing technologies advance, the secure and trustworthy execution of applications has garnered increasing attention. However, recent time-based attacks have severely disrupted trust and pose significant threats to the normal functioning of applications across various fields, especially the safety of real-time systems. This highlights the critical importance of a robust trusted timekeeping infrastructure. We conduct a detailed analysis of the unique challenges in trusted timekeeping systems and propose the `CIAT` model, which integrates the classic Confidentiality, Integrity, and Availability framework by incorporating Timeliness. Within the `CIAT` model, we systematically analyze various threats, including Trust Attacks, Precision Attacks, and Availability Attacks. To address these multifaceted challenges, we introduce the Trusted and Attack-resilient Clock Source (TArCS), a novel framework that leverages TEEs and Remote Attestation (RA) to ensure the confidentiality and integrity of time sources, and employs RDMA to enhance resilience against a wide range of time attacks. We provide rigorous security proofs for TArCS against Trust Attacks and conduct comprehensive evaluations against Precision and Availability Attacks. TArCS achieves 10us-precision in short-link tests and 4ms-precision in long-link tests, while demonstrating 23ms-level bounded precision under intensive precision attacks, outperforming the attack resilience of the state-of-the-art work. Additionally, TArCS exhibits strong scalability and reliability, ensuring consistent performance under varying system loads and network conditions.

Keywords: Trusted timekeeping · Remote direct memory access · Confidential computing

1 Introduction

Trusted Execution Environments (TEEs) such as Intel SGX, AMD SEV, and ARM TrustZone protect code and data through hardware isolation [6,12,21].

L. Eeckhout et al. (Eds.): APPT 2026, LNCS 16693, pp. 498–512, 2027.
https://doi.org/10.1007/978-981-92-4805-6_33

Yet trusted execution still depends on trusted inputs, especially timestamps [3]. Applications such as distributed transactions and telemetry require precise, consistent time, while mainstream TEEs offer little support for trustworthy clock sources [5,23,43].

Time attacks are well documented across control, payment, sensing, and positioning systems [4,26,30,35,40,42]. Existing trusted timekeeping solutions either rely on limited hardware counters [3,5] or suffer from attacks and large precision loss [41].

To systematically analyze these threats, we propose the `CIAT` model. The classic `CIA` model—*Confidentiality* (`C.`), *Integrity* (`I.`), and *Availability* (`A.`)—is a foundation of data and execution security [25]. However, a timestamp is trustworthy only within a bounded time interval; malicious delays can break security even if `CIA` holds [35]. We therefore extend the model with *Timeliness* (`T.`), forming the `CIAT` model, and categorize attacks into *Trust Attacks* (violating `C.`/`I.`), *Precision Attacks* (violating `T.`), and *Availability Attacks* (violating `A.`). We then introduce TArCS, ***a trusted, robust, and attack-resilient clock source framework*** that integrates TEE and remote attestation (RA) for `C.` and `I.`, one-sided RDMA semantics and multi-threaded counting for `T.` resilience, and cryptographic verification with redundant links for network threat mitigation.

TArCS utilizes multiple RDMA-based network connections (each with a control path for RA and an encrypted datapath) and local counting threads, processed by a timekeeping algorithm with time compensation and masking policies. We provide a security proof (Appendix A) showing that TArCS withstands Trust Attackers, limiting adversaries to precision attacks mitigated by our `T.`/`A.` designs. Comprehensive evaluation using real machines and our simulator TArCSim shows 10us-precision on short links, 4ms-precision on long links, successful mitigation of delay attacks with affected ratio $< 50\%$, and 23ms-precision under 50% scheduling attacks, outperforming the 700ms degradation of the state-of-the-art work.[1]

In summary, our main contributions are to:

- Propose the `CIAT` model for time security and categorize threats into *Trust*, *Precision*, and *Availability* attacks.
- Design TArCS, a trusted clock source architecture combining TEE, RA, RDMA, and multi-source timekeeping.
- Prove `C.` and `I.` properties and build TArCSim for controlled evaluation.
- Evaluate precision and attack resilience, showing 23-ms precision under combined delay and scheduling attacks.

2 Background

Confidential computing [33] protects data confidentiality and integrity with *trusted execution environments* (TEEs). Common TEEs include Intel SGX,

[1] Like prior works [5,34], TArCS cannot guarantee absolute `A.` against DoS-level attacks, which are easily detectable [5] and outside the typical threat model.

AMD SEV, and ARM CCA [12,16,21]. *Remote attestation* (RA) lets a verifier check the integrity of a remote TEE and establish trust across hosts; hardware-backed RA generally provides the strongest guarantees [8,10].

RDMA provides direct remote memory access with one-sided and two-sided verbs, bypassing the remote CPU/OS on the data path [37]. It is widely deployed in data centers and is increasingly explored beyond tightly controlled clusters [1, 24,32,44].

Trusted timekeeping spans the whole time stack [3,5]: a *clock source* generates time, and *timestamp transfer* delivers it to applications. Internal sources such as `rdtsc`/`rdtscp` are precise but can be manipulated by privileged software [18,19]; external sources are better synchronized but enlarge the attack surface. PTP/gPTP offer high precision with hardware timestamping [17], while NTP/Chrony typically trade precision for deployability [29,31]. Existing timestamp-transfer defenses still need a trusted clock source and must tolerate delay attacks on delivery [27,34].

3 Motivation and Related Work

The `CIAT` model extends `CIA` with *Timeliness*: a timestamp can preserve `C./I./A.` yet still be security-useless if adversarial delay destroys its value [20]. Existing defenses cover only parts of the time stack, so we briefly position TArCS against them. Prior work falls into two complementary categories: *trusted timestamp transfer* and *trusted clock source*. Secure timekeeping needs both.

TEE-based timestamp-transfer systems resist interruption and delay on the delivery path [15,27,28,34,36]. TimeGuard [34] is the state-of-the-art design, but it still assumes a trustworthy clock source.

Among trusted clock sources, TimeSeal [5] combines `sgx_get_trusted_time` with counting threads, but its precision degrades by over 100 ms under scheduling and delay attacks [34], and the counter is discontinued on Linux [3]. Triad [14] uses `TSC` plus NTPSec, yet CPU-frequency dependence and noisy `RDRAND` enable ±40% timer manipulation [41], and later analysis shows the design is unsafe [9].

Conventional NTP/Chrony and PTP/gPTP target synchronization quality rather than adversarial trustworthiness [17,29,31,38].

TArCS focuses on the missing piece: a *secure clock source*. By combining TEE, RA, and RDMA, it provides stronger trust guarantees than Triad and substantially higher resilience than TimeSeal, reaching 23-ms precision under intensive delay attacks versus 700 ms in the state-of-the-art baseline.

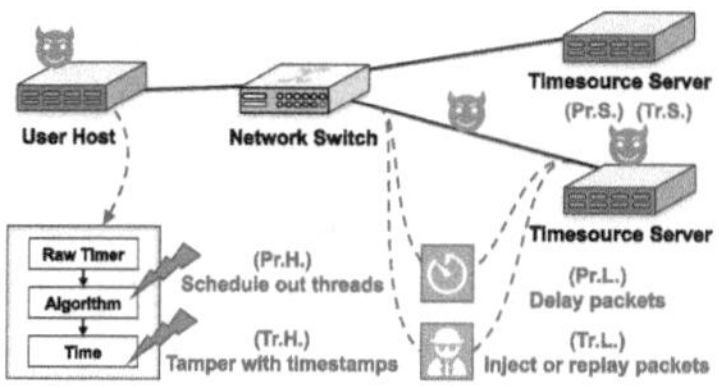

Fig. 1. Threat model of TArCS. Potential attackers include precision (Pr.) and trust (Tr.) attackers, originating from hosts (H.) or links (L.), targeting the trust or precision of the system.

4 Threat Model and Attack Analysis

4.1 Threat Model

We apply our `CIAT` security model. Attackers aim to compromise the sense of time while maintaining stealth [5]. Attackers must break at least one CIAT property: `C./I.` → *Trust Attacks* (Tr.), `A.` → *Availability Attacks* (Av.), and `T.` → *Precision Attacks* (Pr.). Threats can arise from hosts (H.), links (L.), or servers (S.), as illustrated in Fig. 1.

4.2 Attack Analysis

Trust Attackers directly tamper with timestamps or their metadata. **Tr.H.** attackers corrupt the host software stack, **Tr.L.** attackers attempt injection or replay on links, and **Tr.S.** attackers alter server-side timestamps. TArCS defends them with TEE protection, RA, encryption, and sequence numbers; Appendix A gives the proof sketch.

Precision Attackers degrade time accuracy without breaking `C./I.`. **Pr.H.** attackers manipulate scheduling or replay delayed packets from host memory [5]; **Pr.L.** attackers delay or truncate link traffic; **Pr.S.** attackers delay timestamp emission at the server. Such attacks cannot be eliminated in software alone [4], so TArCS uses redundancy and anomaly masking to bound their impact.

For Pr.H. delay attackers, the DMA path from RNIC to MR bypasses the processor and is *immune by design*. For the path from MR to timekeeping threads, the attacker may attempt MR unmapping or replay attacks; both are defended by RDMA NIC's rkey access control and server-side RDMA Read detection (details in Appendix B).

Pr.S. is equivalent to Pr.L. from the host's perspective, so we evaluate *Pr.H. scheduling attacks* and *Pr.L. delay attacks* in Sect. 6.4.

Availability Attackers intensify precision attacks, aiming to disrupt `A.` rather than stealthily perturb time.

Analysis. TArCS uses multi-link and multi-thread redundancy to preserve bounded precision under partial availability loss. Non-TEE components are assumed untrusted and non-confidential; critical secrets remain inside the TEE.

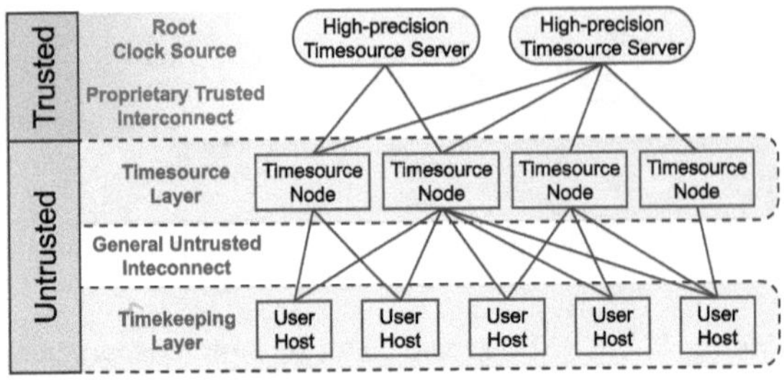

Fig. 2. The overview of the 3-layer architecture of TArCS.

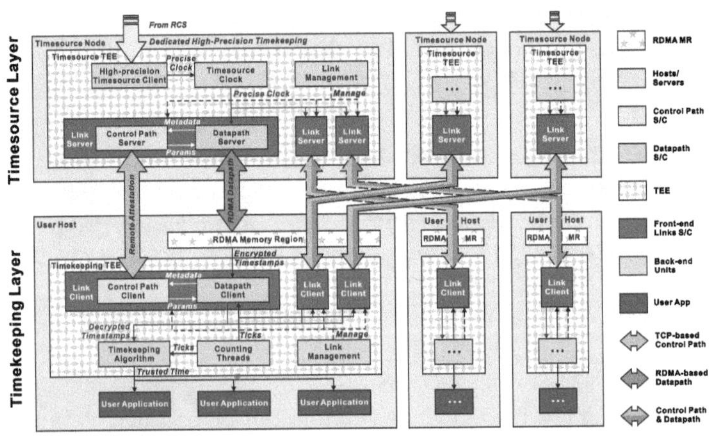

Fig. 3. Framework between the Timesource and Timekeeping Layers. Each link contains a TCP-based control path and an RDMA-based datapath; the Timekeeping TEE fuses timestamps from multiple links and local counting threads.

5 TArCS Framework

Overview. TArCS has three layers (Fig. 2): a high-precision Root Clock Source (RCS), a gPTP-synchronized Timesource Layer, and a Timekeeping Layer at user hosts. Between the latter two, TArCS builds a trusted *control path*, a low-latency *datapath*, and a local *timekeeping algorithm* (Fig. 3).

5.1 TEE Setup and Integration

Most logic resides inside the TEE, including the control path, datapath handlers, and timekeeping backend; total TEE buffers are about 10 KB. The RDMA MR stays outside the TEE, while encryption/verification protect `C.`/`I.` and one-sided writes protect `T.`. The TEE accesses packets through platform-specific shared memory (Appendix C).

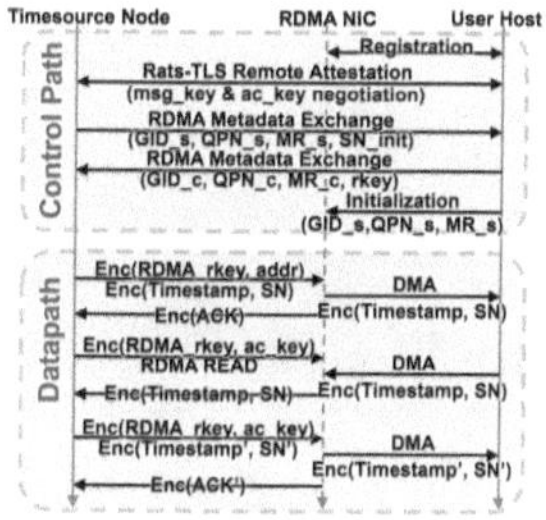

Fig. 4. Communication protocol and parameter exchange.

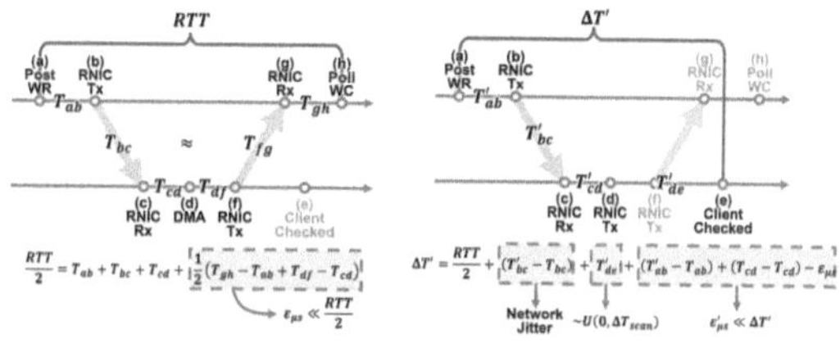

(a) Critical flow for RTT estimation.

(b) Critical flow for time compensation.

Fig. 5. Datapath timing events used for RTT estimation and time compensation $\Delta T'$.

5.2 Control Path

The Control Path performs one-time RA (Rats-TLS [11]) between server and client TEEs, derives encryption keys, exchanges RDMA metadata and TArCS parameters, and then synchronizes startup (Fig. 4). Exchanged data include standard RDMA metadata plus the initial sequence number, address-control parameters, receive window, frequency, and timeout.

5.3 Datapath

The TArCS datapath sends encrypted timestamp packets via one-sided RDMA Write, so the client CPU is bypassed on arrival (Fig. 4). The client polls the MR, verifies valid packets, and enqueues timestamps; the server uses ACKs to confirm arrival and estimate RTT.

Time Compensation. The client corrects two gaps between generation and consumption: link delay (a–d in Fig. 5) with half of the server-maintained RTT, and scanning delay (d–e) with half of ΔT_{scan}.

Address Control. Server and client maintain a shared address window of length K for the next packet positions. Addresses are derived from shared randomness and sequence numbers, hiding packet locations while tolerating up to $K - 1$ consecutive losses.

Failure Detection and Multi-link Design. Excessive scan failures or RTT deviation trigger connection reset through the control path. Many-to-many links improve `A.` and let the client compare paths to filter compromised ones when fewer than half are affected.

Entry Deletion Detection. The server occasionally RDMA-reads previously written entries and compares them with the expected ciphertext to detect host-side replay or deletion.

Table 1. Specifications of Test Environment

Host	Processor	RNIC	RAM	Core	Kernel	TEE
H1	Xeon S4314	CX6	256GB	128	5.15.0	SGX
H2	Xeon P8480+	CX6	1TB	224	6.8.0	SGX
H3/4	EPYC 7513	RXE	128GB	64	5.19.0	SEV

5.4 Timekeeping

Multiple Counting Threads. Counting threads continuously increment local ticks to refine time resolution [5]. The datapath records both the scan period ΔT_{scan} and the tick values observed when valid packets arrive.

Counting Rate and Current Time Estimation. Tpus (ticks per us) is estimated from recent tick/timestamp differences with an exponential window. For each valid packet, the client compensates link and scanning delay, converts tick differences into time, removes outliers across counting threads, and averages across recent packets and datapaths to obtain the final estimate (details in Sect. 6.2).

Quality Evaluation and Masking Policy. TArCS masks datapaths with $D[RTT]_i > D[RTT]_{Threshold}$ and threads with $D[Tpus]_j > D[Tpus]_{Threshold}$, temporarily excluding them from estimation until quality recovers. This mitigates precision attacks with bounded loss when fewer than half of links/threads are compromised.

Re-synchronization. Nodes recover by reestablishing links and counting threads. Each connection keeps independent state, so setup and recovery only add or remove the affected variables; convergence takes a few RTTs.

6 Evaluation

6.1 Experimental Setup

Short-link tests and real-machine stress tests run on the Intel/AMD hosts in Table 1. Long-link and attack-resilience tests use TArCSim, which we validate against real-machine measurements.

6.2 TArCSim Design and Theoretical Analysis

Timestamp Packet Flow. Figure 5 marks the key events from packet posting to client detection and ACK return.

RTT Estimation and Time Deviation. Under link symmetry, $\frac{RTT}{2} \approx T_{ab} + T_{bc} + T_{cd} + \varepsilon_{\mu s}$. The residual deviation is dominated by link fluctuation and scanning error (Appendix D).

(a) Distribution of long-link network delay.

(b) Distribution of counting ticks per us.

Fig. 6. Distributions sampled from real machines and used by TArCSim.

Counting Threads. Under random scheduling, their tick rates are Gaussian-like; to capture real jitter, we sample directly from deployed systems [13].

TArCSim. TArCSim reuses the same timekeeping logic with real-sampled link delays, counting-thread rates, and scan cycles (Fig. 6), plus Gaussian noise for $\varepsilon_{\mu s}$.

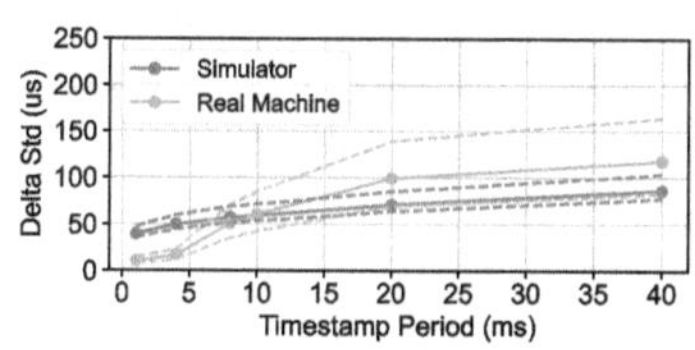

Fig. 7. Precision of TArCS and TArCSim under different timestamp posting frequencies.

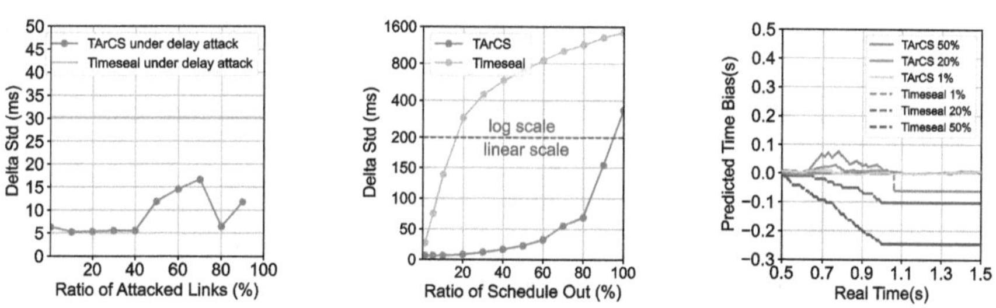

(a) Δstd vs. attacked-link ratio under link delay attack.

(b) Δstd vs. scheduling-out ratio under scheduling attack.

(c) Estimated time bias under host scheduling attack.

Fig. 8. TArCS precision under attack-resilience test.

6.3 Precision Evaluation

We evaluate precision through short-link and long-link tests. The short-link setup uses ConnectX-6 RNICs over short RoCE links with varying server timestamp frequency. Precision is measured by Δstd, the standard deviation of estimated-vs.-actual time differences.

As shown in Fig. 7, TArCSim achieves Δstd close to real tests (10us-level deviation), verifying its reliability. For long-link tests with 10ms-range network delay, Δstd is only 4 ms, highly precise compared to prior work [5].

6.4 Attack-Resilience Test

Link Delay Sttack. Since injection and replay attacks are mitigated by sequence numbers and encryption (Sect. 4), we focus on link delay attacks.

We simulate N servers connected by N links, with n compromised links injecting random delays into a proportion P of timestamp packets. Randomized delay is the strongest stealthy strategy in prior threat models [1,34,35]. When $\rho := \frac{n}{N} \leq 50\%$, TArCS keeps Δstd within a 9.52% fluctuation around 5 ms even as P varies from 0% to 100%.

With $P = 50\%$ fixed, varying ρ from 0% to 90% shows that TArCS maintains precision when $\rho < 50\%$. Beyond this threshold, Δstd rises sharply but stays within twice its baseline value. Compared with TimeSeal [5], TArCS yields lower Δstd across all tested delay-attack scenarios.

This 50% threshold is theoretically grounded in the delay-mixture model: the worst-case deviation grows slowly for $\rho < 0.5$ but increases rapidly once adversarial links become the majority (derivation in Appendix D).

Host Scheduling Attack. We model a compromised OS that stealthily schedules out counting threads for irregular periods while appearing normal otherwise. Let R denote the expected proportion of threads scheduled out.

Figure 8b shows that for small R, Δstd stays below 50 ms, while TimeSeal [5] reaches 280 ms with 20% scheduling out. Figure 8c further shows that TArCS recovers and reconverges within about 2250 ms after the attack starts, whereas TimeSeal still exhibits at least 120 ms sustained error [5].

The low-pass filter parameter α bounds the adversary's maximal induced error to $\alpha\rho\,\Delta T_{\text{Timestamp}}$ (Appendix D).

Combined Attacks. In combined link-delay and host-scheduling attacks, performance is dominated by the host-side delay; adding link delay increases Δstd by only 4.88%. Scalability and stress-test results are summarized in Appendix E.

7 Conclusion

This paper proposes the `CIAT` security model for trusted timekeeping and introduces TArCS, a trusted, attack-resilient, robust, and scalable clock source leveraging TEE, RA, and RDMA. TArCS achieves 10us-precision in short-link tests and 4ms-precision in long-link tests. Its precision does not degrade under link delay attacks with attacked-link ratio < 50%, and remains at 23ms-precision under 50% scheduling attacks, significantly outperforming the state-of-the-art implementation.

Acknowledgments. This work was generously supported by the National Key Research and Development Program of China under Grant (2024YFB4405400), NSFC (No. U24A6009, 62572265), Shenzhen Science and Technology Program (AI2026017), Beijing Municipal Science and Technology Project (No. Z241100004224028), Beijing Natural Science Foundation (L247013). Finally, we thank anonymous reviewers for insightful feedback.

The technical solution and experimental design presented in this paper were independently completed by the authors. AI tools were used solely for language polishing and formatting optimization, and did not participate in the development of the research ideas or core content.

A Security Proof

We summarize the proof obligations used in the paper and show that Trust Attackers can at most delay already generated packets on the datapath.

A.1 Definitions and Preliminaries

Def. 1. A *party* $P = (\mathcal{S}, \mathcal{T}, s_0, p, c)$ is a state machine with states $\mathcal{S}$, transition function $\mathcal{T}$, initial state s_0, parameters p, and local constraints c.

Def. 2. A *connection* $X(A, B) = \langle l2r, r2l \rangle$ maps a subset of $A.p^o$ to $B.p^i$ and a subset of $B.p^o$ to $A.p^i$; $X.p$ denotes the parameters exposed on the connection.

Def. 3. We write $P|_t$ for the state of P at time t. The composition $A \oplus_X B$ combines two parties with connection X, and $A \preceq C$ means that A is a sub-party of C under such a composition.

Def. 4. $\Theta(A).Leak|_t$ denotes the parameters of A leaked up to time t, and $\Theta(A).Attack|_t$ the logical parties derived from those leaks. For a composition, leakage is the span of leaks from both sub-parties and their connecting links.

Def. 5. $Evi_A(B)$ is the evidence about B stored in A.

Def. 6. A party or connection is *inte.* if the attacker cannot modify its protected outputs, and *conf.* if its sensitive parameters are absent from the corresponding leakage set; *secure* means both.

Under this notation, TArCS is modeled as $TArCS = TArCS_{DP} \oplus_{X^S_{Loc} \| X^C_{Loc}} TArCS_{CP}$, where $TArCS_{CP} = C_{TEE} \oplus_{X_{RA}} S_{TEE}$ and $TArCS_{DP} = C_{DP} \oplus_{X_{RDMA}} S_{DP}$. We abstract the underlying RDMA network as a connection whose leakage is no stronger than the link it represents.

A.2 Assumptions and Security Proof

From the threat model in Section 4 and the implementation in Section 5, we use the following assumptions.

Ass. 1. TEE, RA, and local TEE/NEE communication are secure; hence S/C_{TEE}, $X_{RA}(S_{TEE}, C_{TEE})$, and $X_{Loc}(S/C_{TEE}, S/C_{NEE})$ are secure.

Ass. 2. The attacker stealthily corrupts the NEE's sense of time without changing its control flow.[2] Thus the states of S/C_{NEE} remain inte..

[2] Here, stealthiness means that the attacker can only attack in "legal" ways that do not violate the client's constraints.

Ass. 3. Cryptography resists key recovery and plaintext recovery: $K \notin \mathrm{span}(\mathcal{E}_K(M), M)$, and leaking $\mathcal{E}_K(M)$ implies either prior observation of that ciphertext or leakage of K itself.

Ass. 4. The implementation enforces a bounded receive window L: generated packets induce matching ACKs, observed ACKs correspond to previously emitted ciphertexts, and accepted sequence numbers are monotonic at the client.

These assumptions imply that a Trust Attacker cannot forge new valid packets or alter the control flow of the protocol; at most, it can delay packets already emitted on the datapath.

Prop. 1. Confidentiality. $Key \notin \bigcup_{t \in \mathbb{R}} (\Theta(TArCS).Leak)|_t$.

Proof. The key appears only in TEE-protected state and in RA-protected setup traffic. By Asss. 1 and 3, neither location leaks Key, and observing ciphertexts does not reveal the key. Hence Key never enters $\Theta(TArCS).Leak$. □

Lem. 1. Authentication. $\mathcal{E}_{Key}(Seq \parallel T) \in \Theta(TArCS).Leak_t \Rightarrow (Seq \parallel T) \in \bigcup_{\tau \leq t} TArCS.p|_\tau$.

Proof. By Prop. 1, the attacker does not learn Key. Ass. 3 therefore implies that any leaked valid ciphertext must be a ciphertext previously produced inside TArCS. Thus every accepted encrypted packet corresponds to a packet genuinely generated by the server. □

Prop. 2 Integrity. $\forall A \in \Theta(TArCS).Attack|_t$ s.t. $Evic_{C_{DP}}(A \oplus S_{DP}) = Evic_{C_{DP}}(S_{DP})$, $C \oplus S$ and $C \oplus A \oplus S$ have an equivalent execution flow up to a bounded time difference.

Proof. The client authenticates a server by its metadata and ciphertext stream $Evic_{C_{DP}}(S_{DP})$. By Lem. 1, an attacker can only replay or filter packets that were already generated; it cannot fabricate a fresh future packet. Ass. 4 further constrains accepted sequence numbers to a monotonic window of size L, so replay is bounded and cannot change the client's execution except through a timing shift of at most L/f_s. Combined with Ass. 2, the attacker therefore preserves the execution flow and can only introduce bounded delay. □

Prop. 2 shows that attacks on the datapath reduce to delay attacks on valid packets, affecting precision but not `C.` or `I.`. That residual effect is precisely the target of the mitigation evaluated in Section 6.4.

B Pr.H. Attack Defense Details

Pr.H. attackers on the path from the MR to timekeeping threads mainly have two options. In an **MR unmapping attack**, the attacker tries to deregister the victim MR and substitute a malicious one. This fails because RDMA access is controlled by RNIC-managed *rkeys*; once the victim MR is registered, reusing the same valid *rkey* without detection is infeasible.

In a **replay attack**, the attacker races to read, delay, and restore MR entries before the timekeeping threads consume them. TArCS detects this with randomized RDMA Reads of recently written entries: if an attacker removes or rewrites an entry, the server observes a mismatch against the expected ciphertext. Repeated opportunistic interference is therefore exposed with high probability.

C TEE Integration Details

TArCS only requires the TEE to read packets written into an out-of-TEE RDMA MR. In AMD SEV, this maps to shared pages protected by RMP permissions; emerging support such as SEV-TIO further narrows the trusted-I/O gap [2,21]. In Intel SGX, shared unprotected buffers are acceptable because timestamp confidentiality and integrity are still protected by TArCS's encryption and verification [39]. ARM CCA similarly exposes shared buffers between the Realm and the Normal World [7]. These mechanisms allow the same trust boundary to be preserved across today's heterogeneous TEE platforms and future DPU-assisted trusted-I/O designs [22].

D Theoretical Analysis Details

RTT Estimation Derivation. With timestamping events (a)–(h), $RTT = T_{ab} + T_{bc} + T_{cd} + T_{df} + T_{fg} + T_{gh}$. Under approximate link symmetry ($T_{bc} = T_{fg}$), $RTT/2$ estimates the sender-to-client delay up to a sub-microsecond RNIC term. The remaining error in $\Delta T'$ is therefore dominated by link fluctuation and the scan-to-consume delay, matching the Gaussian-plus-uniform model used in Section 6.2.

Delay-mixture Model. Let ρ be the fraction of delayed links and $r = \lambda_{\text{delay}}/\lambda$ the slowdown ratio. Under masking cap q, the worst-case expected deviation is attained at $\rho = q$:

$$\mathbb{E}[\text{err}] = \frac{r\rho \ln \frac{r\rho}{r\rho+1-\rho} - \rho \ln \rho}{(1-\rho)\lambda}.$$

The expression grows slowly for $\rho < 0.5$ and rises sharply once delayed links become the majority, explaining the empirical threshold around 50%.

Low-pass Filter Bound. When a fraction ρ of samples are scheduled out, the filter parameter α bounds the induced error by $\alpha\rho\,\Delta T_{\text{Timestamp}}$. With the typical choice $\alpha = 0.1$, the resulting deviation remains a small fraction of the timestamp period.

E Scalability and Stress Tests

Each server sustains sub-10 ms timing for more than 50 clients, while a single host supports more than 200 servers. A client scales to 220 datapaths and 1500 counting threads, though the precision in Section 6.3–Section 6.4 needs only about 10 datapaths and tens of threads.

Under heavy CPU load, TArCS maintains 3 ms precision on SGX with 10 threads and 2 links, and 2 ms in a single-core SEV-SNP VM under combined memory and I/O stress.

References

1. Abaza, H., et al.: RDMA-based deterministic communication architecture for autonomous driving. In: 2023 IEEE 29th International Conference on Embedded and Real-Time Computing Systems and Applications (RTCSA), pp. 137–146 (2023). https://doi.org/10.1109/RTCSA58653.2023.00025
2. Advanced Micro Devices, Inc.: Amd sev-tio: Trusted i/o for secure encrypted virtualization. Tech. rep., Advanced Micro Devices, Inc. (2023). https://www.amd.com/content/dam/amd/en/documents/epyc-business-docs/white-papers/sev-tio-whitepaper.pdf. white Paper
3. Alder, F., Scopelliti, G., Van Bulck, J., Mühlberg, J.T.: About time: on the challenges of temporal guarantees in untrusted environments. In: Proceedings of the 6th Workshop on System Software for Trusted Execution, pp. 27–33. SysTEX '23, Association for Computing Machinery, New York, NY, USA (2023). https://doi.org/10.1145/3578359.3593038
4. Anwar, F.: Trusted time for untrusted edge systems. In: Proceedings of the 4th International Workshop on Real-time and IntelliGent Edge Computing, pp. 1–6 (2025)
5. Anwar, F.M., Garcia, L., Han, X., Srivastava, M.: Securing time in untrusted operating systems with timeseal. In: 2019 IEEE Real-Time Systems Symposium (RTSS), pp. 80–92 (2019). https://doi.org/10.1109/RTSS46320.2019.00018
6. ARM: Building a secure system using trustzone technology. ARM Technical White Paper, vol. 4 (2009)
7. Arm Limited: Introducing Arm Confidential Compute Architecture Version 4.0 (2025). https://developer.arm.com/documentation/den0125/400/. Accessed 02 May 2025
8. Banks, A.S., Kisiel, M., Korsholm, P.: Remote attestation: a literature review. arXiv:2105.02466 arXiv preprint (2021)
9. Bettinger, M., Ben Mokhtar, S., Simonet-Boulogne, A.: An open-source implementation and security analysis of triad's tee trusted time protocol. In: 2025 55th Annual IEEE/IFIP International Conference on Dependable Systems and Networks - Supplemental Volume (DSN-S), pp. 133–139 (2025).https://doi.org/10.1109/DSN-S65789.2025.00053
10. Coker, G., et al.: Principles of remote attestation. Int. J. Inf. Secur. **10**, 63–81 (2011)
11. Containers, I.: RATS TLS: rats architecture based TLS using librats (2025). https://github.com/inclavare-containers/rats-tls. Accessed 13 Jan 2025
12. Costan, V., Devadas, S.: Intel SGX explained. IACR Cryptol. ePrint Arch. **2016**, 86 (2016)
13. Edition, F., Papoulis, A., Pillai, S.U.: Probability, Random Variables, and Stochastic Processes. McGraw-Hill Europe: New York, NY, USA (2002)
14. Fernandez, G., Brito, A., Fetzer, C.: Triad: trusted timestamps in untrusted environments. In: 2023 IEEE International Conference on Cloud Computing Technology and Science (CloudCom), pp. 169–176. IEEE (2023)
15. Hamidy, G.M., Philippaerts, P., Joosen, W.: T3e: a practical solution to trusted time in secure enclaves. In: Network and System Security: 17th International Conference, NSS 2023, Canterbury, UK, 14–16 August 2023, Proceedings, pp. 305–326. Springer-Verlag, Berlin, Heidelberg (2023). https://doi.org/10.1007/978-3-031-39828-5_17

16. Huang, H., Zhang, F., Yan, S., Wei, T., He, Z.: Sok: a comparison study of arm trustzone and CCA. In: 2024 International Symposium on Secure and Private Execution Environment Design (SEED), pp. 107–118. IEEE (2024)
17. IEEE Standards Association: IEEE standard for a precision clock synchronization protocol for networked measurement and control systems. Standard 1588-2008, IEEE (2008). https://ieeexplore.ieee.org/document/4579760. also known as PTP and gPTP
18. Intel: Intel(r) Software Guard Extensions Software Developer Manual (2016). https://www.intel.com/content/dam/www/public/us/en/documents/manuals
19. Intel: Intel(r) software guard extensions forum TSC discussion topic 743186 (2017). https://software.intel.com/
20. Juffinger, J., Neela, S.R., Gruss, D.: Not so secure TSC. In: 23rd International Conference on Applied Cryptography and Network Security. Springer (2025)
21. Kaplan, D., Powell, J., Woller, T.: Amd memory encryption. Tech. rep., Advanced Micro Devices, Inc. (2021). https://www.amd.com/content/dam/amd/en/documents/epyc-business-docs/white-papers/memory-encryption-white-paper.pdf. white Paper
22. Lal, R., Anderson, J.B., Jackson, A.: Data processing unit's entry into confidential computing. In: Proceedings of the 12th International Workshop on Hardware and Architectural Support for Security and Privacy, pp. 56–63. HASP '23, Association for Computing Machinery, New York, NY, USA (2023). https://doi.org/10.1145/3623652.3623670
23. Lamport, L.: Time, clocks, and the ordering of events in a distributed system. Commun. ACM **21**(7), 558–565 (1978)
24. Le, Y., Stephens, B., Singhvi, A., Akella, A., Swift, M.M.: Rogue: RDMA over generic unconverged ethernet. In: Proceedings of the ACM Symposium on Cloud Computing, pp. 225–236. SoCC '18, Association for Computing Machinery, New York, NY, USA (2018). https://doi.org/10.1145/3267809.3267826
25. Lee, R.B.: Security Basics for Computer Architects. Springer Nature (2022)
26. Li, A., Sudvarg, M., Liu, H., Yu, Z., Gill, C., Zhang, N.: Polyrhythm: adaptive tuning of a multi-channel attack template for timing interference. In: 2022 IEEE Real-Time Systems Symposium (RTSS), pp. 225–239. IEEE (2022)
27. Liang, H., Li, M.: Bring the missing jigsaw back: trustedclock for SGX enclaves. In: Proceedings of the 11th European Workshop on Systems Security. EuroSec'18, Association for Computing Machinery, New York, NY, USA (2018). https://doi.org/10.1145/3193111.3193119
28. Liang, H., Li, M., Chen, Y., Jiang, L., Xie, Z., Yang, T.: Establishing trusted i/o paths for SGX client systems with aurora. IEEE Trans. Inf. Forensics Secur. **15**, 1589–1600 (2020). https://doi.org/10.1109/TIFS.2019.2945621
29. Lichvar, M.: Chrony: a network time protocol (NTP) client and server (2024). https://chrony.tuxfamily.org/. Accessed 13 Jan 2025
30. Mahfouzi, R., Aminifar, A., Samii, S., Payer, M., Eles, P., Peng, Z.: Butterfly attack: adversarial manipulation of temporal properties of cyber-physical systems. In: 2019 IEEE Real-Time Systems Symposium (RTSS), pp. 93–106. IEEE (2019)
31. Mills, D.L., Burbank, J., Barber, W.A., Stone, J.T., Storch, R.J.: Network time protocol version 4: protocol and algorithms specification. Internet Requests Comments (2010). https://rfc-editor.org/rfc/rfc5905.txt
32. Mittal, R., et al.: Revisiting network support for RDMA. In: Proceedings of the 2018 Conference of the ACM Special Interest Group on Data Communication, pp. 313–326. SIGCOMM '18, Association for Computing Machinery, New York, NY, USA (2018). https://doi.org/10.1145/3230543.3230557

33. Mulligan, D.P., Petri, G., Spinale, N., Stockwell, G., Vincent, H.J.: Confidential computing—a brave new world. In: 2021 International Symposium on Secure and Private Execution Environment Design (SEED), pp. 132–138. IEEE (2021)
34. Nasrullah, A., Anwar, F.M.: Trusted timing services with timeguard. In: 2024 IEEE 30th Real-Time and Embedded Technology and Applications Symposium (RTAS), pp. 1–14 (2024). https://doi.org/10.1109/RTAS61025.2024.00009
35. Nasrullah, A., Anwar, F.M.: Sok: state of the time: on trustworthiness of digital clocks. arXiv:2502.09837 arXiv preprint (2025)
36. Raj, H., et al.: FTPM: a software-only implementation of a TPM chip. In: Proceedings of the 25th USENIX Conference on Security Symposium, pp. 841–856. SEC'16, USENIX Association, USA (2016)
37. RDMA Consortium: RDMA over converged ethernet (ROCE) version 2. Specification RoCEv2, RDMA Consortium (2017). https://www.rdmaconsortium.org/. version 2 of the RoCE specification
38. Resner, D., Fröhlich, A.A., Wanner, L.F.: Speculative precision time protocol: submicrosecond clock synchronization for the IoT. In: 2016 IEEE 21st International Conference on Emerging Technologies and Factory Automation (ETFA), pp. 1–8. IEEE (2016)
39. Shen, Y., Chen, Y., Chen, K., Tian, H., Yan, S.: To isolate, or to share? that is a question for intel SGX. In: Proceedings of the 9th Asia-Pacific Workshop on Systems. APSys '18, Association for Computing Machinery, New York, NY, USA (2018). https://doi.org/10.1145/3265723.3265727
40. Tang, A., Sethumadhavan, S., Stolfo, S.: {CLKSCREW}: exposing the perils of {Security-Oblivious} energy management. In: 26th USENIX Security Symposium (USENIX Security 17), pp. 1057–1074 (2017)
41. Trach, B., Faqeh, R., Oleksenko, O., Ozga, W., Bhatotia, P., Fetzer, C.: T-lease: a trusted lease primitive for distributed systems. In: Proceedings of the 11th ACM Symposium on Cloud Computing, pp. 387–400. SoCC '20, Association for Computing Machinery, New York, NY, USA (2020). https://doi.org/10.1145/3419111.3421273
42. Yamashita, K., Cyr, B., Fu, K., Burleson, W., Sugawara, T.: Redshift: manipulating signal propagation delay via continuous-wave lasers. In: IACR Transactions on Cryptographic Hardware and Embedded Systems, pp. 463–489 (2022)
43. Yu, M.: Network telemetry: towards a top-down approach **49**(1), 11–17 (2019). https://doi.org/10.1145/3314212.3314215
44. Yu, W., Rao, N.S., Wyckoff, P., Vetter, J.S.: Performance of RDMA-capable storage protocols on wide-area network. In: 2008 3rd Petascale Data Storage Workshop (2008). https://doi.org/10.1109/PDSW.2008.4811885

Data Efficiency

CRAFT: Exploiting Precharge Cost Asymmetry for Adaptive DRAM Row Buffer Management

Han Xu, Ziyang Liu, Weitong Wang, Yuyangheng Wang, and Fuxin Zhang(✉)

Institute of Computing Technology, Chinese Academy of Sciences, and University of Chinese Academy of Sciences, Beijing, China
{xuhan21b,wangweitong22z,wangyuyangheng22s,fxzhang}@ict.ac.cn, liuziyang20a@mails.ucas.ac.cn

Abstract. DRAM row buffer management presents a fundamental tradeoff between exploiting row buffer locality and minimizing conflict penalties. The optimal policy varies across workloads, execution phases, and individual address ranges. Existing adaptive schemes, however, face a persistent tension between hardware complexity and management effectiveness.

This paper presents CRAFT, a lightweight, cost-aware adaptive timeout scheme for DRAM row buffer management. CRAFT exploits the observation that the two failure modes of speculative precharge incur qualitatively different performance costs, and translates this asymmetry into differentiated per-bank timeout adjustments. Incorrect speculative precharges increase the timeout through exponential backoff, whereas conflicts reduce it with a smaller step proportional to the avoidable overhead. Three precharge-outcome-based refinements further improve adaptation precision without additional hardware. The mechanism requires no prediction tables, feature extraction, or learned models.

We evaluate CRAFT using a cycle-accurate simulator across 12 memory-intensive workloads from graph analytics and scientific computing. CRAFT improves IPC by 7.73%, 3.10%, and 2.84% over ABP, DYMPL, and INTAP, respectively. The total storage overhead is 140 bytes per channel, representing a 24× reduction relative to DYMPL and more than a 140× reduction relative to ABP.

Keywords: DRAM row buffer management · page policy · memory controller · feedback-driven adaptation

1 Introduction

Main memory latency remains a primary performance bottleneck in modern processor systems [7,20,29]. A critical factor governing this latency is how the memory controller manages the *row buffer* in each DRAM bank, the internal

L. Eeckhout et al. (Eds.): APPT 2026, LNCS 16693, pp. 515–530, 2027.
https://doi.org/10.1007/978-981-92-4805-6_34

sense-amplifier array that caches the most recently activated row. Holding a row open (the *open-page* policy) maximizes the chance of serving subsequent accesses to the same row at low latency, but risks expensive conflicts when a subsequent request targets a different row. Closing immediately after each access (the *close-page* policy) eliminates such conflicts but forfeits all potential row locality. This fundamental tradeoff makes row buffer management one of the most extensively studied yet persistently challenging aspects of memory controller design [10,30].

The optimal page policy varies across workloads, execution phases, and address ranges, and neither static policy dominates. Open-page loses up to 11% IPC under frequent row buffer conflicts, while close-page sacrifices up to 28% IPC under high row buffer locality (Fig. 1(a)). Locality also shifts within a single execution. The row buffer hit rate of `mcf` moves from above 90% to below 10%, while `PageRank` follows the inverse trajectory (Fig. 1(b)). It further differs across banks in a channel. Under open-page, `omnetpp` exhibits a per-bank row buffer hit rate coefficient of variation of 1.51. Effective row buffer management should therefore adapt per bank and per execution phase.

Achieving per-bank, phase-adaptive row buffer management with low hardware overhead remains an open problem. Prior adaptive schemes face a tradeoff between hardware complexity and adaptation precision. ABP [3] uses approximately 20 KB per channel for per-row prediction tables. DYMPL [22] uses a 3.39 KB perceptron classifier and requires inference on the critical path. INTAP [4] adjusts a per-bank timeout in approximately 200 bytes per channel, but applies the same fixed step to both incorrect speculative precharges and conflicts, ignoring the distinction between the speculation-induced penalty and the inherent cost of the access pattern.

This paper presents CRAFT, a lightweight, cost-aware adaptive timeout scheme for DRAM row buffer management. Among the four observable outcomes of timeout-based speculative precharge, CRAFT focuses on three feedback-relevant cases: correct speculative precharge, incorrect speculative precharge, and conflict. It translates their asymmetric performance costs into differentiated per-bank timeout adjustments. Incorrect speculative precharges increase the timeout through exponential backoff, whereas conflicts reduce it with a smaller proportional step. The mechanism requires no prediction tables, feature extraction, or learned models. Section 3.1 presents the full cost analysis and design rationale.

The contributions of this paper are as follows:

1. We show that incorrect speculative precharges and conflicts incur qualitatively different performance costs, and we propose CRAFT, a feedback-driven scheme that translates this cost asymmetry into differentiated per-bank timeout adjustments while requiring only 140 bytes per channel, representing more than a 140× storage reduction compared to ABP.
2. Through ablation analysis, we show that precharge outcomes provide an effective basis for timeout adaptation in our evaluated setting, without requiring auxiliary runtime metrics.

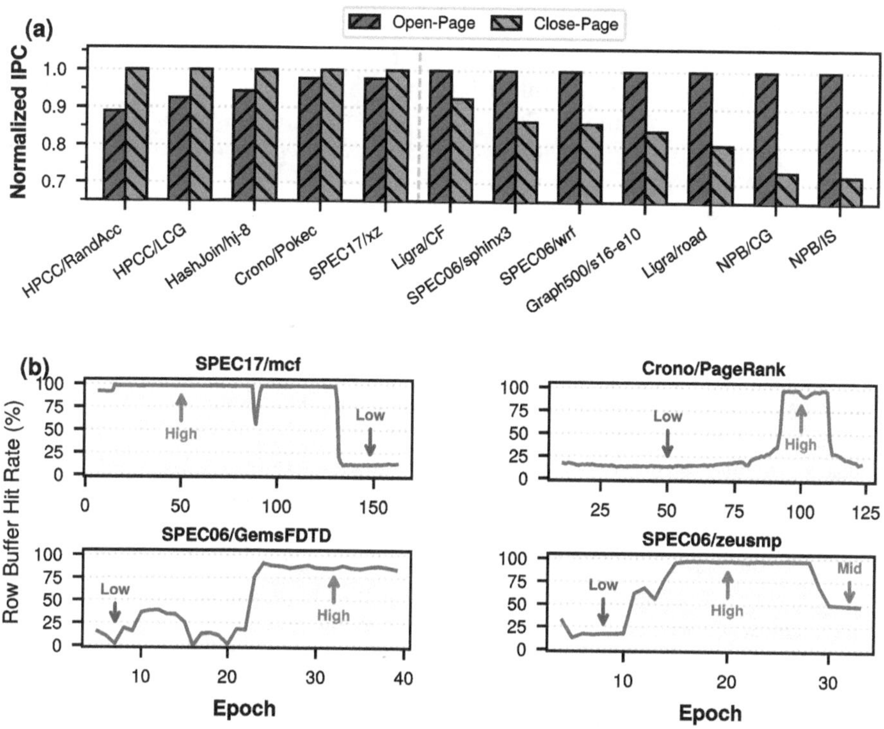

Fig. 1. (a) Normalized IPC of open-page and close-page policies across 12 memory-intensive workloads, normalized to the better static policy per workload. Neither static policy dominates across all workloads. (b) Row buffer hit rate across execution epochs under the open-page policy for four representative workloads. Each workload exhibits distinct phase transitions between high- and low-locality regimes.

3. We evaluate CRAFT on 12 memory-intensive workloads under a DDR5-4800 configuration. CRAFT improves IPC relative to ABP, DYMPL, and INTAP across the evaluated workloads.

2 Background

2.1 DRAM Row Buffer Fundamentals

Modern DRAM organizes each bank around a *row buffer*, an array of sense amplifiers that latches the most recently activated row. As Fig. 2(a) shows, access latency depends on the row buffer state. A hit incurs only t_{CAS}, a miss requires $t_{\mathrm{RCD}} + t_{\mathrm{CAS}}$, and a conflict requires precharge then activation, totaling $t_{\mathrm{RP}} + t_{\mathrm{RCD}} + t_{\mathrm{CAS}}$. An *open-page* policy keeps the row open to exploit hits, whereas a *close-page* policy precharges immediately to avoid conflicts. Neither static policy dominates, as Fig. 1 shows.

Timeout-based Speculative Precharge. Timeout-based policies occupy a middle ground. The controller starts a countdown timer when a row becomes idle, and speculatively precharges the bank if the timer expires before the next request. A short timeout approximates close-page behavior and a long timeout approximates open-page behavior. This speculation produces one of four outcomes, illustrated in Fig. 2(b):

1. **Correct speculative precharge.** The next request targets a different row, so the precharge correctly anticipated the end of locality. The effective cost is zero.
2. **Incorrect speculative precharge.** The next request targets the same row, forcing a reactivation. Both the precharge and the reactivation are unnecessary operations that would not occur if the row were kept open.
3. **Conflict.** The next request targets a different row before the timeout expires. The controller issues an on-demand precharge and then activates the target row. The activation is inherent to the access pattern, and only the opportunity to overlap precharge with idle bank cycles is lost.
4. **Row buffer hit.** The next request targets the same row before the timeout, incurring no additional cost. Because no precharge is issued, CRAFT's feedback loop operates on the first three outcomes only.

2.2 Limitations of Existing Adaptive Schemes

Several adaptive row buffer management schemes have been proposed. Table 1 summarizes three representative baselines.

Table 1. Comparison of adaptive row buffer management baselines.

Scheme	Decision Mechanism	Storage/Ch	Key Limitation
ABP	Per-row access count table	~20 KB	High storage; binary prediction
DYMPL	Perceptron + page row table	3.39 KB	Indirect features; no cost-aware adaptation
INTAP	Mistake counter, fixed step	~200 B	Symmetric step; no cost differentiation

ABP [3] requires approximately 20 KB per channel for a set-associative per-row prediction table, which is impractical for DDR5 controllers with 32 banks per channel. DYMPL [22] employs a perceptron over seven features with a 512-entry page row table at 3.39 KB per channel, and does not directly observe the cost consequences of precharge decisions. INTAP [4] adjusts a per-bank timeout through a mistake counter, but applies symmetric fixed-step adjustments that treat incorrect speculative precharges and conflicts identically.

All three baselines share a deeper deficiency. None distinguishes precharge outcomes by the nature of the waste they produce. This distinction motivates CRAFT's cost-aware timeout adaptation, analyzed in Sect. 3.1.

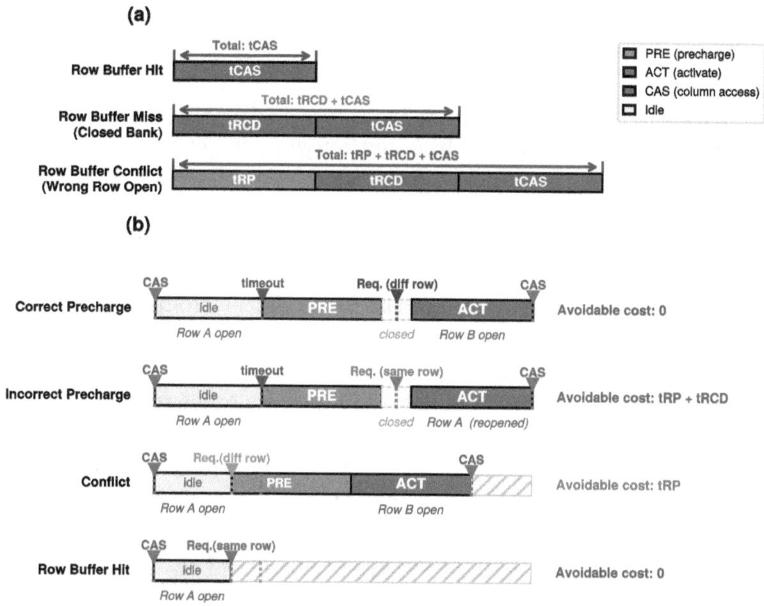

Fig. 2. Row buffer access scenarios and timeout precharge outcomes. (a) Three row buffer states at the time of a memory request. A row buffer hit incurs only t_{CAS}. A closed-bank access requires $t_{\text{RCD}} + t_{\text{CAS}}$. A row buffer conflict pays $t_{\text{RP}} + t_{\text{RCD}} + t_{\text{CAS}}$. (b) Four outcomes of timeout-triggered speculative precharge. CRAFT's feedback loop uses the three outcomes involving a precharge event.

3 CRAFT Design

CRAFT exploits the cost asymmetry of precharge outcomes to adaptively manage DRAM row buffers. It comprises a core feedback loop (Sect. 3.1), three precharge-outcome-based refinements (Sect. 3.2), and a compact hardware implementation (Sect. 3.3).

3.1 Core Feedback Loop

CRAFT maintains a per-bank timeout counter that specifies the number of idle cycles after the last column access before the controller speculatively issues a precharge. It detects the three precharge outcomes at two points. A conflict occurs when a request for a different row arrives before the timeout expires, indicating the timeout is too long. The other two outcomes are identified at the activation following a timeout-triggered precharge. A same-row activation indicates an incorrect speculative precharge and a timeout that was too short, whereas a different-row activation indicates a correct precharge at an appropriate timeout. CRAFT exploits the different performance costs of these outcomes to derive both the direction and the magnitude of each adjustment.

CRAFT adjusts the per-bank timeout value in response to these outcomes according to three design principles.

(a) Cost-driven Asymmetric Step Sizes. Timeout-based speculative precharge serves both sides of the trade-off. Keeping a row open serves same-row accesses as row buffer hits, while a timely precharge overlaps precharge overhead with idle bank cycles and reduces the penalty for subsequent different-row accesses. An incorrect speculative precharge eliminates the first benefit entirely. Both the precharge and the subsequent reactivation are unnecessary operations that would not occur if the row were kept open, so the controller-attributable waste amounts to $t_{RP} + t_{RCD}$.

Conflicts present a different cost model. The target row differs from the buffered row, so the precharge and activation are inherent to the access pattern regardless of the timeout decision, and only the timing is a controller-attributable error. A correctly timed precharge would have overlapped t_{RP} with idle bank cycles, so the avoidable overhead is limited to that missed overlap of t_{RP}.

The ratio of avoidable overhead between these two outcomes is $(t_{RP} + t_{RCD})/t_{RP}$. Under our DDR5-4800 configuration with $t_{RP} = t_{RCD} = 40$ cycles, the ratio is 2:1. CRAFT mirrors this asymmetry in its adjustment magnitudes. The increment for incorrect speculative precharges uses a base value of `BASE_STEP` = 50 cycles, slightly larger than t_{RP}, so each increase produces an observable change in the timeout. The decrement for conflicts is scaled by the factor $t_{RP}/(t_{RP}+t_{RCD})$ and evaluates to 25 cycles under the same configuration.

These magnitudes are not specific to DDR5-4800. Both steps are derived at initialization from t_{RP} and the ratio $t_{RP}/(t_{RP} + t_{RCD})$ rather than being fixed constants. For a DRAM standard with $t_{RP} \neq t_{RCD}$, the same expressions yield a different and automatically computed asymmetry, so porting CRAFT to another timing configuration requires no manual retuning. The design is therefore tied to the form of the timing model rather than to the specific DDR5-4800 values.

This asymmetry creates a deliberate upward bias. Under equal frequencies of incorrect speculative precharges and conflicts, net timeout increases accumulate, reflecting the 2:1 cost ratio. T_{MAX} bounds this bias at 3200 cycles, after which conflicts and reductions following consecutive correct speculative precharges provide downward pressure.

(b) Exponential Backoff. CRAFT applies exponential backoff to consecutive incorrect speculative precharges by left-shifting the base step. Let n denote the number of consecutive incorrect speculative precharges observed so far, capped at $N_{\max} = 7$. The effective step size is

$$s = s_0 \cdot 2^{\min(n,\, N_{\max})} \tag{1}$$

where s_0 = `BASE_STEP` = 50 cycles. A conflict resets the counter to zero. A correct speculative precharge decrements the counter by one (the SD refinement in Sect. 3.2), dampening future backoff without fully erasing it. This enables rapid convergence during sustained high-locality phases, reaching the upper bound within a few feedback events.

(c) Continuous Adjustment Range. The timeout adjusts within $[T_{\mathrm{MIN}}, T_{\mathrm{MAX}}] = [50, 3200]$ cycles. T_{MIN} matches `BASE_STEP` to prevent degeneration to close-page behavior, and T_{MAX} prevents indefinitely open rows.

Algorithm 1 presents the complete pseudocode, including the three refinements described in Sect. 3.2 (annotated [RS], [RW], [SD]).

Algorithm 1 CRAFT Feedback Loop

```
On each incoming bank request (while row open):
if new_row ≠ open_row then                                   ▷ Conflict
    step ← BASE_STEP × tRP/(tRP + tRCD)
    if is_read: step ← 2 × step                              ▷ [RW]
    timeout ← timeout − step                                 ▷ Reduce timeout
    reopen_streak ← 0; right_streak ← 0
    timeout ← clamp(timeout, T_MIN, T_MAX)
end if

On each bank ACT event (following timeout precharge):
if prev_closed_by_timeout then
    if new_row = prev_row then                               ▷ Incorrect speculative precharge
        step ← BASE_STEP ≪ min(reopen_streak, SHIFT_CAP)
        if is_write: step ← step ≫ 1                         ▷ [RW]
        timeout ← timeout + step                             ▷ Increase timeout
        reopen_streak ← min(reopen_streak + 1, 7)
        right_streak ← 0
    else                                                     ▷ Correct speculative precharge
        reopen_streak ← max(reopen_streak − 1, 0)            ▷ [SD]
        right_streak ← min(right_streak + 1, 7)              ▷ [RS]
        if right_streak ≥ 4 then                             ▷ [RS]
            timeout ← timeout − BASE_STEP × tRP/(2 (tRP + tRCD))   ▷ [RS]
        end if
    end if
    timeout ← clamp(timeout, T_MIN, T_MAX)
end if
```

3.2 Precharge-Path Refinements

The core feedback loop provides the primary adaptive capability. The following three refinements exploit additional precharge-outcome information to improve adaptation precision. All three are lightweight and add no hardware structures beyond simple counters.

(a) Timeout Reduction After Consecutive Correct Speculative Precharges (RS). After four or more consecutive correct speculative precharges, the timeout decrements by half the conflict decrement. The threshold of four provides a conservative confirmation that a high-locality phase has ended, so the reduction is not

triggered by isolated correct outcomes from transient access noise. Without RS, a bank leaving a high-locality phase would retain an unnecessarily large timeout until a conflict explicitly triggers a reduction. RS therefore provides a proactive reduction path in the absence of conflict signals, adding three bits per bank for the *right_streak* counter.

(b) Read/Write Cost Differentiation (RW). An incorrect speculative precharge blocking a read stalls the processor pipeline, while one blocking a write is absorbed by the write buffer in the memory controller. CRAFT exploits this asymmetry by halving the increment for write incorrect speculative precharges and doubling the decrement for read conflicts. RW requires no additional storage.

(c) Streak Decay (SD). Each correct speculative precharge decrements *reopen_streak* by one, preventing a historically elevated streak from causing disproportionately large increments later. SD requires no additional storage.

3.3 Hardware Overhead

Each bank maintains five fields totaling 35 bits: a 12-bit timeout value, two 3-bit streak counters, a 16-bit previous-row address, and a 1-bit timeout-precharge flag. For 32 banks per channel, this amounts to 140 bytes per channel. CRAFT requires no specialized hardware structures; the critical path requires only one comparison and one addition or subtraction.

CRAFT operates entirely at the policy layer. It sets the per-bank timeout that determines when an idle row becomes a candidate for speculative precharge, and it does not issue DRAM commands directly. When a timeout expires, the resulting precharge enters the command queue and is issued by the existing command scheduler, which enforces all JEDEC timing constraints. A speculative precharge therefore observes t_{RAS} on the open row and t_{RP} before the subsequent activation, identically to an on-demand precharge. Refresh commands retain priority under t_{REFI} and t_{RFC}, and read-to-write turnaround timing is unaffected. CRAFT changes only the timing of an otherwise legal precharge decision and never overrides protocol constraints.

4 Methodology

4.1 Simulation Infrastructure

We evaluate CRAFT using ChampSim [6] integrated with DRAMSim3 [17], implementing CRAFT and all three baselines within the same infrastructure and DRAM controller model. All schemes share the same processor, cache hierarchy, DRAM timing parameters, address mapping, command queue sizes, traces, and warmup and measurement intervals, summarized in Table 2.

Table 2. Simulation configuration.

Component	Parameter	Value
Processor	Frequency	4 GHz
	Pipeline width	6
	ROB entries	350
Caches	L1 (I/D): Size / Assoc.Latency	32 KB / 8-way / 4 cycles
	L2: Size/Assoc.Latency	1 MB/8-way/10 cycles
	LLC: Size/Assoc.Latency	4 MB/16-way/20 cycles
DRAM	Standard	DDR5-4800
	Channels/Ranks/Banks per channel	4/1/32
	Rows per bank	65,536
	$t_{CAS}/t_{RCD}/t_{RP}$ (DRAM cycles)	40/40/40
	Address mapping	Ro-Ra-Ba-Bg-Ch-Co
	Command queue (per bank)	8 entries

4.2 Workloads

We select 12 memory-intensive workloads from three suites. Graph workloads are drawn from LIGRA [25] and CRONO [1] on three SNAP graphs [16]: roadNet-CA, higgs, and soc-pokec. The scientific workloads are sphinx3 and wrf from SPEC CPU2006 [8]. Representative phases are selected with SimPoint [24] using maxK = 30 and 100M-instruction intervals, with 20M instructions for warmup and 80M for measurement per point. The suite is intentionally biased toward memory-intensive single-core behavior, and we interpret the results within that setting.

4.3 Baselines

We compare CRAFT against ABP [3], DYMPL [22], and INTAP [4]. All baselines are implemented in the same infrastructure under the DDR5-4800 configuration in Table 2. All schemes use the same FR-FCFS command scheduler. The address mapping, queue capacities, and trace inputs also remain fixed across schemes; only the row buffer management logic differs. Unless otherwise noted, the CRAFT configuration evaluated in Sects. 5.1–5.3 includes the core feedback loop and all three precharge-outcome-based refinements (RS, RW, SD) described in Sect. 3.2. Section 5.4 isolates the contribution of each component.

4.4 Metrics

We report three metrics. **IPC** is the primary metric, reported as per-workload improvement over each baseline. **Read row buffer hit rate** is the fraction of read requests served from the activated row; write hit rates are excluded because writes complete in the controller's write buffer. **Average read latency** is the mean DRAM service time for reads in DRAM cycles.

5 Evaluation

5.1 IPC Performance

Figure 3 presents the per-workload IPC improvement of CRAFT over each baseline. CRAFT achieves geometric mean IPC improvements of 7.73% over ABP, 3.10% over DYMPL, and 2.84% over INTAP. CRAFT improves IPC on all 12 workloads relative to all three baselines, with gains ranging from 1.61% to 12.20%.

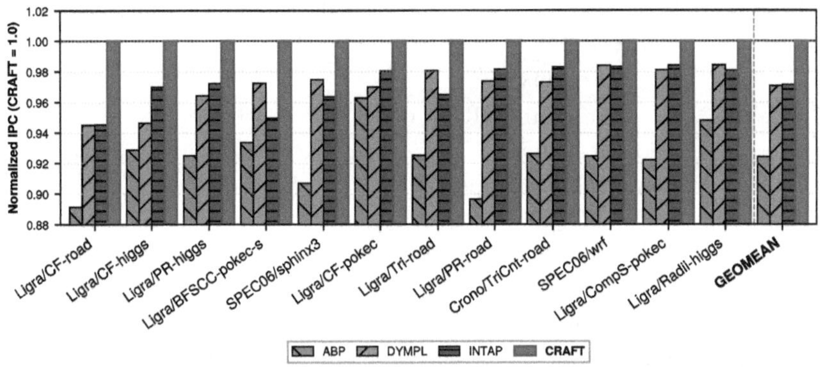

Fig. 3. Normalized IPC across 12 workloads (CRAFT = 1.0). CRAFT improves IPC relative to all three baselines on the evaluated workloads. The geometric mean improvements are 7.73%, 3.10%, and 2.84% over ABP, DYMPL, and INTAP, respectively.

The largest gains over ABP occur in graph traversal workloads such as CF and PageRank (7.1% to 12.2%), where locality changes abruptly across phases. Graph analysis and the two scientific workloads also benefit, indicating that the per-bank feedback loop adapts across several locality regimes.

5.2 DRAM-Level Performance Analysis

Figure 4 presents the per-workload read row buffer hit rate and average read latency for all four schemes. CRAFT achieves the highest read row buffer hit rate (RBHR) on all 12 workloads, surpassing the best baseline by an average of 5.62%, with the largest gains on CF/roadNet-CA (+9.25%), PageRank/roadNet-CA (+9.12%), and sphinx3 (+7.76%). CRAFT also achieves the lowest average read latency, with a mean reduction of 2.74%. The RBHR and latency improvements are correlated, confirming that the IPC gains in Sect. 5.1 originate from improved row buffer management at the DRAM level. Write row buffer hit rates remain nearly identical across all policies, so the gain comes primarily from the read path.

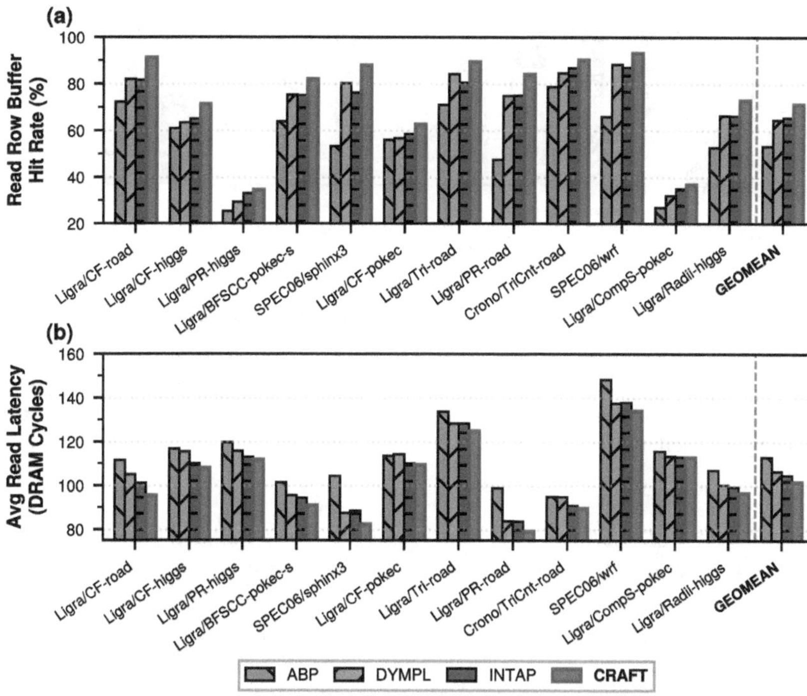

Fig. 4. DRAM-level performance across 12 workloads. (a) Read row buffer hit rate. CRAFT achieves the highest RBHR on every workload, with an average improvement of 5.62% over the best baseline. (b) Average read latency in DRAM cycles. CRAFT achieves the lowest latency on every workload, with a mean reduction of 2.74%.

5.3 Timeout Distribution

Figure 5 presents the timeout value distribution for each workload. We partition the timeout range into Low [50, 800), Mid [800, 2000), and High [2000, 3200]. These ranges correspond to close-page-like, intermediate, and open-page-like behavior. Three adaptation patterns emerge.

In close-page-like workloads, PageRank/higgs concentrates 96.9% of observations in the Low range, with Components-Shortcut/pokec similar. In a gradual transition, CF/higgs spreads values across all three ranges, reflecting a shift from conflict-dominated early phases to locality-rich later phases. In open-page-like workloads, the roadNet-CA cases concentrate in the High range, and PageRank on roadNet-CA yields 90.9% High versus 96.9% Low on higgs, confirming that adaptation reflects the runtime access pattern rather than algorithm identity.

The timeout distribution also evolves over execution progress. CF/roadNet-CA remains dominated by the High range throughout execution, consistent with sustained spatial locality in the road-network graph, whereas CF/higgs begins in the Low range and gradually transitions toward higher timeout values. sphinx3 stays predominantly in the High range but exhibits periodic fluctuations into

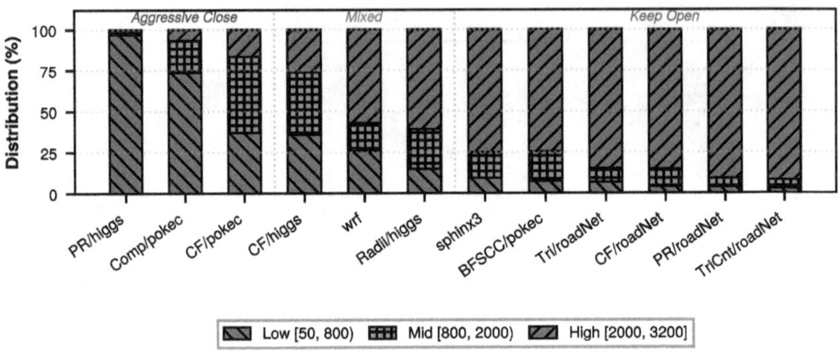

Fig. 5. Timeout value distribution across 12 workloads, sorted from close-page-like (left) to open-page-like (right). CRAFT adapts to three distinct behavioral regimes without any explicit mode selection.

the Low and Mid ranges, indicating brief phases of reduced locality within an overall open-page-like pattern.

5.4 Ablation Study

We quantify the contribution of each design component. Table 3 defines the variants, and Fig. 6 compares eight of them, normalizing each variant's geometric mean IPC gain over the best baseline to the core feedback loop's gain.

Table 3. Ablation study variants.

Variant	Components	Description
BASE	Core loop only	Cost-asymmetric step sizes + exponential backoff
RS	BASE + Right Streak	Timeout reduction after consecutive correct speculative precharges
RW	BASE + Read/Write	Differentiated step sizes by command type
SD	BASE + Streak Decay	Gradual decay of *reopen_streak* on correct speculative precharges
PRECHARGE	BASE + RS + RW + SD	All three precharge-outcome-based refinements combined
PR	BASE + Phase Reset	Reset timeout to initial value on conflict
QDSD	BASE + Queue-Depth	Scale the conflict decrement by queue occupancy
ALL	PRECHARGE + PR + QDSD	All precharge-outcome-based and conflict-based heuristics combined

BASE (cost-asymmetric step sizes + exponential backoff) accounts for 76% of the final improvement, indicating that outcome-aware feedback provides a strong

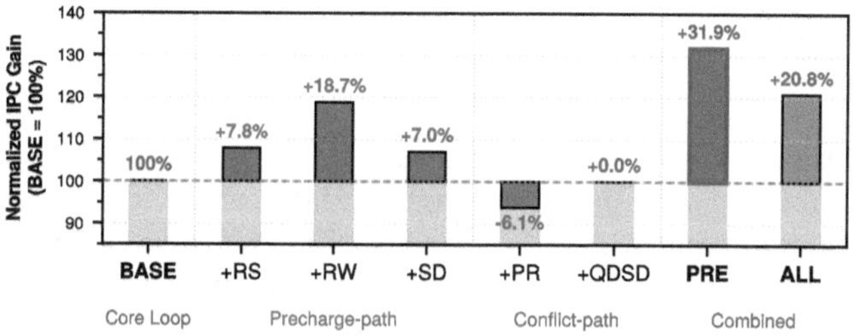

Fig. 6. Ablation study of CRAFT design components. Green bars correspond to the core feedback loop and the PRECHARGE configuration. Blue bars show individual precharge-outcome-based enhancements. Red bars show individual conflict-based heuristics. The dashed line marks the BASE level. (Color figure online)

signal. The PRECHARGE variant (BASE + RS + RW + SD) achieves 131.9% of BASE's gain, with RW strongest at 118.7% and RS and SD reaching 107.8% and 107.0%. Conflict-based heuristics do not help. PR and QDSD individually reach 93.9% and 100.0% of BASE, and the ALL variant reaches 120.8%, an 11.1% drop from PRECHARGE. The three-way precharge outcome classification thus captures most of the useful feedback information.

6 Related Work

Static page policies set a fixed behavior. JEDEC [11] defines per-command auto-precharge, and Minimalist Open-page [12] closes a row after a fixed hit count. Predictor-based schemes infer per-row reuse from history or address signals [3,5], but their storage scales with the number of tracked rows. INTAP [4] adjusts a per-bank timeout through a fixed-step mistake counter, applying identical adjustments to both failure modes. DYMPL [22] applies a perceptron over indirect features, and [9] uses reinforcement learning. Both require auxiliary model state and do not directly observe precharge outcome cost. CRAFT instead distinguishes the two failure modes by cost and sets adjustment magnitudes from this asymmetry without additional model state.

Other work addresses DRAM performance from orthogonal angles. Scheduling algorithms such as FR-FCFS [23], stall-time fair scheduling [21], Thread Cluster Memory Scheduling [13], and Staged Memory Scheduling [2] govern request issue order, and the virtual write queue [26] coordinates write-back with row management. Multi-core interference proposals [19,27] partition bandwidth or estimate slowdown for fairness. At the device level, SALP [14] and Tiered-Latency DRAM [15] reduce access overhead through bank and subarray organization, RAIDR [18] reduces refresh frequency, and Udipi et al. [28] propose energy-aware rank arrangements. These are complementary to CRAFT, which operates at the policy layer and changes neither the DRAM device nor the scheduler.

7 Conclusion

This paper presents CRAFT, a lightweight row buffer management scheme that exploits the cost asymmetry between the two failure modes of speculative precharge, combining asymmetric timeout updates with exponential backoff in only 140 bytes per channel. Across 12 memory-intensive workloads, it improves IPC by 7.73%, 3.10%, and 2.84% over ABP, DYMPL, and INTAP, raises the read row buffer hit rate by 5.62% over the best baseline, and reduces read latency by 2.74%. Broader multi-core and cross-standard validation of these single-core DDR5 results remains future work.

Acknowledgments. This work was supported by the Innovation Project of the Institute of Computing Technology, Chinese Academy of Sciences under Grant E461100.

Disclosure of Interests. The authors have no competing interests to declare.

Use of Generative AI. Artificial intelligence tools, if used, were used only for language organization and figure/table polishing, and did not participate in the generation of the core ideas or technical content.

References

1. Ahmad, M., Hijaz, F., Shi, Q., Khan, O.: CRONO: a benchmark suite for multithreaded graph algorithms executing on futuristic multicores. In: 2015 IEEE International Symposium on Workload Characterization, pp. 44–55 (2015)
2. Ausavarungnirun, R., Chang, K.K.W., Subramanian, L., Loh, G.H., Mutlu, O.: Staged memory scheduling: achieving high performance and scalability in heterogeneous systems. In: 39th International Symposium on Computer Architecture (ISCA 2012), pp. 416–427. IEEE Computer Society (2012)
3. Awasthi, M., Nellans, D.W., Sudan, K., Balasubramonian, R., Davis, A.: Handling the problems and opportunities posed by multiple on-chip memory controllers. In: Proceedings of the 19th International Conference on Parallel Architectures and Compilation Techniques, pp. 319–330 (2010)
4. Dodd, J.M.: Adaptive page management (2006). uS Patent 7,076,617
5. Ghasempour, M., Jaleel, A., Garside, J.D., Luján, M.: HAPPY: hybrid address-based page policy in DRAMs. In: Proceedings of the Second International Symposium on Memory Systems, pp. 311–321 (2016)
6. Gober, N., et al.: The Championship Simulator: Architectural Simulation for Education and Competition (2022)
7. Hennessy, J.L., Patterson, D.A.: A new golden age for computer architecture. Commun. ACM **62**(2), 48–60 (2019)
8. Henning, J.L.: SPEC CPU2006 benchmark descriptions. ACM SIGARCH Comput. Architect. News **34**(4), 1–17 (2006)
9. Ipek, E., Mutlu, O., Martínez, J.F., Caruana, R.: Self optimizing memory controllers: a reinforcement learning approach. In: Proceedings of the 35th Annual International Symposium on Computer Architecture, pp. 39–50 (2008)
10. Jacob, B., Wang, D., Ng, S.: Memory systems: cache, DRAM, disk. Morgan Kaufmann (2010)

11. JEDEC Solid State Technology Association: JEDEC DDR5 SDRAM standard. JESD79-5 (2020)
12. Kaseridis, D., Stuecheli, J., John, L.K.: Minimalist open-page: a DRAM page-mode scheduling policy for the many-core era. In: Proceedings of the 44th Annual IEEE/ACM International Symposium on Microarchitecture, pp. 24–35 (2011)
13. Kim, Y., Papamichael, M., Mutlu, O., Harchol-Balter, M.: Thread cluster memory scheduling: exploiting differences in memory access behavior. In: 43rd Annual IEEE/ACM International Symposium on Microarchitecture (MICRO 2010), pp. 65–76. IEEE Computer Society (2010)
14. Kim, Y., Seshadri, V., Lee, D., Liu, J., Mutlu, O.: A case for exploiting subarray-level parallelism (SALP) in DRAM. In: 39th International Symposium on Computer Architecture (ISCA 2012), pp. 368–379. IEEE Computer Society (2012)
15. Lee, D., Kim, Y., Seshadri, V., Liu, J., Subramanian, L., Mutlu, O.: Tiered-latency DRAM: a low latency and low cost DRAM architecture. In: 19th IEEE International Symposium on High Performance Computer Architecture (HPCA 2013), pp. 615–626. IEEE Computer Society (2013)
16. Leskovec, J., Sosič, R.: SNAP: a general-purpose network analysis and graph-mining library. ACM Trans. Intell. Syst. Technol. **8**(1), 1–20 (2016)
17. Li, S., Yang, Z., Reddy, D., Srivastava, A., Jacob, B.: DRAMsim3: a cycle-accurate, thermal-capable DRAM simulator. IEEE Comput. Archit. Lett. **19**(2), 106–109 (2020)
18. Liu, J., Jaiyen, B., Veras, R., Mutlu, O.: RAIDR: retention-aware intelligent DRAM refresh. In: 39th International Symposium on Computer Architecture (ISCA 2012), pp. 1–12. IEEE Computer Society (2012)
19. Muralidhara, S.P., Subramanian, L., Mutlu, O., Kandemir, M.T., Moscibroda, T.: Reducing memory interference in multicore systems via application-aware memory channel partitioning. In: 44th Annual IEEE/ACM International Symposium on Microarchitecture (MICRO 2011), pp. 374–385. ACM (2011)
20. Mutlu, O.: Memory scaling: a systems architecture perspective. In: 5th IEEE International Memory Workshop, pp. 21–25. IEEE (2013)
21. Mutlu, O., Moscibroda, T.: Stall-time fair memory access scheduling for chip multiprocessors. In: 40th Annual IEEE/ACM International Symposium on Microarchitecture (MICRO 2007), pp. 146–160. IEEE Computer Society (2007)
22. Rafique, M.M., Lin, W.T., Ramanathan, A., Manohar, R.: Dympl: dynamic multi-feature page management policy using perceptron learning. In: Proceedings of the International Symposium on Memory Systems (2022)
23. Rixner, S., Dally, W.J., Kapasi, U.J., Mattson, P.R., Owens, J.D.: Memory access scheduling. In: 27th International Symposium on Computer Architecture (ISCA 2000), pp. 128–138. IEEE Computer Society (2000)
24. Sherwood, T., Perelman, E., Hamerly, G., Calder, B.: Automatically characterizing large scale program behavior. In: Proceedings of the 10th International Conference on Architectural Support for Programming Languages and Operating Systems, pp. 45–57 (2002)
25. Shun, J., Blelloch, G.E.: LIGRA: a lightweight graph processing framework for shared memory. In: Proceedings of the 18th ACM SIGPLAN Symposium on Principles and Practice of Parallel Programming, pp. 135–146 (2013)
26. Stuecheli, J., Kaseridis, D., Daly, D., Hunter, H.C., John, L.K.: The virtual write queue: coordinating DRAM and last-level cache policies. In: 37th International Symposium on Computer Architecture (ISCA 2010), pp. 72–82. ACM (2010)

27. Subramanian, L., Seshadri, V., Kim, Y., Jaiyen, B., Mutlu, O.: MISE: providing performance predictability and improving fairness in shared main memory systems. In: 19th IEEE International Symposium on High Performance Computer Architecture (HPCA 2013), pp. 639–650. IEEE Computer Society (2013)
28. Udipi, A.N., Muralimanohar, N., Chatterjee, N., Balasubramonian, R., Davis, A., Jouppi, N.P.: Rethinking DRAM design and organization for energy-constrained multi-cores. In: 37th International Symposium on Computer Architecture (ISCA 2010), pp. 175–186. ACM (2010)
29. Wulf, W.A., McKee, S.A.: Hitting the memory wall: implications of the obvious. ACM SIGARCH Comput. Architect. News **23**(1), 20–24 (1995)
30. Zhang, Z., Zhu, Z., Zhang, X.: A permutation-based page interleaving scheme to reduce row-buffer conflicts and exploit data locality. In: Proceedings of the 33rd Annual ACM/IEEE International Symposium on Microarchitecture, pp. 32–41 (2000)

Improving Compression Ratio of Lossy Compression for HPC via Modeling-Based Arithmetic Coding

Zhichao Yang, Xiangyu Zou(✉), Wen Xia, and Boou Jiang

Harbin Institute of Technology, Shenzhen, China
zouxiangyu@hit.edu.cn

Abstract. HPC applications generate massive amounts of data that impose significant burdens on both storage and I/O systems. Although lossy compressors have been widely adopted in this scenario to reduce data volume to accelerate data dumps/loads, the SOTA approach fails to fully exploit data redundancy because it relies on separate techniques that operate at incompatible granularity. Their suboptimal compression ratios leave I/O as the dominant bottleneck in data dumps/loads.

We propose MAC, a compression framework that aligns modeling-based arithmetic coding with HPC system characteristics. It exploits a key compute-for-I/O trade-off: (1) Modeling-based arithmetic coding achieves near-optimal compression ratios but is always constrained by processing speed. (2) HPC system relies on compression-assisted I/O, and a higher compression ratio (reduce I/O cost) can largely offset the overhead of slower compression for such I/O-bounded scenario. To fully unlock this trade-off and make it practically efficient, we design several techniques such as structure-aware compaction and structure-based modeling, to mitigate the speed constraints of arithmetic coding. Experimental results show that MAC not only delivers superior compression ratios but also improves data dumping and loading throughput, demonstrating its effectiveness for HPC systems.

Keywords: Data Compression · HPC · I/O acceleration

1 Introduction

High-performance computing (HPC) simulations generate massive volumes of data. For example, climate scientists often run large ensembles of high-fidelity simulations, and estimating even a single ensemble member per simulated day can produce as much as 260 TB of data every 16 s across the ensemble [6,19,24]. Such extreme data rates impose tremendous burdens on the storage and I/O systems of HPC clusters, motivating the use of compression techniques [12,22,27] to alleviate pressure.

Error-bounded lossy compressors have been widely adopted in HPC because they achieve much higher compression ratios while preserving data usability [2,15]. They are often integrated into I/O frameworks of supercomputers

L. Eeckhout et al. (Eds.): APPT 2026, LNCS 16693, pp. 531–546, 2027.
https://doi.org/10.1007/978-981-92-4805-6_35

such as ADIOS2 [8] to reduce storage and I/O overhead. However, despite delivering compression ratios several times higher than lossless compressors, I/O still dominates data dumps/loads, accounting for up to 80% of total runtime [22,27]. This highlights the critical need for further improving compression ratios.

SZ [11,22] is the state-of-the-art lossy compressor. It aims to compress sequences or matrices of floating-point numbers, the main data type in scientific scenario, with both high compression ratios and strict adherence to user-specified error bounds. The workflow of the SZ compressor consists of two main stages: ❶ Delta Computation and Quantization. Differences between adjacent floating-point numbers are quantized into *quantization factors*, with the maximum quantization error limited to the user-specified error bound. ❷ Compression on Quantization Factors. Huffman coding [9] and LZ-based algorithms like Zstd [5] or Gzip [7] are sequentially applied to compress these factors and losslessly exploit their redundancies.

However, our study reveals that the second stage of SZ fails to jointly exploit different redundancies in quantization factors, fundamentally limiting compression effectiveness. Specifically, in this stage, huffman coding leverages symbol-frequency skewness and LZ-based algorithms target repeated bytestreams, but their incompatible processing granularity prevent effective integration (§ 2.4): ❶ Huffman coding converts integer factors into variable-length bitstreams, breaking byte alignment and weakening subsequent byte-level LZ compression; ❷ reversing the order leads to similar inefficiency.

To address this limitation, we discover that modeling-based arithmetic coding can help. Modeling-based arithmetic coding is an entropy coding technique that builds statistical and historical contexts to capture both symbol-frequency skewness and repeated fragments in bit-level. It achieves a deep understanding of data trends, and thus achieves superior compression ratios. However, its modeling step leads to an extremely low throughput (often below 1 MB/s, § 2.5), which confines its use to only academic research in the past.

The opportunity lies in an alignment between HPC system characteristics and modeling-based arithmetic coding: ❶ Modeling-based arithmetic coding offers higher compression ratios but suffers from slow speed. ❷ As mentioned above, in scientific applications, I/O still accounts for more than 80% of the overall runtime even with compressors employed [22,27], meaning that higher compression ratios potentially can offset slower compression by reducing I/O overhead during data dumps/loads.

To fully unlock this trade-off, we propose MAC, an efficient HPC compressor for I/O acceleration. ❶ It integrates the modeling-based arithmetic coding into the SZ compressor, unlocking greater compression potential. ❷ It proposes two techniques to leverage the structural characteristics of scientific data, which hugely reduces the computation overhead in modeling process, and thus, makes modeling-based arithmetic coding practical for HPC scenarios.

The evaluation suggests that MAC-SZ achieves a compression ratio of up to 28% higher compared to the original SZ compressor with a comparable end-to-end throughput in the data dumps/loads. Moreover, our implementation is significantly more efficient than directly applying the fast modeling-based arithmetic coding (LPAQ [14]), with about 3x to 10x throughput.

2 Background and Motivation

2.1 I/O Burden in HPC Applications

Most HPC applications simulate physical, chemical, biological, astronomical and other kinds of processes, while periodically capturing snapshots of the simulation state. They are built to help scientists better understand a scientific phenomenon. These simulations generate a tremendous amount of data, primarily consisting of high-dimensional matrices of floating-point numbers.

To enable further analysis, the generated data must be stored to disk. However, prior studies have identified I/O as a major performance bottleneck in this process [4,11]. This bottleneck arises from both the massive volume and high velocity of data produced by simulation applications, which run on many cores and generate data at rates that often exceed the I/O bandwidth of the underlying cluster. In extreme cases, data can be generated at speeds as high as 16TB/s [6,11], far surpassing the throughput limits of most parallel file systems. To relieve this I/O burden, compression techniques are introduced to the I/O path to reduce the data size. ADIOS2 [8], for example, is an I/O system designed specially for HPC clusters that is able to adaptively run compression/decompression before data dumps/loads.

2.2 Lossy Compression for HPC

Lossless compression is generally ineffective (e.g., with compression ratio usually under 2 or less [2,30]) for scientific datasets. These datasets primarily consist of floating-point numbers, whose mantissas are typically randomly distributed, leaving little redundancy to exploit [11]. As a result, error-bounded lossy compression, is more commonly adopted in HPC clusters [26]. These methods guarantee a user-specified maximum precision loss for each data points and thus enlarge the compressibility among these data accordingly. In doing so, they enable efficient storage while preserving necessary accuracy required for scientific analysis.

SZ compressor [11,22] is the most widely used error-bounded lossy compressor for HPC datasets and has been integrated into ADIOS2 [8], a widely-used I/O adapter for supercomputers. ❶ It first quantifies differences between adjacent floating-point numbers to generate *quantization factors* with a carefully configured quantizer, which ensures the maximum quantization error will not exceed the user-specified error bound. ❷ Subsequently, it compresses these quantization factors (i.e., integer sequences) by sequentially applying Huffman coding and LZ-based algorithms.

In the second step, huffman coding and LZ-based algorithms are designed to exploit different kinds of redundancies among quantization factors. ❶ Specifically, Huffman coding targets the frequency skewness of these factors by assigning short codes to frequent ones and long codes to rare ones; ❷ meanwhile, LZ-based algorithms target repeated sequence fragments by replacing them with references to their previous occurrences. Therefore, these redundancies can be fully eliminated only when the two components operate synergistically.

2.3 Modeling-Based Arithmetic Coding

Arithmetic coding [16–18,25] is a way of exploiting data patterns for compression. It makes static frequency statistics for symbols, and accordingly encodes an entire message into a single fractional number in the interval [0, 1). Due to the static statistics, the upper limit of compression ratio for this approach is also the information entropy.

Modeling-based arithmetic coding is a variant of arithmetic coding. It introduces a dynamic modeling module to analyze historical data streams and predict the next symbol based on previous ones. If the prediction is correct, only a short code is stored, resulting in high compression efficiency; otherwise, a long code is stored.

Because this approach makes predictions according to preceding symbols, it additionally has the ability to capture the redundancies of repeated fragments, thereby simultaneously handling the redundancies targeted by both sHuffman coding and LZ-based algorithms. Therefore, this kind of approach, such as the PAQ series [14,21,29], Cmix [10], and NNCP [1], has achieved significantly higher compression ratios on text datasets.

However, the limitation of this approach also arises from its modeling mechanism. The modeling and prediction operations impose significant computational overhead. Consequently, this approach is rarely adopted in real-world systems and remains primarily confined to academic research.

2.4 Observations

Observation 1: Insufficient Compression in the Existing Approach. As mentioned above, SZ employs Huffman coding and an LZ-based algorithm (e.g., Zstd or Gzip) to exploit two types of redundancy in quantization factors: symbol-frequency skewness and repeated fragments. However, this combination fails to deliver optimal results, as shown in Fig. 1. Both Zstd and Huffman coding individually achieve respectable compression ratios, confirming the coexistence of these redundancy patterns. Yet, combining them (either Huffman+Zstd or Zstd+Huffman) offers marginal additional benefits. The inefficiency stems from mismatched processing granularities: ❶ Huffman operates on four-byte integer units (quantization factors) and produces variable-length codes (with different bit-length); ❷ Zstd operates primarily on byte-level fragments and produces variable-length references (a mix of byte-aligned and bit-aligned data). Therefore, each approach disrupts the working data unit of the other, thereby limiting redundancy elimination. This highlights the need for a better compression method for quantization factors: one that avoids granularity mismatches and achieves materially higher compressibility.

Observation 2: Trading Computation for Better Compression is End-to-End Efficient in HPC Data Dumps and Loads. As studied in previous work [22,27], I/O still accounts for more than 80% of the overall runtime even with the compressors employed. This is because HPC applications incur massive I/O overheads (e.g., generating up to 16 TB of data per second [6,11]), while being computation-rich environments that provide ample processing resources for highly parallel compression. Therefore, it is worthwhile investing in additional computation to obtain higher compression and reduce I/O time, further improving end-to-end throughput.

Together with Observation 1, this motivates adopting a stronger (even more compute-intensive) compressor for quantization factors in HPC scenario.

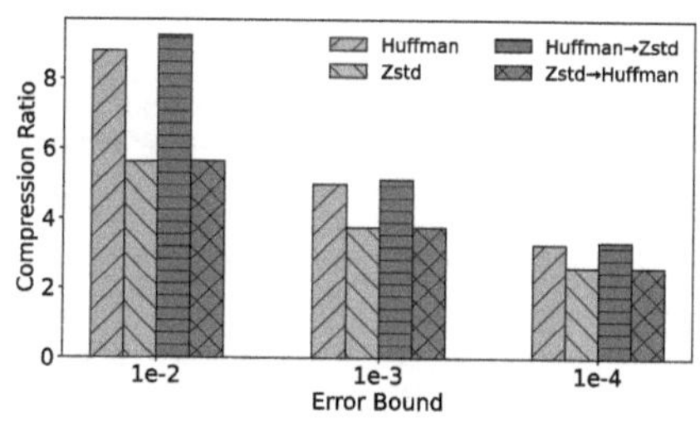

Fig. 1. Although they target different data redundancies, simply combining two approach achieves little improvement in compression ratio compared to their standalone.

Table 1. Modeling-based approach (LPAQ) has better compression ratio (CR) but has worse compression speed (CS, MB/s) and decompression speed (DS, MB/s) on quantization factors.

ErrorBound	Method	CR	CS	DS
1e−2	Huffman	8.68	498	270
1e−2	LPAQ	10.56	0.58	0.56
1e−3	Huffman	4.98	423	186
1e−3	LPAQ	6.06	0.58	0.55
1e−4	Huffman	3.26	387	110
1e−4	LPAQ	3.85	0.54	0.58

2.5 Motivation

We observe that modeling-based arithmetic coding is a promising candidate to achieve the above computation–I/O tradeoff for in-path compression during

HPC data dumps and loads. Modeling-based arithmetic coding is known for delivering near-optimal compression ratios [14], yet it suffers from slow processing speed. Its advantage on compression ratio aligns with Observation 1, while its computational overhead can be compensated by the compute-rich environment described in Observation 2:

❶ Modeling-based arithmetic coding compresses data using context models that capture both kinds of redundancies of the input, as mentioned in Sect. 2.3, and it addresses the limitation identified in Observation 1.

❷ Although modeling-based arithmetic coding incurs significant computational overhead due to frequent updates of numerous context states, its high compression ratio can substantially reduce I/O volume. Hence, in HPC dumps and loads, where computation is abundant but I/O is costly, this tradeoff makes modeling-based arithmetic coding a potential choice, as mentioned in Observation 2.

Challenge: Too Slow Processing Speed of Modeling-Based Arithmetic Coding. Although this scenario tolerates a more computation-intensive yet stronger compressor, existing modeling-based arithmetic coding approaches remain prohibitively slow. As demonstrated in Table 1, although applying the fastest modeling-based arithmetic coding method (LPAQ [14]) to quantization factors yields a higher compression ratio, it incurs a prohibitive degradation in throughput. These results underscore the need for a faster modeling-based arithmetic coding design to effectively balance the computation–I/O tradeoff for in-path compression during HPC data dumps and loads.

3 Design and Implementation

3.1 Overview

In this section, we propose MAC, a structure-aware modeling–based arithmetic coding scheme. It is designed to integrate seamlessly into the SZ compressor, aiming to achieve higher compression ratios on scientific datasets.

As illustrated in Fig. 2, MAC operates on the quantization factors generated by the SZ pipeline. It performs bit-level arithmetic coding while leveraging the inherent structure of quantization factors to accelerate model construction and improve overall throughput. MAC consists of three main modules.

❶**Structure-Aware Preprocessor**: The structure-aware preprocessor aims to reduce the input size for subsequent modeling stages. Leveraging the typically compactable nature of quantization factors, it employs bit-packing techniques to efficiently compact their significant digits. By filtering and retaining only the essential components of the quantization factors for modeling, this preprocessor substantially shrinks the size of the bitstream to be modeled.

❷**Context-Based Modeler**: As shown in Fig. 3, the context-based modeler captures the temporal dependencies and recurring patterns in the compacted

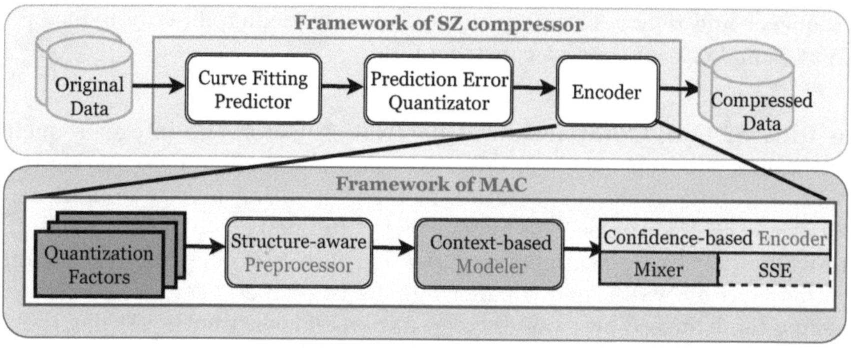

Fig. 2. The overview of MAC-SZ.

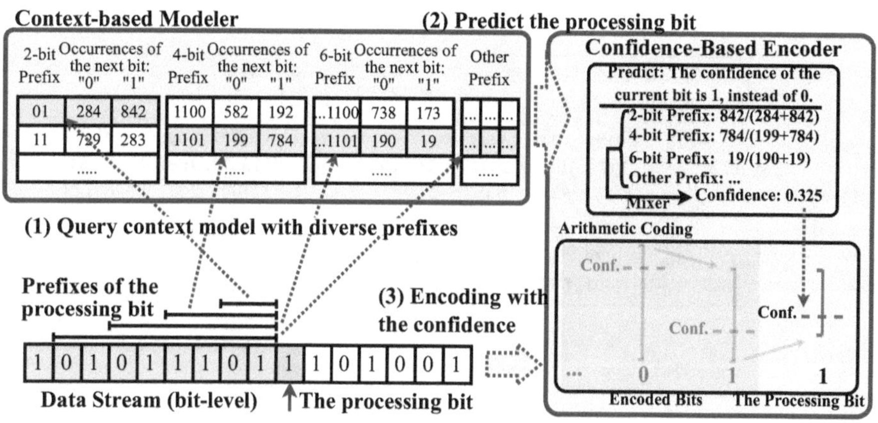

Fig. 3. The workflow of MAC.

quantization factors produced by the preprocessor. By analyzing historical trends and structural regularities, it enables an accurate prediction of data behavior. Through the careful selection of context types tailored to the structure of quantization factors and the application of lightweight machine learning algorithms, the modeler efficiently extracts critical features for bitstream prediction with simplified computation complexity.

❸**Confidence-Based Encoder**: The confidence-based encoder performs the final bitstream encoding on the compacted quantization factors. It applies adaptive arithmetic coding, utilizing the prediction confidence generated by the context-based modeler as the symbol probability. The higher the prediction accuracy, the more effective the resulting compression.

3.2 Structure-Aware Preprocessor

The structure-aware preprocessor converts quantization factors into a compact representation. It identifies structural units within the quantization factor sequence and removes redundant bits before modeling, directly reducing the computational cost of context construction.

The Idea of Our Compaction. Quantization factors are integer sequences whose values are typically concentrated within a small range. As shown in Table 2, over 90% of the quantization factors fall within narrow bounds across datasets and error settings. This explains why Huffman coding has been effective historically. However, since most quantization factors occupy only a fraction of the 4-byte integer width, many higher bits are consistently zero and never used. Modeling these unused bits wastes computation and contributes nothing to compression efficiency.

Table 2. Quantization factors are centralized in a small range.

Datasets	Error bound	90% Central Range	Max Value	Datasets	Error bound	90% Central Range	Max Value
CESM-ATM	1e-2	[121, 134]	255	Hurricane	1e-2	[1022, 1026]	2047
	1e-3	[957, 1091]	2047		1e-3	[16378, 16390]	32767
	1e-4	[7427, 8958]	16383		1e-4	[131005, 131139]	262143
EXAALT	1e-2	[15, 17]	31	Miranda	1e-2	[16, 16]	21
	1e-3	[30, 34]	63		1e-3	[15, 16]	31
	1e-4	[491, 533]	1023		1e-4	[14, 18]	31

The Mechanism of Our Compaction. To address this inefficiency, the preprocessor scans the quantization factor sequence before compression to locate the non-zero bits of each factor and compact them into fixed-size units. All factors are stored using the bit width of the largest value, with leading zeros removed accordingly. This compaction step substantially shortens the bitstream and proportionally reduces the workload of subsequent modeling.

Although more space-efficient formats such as variable-length integers could be used, they are incompatible with bitstream modeling, which requires fixed boundaries to recognize context relationships. Therefore, our compaction approach preserves the fixed-size integer structure while minimizing redundancy, enabling the modeling process to capture contextual probability patterns efficiently without sacrificing the overall compression ratio.

3.3 Context-Based Modeler

The context-based modeler in MAC captures probability patterns within the compacted bitstream and builds prediction models for bitwise compression. It records the likelihood of the next bit being 0 or 1 under different prefix conditions, allowing efficient prediction when the same pattern reappears. However,

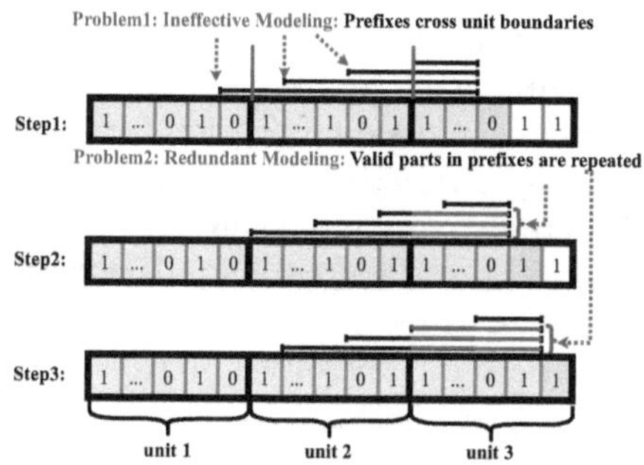

Fig. 4. Inefficiencies of applying traditional modeling on quantization factors.

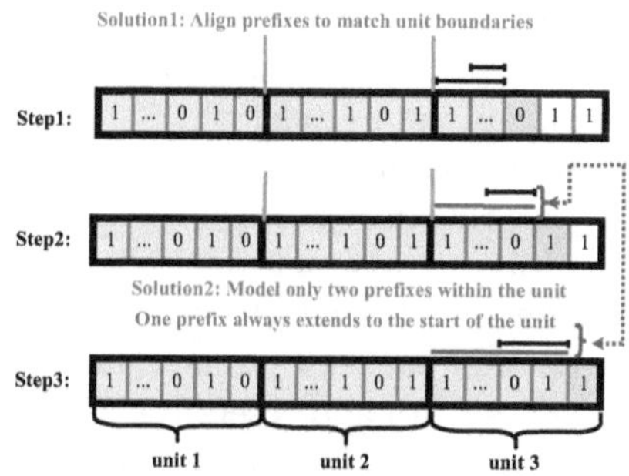

Fig. 5. Modeling in our approach, with fewer but more efficient prefixes.

as discussed in § 2.5, context modeling incurs substantial computational overhead, often becoming a major bottleneck. The key challenge, therefore, is how to perform modeling both effectively and efficiently.

The Idea of Our Modeling. We identify two inefficiencies when directly applying existing modeling-based arithmetic coding to quantization factors (Fig. 4): ❶ Ineffective Modeling. Traditional modeling techniques (e.g., LPAQ series) were mostly developed for byte-aligned data. Yet after the preprocessor, quantization factors lose this feature and this causes cross-boundary context building. In this scenario, the modeler will pack the last few bits of the former quantization factor and the first few bits of the current quantization factor together as the input of the context hash function. Such context building might not contribute to finding the real link between quantization factors, but pollute the hash table of history information instead. ❷ Redundant Modeling. Cross-boundary modeling not only lacks semantic meaning but also introduces redundancy, as the effective parts of many prefixes overlap a lot. This repetition wastes computation without improving prediction accuracy.

To address these issues, MAC introduces structure-guided modeling based on two complementary prefix types (Fig. 5): ❶ Adaptive-length Prefix $p1$ and its history $h1$: $p1$'s length always equals to the finished part in the current quantization factor, while $h1$ are rolling hash result of $p1$. Such a prefix mechanism helps to capture frequency skewness across quantization factors. ❷ 8-bit Prefix $p2$ and its history $h2$: $p2$ serves as an alternative for determining the probability of the next bit being 0 or 1. This prefix also extends to at most the start of the current quantization factor and will not take cross-boundary bits. When updating, $h2$ is set to the value of $p2$ and $p2$ is reset. Each history update happens every one byte. When predicting the next bit, these two prefixes along with their histories are hashed and used as the query index of the statistical table.

The Workflow of Our Modeling:

1. The encoder maintains a table indexed by prefixes' and histories' values.
2. When processing a new quantization factor,
   - Starting with the first bit of the quantization factor, two prefixes are all reset to 0, indicating to the encoder that a new quantization factor is being processed. Prediction of each prefix is made on its own history.
   - Next, both prefixes use the first bit of the quantization factor as the prefix and perform prediction and update.
   - This process continues until one byte out of the quantization factor is processed or it is already the end of the quantization factor. Then the encoder updates the histories and resets the 8-bit prefix.
3. The same procedure is repeated for each subsequent quantization factor until all have been processed.

3.4 Confidence-Based Encoder

The confidence-based encoder is responsible for encoding each bit using the predicted confidence produced by the context model. It consists of two components: *Mixer* and *Secondary Symbol Encoder*.

Mixer. The mixer combines predictions from multiple context-based modelers to generate a unified prediction. It calculates a weighted average of the modelers' outputs, where the weights are dynamically updated based on prediction accuracy and context relevance. Modelers with better past performance under similar contexts are assigned higher weights. The weights are stored in a context-indexed table and updated based on prediction error.

Secondary Symbol Encoder. This component further adjusts the prediction. Basically, if the same contexts have occurred before and the prediction of our model always comes out favoring "1" instead of "0", we will try to eliminate the imbalance by pulling the prediction number a little back to "0" and vice versa.

After these processes, a final prediction and the corresponding confidence are generated. Then, our confidence-based encoder runs arithmetic coding with the prediction and confidence to compress the processing bit.

Table 3. Five Evaluated Datasets.

Name	Size	Dimensions
CESM-ATM	673M	$26 \times 1800 \times 3600$
EXAALT	342M	83×1077290
Hurricane	96M	$100 \times 500 \times 500$
Miranda	288M	$256 \times 384 \times 384$
BrownSamples	257M	33554433×1

Table 4. Compression ratios of evaluated approaches on five evaluated datasets under different error bounds.

Error Bound	Method	Dataset				
		CESM-ATM	EXAALT	Hurricane	Miranda	BrownSamples
1e-2	SZ	9.25	31.48	14.28	202.99	1373.26
	ADT-FSE-SZ	9.24(-0.1%)	31.34(-0.4%)	14.24(-0.3%)	203.41(+0.2%)	1345.74(-2.0%)
	MAC-SZ	10.56(+14.2%)	33.03(+4.9%)	16.06(+12.4%)	207.25(+2.1%)	1549.28(+12.8%)
	LPAQ-SZ	10.27(+11.0%)	33.19(+5.4%)	15.85(+11.0%)	202.84(-0.1%)	1167.78(-15.0%)
1e-3	SZ	5.13	14.04	11.41	146.55	189.19
	ADT-FSE-SZ	5.12(-0.1%)	14.04(0.0%)	11.36(-0.4%)	146.58(+0.0%)	184.38(-2.5%)
	MAC-SZ	5.85(+14.1%)	15.22(+8.4%)	12.53(+9.8%)	149.22(+1.8%)	210.94(+11.5%)
	LPAQ-SZ	5.92(+15.5%)	15.37(+9.4%)	13.23(+16.0%)	146.17(-0.3%)	193.27(+2.2%)
1e-4	SZ	3.33	6.24	8.13	63.55	37.27
	ADT-FSE-SZ	3.33(0.0%)	6.24(0.0%)	8.01(-1.5%)	63.56(+0.0%)	37.24(-0.1%)
	MAC-SZ	3.39(+1.8%)	6.87(+10.3%)	9.34(+14.9%)	64.47(+1.4%)	39.57(+6.2%)
	LPAQ-SZ	3.77(+13.3%)	6.95(+10.8%)	10.18(+25.2%)	71.60(+12.6%)	39.05(+4.8%)
1e-5	SZ	1.73	3.79	6.22	33.50	13.06
	ADT-FSE-SZ	1.73(0.0%)	3.79(0.0%)	6.13(-1.4%)	33.46(-0.1%)	13.05(-0.1%)
	MAC-SZ	1.73(0.0%)	3.84(+1.3%)	7.58(+21.9%)	42.44(+26.7%)	13.74(+5.2%)
	LPAQ-SZ	1.73(0.0%)	4.13(+9.5%)	8.21(+31.9%)	43.01(+28.4%)	13.70(+4.9%)

4 Evaluation

4.1 Experimental Setup

Platform. We run end-to-end evaluations on 128 nodes in the Tianhe-2 supercomputer [23], each with 64 cores. These nodes are all running Linux 5.15.0-78-TH-cn and organized by Slurm work manager [20]. The remaining standalone evaluations that do not involve massive parallel I/O are performed on a server with 64 Intel Xeon(R) Gold 6130 processors @ 2.1G HZ, 128GB memory. The server runs Ubuntu 18.04.1.

Configuration. We evaluate the following four approaches to comprehensively demonstrate the advantages of MAC-SZ:

- Original SZ Compressor [11,22]: The original SZ compressor, which uses Huffman coding and Zstandard to compress quantization factors.

- ADT-FSE-SZ [13]: A version of SZ that combines adaptation table and FSE encoder [3] as its quantization factor encoder.
- LPAQ-SZ: An alternative version of SZ that incorporates LPAQ [14] (the fastest modeling-based arithmetic coding) for compressing quantization factors.
- MAC-SZ: Our proposed approach, which applies MAC to compress quantization factors in SZ.

Datasets. All the datasets we use are downloaded from SDRbench (Scientific Data Reduction Benchmarks) [28]. Specifically, we conducted our tests upon the CESM-ATM, EXAALT, Hurricane ISABEL, Miranda and BrownSamples datasets. They cover a wide range of domains and dimensional sizes. Key information about these datasets is available in Table 3.

Error Bounds and Other Configurations. We test all files with error bounds from 1e-2 to 1e-5 using the *pw_rel* error bound type for all methods. All methods use the maximum compression level in their configurations.

4.2 Compression Ratio of Different Approaches

Table 4 presents the overall file compression ratios for each dataset. As shown in the table, MAC consistently achieves visible improvements across all datasets. Under an error bound of 1e-2, MAC-SZ notably increases the compression ratio of CESM-ATM from 9.25 to 10.56 (+14.2%) and Hurricane from 14.28 to 16.06 (+12.4%) compared to the original SZ. Even under the strict 1e-5 error bound, MAC-SZ maintains superiority, achieving a 7.58 ratio on Hurricane (+21.9% over SZ's 6.22) and a 42.44 ratio on Miranda (+26.7% over SZ's 33.50).

In contrast, ADT-FSE-SZ performs similarly to original SZ, showing slight regressions, such as a 2.5% drop on BrownSamples at 1e-3. Meanwhile, LPAQ delivers higher compression ratios in some cases but sometimes leads to performance degradation. Considering that MAC employs only two models in the modeling stage, compared to six in LPAQ, these results demonstrate the effectiveness of MAC's modeling strategy and the validity of our findings in § 3.3.

4.3 Time Cost of Compression/Decompression

Beyond improving the compression ratio of SZ on HPC datasets, our design also targets minimizing modeling overhead to enhance both compression and decompression throughput. To evaluate this, we measure the runtime of compression and decompression on the same datasets used in the ratio experiments, as shown in Fig. 6.

MAC-SZ significantly outperforms LPAQ-SZ, reducing compression and decompression time by 3–10×. The improvement stems from our structure-aware

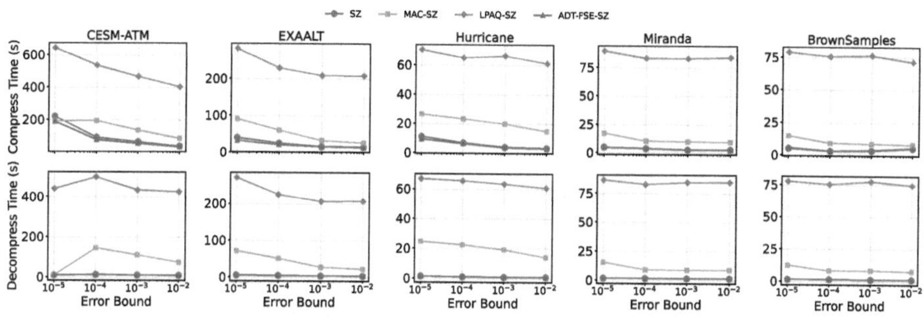

Fig. 6. Average compression (above) and decompression (below) time on five datasets, our approach is significantly faster than directly applying existing modeling-based arithmetic coding (LPAQ).

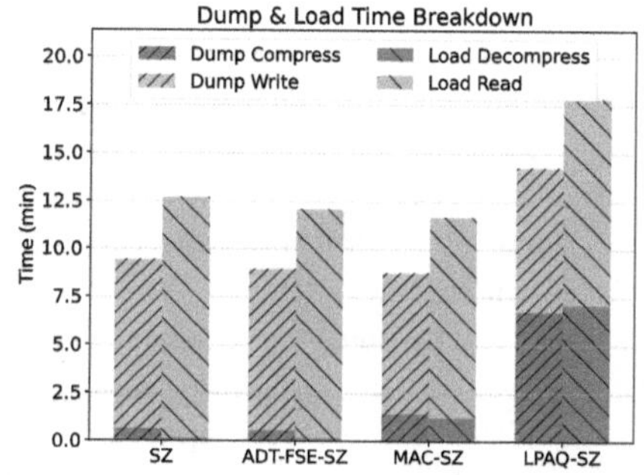

Fig. 7. Time breakdown of data dumps and loads in an 8192-core HPC environment.

compaction and structure-guided modeling, which substantially reduce the computational cost of context construction. Although MAC-SZ introduces higher runtime than the original SZ, its superior compression ratio compensates for this overhead. Overall, MAC-SZ achieves a favorable computation–I/O tradeoff, as further demonstrated in Sect. 4.4.

4.4 Overall Performance

Figures 7 and 8 present a comprehensive comparison of the four evaluated approaches on the Tianhe-2 supercomputer.

As shown, our approach achieves approximately 1.07× and 1.08× the dumping and loading throughput of the original SZ compressor, respectively, while improving the compression ratio by around 1.14×. The time breakdown specifically reveals that although MAC-SZ spends slightly more time in the compression and decompression phases compared to SZ, it significantly slashes the write and read times during I/O operations. By successfully trading computation time for reduced I/O bottlenecks, MAC proves to be a highly effective architectural design for modern HPC workflows.

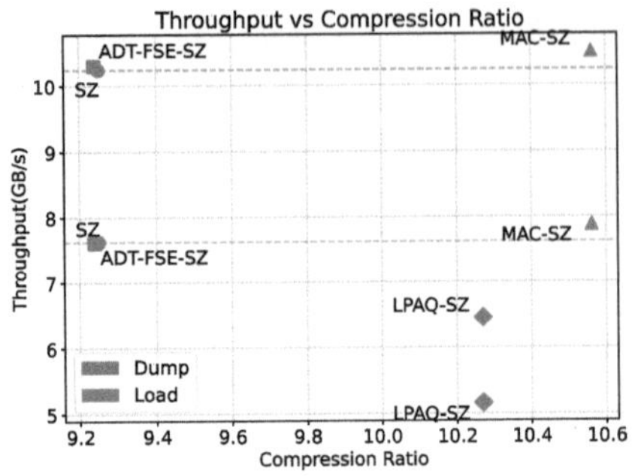

Fig. 8. Comparison between throughput and compression ratio in both dumping and loading scenarios.

5 Conclusion

We present MAC, a structure-aware arithmetic coding scheme designed to improve the compression ratio of SZ for scientific datasets. ❶ It integrates the modeling-based arithmetic coding into the SZ compressor, unlocking greater compression potential. ❷ It introduces two structure-aware techniques that reduce the computational overhead of modeling, making modeling-based arithmetic coding practical in HPC scenarios. Experimental results demonstrate MAC's potential to alleviate I/O and storage bottlenecks in modern HPC workflows.

Acknowledgements. This work was partially supported by the National Natural Science Foundation of China (Grant No. 62502119), the Shenzhen Science and Technology Program (Grant No. GXWD20231128111309001), and the Guangdong Basic and Applied Basic Research Foundation (Grant No. 2023A1515110072).

Declaration. Artificial intelligence tools, if used, were used only for language organization and figure/table polishing, and did not participate in the generation of the core ideas or technical content.

References

1. Bellard, F.: NNCP v2: lossless data compression with transformer (2021). https://bellard.org/nncp
2. Burtscher, M., Ratanaworabhan, P.: FPC: a high-speed compressor for double-precision floating-point data. IEEE Trans. Comput. **58**(1), 18–31 (2009)
3. Collet, Y.: Finite state entropy (2013). https://github.com/Cyan4973/FiniteStateEntropy
4. Di, S., Cappello, F.: Fast error-bounded lossy HPC data compression with SZ. In: International Parallel and Distributed Processing Symposium (IPDPS), pp. 730–739 (2016)

5. Facebook: Zstd (2015). https://github.com/facebook/zstd
6. Foster, I.T., Ainsworth, M., Allen, B., et al.: Computing just what you need: online data analysis and reduction at extreme scales. In: Euro-Par 2017: Parallel Processing, LNCS, vol. 10417, pp. 3–19 (2017)
7. GNU: Gzip (1992). https://www.gzip.org
8. Godoy, W.F., Podhorszki, N., Wang, R., et al.: ADIOS 2: the adaptable input output system. A framework for high-performance data management. SoftwareX **12**, 100561 (2020)
9. Huffman, D.A.: A method for the construction of minimum-redundancy codes. Proc. IRE **40**(9), 1098–1101 (1952)
10. Knoll, B.: Cmix (2014). https://github.com/byronknoll/cmix
11. Liang, X., Di, S., Tao, D., et al.: An efficient transformation scheme for lossy data compression with point-wise relative error bound. In: International Conference on Cluster Computing (CLUSTER), pp. 179–189 (2018)
12. Lindstrom, P.: Fixed-rate compressed floating-point arrays. IEEE Trans. Vis. Comput. Graph. **20**(12), 2674–2683 (2014)
13. Lu, T., Zhong, Y., Sun, Z., et al.: ADT-FSE: a new encoder for SZ. In: Proceedings of the International Conference for High Performance Computing (SC), pp. 45:1–45:13 (2023)
14. Mahoney, M.: LPAQ (2007). http://mattmahoney.net/dc/#lpaq
15. Meister, D., Kaiser, J., Brinkmann, A., et al.: A study on data deduplication in HPC storage systems. In: SC Conference on High Performance Computing Networking, Storage and Analysis, SC '12, Salt Lake City, UT, USA - November 11 – 15, 2012, p. 7 (2012)
16. Moffat, A., Neal, R.M., Witten, I.H.: Arithmetic coding revisited. In: Proceedings of the IEEE Data Compression Conference (DCC '95), pp. 202–211 (1995)
17. Pennebaker, W.B., Mitchell, J.L., Langdon, G.G., Arps, R.B.: An overview of the basic principles of the q-coder adaptive binary arithmetic coder. IBM J. Res. Dev. **32**(6), 717–726 (1988)
18. Rissanen, J., Langdon, G.G.: Arithmetic coding. IBM J. Res. Dev. **23**(2), 149–162 (1979)
19. Shang, H., et al.: Large-scale simulation of quantum computational chemistry on a new sunway supercomputer. In: International Conference for High Performance Computing (SC), pp. 14:1–14:14 (2022)
20. SlurmTeam: Slurm workload manager (2021). https://slurm.schedmd.com
21. Tang, D., Sun, X., Guan, N., et al.: *p*LPAQ: accelerating LPAQ compression on FPGA. In: International Conference on Field-Programmable Technology, ICFPT 2022, Hong Kong, December 5–9, 2022, pp. 1–6 (2022)
22. Tao, D., Di, S., Chen, Z., et al.: Significantly improving lossy compression for scientific data sets based on multidimensional prediction and error-controlled quantization. In: International Parallel and Distributed Processing Symposium (IPDPS), pp. 1129–1139 (2017)
23. TianHeTeam: Tianhe supercomputer (2013). https://en.wikipedia.org/wiki/Tianhe-2
24. Wan, W., et al.: 69.7-PFlops extreme scale earthquake simulation with crossing multi-faults and topography on sunway. In: Proceedings of the International Conference for High Performance Computing (SC), pp. 10:1–10:15 (2023)
25. Witten, I.H., Neal, R.M., Cleary, J.G.: Arithmetic coding for data compression. Commun. ACM **30**(6), 520–540 (1987)

26. Yu, X., Di, S., Zhao, K., et al.: Ultrafast error-bounded lossy compression for scientific datasets. In: International Symposium on High-Performance Parallel and Distributed Computing (HPDC), pp. 159–171 (2022)
27. Zhao, K., Di, S., Liang, X., et al.: Significantly improving lossy compression for HPC datasets with second-order prediction and parameter optimization. In: International Symposium on High-Performance Parallel and Distributed Computing (HPDC), pp. 89–100 (2020)
28. Zhao, K., et al.: SDRBench: scientific data reduction benchmark for lossy compressors (2021). https://sdrbench.github.io
29. Zhu, W., Tong, W., Ge, H., et al.: LpaqHP: a high-performance FPGA accelerator for LPAQ compression. In: Proceedings of the 53rd International Conference on Parallel Processing, ICPP 2024, Gotland, Sweden, August 12–15, 2024, pp. 898–907 (2024)
30. Zou, X., et al.: Performance optimization for relative-error-bounded lossy compression on scientific data. IEEE Trans. Parallel Distrib. Syst. **31**(7), 1665–1680 (2020)

VecTEE: Compact TEE Metadata Caching for Efficient Secure Vector Computing

Husheng Han[1], Di Huang[1,3], Tianyun Ma[2], Xinyao Zheng[1,3,4], Jianan Mu[1], Zidong Du[1,3], Xing Hu[1,3](✉), and Qi Guo[1,3]

[1] State Key Lab of Processors, Institute of Computing Technology, Chinese Academy of Sciences, Beijing, China
{hanhusheng,huangdi,zhengxinyao22s,mujianan,duzidong,huxing,guoqi}@ict.ac.cn
[2] Institute of AI for Industries, Chinese Academy of Sciences, Beijing, China
tyma@iaii.ac.cn
[3] University of Chinese Academy of Sciences, Beijing, China
[4] Cambricon Technologies Co., Ltd., Beijing, China

Abstract. Vector computation on Neural Processing Units (NPUs), such as in embedding layers, offers strong feature representation capabilities and has been widely adopted in privacy-sensitive applications, including deep learning-based recommendation systems (DLRM) and large-scale model inference. To protect user inputs and behavioral features, Trusted Execution Environments (TEEs) have emerged as a promising approach, benefiting from hardware-based security guarantees and low computational overhead. However, ensuring memory data confidentiality in TEEs requires frequent access to substantial off-chip metadata, which, combined with the random access patterns of vector computation, incurs significant memory performance overhead.

To address this issue, we propose VecTEE , an efficient NPU-oriented TEE design that leverages a compact metadata caching mechanism to improve vector memory access performance. Specifically, VecTEE employs: (1) vector-granularity management to reduce metadata size; (2) compacted management of high-access-frequency metadata to enhance temporal locality; and (3) a version-number-least cache replacement policy to improve hot metadata residency. Evaluation of representative workloads shows that VecTEE achieves up to 68% performance improvement, with an average gain of 50%.

Keywords: vector computing · trusted execution environment · hardware architecture · neural processing unit

1 Introduction

Vector computing has drawn increased attention for its feature representation capability and has been widely used in applications like deep-learning-based recommendation systems (DLRM) [19,22], Retrieval-Augmented-Generation (RAG) [9,23] and large language models (LLMs) [25]. For example, DLRM is

L. Eeckhout et al. (Eds.): APPT 2026, LNCS 16693, pp. 547–561, 2027.
https://doi.org/10.1007/978-981-92-4805-6_36

widely adopted in industrial environments, occupying nearly 25% of Google's training and inference TPUs, in which the core and representative vector computing operator, embedding layer, often becomes the performance bottleneck due to large storage requirements and random access patterns [16,19,27].

In privacy-sensitive applications like DLRM and RAG, user inputs or knowledge bases often contain sensitive information, requiring security guarantees [10,30]. Compared to other confidential computing approaches [2,15,20,28], Trusted Execution Environments (TEEs) have gained widespread attention for their relatively low performance overhead and strong security guarantees. TEEs assume that only the chip itself is secure, while the connected external memory such as GDDR is vulnerable to privileged software attacks or physical attacks. TEEs employ encryption and verification mechanisms to protect memory data. This paper focuses on GDDR rather than HBM due to its lower cost and widespread adoption, following existing works [1,13,21].

TEEs ensure memory data security by encrypting and verifying data during memory access, using metadata composed of a version number (VN) and message authentication code (MAC) for decryption and integrity checking. The VN tracks updates at a memory address, while the MAC records the hash of data and related information; both are updated upon data writes. **Existing NPU TEEs mainly support scalar (cacheline-grained metadata) or tensor data (tensor-grained metadata) but perform poorly in vector computing**. The tensor-grained mechanism stores tensor-level metadata on-chip for efficiency [13] but fails under the random access patterns of vector computing. The cacheline-grained mechanism supports vector operations by storing VN and MAC per cacheline, yet incurs high memory and performance overheads (35% additional access amount and 52% performance overhead) even with dedicated metadata caches.

Since the metadata has to be stored off-chip in vector computing, *fully utilizing the existing on-chip metadata cache* is the most promising solution. However, we identify that the metadata cache faces the following challenges on vector computing (Fig. 1). **C1: the substantial metadata volume** (9.4% memory occupation) makes it challenging for the limited capacity of the metadata cache, leading to frequent cache thrashing. **C2: the discrete distribution of hot vectors compromises the temporal locality of hot metadata.** The skew access characteristic that few frequently accessed vectors occupy the majority of memory accesses could leverage temporal locality to reduce off-chip requests for their related metadata. Despite its potential, considering that a single cacheline can hold multiple metadata entries (e.g., 32), the discrete access distribution results in only a few metadata in the cacheline being frequently accessed, diminishing their temporal locality and hurting the cache efficiency.

To address the issues, we propose VecTEE to reduce metadata access overhead via compact metadata caching. **1) Vector-grained metadata**. We develop a flexible, vector-grained off-chip metadata mechanism to reduce the metadata volume and mitigate the cache capacity pressure. To support multiple granularities due to the NPU requirements, we propose an efficient metadata

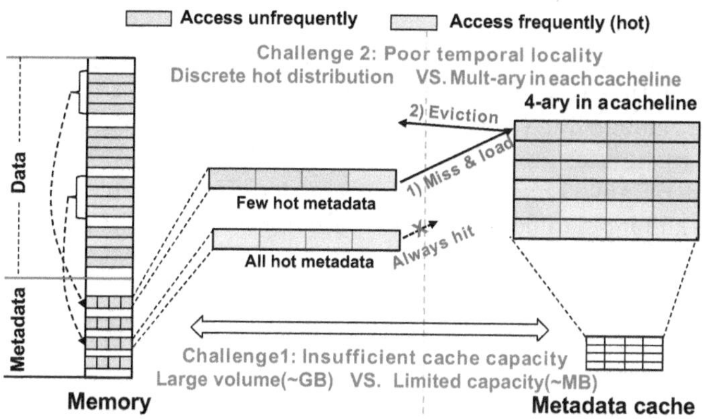

Fig. 1. Challenges for efficient secure memory access. Off-chip memory organizes data and manages metadata at cacheline granularity, resulting in large metadata volume. Due to metadata scale, random access, and discrete hot metadata distribution, the on-chip metadata cache struggles to achieve high hit rates, leading to frequent memory reads and write-backs, forming a memory bottleneck.

checking and routing mechanism via segment-based memory isolation. **2) Compacting hot metadata**. Observing that vector computing typically has prior knowledge of access frequencies, we propose a frequency-based arrangement of hot vectors. This compacts hot metadata in a few cachelines, increasing caching efficiency through the improved temporal locality. **3) VN-least replacement policy**. Observing the VN tracks long-time write-back counts, we propose the VN-least replacement policy and merged metadata cache to prioritize the retention of hot data, thus increasing cache effectiveness.

Our main contributions are as follows:

- We perform detailed performance analysis on secure vector computing, identifying that the main performance challenge lies in the inefficiency of metadata caching.
- We propose VecTEE to enhance the metadata caching by vector-grained metadata management, compact hot metadata layout and VN-least replacement policy, with negligible hardware cost.
- We conduct cycle-accurate simulation with enhanced Ramulator and the results show significant improvements in performance (50%) and metadata hit rate (from 84% to 95%).

2 Background and Motivation

2.1 Vector Computing

Vector computing, represented by embedding operations, transforms categorical features into dense vector representations, serving as the primary storage and computation component in these systems. In production-scale models, embedding tables can reach hundreds of GB or even TB [27], occupying over 60% of total execution time [22]. **Vector computing exhibits two access characteristics**. First, embedding operations follow index-based random access patterns (Fig. 2(a)), where user inputs trigger unpredictable accesses to embedding table entries, undermining cache prefetching and locality principles. Second, access frequency exhibits significant hot-cold distribution (Fig. 2(b)), where a small number of hot vectors account for the majority of access requests. For example, in the Criteo dataset [6], 1% of vectors contribute 95% of access frequency. These characteristics provide optimization opportunities for system design.

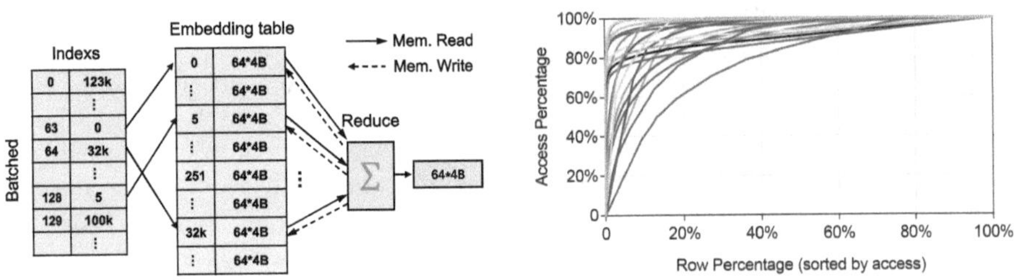

(a) Embedding operation flowchart. (b) Hot-cold access distribution.

Fig. 2. Vector computing characteristics: (a) shows typical vector-grained random access pattern in embedding operations; (b) illustrates the long-tail distribution where a small fraction of vectors account for majority of accesses. The 10 curves represent the frequency results of 10 embedding tables.

2.2 Memory Protection

To protect the security of off-chip memory data, existing research typically implements secure memory access based on TEE memory protection mechanisms [5,13,18,24]. For off-chip memory security, TEEs employ data encryption (ensuring confidentiality), verification via MAC (ensuring integrity), and version numbers (ensuring freshness against replay attacks). As shown in Fig. 3, VN and MAC serve as metadata that must be accessed for each data access: VN participates in encryption/decryption with the physical address, while MAC verifies data integrity. Besides, the metadata is typically stored off-chip due to their large volume, requiring Merkle Trees for integrity protection, which introduces additional storage and recursive access overhead.

Existing works in CPU and NPU have different protection granularities. CPU TEEs typically adopt cacheline-grained metadata (Fig. 3(a)), where each cacheline requires independent VN, resulting in significant storage overhead (e.g., 11% for 56-bit VN per 64B cacheline). In contrast, NPU TEE designs leverage tensor access patterns to use tensor-grained VN (Fig. 3(b)), storing unified metadata on-chip to eliminate off-chip access and Merkle Tree dependency [13,21,24].

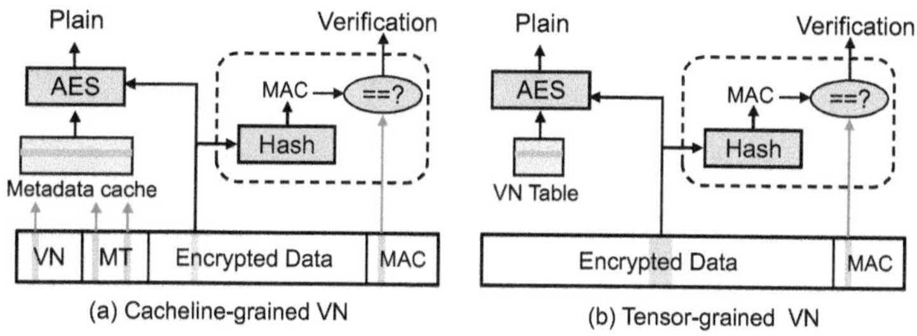

Fig. 3. TEE memory protection mechanisms and two protection granularities.

However, vector computing's random access pattern conflicts with tensor-grained assumptions, motivating new metadata management approaches.

2.3 Motivation

In vector computing, metadata must be stored off-chip due to its large volume, requiring frequent metadata access during memory operations. Fully utilizing the on-chip metadata cache is a promising optimization direction, but we identify two key challenges (see Fig. 1): **C1**: Metadata occupies 9.4% of memory, leading to frequent cache thrashing; **C2**: Discrete hot vector distribution weakens temporal locality of metadata cachelines.

Inefficient Metadata Granularity: Current metadata management mechanisms face a granularity dilemma. Cacheline-grained schemes support arbitrary random access but require independent metadata per cacheline, causing significant overhead (metadata access occupies over 35% of off-chip access volume, causing up to 52% performance loss in Fig. 4(a)). Tensor-grained schemes [13, 18] store unified metadata on-chip but rely on structured access patterns, conflicting with vector computing's index-based random access. This motivates a new granularity that balances flexibility and efficiency for vector computing.

Limited Temporal Locality: Vector computing uses index-based random access, which breaks spatial locality. As a result, the metadata cache mainly depends on temporal locality, keeping frequently accessed hot data in cache to improve efficiency. Prefetching is not effective here, but maintaining hot data in cache can increase the overall hit rate. In vector computing, access patterns show strong hot-cold behavior: a small number of vectors receive most of the accesses. For example, in the Criteo dataset, 1% of vectors account for 95% of access frequency (Fig. 2b). Therefore, metadata for these hot vectors should stay in cache to reduce expensive off-chip memory accesses.

To further improve cache efficiency, hot metadata should be clustered within the same cachelines to avoid frequent replacements caused by limited cache capacity. However, in practice, hot metadata is often scattered, reducing temporal locality. For instance, under a 32-entry-per-cacheline configuration, more than 95% of cachelines contain fewer than three hot metadata entries (Fig. 4b), meaning hot data is poorly concentrated. This weakens temporal locality and motivates compact hot metadata management methods.

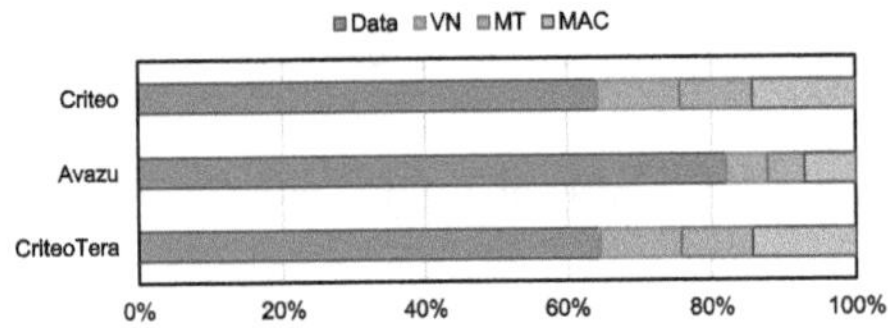

(a) Memory access breakdown.

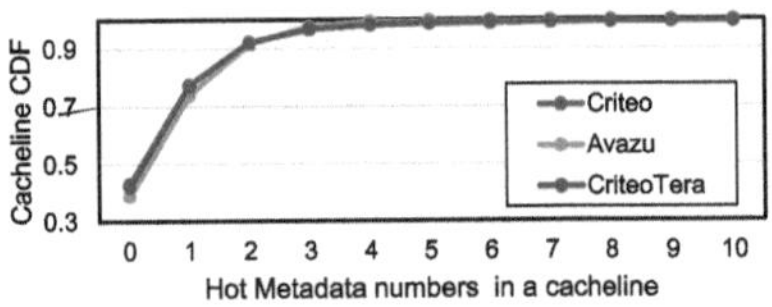

(b) Hot metadata distribution.

Fig. 4. Motivation experiments: (a) shows metadata access overhead under cacheline-grained protection; (b) illustrates discrete distribution of hot metadata within cachelines.

3 VecTEE Architecture

In this paper, we propose VecTEE for efficient secure NPU vector computing. 1) Vector-grained metadata management. To reduce the volume of metadata, we observe that the uniform vector length characteristic in vector tasks allows for the construction of task-specific vector-grained metadata management, reducing the metadata amount by several times. 2) Compact hot metadata. To address the issue of frequent cache evictions caused by discrete hot metadata, we propose a frequency-based hot vector arrangement method to facilitate compact hot metadata. 3) VN-least replacement policy. Noting that VN reflects data access activity over a longer time window, we propose the VN-least cache replacement policy to retain hot data on-chip as much as possible.

3.1 Vector-Grained Metadata Management

Vector computing applications typically use fixed vector sizes [19,22,26], enabling direct mapping from vector index to metadata address. And due to the vector-grained access pattern, all cachelines within a vector can share the same metadata. These characteristics provide basis for designing vector-grained metadata management, which can reduce storage by several times compared to cacheline-grained approach (Fig. 5b).

However, vector-grained management faces two challenges: (1) supporting multiple granularities (vector, tensor, cacheline) across diverse data types increases the complexity of memory allocation and access mechanisms; and (2) metadata address generation must account for varying vector sizes among different applications, even though each application uses a fixed vector size. For

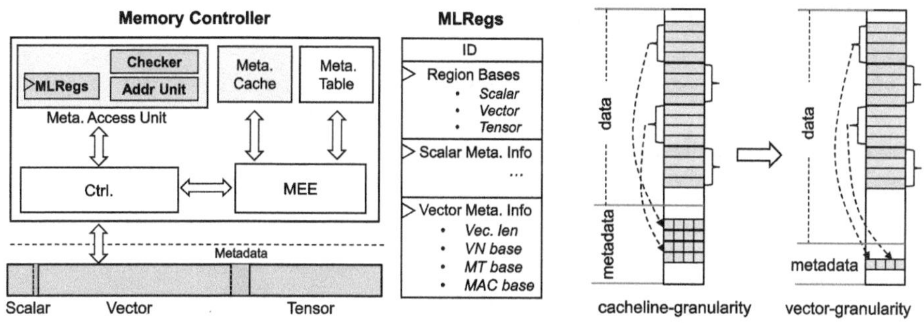

(a) VecTEE architecture overview. (b) Vector-grained VN.

Fig. 5. (a) Metadata management unit and three-granularity memory layout; (b) Vector-grained VS. cacheline-grained VN storage.

cacheline granularity, since cacheline size is fixed and known, metadata address can be derived from metadata region start address and data cacheline address, but this method is difficult to directly apply to variable-sized vector computing scenarios. For tensor granularity, tensor index is used to lookup corresponding tensor metadata in on-chip storage. Since tensor quantity is minimal, content-addressable storage can be used, but vector metadata cannot adopt this approach due to large volume and off-chip memory location.

To support multiple granularities, we design a Metadata Access Unit (Fig. 5a) with segment-based memory isolation. The unit partitions memory into three regions (scalar, vector, tensor), with Metadata Layout Registers (MLRegs) that records region base addresses and vector lengths. During access, the Checker determines data type via base address comparison, and the Address Unit generates metadata addresses accordingly. Then, the Memory Encryption Engine (MEE) obtains metadata to perform encryption, decryption, or verification operations. For scalar or vector data, metadata is obtained from metadata cache (on hit) or off-chip memory (on miss) based on cache hit status. For tensor data, the memory controller reads tensor-grained metadata from on-chip metadata table [13]. We adopt virtual address for encryption to eliminate the irregularity of physical memory caused by the operation system and further enable the segment-based isolation.

When a vector data access occurs, the hardware needs to compute the vector index efficiently, then locates and retrieves the corresponding metadata. To enable efficient index calculation, MLRegs store both the vector length and the base address of the vector data, allowing fast and flexible metadata address generation. The main process is:

1. **Index calculation:** The vector length is used to compute a vector index, which also serves as a metadata index. For lengths that are powers of two, this can be done through simple shift operations. Otherwise, since the vector size is fixed within the application, we apply the fast division optimization method

[11] with precomputed constants to replace division with a multiplication and a shift operation.
2. **Metadata address generation:** Combine the metadata index with the metadata base address to obtain the final metadata address.
3. **Merkle Tree address generation:** The Merkle Tree mapping for vector-grained metadata follows cacheline-level strategy [12], so all required node addresses can be derived once the index is known.

3.2 Compact Hot Metadata Layout

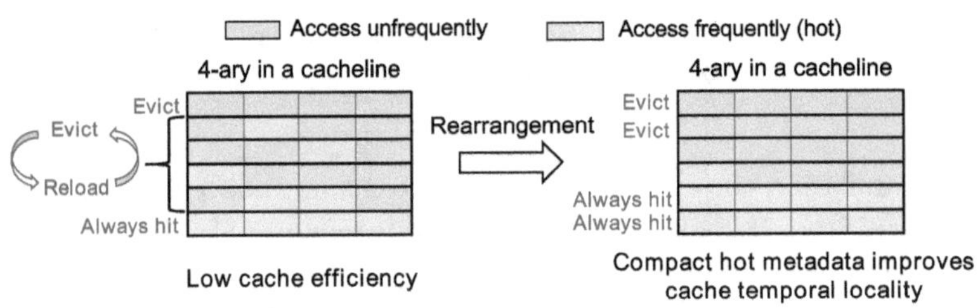

Fig. 6. Compact hot data storage improves metadata cache efficiency.

To improve cache efficiency, hot metadata should be compactly stored in as few cachelines as possible (Fig. 6) to improve temporal locality and reduce off-chip memory access. *Since metadata and vectors correspond one-to-one, this can be achieved through two approaches.* **Simply compact hot metadata**: This approach remaps hot metadata to a compact region at runtime. However, it requires large mapping tables similar to page tables, breaking the simple address mapping between data and metadata. Although the remapping can be optimized by hardware cache (like TLB), the vector granularity is far smaller than 4KB pages, requiring more storage and making it impractical. Thus, we adopt the more efficient compact hot vector storage instead.

Compact Hot Vectors : We propose frequency-based vector rearrangement to compact the hot vectors and further the hot metadata with three steps: (1) Frequency collection: Collect vector access frequencies via offline or online methods. (2) Vector sorting: Reorder vectors by access frequency. (3) Mapping reconstruction: Construct index mapping to compactly store hot vectors together. For frequency collection, we offer offline and online approaches. In the offline approach, based on the static dataset statistics in vector computing training tasks, vector access frequency can be obtained offline by counting samples per feature element. Online approach can further be divided into software and hardware schemes. The software scheme introduces a warm-up phase to initialize frequency tables; the hardware scheme leverages the characteristic that VN records the vector write counts, thus introducing a *CopyVN* instruction to copy and regard VN metadata as access frequency and trigger rearrangement.

To adapt to potential variations in workload access patterns, we employ a runtime rearrangement mechanism. The rearrangement of n vectors is uniquely characterized by a decomposition into several disjoint cyclic chains, which represent the canonical cycle structure of the corresponding permutation. Each chain can be efficiently reorganized using only one vector buffer. Based on the capacity of additional storage resources, the rearrangement strategies are classified as follows: (1) Limited buffer (e.g., one vector): in-place swapping along cyclic chains is conducted with state tracking (pending, in cache, moving, completed) to guarantee consistency. (2) k buffers: up to k chains can be rearranged in parallel. (3) Sufficient storage: all data movements are executed in parallel. Thus, our proposed mechanism achieves online, adaptive hot metadata rearrangement while ensuring data consistency.

3.3 VN-Least Replacement Policy

To reduce the metadata off-chip memory access, the cache is proposed to minimize the eviction of hot metadata. Observing that in write-intensive training workloads, VN can represent the temporal locality of metadata well, which inspires us to design the VN-least replacement policy.

The VN-least replacement policy faces challenges arising from the split-counter multi-ary format [29], where each cacheline stores multiple narrow-bitwidth minor VNs (incrementing per write-back) and one shared wide-bitwidth major VN (incrementing when any minor VN overflows). First, interference among VNs within a cacheline leads to discrepancies between VN and actual write frequencies. When a minor VN overflows, it resets all minor VNs to zero and increments the shared major VN, causing cold data to appear hotter than it is. Second, access frequency information is unavailable at the cacheline granularity. Since replacement occurs at cacheline level, the multi-ary VNs within a cacheline should be summed and stored, introducing latency and area overhead.

The proposed VN-least policy addresses these challenges using compact hot-data placement and the major VN. Compactly grouping hot data reduces VN interference, mitigating the effect of global resets, since VNs within a cacheline have similar values. Moreover, in the split-counter format, the major VN naturally captures the write frequency of the entire cacheline, providing cacheline-level access information without extra storage. Despite that, adding a few bits for simple reductions on minor VNs further refines this replacement.

Besides, we also propose merging the VN and Merkle Tree caches to improve efficiency and flexibility. The hierarchical dependencies of Merkle Trees create dynamic caching demands; the merged cache adaptively allocates capacity between the two metadata types at runtime. Since both share similar split-counter and multi-ary structures, the VN-least policy can manage both efficiently (Fig. 7).

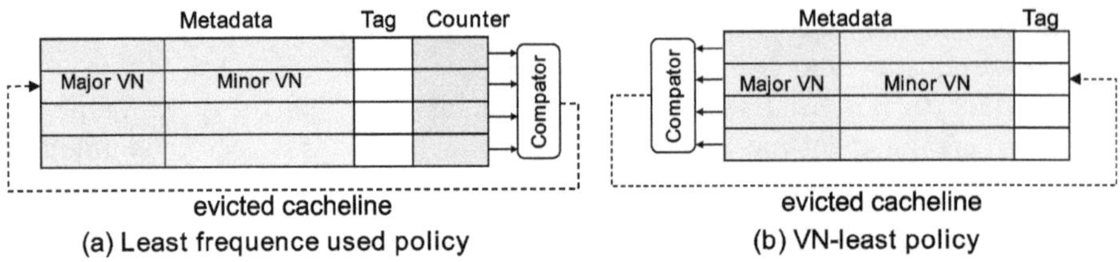

Fig. 7. Replacement policy comparison. VN-least requires no extra storage or counter logic compared to LFU.

3.4 Security Discussion

VecTEE fully inherits TEE's security model without changing core mechanisms—encryption ensures confidentiality, MAC and Merkle Tree guarantee data and VN integrity, and VNs defend against replay attacks. The vector-grained management and VN-least replacement only adjust granularity and caching, without affecting security guarantees. Memory access pattern side-channel issues are orthogonal to TEE protection, while VecTEE 's data rearrangement may even mitigate the risk.

4 Experiments

4.1 Experimental Methodology

We evaluate VecTEE on embedding operations and vector database. Vector length defaults to 32 (varying 16–64), batch size is 64. Since public TEE schemes (e.g., Intel SGX) target CPUs without NPU implementations, we use Ramulator [17], a widely-adopted memory simulator in TEE research [13], for cycle-accurate evaluation with TEE mechanisms implemented in the memory controller. Comparison methods include:

- BL (baseline): Cacheline-grained metadata with AES-256 encryption, GMAC-based MAC verification, Merkle Tree integrity protection, split-counter VN format [29], and LRU replacement.
- BL+Vec: Baseline with vector-grained metadata management.
- BL+Comp: Baseline with compact hot metadata storage.
- BL+VNL: Baseline with VN-least cache replacement policy.
- VecTEE: All three optimizations combined.

Hardware overhead is evaluated via RTL synthesis on SMIC 12nm process and CACTI 7.0 [4] for cache modeling. Table 1 shows the hardware configurations used in our evaluation.

4.2 Performance Results

The embedding evaluation are performed on three benchmark datasets: Criteo Kaggle [6], Avazu [3], and Criteo Terabyte [7], as shown in Fig. 8. VecTEE achieves maximum 68% and average 50% performance improvement across three benchmarks. Key observations: (1) All three methods bring additive improvements and when applied sequentially, they provide 8.2%, 28.6%, and 11.3% gains respectively. (2) Compact hot data storage contributes the largest improvement, indicating that discrete hot data distribution significantly affects metadata cache efficiency. (3) Performance gains vary across benchmarks due to different hot data distributions and workload characteristics.

Table 1. Hardware configurations

Component	Configuration
VN&MT Cache	128 KB, 8-way, VNL/LRU
MAC Cache	64 KB, 8-way, LRU
AES/Hash Lat.	40 cycles
GDDR5 Memory	16 GB, 6000 MT/s

The hit rate analysis (Fig. 8(b)) shows improvement from 84% to 95%. The three methods independently improve cache efficiency with additive effects. They prioritize caching VN and lower-level Merkle Tree nodes, reducing access to higher-level nodes. The merged VN and Merkle Tree cache enables dynamic capacity allocation, improving overall flexibility—VN hit rate gains may accompany Merkle Tree hit rate changes.

The access volume breakdown (Fig. 8(c)) on Criteo dataset shows metadata access ratio drops from 58% (baseline) to 42%, 16%, and finally 12% as optimizations are progressively applied, demonstrating each method's effectiveness.

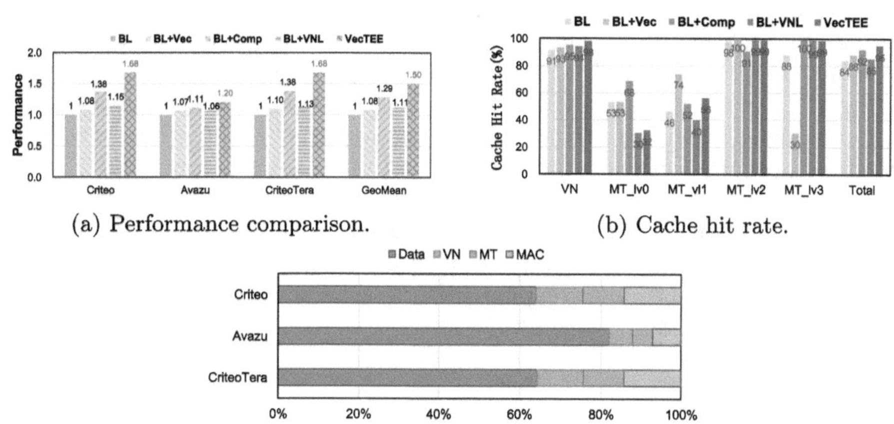

(a) Performance comparison.

(b) Cache hit rate.

(c) Access volume breakdown.

Fig. 8. Performance evaluation: (a) speedup across benchmarks; (b) cache hit rate improvement; (c) metadata access reduction on Criteo.

Figure 9 shows sensitivity analysis. For vector length (Fig. 9(a)), performance gain decreases from 85% to 52% as length increases from 16 to 64. For cache capacity (Fig. 9(b)), VecTEE maintains 50% improvement across 64KB–512KB.

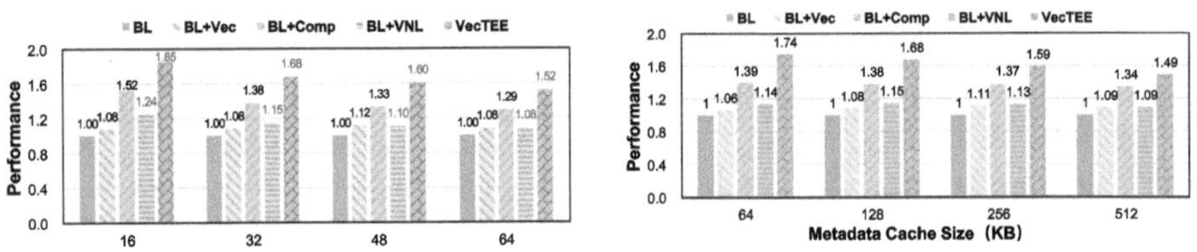

(a) Vector length sensitivity. (b) Cache capacity sensitivity.

Fig. 9. Sensitivity analysis on Criteo dataset: (a) various vector lengths; (b) various cache sizes.

4.3 Vector Database Evaluation

To further verify VecTEE 's generality, we conduct experimental evaluation based on vector database scenario. Specifically, we use SIFT1M dataset, which is widely used for nearest neighbor retrieval evaluation (containing 1 million vectors with dimension 128) [14], and generate 50,000 random queries based on FAISS framework [8], each query retrieving the nearest 100 data vectors. Experiments compare baseline scheme, two individual optimization schemes, and combined optimization scheme performance (VN-least replacement policy shows no significant advantage, configured as baseline LRU replacement policy). Our results in Fig. 10 show that both vector-grained metadata management and compact metadata management can significantly improve memory access efficiency, with combined optimization achieving approximately 19% performance improvement, and metadata cache hit rate improving from 82% to 99%. This additional experiment further verifies VecTEE 's effectiveness and extensibility in vector database scenarios, demonstrating its ability to maintain significant performance advantages not only in embedding computation of specific models but also in broader vector computing tasks.

4.4 Hardware Cost

VecTEE requires only lightweight logic at the memory controller (MLRegs, VN-least comparator, address checking), without modifying computing cores or instruction sets. First, the vector-grained metadata management only adds MLRegs on-chip (less than 1KB) and address checker with the area of 1296 μm^2. Second, the compact management of hot data require negligible hardware modifications. Finally, the VN-least replacement policy utilizes existing major VNs, requiring no additional state storage units, and lightweight three-stage pipelined

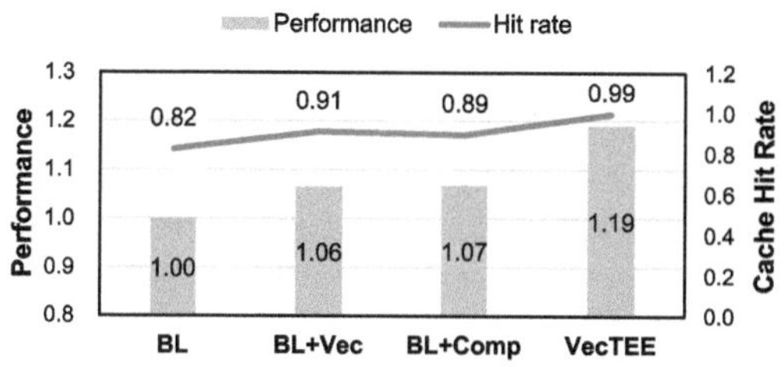

Fig. 10. Vector database query experiment results (SIFT1M dataset, comparing two individual methods and combined method).

comparison tree for comparator (446.7 μm^2). Therefore, the design is portable across NPU architectures. For example, TPU adaptation requires only extending the controller with MLRegs and metadata cache.

5 Conclusion

In this paper, we propose VecTEE to secure NPU vector computing that reduces TEE overhead with compact metadata caching. We propose vector granularity to reduce metadata volume, compact hot metadata to improve metadata temporal locality, and employ a VN-least replacement policy to retain hot data on-chip. Evaluations show that VecTEE enhances the support for vector computing in NPU TEE and effectively improves performance.

Acknowledgment. This work is partially supported by the Strategic Priority Research Program of the Chinese Academy of Sciences (Grants No. XDB0660300, XDB0660301, XDB0660302), Science and Technology Major Special Program of Jiangsu (Grant No. BG2024028), the NSF of China (Grants No. U22A2028, 62341411, 6240073476), CAS Project for Young Scientists in Basic Research (YSBR-029) and Youth Innovation Promotion Association CAS.

Artificial intelligence tools, if used, were used only for language organization and figure/table polishing, and did not participate in the generation of the core ideas or technical content.

References

1. Abdullah, R., Zhou, H., Awad, A.: Plutus: bandwidth-efficient memory security for GPUs. In: Proceedings of the IEEE International Symposium on High-Performance Computer Architecture (HPCA), pp. 543–555 (2023)
2. Akimoto, Y., Fukuchi, K., Akimoto, Y., Sakuma, J.: Privformer: privacy-preserving transformer with MPC. In: 2023 IEEE 8th European Symposium on Security and Privacy (EuroS&P), pp. 392–410. IEEE (2023)
3. Avazu: Avazu mobile ads CTR. https://www.kaggle.com/c/avazu-ctr-prediction

4. Balasubramonian, R., Kahng, A.B., Muralimanohar, N., Shafiee, A., Srinivas, V.: Cacti 7: new tools for interconnect exploration in innovative off-chip memories. Trans. Archit. Code Optim. (TACO) **14**(2), 1–25 (2017)
5. Costan, V., Devadas, S.: Intel SGX explained. Cryptology ePrint Archive (2016)
6. Criteo: Criteo display ad challenge. www.kaggle.com/c/criteo-display-ad-challenge
7. Criteo: Terabyte click logs. https://huggingface.co/datasets/criteo/CriteoClickLogs
8. Douze, M., et al.: The Faiss library. IEEE Trans. Big Data (2025)
9. Gao, Y., et al.: Retrieval-augmented generation for large language models: a survey. arXiv preprint arXiv:2312.10997 (2023)
10. Ghazi, B., et al.: Sparsity-preserving differentially private training of large embedding models. In: Proceedings of the Advances in Neural Information Processing Systems (2024)
11. Granlund, T., Montgomery, P.L.: Division by invariant integers using multiplication. In: Proceedings of the ACM SIGPLAN 1994 Conference on Programming Language Design and implementation, pp. 61–72 (1994)
12. Gueron, S.: A memory encryption engine suitable for general purpose processors. IEEE Secur. Priv. **14**(6), 54–62 (2016)
13. Hua, W., Umar, M., Zhang, Z., Suh, G.E.: MGX: near-zero overhead memory protection for data-intensive accelerators. In: Proceedings of the Annual International Symposium on Computer Architecture (ISCA), pp. 726–741 (2022)
14. Jegou, H., Douze, M., Schmid, C.: Product quantization for nearest neighbor search. TPAMI **33**(1), 117–128 (2010)
15. Jiao, D., et al.: Neo: towards efficient fully homomorphic encryption acceleration using tensor core. In: Proceedings of the 52nd Annual International Symposium on Computer Architecture, pp. 107–121 (2025)
16. Jouppi, N., et al.: TPU v4: an optically reconfigurable supercomputer for machine learning with hardware support for embeddings. In: Proceedings of the Annual International Symposium on Computer Architecture (ISCA), pp. 1–14 (2023)
17. Kim, Y., Yang, W., Mutlu, O.: Ramulator: a fast and extensible dram simulator. IEEE Comput. Archit. Lett. (CAL) **15**(1), 45–49 (2015)
18. Lee, S., Kim, J., Na, S., Park, J., Huh, J.: TNPU: supporting trusted execution with tree-less integrity protection for neural processing unit. In: Proceedings of the IEEE International Symposium on High-Performance Computer Architecture (HPCA), pp. 229–243 (2022)
19. Liu, H., et al.: Accelerating personalized recommendation with cross-level near-memory processing. In: Proceedings of the Annual International Symposium on Computer Architecture (ISCA), pp. 1–13 (2023)
20. Mu, J., et al.: Alchemist: a unified accelerator architecture for cross-scheme fully homomorphic encryption. In: Proceedings of the 61st ACM/IEEE Design Automation Conference, pp. 1–6 (2024)
21. Na, S., Lee, S., Kim, Y., Park, J., Huh, J.: Common counters: compressed encryption counters for secure GPU memory. In: Proceedings of the High-Performance Computer Architecture (HPCA), pp. 1–13 (2021)
22. Naumov, M., et al.: Deep learning recommendation model for personalization and recommendation systems. arXiv preprint arXiv:1906.00091 (2019)
23. Quinn, D., et al.: Accelerating retrieval-augmented generation. In: Proceedings of the 30th ACM International Conference on Architectural Support for Programming Languages and Operating Systems, vol. 1, pp. 15–32 (2025)

24. Shrivastava, N., Sarangi, S.R.: Securator: a fast and secure neural processing unit. In: Proceedings of the IEEE International Symposium on High-Performance Computer Architecture (HPCA), pp. 1127–1139 (2023)
25. South, T., Zuskind, G., Mahari, R., Hardjono, T.: Secure community transformers: private pooled data for LLMs (2023)
26. Touvron, H., et al.: LLaMA: open and efficient foundation language models. arXiv preprint arXiv:2302.13971 (2023)
27. Wang, Z., et al.: OPER: optimality-guided embedding table parallelization for large-scale recommendation model. In: Proceedings of the USENIX Annual Technical Conference (USENIX ATC), pp. 667–682 (2024)
28. Watson, J.L., Wagh, S., Popa, R.A.: Piranha: a GPU platform for secure computation. In: USENIX Security Symposium (USENIX Security), pp. 827–844 (2022)
29. Yan, C., Englender, D., Prvulovic, M., Rogers, B., Solihin, Y.: Improving cost, performance, and security of memory encryption and authentication. ACM SIGARCH Comput. Archit. News **34**(2), 179–190 (2006)
30. Zheng, X., et al.: InputSnatch: stealing input in LLM services via timing side-channel attacks. arXiv preprint arXiv:2411.18191 (2024)

Poster Papers

AMXStencil: Boosting the Performance of Stencil Computations on AMX-Powered CPUs via Fusion

Zitong An, Kangkang Chen, Huayou Su(✉), Jinwei Xu, and Xi Yang

National University of Defense Technology, Changsha 410073, China
{anzitong,chenkangkang,shyou,xujinwei13,yangxi1016}@nudt.edu.cn

Abstract. Stencil computation is a fundamental operator in scientific computing. Recent matrix-multiplication-based methods exploit GPU Tensor Cores, but directly adapting them to Intel Advanced Matrix Extensions (AMX) incurs layout transformation overhead, off-chip memory accesses, and low tile utilization. This paper presents AMXStencil, a fusion-based framework for accelerating stencil computations on AMX-powered CPUs. AMXStencil integrates layout transformation with precision conversion, fuses multiple matrix-chain multiplications within AMX tile registers to improve hardware utilization and reduce memory traffic. Experimental results demonstrate that AMXStencil achieves speedups of up to 36.41×, 12.94×, and 4.06× over unoptimized Conv-based, LoRA-based, and AVX-based implementations, respectively.

Keywords: Stencil Computation · Intel AMX · Fusion · Matrix Multiplication

1 Introduction

Stencil computation is a fundamental computational pattern in scientific computing. It updates each grid point using neighboring values and is widely used in physical simulation, numerical solvers, and learning-based scientific workloads. Due to its regular data access pattern and high computational intensity, stencil computation has been extensively optimized on CPUs and GPUs through tiling [1,8,11], vectorization [6,10], and temporal blocking [5].

Recent AI accelerators provide new opportunities for stencil acceleration. In particular, Tensor Core-based methods [2,7,9] transform stencil computation into matrix multiplication to exploit high-throughput matrix engines. Recent Intel CPUs integrate Advanced Matrix Extensions (AMX), a built-in matrix accelerator. However, directly adapting these methods to Intel Advanced Matrix Extensions (AMX) [3] is inefficient, because AMX differs from GPU Tensor Cores in tile dimensions, data layout requirements, on-chip storage capacity, and memory access behavior.

In this paper, we propose AMXStencil, a fusion-based framework for accelerating stencil computation on AMX-powered CPUs. To the best of our knowledge,

L. Eeckhout et al. (Eds.): APPT 2026, LNCS 16693, pp. 565–571, 2027.
https://doi.org/10.1007/978-981-92-4805-6_37

this constitutes the first effort dedicated to stencil computation optimization leveraging Intel AMX. AMXStencil integrates data fusion and operator fusion to reduce layout transformation overhead and avoid unnecessary memory accesses. We evaluate AMXStencil on two AMX-enabled Intel CPUs. Experimental results show that AMXStencil achieves speedups of up to 36.41×, 12.94×, and 4.06× over Conv-based, LoRA-based, and AVX-based implementations, respectively.

2 Background and Motivations

2.1 Stencil Computation

Stencil is a fundamental computation in the fields of scientific computing and artificial intelligence. It typically involves executing the same computational process on all points within a regular grid. In each time step, the point to update is calculated from the old values of itself and its neighbors using a fixed, identical stencil function. Algorithm 1 illustrates the iterative update process of Box-2D9P stencil computation, where the value of the point (i,j) at the current time step t is computed from predefined calculations using values of point (i,j) and its surrounding eight points from the previous time step $t-1$.

Algorithm 1. Box-2D9P Stencil

Require: mesh A_0, weight $w_{11} \sim w_{33}$
Ensure: mesh *output*
for $t = 1$ to *times* **do**
  for each $A_t[i][j]$ in A_t **do**
    $A_t[i][j] = A_{t-1}[i-1][j-1] \times w_{11} + A_{t-1}[i-1][j] \times w_{12} + A_{t-1}[i-1][j+1] \times w_{13} + A_{t-1}[i][j-1] \times w_{21} + A_{t-1}[i][j] \times w_{22} + A_{t-1}[i][j+1] \times w_{23} + A_{t-1}[i+1][j-1] \times w_{31} + A_{t-1}[i+1][j] \times w_{32} + A_{t-1}[i+1][j+1] \times w_{33}$
  end for
end for
output $= A_{times}$

2.2 Motivations

Intel AMX is a dedicated matrix acceleration unit built into the 4th Gen Intel Xeon Scalable Processors (codenamed Sapphire Rapids) and subsequent generations, supporting the fast execution of the operation $C = A \times B + C$. When AMX performs matrix multiplication calculations $C = A \times B + C$, the matrix B is required to comply with a specific data layout. This transformation groups the original row-major matrix into row pairs and packs their elements column-wise into sequential 2-element blocks.

Stencil computation based on AMX requires transforming stencils into a matrix multiplication pattern. We first directly map two classic Tensor Core-oriented stencil optimization methods, ConvStencil and LoRAStencil to AMX, denoting them as Conv-based implementation and LoRA-based implementation, respectively. We identify three factors affecting performance. The first one is substantial layout transformation overhead. The layout transformation accounts for a significant fraction of execution time, exceeding 50% in the worst case. The second one is the frequent off-chip access of intermediate results. The interface provided by oneDNN [4] follows a memory-to-memory pattern, which results in significant data movement overhead. The third one is the low hardware utilization. The utilization rates of the AMX tile registers corresponding to baseline implementation are not exceeded, with the maximum not exceeding 34% and the minimum below 6%.

3 AMXStencil Design

To address the above issues, we propose AMXStencil, a fusion-based method for accelerating stencil computations on AMX processors. Given a stencil kernel, AMXStencil first decomposes it into a set of low-rank matrix components. For each input tile, the computation is expressed as a sequence of MCMs in the form of $U_i \times X \times V_i$, where X denotes the input sub-block and U_i, V_i are weight matrices derived from the stencil kernel. AMXStencil then applies two fusion techniques to improve the performance of stencil computations. To improve hardware utilization, we also performed time-step unrolling for stencil computations.

3.1 Data Fusion

AMX tile matrix multiplication requires the right-hand-side operand to follow a blocked interleaved layout. Under the original computation order $(U_i \times X) \times V_i$, AMX requires two layout transformations for X and one for V_i to satisfy the layout constraint of the right-hand-side operand, as shown in Fig. 1(a). In addition, because the intermediate result of $U_i \times X$ is generated in FP32, an extra precision compression to BF16 is required before multiplication with V_i.

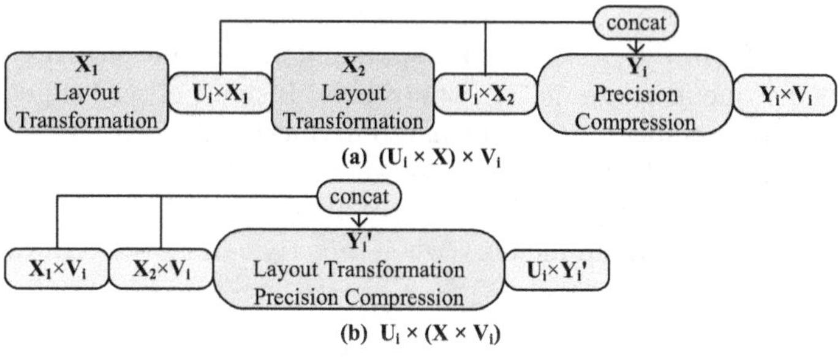

Fig. 1. Data fuser for MCM based on computation reordering.

To reduce this overhead, we reorder the computation as $U_i \times (X \times V_i)$. Under this order, only one layout transformation is needed for V_i, and the intermediate result of $X \times V_i$ requires only one fused transformation before reuse, as shown in Fig. 1(b). Furthermore, since the result of $X \times V_i$ must still be compressed from FP32 to BF16, we fuse layout transformation and precision conversion into a single kernel, replacing separate operations and eliminating redundant transformations of X. In this way, AMXStencil removes redundant transformations and reduces memory traffic before matrix multiplication.

3.2 Operator Fusion

Since the interface provided by oneDNN follows a memory-to-memory pattern, the intermediate results of the $r + 1$ MCMs need to be written back to main memory, and the input data X needs to be reloaded repeatedly, resulting in frequent access overhead.

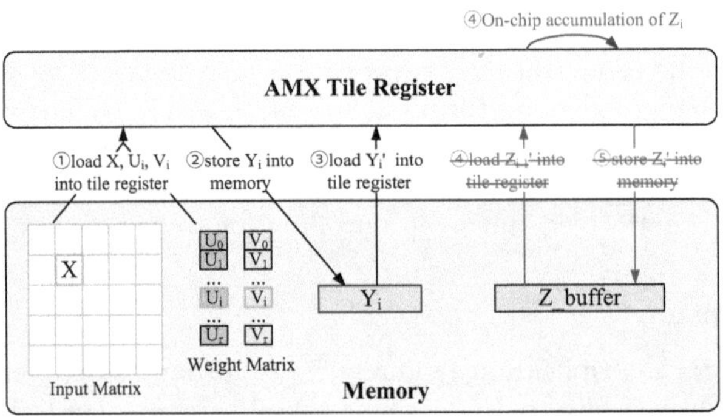

Fig. 2. Operator fuser of MCM in AMXStencil, the input X needs to be loaded only once, and the results of each MCM can be held in the tile registers.

To address this issue, AMXStencil proposes an operator fusion method that implements on-chip fusion of $r+1$ MCM computations based on tile registers. It fuses multiple MCMs of $U_i \times X \times V_i$ corresponding to multiple rank-1 components with their subsequent accumulation operations. Instead of writing each partial result Z_i back to memory, it is immediately reduced with the preceding partial sums retained in the tile registers, as shown in Fig. 2. Meanwhile, we keep the input matrix X resident in the tile registers of AMX, which avoids the need to repeatedly load X from main memory when directly calling the GEMM interface provided by oneDNN (Fig. 3).

4 Experiments

We evaluate AMXStencil on two AMX-enabled Intel CPUs: Intel Gold 6434 (Gold 6434) and Intel Xeon Max 9462 (Max 9462). Gold 6434 has 8 physical cores and 45 MiB L3 cache, while Max 9462 provides 32 physical cores and 75

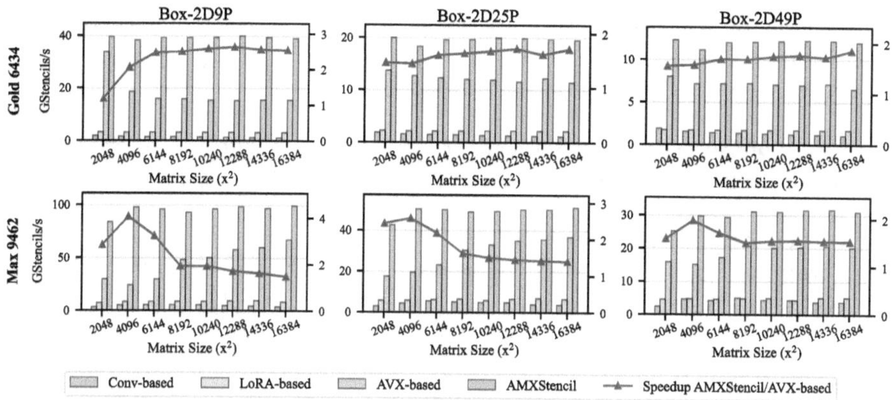

Fig. 3. Performance and speedup comparison on Gold 6434 (8 cores) and Max 9462 (32 cores). The speedup denotes the relative throughput improvement of AMXStencil over each baseline. Outsized speedups over Conv-based and LoRA-based methods are excluded to preserve axis scaling.

MiB L3 cache. To assess effectiveness, we compare AMXStencil with Conv-based and LoRA-based implementations, as well as the classic stencil computation implemented on AVX vector units. Performance is measured in GStencils/s, defined as the number of updated grid points per second divided by 10^9.

In this section, we evaluate the performance of AMXStencil and the baselines across different 2D box stencil computations and problem sizes. The evaluated stencil kernels include Box-2D9P, Box-2D25P, and Box-2D49P. For each kernel, we vary the input size and execute each configuration for 50 iterations. Specifically, AMXStencil achieves average speedups of 1.87× and 1.93× over the AVX-based implementation on the Gold 6434 and Max 9462, respectively, while reaching maximum speedups of 2.63× and 4.06× on the two platforms. When compared to the unoptimized Conv-based and LoRA-based implementations, AMXStencil yields even more substantial speedups: up to 36.41× and 12.94× on the Gold 6434, and 26.65× and 11.85× on the Max 9462, respectively.

5 Conclusion

To address the performance challenges of stencil computation on CPUs, this paper proposes AMXStencil, an efficient stencil computation method with data fusion and operator fusion for AMX. By fusing layout transformation and precision conversion within matrix chain multiplication (MCM), AMXStencil significantly reduces layout transformation overhead. Secondly, it leverages tile registers to fuse $r + 1$ MCMs on-chip through operator fusion, avoiding frequent off-chip accesses to intermediate results. Extensive evaluations demonstrate that AMXStencil significantly outperforms existing approaches.

Acknowledgments. This work is supported by the National Key R&D Program of China (No.2022YFB4501400) and Furong Program Young Talent (Science & Technology Innovation No.2025RC3126.)

Disclosure of Interests. The authors have no competing interests to declare that are relevant to the content of this article.

Use of Artificial Intelligence Tools. The technical solution and experimental design presented in this paper were independently completed by the authors. AI tools were used solely for language polishing and formatting optimization, and did not participate in the development of the research ideas or core content.

References

1. Bondhugula, U., Bandishti, V., Pananilath, I.: Diamond tiling: tiling techniques to maximize parallelism for stencil computations. IEEE Trans. Parallel Distrib. Syst. **28**(5), 1285–1298 (2016)
2. Chen, Y., Li, K., Wang, Y.: Convstencil: transform stencil computation to matrix multiplication on tensor cores. In: Proceedings of the 29th ACM SIGPLAN Annual Symposium on Principles and Practice of Parallel Programming, pp. 333–347 (2024)
3. Corporation, I.: Intel® intrinsics guide. https://www.intel.com/content/www/us/en/docs/intrinsics-guide/index.html (2024). Accessed 20 Aug 2025
4. Corporation, I.: Intel® oneapi deep neural network library (onednn). https://www.intel.com/content/www/us/en/developer/tools/oneapi/onednn.html (2026). Accessed 13 Jun 2026
5. Grosser, T., Cohen, A., Kelly, P.H.: Split tiling for GPUS: automatic parallelization using trapezoidal tiles. In: Proceedings of the 6th Workshop on General Purpose Processor Using Graphics Processing Units, pp. 24–31 (2013)
6. Li, K., Yuan, L., Zhang, Y.: Reducing redundancy in data organization and arithmetic calculation for stencil computations. In: Proceedings of the International Conference for High Performance Computing, Networking, Storage and Analysis, pp. 1–15 (2021)
7. Liu, X., et al.: Toward accelerated stencil computation by adapting tensor core unit on GPU. In: Proceedings of the 36th ACM International Conference on Supercomputing, pp. 1–12 (2022)
8. Oh, C., Zheng, Z., Shen, X.: Gopipe: a granularity-oblivious programming framework for pipelined stencil executions on GPU. In: Proceedings of the ACM International Conference on Parallel Architectures and Compilation Techniques, pp. 43–54 (2020)
9. Zhang, Y., Li, K., Yuan, L.: Lorastencil: low-rank adaptation of stencil computation on tensor cores. In: Proceedings of the SC24: International Conference for High Performance Computing, Networking, Storage and Analysis, pp. 1–17 (2024)

10. Zhang, Y., Li, K., Yuan, L.: Jigsaw: toward conflict-free vectorized stencil computation by tessellating swizzled registers. In: Proceedings of the 30th ACM SIGPLAN Annual Symposium on Principles and Practice of Parallel Programming, pp. 481–495 (2025)
11. Zhao, T., Basu, P., Williams, S.: Exploiting reuse and vectorization in blocked stencil computations on CPUS and GPUS. In: Proceedings of the International Conference for High Performance Computing, Networking, Storage and Analysis, pp. 1–44 (2019)

S^2M: Spatiotemporal-Cooperative Symbiotic Memory for Heterogeneous PQC Acceleration

Sizhao Li[1,2(✉)], Zili Zhou[2(✉)], Wei Li[3], Chenyu Zhai[2], Bingrui Guo[4], and Donghui Guo[5]

[1] College of Integrated Circuits, Harbin Engineering University, Harbin, China
sizhao.li@hrbeu.edu.cn
[2] College of Computer Science and Technology, Harbin Engineering University, Harbin, China
{lizi_zhou,luciderpluto}@hrbeu.edu.cn
[3] Xinli Technology Innovation Center Co., Ltd, Beijing, China
liwei@xinitech.com
[4] School of Computer Science, Peking University, Beijing, China
bguo9894@stu.pku.edu.cn
[5] School of Electronic Science and Engineering, Xiamen University, Xiamen, China
dhguo@xmu.edu.cn

Abstract. Post-Quantum Cryptography (PQC) algorithms such as ML-KEM and ML-DSA are essential for quantum-resistant security, but acceleration remains constrained by memory traffic, bank conflicts, and short-lived intermediate data. Existing accelerators mainly optimize arithmetic datapaths or fixed access patterns, making it difficult to efficiently support ML-KEM's streaming phases together with ML-DSA's irregular transient data. This paper proposes S^2M, a spatiotemporal-cooperative memory architecture for heterogeneous PQC acceleration. S^2M uses an Algorithm-Aware Lifetime Analyzer (ALA) to identify reusable lifetime intervals and a Dedicated Address Allocator (DAA) for conflict-free placement in banked SRAM. By combining temporal SRAM reuse with spatial bank-conflict avoidance, S^2M provides a unified memory substrate for heterogeneous PQC workloads. RTL synthesis in a 28nm process and cycle-accurate simulation show that S^2M operates at 200 MHz, completes the evaluated ALA–DAA scheduling phase in 168 cycles, and achieves zero memory conflicts with 9.17 million memory accesses per watt. Among the compared PQC accelerators, S^2M achieves the lowest area and power with competitive latency and throughput, reducing area and power by at least 1.66× and 1.75×, respectively.

Keywords: Post-Quantum Cryptography · Spatiotemporal cooperation · Symbiotic memory · Lifetime scheduling · Bank interleaving

L. Eeckhout et al. (Eds.): APPT 2026, LNCS 16693, pp. 572–578, 2027.
https://doi.org/10.1007/978-981-92-4805-6_38

1 Introduction

Quantum computers threaten widely deployed public-key cryptosystems such as RSA and ECC, since Shor's algorithm solves integer factorization and discrete logarithms in polynomial time [1]. NIST has therefore standardized lattice-based ML-KEM and ML-DSA for quantum-safe key encapsulation and digital signatures [2,4]. Although NTT/INTT engines reduce polynomial arithmetic cost, practical PQC accelerators remain limited by memory traffic, bank conflicts, and numerous short-lived intermediate values [4,5].

A central challenge is the divergent memory behavior of ML-KEM and ML-DSA. ML-KEM largely follows deterministic streaming dataflows, whereas ML-DSA involves rejection sampling and transient vectors such as z, w, and c. Existing accelerators and PIM-oriented designs optimize arithmetic datapaths or fixed conflict-free access patterns, but still bind logical data objects to static physical buffers [6–10]. Such mapping either over-reserves SRAM for worst-case ML-DSA lifetimes or underutilizes banks during regular ML-KEM phases.

This paper proposes S^2M, a spatiotemporal-cooperative memory architecture for heterogeneous PQC acceleration. S^2M formulates PQC memory management as lifetime-aware bank allocation: objects with non-overlapping lifetimes reuse the same SRAM chunk, while overlapping or concurrently accessed objects are separated across banks or offsets. S^2M realizes this through an Algorithm-Aware Lifetime Analyzer (ALA), which derives lifetime compatibility from algorithm-level events, and a Dedicated Address Allocator (DAA), which maps logical objects to conflict-free physical SRAM chunks. The main contributions are:

- We formulate heterogeneous PQC memory management as lifetime-aware bank allocation for temporal reuse and spatial conflict avoidance.
- We propose an ALA–DAA scheduling pipeline with a unified bank-interleaved SRAM organization for both streaming ML-KEM and irregular ML-DSA phases.
- We implement S^2M in 28nm RTL, achieving 168 scheduling cycles, zero memory conflicts, 9.17 million memory accesses per watt, and the lowest area and power among the compared PQC accelerators.

2 S^2M Architecture and Lifetime-Aware Scheduling

Figure 1 shows the proposed S^2M architecture, which consists of an Algorithm Execution Orchestrator, an Algorithm-Aware Lifetime Analyzer (ALA), a Dedicated Address Allocator (DAA), and a unified banked SRAM array. The orchestrator serves as the interface between PQC datapaths and the memory scheduler. It monitors completion, sampling, and phase-transition events from algorithm modules such as NTT and sampling units. Each event is first synchronized to the global clock and converted into a single-cycle trigger pulse. The pulse then activates an FSM to latch the current cycle count and module metadata. The

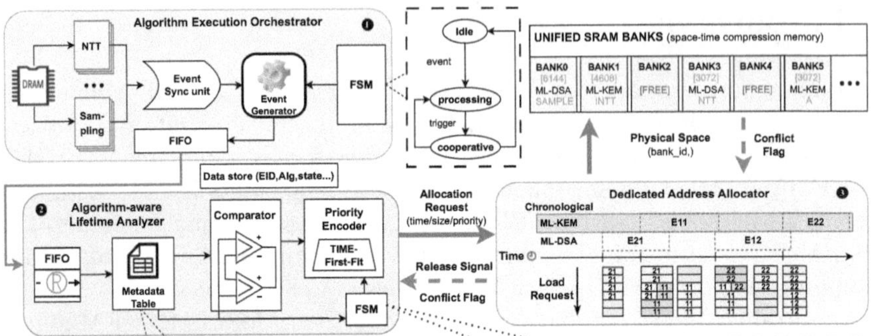

ID	Algorithm	Phase	Module	State	DataTag	BitLength	StartCycle	EndCycle
E11	ML-KEM	enc	INTT	A_INTT	st_NTT_ MUL_A00_r0	4608	700	830
E21	ML-DSA	keygen	SAM PLE	SAMPLE Secret	KG_ SAMPLE_S1	6144	0	260
E12	ML-KEM	dec	A	A_ SAMPLE	A_gen_ st_A00	3072	200	470
E22	ML-DSA	sign	NTT	NTT	SG_ NTT_S2	3072	430	600

Fig. 1. Overview of S^2M architecture. ❶ denotes the Algorithm Execution Orchestrator, which controls execution through an FSM and Event Pulse Generator to synchronize data collection; ❷ represents the **ALA**, which uses FIFO and ROM for metadata storage and analyzes temporal overlaps using a Comparator; ❸ illustrates the **DAA**, which manages allocation requests and physical address mapping while checking conflicts in the Unified SRAM Banks.

captured information is packed into a compact FIFO entry containing the algorithm type, execution phase, source module, status, data label, object size, and lifetime window.

The ALA performs lifetime-aware temporal scheduling. It dequeues event packets, registers object metadata into a lifetime table, and uses a comparator array to detect temporal overlap between each incoming lifetime interval and active entries. Objects with non-overlapping lifetimes are eligible to reuse the same physical SRAM chunk, whereas overlapping objects must be separated spatially. This mechanism converts short-lived PQC intermediates into reusable storage intervals without modifying the cryptographic dataflow.

To determine allocation order, the ALA adopts a priority-first-fit policy. Each request is represented by its priority and size. Requests are first sorted by execution-phase priority and then by object size when priorities are identical. Each request is assigned to the first bank chunk that satisfies both lifetime and capacity constraints. This priority-aware ordering favors phase-critical data and reduces fragmentation caused by irregular short-lived objects.

The DAA performs physical address allocation and bank-state management. Given an ALA request tuple $(priority, size, start, end)$, the DAA scans bank timelines to find a contiguous SRAM chunk satisfying both spatial capacity and temporal availability constraints. A successful allocation returns a physical address consisting of a bank identifier and a local offset; otherwise, a conflict flag is raised. Each bank is tracked as idle, allocated, conflicting, or pre-allocated, enabling look-ahead reservation for dependent phases. When an object's lifetime expires, the corresponding bank chunk is released for subsequent reuse.

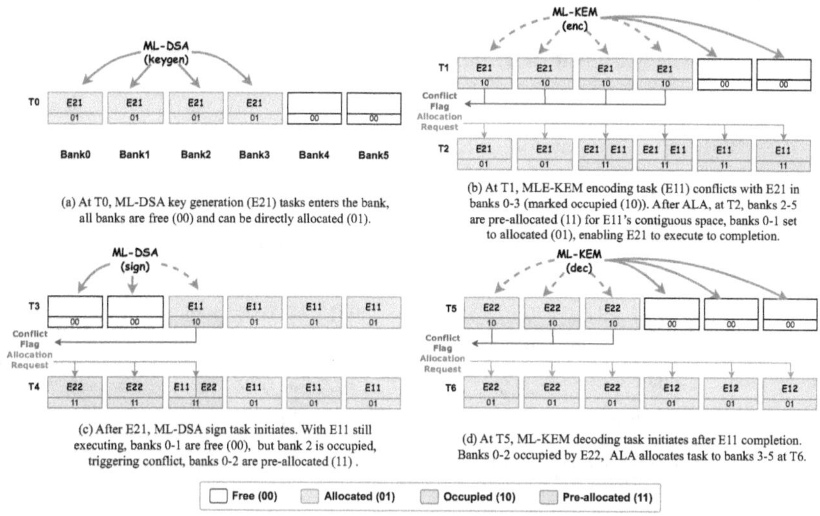

(a) At T0, ML-DSA key generation (E21) tasks enters the bank, all banks are free (00) and can be directly allocated (01).

(b) At T1, MLE-KEM encoding task (E11) conflicts with E21 in banks 0-3 (marked occupied (10)). After ALA, at T2, banks 2-5 are pre-allocated (11) for E11's contiguous space, banks 0-1 set to allocated (01), enabling E21 to execute to completion.

(c) After E21, ML-DSA sign task initiates. With E11 still executing, banks 0-1 are free (00), but bank 2 is occupied, triggering conflict, banks 0-2 are pre-allocated (11).

(d) At T5, ML-KEM decoding task initiates after E11 completion. Banks 0-2 occupied by E22, ALA allocates task to banks 3-5 at T6.

Fig. 2. DAA bank-state evolution, illustrating bank-time reuse, conflict redirection, and look-ahead pre-allocation across heterogeneous PQC tasks.

S^2M therefore exploits temporal reuse and spatial conflict avoidance within a unified SRAM substrate. For ML-KEM, the DAA can generate bank mappings suitable for regular streaming dataflows. For ML-DSA, the ALA and DAA can aggressively reclaim short-lived storage produced by rejection sampling and transient vectors such as z, w, and c. As illustrated in Fig. 2, when ML-KEM and ML-DSA tasks occupy disjoint bank-time regions, they can share the same physical SRAM banks across different time intervals. When access or lifetime conflicts occur, requests are redirected to available bank-time regions, and successor phases can be pre-allocated while preserving data dependencies. Consequently, S^2M avoids static per-phase buffer reservation and provides a compact, conflict-aware memory substrate for heterogeneous PQC workloads.

3 Implementation and Evaluation

S^2M is implemented in Verilog RTL, simulated with VCS, and synthesized using Synopsys Design Compiler under an SMIC 28nm PDK. The design operates at 200 MHz. Validation is performed with cycle-accurate tests using 2^{16} vectors generated from NIST-standard PQC workloads. The evaluation focuses on the ALA–DAA memory-scheduling phase to isolate the contribution of lifetime-aware address allocation and bank-conflict avoidance.

Table 1 compares S^{2}M with related designs. S^{2}M achieves the lowest area and power while maintaining competitive latency and throughput. Compared with PQC PIM baselines, it reduces area by at least 1.66× and power by at least 1.75×. These results indicate that the efficiency improvement comes primarily from lifetime-aware SRAM reuse and compact scheduling logic, rather than from simply increasing arithmetic parallelism.

Table 1. Comparison of S^{2}M with state-of-the-art solutions.

Design*	Max f (MHz)	Latency t_l (μs)	Tput. (KP/s)	Area (mm^2)	Power (μW)
MB [4]	202	1.3	47.5	0.103	273
KCF [5]	200	23.8	39.3	0.086	834
BP [10]	3.8K	61.9	183.4	0.063	340
CF [7]	213	1.27	189.5	0.072	725
SR [8]	200	1.57	106.9	0.124	518
RISC-V1 [11]	1.25K	0.18	2.4K	/	11.3K
RISC-V2 [12]	1K	85	1.8K	6.639	14.9K
S^{2}M	200	1.31	160.4	**0.038**	**156**

* All technology nodes are projected to 28nm.

Table 2 further evaluates memory-scheduling capability. S^{2}M is the only compared design that simultaneously supports multi-algorithm scheduling, DAA-based address allocation, an N storage footprint, and zero-conflict access. Compared with CF and MM, which also achieve zero conflicts, S^{2}M reduces scheduling cycles to 168 through explicit dynamic address allocation. Compared with PQCPIM, Ro, and ConPQC, it avoids bank-conflict penalties while maintaining a compact storage footprint, and achieves the highest memory-access efficiency of 9.17 million accesses per watt. These results directly reflect the ALA–DAA scheduling effect: lifetime-aware reuse reduces SRAM over-reservation, while

Table 2. Memory performance comparisons with related works.

Work	Multi-alg.	DAA	Storage	Cycles	Conflict num./K	Mem. Acc num./mW ↑
CF [7]	✓	✗	N	270	0	3.05
MM [9]	✓	✗	N	276	0	8.50
PQCPIM [6]	✓	✗	$2N$	313	12.5	6.82
Ro [13]	✗	✗	$2N$	385	23.1	5.37
ConPQC [14]	✗	✗	$\lg N$	569	18.4	4.88
S^{2}M	✓	✓	N	**168**	0	**9.17**

bank-aware mapping eliminates conflict-induced stalls without increasing the storage footprint beyond N.

4 Conclusion

S^{2}M presents a spatiotemporal-cooperative memory architecture for heterogeneous PQC acceleration. It combines ALA-based lifetime analysis and DAA-based address mapping to enable temporal SRAM reuse and spatial conflict avoidance across ML-KEM and ML-DSA phases. In 28nm RTL evaluation, S^{2}M achieves zero memory conflicts, 168 scheduling cycles, 9.17 million memory accesses per watt, and the lowest area and power among the compared PQC accelerators. These results show that lifetime-aware memory scheduling is an effective substrate for compact multi-algorithm PQC acceleration.

Acknowledgments. This work is supported by the National Key R&D Program of China (No.2022YFB4400703), the National Key R&D Program of Heilongjiang Province (2024ZXDXA12) and the Fundamental Research Funds for the Central Universities (3072026XK0801).

Disclosure of Interests. All authors disclosed no relevant relationships.

References

1. Shor, P.W.: Algorithms for Quantum Computation: Discrete Logarithms and Factoring. In: Annual Symposium on Foundations of Computer Science, pp. 124-134, Santa Fe, NM, USA (1994). https://doi.org/10.1109/SFCS.1994.365700
2. FIPS Homepage. https://csrc.nist.gov/pubs/fips/203/final. Accessed 13 Aug 2024
3. FIPS Homepage. https://csrc.nist.gov/pubs/fips/204/final. Accessed 13 Aug 2024
4. Chen, X.: Efficient access scheme for multi-bank based NTT architecture through conflict graph. In: Proceedings of the ACM/IEEE Design Automation Conference (DAC), pp. 91–96., San Francisco, CA, USA (2022). https://doi.org/10.1145/3489517.3530656
5. Guo, W., Li, S.: Highly-efficient hardware architecture for crystals-kyber with a novel conflict-free memory access pattern. IEEE Trans. Circuits Syst. I Regul. Pap. **70**(11), 4505–4515 (2023). https://doi.org/10.1109/TCSI.2023.3306347
6. Park, J., Lee, S., Lee,J.: NTT-PIM: row-centric architecture and mapping for efficient number-theoretic transform on PIM. In: Proceedings of the ACM/IEEE Design Automation Conference (DAC), pp. 1–6, San Francisco, CA, USA (2023). https://doi.org/10.1109/DAC56929.2023.10247747
7. Chen, X., Yang, B., Yin, S., Wei, S., Liu, L.: CFNTT: scalable radix-2/4 NTT multiplication architecture with an efficient conflict-free memory mapping scheme. IACR Trans. Cryptographic Hardware Embed. Syst. 94–126 (2022). https://doi.org/10.46586/tches.v2022.i1.94-126
8. Guo, W., Li, S.: Split-radix based compact hardware architecture for crystals-kyber. IEEE Trans. Comput. **73**(1), 97–108 (2024). https://doi.org/10.1109/TC.2023.3320040

9. Zhao, Y., Liu, X., Hu, Y., Xiao, H.: Design of an efficient NTT/INTT architecture with low-complex memory mapping scheme. IEEE Trans. Circuits Syst. II Express Briefs **71**(1), 400–404 (2024). https://doi.org/10.1109/TCSII.2023.3296492
10. Zhang, J., Imani, M., Sadredini, E.: BP-NTT: fast and compact in-SRAM Number theoretic transform with bit-parallel modular multiplication. In: Proceedings of the ACM/IEEE Design Automation Conference (DAC), pp. 1–6., San Francisco, CA, USA (2023). https://doi.org/10.1109/DAC56929.2023.10247691
11. Kuang, H., Zhao, Y., Han, J.: A high-speed NTT-based polynomial multiplication accelerator with vector extension of RISC-V for saber algorithm. In: Proceedings of the IEEE Asia Pacific Conference on Circuits and Systems (APCCAS), pp. 592–595., Shenzhen, China (2022). https://doi.org/10.1109/APCCAS55924.2022.10090293
12. Paludo, R., Sousa, L.: NTT architecture for a Linux-ready RISC-V fully-homomorphic encryption accelerator. IEEE Trans. Circuits Syst. I Regul. Pap. **69**(7), 2669–2682 (2022). https://doi.org/10.1109/TCSI.2022.3166550
13. Feng, X., Li, S., Xu, S.: RLWE-oriented high-speed polynomial multiplier utilizing multi-lane stockham NTT algorithm. IEEE Trans. Circuits Syst. II Express Briefs **67**(3), 556–559 (2020). https://doi.org/10.1109/TCSII.2019.2917621
14. Banerjee, U., Ukyab, T.S., Chandrakasan, A.P.: Sapphire: a configurable crypto-processor for post-quantum lattice-based protocols. IACR Trans. Cryptographic Hardware Embed. Syst. 17–61 (2019). https://doi.org/10.13154/tches.v2019.i4.17-61

WaferSim: A Simulation Infrastructure for LLM Service on Wafer-Scale Chips

Zheng Xu[1], Jiaxin Liu[1], Dehao Kong[1], Jiamu Fu[1], Xu Dai[2], Lei Wang[2], Jian Weng[3], Jinyi Deng[1], Yang Hu[1](✉), and Shouyi Yin[1,2]

[1] Tsinghua University, Beijing, China
hu_yang@tsinghua.edu.cn
[2] Shanghai Artificial Intelligence Laboratory, Shanghai, China
[3] King Abdullah University of Science and Technology, Thuwal, Saudi Arabia

Abstract. This work proposes WaferSim, a simulation infrastructure for LLM service on wafer-scale chips. It introduces comprehensive inter-instance simulation, previously absent in existing tools, through unified multi-instance request management and inter-instance communication modeling. In addition, WaferSim introduces Lookup Table (LuT) and result reuse mechanisms at the intra-instance simulation level, achieving high accuracy while significantly accelerating simulation, and overcoming the inefficiency of prior works that fail to meet the real-time requirements of LLM service. Our experiments demonstrate that WaferSim accurately captures real-system performance with less than 9.67% error and achieves up to 522.66× speedup over existing NPU-based distributed simulators.

1 Introduction

The rapidly increasing parameter scale of large language models (LLMs) imposes significant demands on compute, memory, and communication resources. Wafer-scale integration [6], enabled by advanced packaging, can connect tens of NPU dies through high-bandwidth Die-to-Die (D2D) links and is therefore a promising hardware solution for LLM serving. Despite this potential, research in this direction remains severely under-explored due to the lack of dedicated simulation infrastructure for LLM service on wafer-scale chips.

By combining existing simulators, intra-instance simulation on multi-NPU systems can be achieved. For example, single-NPU simulators such as GeneSys [5] estimate each sub-operator latency, while multi-NPU estimation frameworks like LLMServingSim [3] aggregate these latencies and add collective communication costs to obtain operator-level latency. Summing the latency of all operators in LLMs yields the per-iteration latency of a request. However, this approach remains insufficient for simulating wafer-scale LLM serving.

First, as shown in Fig. 1, the inter-instance simulation level is absent. A 12-inch wafer-scale chip can integrate dozens of NPU dies and partition them into multiple instances that process different requests concurrently. This requires unified instance management for request allocation and support for heterogeneous

L. Eeckhout et al. (Eds.): APPT 2026, LNCS 16693, pp. 579–585, 2027.
https://doi.org/10.1007/978-981-92-4805-6_39

instances in disaggregated scheduling (***Challenge 1***). Moreover, disaggregated scheduling introduces inter-instance KV cache transfers, which share D2D links with intra-instance collectives and may cause communication contention, requiring unified D2D link modeling (***Challenge 2***). Second, existing intra-instance simulation relies on slow per-operator modeling based on single-NPU simulators, making it difficult to meet the real-time requirements of online LLM serving. Therefore, fast and accurate NPU-level simulation is needed (***Challenge 3***).

To address these challenges, we propose WaferSim, a simulator specifically designed for LLM service on wafer-scale chips. Our contributions are summarized as follows:

- WaferSim introduces unified instance-level request management to support diverse LLM serving strategies, thereby addressing Challenge 1.
- WaferSim supports flexible intra-instance parallel strategies and jointly models inter-instance KV cache transfers with intra-instance collective communication on shared D2D links, enabling contention-aware communication analysis and addressing Challenge 2.
- WaferSim introduces Lookup Table and result reuse mechanisms to enable fast and accurate NPU-level simulation, thereby addressing Challenge 3.
- Compared with the real NPU-based hardware system, WaferSim achieves average error rates below **3.49%** for intra-instance simulation and **9.67%** for LLM service simulation, while providing up to a **522.66**$\times$ simulation speedup over existing simulators.

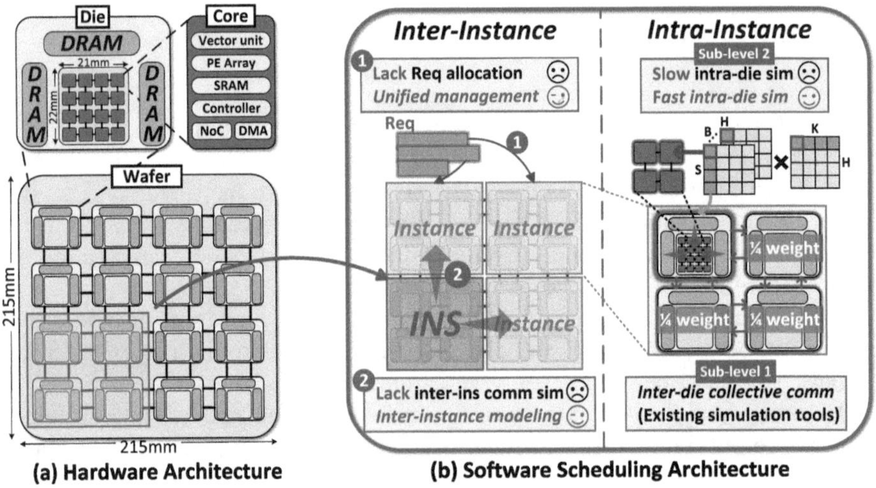

Fig. 1. Hierarchical Hardware and Software Architecture for Wafer-Scale Chips.

2 Background

2.1 LLM Inference and Serving Systems

LLM inference consists of a computation-intensive prefill phase and a memory-intensive decode phase. LLM serving systems mainly adopt either unified scheduling [2], which suffers from prefill-decode interference, or disaggregated scheduling [7,9], which mitigates such interference by separating the two phases on different instances, at the cost of inter-instance KV cache transfer overhead.

2.2 Wafer-Scale Chips

Figure 1 illustrates the hardware and software scheduling hierarchy for wafer-scale chips. The hardware adopts a three-level architecture: wafer, die, and core. Dies are connected by a 2D-mesh high-speed D2D network and each die integrates compute cores, DRAM, and D2D interfaces. Correspondingly, the software stack comprises an inter-instance level for request allocation and inter-instance communication, and an intra-instance level for inter-die parallelism with collective communication and intra-die dataflow.

3 WaferSim Framework

Figure 2 summarizes WaferSim, which takes requests as input and outputs system-level metrics such as end-to-end (E2E) latency. E2E latency consists of execution time from intra-instance simulation and waiting time from queuing and inter-instance KV transfers. WaferSim consists of five components: Request

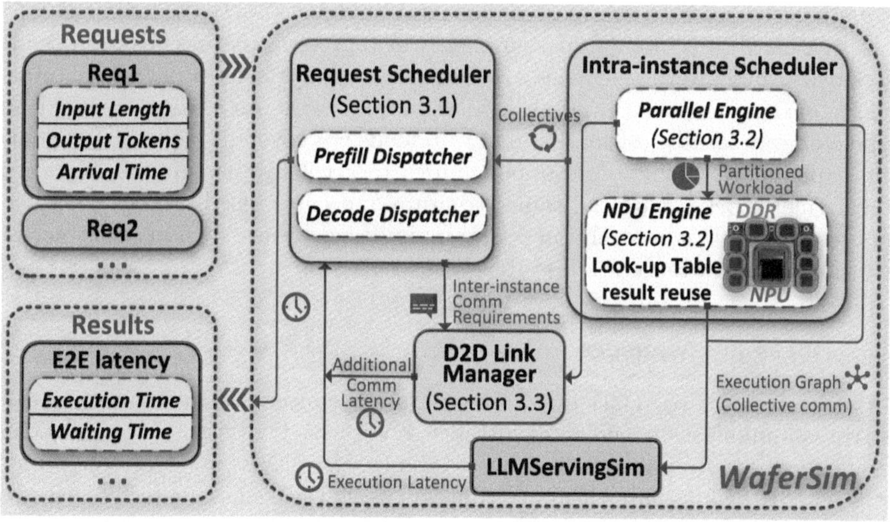

Fig. 2. WaferSim Framework.

Scheduler, Parallel Engine, NPU Engine, LLMServingSim [3], and D2D Link Manager.

3.1 Request Scheduler

The Request Scheduler allocates requests across instances and maintains both prefill and decode queues, enabling support for diverse LLM serving strategies. In unified serving, each instance maintains coupled prefill and decode queues with a consistent batching policy. In disaggregated serving, each instance activates either prefill or decode queues, which also requires inter-instance communication management. By flexibly configuring queue numbers, coupling, and whether inter-instance communication is required, WaferSim can support additional LLM scheduling variants [10].

3.2 Parallel Engine and NPU Engine

The Parallel Engine partitions each request across multiple dies within an instance according to splitting configurations, enabling WaferSim to support diverse parallel strategies. It exposes configurable splitting dimensions (B, S, K, H, $Block$), where B, S, K, and H control batch, sequence, and tensor parallelism, and $Block$ controls pipeline parallelism. The Parallel Engine then dispatches partitioned sub-tasks to the NPU Engine and forwards the derived collective communication requirements to LLMServingSim [3], which integrates the resulting communication requirements with NPU execution results to simulate intra-instance performance and return the request execution time.

The NPU Engine estimates die-level sub-task execution. It adopts a hybrid technique that combines the Lookup Table (LuT) with result reuse mechanisms to minimize simulation overhead while maintaining accuracy. We build the LuT from real-hardware latency measurements of representative prefill and decode workloads, then use these entries to calibrate the analytical simulator by capturing system overheads. At runtime, WaferSim queries the LuT based on workload characteristics for fast estimation. For workloads not covered by the LuT, WaferSim exploits two result reuse opportunities to accelerate simulation: repeated transformer blocks share the same structure and can reuse block-level simulation results, while non-attention operators in decode phase remain stable across iterations and can reuse the first-iteration result.

3.3 D2D Link Manager

On wafer-scale chips, D2D link communication consists of intra-instance collective communication and inter-instance KV cache transfers. Since collective communication directly affects request latency, the D2D Link Manager prioritizes it and schedules inter-instance transfers using the remaining bandwidth. To jointly model these two types of traffic, it represents dies as graph vertices and assigns link weights according to current collective-communication occupancy.

Inter-instance KV transfer is then formulated as a shortest-path problem, and solved via the Dijkstra algorithm [4] to select transmission paths.

Given the source die, destination die, transfer volume, and D2D bandwidth, the D2D Link Manager estimates the equivalent bandwidth along the selected path under time-division multiplexing rule and computes the corresponding transfer latency. It also updates link weights during the transfer to reflect contention and restores them after completion.

4 Evaluation

4.1 Experimental Setup

We compare WaferSim with both a real NPU-based system (Real) and a simulator baseline combining LLMServingSim [3] with GeneSys [5] (L+G). The real system has a 2 × 2 array of TsingMicro TX81 (as shown in Fig. 2). For LLM models, we choose LLaMA2-7B, LLaMA2-13B, and LLaMA2-70B [8].

4.2 Simulation Accuracy and Simulation Time

Figure 3 presents the intra-instance simulation accuracy. We set the instance sizes of LLaMA2-7B, LLaMA2-13B, and LLaMA2-70B as 1, 2, and 4 NPU dies, respectively, and evaluate one-iteration latency. For prefill, the sequence length ranges from 512 to 8192. For decode, the batch size ranges from 1 to 16 with KV lengths of 1024. WaferSim achieves average error rates of 2.98% and 3.49% for prefill and decode, respectively.

Figure 4(a) presents the system-level simulation accuracy. We evaluate both unified and disaggregated scheduling using a one-minute conversational workload [1], with E2E latency as the metric. LLaMA2-7B uses four 1-die instances, while LLaMA2-13B uses two 2-die instances. In disaggregated scheduling, they are evenly split into prefill and decode instances. We also approximate larger configurations (2 × 4, 4 × 4, and 6 × 6 dies) by running sampled workloads on Real. WaferSim achieves average error rates of 5.18% under unified scheduling and 9.67% under disaggregated scheduling.

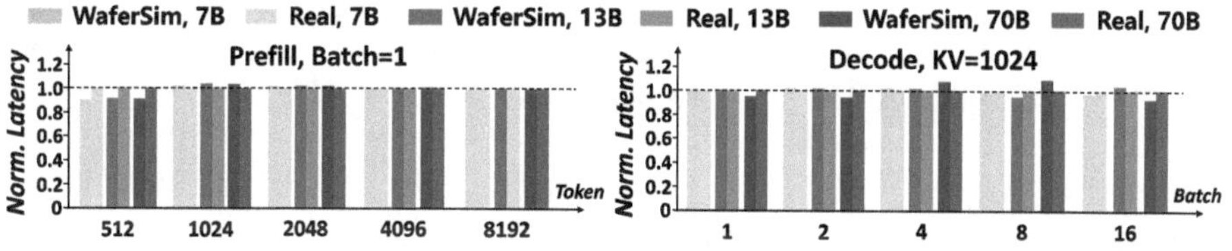

Fig. 3. Intra-Instance Simulation Accuracy Comparison.

Figure 4(b) compares the simulation time between WaferSim and L+G. We measure one iteration simulation time for prefill (batch size 4, sequence length

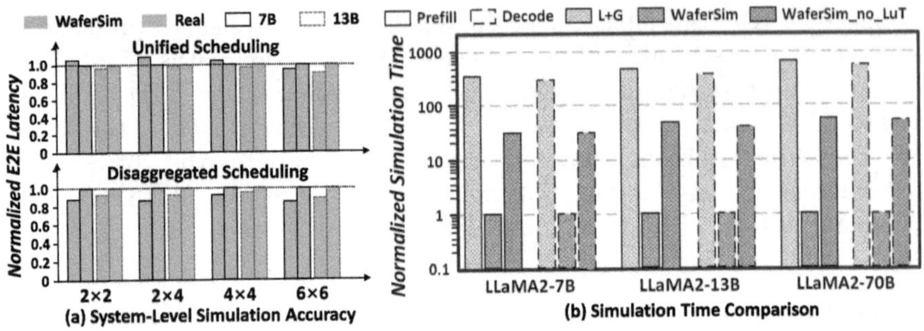

Fig. 4. System-Level Simulation Accuracy and Simulation Time Comparison.

2048) and decode (batch size 4, KV length 2048) workloads. With LuT hits, WaferSim achieves average speedups of 522.66× for prefill and 441.98× for decode over L+G; without LuT hits, WaferSim still achieves 45.06× and 41.70× speedups, respectively.

5 Conclusion

WaferSim is the first simulator for LLM serving on wafer-scale chips. It introduces unified multi-instance request scheduling management, adopting a lightweight NPU Engine with LuT and result reuse, and accurately modeling inter-instance KV cache transfers. Experiments show that WaferSim preserves accuracy while providing large simulation speedups, making it a practical infrastructure for advancing LLM serving research on wafer-scale chips.

Acknowledgements. This work was supported in part by the National Science and Technology Major Project under Grant 2022ZD0115200; by NSFC under Grant 92464302, Grant 62125403, Grant U24B20164, Grant U24A20234 and Grant 62502255; in part by the Beijing S&T Project Z251100008425010; Shanghai Municipal Science and Technology Major project; the Natural Science Foundation of Jiangsu Province Basic Research Program under Grant BK20243042; the BNRist; and the Beijing Advanced Innovation Center for Integrated Circuits. The technical solution and experimental design presented in this paper were independently completed by the authors. AI tools were used solely for language polishing and formatting optimization, and did not participate in the development of the research ideas or core content.

References

1. Azurepublicdataset. https://github.com/Azure/AzurePublicDataset/tree/master (2023)
2. Agrawal, A., et al.: Sarathi: efficient LLM inference by piggybacking decodes with chunked prefills. arXiv preprint arXiv:2308.16369 (2023)

3. Cho, J., et al.: Llmservingsim: a HW/SW co-simulation infrastructure for LLM inference serving at scale. In: Proceedings of the 2024 IEEE International Symposium on Workload Characterization (IISWC) (2024)
4. Dijkstra, E.W.: A note on two problems in connexion with graphs. In: Edsger Wybe Dijkstra: his life, work, and legacy, pp. 287–290 (2022)
5. Ghodrati, S., et al.: Tandem processor: grappling with emerging operators in neural networks. In: Proceedings of the 29th ACM International Conference on Architectural Support for Programming Languages and Operating Systems (2024)
6. Hu, Y., et al.: Wafer-scale computing: advancements, challenges, and future perspectives. IEEE Circuits Syst. Mag. (2024)
7. Patel, P., et al.: Splitwise: efficient generative LLM inference using phase splitting. In: Proceedings of the 2024 ACM/IEEE 51st Annual International Symposium on Computer Architecture (ISCA) (2024)
8. Touvron, H., et al.: Llama 2: open foundation and fine-tuned chat models. arXiv preprint arXiv:2307.09288 (2023)
9. Xu, Z., et al.: WSC-LLM: efficient LLM service and architecture co-exploration for wafer-scale chips. In: Proceedings of the 52nd Annual International Symposium on Computer Architecture (ISCA) (2025)
10. Xu, Z., et al.: Face: fully overlapped pd scheduling and multi-level architecture co-exploration on wafer. In: Proceedings of the 2026 IEEE International Symposium on High Performance Computer Architecture (HPCA) (2026)

OrbitGuard: Hierarchical Orbit-Aware Runtime for Spaceborne LLM Inference

Han Yang[1], Xiaofeng Hou[1(✉)], Jiacheng Liu[2], Xiaozhi Zhu[1], and Chao Li[1]

[1] Shanghai Jiao Tong University, Shanghai, China
hou-xf@cs.sjtu.edu.cn
[2] The Hong Kong University of Science and Technology, Hong Kong, China

Abstract. Deploying large language model inference in low Earth orbit faces dynamic radiation risks: high-energy particles can induce hardware bit flips, leading to inference errors. Traditional static redundancy wastes energy during radiation-safe windows while failing to handle sudden faults during high-radiation passes, causing service unavailability. To address this, we propose OrbitGuard, a hierarchical runtime system that perceives and adapts to orbital radiation risks. At the macro-scheduling level, an orbit-aware scheduler monitors orbital risk status and defers long-generation requests away from high-risk windows, thereby reducing exposure for the most vulnerable workloads. At the micro-execution level, a token-level early-exit mechanism compares dual decoding replicas and triggers an immediate fallback upon the first sign of divergence. Evaluations show that OrbitGuard improves exact match by 1.90%, reduces failure rate by 65%, and cuts the cost of dual-modular redundancy from 2.13× to 1.28×.

Keywords: Spaceborne Computing · LLM Inference · Fault Tolerance

1 Introduction

Advances in radiation-hardened COTS devices and heterogeneous computing enable onboard intelligent computing, requiring algorithm–architecture–environment co-optimization under space constraints [7]. However, the space environment is dynamic: energetic particles cause logic errors, bit flips, and permanent failures. Radiation flux varies with orbital phase, creating risk windows [11]. These dynamics challenge LLM inference: autoregressive generation can amplify a single upset via attention, leading to collapse or errors [2]. Late detection wastes computation, unacceptable for power-constrained platforms. Existing fault-tolerance treats radiation as constant noise, ignoring orbit-dependent dynamics [8,9].

We analyze these issues from two perspectives. First, macro-scheduling: generation length has a nonlinear positive correlation with failure probability. Long requests incur larger exposure windows, and late fault detection leads to costly

L. Eeckhout et al. (Eds.): APPT 2026, LNCS 16693, pp. 586–591, 2027.
https://doi.org/10.1007/978-981-92-4805-6_40

waste. Second, micro-execution: coarse-grained redundancy is inefficient. Conventional request-level Dual Modular Redundancy requires both replicas to fully execute the entire sequence before comparison, potentially incurring the overhead of two complete long responses.

To address these challenges, we propose **OrbitGuard**, a hierarchical, orbit-aware runtime that adapts fault-tolerance to time-varying radiation. At the macro level, OrbitGuard dynamically defers long-generation tasks from high-radiation windows to minimize exposure risks. At the micro level, it introduces a token-level early-exit DMR mechanism that compares dual replicas at each decoding step, triggering fallback recovery at the first token divergence to eliminate redundant downstream computation. By bridging environmental awareness with fine-grained execution control, OrbitGuard minimizes ineffective computation and achieves an optimal resource-energy trade-off for the micro AI data center [3] in space. The main contributions of this work are summarized as follows:

- We propose OrbitGuard, the first hierarchical runtime that jointly optimizes macro-scheduling and micro-execution for fault-tolerant LLM inference under LEO's dynamic radiation environment.
- We design an orbit-aware scheduling (OAS) mechanism with a three-state risk model for risk- and deadline-aware request dispatch.
- We introduce a dual-track token-level early-exit (TLEE) mechanism that monitors replica agreement at every decoding step.
- Evaluated on five NLP benchmarks under three fault-severity levels, OrbitGuard achieves 98.80% of full DMR's output quality while reducing computational cost by 39.70%.

2 Related Work

Neural-network fault studies show that bit-flip vulnerability is highly structured. In LLMs, FlipGuard [1] analyzes bit-flip sensitivity and proposes exponent-bit protection; GoldenTransformer [4] provides a modular fault-injection framework; and RoR [6] links vulnerability to the interaction between sensitive bits and activation outliers. These works identify where faults matter and how to defend specific structures, but they typically assume static fault exposure.

System-level adaptive protection has been explored for space processors and accelerators. Safe-NEureka uses separate performance and redundancy modes for on-board DNN acceleration [10]. Logical Maneuvers studies detection and recovery from adversarial hardware faults in space platforms [5]. These efforts establish the engineering value of adaptive reliability, but they do not study LLM request scheduling, long-vs-short generation asymmetry, or token-level fail-fast execution.

Table 1. Operational policy used in the current prototype.

Orbit State	Execution Mode		Scheduling Action
	Short Tasks	Long Tasks	
Safe	Fast	Fast	Drain backlog (prioritize long jobs)
Elevated	Fast	Safe	Keep short jobs fast; protect long jobs
Critical	Safe	Safe	Defer long jobs; protect all admitted

3 OrbitGuard: Hierarchical Orbit-Aware Runtime

3.1 Overview

Figure 1 illustrates OrbitGuard's hierarchical runtime, which operates at two time scales. The macro control loop uses orbit state, queue state, and request metadata to decide whether to launch a request immediately or defer it to a safer window. The micro control loop selects an execution mode for each admitted request and, in the protected path, monitors replica agreement at token granularity to enable early abandonment of redundant decoding. Together, OAS avoids high-risk exposure at the source, while TLEE ensures low-cost reliability during execution, enabling the system to balance inference throughput and hardware fault tolerance in harsh on-orbit environments.

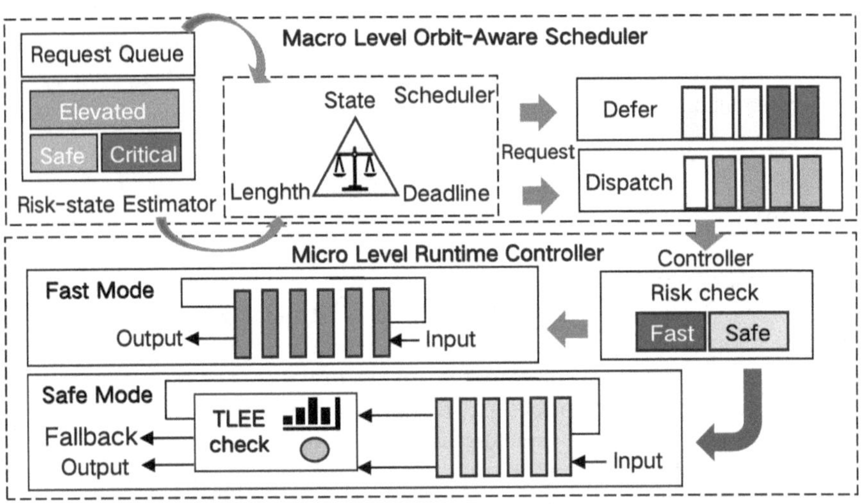

Fig. 1. Overview of OrbitGuard.

3.2 Macro Level: Orbit-Aware Scheduling

In our design, we abstract orbital conditions into three states: `safe`, `elevated`, and `critical`, representing a progressive risk hierarchy. This abstraction captures the key runtime property that orbital risk is time-varying, enabling differentiated responses.

Table 1 concretizes this rule. A core design principle of OAS is the separation of two distinct decisions: *dispatch*, which determines whether to launch a task immediately, and *protection*, which selects the appropriate execution mode. For example, a long request occurring within a critical window is first a scheduling question regarding whether it should be deferred, and only subsequently an execution-mode question. Because the policy is intentionally lightweight, it requires neither precise particle-rate prediction nor preemption. It relies only on a coarse orbital state signal and a request-length estimate, making it highly practical for resource-constrained spaceborne platforms.

3.3 Micro Level: Dual-Track Token-Level Early Exit

When a request must execute within a risk window, the runtime enters protected mode using two decoding replicas. TLEE checks consistency token by token during decoding and aborts immediately upon divergence. Core principle: fail fast at the first trustworthy sign of divergence.

As shown in Fig. 2, TLEE provides two checking tracks. For deterministic decoding ($T = 0$), it uses exact matching: compares token IDs from two replicas at each step and falls back on any mismatch. For non-deterministic decoding ($T > 0$), it uses distribution comparison: compares probability distributions over the next token and triggers a fallback when divergence (e.g., KL divergence) exceeds a threshold θ. In both tracks, TLEE fails fast at the first trustworthy sign of replica disagreement, minimizing redundant execution overhead while ensuring reliability. Regardless of which checking track is used, TLEE consistently follows the same overarching principle: fail fast and fall back at the first trustworthy sign of replica disagreement, thereby minimizing the time and computational cost of redundant execution while ensuring reliability.

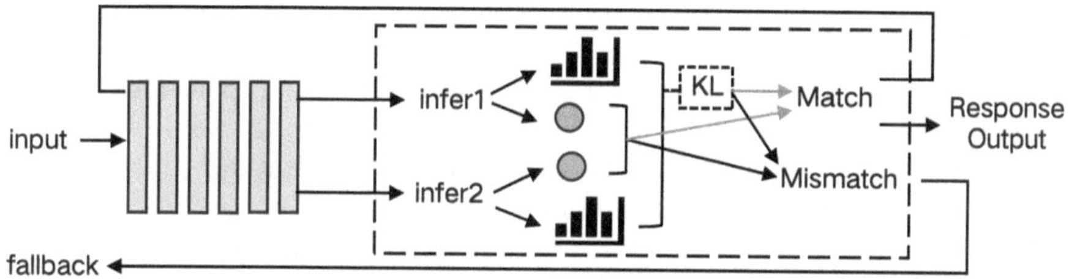

Fig. 2. Mechanism of TLEE.

4 Evaluation

4.1 Experimental Setup

We evaluate OrbitGuard using `Qwen2.5-1.5B-Instruct` [12] on five NLP benchmarks. We process the full validation splits across five random seeds, yielding

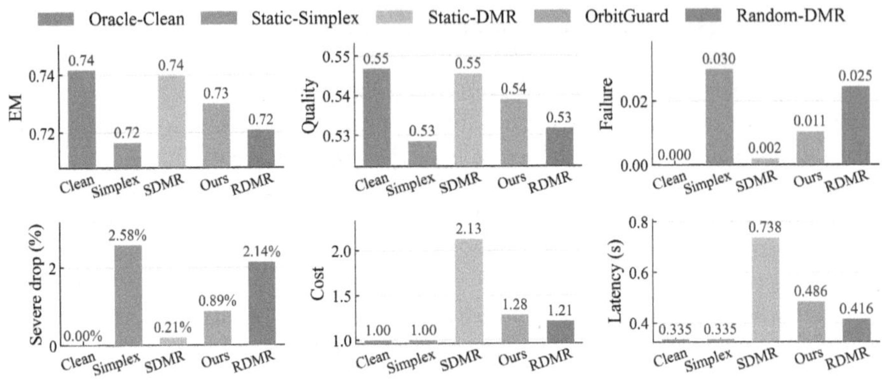

Fig. 3. Main results on `Qwen2.5-1.5B-Instruct`.

7,165 requests per policy. To emulate orbit transits, we cyclically map requests to a sequence of risk states $\Sigma = \{\texttt{safe}, \texttt{elevated}, \texttt{critical}\}$. We employ a trace-driven methodology to ensure tightly controlled comparisons and measure quality, failure rate, latency, and relative computational cost.

We compare against three baselines: Static-Simplex uses single inference with the lowest overhead but no fault tolerance; Static-DMR applies fixed dual-modular redundancy to all requests; Random-DMR selects requests for protection randomly, independent of radiation risk. It serves as a control baseline that matches the number of protected requests to OrbitGuard within each random seed, isolating the effect of risk awareness from protection quantity and sampling variance. We measure quality, failure rate, latency, and relative computational cost. The relative cost counts inference passes as 1 for simplex, 2 for protected execution without rollback, and 3 for protected execution with clean fallback.

4.2 Performance Evaluation

We first conduct an end-to-end performance evaluation of OrbitGuard, comparing it against three baseline strategies: Static-Simplex, Random-DMR, and Static-DMR. As shown in Fig. 3, on the full test-set evaluation, the three-state OrbitGuard controller clearly outperforms both Static-Simplex and Random-DMR. Specifically, it improves EM accuracy by 1.90%, reduces failure rate by 65%, cuts severe quality drops to 0.89%, and requires only 1.28× relative cost. While Static-DMR naturally provides the highest request-level robustness, its 2.13 × cost is often prohibitive for resource-constrained space platforms. OrbitGuard acts as a highly efficient execution baseline, cutting 39.70% of Static-DMR's redundancy cost while retaining 98.80% of its average quality. The per-state behavior also shows that the three-state design is meaningful rather than cosmetic. The mean relative cost is 1.00 × in safe windows, 1.56 × in elevated windows, and 2.44 × in critical windows. This remaining gap is exactly what motivates the macro and micro layers of the hierarchical runtime.

5 Conclusion

We presented OrbitGuard, an orbit-aware runtime that shifts LLM fault-tolerance under variable LEO radiation from static protection to dynamic adaptation. By coordinating macro-scheduling and micro-execution, OrbitGuard balances active avoidance, fine-grained protection, and fast recovery. While currently validated via trace-driven simulation, future work will focus on physical hardware deployment, real-time telemetry integration, and multi-satellite task migration.

Acknowledgment. We sincerely thank all the anonymous reviewers for their valuable comments and feedback. This work was supported by the National Natural Science Foundation of China (No. 62502302) and the STCSM International S&T Cooperation Project (23510713200).

References

1. Chen, Y., et al.: Bit-flip error resilience in LLMs: a comprehensive analysis and defense framework. In: EMNLP (2025)
2. Das, S., et al.: One bit-flip away from collapse: Security and safety in AI models and accelerators. In: 2025 First ICEdge (2025)
3. Guo, J., Wang, X., Wang, J., Hou, X., Li, C., Guo, M.: TriCooling-sim: efficient thermal simulation for high-density micro ai data centers. In: NPC (2025)
4. Howard, L.: GoldenTransformer: a modular fault injection framework for transformer robustness research. arXiv preprint (2025)
5. Dana, K., Khalaj Monfared, F., Tajik, S., S.: Logical maneuvers: detecting and mitigating adversarial hardware faults in space. In: NDSS (2025)
6. Liu, D., Chen, S.: Rotated robustness: a training-free defense against bit-flip attacks on large language models. arXiv preprint (2026)
7. Liu, H., et al.: Edge intelligence from space: a survey and future challenges. Authorea Preprints (2025)
8. Rech, P.: Artificial neural networks for space and safety-critical applications: reliability issues and potential solutions. TNS (2024)
9. Shao, C., Guo, J., Wang, P., Wang, J., Li, C., Guo, M.: Oversubscribing GPU unified virtual memory: implications and suggestions. In: ICPE (2022)
10. Tedeschi, R., et al.: Safe-neureka: a hybrid modular redundant DNN accelerator for on-board satellite ai processing. JETC (2026)
11. Xapsos, M.: The single event effects environment of space. Presentation/Bootcamp Material 20205011676, NASA (2021). Texas A&M University Bootcamp. Available at NTRS
12. Yang, A., et al.: Qwen2. 5 technical report. arXiv preprint arXiv:2412.15115 (2024)

MV-BSD: Multi-variable Speculation Diagrams for Compact Automated Logic Design

Xiangtao Guan[1,2], Shuyao Cheng[2], Rui Zhang[2], and Zidong Du[2](✉)

[1] University of Science and Technology of China, Hefei 230027, China
guanxt@mail.ustc.edu.cn

[2] State Key Lab of Processors, Institute of Computing Technology, Chinese Academy of Sciences, Beijing 100190, China
{chengshuyao,zhangrui,duzidong}@ict.ac.cn

Abstract. Automated logic design aims to reduce human effort in chip design, where logic design and verification remain labor-intensive stages. Binary Speculation Diagram (BSD) constructs circuits through speculative decision expansion and has demonstrated effectiveness on large-scale designs, including RISC-V CPUs with over four million gates. However, BSD-based automated design still inherits one-variable branching, which causes excessive graph expansion on circuits with strong multi-variable dependencies. We propose Multi-Variable Binary Speculation Diagram (MV-BSD), which generalizes each decision node to branch on a multi-variable Boolean function. This allows patterns such as partial products and carry chains to be captured directly within individual nodes. We further introduce suffix-equivalence merging, a hash-based rule that removes redundant nodes under multi-variable branching. Experiments on ISCAS and EPFL benchmark circuits show that 2-variable MV-BSD reduces DAG node counts by 79.5% on average compared with A-BSD. For multiplier construction, MV-BSD reaches zero validation error up to 10 bits and reduces the 8-bit multiplier node count by 63.8%.

1 Introduction

Logic design and verification remain among the most labor-intensive stages in chip design. Automated approaches such as circuit learning [3,9] have improved Boolean function modeling, but their accuracy remains limited on general logic. Binary Speculation Diagram (BSD) achieves higher accuracy by learning circuit structure from input-output examples [5], and has been extended to superscalar processor design, area optimization, and automatic pipelining [4,6,7].

Despite this progress, BSD and A-BSD inherit the single-variable branching paradigm of classical Binary Decision Diagrams (BDDs) [1]: each internal node tests exactly one Boolean variable. When the target function contains strong multi-variable interactions, such as multiplier partial products and carry propagation, the diagram must express these interactions through deep cascades of

L. Eeckhout et al. (Eds.): APPT 2026, LNCS 16693, pp. 592–598, 2027.
https://doi.org/10.1007/978-981-92-4805-6_41

nodes. Bryant's lower bound for multiplication shows that this barrier is structural rather than merely an ordering problem [2]. In practice, BSD and A-BSD both exhibit rapid growth on multiplier circuits even with search-based ordering.

This paper proposes Multi-Variable BSD (MV-BSD), a decision diagram structure that replaces single-variable branching with multi-variable Boolean decision nodes. A node can branch on a function such as $a_i \wedge b_j$, directly capturing partial products that single-variable diagrams must enumerate. To keep the graph compact after wider branching, MV-BSD introduces suffix-equivalence merging, which merges nodes that impose no conflicting output requirements on shared remaining suffixes. The construction remains automatic: each layer greedily selects a high-quality decision function, expands active nodes, and then merges compatible suffix behavior.

Our experiments show that MV-BSD provides clear advantages on both arithmetic and general logic benchmarks. On 30 circuits from the ISCAS and EPFL suites, 2-variable MV-BSD achieves a 79.46% geometric-mean node reduction compared with A-BSD. On the 8-bit multiplier, it reaches 0% validation error with 134,381 nodes, a 63.8% size reduction and a 33.74%-point accuracy improvement over A-BSD.

The main contributions are:

- We propose MV-BSD with multi-variable decision nodes.
- We develop automatic candidate selection and suffix-equivalence merging for compact construction.
- We demonstrate substantial node-count reductions on ISCAS/EPFL circuits and exact multiplier construction up to 10 bits.

2 Related Work

Automated Design. Automated circuit design has long relied on Boolean function representations and search. Modern circuit-learning methods construct decision trees or graphs from input-output examples [3,9], while recent LLM-based HDL generation explores a higher-level automation path [8]. These approaches operate at different abstraction levels; decision-diagram-based methods still rely on branching structures to represent the learned logic.

BSD-Based Methods. BDDs provide canonical Boolean function representation under fixed variable ordering [1], but their size depends heavily on ordering [11]. For multiplication, every BDD requires $\Omega(2^n)$ nodes regardless of ordering [2]. BSD extends BDDs for automated logic design by introducing speculation nodes that trade accuracy for compactness [5]. A-BSD improves area with Monte-Carlo tree search [4], while related BSD work targets automatic pipelining [6]. These methods improve search and optimization, but the branch predicate remains a single variable.

Decision Expressiveness. Multi-input gates have been studied for logic synthesis [10]. We use the same observation at the decision-diagram level: allowing a

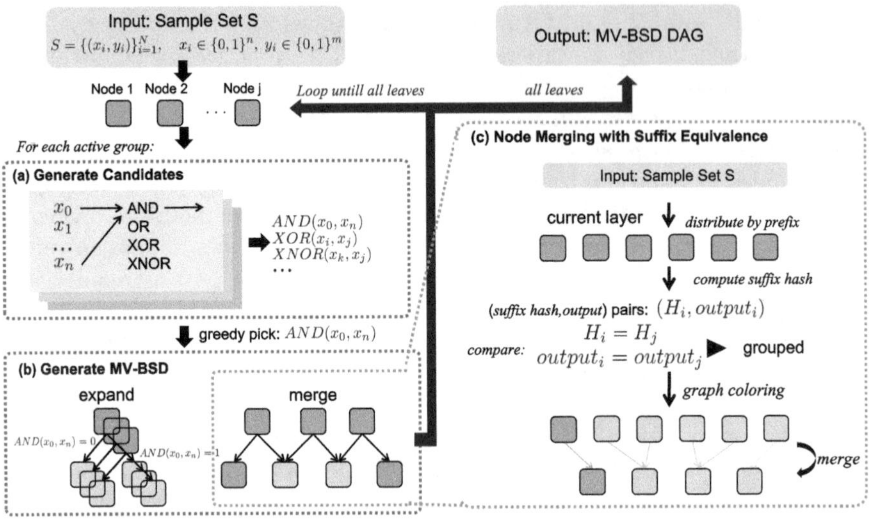

Fig. 1. Method overview. Given a sample set S, the MV-BSD construction iterates through three phases at each layer: (a) candidate generation and greedy selection of a multi-variable branching function; (b) decision diagram expansion that partitions samples according to the selected function; and (c) suffix-equivalence merging that collapses nodes with identical future behavior. The loop terminates when all leaves hold constant values.

branch predicate to depend on multiple variables increases expressiveness. MV-BSD uses NPN equivalence to keep the candidate space tractable. Two-variable functions have 4 nondegenerate NPN classes, including AND, OR, and XOR; three-variable functions have 14. We focus on two-variable branching because AND directly captures multiplier partial products $a_i \cdot b_j$ and the smaller search space makes greedy construction reliable.

3 Methodology

MV-BSD constructs a decision diagram from input-output samples through iterative layer expansion. Each layer has three phases: candidate multi-variable branch functions are generated and greedily selected, active nodes are expanded by sample partitioning, and redundant children are merged by suffix equivalence.

Multi-variable Decision Nodes. In a classical BDD, each internal node tests one input variable. MV-BSD generalizes this mechanism by storing an ordered variable set and a compact truth table, as shown in Fig. 1. For a set such as $\{v_1, v_2, v_3\}$, the sampled values form an index into the truth table, and the selected bit determines which child to follow. This representation strictly contains single-variable branching: a truth table can ignore all but one variable, but it can also realize predicates such as $a_i \wedge b_j$, which capture multiplier partial products in one step. As in BSD, all nodes at the same depth share the same

Table 1. Node Count and Error Rate for 8-bit Multiplier Construction

Method	Nodes	Error Rate
A-BSD	371,676	33.74%
MV-BSD (2-variable)	134,381	0%

branching function. This ordered property ensures that nodes at the same depth face the same future branch sequence, which is required for suffix-equivalence merging.

Candidate Generation and Selection. The search space is pruned by an activity score measuring how well each input variable distinguishes samples with different output values in the current active nodes. Only the top K variables are retained. For two-variable branching, MV-BSD forms $\binom{K}{2} \times 4$ candidates using the 4 nondegenerate NPN classes; for three-variable branching, it forms $\binom{K}{3} \times 14$ candidates. Each candidate is represented as a variable set and truth table.

Each candidate function f is simulated on active nodes and scored by

$$Q(f, S) = \alpha L + \beta \Delta H, \tag{1}$$

where L counts newly formed constant leaves and ΔH is entropy reduction. We set $\alpha = 10$ and $\beta = 100$, biasing selection toward balanced partitions with more downstream merging opportunities.

Expansion and Suffix-Equivalence Merging. After selecting f^*, each non-constant active node splits into two children according to the branch output. A child becomes a leaf if all samples reaching it share the same output. The remaining children are merged when they impose no conflicting output requirement on any shared suffix. This relaxes standard BSD's identical-sample-set condition: two nodes may differ in their sample sets, but can still be merged if their future suffix behavior is compatible. The implementation hashes suffix-output maps and greedily assigns children to compatible merge classes, giving $O(N)$ merging time per layer.

Multiplier Specialization and Complexity. For multipliers, AND predicates over (a_i, b_j) directly form partial products, and suffix-equivalence merging recovers sharing in carry-related suffixes. The same framework also applies without domain knowledge through greedy search. Per layer, variable profiling costs $O(Nn)$, candidate evaluation costs $O(K^3 N)$ for fixed K, and merging costs $O(N)$. For depth D, construction is $O(DNn)$; for n-bit multipliers with $D = O(n)$, this becomes $O(n^2 N)$ over sampled data, contrasting with the exponential BDD lower bound.

4 Evaluation

We evaluate MV-BSD on structured arithmetic circuits and general logic benchmarks. For multiplier construction, each bit width uses 5,000,000 training sam-

Table 2. Comparison on ISCAS and EPFL Benchmarks

benchmark	circuit	A-BSD		MV-BSD(2 var)			MV-BSD(3 var)		
		# nodes	runtime(s)	# nodes	ratio(%)	runtime(s)	# nodes	ratio(%)	runtime(s)
ISCAS	c1355	270	11.97	**125**	46.30%	14.52	149	55.19%	23.64
	c17	14	0.16	**8**	57.14%	0.48	10	71.43%	0.73
	c1908	331	31.33	**219**	66.16%	60.53	497	150.15%	113.85
	c2670	11101	1182.60	**1721**	15.50%	344.60	2718	24.48%	274.34
	c3540	15995	2176.27	**1794**	11.22%	191.12	2761	17.26%	197.43
	c432	171	0.62	**123**	71.93%	7.38	190	111.11%	2.45
	c499	147	5.86	**131**	89.12%	16.86	149	101.36%	17.01
	c5315	13525	234.50	**3530**	26.10%	431.85	8505	62.88%	479.39
	c6288	16231	1360.83	**4264**	26.27%	2297.63	7351	45.29%	2576.65
	c7552	22539	467.87	**4283**	19.00%	619.46	13622	60.44%	647.02
	c880	9796	885.85	**411**	4.20%	44.87	646	6.59%	67.44
EPFL	cavlc	4645	26.77	**1971**	42.43%	149.89	3161	68.05%	130.84
	ctrl	506	3.55	**303**	59.88%	29.94	467	92.29%	26.60
	dec	20263	230.36	**1098**	5.42%	87.24	2074	10.24%	79.67
	div	10137	17.47	**694**	6.85%	102.07	3672	36.22%	123.87
	i2c	52960	758.11	**3607**	6.81%	630.71	9208	17.39%	576.08
	int2float	2015	15.63	**784**	38.91%	51.85	1236	61.34%	45.21
	log2	**1000**	18.69	**1000**	100.00%	50.06	1644	164.40%	74.23
	max	10781	92.94	**1815**	16.84%	148.21	3795	35.20%	121.43
	memctrl	84896	8011.57	**8015**	9.44%	2849.25	16604	19.56%	3155.78
	multiplier	35305	3828.23	**5398**	15.29%	4481.00	8147	23.08%	4906.76
	router	4277	65.79	**686**	16.04%	143.86	1171	27.38%	137.71
	sin	4523	961.46	**378**	8.36%	86.66	607	13.42%	66.29
	sqrt	9220	214.58	**1588**	17.22%	449.70	4264	46.25%	482.48
	square	46466	5800.65	**4020**	8.65%	830.49	5801	12.48%	800.19
	voter	153625	336.43	**12183**	7.93%	551.65	29013	18.89%	680.53
	Priority	4764	817.45	**686**	14.40%	94.52	1759	36.92%	88.65
	adder	155	15.80	**49**	31.61%	28.60	90	58.06%	28.30
	arbiter	69588	224.35	**10132**	14.56%	766.49	27966	40.19%	715.44
	bar	8258	51.34	**2899**	35.11%	224.68	4420	53.52%	189.45
Geomean		4781.31	115.23	982.06	20.54%	137.50	1843.58	38.56%	140.01

ples and 100,000 validation samples, uniformly sampled, targeting the middle output bit. For general logic, we use 30 circuits from the ISCAS and EPFL suites, extracting up to 1,000 logic cones per circuit. Each cone uses 5,000,000 training samples and 100,000 validation samples. The baseline is A-BSD [4]; metrics are node count, validation error rate, and construction time. Experiments run on CentOS 7.8 with an Intel Xeon Gold 6254 CPU and 1.5 TB memory.

Multiplier Construction. Table 1 reports the 8-bit multiplier result from the submission. A-BSD produces 371,676 nodes and 33.74% validation error, while 2-variable MV-BSD reaches 0% error with 134,381 nodes. This is a 63.8% node reduction and shows that multi-variable branching can directly capture partial products that single-variable decomposition must enumerate.

ISCAS and EPFL Benchmarks. Table 2 shows that across 30 benchmark circuits, A-BSD requires a geometric-mean 4,781.31 nodes. The 2-variable MV-BSD configuration reduces this to 982.06 nodes, corresponding to a 79.46% node reduction, while runtime increases from 115.23 s to 137.50 s. The 3-variable configuration still reduces size relative to A-BSD, with a geomean 1,843.58 nodes, but underperforms the 2-variable variant because the larger Boolean-function search space makes greedy selection less reliable.

Scalability and Ablation. For 4–10 bit multipliers, A-BSD exhibits steep exponential growth and becomes impractical beyond modest sizes. MV-BSD grows more slowly and remains exact up to 10 bits, although it also fails to complete beyond 10 bits within available memory because the shift-and-add multiplier structure itself requires many nodes. Disabling suffix-equivalence merging causes a sharp node-count increase, confirming that compactness depends on merging compatible suffix behavior after multi-variable expansion.

5 Conclusion

This paper proposes Multi-Variable BSD (MV-BSD), a decision diagram framework that generalizes single-variable branching to multi-variable Boolean function branching. By capturing multi-bit interactions, such as partial products and carry-related patterns, inside individual nodes, MV-BSD achieves substantially more compact representations than single-variable approaches. Experiments demonstrate a 63.8% node reduction with exact validation on the 8-bit multiplier and a 79.5% geometric-mean reduction on 30 ISCAS/EPFL benchmarks. These results indicate that extending the branching mechanism is an effective way to address the expressiveness limitation of single-variable decision structures.

Acknowledgements. This work is partially supported by the NSF of China (Grants No. 62341411, 62502504), Strategic Priority Research Program of the Chinese Academy of Sciences (Grants No. XDB0660200, XDB0660201, XDB0660202), CAS Project for Young Scientists in Basic Research (YSBR-029) and Youth Innovation Promotion Association CAS.

Use of AI. The technical solution and experimental design presented in this paper were independently completed by the authors. AI tools were used solely for language polishing and formatting optimization, and did not participate in the development of the research ideas or core content.

References

1. Bryant, R.E.: Graph-based algorithms for Boolean function manipulation. IEEE Trans. Comput. C **35**(8), 677–691 (1986)
2. Bryant, R.E.: On the complexity of VLSI implementations and graph representations of Boolean functions with application to integer multiplication. IEEE Trans. Comput. **40**(2), 205–213 (1991)
3. Chen, P.W., Huang, Y.C., Lee, C.L., Jiang, J.H.R.: Circuit learning for logic regression on high dimensional Boolean space. In: 2020 57th ACM/IEEE Design Automation Conference (DAC), pp. 1–6. IEEE (2020)
4. Cheng, S., Guan, X., Du, Z.: Area-efficient automated logic design with Monte-Carlo tree search. In: International Symposium on Advanced Parallel Processing Technologies, pp. 47–58. Springer (2025)
5. Cheng, S., et al.: Automated CPU design by learning from input-output examples. In: IJCAI, pp. 3843–3853 (2024)
6. Cheng, S., et al.: Revisiting automatic pipelining: gate-level forwarding and speculation. In: Proceedings of the 61st ACM/IEEE Design Automation Conference, pp. 1–6 (2024)
7. Cheng, S., et al.: Automated superscalar processor design by learning data dependencies. In: Proceedings of the Thirty-Fourth International Joint Conference on Artificial Intelligence, pp. 4932–4939 (2025)
8. Fu, Y., et al.: GPT4AIGChip: towards next-generation AI accelerator design automation via large language models. In: 2023 IEEE/ACM International Conference on Computer Aided Design (ICCAD), pp. 1–9. IEEE (2023)
9. Huang, Y.S., Jiang, J.H.R.: Circuit learning: from decision trees to decision graphs. IEEE Trans. Comput. Aided Des. Integr. Circuits Syst. **42**(11), 3985–3996 (2023)
10. Marakkalage, D.S., Testa, E., Riener, H., Mishchenko, A., Soeken, M., De Micheli, G.: Three-input gates for logic synthesis. IEEE Trans. Comput. Aided Des. Integr. Circuits Syst. **40**(10), 2184–2188 (2020)
11. Rudell, R.: Dynamic variable ordering for ordered binary decision diagrams. In: Proceedings of 1993 International Conference on Computer Aided Design (ICCAD), pp. 42–47. IEEE (1993)

RV-CIM: Energy–Delay Optimized Mapping and Architecture Co-Design for a RISC-V Multi-core SoC with Configurable DCIM Cluster

Ninghui Shang[1], Ying Liu[2], Zecheng Zhou[1], Jiyong Hu[1], Zhiqiang Guo[2], Zhiyuan Chen[1], Wentao Zhao[1], Guoxiang Li[1], Peiyu Chen[2], Yufei Ma[1(✉)], and Le Ye[1,2(✉)]

[1] Peking University, Beijing, China
yufei.ma@pku.edu.cn
[2] Advanced Institute of Information Technology, Peking University, Hangzhou, China
yele@pku.edu.cn

Abstract. For various edge AI scenarios, the hardware accelerator necessitates high flexibility, high energy efficiency, and low latency. To meet these requirements, this work proposes RV-CIM, a heterogeneous RISC-V multi-core SoC integrating a configurable digital compute-in-memory (DCIM) cluster and a co-designed mapping framework. At the hardware level, we introduce a versatile accelerator architecture built on a configurable DCIM cluster and complement it with a comprehensive set of RISC-V instruction extensions. At the software level, we propose a two-level mapping framework: (1) an adaptive inter-core workload allocator to minimize synchronization-induced tail latency, and (2) intra-core tiling and scheduling, jointly improving the energy efficiency and latency. Experimental results show that RV-CIM achieves a 1.45× and 1.25× reduction in latency, and 1.9× and 2.16× improvement in energy consumption for ResNet-34 and ModernBERT-large.

Keywords: DCIM · Mapping · AI Accelerator · RISC-V

1 Introduction

Nowadays, deep neural networks (DNNs) remain the dominant AI solutions. These primarily encompass convolutional neural networks (CNNs) and transformer-based models, exhibiting highly diverse topologies, operator types, and computational patterns. This demands AI accelerators with strong programmability and versatility to support end-to-end deployment across heterogeneous models. Meanwhile, edge devices are typically battery-powered, requiring

---

N. Shang and Y. Liu—These authors contributed equally to this work.

L. Eeckhout et al. (Eds.): APPT 2026, LNCS 16693, pp. 599–606, 2027.
https://doi.org/10.1007/978-981-92-4805-6_42

AI accelerators to provide such versatility while satisfying strict energy constraints.

Digital compute-in-memory (DCIM), by eliminating the data-movement bottleneck of the von Neumann paradigm, has been introduced as processing engines(PEs), enabling massively parallel multiply-and-accumulate (MAC) operations without compromising accuracy, energy efficiency, and configurability. Nevertheless, recent DCIM-based AI accelerators [4] have primarily excelled in specific applications by tailoring the computation dataflow and execution schedule, sacrificing the versatility required for diverse scenarios.

As edge AI workloads continue to scale in complexity and throughput demand, modern SoCs increasingly deploy multiple NPU engines rather than a single accelerator [1]. While this solution appears promising, existing works face several important challenges: (1) Multi-core NPUs share a global external memory interface, where uniform workload splitting causes severe tail latency, degrading overall performance. (2) The diverse tensor shapes and operator patterns of modern DNNs make fixed tiling and scheduling highly inefficient. (3) A unified and comprehensive RISC-V–based instruction and architecture framework is still absent from current designs.

To address these issues, this work proposes a heterogeneous multi-core RISC-V SoC, named RV-CIM, achieving both low energy consumption and latency for various DNN models through hardware-software co-optimization. The key contributions of this work are summarized as follows:

- At the hardware level, we introduce a heterogeneous DCIM-based RISC-V SoC integrated with customized RISC-V ISA extensions.
- At the software level, we propose a two-level mapping strategy to minimize EDP.
- To validate the efficacy of RV-CIM and software mapping strategies, we have developed an RV-CIM simulator to emulate hardware behavior.

The experiments reveal that, in the case of ResNet-34 and ModernBERT-large, the optimized mapping strategies result in a latency reduction of 1.45× and 1.25×, respectively, and an EDP improvement of 1.9× and 2.16×.

2 Background and Motivation

2.1 Flexibility Analysis of Digital CIM

The DCIM macros implement vector–matrix multiplication (VMM) by broadcasting the input vector across the stored weight matrix and producing the output vector through parallel multiplier cells followed by adder trees. To increase memory density, recent DCIM designs adopt a multi-subarray structure, where each subarray stores multi-bit weights into pages and shares one computation unit [2]. For each operation, a single page is selected to perform MAC with the input. The CIM cluster further provides configurability in the supported VMM dimensions. The combination of multi-page weight storage and flexible VMM sizing enables a wide design space for workload mapping.

2.2 Mapping Challenges of Multi-core SoC

On the one hand, according to [3], synchronization among multiple cores can lead to significant latency overhead. The global external memory, functioning as a slave to the bus, is accessed by each master NPU core sequentially, resulting in increased latency determined by the last core to finish, known as tail latency, and leading to degraded temporal utilization. On the other hand, fixed tiling may lead to suboptimal tiling size and order, resulting in worse EDP. Besides, considering that CPU control overhead is non-negligible in real deployment and limits accelerator efficiency, traditional sequential scheduling may further reduce hardware parallelism due to delayed instruction dispatch, leading to low spatial utilization.

3 Heterogeneous DCIM-Based RISC-V Core

We start by introducing our hardware architecture, which is designed to support a wide variety of workloads. By integrating multiple AI specific functional units with a customized instruction set, the design supports both DCIM configurability and run-time programmability.

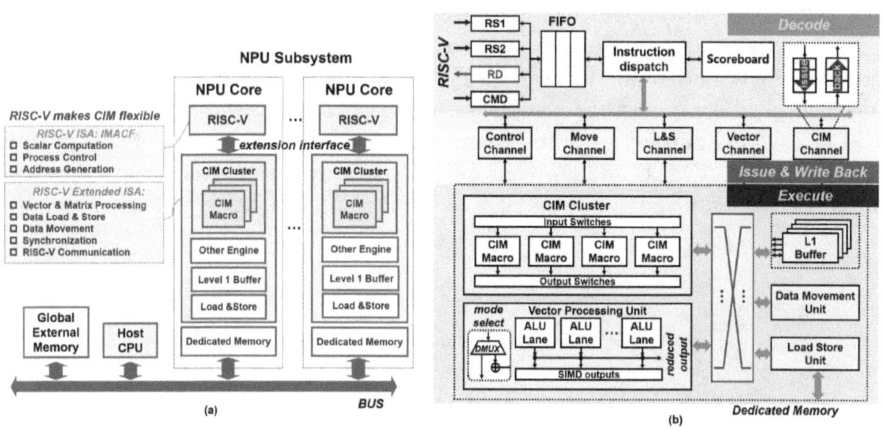

Fig. 1. (a) The overview of NPU subsystem. (b) The hardware architecture of NPU Core.

3.1 Hardware Architecture of RV-CIM

The overall hardware architecture of the RV-CIM NPU subsystem is depicted in Fig. 1(a) with multiple NPU cores. Each NPU core has sequential access to the shared global external memory. Figure 1(b) illustrates the detailed architecture of our NPU core. Within each NPU core, a RISC-V processor is heterogeneously coupled with an AI accelerator. The extension interface follows the RISC-V custom-instruction specification, with industrial extensions such as Nuclei's NICE, enabling the RISC-V core to dispatch custom operations to accelerator and control the execution. Leveraging the original scalar ISA of RISC-V, the NPU alleviates the design complexities associated with handling control signals, thereby achieving greater flexibility. The FIFO queue buffers instructions that cannot be processed promptly. The instruction dispatch module decodes and issues instructions to the corresponding function unit channel. The CIM cluster consists of four DCIM macros, which can be flexibly combined with input and output switches, facilitating MAC operations. The VPU is responsible for element-wise operations and activation functions, such as softmax and quantization. The Load & Store (L&S) channel controls off-chip data access for the L&S unit.

3.2 Extended RISC-V-Based ISA

The extended RISC-V ISA customized for CIM operation is divided into five categories, namely *control*, *vector*, *matrix*, *movement*, and *off-chip access primitives.*

Control Primitives are used for NPU configuration, with the *sync* instruction specifically ensuring NPU idleness to enable efficient multicore synchronization. ***Vector Primitives*** have four extended instructions: *vv_v*, *vs_v*, *v_s*, and *v_v*, where v and s denote vector and scalar, respectively. It is designed to perform SIMD and reduction operations, supporting nonlinear operations and quantization during network acceleration. ***Matrix Primitives*** are designed to drive the DCIM cluster for MAC operations, including matrix-matrix multiplication (MMM), VMM, and convolution. ***Movement Primitives*** are designed to manage on-chip data movement and processing, including transpose opera-

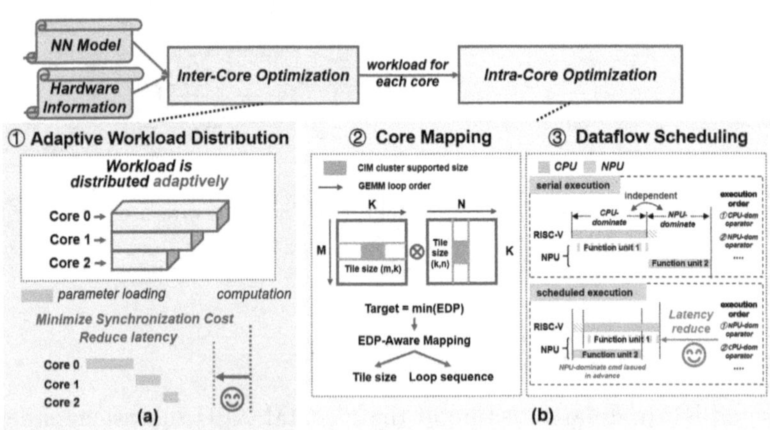

Fig. 2. Two-level mapping strategy optimization: (a) inter-core adaptive workload allocation and (b) intra-core energy-delay co-optimization.

tion to support attention. ***Off-chip Primitives*** handle off-chip data access, including *load* and *store* operations.

4 Mapping Strategy Optimization

4.1 Inter-Core Adaptive Workload Allocation

To mitigate the tail latency and improve spatial utilization, an adaptive workload allocation strategy is employed, as shown in Fig. 2(a), which assigns varying workloads to each core, so that all NPU cores complete their assigned computations at approximately the same time.

For operators involving MMM between matrix A and matrix B, multiple partitioning dimensions are possible. Since different layers exhibit MMMs of different sizes, their feasible partitioning options also vary. Consequently, each layer provides numerous candidates for multi-core allocation, making brute-force enumeration impractical for identifying the optimal solution. In this work, we employ a genetic algorithm to implement adaptive workload allocation. The algorithm selects the search space based on layer information and randomly generates an initial population, where each individual represents the workload allocation across multiple cores. The algorithm evaluates the fitness of each individual by assessing latency and applying a penalty function that accounts for memory constraints. It then generates a new population, gradually optimizing the workload allocation according to the fitness values.

4.2 Intra-Core Mapping and Scheduling

1) **Energy-Delay-Aware Mapping**. Although the CIM architecture can reduce data-movement overhead by storing weights in situ, the constrained hardware resources prevent the execution of a full-scale matrix MAC when the MMM size becomes too large, forcing the matrix to be partitioned into tiles. In this work, the DCIM cluster with multiple DCIM macros and weight pages enables substantial mapping space to explore the optimal tile size in DCIM cluster. Weight pages in DCIM are divided into N groups. These groups are concatenated to increase the supported k, while the pages within each group expand the n dimension.

To achieve a complete MMM with dimensions M, N, and K, tiled MMM operations use a triple loop over M, N, and K directions. The order of this triple loop impacts data reuse, energy consumption, bandwidth and throughput utilization, and execution latency. To determine the optimal tiling strategy, we develop a detailed simulator, which simulates the data movement and computation flow, selecting the mapping configuration that yields the lowest EDP.

2) **Delay-Aware Scheduling**. Operators are categorized as CPU-dominated or NPU-dominated based on their relative execution cycles. NPU-dominate operators require significantly fewer cycles for RISC-V processor control compared to NPU data processing. Conversely, CPU-dominate operators involve RISC-V more closely, requiring the breakdown of 2D matrices or 3D tensors into vectors

or scalars, like non-linear operations. For these, the multi-level loops and control overhead cause the CPU to dominate the overall system runtime.

Figure 2(b) illustrates the principle and impact of delay-aware mapping. When a CPU-dominate operator is followed by an independent NPU-dominate operator, RISC-V's busy state during CPU-dominate execution delays the dispatch of NPU-dominate instructions. To address this, our delay-aware mapping scheduling strategy adjusts the execution order, leveraging NPU parallelism to reduce total latency. By analyzing the network topology to identify CPU-dominated operators followed by independent NPU-dominated operators and adjusting their order, our optimization strategy effectively reduces overall latency.

5 Application and Evaluation

5.1 Experiment Setup

To assess the benefits of our proposed software-hardware co-optimization, we implemented RV-CIM and tested the performance on AlexNet, ResNet and ModernBERT-base/large. We set the baseline by uniformly distributing the workload across cores for inter-core execution. Within each core, we adopt a fixed CIM-cluster configuration of $1 \times \text{channel}_{\text{in}}$ with a 2-page group for matrix tiling, and the NKM loop order strategy following prior work [5].

We developed a cycle-accurate simulator to estimate energy and latency for each strategy, based on the hardware configurations outlined in Fig. 3(a). The energy of on-chip SRAM components is evaluated using the Arm Artisan Memory Compiler, and the off-chip memory energy is estimated with [6] under a typical LPDDR4 configuration. The vector processing energy is obtained by synthesizing the unit under commercial 22nm technology with Synopsys Design Compiler. The CIM macro is designed and simulated at the transistor level using Cadence Virtuoso for precise power estimation.

5.2 Experimental Results

(1) **Implementation Results.** The synthesis results exhibit that the area of the NPU core is 1.83 mm^2. The DCIM and the L1 buffer (SRAM) occupy the vast majority of the total area, accounting for 43.7% and 34.9%, respectively.

(2) **Efficiency Evaluation for Models.** Figure 3(b)(c) show latency and EDP results for ResNet34 layers under various strategies. Compared to the baseline, adaptive workload allocation improves latency by 1.19× on average. When combined with intra-core optimization, further improvements of up to 1.45× are achieved. The EDP is improved by 2.55× to 3.44× across different layers. Figure 3(d)(e) shows the normalized latency and energy improvement for AlexNet, ResNet-18, ResNet-34, ModernBERT-base and ModernBERT-large. For Attnetion-based DNNs, the sequence length is set to 1024. Regarding the end-to-end transformer-base model, our proposed strategies lead to approximately a 1.22× reduction in latency and a 2.13× reduction in energy consumption.

Table 1. Hardware Configurations

Component	*Parameter*
Core Number	4
CIM Macro Number	4
CIM Macro Size	64×256
Weight Page Number	16
Memory Size	512MB
L1 Buffer	128kB
Offchip Bandwidth	12.8GB/s
ALU Lane Number	64

(a)

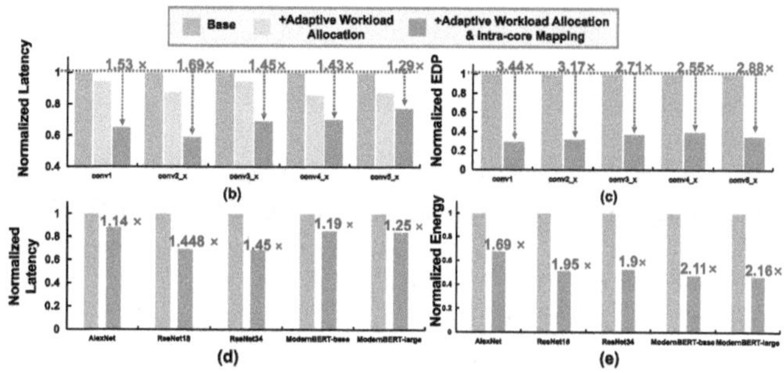

Fig. 3. (a) Hardware configuration table. Comparison between the baseline and the proposed optimization strategies. (b) latency and (c) EDP for ResNet layers. End-to-end evaluation results of (d) latency normalized to baseline and (e) energy results normalized to baseline.

6 Conclusion

In this paper, we present RV-CIM, a heterogeneous DCIM-based RISC-V SoC with configurable CIM cluster. At the hardware level, an extended RV-based CIM ISA is utilized to realize efficient data processing. At the software level, an adaptive workload allocation strategy for inter-core mapping as well as the EDP-aware tiling and scheduling for intra-core mapping are proposed to enhance the utilization. Experiments demonstrate that, for ResNet-34 and ModernBERT-large respectively, the optimized mapping strategies can achieve a 1.45× and 1.25× reduction in latency, and a 1.9× and 2.16× improvement in energy consumption.

Acknowledgments. This work is supported by Beijing Natural Science Foundation (No. L257017), National Key Research and Development Program of China (Grant 2023YFB4404603), and National Natural Science Foundation of China (Grant No. U24A20287, No. 62225401, No. 62574011 and No. 92464301). Artificial intelligence tools, if used, were used only for language organization and figure/table polishing, and did not participate in the generation of the core ideas or technical content.

References

1. Chen, T., et al.: PipeCIM: a high-throughput computing-in-memory microprocessor with nested pipeline and RISC-V extended instructions. IEEE Trans. Circuits Syst. I Regul. Pap. **71**(7), 3214–3227 (2024)
2. Fujiwara, H., et al.: 34.4 A 3nm, 32.5 TOPS/W, 55.0 TOPS/mm 2 and 3.78 Mb/mm 2 fully-digital compute-in-memory macro supporting INT12× INT12 with a parallel-MAC architecture and foundry 6T-SRAM bit cell. In: 2024 IEEE International Solid-State Circuits Conference (ISSCC). vol. 67, pp. 572–574. IEEE (2024)
3. Jung, H., et al.: Accelerating deep neural networks on mobile multicore NPUs. In: Proceedings of the 21st ACM/IEEE International Symposium on Code Generation and Optimization, pp. 236–248 (2023)

4. Shih, M.E., et al.: 20.1 NVE: A 3nm 23.2TOPS/W 12b-Digital-CIM-based neural engine for high-resolution visual-quality enhancement on smart devices. In: 2024 IEEE International Solid-State Circuits Conference (ISSCC). vol. 67, pp. 360–362 (2024)
5. Tu, F., et al.: SDP: Co-Designing Algorithm, Dataflow, and Architecture for In-SRAMSparse NN Acceleration. vol. 42, pp. 109–121 (2023)
6. Wu, Y.N., et al.: Accelergy: an architecture-level energy estimation methodology for accelerator designs. In: IEEE/ACM International Conference on Computer-Aided Design (ICCAD) (2019)

LLM-SYCL: Automated SYCL Generation from CUDA via Search-Driven LLM Translation

Shuai Yuan[1,2], Zhou Li[1,2], Yuanbo Wen[1,2], En Shao[1,2](✉), and Guangming Tan[1,2]

[1] University of Chinese Academy of Sciences, Beijing 100049, China
{yuanshuai251,lizhou23}@mails.ucas.ac.cn,
{wenyuanbo,shaoen,tgm}@ict.ac.cn

[2] State Key Lab of Processors, Institute of Computing Technology, CAS, Beijing 100190, China

Abstract. CUDA-to-SYCL translation is important for performance portability, yet rule-based migration tools often struggle to preserve parallel hierarchy, locality, and CUDA-specific optimization structure. We present LLM-SYCL, a search-driven SYCL generation backend for QiMeng-Xpiler. Starting from a normalized loop representation recovered from CUDA code, LLM-SYCL reconstructs SYCL thread binding, local-memory tiling, and subgroup-oriented arithmetic using target-aware prompts, guarded post-processing, and compile-and-run validation. On NVIDIA A100, all 20 regular GEMM cases compile, run, and pass correctness, with type-level geometric-mean retention of 67.5%–78.0% relative to CUDA and performance close to DPCT. On three WMMA/Tensor Core challenge cases, LLM-SYCL passes all cases while DPCT fails all of them. The generated SYCL kernels also run on AMD MI210 with comparable type-level throughput, showing that search-driven LLM translation can provide practical CUDA-to-SYCL portability.

Keywords: SYCL · Code Transcompiler · LLM-Driven Code Generation · Heterogeneous Computing

1 Introduction

SYCL provides a standard C++ model for heterogeneous programming while preserving device queues, hierarchical parallelism, local memory, and vendor-independent execution. These properties make SYCL an attractive target for migrating CUDA-centric software toward portable GPU execution [1].

The most visible practical baseline is Intel's DPC++ Compatibility Tool (DPCT), a rule-based CUDA-to-SYCL translator [2]. DPCT is useful for quickly producing compilable SYCL baselines, but syntactic migration alone is often not enough for performance-sensitive kernels. Prior evaluation reports that DPCT

L. Eeckhout et al. (Eds.): APPT 2026, LNCS 16693, pp. 607–612, 2027.
https://doi.org/10.1007/978-981-92-4805-6_43

can migrate a large fraction of benchmark code, while still requiring manual intervention and leaving performance gaps [3]. The hard cases are exactly those where CUDA constructs encode optimization intent: thread hierarchy, shared-memory tiling, subgroup behavior, and Tensor Core style programming.

LLM-assisted transcompilation provides a complementary route. QiMeng-Xpiler combines LLM-guided transformations, symbolic repair, and hierarchical search for tensor-program translation [4], but it does not provide a SYCL back-end. We extend this framework with LLM-SYCL, a search-driven pipeline for automated CUDA-to-SYCL generation. Rather than treating migration as one-shot text rewriting, LLM-SYCL uses intermediate program states, target-specific prompts, and execution feedback to recover both correctness and optimization structure.

This paper makes three contributions. First, we add a SYCL generation backend to QiMeng-Xpiler, enabling automatic migration from CUDA-derived loop code to portable SYCL kernels. Second, we design target-aware prompting and guarded validation for reconstructing thread binding, local-memory tiling, and subgroup-oriented arithmetic. Third, we evaluate regular GEMM kernels, WMMA/Tensor Core challenge kernels, and cross-vendor execution on NVIDIA A100 and AMD MI210.

2 Methodology

2.1 System Overview

Figure 1 shows the LLM-SYCL workflow. The inherited QiMeng-Xpiler front end first lowers CUDA kernels into a normalized CPU-style loop representation. This representation removes some CUDA-specific syntax while retaining the loop structure needed to recover matrix-multiplication semantics. Our contribution is the CPU-to-SYCL backend, which regenerates target code through search rather than committing to a single direct translation.

The backend follows three stages. Thread binding lifts loop nests into SYCL `q.submit` and `parallel_for` forms. Local-memory conversion promotes suitable matrix-multiplication regions into tiled kernels using `local_accessor`. Tensorization then refines arithmetic toward subgroup-aware and fused-multiply-add style implementations. MCTS explores both pass choices and pass-local parameters, using compilation, correctness, and timing feedback to guide the search.

2.2 Prompting, Validation, and Fallback

The SYCL backend reuses QiMeng-Xpiler's transformation framework, but the prompts and guards are target-specific. Thread-binding prompts constrain the model to use core SYCL kernel forms and to respect the distinction between `item` and `nd_item`. Cache and tensorization prompts operate on annotated matrix-multiplication regions, and are augmented with workload shape, target-device context, preferred subgroup size, and compatibility hints. This conditioning

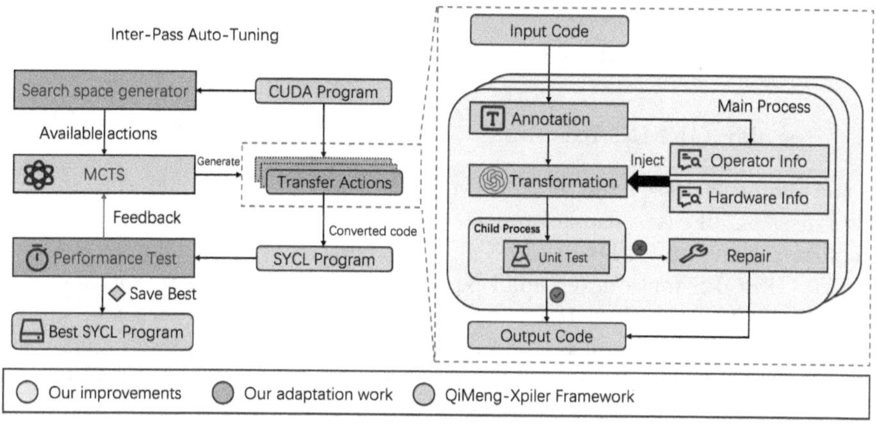

Fig. 1. System overview of LLM-SYCL. The inherited semantic recovery stage produces normalized loop code; the new SYCL backend reconstructs parallel hierarchy, local-memory use, and arithmetic structure through search-guided transformations.

is important because tiling and subgroup choices are strongly workload- and backend-dependent.

Model output is checked before it enters performance evaluation. The backend removes markdown artifacts, repairs common subgroup-lambda syntax errors, and rejects candidates that violate complete-function, core-SYCL, or local-memory-safety constraints. If a prompt-based cache or tensorization pass is missing, malformed, or semantically weak, deterministic fallbacks construct tiled kernels or promote cached kernels into subgroup-style arithmetic forms. Final candidates are compiled and executed in isolated temporary harnesses that record compile success, runnable status, correctness, and latency. These guards do not eliminate model uncertainty, but they reduce silent failures and make the search loop practical.

3 Evaluation

3.1 Setup

We evaluate two GEMM-derived benchmark suites. The regular suite contains 20 FP32 cases grouped into square (S), small-K (K), wide-N (N), and tall-M (M) workload types, with five cases per type. Each regular case is measured in three forms: the original tiled CUDA kernel, the corresponding DPCT-generated SYCL kernel, and the LLM-SYCL-generated SYCL kernel. The advanced suite contains three WMMA/Tensor Core kernels covering square, deep-K, and small-K profiles.

The main experiments run on NVIDIA A100. For each kernel, the harness compiles a temporary benchmark shared object, invokes a timed entry function, records five repeats, and reports median latency-derived GFLOPS. Correctness is checked against a reference GEMM result. To test portability, the regular LLM-SYCL kernels are also evaluated on AMD MI210.

3.2 Regular GEMM Results

On the regular 20-case suite, both LLM-SYCL and DPCT compile, run, and pass correctness on all cases. Table 1 reports type-level geometric-mean GFLOPS and retention relative to CUDA. LLM-SYCL reaches 1760.76, 2623.80, 3388.63, and 3504.79 GFLOPS for square, small-K, wide-N, and tall-M cases, corresponding to 67.5%–78.0% retention. It is slightly behind DPCT on square and wide-N, and slightly ahead on small-K and tall-M. The strongest individual regular cases exceed 3.7 TFLOPS, showing that the backend recovers a substantial fraction of CUDA throughput without relying on one-to-one syntactic mappings.

Table 1. Type-level summary on the regular GEMM suite. GFLOPS and retention values are geometric means over five cases in each type.

Type	CUDA Baseline	DPCT	LLM-SYCL
Square (S)	2609.39	1798.22 (68.9%)	1760.76 (67.5%)
Small-K (K)	3660.53	2597.14 (70.9%)	2623.80 (71.7%)
Wide-N (N)	4604.28	3588.27 (77.9%)	3388.63 (73.6%)
Tall-M (M)	4491.39	3498.67 (77.9%)	3504.79 (78.0%)

3.3 Advanced and Cross-Platform Results

The advanced challenge set highlights the benefit of search-driven regeneration on CUDA-specific kernels. As shown in Table 2, LLM-SYCL compiles, runs, and passes correctness on all three WMMA/Tensor Core cases, while DPCT fails on all three translations. The generated SYCL kernels do not match the Tensor Core CUDA baseline, but they remain viable and portable where direct rule-based conversion breaks down.

Table 2. Advanced WMMA/Tensor Core challenge set on NVIDIA A100. DPCT is omitted because all three translations fail.

Case	CUDA Baseline		LLM-SYCL	
	GFLOPS	%Peak	GFLOPS	%Peak
A1	18817.24	96.50	3508.89	17.99
A2	17468.99	89.58	3483.05	17.86
A3	18922.83	97.04	3557.71	18.24

Cross-vendor results further show that the generated kernels are not narrowly tied to one backend. Table 3 reports type-level performance on A100 and MI210. The absolute throughput is close in the K and N types, while tall-M is stronger on A100 and wide-N is stronger on MI210. Overall, the workload-type pattern is consistent across vendors.

Table 3. Cross-platform type-level summary of LLM-SYCL. Values are geometric means over five regular cases in each type.

Type	NVIDIA A100 GFLOPS	AMD MI210 GFLOPS
Square (S)	1760.76 (9.03% peak)	1670.20 (7.26% peak)
Small-K (K)	2623.80 (13.46% peak)	2605.70 (11.33% peak)
Wide-N (N)	3388.63 (17.38% peak)	3555.90 (15.46% peak)
Tall-M (M)	3504.79 (17.97% peak)	3126.95 (13.60% peak)

These results suggest that LLM-SYCL is not uniformly stronger than DPCT on conventional GEMM kernels, but it is competitive while covering difficult CUDA-specific cases that DPCT cannot handle. The remaining gap to native CUDA is mainly a kernel-efficiency issue rather than a correctness or portability failure.

4 Conclusion

LLM-SYCL extends QiMeng-Xpiler with a search-driven SYCL backend for CUDA migration. By combining target-aware prompts, guarded validation, and isolated execution feedback, it reconstructs parallel hierarchy, local-memory use, and arithmetic structure in portable SYCL code. The regular suite shows competitive performance against DPCT, the advanced suite shows robustness on WMMA/Tensor Core kernels, and the AMD MI210 results demonstrate meaningful cross-platform portability. Future work will broaden the evaluation beyond GEMM and improve hardware-aware subgroup and tensorization generation.

Disclosure of Interests. The authors have no competing interests to declare that are relevant to the content of this article.

Declaration on AI Use. The technical solution and experimental design presented in this paper were independently completed by the authors. AI tools were used solely for language polishing and formatting optimization, and did not participate in the development of the research ideas or core content. Artificial intelligence tools, if used, were used only for language organization and figure/table polishing, and did not participate in the generation of the core ideas or technical content.

References

1. Reinders, J., Ashbaugh, B., Brodman, J., Kinsner, M., Pennycook, J., Tian, X.: Data Parallel C++: Mastering DPC++ for Programming of Heterogeneous Systems using C++ and SYCL. Apress, Berkeley, CA (2021). https://doi.org/10.1007/978-1-4842-5574-2
2. Intel Corporation: Intel DPC++ Compatibility Tool. https://www.intel.com/content/www/us/en/developer/tools/oneapi/dpc-compatibility-tool.html. Accessed 04 Apr 2026
3. Castaño, G., Faqir-Rhazoui, Y., García, C., Prieto-Matías, M.: Evaluation of Intel's DPC++ compatibility tool in heterogeneous computing. J. Parallel Distributed Comput. **165**, 120–129 (2022). https://doi.org/10.1016/j.jpdc.2022.03.017
4. Dong, S., et al.: QiMeng-Xpiler: transcompiling tensor programs for deep learning systems with a neural-symbolic approach. In: 19th USENIX Symposium on Operating Systems Design and Implementation (OSDI '25), pp. 239–256 (2025)

Characterizing and Mitigating I/O Bottlenecks in LLM Inference on Disaggregated HPC Systems

Qin Zhu[1], Fanzi Zeng[1(✉)], Kenli Li[1], Hai Tan[2], Mengyuan Zhang[4], Haoran Kong[1], Longbao Dai[1], Wenlong Liu[1], and Xiang Zhu[3]

[1] College of Computer Science, Hunan University, Changsha, China
{B251000750,lkl,konghaoran,longbaodai00,B251000792}@hnu.edu.cn, zengfanzi@126.com

[2] School of Information Engineering, Nanjing Audit University, Nanjing, China
270602@nau.edu.cn

[3] College of Information, Mechanical and Electrical Engineering, Shanghai Normal University, Shanghai, China
1000552527@smail.shnu.edu.cn

[4] School of Computer Science and Technology, Tongji University, Shanghai, China
2341065@tongji.edu.cn

Abstract. Storage-compute disaggregation is the prevailing architecture in modern HPC systems, yet its impact on LLM inference remains poorly understood. We present a large-scale I/O characterization on a disaggregated cluster with up to 512 nodes, revealing that I/O contributes over 99% of run-to-run latency *variance* despite accounting for only 41% of mean latency. We propose a three-phase I/O model validated across 11 architectures, 7 storage back-ends, and 2 topologies (MAPE$\leq$ 7.5%). Guided by this model, our I/O-aware optimizations achieve up to 3.7$\times$ throughput improvement while reducing 24-hour degradation from 28.5% to 6.8%.

Keywords: HPC · I/O bottleneck · LLM inference · disaggregation · performance modeling

1 Introduction

Modern HPC systems increasingly adopt storage-compute disaggregation [1], yet the impact on LLM inference remains unquantified. Our experiments reveal: $\text{Var}(T_{I/O})/\text{Var}(T_{total}) = 99.2\%$ (60-min trace, 70M records). Although mean I/O accounts for ~41% of total latency, it dominates run-to-run *fluctuation* while GPU computation remains stable.

We make four contributions. **C1.** A three-phase I/O model with model-parallelism extension (MAPE$\leq$ 7.5%). **C2.** Non-intrusive LD_PRELOAD monitoring (<1.1% overhead). **C3.** First I/O characterization across 11 architectures (5 MoE gating variants, 175B model-parallel), 7 storage back-ends, and

L. Eeckhout et al. (Eds.): APPT 2026, LNCS 16693, pp. 613–618, 2027.
https://doi.org/10.1007/978-981-92-4805-6_44

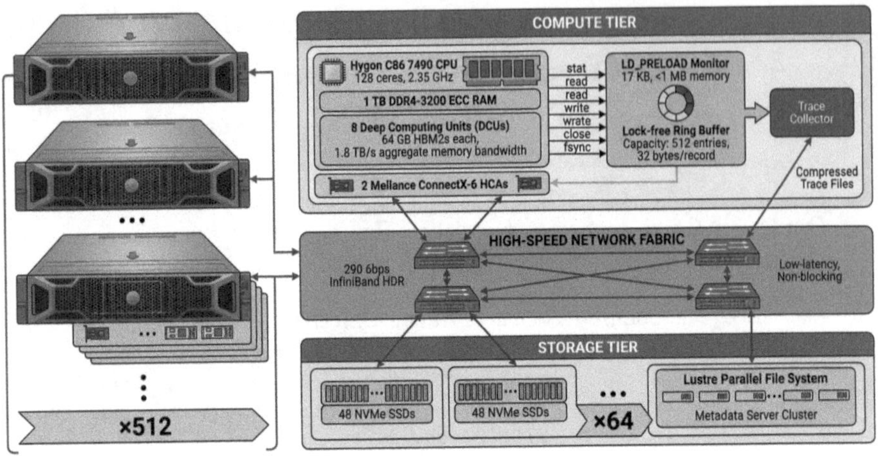

Fig. 1. Disaggregated HPC architecture with non-intrusive I/O monitoring.

512 nodes. **C4.** I/O-aware optimizations achieving 3.7× throughput, reducing 24-hour degradation by 76%.

2 Related Work

GPU optimizations (vLLM [2], TensorRT-LLM [3], DeepSpeed [4]) assume weights already reside in GPU memory, overlooking I/O overhead on disaggregated systems. HPC I/O tools (Darshan [5], ROMIO [6]) provide profiling for traditional workloads but lack LLM-specific characterization; strace incurs 5–300% overhead. Classical models (LogGP [7], $M/G/k$ queueing [8]) capture network and storage costs but do not account for the bimodal hot/cold-path latency unique to LLM inference. Disaggregated storage [9], RDMA [10], burst buffers [11], and parallel file systems [12] are well studied for conventional HPC but LLM-specific I/O remains unexplored. Our work bridges this gap with a phase-decomposed model and non-intrusive monitoring.

3 Methodology

System Architecture. Up to 512 compute nodes (8 DCUs each, 64 GB HBM2e) access shared storage via 200 Gbps InfiniBand (Fig. 1). Our LD_PRELOAD monitor intercepts six POSIX I/O calls with 0.8% overhead.

Three-phase I/O Model. We decompose inference I/O into: *Phase 1 (Loading):* $T_{load} = M_{active}/R_{storage} \times (1 - P_{cache\_hit})$, where M_{active} is active model size ($M_{shared} + k \cdot M_{expert}$ for MoE). For model-parallel: $T_{load}^{MP} = M/(P \cdot R_{storage}) \times (1 - P_{cache\_hit}) + T_{allgather}(M, P)$. *Phase 2 (KV Cache):* $T_{cache} = \sum_{t=1}^{N} T_{cache}^{(t)}$. *Phase 3 (Persistence):* $T_{persist} = N \cdot S_{token}/R_{storage}$.

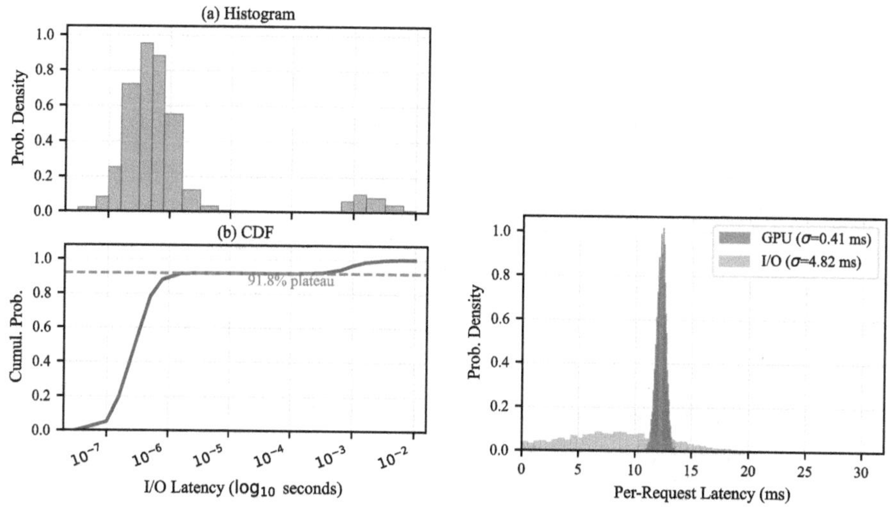

Fig. 2. Left: bimodal I/O latency. Right: GPU vs. I/O variance ($s^2_{I/O}/s^2_{total} = 99.2\%$).

Total: $T_{I/O} = T_{load} + T_{cache} + T_{persist}$; throughput $\Theta = N/\max(T_{compute}, T_{I/O})$. Validation: single-request MAPE 4.2%, batching MAPE 7.5%, loading-only MAPE 2.1%, all $p < 0.001$.

Setup. 7 storage back-ends (NVMe+Lustre, NFS, BeeGFS, CephFS, Burst-Buffer, Spectrum Scale). 11 models: Dense (Qwen3-4B/14B/32B, LLaMA-2-70B, etc.), MoE with 5 gating strategies (Mixtral top-2, DeepSeek top-6, Switch top-1, expert-choice [13], hash [14]), and OPT-175B (8-way TP). Frameworks: vLLM, DeepSpeed, HF Accelerate, TensorRT-LLM. All $N = 10$, $p < 0.001$, Cohen's $d > 1.2$.

4 Empirical Findings

Finding 1: Bimodal I/O Latency. Qwen3-14B shows 91.8% hot-path ($< 1\,\mu$s) vs. 8.2% cold-path (> 1 ms) operations (Fig. 2). GPU CV $= 3.3\%$ vs. I/O CV $= 56.7\%$, yielding $s^2_{I/O}/s^2_{total} = 99.2\%$ (Levene's $F = 2{,}847$).

Finding 2: Scale and Gating Diversity. Table 1 shows small dense models (<16 GB) are KV-cache-dominant while large models (>32 GB) are loading-dominant. Among MoE gating strategies, expert-choice and hash achieve highest hot-path ratios (87.5%, 89.2%) and cache hits (85.2%, 87.8%), while Switch top-1 is worst (81.5%, 72.3%) due to routing diversity destroying cache locality.

Finding 3: 175B Model-Parallel. OPT-175B (325 GB, 8-way TP, 40.6 GB/device): loading dominates at $91.2 \pm 1.5\%$, all-gather synchronization adds $12.5 \pm 1.8\%$, and hot-path drops to $78.5 \pm 2.2\%$—the lowest across all configurations. Cold TTFT reaches $\sim$28.5 s; warm TTFT is 185 ± 12 ms. Preloading

Table 1. Model I/O Characterization ($N = 10$)

(a) Dense Transformers

Metric	4B	14B	32B	70B
Active Size (GB)	8	28	64	130
KV Cache / Loading %	78/22	55/45	32/68	18/82
Hot path %	94.2 ± 0.8	91.8 ± 0.7	88.5 ± 1.2	83.2 ± 1.5

(b) MoE Models (5 Gating Strategies)

	Mixtral *top-2*	DS-MoE *top-6*	Switch *top-1*	EC-MoE *EC*	Hash *hash*
Hot %	86.8 ± 1.8	84.2 ± 2.3	81.5 ± 3.1	87.5 ± 1.5	89.2 ± 1.2
Cache hit %	82.5 ± 2.1	78.8 ± 2.8	72.3 ± 3.5	85.2 ± 1.8	87.8 ± 1.5

reduces cold TTFT by 71% to ~8.2 s. The I/O variance ratio remains above 98%, confirming that disaggregated storage is the dominant performance bottleneck even at extreme model scale.

Finding 4: MPI Scalability (1–512 Nodes). Single-node optimal MPI process range is 16–32 (>80% efficiency), compressing to 4–8/6–10 (fat-tree/dragonfly) at 128 nodes and 2–4/4–6 at 512 nodes. Dragonfly consistently outperforms fat-tree beyond 32 nodes (32% vs. 24% efficiency at 512 nodes, 4,096 DCUs). At 512 nodes, `MPI_Allreduce` constitutes 72% (fat-tree) and 58% (dragonfly) of total MPI overhead. Fat-tree's higher hop count (3.8 vs. 2.1) disproportionately penalizes latency-sensitive collective operations.

5 Optimization

Three strategies: (1) *Preloading* via `mmap` pre-loads model weights into OS page cache, yielding 51.6% cold-start TTFT reduction for Qwen3-14B (2,325 → 1,125 ms) at 11% memory overhead; (2) *Dynamic MPI scheduling* selects process count $N_{opt} = \min(N_{crit}(nodes, topo), \lfloor B \cdot S/M \rfloor)$, where N_{crit} is the topology-aware critical count from scalability analysis and the second term ensures sufficient parallelism; (3) *Adaptive cache refresh* monitors miss rate in real time and triggers refresh when it exceeds $\theta = 15\%$ (selected from $\{5\%, \ldots, 25\%\}$ on 12-hour runs), triggering ~8 events in 24 h with 6 min total downtime.

Table 2 shows our combined approach achieves 3.7× throughput over no-optimization baseline, outperforming all six alternatives. Cross-model improvements range from 3.1× (OPT-175B) to 3.7× (Qwen3-14B), all with $p < .001$. Cross-framework results are consistent: vLLM (3.7×), DeepSpeed (3.4×), HF Accelerate (3.3×). At larger scales, improvement narrows from 3.7× at 1 node to 2.4–2.8× at 512 nodes due to MPI overhead, with dragonfly consistently outperforming fat-tree; topology-aware scheduling recovers 18–25% efficiency. 24-hour

Table 2. Optimization Comparison (Qwen3-14B, $N = 10$)

Strategy	Tput (req/s)	TTFT (ms)	Impr.
No optimization	4.15 ± 0.11	$2{,}325 \pm 108$	1.0×
Quiver [15]	13.80 ± 0.35	$1{,}450 \pm 85$	3.3×
RDMA Prefetch	12.25 ± 0.42	$1{,}680 \pm 92$	3.0×
Round-Robin MPI	14.10 ± 0.30	$2{,}310 \pm 110$	3.4×
Hier. KV Cache	13.20 ± 0.32	$2{,}150 \pm 98$	3.2×
TRT-LLM Dist. Load	14.50 ± 0.28	$1{,}350 \pm 78$	3.5×
Ours (combined)	$\mathbf{15.42 \pm 0.22}$	$\mathbf{1{,}125 \pm 62}$	**3.7×**

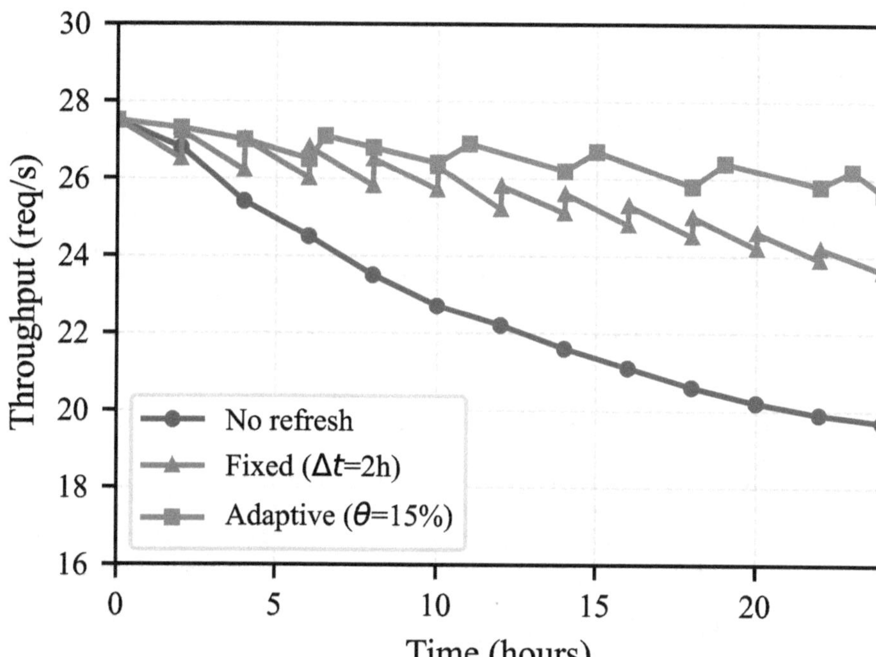

Fig. 3. 24-hour throughput: adaptive refresh limits degradation to 6.8%.

stability: degradation reduced from 28.5% (no refresh) to 14.2% (fixed $\Delta t = 2\,\text{h}$) to **6.8%** (adaptive $\theta = 15\%$, Fig. 3).

6 Conclusion

We present the first I/O behavior model for LLM inference on disaggregated HPC, validated across 11 architectures (5 MoE gating variants, 175B model-parallel), 7 storage back-ends, and up to 512 nodes under fat-tree and dragonfly topologies. The bimodal I/O pattern generalizes across all configurations (hot-path 78.5–94.2%). Gating strategy emerges as a first-order I/O determinant: expert-choice and hash routing achieve 85–88% cache hit rates, while Switch top-1 degrades to 72%. Combined optimization achieves 3.1–3.7× throughput over six baselines, with adaptive refresh reducing 24-hour degradation from 28.5% to 6.8%.

Limitations. OPT-175B is tested with pseudo-random weights. Fine-tuning, long-context (>32K) workloads, and CXL-based disaggregation remain future work. All data and monitoring tools will be open-sourced upon publication.

AI Use Statement. The technical solution and experimental design were independently completed by the authors. AI tools were used solely for language polishing and formatting optimization.

References

1. Gao, P.X., et al.: Network requirements for resource disaggregation. In: Proceedings of USENIX OSDI, pp. 249–264 (2016)
2. Kwon, W., et al.: Efficient memory management for large language model serving with PagedAttention. In: Proceedings of ACM SOSP, pp. 611–626 (2023)
3. NVIDIA.: TensorRT-LLM (2023). https://github.com/NVIDIA/TensorRT-LLM
4. Aminabadi, R.Y.: DeepSpeed inference: enabling efficient inference of transformer models at unprecedented scale. In: Proceedings of IEEE SC, pp. 1–15 (2022)
5. Carns, P., et al.: Understanding and improving computational science storage access through continuous characterization. ACM Trans. Storage **7**(3) (2011)
6. Thakur, R., Gropp, W., Lusk, E.: Data sieving and collective I/O in ROMIO. In: Proceedings of IEEE Symposium Frontiers Massively Parallel Computer, pp. 182–189 (1999)
7. Alexandrov, A., et al.: LogGP: incorporating long messages into the LogP model. J. Parallel Distrib. Comput. **44**(1), 71–79 (1997)
8. Varki, E., Merchant, A., Xu, J., Qiu, X.: Issues and challenges in the performance analysis of real disk arrays. IEEE Trans. Parallel Distrib. Syst. **15**(6), 559–574 (2004)
9. Shan, Y., Huang, Y., Chen, Y., Zhang, Y.: LegoOS: a disseminated, distributed OS for hardware resource disaggregation. In: Proceedings of USENIX OSDI, pp. 69–87 (2018)
10. Kalia, A., Kaminsky, M., Andersen, D.G.: Using RDMA efficiently for key-value services. In: Proceedings of ACM SIGCOMM, pp. 295–306 (2014)
11. Liu, N.: On the role of burst buffers in leadership-class storage systems. In: Proceedings of IEEE MSST (2012)
12. Schmuck, F., Haskin, R.: GPFS: a shared-disk file system for large computing clusters. In: Proceedings of USENIX FAST (2002)
13. Zhou, Y., et al.: Mixture-of-experts with expert choice routing. In: Proceedings of NeurIPS (2022)
14. Roller, S., Sukhbaatar, S., Szlam, A., Weston, J.: Hash layers for large sparse models. In: Proceedings of NeurIPS (2021)
15. Kumar, A.V., Sivathanu, M.: Quiver: an informed storage cache for deep learning. In: Proceedings of USENIX FAST, pp. 283–296 (2020)

A Bottom-Up Approach for Die-to-Die Interconnect Optimization: From PHY Latency Reduction to System-Level Design Implications

Jinfei Hu[1,2,3], Liqiong Yang[1,2], Jingyi Wang[1,2], and Jian Wang[1,2,3](✉)

[1] State Key Lab of Processors, ICT, CAS, Beijing 100190, China
hujinfei22@mails.ucas.ac.cn, {yangliqiong,wangjingyi,jw}@ict.ac.cn
[2] Institute of Computing Technology, CAS, Beijing 100190, China
[3] University of Chinese Academy of Sciences, Beijing 100049, China

Abstract. As chiplet-based architectures emerge as a promising solution for scaling performance beyond monolithic die limitations, advances in packaging technology enable short-reach co-packaged die-to-die interconnects with significantly improved channel conditions, creating new opportunities to re-optimize the PHY layer originally designed for longer-reach communication. However, the relationship between such low-level optimization and its system-level impact remains poorly understood. In this paper, we take a bottom-up approach for die-to-die interconnect optimization, bridging circuit-level design and system-level analysis. At the PCS (Physical Coding Sublayer) level, our symmetric optimization reduced end-to-end PHY latency by approximately 47.3%. We then develop xLinkx, a die-to-die link simulator supporting PCIe Gen4/5, and CXL 2.0, across ring, mesh, and IO-die topologies. Experiments characterize the workload sensitivity of PHY latency optimization, revealing how memory-level parallelism and payload size determine its effective region. We evaluate optimization benefits across multiple topologies and system scales. Results show that ring topology benefits the most, with transaction latency reduced by up to 28%, while optimization gains exhibit clear diminishing marginal returns as the number of dies increases.

Keywords: Latency Optimization · Chiplet · Performance Evaluation

1 Introduction

As Moore's Law slows, chiplet integration has become a promising alternative to monolithic SoCs for addressing yield, thermal, and cost limits. AMD EPYC demonstrated its commercial viability [1], and packaging advances from 2D substrates to 2.5D interposers and 3D stacking [2] have shortened die-to-die links to millimeters, creating opportunities to re-optimize PHY for short-reach communication. Prior work has optimized interconnects across layers, including NoC-controlled PHY [6], low-latency PCIe retimers [4], and CXL memory/device

L. Eeckhout et al. (Eds.): APPT 2026, LNCS 16693, pp. 619–624, 2027.
https://doi.org/10.1007/978-981-92-4805-6_45

characterization [3,5]. However, circuit- and system-level studies remain largely separated, and how circuit-level latency reductions translate into protocol- and workload-level performance gains remains unclear.

To bridge this gap, we present a bottom-up circuit-to-system study that connects PCS-layer latency optimization with xLinkx-based system-level evaluation. The main contributions of this paper are as follows: (1) We co-optimize asynchronous FIFO, elastic buffer, and synchronous clock-domain logic in the PCS layer, reducing end-to-end PHY latency by 47.3%. (2) We develop xLinkx, a specification-level die-to-die link simulator for PCIe Gen4/5 and CXL 2.0, modeling credit-based flow control, reliable transport, and flit packing across ring, mesh, and IO-die topologies. (3) We quantify the workload-, topology-, and scale-dependent benefits of PHY latency optimization, deriving design guidance for chiplet interconnects.

2 Background and Motivation

PCIe uses a layered stack consisting of the Transaction, Data Link, and Physical Layers. The PCS performs encoding, scrambling, clock domain crossing (CDC), elastic buffering, and lane deskewing, whereas the PMA(Physical Medium Attachment) mainly handles serialization and low-level physical-interface functions. CXL 2.0 reuses the PCIe Physical Layer. CDC is a major source of PCS latency and the transmitter–receiver clock relationship depends on whether they share a common source and whether their frequencies match.

In co-packaged scenarios, both ends can share the same reference clock source, reducing frequency offsets to near zero and rendering the frequency compensation function of the elastic buffer largely unnecessary. Furthermore, improved channel conditions allow simplified PMA analog circuits, and the resulting adjustment in serialization ratio enables integer-multiple clock relationships in the PCS. These changes collectively open significant optimization space for reducing CDC latency in the Physical Layer. At the same time, how such PHY latency reduction translates into system-level performance remains unclear. This motivates the study in the rest of paper.

3 Design and Implementation

3.1 PHY Latency Optimization

We iteratively optimize the Loongson Coherent Link and PCIe interconnect. Figure 1 shows the data and clock architectures of the 16-lane link, with colors indicating clock sources; in each TX/RX channel, the left and right sides denote the original and optimized designs, respectively.

On the PCS transmit side, we redesign the data-width conversion module to convert 32-bit input to 16-bit output, enabled by corresponding analog-circuit modifications. This turns clock conversion into a 2× relationship, reduces data conversion to a single-cycle register split, and moves synchronization to the higher-frequency clock domain. The receive side follows the same

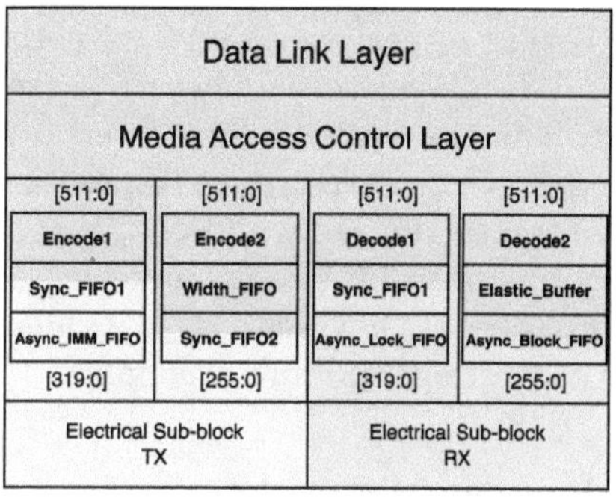

Fig. 1. Link architecture

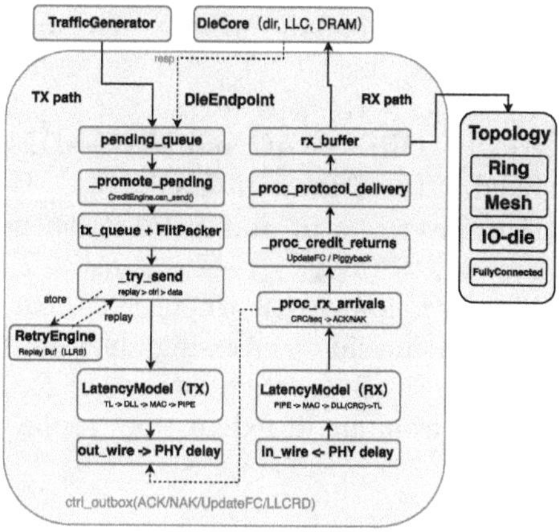

Fig. 2. simulation stack of xLinkx

symmetric 16-bit datapath and synchronization design. The elastic buffer is retained for reliability but with compressed depth, and the maximum depth is $EB\_Depth = \frac{MaxSymbolTimes+MaxInterval}{10^6/(ppm_1+ppm_2)} \times 2$, where $MaxSymbolTimes = \frac{MaxPayloadSize+PktOverhead}{LinkWidth}$. The factor of 2 covers worst-case overflow and underflow compensation.

On the PMA side, we adapt the internal loopback and PRBS test paths and replace the transmitter serializer with a 16-4-2-1 architecture. The receiver is modified symmetrically, with CDR, DFE, and symbol detection/alignment adjusted for the 16-bit datapath.

3.2 Die-to-Die Link Simulator

Overall Architecture. We develop xLinkx, a cycle-approximate chiplet link simulator targeting chiplet interconnects. By modeling specification-level protocol-stack details—flow control, reliable transport, flit packing, and transfer widths—xLinkx captures bottlenecks beyond simple bandwidth–latency pipe models. Each die-to-die link comprises two symmetric protocol stack paths for the transmit and receive directions. The software simulation stack, shown in Fig. 2, employs a unified scheduling framework in which different protocol engines independently manage their own credit, retry, and packing mechanisms. Switching protocols requires only replacing the engine module. The simulator uses the PIPE clock as the global timebase, with each layer having an independent data width and corresponding clock frequency.

$$T_{\text{layer}} = \left\lceil \frac{B_{\text{pkt}}}{W_{\text{layer}}} \right\rceil \times T_{\text{beat}} \quad (1) \qquad T_{\text{txn}} = \sum_{i=1}^{S} T_{\text{one\_way},i} + \sum_{j=1}^{S-1} T_{\text{home},j} \quad (2)$$

Latency Model. xLinkx decomposes latency into size-dependent pipeline delay and fixed PHY traversal delay. For each packet, the one-way latency is $T_{\text{one\_way}} = T_{\text{tx\_pipe}} + T_{\text{phy}} + T_{\text{rx\_pipe}}$, where the TX/RX pipelines correspond to TL→DLL→MAC and MAC→DLL(CRC)→TL, respectively, and T_{phy} is the fixed PHY latency. In Eq. 1, B_{pkt}, W_{layer}, and T_{beat} denote the on-wire packet size, layer width, and PIPE ticks per beat. The transmit pipeline latency is $T_{\text{tx\_pipe}} = (T_{\text{beat,TL}} + T_{\text{beat,DLL}} + T_{\text{beat,MAC}}) + (N_{\text{bn}} - 1)T_{\text{beat,bn}}$. Transaction latency follows Eq. 2, where S is the number of transaction steps and $T_{\text{home},j}$ captures home-side processing such as directory lookup, LLC access, and DRAM access. Finally, system latency is $T_{\text{system}} = T_{\text{queue}} + T_{\text{txn}}$, where T_{queue} includes delays from credit exhaustion, replay-buffer congestion, and link occupancy.

Engine. PCIe Gen4/5 share a common TLP-mode model, with traffic injected through AXI-to-PCIe TLP mapping. Transmission is gated by both six credit pools and retry-buffer availability, while reliability is modeled using ACK/NAK DLLPs and a replay buffer under strict-priority scheduling. CXL 2.0 is modeled with fixed 68B flits, supporting CXL.cache/mem message packing, two-flit rollover for 64B cacheline data, piggybacked credit returns, and standalone LLCRD flits when reverse traffic is unavailable. Its transmit path similarly applies slot-credit and LLRB-space gating, with receiver-initiated LLR reliability and priority scheduling of replay, control, and new data flits.

Topology Layer. The topology layer organizes multiple die nodes and links into specific interconnect. Each die node contains a traffic generator, a local processing unit (DieCore), and one or more link endpoints. The DieCore models differentiated processing latency, multi-hop routing uses shortest-path algorithms with per-protocol route tables, and intermediate nodes perform store-and-forward.

4 Experiments

4.1 Experimental Setup

RTL validation uses UVM 1.1d to issue AXI requests, with analog circuits abstracted by SMIC 12-nm behavioral models. System-level experiments run on xLinkx with a 16 GT/s lane rate, 16 lanes, a 64 B MAC width, and BER=1×10^{-15}. Credit pools are sized to the BDP under the baseline PHY latency of 31.7 ns and kept fixed across both PHY settings. Workloads follow a closed-loop pointer-chase pattern that maintains a target MLP, reissuing each completed request after an exponentially distributed think time.

4.2 RTL Circuit Delay

The optimized transmitter and receiver are referred to as New TX and New RX, respectively. When both sides adopt the optimized design, the end-to-end PIPE-to-PIPE latency is reduced from 31.7ns to 16.7ns, a reduction of approximately

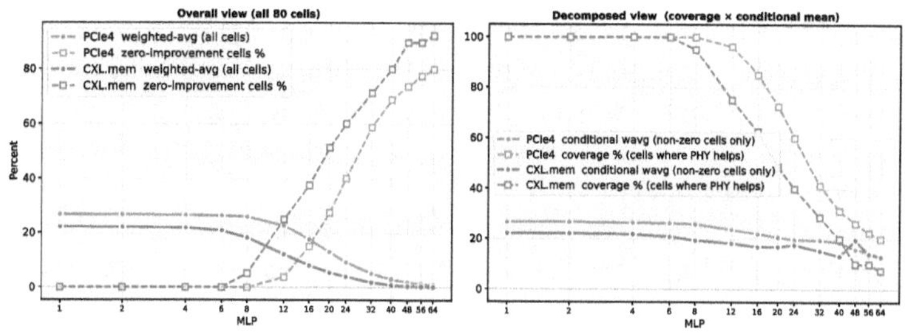

Fig. 3. Average latency – PHY 16.7 vs 31.7 summary across all cells

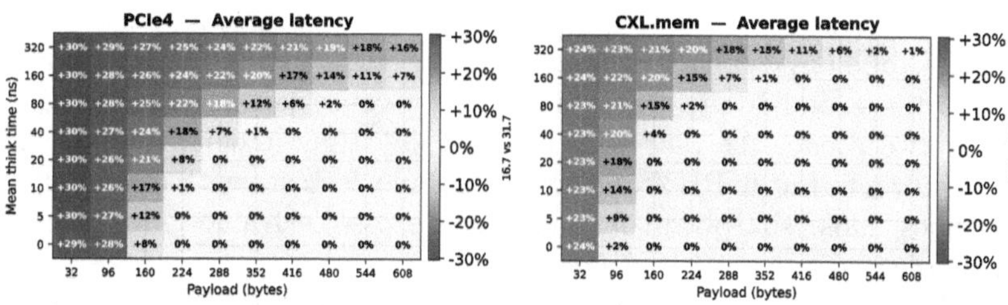

Fig. 4. Average latency – PHY 16.7ns improvement over 31.7ns

47.3%. The optimized transmitter and receiver maintain backward compatibility with the standard PCIe PIPE layer and can be deployed independently. Furthermore, by adjusting the PLL frequency division ratio, we conduct a derivative experiment at 20GT/s, achieving a latency of 14.4ns, a reduction of 54.5%.

4.3 Load Sensitivity Analysis of Latency Optimization Benefits

This experiment sweeps read requests across 10 payload sizes, 14 MLP levels, and 8 think times. As shown in Fig. 3, PHY-latency benefits are increasingly masked as MLP grows. Still, under a 1% improvement threshold, 20% of PCIe workloads and 7.5% of CXL.mem workloads remain beneficial at MLP=64, achieving

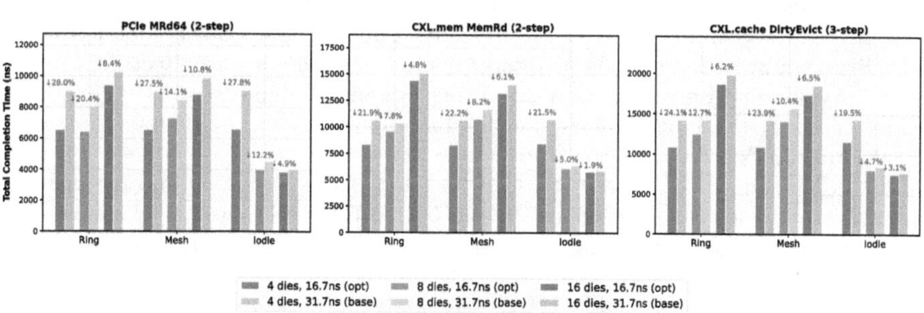

Fig. 5. Total Completion Time vs Topology x Die Count x PHY

average gains of 14.1% and 14.4%, respectively. Since MLP=8 marks the upper end of the improvement plateau, we fix MLP=8 for the extended payload sweep in Fig. 4. Larger payloads saturate the link earlier and mask the optimization effect, while longer think times lower the injection rate and push the benefit toward its theoretical upper bound.

In summary, for sustained high-throughput transfers, the impact of PHY latency is limited; for burst transfers and memory access patterns with request dependencies, latency optimization still yields significant system-level benefits.

4.4 Scalability Analysis of Latency Optimization Across Multi-Die Topologies

To quantify topology-dependent benefits, we evaluate Ring, Mesh, and IODie systems at 4-, 8-, and 16-die scales. The pointer-chase workload issues 512 read requests between each die pair with a 5 ns think time under three parallelism levels. As shown in Fig. 5, PHY-optimization gains decrease with die count across all topologies, most sharply in IODie, where cross-die traffic converges at the central IO die and creates a bottleneck.

Overall, PHY optimization is most effective for simpler, smaller-scale, and lower-parallelism systems. For large-scale IODie designs, marginal returns are limited, suggesting that load balancing at the central IO die or bandwidth expansion should be prioritized.

Acknowledgments. This work was supported by the Innovation Project of the ICT, Chinese Academy of Sciences under Grant E461100.

Use of Generative AI. Artificial intelligence tools, if used, were used only for language organization and figure/table polishing, and did not participate in the generation of the core ideas or technical content.

References

1. Burd, T., Beck, N., White, et al.: zeppelin: an soc for multichip architectures. IEEE J. Solid-State Circ. **54**(1), 133–143 (2018)
2. Lau, J.H.: Recent advances and trends in advanced packaging. IEEE Trans. Components, Packaging Manuf. Technol. **12**(2), 228–252 (2022)
3. Li, H., Berger, et al.: Pond: CXL-based memory pooling systems for cloud platforms. In: Proceedings of the 28th ACM International Conference on Architectural Support for Programming Languages and Operating Systems, Volume 2, pp. 574–587 (2023)
4. Liu, et al.: A low-latency, low-jitter RETIMER circuit for PCIE 6.0. Electronics **12**(14), 3102 (2023)
5. Liu, J., Hadian, et al.: Systematic CXL memory characterization and performance analysis at scale. In: Proceedings of the 30th ACM International Conference on Architectural Support for Programming Languages and Operating Systems, Volume 2, pp. 1203–1217 (2025)
6. Sharma, D.D., Pasdast, et al.: Universal Chiplet interconnect express (UCIE): an open industry standard for innovations with Chiplets at package level. IEEE Trans. Components, Packaging Manuf. Technol. **12**(9), 1423–1431 (2022)

EcoVLA: Energy-Efficient Device-Edge Co-inference for Vision-Language-Action Models Under Real-Time Constraints

Ao Zhou[1], Bo Dai[1], Le Yu[1], Xingyu Liu[2], Zeyu Hao[1], Lingkun Long[1], Chunming Hu[1], and Jianlei Yang[1](✉)

[1] Beihang University, No.37 Xueyuan Road, Beijing, China
{aozhou,jianlei}@buaa.edu.cn
[2] Beijing University of Technology, No.100 Pingleyuan Road, Beijing, China

Abstract. Vision-Language-Action (VLA) models are a promising foundation for Embodied AI, but their high inference cost hinders robotic deployment. On-device inference is limited by compute and energy budgets, while full edge offloading is sensitive to network fluctuations and edge contention. Device-edge co-inference is a flexible alternative, but existing designs lack unified support for heterogeneous VLA paradigms and energy-aware scheduling. We propose EcoVLA, an adaptive device-edge co-inference framework for VLA models that maximizes system energy efficiency under real-time constraints. It abstracts VLA models into a unified stage-level co-inference space, estimates latency and energy from offline profiling and online sensing, and dynamically selects the most energy-efficient real-time scheme, with a lightweight transmission mechanism reducing communication overhead. Experiments show that EcoVLA improves energy efficiency by up to 236% over existing approaches under a 20 Hz constraint while consistently satisfying the real-time service-level objective (SLO).

Keywords: Vision-Language-Action Models · Device-Edge Co-Inference · Real-Time Inference · Energy Efficiency · Adaptive Scheduling.

1 Introduction

Vision-Language-Action (VLA) models integrate visual perception and language understanding into action generation, achieving strong performance across Embodied AI tasks [1]. However, their prohibitive computational cost is mismatched with the limited compute and energy budgets of robot devices. Recent VLA acceleration mainly optimizes on-device execution or relies on full edge offloading. ActionFlow [3] improves hardware utilization via cross-request pipelining, and RealtimeVLA [7] applies system optimizations such as *CUDA*

A. Zhou and B. Dai—Contributed equally to this work.

L. Eeckhout et al. (Eds.): APPT 2026, LNCS 16693, pp. 625–631, 2027.
https://doi.org/10.1007/978-981-92-4805-6_46

Graph, yet both remain bounded by on-device resource and energy limits. Full edge offloading instead treats the robot as a thin client [1], but is sensitive to network fluctuations and multi-robot contention, making real-time latency hard to guarantee.

As an emerging paradigm, device-edge co-inference provides a more flexible alternative by partitioning model execution between the robot and edge server [11]. Although co-inference has been studied for DNNs and LLMs [10], existing designs are not directly applicable to VLA models because they overlook heterogeneous VLA execution paradigms and embodied-control constraints. Moreover, robotic control does not benefit from finishing inference much earlier than the action-execution period, since the system still waits before issuing the next command, as also noted by VLASH [9]. This shifts the optimization goal from throughput maximization to energy-efficiency maximization under strict real-time service-level objective (SLO) constraints.

To this end, we propose EcoVLA, the first adaptive device-edge co-inference framework for VLA models that maximizes actions per joule (Actions/J) under real-time constraints. EcoVLA decouples VLA computation into a stage-level execution graph, enabling architecture-agnostic execution and communication across heterogeneous paradigms. It further builds a joint latency-energy model for fast runtime evaluation and uses energy-priority scheduling to select the most efficient SLO-feasible scheme, with lightweight transmission reducing communication cost. The main contributions are as follows:

- **Framework.** We present EcoVLA, the first adaptive device-edge co-inference framework that maximizes VLA energy efficiency under real-time constraints.
- **System-Aware Scheduling.** We build a system performance model with over 95% prediction accuracy within a 20% error bound, guiding dynamic scheduling toward the energy-optimal configuration in the SLO-feasible space.
- **Evaluation.** Experiments across diverse VLA models and system configurations show that EcoVLA improves energy efficiency by up to 236% over fixed co-inference baselines under a 20 Hz constraint.

2 Motivation and Overview

2.1 Why VLA Co-inference is Challenging

Building efficient device-edge co-inference for VLA models requires addressing three challenges. **(1) Heterogeneous VLA paradigms lack unified co-inference support.** As shown in Fig. 1(a), autoregressive VLAs such as OpenVLA [5] and diffusion-based VLAs such as π_0 [1] differ in execution flow and stage boundaries, making model-specific splits hard to generalize. **(2) Dynamic runtime conditions make static deployment unreliable.** VLA systems face changing network conditions and edge workloads. As illustrated in Fig. 1(b), full edge offloading and fixed partitioning [4] may become inefficient or violate real-time constraints when bandwidth drops or edge contention increases. **(3)**

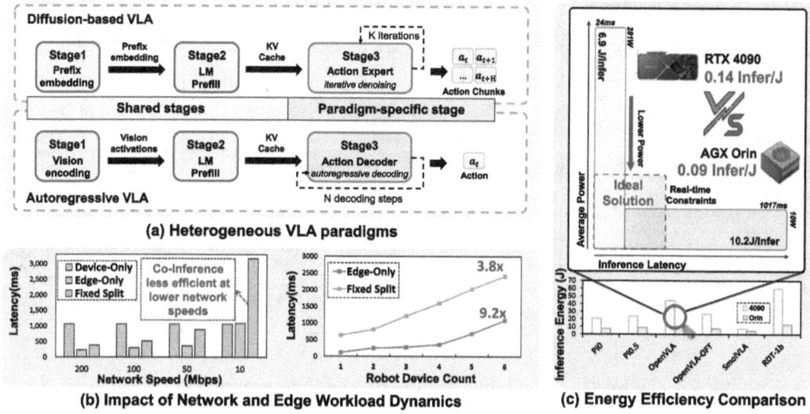

Fig. 1. Challenges and motivation of EcoVLA.

Energy efficiency requires joint system-level evaluation. Robotic energy efficiency depends on both latency and power. A low-power device such as Jetson is not necessarily more energy-efficient, since longer execution can increase energy per action or violate the SLO, as shown in Fig. 1(c).

2.2 EcoVLA Overview

Figure 2 shows the overview of EcoVLA. EcoVLA first abstracts heterogeneous VLA models into a unified stage-level execution graph, enabling paradigm-agnostic co-inference across autoregressive and diffusion-based models. A system performance model combines offline stage-level profiling with online sensing of network and edge workload conditions to estimate latency and energy for candidate schemes. An SLO-constrained energy-priority scheduler then selects the most energy-efficient feasible plan, which is enforced by a stage-aware runtime and lightweight communication middleware. In this way, EcoVLA turns VLA co-inference from static model partitioning into dynamic runtime optimization.

3 EcoVLA Methodology

3.1 Unified Stage-Level Co-inference Space

EcoVLA abstracts each VLA inference as a stage-level directed acyclic graph, where each node is an independently deployable computation unit and each edge represents an inter-stage data dependency. Compared with operator-level partitioning, this abstraction better matches VLA semantics and reduces runtime overhead. Each stage is *serializable*, *relocatable*, and *independently executable*, enabling autoregressive and diffusion-based VLAs to share a unified representation. EcoVLA further defines a unified intermediate-state interface on each stage edge, which packages stage inputs, outputs, and incremental context. By

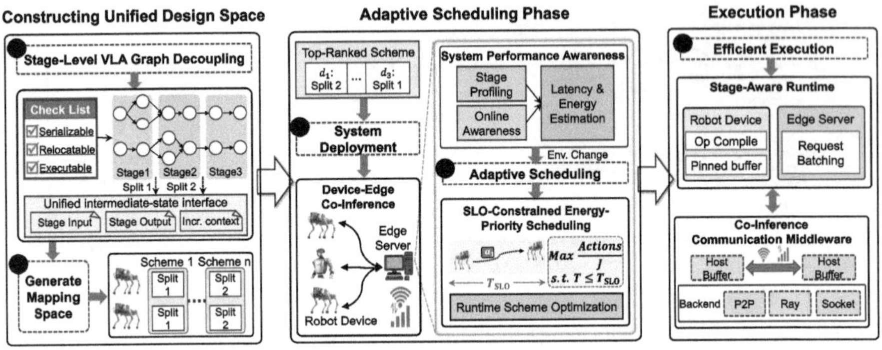

Fig. 2. Overview of the EcoVLA framework.

exposing packet size and stage attributes, EcoVLA can explicitly model communication cost while keeping scheduling independent of model-specific details. Finally, EcoVLA defines a mapping space that assigns each stage to the device or edge, filtering infeasible mappings by memory, operator support, and residency constraints.

3.2 System Performance Awareness

Efficient scheduling requires estimating candidate plans without online execution. EcoVLA therefore builds a lightweight performance module that combines offline profiling, online sensing, and feedback-based calibration. It profiles per-stage latency and power on each device, including computation and stage-boundary overheads such as packet processing, dispatch, queuing, and send-side operations. Transmission cost is estimated from packet size and online network probing, while edge-side queuing delay is inferred from request arrivals, queue states, and SLO constraints. For each candidate mapping, EcoVLA aggregates stage execution, transmission, and queuing delay along the dependency graph, accumulates computation and communication energy, and reports efficiency as Actions/J.

3.3 Adaptive Scheduling and Execution

For each request, EcoVLA derives a latency budget from the target frequency and action chunk length, evaluates feasible mappings via the performance-awareness module, and selects the SLO-satisfying plan with the highest predicted Actions/J, falling back to the lowest-latency plan when none is feasible. Each decision yields a complete stage-level plan covering placement, communication paths, and batching. For batching-capable edge stages, it batches compatible requests within the SLO slack, refines their latency and energy estimates, and reserves node-occupancy intervals so that later requests account for committed load. Observed latency, stage time, and communication cost are fed back to calibrate the model, letting EcoVLA adapt without a static lookup table. At runtime, a schedule-preserving executor keeps stage boundaries, queue semantics, and batching consistent with the scheduler, while a lightweight middleware transmits the structured intermediate packet as its basic unit. Pinned memory, pre-allocated buffers, asynchronous transfers, and graph-level compilation reduce fixed overhead and overlap communication with computation.

4 Experimental Evaluation

4.1 Experimental Setup

We evaluate EcoVLA on five VLA models: the autoregressive OpenVLA [5] and four diffusion-based models: π_0 [1], $\pi_{0.5}$ [2], SmolVLA [8], and RDT-1b [6], with action chunk size 20 for diffusion-based models. Using official implementations, we compare EcoVLA against three baselines: local robot-side execution (*Device-Only*), full edge offloading (*Edge-Only*), and static device-edge partitioning (*Fixed Split*) [4]. Our testbed pairs an NVIDIA Jetson AGX Orin 32GB (robot device) with an NVIDIA RTX 4090 (edge server). EcoVLA uses `Ray RPC` for control messages and `torch.distributed` with `Gloo` for tensor transmission. Energy is measured at the system level, covering both device and edge.

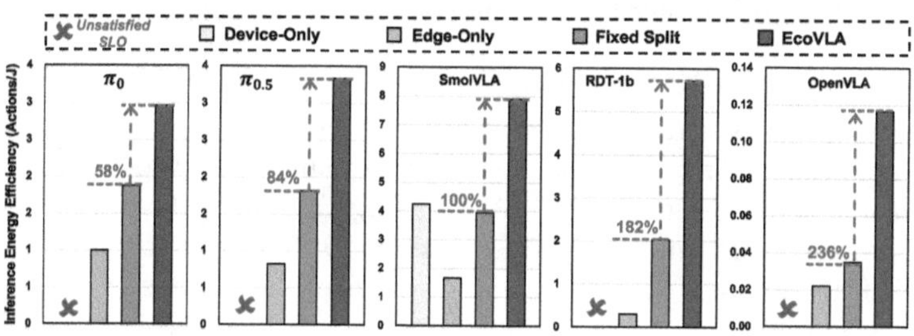

Fig. 3. Energy efficiency comparison. ✗ (Color figure online) indicates SLO violation.

4.2 Experimental Results

EcoVLA vs. Existing Approaches. Following prior real-time VLA settings [3], we set the target action-output frequency to 20 Hz. For diffusion-based models with an action chunk size of 20, this corresponds to a 1 s per-inference latency budget. As shown in Fig. 3, EcoVLA attains the highest energy efficiency among SLO-satisfying schemes, improving Actions/J over *Fixed Split* by up to 236% on OpenVLA. *Device-Only* occasionally shows competitive raw efficiency but violates the SLO on four models, confirming that on-device execution alone cannot reliably support VLA deployment. The gain stems from selecting the most energy-efficient plan within the SLO-feasible region rather than a fixed split.

Evaluation Under Network and Edge-Workload Variability. As shown in Fig. 4, *Fixed Split* degrades sharply as its static communication pattern mismatches the reduced bandwidth, while *Edge-Only* suffers from higher offloading cost. EcoVLA detects the change and switches to a device-heavier plan, stabilizing latency around 0.1 s and sustaining 2.43 Actions/J during the degraded phase, compared with 1.78 for *Edge-Only* and 1.11 for *Fixed Split*. Across different edge-load regimes, EcoVLA reduces latency and energy by up to 35.9% and 31.8% over *Fixed Split*, and by 26.8% and 24.6% over *Edge-Only*.

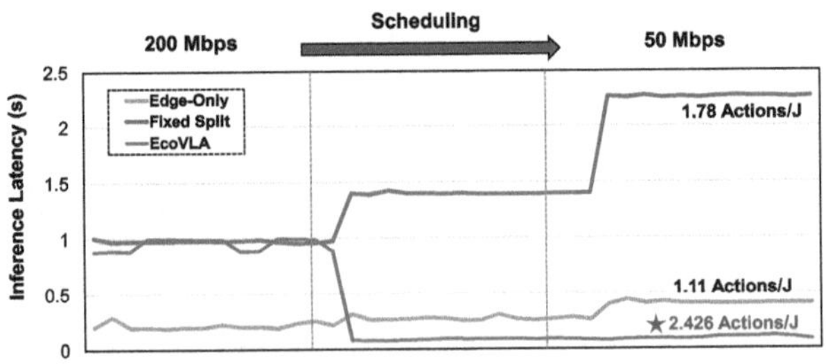

Fig. 4. Runtime adaptation under network deterioration.

Evaluation of System Performance Awareness. Across the candidate schemes explored during scheduling, the latency and energy predictors achieve Mean Absolute Percentage Error (MAPE) of 6% and 3.8%. Over 80% of predictions fall within ±10% and over 95% within ±20%, accurate enough to distinguish SLO-feasible plans and select energy-efficient candidates.

5 Conclusion

This paper presented EcoVLA, a device-edge co-inference framework for energy-efficient real-time VLA deployment. EcoVLA unifies heterogeneous VLA models through a stage-level abstraction and dynamically selects the most energy-efficient SLO-feasible plan via system-aware estimation. Experiments on five representative VLA models using a Jetson AGX Orin-RTX 4090 testbed show that EcoVLA improves energy efficiency by up to 236% over fixed co-inference baselines under a 20 Hz action-output constraint while consistently satisfying the SLO.

Acknowledgments. This work is supported in part by the Beijing Natural Science Foundation (Grant No. L243031), the National Natural Science Foundation of China (Grant No. 62572036), and the National Key R&D Program of China (Grant No. 2023YFB4503704 and 2024YFB4505601).

References

1. Black, K., et al.: π_0: a vision-language-action flow model for general robot control. arXiv preprint (2024)
2. Black, K., et al.: $\pi_{0.5}$: a vision-language-action model with open-world generalization. In: arXiv preprint (2025)
3. Dai, Y., et al.: ActionFlow: a pipelined action acceleration for vision language models on edge. arXiv preprint (2025)
4. Jiang, W., et al.: How fast can I run my VLA? Demystifying VLA inference performance with VLA-Perf. arXiv preprint (2026)
5. Kim, M.J., et al.: OpenVLA: an open-source vision-language-action model. arXiv preprint (2024)
6. Liu, S., et al.: RDT-1B: a diffusion foundation model for bimanual manipulation. In: Proceedings of ICLR (2025)
7. Ma, Y., et al.: Running VLAs at real-time speed. arXiv preprint (2025)
8. Shukor, M., et al.: SmolVLA: a vision-language-action model for affordable and efficient robotics. arXiv preprint (2025)
9. Tang, J., et al.: VLASH: Real-time VLAs via future-state-aware asynchronous inference. arXiv preprint (2025)
10. Yuan, C., et al.: Task-oriented feature compression for multimodal understanding via device-edge co-inference. IEEE TMC (2025)
11. Zhou, A., et al.: Graph neural networks automated design and deployment on device-edge co-inference systems. In: Proceedings of DAC (2024)

COMET: An FP32 Matrix Multiplication Accelerator by Extending INT8-Based Arrays

Xia Ruiyang[1,2], Hao Yifan[1,2](✉), Zhao Yuming[1,3], Liu Yang[1,2], Zhao Yongwei[1,2], Du Zidong[1,2], Hu Xing[1,2], Li Wei[1,2], and Guo Qi[1,2]

[1] State Key Laboratory of Processors, Institute of Computing Technology, Beijing, China
xiaruiyang19@mails.ucas.ac.cn,
{haoyifan,liuyang22z1,zhaoyongwei,duzidong,huxing,liwei2017, guoqi}@ict.ac.cn, yumingzhao@mail.ustc.edu.cn

[2] University of Chinese Academy of Sciences, Beijing, China

[3] University of Science and Technology of China, Hefei, Anhui, China

Abstract. FP32 matrix multiplication remains important for numerically sensitive deep learning and scientific workloads, but modern accelerators devote most compute resources to low-bitwidth arrays. This paper presents COMET, an FP32 matrix multiplication accelerator that extends INT8-based arrays instead of adding a separate FP32 array. COMET uses Toom-Cook-3 to reduce sliced integer matrix products from 9 to 5, and introduces a matrix-level Interpolation & Accumulation Unit to lower accumulation and normalization cost. RTL evaluation shows that COMET preserves FP32 numerical fidelity while achieving 2.57× speedup, 3.34× energy-efficiency improvement, and only 18.01% area overhead over an INT8-native array.

Keywords: FP32 matrix multiplication · accelerator architecture · INT8 array reuse · Toom-Cook decomposition

1 Introduction

Modern AI and scientific workloads still rely on FP32 matrix multiplication. FP32 remains important for numerically sensitive training [1,9,10,18] and AI-for-science applications such as DeepMD [14,15,17]. These workloads need high FP32 throughput with predictable numerical behavior.

This requirement is mismatched with modern accelerator organization. GPUs and domain accelerators devote most compute density to low-bitwidth matrix arrays, while FP32 support is typically provided by smaller, separate units [5, 11,12]. As a result, abundant INT8/Tensor-Core-style resources cannot directly serve FP32 matrix multiplication [3,4].

Reusing low-bitwidth arrays for FP32 is attractive but not automatic. Slicing each FP32 mantissa into three low-bitwidth fragments creates 9 schoolbook

L. Eeckhout et al. (Eds.): APPT 2026, LNCS 16693, pp. 632–637, 2027.
https://doi.org/10.1007/978-981-92-4805-6_47

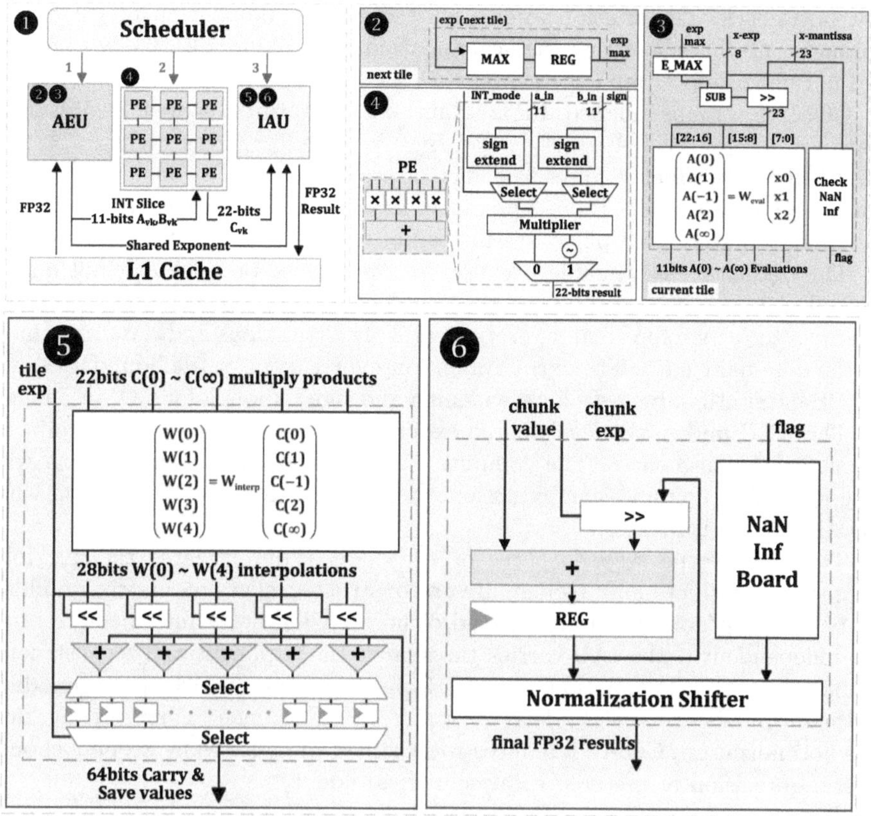

Fig. 1. COMET architecture overview. The AEU evaluates Toom-3 points, the extended INT8-based array computes five integer matrix products, and the IAU interpolates and accumulates results at matrix granularity.

integer products [7,8], and naive accumulation can be dominated by alignment, shifting, and normalization. The core challenge is to make both multiplication and accumulation preserve the savings of INT8-array reuse.

We propose COMET, an FP32 matrix multiplication accelerator that extends INT8-based arrays. COMET uses matrix-level Toom-Cook-3 [2,13] to reduce integer matrix products from 9 to 5, and a matrix-level Interpolation & Accumulation Unit (IAU) to move exponent alignment and accumulation away from scalar products. RTL and workload evaluation show FP32 numerical fidelity, 2.57× speedup, and 3.34× energy-efficiency gains over GPU FP32 cores.

2 COMET Architecture

Figure 1 shows the COMET datapath. COMET is designed to reuse the dense low-bitwidth array without turning the surrounding FP32 support logic into the new bottleneck. The multiplication path reduces the number of integer matrix products entering the array; the accumulation path reduces FP32-style shifting and normalization around the array.

COMET groups aligned FP32 mantissas into three signed low-bitwidth matrices, $A(x) = A_0 + A_1x + A_2x^2$ and $B(x) = B_0 + B_1x + B_2x^2$, where $x = 2^{-8}$. A schoolbook product requires 9 coefficient products. COMET instead evaluates both polynomials at five Toom-3 points, 0, 1, -1, 2, and ∞, so the array performs five integer matrix multiplications instead of nine.

This reduction is valuable because each pointwise product is a full matrix multiplication, not a scalar operation hidden in control logic. Moving from 9 products to 5 therefore removes repeated array activations and data movement on the dominant path. The extra evaluation logic is kept at tile boundaries, and the PE datapath only needs local widening and sign handling for COMET mode.

The AEU finds a tile-level shared exponent, aligns mantissas, and emits 11-bit signed Toom-3 slices. The compute array then reuses the INT8 path with only local widening and sign extension, preserving native INT8 execution when COMET mode is disabled.

The IAU is the second source of efficiency. It interpolates the five integer matrix products and accumulates reconstructed slices at matrix granularity before final normalization. Instead of normalizing every intermediate product independently, the IAU carries the shared tile exponent and reconstructed chunks through accumulation, then performs rounding and exception handling at the output boundary. By delaying scalar-style alignment, carry propagation, and normalization, COMET reduces wide shifter pressure while keeping enough internal precision to preserve FP32 numerical fidelity.

The key reason to move accumulation to matrix granularity is the cost of exponent alignment. If alignment is performed after each partial product, an $n \times n$ matrix multiplication requires $O(n^3)$ shifts and wide additions. COMET instead aligns operands before they enter the array, reducing this work to $O(n^2)$ tile preparation. The resulting matrix products share an alignment domain, so shifting, accumulation, and normalization can be batched and reused across the tile.

3 Evaluation

We implement COMET and baselines in SystemVerilog RTL, synthesize them in a TSMC 12nm FinFET technology at 0.9V and 1.0 GHz, and estimate power with PrimeTime. Baselines include an INT8-native array, an FP32-FMA array, a schoolbook FP32-over-INT8 design, and a process-normalized NVIDIA A100 reference [11]. We report both numerical and hardware metrics because COMET only succeeds if INT8-array reuse does not trade away FP32 semantics.

3.1 Numerical Fidelity

COMET's Toom-3 path is not approximate: evaluation and interpolation reconstruct the sliced product before final FP32 normalization. We compare COMET

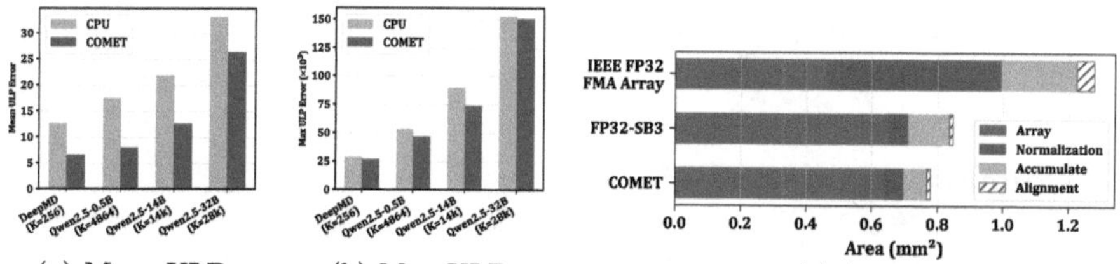

(a) Mean ULP (b) Max ULP (c) Area

Fig. 2. Numerical fidelity and post-synthesis area comparison.

with a Kulisch-accumulator golden model [6] and a CPU implementation using FP64 accumulation. The ULP measurements include the final rounding path, so they cover the combined effect of slicing, interpolation, accumulation, and normalization.

For LLM and DeepMD workloads [15–17], Fig. 2 shows that COMET maintains FP32 numerical fidelity. COMET has lower mean/max ULP error than the CPU baseline on the tested cases, and MSE remains below 1×10^{-10}. These results indicate that the matrix-level exponent sharing and delayed normalization do not introduce the error amplification that would be expected from an approximate low-bitwidth emulation path.

3.2 Hardware Results

Figure 2c shows that COMET adds only 18.01% area over the INT8-native array while adding FP32 matrix multiplication. Most of the added cost is outside the dense array, in normalization, accumulation, and alignment support. Compared with a conventional FP32-FMA array, COMET occupies 60.95% of the area, a 39.05% reduction, because it avoids replicating full FP32 multiply-accumulate logic in every PE.

Figure 3 shows the throughput and energy gains. The average speedup follows from reducing the dominant matrix products and keeping the reused array highly utilized; the energy gain additionally comes from fewer array invocations and less scalar-style normalization traffic. By combining 5-product Toom-3 execution

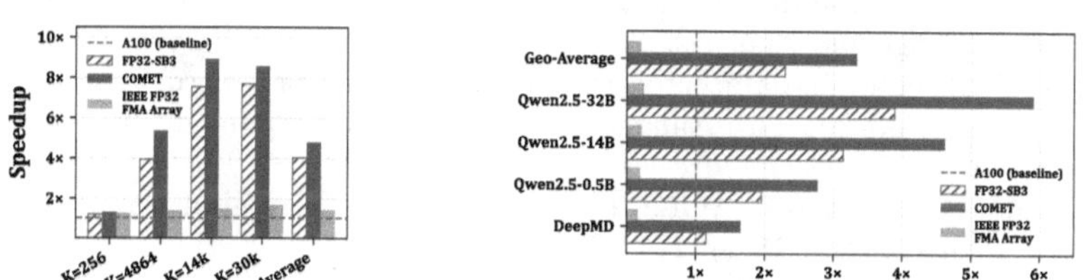

(a) Performance (b) Energy efficiency

Fig. 3. Performance and energy-efficiency gains over FP32 baselines.

with matrix-level accumulation, COMET is 2.57× faster and 3.34× more energy-efficient than GPU FP32 cores, with a peak GEMM speedup of 8.92×.

4 Conclusion

COMET demonstrates that INT8-based arrays can be extended to support efficient FP32 matrix multiplication. Toom-3 reduces integer matrix products from 9 to 5, while the IAU lowers accumulation overhead at matrix granularity. The resulting design improves speed and energy efficiency with modest area overhead, making it suitable for scientific AI and high-precision deep learning workloads.

Acknowledgments. This work is partially supported by the NSF of China (Grants No. 62341411, 62302478, U22A2028), Strategic Priority Research Program of the Chinese Academy of Sciences (Grants No. XDB0660300, XDB0660301, XDB0660302), CAS Project for Young Scientists in Basic Research (YSBR-029), and Youth Innovation Promotion Association CAS. The technical solution and experimental design presented in this paper were independently completed by the authors. AI tools were used solely for language polishing and formatting optimization, and did not participate in the development of the research ideas or core content.

Disclosure of Interests. The authors have no competing interests to declare that are relevant to the content of this article.

References

1. Abdelaziz, H., Shin, J.H., Pedram, A., Hassoun, J., et al.: Rethinking floating point overheads for mixed precision DNN accelerators. Proc. Mach. Learn. Syst. **3**, 223–239 (2021)
2. Cook, S.A., Aanderaa, S.O.: On the minimum computation time of functions. Trans. Am. Math. Soc. **142**, 291–314 (1969)
3. Fu, Y., Bolotin, E., Chatterjee, N., Nellans, D., Keckler, S.W.: GPU domain specialization via composable on-package architecture. ACM Trans. Architecture Code Optimization (TACO) **19**(1), 1–23 (2021)
4. Ha, D., Zhang, Y., Kao, C.C., Hughes, C.J., Ro, W.W., Tseng, H.W.: M 3 xu: achieving high-precision and complex matrix multiplication with low-precision MXUS. In: SC24: International Conference for High Performance Computing, Networking, Storage and Analysis, pp. 1–16. IEEE (2024)
5. Jouppi, N.P., et al.: In-datacenter performance analysis of a tensor processing unit. In: Proceedings of the 44th Annual International Symposium on Computer Architecture, pp. 1–12 (2017)
6. Kulisch, U.W., Miranker, W.L.: The arithmetic of the digital computer: a new approach. SIAM Rev. **28**(1), 1–40 (1986)
7. Lin, Z., Sun, A., Zhang, X., Lu, Y.: Mixpert: Optimizing mixed-precision floating point emulation on GPU integer tensor cores. In: Proceedings of the 25th ACM SIGPLAN/SIGBED International Conference on Languages, Compilers, and Tools for Embedded Systems, pp. 34–45 (2024)

8. Ma, Z., et al.: Efficiently emulating high-bitwidth computation with low-bitwidth hardware. In: Proceedings of the 36th ACM International Conference on Supercomputing, pp. 1–12 (2022)
9. Mudigere, D., et al.: Software-hardware co-design for fast and scalable training of deep learning recommendation models. In: Proceedings of the 49th Annual International Symposium on Computer Architecture, pp. 993–1011 (2022)
10. Noh, S.H., Koo, J., Lee, S., Park, J., Kung, J.: Flexblock: a flexible DNN training accelerator with multi-mode block floating point support. IEEE Trans. Comput. **72**(9), 2522–2535 (2023)
11. NVIDIA Corporation: NVIDIA A100 Tensor Core GPU Architecture: Unprecedented Acceleration at Every Scale. Whitepaper, NVIDIA Corporation, US (2020)
12. NVIDIA Corporation: NVIDIA H100 Tensor Core GPU Architecture: Exceptional Performance, Scalability, and Security for The Data Center. Whitepaper, NVIDIA Corporation, US (2022)
13. Toom, A.L.: The complexity of a scheme of functional elements realizing the multiplication of integers. Soviet Math. Doklady **3**, 714–716 (1963)
14. Valero-Lara, P., Jorquera, I., Lui, F., Vetter, J.: Mixed-precision s/DGEMM using the tf32 and tf64 frameworks on low-precision ai tensor cores. In: Proceedings of the SC'23 Workshops of the International Conference on High Performance Computing, Network, Storage, and Analysis, pp. 179–186 (2023)
15. Wang, H., Zhang, L., Han, J., et al.: Deepmd-kit: a deep learning package for many-body potential energy representation and molecular dynamics. Comput. Phys. Commun. **228**, 178–184 (2018)
16. Yang, A., et al.: Qwen2.5 Technical report. arXiv preprint arXiv:2412.15115 (2024)
17. Zhang, L., Han, J., Wang, H., Car, R., E, W.: Deep potential molecular dynamics: a scalable model with the accuracy of quantum mechanics. Phy. Rev. Lett. **120**(14), 143001 (2018)
18. Zhang, S.Q., McDanel, B., Kung, H.: Fast: DNN training under variable precision block floating point with stochastic rounding. In: 2022 IEEE International Symposium on High-Performance Computer Architecture (HPCA), pp. 846–860. IEEE (2022)

Author Index

L. Eeckhout et al. (Eds.): APPT 2026, LNCS 16693, pp. 639–642, 2027.
https://doi.org/10.1007/978-981-92-4805-6